BRITISH
ENGLISH
A TO ZED

BRITISH ENGLISH A TO ZED

A Definitive Guide to the Queen's English

NORMAN W. SCHUR
REVISED BY EUGENE EHRLICH
AND RICHARD EHRLICH

Skyhorse Publishing

Skyhorse Publishing books may be purchased in bulk at special
discounts for sales promotion, corporate gifts, fund-raising, or
educational purposes. Special editions can also be created to
specifications. For details, contact the Special Sales Department,
Skyhorse Publishing, 307 West 36th Street, 11th Floor, New
York, NY 10018 or info@skyhorsepublishing.com.

Skyhorse® and Skyhorse Publishing® are registered trademarks
of Skyhorse Publishing, Inc.®, a Delaware corporation.

Visit our website at www.skyhorsepublishing.com.

10 9 8 7 6 5 4 3 2 1

Library of Congress Cataloging-in-Publication Data is available
on file.

ISBN: 978-1-62087-577-3

Printed in the United States of America

CONTENTS

FOREWORD

Over 25 years have passed since the first edition of *British English A to Zed* was published, and five since its second edition. Over those two and a half decades, and even in the decade or so since the second edition, there have been significant changes in British English—and in British life. This edition aims at taking stock of those changes.

Most important, this edition adds more than 500 new words and terms that have come into common use since the previous edition was published. The additions are by no means comprehensive, but they include some of the most prominent new locutions in a language that has grown increasingly rich. The Queen's English, often regarded as a paradigm of correct and "proper" usage, has been busy absorbing words and phrases from diverse sources—some reflecting new political alignments, some from overseas, many from the argot of the street. No lexicon of British English can ignore these, as Norman Schur recognized when he wrote the first edition of *British English A to Zed,* and this edition continues with that work.

This new edition also adds a gloss on the work of the earlier editions. Some of the words given as standard usage in the first edition are now rarely used, and those entries have been duly amended to take account of the change. Some old words have changed their meanings, and those changes, too, are included. It should also be noted that some fundamental changes in British life—in areas as diverse as education and telecommunications—have occurred since Norman Schur wrote his first edition. This edition attempts to track those changes, both in amended entries and in new entries.

Any language is in a constant state of development. When this book is next updated, whether in five or in 20 years, the incessant process of linguistic and social change will require still further additions and emendations. This edition, though compiled with utmost care, can be regarded only as a work in progress. And that is true also of the English language itself.

We thank Emma Dally, of London, England, for her invaluable assistance with many editorial tasks. Likewise, Rebecca, Alice, and Ruth Ehrlich all gave valuable advice on contemporary slang.

Eugene Ehrlich
Mamaroneck, New York

Richard Ehrlich
London, England

PREFACE TO THE FIRST EDITION

The book is essentially a glossary of Briticisms for the guidance of Americans caught in the entrapment of a common language. I have seen fit to include certain terms and expressions which, though they may be fading from current British use, or may even have disappeared completely from most people's everyday conversation, an American might run up against in the literature of a few years ago, or quite possibly in the conversation of an elderly person, especially in the more remote parts of the British countryside. In some instances, I have expanded the discussion in an effort to demonstrate not only peculiarities of the language of Britain, but also aspects of her culture as reflected by her language.

What began as a pastime took on tangible form and, somewhat to my own surprise, has emerged as a serious compilation. I would be grateful if (in addition to omissions and possible erroneous inclusions and definitions) new items which appear from time to time were called to the attention of the publisher. Not the least of my rewards has been the volume and tenor of the response I have received from scholars and aficionados in many parts of the world who have written letters ranging from a few words of appreciation to essays full of valuable information and comments. Many of the entries must evoke some controversy and even censure. "A dictionary-maker," said H. W. Fowler in his preface to the *Concise Oxford Dictionary* (reprinted in the sixth edition of that admirable work, 1976), "unless he is a monster of omniscience, must deal with a great many matters of which he has no first-hand knowledge. That he has been guilty of errors and omissions in some of these he will learn soon after publication, sometimes with gratitude to his enlightener, sometimes otherwise."

—Norman Schur
1987

EXPLANATORY NOTES

For a full discussion of the criteria used in assembling the Briticisms and their American equivalents the reader is referred to the Introduction. The following are brief notes on how to use the dictionary.

Entries
Briticisms, listed alphabetically, are set in boldface on the left-hand side of each entry. American equivalents are set in boldface on the right, opposite the British headword. When there is no American equivalent, SEE COMMENT refers the reader to the comment under the headword.

Labels
Parts of speech are set in italics, immediately following the British headword. Usage labels: when a Briticism is nonstandard this is indicated in italics, either at the beginning of the comment or, when there is no comment, immediately following the function label. The labels used are: *Rhyming slang, Slang, Inf.* (Informal), *Old-fash.* (Old-fashioned), and *Rare.* American equivalents are similarly labeled. Though it has been the policy to attempt to provide American equivalents of the same usage level, that has not always been possible, and in such cases a comment always follows the headword. When the American equivalent is only an approximation of its British counterpart, it is preceded by *approx.*

Pronunciation
When the pronunciation of a Briticism is idiosyncratic, i.e., not ascribable to general differences between British and American pronunciation, a phonetic transcription in small capital letters is given at the beginning of the comment, following the usage label. The system of notation used is too simple to merit a table of its own.

Sense Distinctions
Arabic numerals separate the senses of a headword, both in the American equivalent and in the comment. Divisions are based on usage rather than strict semantic distinctions.

Comment
Examples of typical usage are set in italics, as are British and American terms that are used to illustrate meaning. Glosses of Briticisms are set in single quotes. Briticisms used in the comments which appear in the alphabetical listing are set in **boldface** when it is felt that referring to them would add to the understanding of the comment.

Cross-References
See, See also, and *See under* refer the reader to other entries and to the Appendices. Cross-reference is based on various criteria: related meanings (similarity and contrast), related subject matter (e.g., pub terms, telephone terminology—in such cases the reader may be referred to the Appendices), morphological similarity (in

xii   British English A to Zed

several cases the American equivalent is itself an entry, e.g., *vest* is the equivalent of the British *waistcoat* and is also a Briticism of which the American equivalent is *undershirt*). Readers are also referred to the Appendices that deal with general differences between British and American English, when they have bearing on the entry. Words appearing in **boldface** type in the text of a comment have their own entries in proper alphabetic sequence.

Appendices
The Appendices are of two kinds: the first section contains short notes on general differences between British and American English. These are far from comprehensive, but the reader is referred to works that deal more fully with the topics discussed.

The second section contains tables and glossaries of terms whose meaning and use are best shown when the terms are grouped together (e.g., currency, measures) and lists of specialized slang terms of which only a few are included in the A–Z section.

Index of American Equivalents
This addition to the new edition of the book should be of special help to users searching for British equivalents of particular American words and phrases. The American equivalents given in the main, A–Z section of the book are listed alphabetically in the Index, together with the equivalent Briticisms, which the reader will find treated in full in the main section.

Abbreviations

abbrev.	abbreviation	*n.*	noun
adj.	adjective	*offens.*	offensive
adv.	adverb	*pl.*	plural
approx.	approximate	*prep.*	preposition
conj.	conjunction	*TM*	trademark
derog.	derogatory	*v.i.*	verb, intransitive
inf.	informal	*v.t.*	verb, transitive
interj.	interjection		

BRITISH
ENGLISH
A TO ZED

INTRODUCTION

According to Marcus Cunliffe, in *The Literature of the United States*, a chauvinistic delegate to the Continental Congress moved that the new nation drop the use of the English language entirely; William Morris, in *Newsbreak* (Stackpole, New York, 1975), reports that the more violently anti-British leaders moved to reject English as the national language in favor of Hebrew, until it was pointed out that very few Americans could speak it; and another delegate proposed an amendment providing that the United States retain English and make the British learn Greek!

American claims to the English language are far from being left unanswered. In April 1974, Jacques Chastenet of the Académie française, suggesting Latin as the most suitable official tongue for the European Economic Community, expressed the concern that "English, or more exactly American, might otherwise take over." He characterized "American" as "not a very precise idiom." Frederick Wood's attempt at consolation in his preface to *Current English Usage* (Macmillan & Co. Ltd., London, 1962) might seem even more offensive: "Certain words and constructions have been described as Americanisms. This does not necessarily mean that they are bad English." In "An Open Letter to the Honorable Mrs. Peter Rodd (Nancy Mitford) On A Very Serious Subject," Evelyn Waugh, discussing the American influence, writes: ". . . American polite vocabulary is different from ours. . . . [It] is pulverized between two stones, refinement and overstatement." Cyril Connolly went pretty far in *The Sunday Times* (London) of December 11, 1966: ". . . the American language is in a state of flux based on the survival of the unfittest."

Whatever the relationship may be, and however strongly opinions are voiced, it seems clear that in the jet age, what with the movies (the *cinema*), TV (the *telly*), and radio (the *wireless* still, to many Britons), linguistic parochialism is bound to diminish. In *Words in Sheep's Clothing* (Hawthorn Books, Inc., New York, 1969), Mario Pei, after referring to the different meanings given to the same word in the two countries, writes: ". . . In these days of rapid communication and easy interchange, such differences are less important than you would think." The latest edition of the *Pocket Oxford Dictionary* includes a fair number of American terms not found in earlier editions: *teen-age, paper-back, T-shirt, supermarket, sacred cow, sick joke,* and many others. And in their recorded dialogue, published under the title *A Common Language, British and American English* in 1964 by the British Broadcasting Corporation and the Voice of America, Professors Randolph Quirk of University College, London, and Albert H. Marckwardt, of Princeton University, agreed, according to the Foreword, that ". . . the two varieties of English have never been so different as people have imagined, and the dominant tendency, for several decades now, has been clearly that of convergence and even greater similarity." And in a similarly optimistic mood, Ronald Mansbridge, manager emeritus of the American branch of the Cambridge University Press, in his foreword to *Longitude 30 West* (a confidential report to the Syndics of the Cambridge University Press by Lord Acton), refers to the two countries as "strongly linked together—let us reject the old joke 'divided'—by the English language."

1

Welcome or not, the process of convergence is slow, and the differences linger. Herbert R. Mayes, in his London Letter in the *Saturday Review* of November 14, 1970, wrote: ". . . There are enough archaisms here to keep an American off balance. . . . The British are stubborn. . . ." And Suzanne Haire (Lady Haire of Whiteabbey, formerly with the BBC, then living in New York), writing in *The New York Times* of January 11, 1972, of her "Study of 'American-English' at its source," mentioned the "bizarre misunderstandings [which] can result from expressions which have different meanings on the two sides of the Atlantic." The example she selected was the informal noun *tube*, meaning *subway* in Britain and *television* in the United States.

When we get away from standard English and are faced with the ephemeralness of slang and informal terms, the division widens. In a letter to *The Times* published July 12, 1974, the literary critic and translator Nicholas Bethell, answering objections to his review of an English translation of *The Gulag Archipelago*, wrote: ". . . What I was objecting to was the use of words like 'bums' and 'broads' in a translation. They are too American. 'Yobbos' and 'birds' would be equally inappropriate. They are too British. It is a problem that translators are often faced with, how to render slang without adding confusing overtones. One has to try to find a middle way." To a Briton, a *bum* is a *behind*, and a *broad* a *river-widening*. To an American, *yobbo* (an extension of *yob*, backslang—reverse spelling—for *boy*, meaning *lout* or *bum*) would be unintelligible, as would *bird*, in its slang sense, a 'character,' in the sense of an *eccentric*, as in *He's a queer bird!*

Whether standard, informal, or slang, and despite the "convergence" theory, the differences are still many and confusing. Bearing a London dateline, Russell Baker's column in *The New York Times* of September 15, 1970, began: "One of the hardest languages for an American to learn is English," and the language he was referring to was British English. About a year later, Henry Stanhope's review of *Welcome to Britain* (Whitehall Press, London, 1971) in the September 3, 1971, [London] *Times* referred to a glossary in the book as going ". . . some way towards bridging the linguistic gulf, broader than the Atlantic Ocean, which still separates our cultures." And on an arrival a few years ago at Heathrow Airport, London, I picked up a copy of *Welcome*, a newspaper available without charge to passengers, and read Sylvia Goldberg's article headed "Perils of the Spoken Word," which began: "One thing American visitors to Britain are seldom warned about is the 'language problem,'" and continued with the observation that the ". . . most mundane negotiation, the simplest attempt at communication with the natives can lead to unutterable confusion."

Whatever the future may hold in store, I have found that many facets of British English are still in need of clarification and interpretation. For despite occasional deletions because the American equivalent has all but taken over, my list of Briticisms has expanded substantially. Briticisms fall into three main categories:

1. Those that are used in both countries to mean different things. Thus, *davenport* means 'small writing desk' in Britain and 'large sofa' in America. Some words and phrases in this category have diametrically opposite meanings in the two countries. *Bomb* in Britain is slang for 'dazzling success'; in America it generally means 'dismal flop.' The verb *table* is an example of the same phenomenon.
2. Those that are not used at all in America, or extremely rarely, like *call box* and *kiosk* for 'telephone booth'; *hoarding* for 'billboard'; *dustman* for 'garbage man.'
3. Those that are not used (or if used at all, used differently) in America for the simple reason that their referent does not exist there. Examples abound:

beefeater; commoner; during hours; Oxbridge. Often these refer to social and cultural institutions and have taken on connotative meanings which may have approximate American counterparts: *Chelsea; Bloomsbury; redbrick.*

Some terms qualify as Briticisms not because they are exclusively British but because they have a peculiarly British flavor. I lump such terms under the general heading "preferences." For example, if a British girl and an American girl were out shopping together, the British girl, pointing to a shop window, might say, "I'd like to go into that shop and look at that frock," while her friend would more likely say, "I'd like to go into that store and look at that dress." The British girl might have said *dress* but would not have said *store*. The American girl might have said *shop* but would never have said *frock*. And the person who waited on them would be a *saleswoman* or *salesman* to the American girl, but a *shop assistant* to her British friend. It is all rather delicate and subtle, and these preferences keep shifting. Here is a sample list of mutually intelligible terms which qualify as preferences:

BRITAIN	AMERICA
blunt (e.g., of a pencil)	*dull*
crash (automobile, train)	*collision*
engaged (busy)	*tied up*
fancy (verb)	1. *like* 2. *suppose*
motor-car	*automobile*
position (the way things stand)	*situation*
queer (peculiar)	*funny*
sea	1. *ocean* 2. *beach*
snag (describing a troublesome situation)	*trouble, problem, catch, hitch*
tablet	*pill*
tidy	*clean, orderly, neat*
trade	*business*
wager	*bet*
wretched (e.g., of weather, person, luck)	*awful, terrible*

In addition to matters of preference, there is a category that may best be described by the term *overlaps*, to describe the situation where the British also use the American equivalent, but the Americans do not (or usually do not) use the British equivalent. The British, for example, say both *crackers* and *nutty* (meaning 'crazy'), but Americans do not use *crackers* in that sense. Many American terms are by now used more frequently in Britain than the parallel Briticism, which has become old-fashioned. I have preferred to include such entries, but in such cases, I have mentioned the increasing use of or total takeover by the American equivalent. See, for example, *aisle; flicks.*

Conversely, Briticisms which may be familiar to many Americans have been included where in my opinion they have not gained sufficient currency in America to be considered naturalized. In years to come, as jets become bigger and faster and the world continues to shrink, many such items will undoubtedly acquire dual citizenship. In this area, too, inclusion was the rule.

Most Briticisms have precise American equivalents, in which case they are given in boldface. Occasionally, however, this has not been possible. This applies to terms with figurative meanings; here we are on the slippery ground of connotations, implicit references, social context, and cultural implications. Many of these are slang and informal expressions that are too closely tied to British social and cultural institutions to have American equivalents, and in such cases it has been our policy not to attempt to invent one, but instead, to refer the reader to a comment providing a definition and illustrations of the uses and connotations of the British term. This policy is also followed in the case of encyclopedic entries, like *the Commons; beefeater; Dame*. (The phrase SEE COMMENT in place of an American equivalent refers the reader to the text immediately below the entry.)

On the other hand, there are a good many Briticisms that have close or approximate equivalents in American English. These are cases where the referents may be different, but the connotative meanings, based on the social or cultural backgrounds of the referents, or the referents themselves, may be similar enough to render the parallel terms approximate equivalents. Thus, though *the City* and *Wall Street* have different referents, it is reasonable to assume that in most contexts in which a Briton would refer to *the City*, an American would say *Wall Street*.

Many terms have "shared senses," meanings common to both countries. The noun *note*, for instance, can mean 'musical note' (do, re, mi), 'written evidence of debt' (promissory note), 'memorandum' (he made a note of it), 'message' (he passed her a note), and so on. In Britain it has an additional sense that it does not possess in America: a 'piece of paper money' (a one-pound note, a banknote). The American equivalent in that sense is *bill* (a one-dollar bill, a five-dollar bill). Correspondingly, the word *bill* has a multiplicity of senses; the *beak* of a bird, the *draft* of a proposed law, etc. It would unduly lengthen the discussion to list or refer to all shared meanings. It is therefore to be assumed that in the case of terms with more than one sense, those not dealt with are common to both countries.

It has been difficult to apply precise criteria of inclusion and exclusion. Many slang and informal terms have been included but others omitted because they seemed too ephemeral or too narrowly regional. A *roke* is a *ground fog*, but only in Norfolk. In certain parts of Surrey they eat *clod and stickin*, an unattractive-sounding stew, but if you asked for it outside of that area you would be met with a totally uncomprehending stare. It is well to avoid Lancashiremen and Yorkshiremen who are *razat*: they're *sore* at you. In parts of Yorkshire a donkey is a *fussock* or a *fussenock*, in Lancashire a *bronkus* or a *pronkus*. Such narrowly restricted dialectal terms, though amusing enough, have been reluctantly passed by. In the Appendix section, however, we have included certain lists of localized slang.

Pronunciation has been indicated by reference to common words presumably familiar to the general reader, rather than through the use of phonetic symbols which remain an unbroken code to all but specialists. There is an index of American terms for the benefit of those seeking British equivalents. There are appendices dealing with general aspects of British English, and special glossaries of related terms better presented in that fashion than as separate headwords.

A separate section, "Explanatory Notes," is devoted to instructions for the most efficient use of the book.

A.A. Automobile Association
Opposite number to America's *A.A.A. (American Automobile Association)*. Just about everybody in Britain who drives a car is a member of the *A.A.* or of the *R.A.C.*, which is short for *Royal Automobile Club.*

A.A.A. SEE COMMENT
1. See **A.A.**
2. Amateur Athletic Association.

abandonment, *n.* abandon
In the sense of 'uninhibited conduct.' *Abandon* is used in Britain as well.

about, *adv.* around
Used as an adverb indicating place, meaning 'near' or 'in the vicinity,' as in, *Is your father about?* In the sense of 'approximately' Americans use both terms interchangeably, but the British much prefer *about*. See also **Appendix I.A.1.**

above the salt SEE COMMENT
Long ago, when the family saltcellar among the powerful and wealthy was a massive silver container, it was placed in the middle of the dining table and marked the boundary between the classes when people dined together. Those seated *above the salt* were members of the higher classes, the family and their peers; those *below the salt* were seated among the inferior guests. Today, of course, these terms are used only metaphorically. At a banquet or formal dinner, however, to sit *above the salt* is to sit in a position of distinction.

absolutely sweet delightful
Usually applied to people, but it can refer to almost anything.

academicals, *n. pl.* cap and gown
Also known as "academic costume" and the hat being called informally a "mortarboard," a term shared with the United States.

Academy, *n.* SEE COMMENT
Royal Academy of Arts. The Academy is usually so understood; *academician* refers especially to that institution. The initials *R.A.* after a name mean that the artist is a member of the institution.

accelerator, *n.* gas pedal

accept, *v.i.* agree
For instance, *I cannot accept that you have met the conditions of the contract.* A common use in Britain. See discussion under **agree.**

access, *n.* visitation
Term used in matrimonial law, referring to the rights of the parent without custody to visit the children of the marriage. See a different usage in **except for access;** and

note an unrelated use in *Access,* the name of a credit card formerly issued by Lloyds Bank Limited.

Staying access means 'temporary custody,' as when the party with visitation rights is authorized to have the minor child stay with him or her for limited periods, e.g., during every other weekend or on certain holidays.

accident and emergency   **ER department**

accident tout   **ambulance chaser**
Both *Slang.*

acclimatize, *v.t.*   **acclimate**

accommodation, *n.*   **accommodations**
In the sense of 'food and lodgings,' the British use the singular. They seem not to use the word at all as the Americans do to include travel facilities, such as train and ship staterooms, plane seats, etc.

accommodation address   **temporary mailing address**
Used in Britain chiefly by persons who do not wish to reveal their home address. See also ***poste restante.***

according to Cocker   **according to best usage**
Inf. Cocker was a popular 17th-century writer on arithmetic. This expression is synonymous with *according to Hoyle,* a term used in both countries. Hoyle was an 18th-century authority on card games.

account, *n.*   **1. bill**
                                        2. charge account
1. Notification of an amount owing.
2. The term *charge account* is not used in Britain.

accountant. See **chartered accountant; commission agent; turf accountant.**

accumulator, *n.*   **battery**
Battery is now commonly used in Britain, but *accumulator* was long generally reserved for *storage battery. Accumulator* is also used to describe a type of horse-racing bet.

act for   **represent**
Lawyers, accountants, and other professionals in Britain *act for,* rather than *represent,* their clients.

action man   *Inf.* SEE COMMENT
A man who enjoys dangerous, physically demanding pastimes. The name comes from a toy figurine popular in the 1960s and 1970s.

action replay   **instant replay**
TV term.

actually, *adv.*   **as a matter of fact; to tell the truth**
A pause-word, like *well* . . . , *you see* . . . , etc; perhaps intended to lend importance to what follows, but in reality meaningless. Some Britons use it repeatedly in flowing discourse. Sometimes *actually* is also used in mock-modesty: *Are you the*

champion? Well yes, I am, actually. It can also be used in veiled reproof: *Actually, we don't do things that way.* Here the idea is *since you force me to say it.*

Adam and Eve, *v.t, Rhyming slang.*   **believe**
I don't Adam and Eve it.

adapter, *n.*   **multiple plug**
A double or triple (perhaps even more) plug transforming a single wall outlet into a multiple one so that two or several lamps, appliances, etc., can be plugged into the one outlet.

A.D.C.   **time and charges**
These letters stand for *Advice of Duration and Charges,* and are what one says to the long-distance operator in order to learn the cost of a call. Now seldom used, since few calls go through the operator. As in America, A.D.C. also means 'aide-de-camp.'

admass, *n.* Also written **ad-mass.**   **mass-media public**
(Accent on the first syllable.) The gullible section of the public (mass) that is most easily influenced by mass-media advertising (ads); especially persons addicted to TV.

Admiralty, *n.*   SEE COMMENT
The Department of the Navy in the Government, now merged in the Ministry of Defence.

adopt, *v.t.*   **nominate**
At caucuses and conventions Americans *nominate* candidates who *run* for election. The British nominate *potential candidates* and finally *adopt* the ones who are going to **stand** for election.

adversarial, *adj.*   **adversary**
A legal term. An *adversarial* (*adversary,* in America) proceeding is a lawsuit involving actual opposing interests, as opposed to a request for a declaratory judgment.

advert, *n.*   *Inf.* **ad**
Inf. (Accent on the first syllable.) Informal abbreviation of *advertisement.*

advice of receipt; advice of delivery. See **recorded delivery.**

advocate, *n.*   SEE COMMENT
An *advocate* is a Scottish **barrister.** It is also the title of a lawyer in some of the Channel Islands, reflecting the influence of the French, who call a lawyer an *avocat.*

aeger, *n.*   **sick note**
(Pronounced EE'-JER or EYE'-GHER.) *Aeger* is Latin for 'sick'; the adjective is here used as a noun, in some university circles. When the student is too sick to take an examination, he is given an *aegrotat* (Latin for 'he is sick'; pronounced EE'-GRO-TAT or EE-GRO'-TAT, the latter being the correct stress in Latin), an official certification of illness testifying that he is unable to attend lectures or take an exam. The same word designates a degree granted a student who has completed all other requirements but was too ill to take the final exams.

aerial, *n.* **antenna**
The British don't use *antenna* except as applied to insects, or figuratively in the plural.

aerodrome, *n.* **airfield**

aeroplane, *n.* **airplane**
Airplane is now just as common.

aesthete, *n.* *Slang.* **grind**
Inf. A special university term, somewhat pejorative, for a studious student; the very antithesis of a **hearty,** in America a *jock.* See **Appendix I.B.1.**

affiliation order SEE COMMENT
In a paternity suit, an order of the court requiring the putative father to support or contribute to the support of the child.

afters, *n. pl.* **dessert**
Inf. Thus: *What's for afters?*

after the break SEE COMMENT
This is the dreadful pronouncement made by British **newsreaders** on stations that allow commercials, and is the equivalent of "after these messages" or words to that effect, *message* being one of the most hateful of euphemisms, foreshadowing a recital of all the advantages of the products one cannot live without.

against the collar **tough going**
Inf. One meaning of *collar* is the roll around a horse's neck. This meaning gives rise to the colloquial phrases *against the collar* and *collar-work,* both of which indicate *uphill effort.*

agency, *n.* SEE COMMENT
A special usage, in signs seen at service stations all over Britain. It means that trucks can fill up at a station displaying that sign and have the fuel billed directly to the company owning or operating the truck. The driver simply signs a form, and no money changes hands.

agent, *n.* See **commission agent; estate agent; turf accountant.**

aggro, *n.* **1. aggravation**
2. aggressiveness
3. trouble
1. *Slang.* In the sense of deliberate 'exasperation,' 'annoyance.'
2. *Slang.* A tendency to violence, a readiness to boil over and commit violent acts on the slightest, if any, provocation, e.g., the emotional imbalance that causes the rioting of a **football** (soccer) crowd or the destructive tendencies of a gang.
3. Violent disturbance, especially in a public place; *the gang went out looking for aggro.*

A.G.M. See **Annual General Meeting.**

agree, *v.t.* **agree to; concede**
Except when used intransitively (*You say it's a good painting: I agree; You want $100 for that old car? I agree*), this verb is followed in American usage by *that* (*I*

agree that it is so) or by *to (I agree to your terms; I agree to go away)*. Those constructions are equally common in Britain, but one British usage not found in America is *agree* followed by a direct object, where Americans would use *concede, admit, accept,* or *approve of,* e.g., *I agree the liability for income tax; I agree the claim for damages; I agree the price; I agree your proposal; I agree your coming tomorrow.* There is a curious relationship between the British uses of *agree* and *accept,* which are more or less the reverse of the American uses, since *agree* is used in Britain where an American would normally say *accept (I agree the liability for damages)* and *accept* is used there in the way in which Americans use *agree (I accept that he is an honest man).*

agreed verdict   **consent decree**
Legal term.

agricultural labourer   **farmhand**

agricultural show   **state or county fair**
An *agricultural show* represents roughly the same aspect of British life as an American *state fair* or *county fair.* The Tunbridge Wells Agricultural Show serves about the same cultural and economic purposes as, for example, the Kansas State Fair or the Great Barrington Fair in Massachusetts.

air bed. See **li-lo.**

air hostess, *n.*   **stewardess**
Performing the same functions as her American counterpart—often willingly, sometimes grudgingly.

airy-fairy, *adj.*   *approx.* **fey**
Inf. In its original sense *airy-fairy* meant 'light and delicate.' It has now acquired a disparaging meaning: 'insubstantial,' 'superficial,' perhaps with connotations of whimsy, artiness, pretentiousness: *This New Age medicine is a lot of airy-fairy nonsense.* There would appear to be no precise American colloquial counterpart.

aisle, *n.*   **church aisle**
Americans use *aisle* generically. In Britain, out of context, it refers to churches, although it is now more and more being used for shops and theaters as well.

albert, *n.*   **watch chain**
Also called an *Albert chain;* if used alone, the *A* drops to lower case. Based on the sartorial habits of Queen Victoria's Prince Consort.

Alcopop, *n.*   **flavored alcoholic beverage**
Inf. A mixture of liquor and water, fruit juices and (sometimes) flavourings, sold in bottles or cans, usually at a strength around that of beer.

A-levels, *n. pl.*   SEE COMMENT
Tests on specific subjects, usually taken by students in the final two years of secondary school education. They are often required for admission to a university. Oxford and Cambridge have additional examinations of their own, as do several other universities.

alight, *v.i.*   **dismount**
Seen in notices at railroad stations and bus stops in Britain.

all in   **1.** *Inf.* **everything thrown in**
                                        2. *Inf.* **anything goes; no holds barred**
                                                                  3. exhausted
1. *Inf. All included,* as in, *The holiday cost us £100 all in* (i.e., travel, **accommoda-tion,** and all other expenses included).
2. *Inf.* As in the phrase, peculiar to American ears, *all-in wrestling* in which the gladiators are permitted to do just about anything except resort to weapons.
3. Common to British and American vocabularies is the adverbial *all in,* meaning 'exhausted.'

all mod cons   SEE COMMENT
All modern conveniences. Originally used by real estate agents to describe any accommodation that has all the expected fixtures and fittings. Now used more widely, often in a jocular or ironic way. See also **amenities.**

all my eye and Betty Martin!   *Inf.* **baloney!**
Inf. Various derivations proposed. The most likely would seem to be *Mihi beata mater* (which appears to be Latin for something like 'Grant to me, blessed Mother'). According to one legend, it was a far from perfect rendition of an invocation to St. Martin, a patron saint of soldiers.

allotment, *n.*   **small rented garden area**
Owned by the local council, and rented to local residents for the raising of vegetables for personal consumption and flowers for personal delight.

all over the shop   *Inf.* **in a mess; in wild disorder**
Inf. His explanation was all over the shop!

allowance, *n.*   **deduction**
Income tax terminology, referring to the amounts allowed per taxpayer, dependent, etc.

all-round, *adj.*   **all-around**

all-rounder, *n.*   SEE COMMENT
A sports term, especially in cricket, denoting a versatile player; in cricket, one good at bowling, fielding, and batting.

all Sir Garnet   *Slang.* **well done!**
An old-fashioned British army phrase. Sir Garnet Wolseley (1833–1913) was a famous military man who wrote the *Soldier's Pocket Book.* Anything described as *all Sir Garnet* is O.K., done by the book.

all the best   **best wishes**
Used at the end of a telephone conversation or e-mail or another informal communication, by way of saying *goodbye and good luck.*

all the fun of the fair   **great fun**
Inf. More damn fun! Often used ironically to describe a tight situation.

almshouse, *n.*   **old people's home**
Originally a charitable home for the poor, the *almshouse* in Britain is today a sub-
sidized home for old folk who live in small apartments at nominal rent, which
often includes a garden **allotment.**

alpha (beta, gamma, *etc*)**.**   **A (B, C, etc.)**
Symbols sometimes used by teachers in marking grades at universities generally. The Greek letters are preferred in some institutions. A first-class mark in an
examination is *alpha*. See also **query, 2.**

Alsatian, *n.*   **German shepherd dog**

aluminium, *n.*   **aluminum**

amber (of traffic lights), *adj.*   **yellow**

ambulance, *n.*   SEE COMMENT
Although there are ambulances in Britain similar to those seen in America, the same
term is applied to small buses that are used, under the National Health system, to
transport ambulatory patients, free of charge, to and from doctors' offices or hospitals for visits. These are sit-up affairs, for those who have no car or who, for financial
or physical reasons, can't manage with regular public transportation.

amenities, *n. pl.*   **conveniences**
Referring to household facilities. (*Amenities* in the American sense is *civilities* in
Britain.) The American term *conveniences* is also used and is found in the abbre-
viated phrase, **all mod cons,** which stands for *all modern conveniences.* Another
British equivalent is **offices.**

American cloth   **oilcloth**
Rare

amongst, *prep.*   **among**
Not quite so common as *whilst* for *while.* But also given as *among.*

and pigs might fly!   *Inf.* **Yeah, sure!**
Inf. Expression of disbelief in response to a prediction, also translated as "Never."

angel on horseback   **oyster wrapped in bacon**
Served on toast in the English version. The Scottish version substitutes smoked
haddock for the oyster. See also the less glamorous **devil on horseback.**

anglepoise lamp   **adjustable reading lamp**
A trademark. The term describes a table lamp with a base built of a series of
hinged arms with springs and counter-weights that adjust the height, beam
direction, and so on.

Annual General Meeting   **Annual Meeting of Shareholders**
                                                              (Stockholders)
Usually abbreviated *A.G.M.* What the British call an *Extraordinary General Meeting*
is called a *Special Meeting of Shareholders (Stockholders)* in America.

anorak, *n.*   **1. light waterproof jacket**
                                                    Slang. **2.** SEE COMMENT
1. An Eskimo word, stressed on the first syllable.
2. a socially awkward person who is obsessive about a particular hobby or subject (e.g. bird-watching or wine connoisseurship). A mild pejorative, often used jocularly.

another pair of shoes   **a horse of a different color**

another place   SEE COMMENT
This is the way the House of Commons refers to the House of Lords, and it works the other way around. Incidentally, *another place* was a Victorian euphemism for *hell*.

answer, *v.i.*   **work**
Inf. In phrases indicating inappropriateness: *It won't answer; It didn't answer.* For example, a person reads an advertisement of the houses-for-rent variety, goes to investigate, finds the situation unsatisfactory, and in answer to a friend's question says, *It didn't answer.* An American might have said, *It wasn't for me.*

answerphone, *n.*   **answering machine**

ante-natal, *adj.*   **prenatal**

anti-clockwise, *adj., adv.*   **counterclockwise**

Any more for the Skylark?   SEE COMMENT
Rare. When mother was a girl, people went to resorts like Southend and Blackpool and took rides on the little excursion boats, one of which was bound to be called the SKYLARK. As the SKYLARK was ready to depart, with a few empty seats, the attendant would cry out, *Any more for the Skylark?* This became a cliché in Britain which eventually became applicable to any situation where a last summons for action was indicated.

apartment, *n.*   **single room**
Especially in a stately home.

APEX fare   **cheap train fare**
Requiring advance purchase, and standing for Advanced Purchase Excursion.

appeal, *n.*   **fund-raising campaign**
One is frequently asked to contribute to the *appeal* of, e.g., Canterbury Cathedral for construction repair, or Ely Cathedral to fight the woodworm. *Appeals* also issue from hospitals, schools, charitable institutions and other worthy causes.

apples and pears, *Rhyming slang.*   **stairs**

appointed to a cure of souls, *Inf.*   **made vicar**

approach, *v.t.*   **service**
A euphemism hard to match. It manages to obscure what a ram does to a ewe under appropriate conditions.

approved school   **reform school**
See also **Borstal.** Little used

A.R. See **recorded delivery.**

archies, *n.*   *Slang.* **ack-ack**
Slang. World War I for *anti-aircraft guns. Ack-ack* became World War II slang in both countries for both the guns and the fire.

argue the toss   *Slang.* **squabble**
Slang. Dispute needlessly.

argy-bargy   **a dispute**
Inf. A noisy wrangle. Also used as a verb: *I grew accustomed to hearing them argy-bargy.*

Army and Navy Stores   SEE COMMENT
Army and Navy store in America is a generic term for a type of shop selling low-priced work and sports clothes, sports and camping equipment, and the like. In London, it is the name of a particular department store selling general merchandise. Usually shortened to *Army and Navy.*

arrow, *n.*   *Inf.* **a single dart**

arrows, *n.*   *Inf.* **the game of darts**
Let's go to the pub and play some arrows.

arse, *n.*   *Slang.* **ass**
Slang. The anatomical, not the zoological designation. Neither term is in polite use.

arsed   *Slang.* **bothered**
Usually used in the negative sense, as in *I can't be arsed to do the laundry today.*

arse over tip, *Slang.*   *Inf.* **head over heels**

arsy-tarsy, *Slang.*   *Slang.* **ass-backwards**

arsy-versy, *adv., Slang.*   **vice versa; backwards**

arterial road   **main road**
Synonymous with *major road* and *trunk road.*

articled clerk. See **articles.**

articles, *n. pl.*   **written agreement**
Usually expanded to *articles of agreement.* A common use, in this sense, is in the term *articles of apprenticeship.* As a verb, to *article* is to *bind by articles of apprenticeship,* from which we get the term *articled clerk,* meaning 'apprentice.' That is the common term in the legal profession in Britain (see **clerk, 1**). When one's apprenticeship is ended, one *comes out of articles.* Accountants, too, have *articled clerks,* who, like those in law offices, are on their way to gaining full professional status.

articulated lorry   **trailer truck**
The verb *articulate* has been used so widely as an intransitive verb meaning 'speak clearly' that most people have forgotten that it is also a transitive verb meaning 'connect by joints.' In truck drivers' vernacular, often shortened to *artic* (accented on the second syllable).

ASBO *n.*   SEE COMMENT
Acronym for Anti-Social Behaviour Order. A legal order issued by a magistrate, which places restrictions on someone's movements, in order to prevent further anti-social behaviour from that person. ASBOs are intended to serve as an alternative to harsher punishment, but failure to comply can result in a fine or imprisonment.

as bright as a new penny, *Inf.*   *Inf.* **as bright as a button**

as cold as charity   **biting cold**
Inf. Often applied to human attitudes, the allusion being to the coldness of the administrative procedures of many charitable organizations. See also **monkey-freezing.**

as dead as mutton   *Inf.* **as dead as a doornail**
Quite dead.

Asdic, *n.*   **sonar**
Stands for *Anti-Submarine Detection Investigation Committee.* Used in finding and locating submarines and submarine objects.

as dim as a Toc H lamp   *Inf.* **thick-headed**
Inf. Rare. Toc H (initials of Talbot House) is an organization for social service and fellowship; so called because it originated at Talbot House, a rest center for soldiers at Poperinghe, Belgium. Talbot House was named for Gilbert Talbot, who was killed in action in 1915. In front of each Toc H location hangs a lamp which is always dimly lit. Sometimes a sign with a lamp replaces the lamp itself. The *dim* in this phrase is short for *dim-witted. Toc* is the pronunciation of *t* in military signaling.

as easy as kiss your hand, *Inf.*   *Inf.* **as easy as pie**
Rare.

as from   **as of**
As from such-and-such a date, e.g., *The fares will be increased by 10 pence as from December 9.*

(the) Ashes, *n. pl.*   SEE COMMENT
Inf. This is a symbolic term meaning 'victory' in test cricket with Australia (see **Test Match**). Thus we have the expressions *win the Ashes, retain (or hold) the Ashes, bring back* (or *win back* or *regain) the Ashes,* etc., depending upon circumstances. When England and Australia play in a test series for *the Ashes* no physical trophy changes hands. Yet after the term came into use, the abstraction did materialize into a pile of physical ashes which are contained in an urn which is in turn contained in a velvet bag, now resting permanently at Lord's Cricket Ground in London.

as near as dammit   *Inf.* **just about**

Slang. Almost exactly; give or take a bit; very close! We'll get there at seven, as near as dammit. Or, *Can we make it in two hours? As near as dammit.* The origin of the phrase is *as near as 'damn it' is to swearing.*

as near as makes no odds   *Inf.* **just about**
Inf. Sometimes *as near as makes no matter.* Either is the equivalent of *give or take a bit.* For example: *I'll get there at nine, as near as makes no odds,* i.e., so near that it makes no difference.

as nice as ninepence   *Inf.* **as nice as pie**
Inf. Unexpectedly pleasant and helpful.

as safe as a bank, *Inf.*   **perfectly safe**

as safe as houses, *Inf.*   **perfectly safe**

assessor, *n.*   **adjuster**
One who appraises the value of property in an insurance claim.

assistant, *n.*   **clerk; salesman; saleslady**
Assistant, in this British use, is short for *shop assistant,* which usually means a 'salesperson' or 'salesclerk,' but can also mean in a more general sense a 'shop attendant' who may not be there to sell you anything but to help out generally.

assisting the police   **held for questioning**
Sometimes *assisting in the inquiry.* These euphemisms are coupled with the practice of withholding names in newspaper reports until the persons involved are formally charged.

assizes, *n. pl.*   **court sessions**
The periodic sessions of the judges of the superior courts in each county of England and Wales for administering civil and criminal justice.

Association football (soccer). See football.

as soon as look at you, *Inf.*   *Inf.* **before you can say 'Jack Robinson'**

as soon as say knife, *Inf.*   *Inf.* **before you can say 'Jack Robinson'**
Also *before you can (could) say knife.*

assurance, *n.*   **(life) insurance**
Assurance, not insurance, is the usual term in Britain. The person or firm covered is *the assured,* and the insurance company is the *assurance society.* Insurance and insured are becoming increasingly common.

as under   **as follows**
For instance, at the top of a bill for services, one might see, *For professional services as under.*

as well   **too**
Mostly a matter of preference. *She speaks French as well* would be usual in Britain; *She speaks French, too,* would be more likely in America.

asylum seeker   **refugee**
The term covers those who are merely seeking employment as well as those fleeing hardship or oppression in their own country.

at best   SEE COMMENT
When a stockbroker takes instructions to buy or sell shares without receiving a stipulated price from the customer, he is undertaking to buy / sell 'at best.' In other words, at the market price prevailing at the time the transaction goes through.

at close of play   *Inf.* **when all is said and done**
Inf. More concretely, this phrase can refer to the end of a certain period or to the conclusion of a situation: *Let me have the memorandum by close of play on Wednesday.* One of many expressions taken over from cricket. See also **at the end of the day.**

at half-cock   *Inf.* **half-cocked**
Inf. As in the expression *go off at half-cock,* meaning 'take action when only partially ready.'

athletics, *n. pl.*   **sports**
Athlete, though used in the broad sense, generally connotes participation in track and field. In a British school one goes *in* for *athletics,* rather than *out* for *sports.*

at risk   **in danger**
E.g., *If we let this slip by, the whole project will be at risk.*

at the crunch   *Inf.* **in the clutch**
Inf. When the chips are down.

at the end of the day   **when all is said and done**
Expressing the ultimate effect or result of foregoing activity or discussion: *Large housing units may be more efficient, but at the end of the day people want their separate homes. Hard feelings were expressed by both sides, but at the end of the day, they parted friends.* See also **at close of play.**

at the side of   *Inf.* **alongside; beside**
Inf. Used in odious comparisons: *She's ugly at the side of her cousin Betty.*

attract, *v.t.*   **involve; entail; incur**
A British bank, answering a customer's letter about its rendering a certain service, wrote: *The work on your enquiry will attract a small charge.* Also used in tax terminology: *This stock will attract capital gains tax rather than income tax. Those wishing to pass on capital to their families without attracting any liability to tax. .-.-.-* (Note *to* tax rather than *for* tax; see **Appendix I.A.1.** on preposition usage in Britain.) In this last example, *incur* may be a preferable equivalent and the author of the tax advice might have been better advised to use the word *incurring,* because it is the thing or operation which *attracts* the tax, not the person.

aubergine, *n.*   **eggplant**

au fait   *Inf.* **conversant**
Fairly common in Britain; sometimes used in America: *he wanted to be made au fait with our condition.*

Aunt Edna   *Inf.* **little old lady from Dubuque**
Inf. Aunt Edna is the invented prototypically provincial nice old lady with whom one must be very careful when suggesting reading matter or theatrical entertainment. See also **Wigan.**

Auntie, *n.*   SEE COMMENT
Slang. The affectionate nickname for the BBC, synonymous with **the Beeb.** *Auntie* used to be short for *Auntie Times,* meaning *The Times* (of London).

Auntie Times. See **Auntie.**

Aunt Sally   **1. target**
                                                   2. *Inf.* **trial balloon**
1. *Inf.* An *Aunt Sally* is a *butt,* an object of ridicule. The term is derived from the carnival game in which one throws balls at a figure known as *Aunt Sally.*
2. *Inf.* Since *Aunt Sally* is something set up to be knocked down, it has acquired the meaning of 'trial balloon,' a proposal submitted for criticism.

au pair   **1.** SEE COMMENT.
                                 2. giving services for board and lodging
1. (Pronounced OH-PAIR.) This term from French applies generically to service bartering arrangements between two parties, with little or no money changing hands. Two professionals might thus make an *au pair* arrangement. British families also exchange children with foreign families in order to broaden the children's experience, this being another type of *au pair* arrangement.
2. The term is heard most often in the expression *au pair girl* (often called just an *au pair*) and refers to the British custom of a family giving a home to a girl from abroad who helps with the children and the housekeeping. Becoming common in the United States.

autocue, *n.*   **TelePrompTer**
Essential devices enabling news-readers (British) and anchorpersons (American) to do their jobs.

awkward, *adj.*   **troublesome; annoying**
Often used in Britain to mean 'difficult,' in the sense of 'hard to deal with,' referring to people who are not easy to get along with.

B

baby-watcher, *n.*   **babysitter**
And *baby-watching* is *babysitting.* **Cf. child-minder.** Obsolete.

back bacon   *approx.* **Canadian bacon**
Back bacon comprises the loin (as in Canadian bacon) attached to a strip of very fatty back meat.

back bench, *n.*   SEE COMMENT
Occupied by Members of Parliament not entitled to a seat on the front benches, which are occupied by ministers (cabinet members) and other members of the government and oppostion leaders. See also **front bench; cross bench.**

backhander *Slang.*   **graft**
Headline *Evening Standard* (London) June 14, 1973:
"'Corruption' trial hears of payments to officials: Ex-Mayor Tells of Backhanders to Councillors." **Councillors** *are councilmen,* demonstrating that Americans did not invent payments under tables.

backlog, *n.*   **overstock**
To a British businessman, *backlog* can mean 'overstocked inventory,' an unhappy condition, as well as a heartening accumulation of orders waiting to be filled.

back passage, *n.*   *Inf.* **rectum**

back-room boy. See **boffin.**

back slang   SEE COMMENT
Slang created by spelling words backwards, a British pastime. Example: *ecilop* is back slang for 'police' and the origin of the slang noun *slop* meaning 'police.'

back to our muttons   *Inf.* **back to business**
Slang. After an extended digression during a serious discussion: *Well now, back to our muttons,* i.e., 'Let's get back to the subject.'

backwardation, *n.*   **penalty for delayed delivery**
A London Stock Exchange term. It consists of a percentage of the selling price payable by the seller of shares for the privilege of delaying delivery of the shares.

backwoodsman, *n.*   SEE COMMENT
Inf. The literal use of this word in Britain is the same as the American an *uncouth person.* Figuratively, a *peer* who rarely, if ever, attends meetings of the House of Lords.

bad hat, *Inf.*   *Inf.* **bad egg**
Bad egg is now also heard in Britain to mean an 'immoral person.'

bad patch   *Inf.* **rough time**

18

Inf. When things are not going well with someone, the British say that he is in or going through a *bad patch;* in America he would be described as having a *rough time* (of it). For other idiomatic uses of *patch,* see **patch** and **not a patch on.**

bad show!   **1.** *Inf.* **tough luck!**
                                                                          2. *Slang.* **lousy!**
1. *Inf.* A show of sympathy.
2. *Inf.* A rebuke for a poor performance. *A ghastly show* is a *terrible mess.* See also **good show!**

bag a brace. See **duck.**

bagging-hook, *n.*   **small scythe**
A rustic term synonymous with **swop.**

bagman, *n.*   **traveling salesman**
This old-fashioned term does not have the abusive meaning of *graft collector,* as in America. In Britain synonymous with **commercial traveller.**

bags, *n. pl.*   **slacks**
Inf. Oxford *bags* were a 1920s style characterized by the exaggerated width of the trouser legs.

bags I!   *Slang.* **Dibs on . . . ! I dibsy! I claim!**
Schoolboy slang. Sometimes *I bag!* or *I Bags!* or *baggy!* or *bagsy! Bags, first innings!* is another variant. *First innings* in this context means a 'first crack at something.' See **first innings.** Examples: *Baggy, no washing up!* (see **wash up**) which would be shouted by a youngster trying to get out of doing the dishes, or *I bag the biggest one!* proclaimed by one of a group of children offered a number of apples or candies of unequal size. **Fains I!** is the opposite of *Bags I!*

bags of . . .   *Inf.* **piles of . . .**
Inf. Usually in the phrase *bags of money.*

bail. See **wicket; up stumps.**
A cricket term.

bailiff, *n.*   **1. sheriff's assistant**
                                                                   2. estate or farm manager
1. A British *bailiff* is one employed by a sheriff to serve legal papers, recover property to pay off debts, and make arrests. An American *bailiff* is a minor court functionary in the nature of a messenger, usher, etc.

bait, *n.*   *Slang.* **grub (food)**
Food that will entice a wild animal.

baked custard. See **custard.**

bakehouse, *n.*   **bakery**
Where bread is baked, not sold. In Britain, a *bakery* is a place where bread and other baked goods are sold.

bakers knee   **knock-knee**
Inward curvature of the legs, once said to have been caused by the constrained
position bakers had to take when kneading bread.

balaam, *n.*   *Slang.* **fillers**
Newspaper slang. Miscellaneous items to fill newspaper space; set in type and kept
in readiness, in a *Balaam-box.* The prophet Balaam could not meet the requirements of Balak, king of Moab, when commanded to curse the Israelites, and the
curse became a blessing instead (Num. 22–24). Balaam thus became the prototype
of the disappointing prophet or ineffective ally. Obsolete.

Balaclava, *n.*   **woolen helmet**
Short for *Balaclava helmet,* which is made of wool and pulled over the head, leaving
the face exposed. Balaclava was the site of an important battle of the Crimean War.
That war made two other contributions to fashion; the sleeve named for Lord Raglan, who occupied the town of Balaclava, and the sweater which was the invention
of the seventh Earl of Cardigan, commander of the famous Light Brigade.

ball and chain *Slang, derog.*   **girlfriend or wife**

ballocks, *n. pl.*   *Vulgar.* **balls**
Vulgar. Also bollochs. Probably the origin of the phrase *all ballocksed* (also *bollixed*)
up, a variation on *all balled up.*

balls, *n. pl.*   **1.** *Slang.* **crap (nonsense)**
                                                              2. *Inf.* **mess**
1. *Slang.* This word is used by itself, as a vulgar expletive, in America. In Britain
it appears in expressions like *That's a lot of balls,* i.e., *stuff and nonsense.*
2. *Slang.* To make a *balls* of something is to make a *mess* of it, to *louse it up.* A variant of *balls* in this sense is *balls-up.* The familiar expressions to *ball up* (a situation)
and *all balled up* are echoes of this usage. Synonymous with *balls* and *balls-up* in
this sense are **cock** and **cock-up.**

(The) ball's in your court   *Inf.* **It's up to you**
Inf. The ball's in your court means 'It is your move now.' A variant is *The ball's at
your feet.*

balls to the wall   **at a disadvantage**
He had me balls to the wall over that contact.

bally, *adj., adv.*   *Slang.* **damned**
Slang. (Rhymes with SALLY.) Expressing disgust, like **bloody.** But it can, by a kind
of reverse English, express the exact opposite, i.e., satisfaction, as in: *We bet on
three races and won the bally lot. Bally* is virtually obsolete.

balmy, *adj.*   **mild, soothing**

band, *n.*   **bracket**
Tax term.

B & B   SEE COMMENT
Inf. Short for *Bed and Breakfast.* Sight seen on British roadsides pointing the way,
most often, to pleasant and inexpensive lodgings and a satisfying meal next

morning, including (if you are lucky) amiable chatter. Increasingly seen in the U.S.

bandit-proof, *adj.*   **bulletproof**
Bulletproof is also used in Britain.

bandy-legged, *adj.*   *Inf.* **bowlegged**
Inf. Referring to persons, and occasionally used also in America. When describing furniture, the British use *bowlegged.*

bang, *adv.*   **absolutely**
"She was *bang* wrong." See also **bang on.**

banger, *n.*   **1. sausage**
                                                                        2. *Slang.* **jalopy**
                                                                        3. firecracker
1. *Slang.* Derived from the tendency of sausages to burst open with a *bang* in the frying pan. See also **slinger.**
2. *Slang.* Derived from the backfire emitted by old heaps.
3. *Schoolboy slang.*

bang off, *Slang*   *Inf.* **pronto**
Immediately; right now.

bang on, *vi, v.t*   *Inf.* **right on the nose**
                                                            Slang. **talk incessantly (about)**
1. *Slang.* Exactly as planned or predicted. Literally, *bang on target,* of World Wars I and II vintage. Synonymous with **dead on.** See also **bang; dead on; spot-on.**
2. *I couldn't stand the way he kept banging on. Stop banging on about the government!*

bang to rights   *Slang.* **red-handed**
You might often hear someone say, *They got him bang to rights.*

bang-up, *adj.*   **swell**
Fine, first-rate: *"They did a bang-up job."*

(the) Bank, *n.*   SEE COMMENT
Always capitalized, it means the 'Bank of England,' Britain's central bank, which presides over the financial system as a whole.

banker's draft, *n.*   **bank check**
A check made out to a creditor by the debtor's bank. Considered to be more secure than a personal check and therefore perceived as cash and more acceptable.

bank holiday, *n.*   **legal holiday**
Also used as an adjective, as in *bank-holiday Monday. Bank holidays* were introduced in 1871.

bank note. See note.

bant, *v.i.*   **diet**
To *bant* is to *diet*. Dr. W. Banting, who died in 1878, originated a treatment for overweight based on abstinence from sugar, starch, etc. His name became and remained the name of this dieting procedure. Very rare today.

bap, *n.*   **bun**
Somewhat larger than the customary American hamburger bun. Originated in Scotland and the North Country; now common in other areas of the country. The roll is slightly sweet, large enough to be cut in strips for toasting, and usually dusted with flour after baking.

bar, *n.* See **lounge bar; pub.**

bar, *v.t.*   *approx.* **loathe**
Slang. When you *bar* something, you exclude it from consideration.

bar, *prep.*   **but; except**
Heard especially in *bar none,* meaning excepting none.
  A special usage is found in horse racing, where, after the favorites' odds are posted, they put up an entry headed BAR, followed by odds, e.g., BAR 20/1. Here, *bar* is short for *bar the favorites* and means that each of the remaining horses in the rest of the field is at 20 to 1. Sometimes one sees *20/1 bar one* or, *20/1 bar two* (or *three,* etc.) which means the field are all at 20 to 1, and you then have to inquire about the *one* or *two* (or *three,* etc.) who are not in the field, i.e., the favorites, and get their odds from those in charge.

bar billiards. See **billiard-saloon.**

Barbour jacket, *n.*   SEE COMMENT
A waxed, waterproof jacket often worn by people in the countryside. Named after the inventor, John Barbour, whose drapery business supplied oilskins and other protective clothing to sailors and fishermen.

bargain, *n.*   **stock market transaction**
The ominous phrase *unable to comply with their bargains,* usually found in newspaper and radio reports of bankruptcies (especially in the matter of stock exchange firms), comes out in America as *unable to meet their debts.* However it's said, it's extremely bad news.

barge-pole, *n.*   **ten-foot pole**
A Briton who wishes to express an aversion toward another person or a business proposal *would not touch it or him with a barge-pole.* Another object left unused by the British in the same connection is a *pair of tongs.*

barking, *adj.*   *Inf.* **mad**
Short for 'barking mad.' *You can tell she's barking just by looking at her eyes.*

barman   **bartender**
The British also say *bartender.* The female British counterpart is a *barmaid.*

barmcake, *n.*   *Slang.* **an idiot**

barmy, *adj.*   *Inf.* **balmy**
Slang. Off one's rocker.

barney *n., Slang.*   squabble

baronet, *n.*   **(hereditary) knight**
Member of the lowest hereditary order. *Sir* precedes the name; *Baronet* (usually abbreviated to *Bart.,* sometimes *Bt.*) follows it: *Sir John Smith, Bart.* See also **Dame; Lady; K.; Lord.**

baron of beef, *n.*   **see comment**
Two sirloins in one roast, a *baron* being much bigger than a simple *Sir.*

barrack   **1.** *Slang.* **boo**
                                                                   2. root for
1. *Slang.* To demonstrate noisily in a public place, like a stadium or a theater, against a team, a player, or a performer; to *jeer;* to *hoot.*
2. *Slang.* In the proper context, *barrack* can mean just the opposite, i.e., to 'root for' a team or player.

barrage, *n.*   **dam**
The two countries share the other more common meanings, military and figurative, of this word, but even in those cases the British accent the first syllable, as they do in *garage,* and soften the *g* to ZH. In the special British meaning of a 'dam in a watercourse,' the accent stays the same but the *g* sound is hardened to *J,* as in *jump.*

barrage balloon   SEE COMMENT
A large balloon tied to the ground by ropes. Used by the military during World War I and World War II to deter low-flying aircraft.

barrel, *n.*
Weight unit. See **Appendix II.C.1.a.**

barrier, *n.*   **gate**
Railroad term meaning the 'gate' through which one passes to and from the platform. A guard standing at the *barrier* collects your ticket (or glances at it again if it is a *season ticket* or round-trip ticket) as you leave. Occasionally, a *ticket inspector* will range through the compartments to check or sell the tickets.

barrister, *n.*   **trial lawyer**
A *barrister* is also known as *counsel.* Apart from serving as *trial lawyers, barristers* are resorted to by **solicitors** (*general practitioners*) for written expert opinions in special fields of the law. The *solicitor* is the person the client retains. The *solicitor* retains the *barrister* or *counsel.* The *solicitor* can try cases in certain inferior courts. The *barrister-solicitor* dichotomy is a legal institution in Britain, though less rigid now than it once was. It exists in practice in America, where, technically, any attorney may try cases, but most practitioners resort to trial counsel in litigated matters. See also **brief; called to the bar; chambers; solicitor.**

barrow, *n.*   **pushcart**
This word means 'pushcart' when referring to a street vendor. In gardening, it is the equivalent of *wheelbarrow,* which is also used in Britain. See also **trolley. Pushcart** is sometimes used in Britain to mean 'baby carriage'; but usually means 'handcart.'

Barry White   **rubbish**
Rhyming slang. Rhyming slang for shite (shit). Barry White was a soul singer famous in the 1970s.

Bart. See **Baronet.**

base rate   **prime rate**
Banking term.

bash, *n., v.t.*   *Inf.* **bang (hit)**
1. *Inf.* All too common in the extremely unpleasant terms *Paki-bashing* and *wogbashing.* See **Paki** and **wog.** See also the amusing usage of the word in **have a bash at.** The term is also used, as in America, for a party.
2. a big party

basin, *n.*   **sink**
Basin is used when referring to the fixture in any room other than the kitchen. **Sink** is used in Britain when referring to a kitchen fixture. Sometimes *wash-basin.*

basket, *n.*   *Slang.* **bastard**
Slang. A euphemism, especially when addressing someone, and in the phrase *little basket,* describing a particularly naughty child.

bat.   SEE COMMENT
1. See **carry one's bat; off one's own bat; play a straight bat; batsman.**
2. Ping-Pong paddle

bat first   **go first**
Inf. Start the ball rolling; a term borrowed from cricket. Synonymous with **take first knock.**

bath, *n., v.t., v.i.*   **1. bathtub**
                                                       2. bathe
1. In Britain, as in America, one can *take a bath,* although in Britain one usually *has,* rather than *takes,* a *bath.* One sits or soaks in the *bath* in Britain rather than in the *bathtub,* as in America.
2. As a verb, *bath* is used like *bathe* in America: one can *bath* the baby (give it a bath) or, simply *bath* (take a bath). See also **bathe.**

bath bun   SEE COMMENT
A type of *sweet bun* which is filled with small seedless raisins called **sultanas** and candied citrus rinds, and has a glazed top studded with coarse grains of white sugar. The term occasionally has the slang meaning of 'old bag,' i.e., 'crone.'

bath chair, *n.*   **wheelchair**
Rare. Sometimes the *b* is capitalized, showing derivation from the city of Bath where they originated. Also called **invalid's chair** and **wheeled chair.**

bath chap   SEE COMMENT
A butcher's term for a portion from a pig's cheek served as a chop. *Chap* is a variant of *chop.* The pig's cheek is usually smoked or brined.

bathe, *n.*   **swim**
In Britain one *swims* in the sea, but one also *bathes* in the sea where Americans used to have a dip. See also **bath; front; sea.**

bathing costume   **bathing suit**
Sometimes *bathing dress* or *swimming costume*. *Bathing dress* used to be confined to
women's outfits. All these terms are rather old-fashioned. In Britain today *bathing
suit* and *swimsuit* are generally used and apply to either sex.

Bath Oliver   SEE COMMENT
A type of cookie or **biscuit** invented by Dr. W. Oliver (d. 1764) of the city of Bath.
It is about an eighth of an inch thick, dry and sweetish, and usually eaten with
cheese. See also **biscuit; digestive biscuits.**

batman, *n.*   **military officer's servant**

baton, *n.*   *Inf.* **billy; nightstick**
(Accent on the first syllable.) Also called a **truncheon.** Carried by policemen.

baton round, *n.*   **plastic bullet**

batsman, *n.*   **(baseball) batter**
Cricket vs. baseball. The British say *fielder* or *fieldsman,* but never *batter*. Generally,
batsman is shortened to *bat: Clive is a fine bat!* See also **bat first; carry one's bat; off
one's own bat; play a straight bat.**

Battersea box   SEE COMMENT
Cylindrical or bottle-shaped little enameled copper case with decorated hinged
top, typically for perfume, bonbons, etc. The authentic antique boxes were produced at Battersea, a part of London, for only a few years (1753–56) and are rare
and expensive. Good copies are being made today with traditional or new designs.

battle cruiser, *n.*   *Rhyming slang.* **boozer**

BBC English   SEE COMMENT
The reference is to the speech of the announcers which was once considered by
some to be the standard pronunciation of English. This situation has changed
since the BBC started employing announcers from different parts of the country,
especially the Midlands and Scotland, who don't necessarily speak *R.P.,* which
stands for **Received Pronunciation.** The label *BBC English* can, in certain contexts, be pejorative. To say of someone that he has a BBC accent may imply that
he has worked very hard to lose his own, indicating social climbing.
See also **Received Pronunciation.**

BBE, *abbrev.*   **Best Before End**
BBE is printed on food labels with the date indicating the point after which the
contents should no longer be eaten. Often referred to (erroneously) as the Sell By
date. In a well-run retailer, foods may be taken off the shelf before their BBE date.
In a badly run store, they may sit there when the date is long past—or have a false
BBE stamped over the correct one.

beach, *n.*   **gravel**
When a Briton wants to close up a ditch with *fill* or *gravel* he may use *beach*.
(When he wants to swim at the beach, he goes to the **sea** or *seaside*.) Rare nowa-
days; gravel is more commonly used.

beadle. See **bumble.**

beak, *n.*   1. schoolmaster
                                                                           2. magistrate
Slang. No precise American slang for either meaning.

beaker, *n.*   cup or mug
In both tongues, a *beaker* is also a favorite piece of glassware for chemists and
chemistry students. But in everyday parlance, a man who asked for a refill of his
cup or *mug* would be in a United States diner, not in Great Britain. Now rare.

bean, *n.*   1. *Inf.* cent
                                                                           2. *Slang.* pep
                                                                           3. *Slang.* hell
                                                                           4. *Slang.* guy; fellow
1. *Slang. I haven't a bean* means 'I'm broke.'
2. *Slang. Full of beans* means 'full of pep.'
3. *Slang.* To *give someone beans* is to *give someone hell* or to *punish him.*
4. *Slang.* In the expression *old bean*, rather outmoded and more likely to be
encountered in P. G. Wodehouse than in current speech.

bean-feast, *n.*   company picnic
Inf. Also called a **beano** *(slang).* Apparently, pork and beans (in Britain **beans
and bacon**) were considered an indispensable element of the annual company
celebration. The term has been extended to mean informally any merry occasion.

beano. See **bean-feast.**

beans and bacon   pork and beans

bearskin, *n.*   SEE COMMENT
High fur hat worn by the Brigade of **Guards;** much higher than a **busby.** Also any
article of clothing made of fur.

beastly, *adj., adv.*   1. unpleasant
                                                                           2. terribly (very)

beat up   *Inf.* **pick up**
Inf. In the sense of 'picking somebody up,' by prearrangement, to go somewhere
together. Thus an official might *beat up* recruits in a town in order to supply his
quota of new troops. You and I might also decide to *beat up some grub at the diner,*
that is, go to the railway dining-car for dinner.

beck, *n.*   brook

bed and breakfast   *Slang.* **wash sale**
Slang. In addition to its standard meaning of 'sleeping accommodations with
breakfast thrown in,' this term has a slang meaning in tax law, describing the sale
of securities to establish a tax loss followed by an immediate repurchase of the
same securities. This wash sale scheme was ruled out in American capital gain
taxation years ago, but not until April 1975 in Britain.

bed bath   sponge bath
Synonymous with **blanket bath.**

bed-board, *n.*   headboard

bedding plant, *n.*   annuals
Americans are occasionally surprised to see *bedding* advertised for sale in plant
nurseries. Also used as an adjective, as in *bedding plants.*

bed-sitter, *n.*   one-room apartment
Inf. Bed-sitting room, meaning a 'combination bedroom-living room'; usually
called *bedsit.* It does not have its own bathroom. If one is included, the unit
becomes a *studio.* Bedsits bespeak hard times, a transient's existence, poverty,
student and artist life. *Bedsit* is also a verb, meaning to 'occupy a bedsit.'

(the) Beeb, *n.*   SEE COMMENT
Inf. Affectionate nickname for the BBC, synonymous with **Auntie.**

beefburger, *n.*   hamburger

beefeater, *n.*   SEE COMMENT
A *warder* (guard) of the Tower of London. They are dressed in ornately decorated red uniforms and distinctively shaped top hats, dating from the fifteenth
century. For illustration (if you can't get to the Tower), see the label on a bottle
of a popular gin. The Tower of London, originally a royal fortress and palace,
became a prison and the *warders* thus became *jailers.* Nowadays, the Tower, a
huge collection of buildings housing many objects of historical interest, including the crown jewels, is crawling with tourists, and the *beefeaters* are its official
guides, knowledgeable and literate, who take groups around, dispensing history and wit in large doses.

beer and skittles   *Inf.* **a bed of roses**
Inf. Skittles being, literally, a ninepins game, *beer and skittles* would seem to be an
apt phrase for *fun and games, high amusement.* Almost always used in the negative:
Life is not all beer and skittles, or, *This job is not all beer and skittles.*

beetle, *n.*   bug

beetle-crusher, *n.*   large boot

beetle off   *Inf.* **take off**
Slang. Sometimes without the *off: It was warm, so we beetled (off) to the sea.*

beetroot, *n.*   beet(s)
The table vegetable known in America as *beet* is always called *beetroot* in Britain.
Beetroot does not add an *s* in the plural. *Beet,* in Britain, describes a related plant,
the root of which is white, not red, used for either the feeding of cattle or the making of sugar, and usually called *sugar beet.*

before you can say knife. See **as soon as say knife.**

beggar, *n.*   *Slang.* **guy; son of a gun**
Slang. The British use *beggar* literally, as we do. They also use it figuratively, in
a pejorative sense, to describe an unsavory character, as in, *a miserable beggar;* or
favorably, to convey admiration, as in, *a plucky little beggar.*

begging for it   SEE COMMENT
Slang. A reference to a person's supposed longing for sexual contact. *She was clearly begging for it.* See also **gagging for it.**

behindhand, *adj.*   **behind**
As in, *a maid behindhand with her housework.* Also *behindhand in my mortgage payments.*

Belisha beacon   **street crossing light**
(Pronounced BE-LEE'-SHA). Ubiquitous post topped by a flashing yellow globe to designate pedestrian crossing. They come in pairs, one on each side of the street, usually reinforced by stripes running across the road (see **zebra**).

bell, *n.*   *Inf.* **ring**
Slang. To *give someone a bell* is to *give him a ring,* i.e., call him up. Criminal and police cant.

below the salt. See **above the salt.**

belt, *n.*   **girdle**
Belt started out as a shortening of what in America would be known as a *garter belt* and in Britain as a *suspender belt* (see **braces; suspenders**). But then *belt* became generic for anything used by ladies to support bulging parts of the anatomy and the equivalent of the American term *girdle,* which is now the accepted term in Britain.

belted earl (*or* **knight)**   SEE COMMENT
Rare. All earls and knights are *belted,* i.e., theoretically they wear sword belts. These are affectionate terms, like *noble lord* (all lords are *noble*) and *gracious duke* (all dukes are *Your Grace.*)

belt up!   *Slang.* **shut up!**
Slang. The British also say **pack it up!** or **put a sock in it!**

be mum   **pour (the tea)**
Inf. Or the coffee. *I'll be mum* or, *Who's going to be mum?* evokes the image of cozy family groups, with a kindly, beaming mom officiating, but it is used jocularly in entirely male groups and even in such strongholds of masculinity as the wardroom of an oil tanker. Also, *be mother.*

bend, *n.*   **curve**
Referring to roads and used on road signs. A *double bend* is an *S curve.* For a different use, see **round the bend.**

bender, *n.*   **1.** SEE COMMENT
                                                           2. trailer truck
1. *Slang.* The old *sixpence.* See **Appendix II.A.**
2. *Slang.* Synonymous with *artic,* short slang for **articulated lorry.**

bend the elbow, *Slang.*   **to have an alcoholic drink**

benefit   **welfare**
Especially in the phrases *on benefit, living on benefit,* etc.

bent, *adj., Slang.*   **1. crooked; dishonest**
                                                                 2. homosexual

be quiet! *interj.*   *Inf.* **keep still!**
In this context, the British do not use *still* in the sense of 'keeping one's mouth
shut.' *Keep still* would be understood to mean 'Don't move.'

berk, *n.*   *approx. Slang.* **dope**
Slang. A fool who is also unpleasant. It is a shortening of *Berkeley* (pronounced
Barkley), which is short for *Berkeley Hunt,* which is rhyming slang for *cunt.*

berm, *n.*   **shoulder**
Of a road. Originally, a terrace between a moat and the bottom of a parapet. See
also **verge.**

Berwick cockles   SEE COMMENT
Not cockles at all, but shell-shaped mints made at Berwick-on-Tweed since 1801.

be sick   **throw up**
See **sick.**

besot, *v.t.*   **1. stupefy; muddle**
                                                                 2. infatuate
In America, the principal meaning of *besot* is to 'get (someone) drunk,' to 'intox-
icate,' so that *besotted* would usually be taken to mean 'drunk' or 'druken.' The
context of intoxicating liquor is absent in the British usage.

bespoke, *adj.*   **made to order; custom made**
Used in the phrases *bespoke clothes, bespoke tailor,* etc.

best   SEE COMMENT
Short for *best bitter,* the order you give in a pub when you want the best beer in
the house.

(the) best of British luck!   *Inf.* **lotsa luck!**
Inf. Said with heavy irony and implying very bad times ahead indeed.

best offer   **at the market**
When you want to tell your stockbroker to sell *at the market* in England, you tell
him to sell **best offer.** This instruction permits him to unload at the bid price.

bethel, *n.*   **chapel**
A **dissenters'** *chapel:* also their meeting-house; sometimes *seamen's church,*
whether afloat or on *terra firma.* Also called, at times, a *bethesda* or a *beulah.*

betterment levy   **improvement assessment**
Increase in your property taxes (**rates**) when you improve your property. Obsolete.

between whiles   **in between**
In the interval between other actions.

bevvied up, *adj.*   *Slang.* **drunk**
Having had too much bevvy.

bevvy, *n.*   **an alcoholic drink**
Slang. Abbrev. of beverage.

beyond the next turning. *See* **block.**

b.f.   *Slang.* **goddamned fool**
Slang. Stands for *bloody fool* (See **bloody.**) The *b.f.* is not to be confused with the proofreaders' mark for *boldface,* which is simplified to *bold* in Britain.

bib-overall, *n.*   SEE COMMENT
Overalls with a solid front top, known as a 'bib.'

bickie, *n.*   **cracker**
Inf. Nursery word for **biscuit.**

Biddy, *n.*   *Derog.* **a woman**
Diminutive of the name Bridget. Often used with 'old', as in *This old biddy appeared at the door.*

biff, *v.t*   *Slang.* **hit**
I biffed him in the nose.

big bug. See **insect.**

big dipper   **roller coaster**
Synonymous with **switchback.**

big pot. See **pot, 3.**

bike. *See* **motor-bike.**

bill, *n.*   **check**
In Britain one asks the waiter for his *bill,* rather than his *check.* (The Briton might pay his *bill* by **cheque.**)

bill broker   **discounter; factor**
One engaged in the business of discounting notes and other negotiable instruments.

billiard-saloon, *n.*   *approx.* **billiard parlor; poolroom**
The game of *pool* in Britain has a set of rules quite different from *pool* (or *straight pool*) as the term is understood in America, where there are many variations of the game, each with its own set of rules. *Bar billiards* is a British game, played with balls and cues, on a table much smaller than a standard American table, and a bar-billiards table is a frequent and thoroughly enjoyable adornment of British pubs.

billingsgate, *n.*   **coarse invective**
Foul language characteristic of a person known as *fishwife.* The term, like the word *fishwife* in the derogatory sense, stems from Billingsgate Market, the former London fish market famous for its foul language.

billion, *adj., n.* See **Appendix II.D.**

bill of quantity   **cost estimate**
Especially in the building contracting business.

Billy Butlin's. See Butlin's.

billycock. See bowler, 1.

bin, *n.*   **hop sack**
Made of canvas and used in hop-picking. But *bin* has many other uses: see **bread bin; orderly bin; waste bin; litter bin; dustbin; skivvy-bin; bin ends.**

bind, *n., v.t., v.i*   *n., v.t.,* **bore**
Inf. A *bind* is a *bore*, whether referring to a person or a job. As a *v.t.*, to *bind* some-one is to *bore him stiff*. In Britain, the victim can be said to be bored *stiff, solid,* or *rigid*.

bin ends   SEE COMMENT
Wine merchants keep their supplies of bottled wine in separate *bins* according to label. When the contents of a number of bins run low, suppliers often offer bar-gains in *bin ends*, i.e., the few remaining cases of certain labels in order to empty those bins and refill them with the same or other labels.

bint, *n.*   **girlfriend**
Slang. From the Arabic word for *daughter,* adopted by British soldiers in the Middle East in World War I. It can also mean 'floozy,' in British spelled *floozie* or *floosie*. See **bird.**

bird, *n.*   *Slang.* **dame**
Slang. Now much more commonly used than **bint.** Synonyms **bint; bit of fluff; Judy.** For a wholly unrelated use, see **give (someone) the bird.**

birl, *v.t., v.i.*   **spin**
Birling is a lumberjack's game which tests the players' ability to stay afloat in a river on logs rotated by their feet. In America, to *birl* is to make the log rotate, but in Britain it has the more general meaning of causing something to rotate, i.e., to spin it, or just to move it quickly. The British use *birl* as an informal noun to mean 'try' or 'gamble,' like *whirl* in the expression *give it a whirl*.

biro, *n.*   **ball-point pen**
Inf. (Pronounced BUY'-RO.) A generic use of the trademark of the original ball-point pen, named after its Hungarian inventor.

Birthday Honours   SEE COMMENT
A miscellany of titles and distinctions, hereditary and otherwise, conferred on the sovereign's birthday, including *knight* (the female equivalent is *dame*), *baron,* O.B.E. *(Officer of the Order of the British Empire),* M.B.E. *(Member of the Order of the British Empire),* C.H. *(Companion of Honour),* P.C. *(Privy Councillor)*. In the case of Elizabeth II, Birthday Honours are conferred on her *official birthday,* June 13. Her real birthday is April 21, but to provide (presumably) more clement weather for outdoor royal festivities, particularly **trooping the colour(s)** at the Horse Guards in London, it was shifted to June 13. Titles are also conferred on New Year's Day and at other times at the request of a retiring prime minister.

biscuit, *n.*   **cracker; cookie**
Biscuit, in Britain, covers both *cookie* and *cracker,* depending upon the circumstances. One is offered *sweet biscuits* (cookies) with tea, and unsweetened ones (crackers) with cheese. To get cookies in Britain, specify *sweet biscuits, tea biscuits,* or even *petits fours.* If you ask for *crackers,* you may get firecrackers, or explosive bonbons or snappers, the kind used at children's parties.

(a) bit missing   *Inf.* **not all there**
Slang. In the sense of 'feeble-minded'; lacking certain of one's marbles.

bit of a knock, *Slang.*   *Slang.* **tough break**

bit of fluff   *Slang.* **piece of ass**
Bit of is prefixed to various slang terms for *available woman,* which is probably the origin of the elliptical use of *bit* to mean *gal.* See also **bit of goods; bit of stuff.**

bit of goods   *Slang.* **number**
Slang. An attractive *bit of goods* in Britain would be *quite a number* or *quite a dish* in America. See **bit of fluff.**

bit of rough, *Inf.*   SEE COMMENT
Said—without implied criticism—of a man whose appearance or demeanor might be described as uncouth, ungentlemanly, or simply unshaven. *She likes a bit of rough.*

bit of spare   **sex session**
Slang. Used in expressions like *he was always after a bit of spare.*

bit of stuff. See bit of fluff.

bitter, *n.*   SEE COMMENT
Bitter is used as a noun to mean beer with a higher hops content, and therefore a somewhat bitter taste (as opposed to mild beer). See also **pint.**

(a) bit thick, *adj.*   *Slang.* **going too far**
Slang. The expression *a bit thick* appears in America sometimes as *a bit much,* but the more common expression in America is *going too far.*

black, *v.t.*   **1. shine**
                                                  2. boycott
1. Referring to shoes. See also **boot.**
2. *Slang.* Describes the interference, presumably on union instructions, by employees of one company with the industrial activities of another company in order to exert pressure in labor disputes. To *black* a firm is to refuse to handle its goods or deliver to it. The term is derived from *blacklist.*

black-beetle, *n.*   **cockroach**
Entomologically speaking, a black-beetle is not a beetle at all.

blackleg, *n., Slang.*   *Slang.* **scab (strikebreaker)**

Black or white?   **Black or regular?**
How do you take your coffee? *Black* needs no explanation; *white* in Britain means 'mixed with milk.' Americans who don't want it *black* add cream or milk (cold in

either case) to their coffee. The British hostess or waitress usually holds the pot of coffee in one hand and the pitcher (**jug,** in Britain) of milk in the other, and inquires, *Black or white?* The British system would appear to be universal outside North America. An American hostess might ask, *With or without?* instead of, *Black or regular?*

Black Paper. See **Paper.**

Blackpool, *n.*   SEE COMMENT
Blackpool is a seaside resort reminiscent of Coney Island, and used symbolically in the same way. Also famous for **T.U.C.** (Trades Union Congress) and political party annual conferences often held there.

Black Rod, *n.*   SEE COMMENT
The senior official responsible for the day-to-day management of the House of Lords. At the State Opening of Parliament each year, he summons the Commons into the House of Lords to hear the Queen's Speech by banging his black rod on the door of the House of Commons.

black spot   **1. accident spot**
           2. trouble spot
Sometimes spelled *blackspot.* This is, unfortunately, a common road sign now and also used metaphorically to mean a 'danger area' or 'trouble spot.' Thus, in a discussion of the unemployment situation, the reporter referred to a certain industry as a *black spot.*

bladdered, *adj.*   *Slang.* **drunk**

Blairite, *n.*   SEE COMMENT
Slang. A follower of Prime Minister Tony Blair and his policies.

blanco, *n.*   **whitener**
Inf. A dressing for buckskin or canvas shoes or sneakers. Also for military webbing equipment, like belts. In the army, it can come in various shades of buff or khaki. In the other services, it is white. It comes in the form of a solid dusty block, which is moistened and then rubbed on whatever needs smartening. White *blanco* is still used by the **Guards** regiment before ceremonial occasions for cleaning belts and rifle slings. See also **clean.** *Blanco* is also used as a verb.

blanket bath   **sponge bath**
A bath given to one who is bedridden. Also called **bed bath.**

blast!, *interj.*   *Slang.* **damn it!; rats!**
Slang. See **bother.**

blather (blether), *v.i.*   **talk nonsense on and on**
With an *-s* added, it becomes a plural noun meaning 'nonsense.' The vowel changes to *i* in *blithering idiot,* a hopeless fool. See also **haver; waffle.**

blaze, *v.i.*   *Slang.* **to smoke marijuana/a joint**

bleeder, *n.*   *Slang.* **an unpleasant person**

bleeding, *adj.*   *Slang.* **damned; goddamned**
Slang. One of the many vulgar euphemisms for the vulgar **bloody**. *See* **blooming; blinking; bally; ruddy; flipping; flaming.**

blighter, *n.*   *Slang.* **character; pain; pest**
Slang. This word originally described a person of such low character as to *blight* his surroundings; now not quite so pejorative, it has its approximate equivalent in a number of American slang terms of which the above are only a few. Can be used in a favorable sense, as in *lucky blighter.*

blighty, *n.*   *approx.* **God's country**
Slang. British soldiers used this word to mean 'back home,' especially after military service abroad, in the same way that the Americans are glad to get back to *God's country* after being abroad. It is derived from *bilayati*, a Hindustani word meaning 'foreign' and was brought back to their own *blighty* by British soldiers returning from service in India. In World War I it was also used to describe a wound serious enough to warrant a soldier's return home: a *blighty* one.

blimey!, *interj.*   *Slang.* **holy mackerel!**
Slang This vulgar interjection is a contraction of *Cor blimey!* or *Gor blimey!* which are distortions of *God blind me!* See also **lumme!**

blimp, *n.*   *Inf.* **stuffed shirt**
Inf. A pompous, elderly stick-in-the-mud, from a David Low cartoon character, Colonel Blimp, a retired officer.

blind, *n., v.i., adj.*   **1.** *n.,* **window shade**
                                                       2. *n., Slang.* **bender**
                                                       3. *adj., Slang.* **damned**
1. In America, *blind* is usually restricted to a venetian blind or some type of shutter.
2. *n., Slang.* A session of excessive drinking.
3. *adj., Slang.* As in *I don't know a blind thing about it!* i.e. *I know nothing about it.*

blinder, *n.*   *Slang.* SEE COMMENT
An extraordinary thing or person; something that is blinding.

blinkers, *n., pl.*   **blinders**

blinking, *adj., adv.*   *Slang.* **damned**
Slang. Euphemism for **bloody:** *He's a blinking fool.*

bloater   SEE COMMENT
1. *n.* a large, lightly smoked herring or mackerel
2. *n. derog.* A fat person

block, n.   **large building**
A block of flats is an *apartment house;* an *office block* is an *office building;* a *tower block* is a *high rise.* In America, *block* is used to describe an area, usually rectangular, bounded by four streets. *In the next block,* to a Briton, would mean *in the next apartment house* or *office building.* In giving directions, the British equivalent would be *beyond the next turning.* It appears, however, that the influence of Amer-

ican visitors is having an increasing effect in bringing *block,* in the American sense, into British usage. See also **apartment; flat.**

block of ice   **ice cube**
Obsolete. The American term, sometimes hyphenated, appears to have won out.

bloke, *n.*   *Slang.* **guy**
Slang. See also **chap; guy.** *My bloke* means *my boy friend; my fellow.*

bloody, *adj., adv.*   **1.** *adj., Slang.* **lousy; contemptible**
                                                2. *adv., Slang.* **damned; goddamned**
Slang. This word is now commonly used as an adverb intensifier modifying either a pejorative adjective, as in *It's bloody awful,* or a flattering adjective, as in *This is bloody marvelous.* Used as an adjective, its nearest equivalent in America would be *lousy,* as in the phrase *a bloody shame. Bloody,* once regarded as a lurid oath, was formerly proscribed in mixed company, but that sort of inhibition is waning nowadays. Despite popular belief, there is no sound reason to suppose that it is derived from *by Our Lady. See* **bleeding; blooming; blinking; bally; ruddy; flipping; flaming.** As to British swearing habits generally, *damn* is less objectionable in Britain than in America, in polite circles, and *darn* is practically obsolete in Britain. Americans are freer with religious names like *Christ* and *Jesus* and deformations like *Jeez,* but *Crikey* (from *Christ*), originally an oath, is now common as an exclamation of surprise, and sometimes of admiration.

bloody-minded, *adj.*   *Inf.* **pigheaded; stubborn**
Inf. Willfully difficult; stubbornly obstructive; cantankerous. An awkward but useful adjective to describe persons you simply can't cope with.

bloomer, *n.*   **1.** *Slang.* **booboo**
                                                       2. SEE COMMENT
1. *Slang.* Synonymous with *blunder,* and sounds like the American slang term *blooper,* which, however, is generally reserved for an embarrassing public *booboo.*
2. *n.* A large loaf of bread, glazed and slashed on top before baking.

blooming, *adj., adv.*   *Inf.* **damned**
Inf. Euphemism for the intensifier **bloody,** like **blinking, bally, ruddy,** etc.

Bloomsbury, *n., adj.*   **1.** SEE COMMENT
                                                      2. *approx.* **highbrow**
1. Bloomsbury is the name of a section of Central London where writers and artists, students and aesthetes generally lived and gathered in the early part of this century. There was a *Bloomsbury set* which included people like Virginia and Leonard Woolf and Lytton Strachey, and others in or on the fringes of the arts, and there was a *Bloomsbury accent.*
2. The name became generally descriptive of that sort of person and atmosphere, and developed into an adjective roughly equivalent to *intellectual* or *highbrow.*

blot one's copybook   *Inf.* **spoil one's record**
Inf. To mar an otherwise perfect record by committing an act of indiscretion.

blower, *n.*　　　　　　　　　　　　　　　　　　**telephone**
Slang. Sometimes referred to in American slang as the *horn*. *Blow* is sometimes used as a noun meaning a 'call' or 'ring' on the telephone as in *If you have any trouble, just give me a blow.*

blowlamp, *n.*　　　　　　　　　　　　　　　　　**blowtorch**
Sometimes *blowflame*. Also called **brazing lamp.**

(be) blown, *v.*　　　　　　　　　　　　　　　**(be) found out**
Inf. Can be said of a person, as well as a spy's cover or any spurious identity.

blow the gaff. See **gaff.**

blow (someone) up　　　　　　　　　**blow up at (someone)**
To *blow* someone *up* is to *blow up at* someone, or to *let him have it,* and a *blowing-up* is what you let him have!

blub, *v. Inf.*　　　　　　　　　　　　　　　　　　　　**sob**

blue, *n.*　　　　　　　　　　　　　　　**letter; letter man**
A man who wins his *letter* and becomes a *letter man* in America wins his *blue* and becomes a *blue* at Oxford or Cambridge. At London University he wins his *purple* and becomes a *purple,* and it appears that other universities award other colors; but neither *purple* nor any other color compares even faintly with the distinction of a *blue.* Oxford *blue* is dark blue; Cambridge *blue* is light blue. A *double-blue* is a *two-letter man;* a *triple-blue* is a *three-letter man.* The sport in which the British athlete represents his university (makes the team, in America) determines whether he earns a *full blue* or *a half blue.* Cricket, crew, rugger, and soccer are *full blue* sports. Tennis, lacrosse, and hockey are half blue sports. A *blue* can be a *full blue* or a *half blue.*

blue, *v.t.*　　　　　　　　　　　　　*Slang.* **blow (squander)**
Slang. Past tense is *blued,* in America *blew. Blue* is apparently a variant of *blow,* which is used as well in Britain for *squander.*

blue book　　　　　　　　　　　　　　　　**legislative report**
In Britain, a parliamentary or privy-council publication. See also **Hansard.**

blue-eyed boy, *Inf.*　　　　　　　　　　　*Inf.* **fair-haired boy**

Blue Paper. See **Paper.**

blue rinse, *adj.*　　　　　　　　　　　　　　　SEE COMMENT
Derog. Used to describe genteel **pensioners** who have a habit of putting a pale blue tint in their white hair.

BM　　　　　　　　　　　　　　　　　　　　SEE COMMENT
The *British Museum,* very frequently abbreviated thus (without periods). The great BM library is now officially called the *British Library.*

BNP　　　　　　　　　　　　　　**British National Party**
Acronym. The leading far-right political party, campaigning mainly on issues of immigration and race.

board, *n.*   **sign**
For instance, a TO LET *board*. See also **notice board; hoarding.**

boarder, *n.*   **resident student**
As opposed to a *day student,* who lives at home. It applies to secondary school, not university. *Boarder* in the American sense is *lodger* in Britain. Cf. **P.G.**

boater, *n.*   **straw hat**

(the) Boat Race   SEE COMMENT
The annual rowing race between Oxford and Cambridge. A sporting event of interest to the British public generally, including many who have not had the benefit of any university attendance. There are lots of boat races, but *The* Boat Race is so understood as the race between Oxford and Cambridge.

bob, *n.*   SEE COMMENT
Slang. One shilling, the former British monetary unit until decimalization. See **Appendix II.A.**

bob-a-job?   **any odd job?**
British Boy Scouts came to the door once a year during Bob-a-Job-Day and asked *Bob-a-job?* You were supposed to find (or invent) a household chore the good young man or men would perform for a *bob* (slang for *shilling*). The proceeds were turned over to the organization for the doing of good works. To indicate the effects of monetary inflation, the special day has now become a week in length.

bobby, *n.*   *Slang.* **cop**
Slang. Named for Sir Robert (Bobby) Peel, Home Secretary, who founded the Metropolitan Police Force in 1829. A former slang term in Britain for *cop,* also named after Sir Robert, was *peeler,* which is, however, still heard in Ireland. *Copper* is another less common slang term for *cop,* which is also used in America but seems to have gone out of fashion. *Robert* (from the same Sir Robert) was another British term for *cop.* See **constable; P.C.; bogey; busies; pointsman; slop.**

bobby-dazzler, *n.*   **something special**
Inf. Anything or anybody outstanding; often applied to a particularly spiffy dresser.

Bob's your uncle!   *Inf.* **there you are! you're done!**
Inf. An expression used at the end of instructions such as road directions, recipes, and the like. For example: *Go about 100 yards, take the first turning on your right, then straight on through a little gate; go 40 yards to a gate on your left marked Main Entrance, but that's not really the main entrance (they just call it that, I haven't a clue why), but 20 yards farther on there's a small gate on your right that really is the main entrance; go through that, you'll see a dismal brown building on your left and—Bob's your uncle!* Or: *. . . add a few cloves, stir for five minutes, turn down the flame, let simmer for an hour or so, and—Bob's your uncle!* One explanation of this curious phrase is its alleged use in Robert Peel's campaign for a seat in Parliament. He was a "law and order" man nicknamed *Bob* (see **bobby**) and *uncle* was used as a term implying benefaction and protection: *Vote for Bob—Bob's your Uncle!* Maybe.

bod, *n.*   *Slang.* **character**
Slang. An abbreviation of *body* and somewhat pejorative. Example: *I saw somebody who seemed to be a night watchman or some other type of lowly bod about the premises.*

bodkin, *n.*   **tape needle**
In Britain the commonest meaning is that of a thick, unpointed needle having a
large eye for drawing tape or ribbon through a hem or a loop. Another meaning
in Britain and America is to designate a large and elaborate hatpin, but most of
those went out of fashion in Edwardian times.

bodyline, *adj.*   SEE COMMENT
Usually in the expression *bodyline bowling.* In **cricket,** *bowling* is the overhand
delivery of the ball (see **bowler, 2.**) to the **batsman** (*batter*), who must defend
his **wicket** (keep the ball from knocking the horizontal pegs (called *bails*) off
the vertical supports (called *stumps*). In *bodyline* bowling, the bowler aims at the
batsman, rather than the wicket, not so much to hurt him as to frighten him, thus
causing him to duck away and so fail to defend his wicket, especially from a ball
with **spin** (*English*) on it sufficient to make it swing in or out as it hits the ground
in front of the batsman and hit the wicket.

boffin, *n.*   **research scientist; expert, especially in science**
Slang. Synonymous with *back-room boy,* referring to a person who during World
War II worked as a scientist for the war effort, as, for instance, in the develop-
ment of radar. Jack Rayner of Muswell Hill, a research scientist in the employ
of the General Post Office, is of the opinion that he may be the original *boffin* to
whom this bit of R.A.F. World War II slang for 'civilian scientist' was applied.
Early in 1943 Mr. Rayner worked with a scientist who liked to give his colleagues nicknames out of Dickens, and the future Mrs. Rayner was his assistant.
The name-giver called her *Mrs. Boffin,* after the character in *Our Mutual Friend.*
By association Mr. Rayner became *Mr. Boffin,* and was thus addressed by his
colleagues on a visit to Fighter and Bomber Command Headquarters soon thereafter. The term is now used more generally for scientists or mathematicians of
high distinction.

bog, *n.*   *Slang.* **john (toilet)**
Slang. Vulgar slang, used usually in the plural to refer to a communal latrine, as
at school or in the service. See **loo.**

bogey (bogy), *n.*   **1.** *Slang.* **cop**
                                                             2. *Slang.* **booger, snot**
1. (Hard G.) *Slang.* This old-fashioned word literally means *bugbear,* which should
explain its slang use among the criminal element.
2. *n.* The term originates in children's speech but is widely used by adults as well
as children.

bogeyman, *n.*   **boogieman**
A frightening imaginary person used to scare children. *If you don't behave, the
bogeyman will come and get you.*

bogie, *n.*   **truck (non-driving locomotive wheels)**
(Hard G.) Railroad term. *Truck* is a British railroad term meaning 'gondola car'
(open freight car). See **bogey.**

bog-standard, *adj.*   *Slang.* **average**
Used almost invariably as a pejorative.

boiled sweets   **hard candy**
Sweets, as a general term, is the British equivalent of the American general term *candy. Boiled sweets* always means the kind of candy that is usually sucked rather than chewed. See, however, **sweet.**

boiler. See **chicken.**

boiler suit   **coverall**

boiling, *n.*   *Slang.* **shooting-match**
Slang. The *whole boiling,* referring to a group of people, means the 'whole *mob* of them' but *boiling* can refer to the *whole lot* of anything.

bollard, *n.*   **traffic post**
A *bollard* in both countries is a post on a ship or dock around which hawsers are tied. An exclusively British meaning is 'traffic post,' i.e., a short post on a traffic island, to regulate traffic by barring passage in certain directions.

bollick, *v.t.*   *Slang.* **bawl out**
Slang. It is a curious coincidence that this word resembles *bollocks* (see **ballocks**) and *bollixed* (as in, *all bollixed up*). Those words and phrases have to do with the noun *ball,* usually found in the plural, whereas *bollick* happens to be associated with the verb *bawl,* in its meaning of 'shout' rather than 'weep.'

bollocks. See **ballocks.**

bolshy, also bolshie, *n., adj.*   *approx.* **unconventional and uncooperative**
Inf. Literally *Bolshevik,* but applied by older folk to any unconventional act or person. To *go bolshie* is to go one's own unconventional way, to engage in anti-Establishment behavior; to disregard the accepted form; to do one's own thing. The general sense of the term is 'mutinous' (socially speaking); 'acting in defiance of good form.' Some use it to mean 'obstreperous,' and apply the term to any trouble-maker. The *Concise Oxford Dictionary* calls it merely 'uncooperative.'

bolter, *n.*   *Inf.* SEE COMMENT
A person (especially male) who is likely to abandon the family home for the smallest of reasons. *I knew he was no good—he was a real bolter.*

bolt-hole, *n.*   **hideaway**
Inf. A pied à terre. Used by exurbanites in *I have a little bolt-hole in Chelsea* and by Londoners in *I have a little bolt-hole in Dorset. The Bolt-Hole* is a jocular name given to the Channel Islands, reputed to be a tax haven. All derived from the rabbit's *bolt-hole.*

bomb, *n.*   1. *Slang.* **smash hit**
                                               2. **fortune**
1. *Slang. A dazzling success*—the exact opposite of its meaning in America: a *dismal flop!* To *go down a bomb* in Britain is to *make a smash hit.* See **knock.**
2. *Slang.* To *make a bomb* is to *make a fortune. It costs a bomb* means it costs 'a fortune' or 'an arm and a leg.'

bonce, *n.*   1. **agate**
                                               2. *Slang.* **noodle**
1. *Slang.* A large playing marble.
2. *Slang.* A rare usage, usually in the expression *biff on the bonce,* a shot on the head.

bone, *v.t.*   *Slang.* **swipe**
Slang. To steal something; evoking the image of a dog skulking off with a bone.

bone. See **when it comes to the bone.**

bone-idle, *adj.*   **extremely lazy**

Bonfire Night   SEE COMMENT
A night on or near November 5th, the anniversary of the **Gunpowder Plot.** Traditionally, families have parties with bonfires and fireworks, and an effigy of **Guy Fawkes** is burned.

bonk, 1. *v.t.,* 2. *n.*   **1.** *Slang.* **have sexual intercourse with**
                                     2. *Slang.* **sexual intercourse**

bonkers, *adj.*   *Slang.* **nuts; goofy**
Slang. Also, **certified; doolally; crackers; dotty.**

bonnet, *n.*   **Car hood**
Automobile term. See **Appendix II.E.**

bonus issue (bonus share)   **stock dividend**

boob, *n., v.t., v.i., Slang.*   **1. goof**
                                                      2. jail
                                                      3. jug
1. Though Americans don't use *boob* as a verb, they commonly use *booboo* to indicate the result.
2. To *get boobed* is to *be imprisoned or apprehended.*
3. In the plural, a *woman's breasts.*

book, *v.t.*   **1. reserve**
                                                    2. charge
1. In Britain one *books* or *reserves* a table, theater seats, hotel rooms, rental cars, etc. A *booking* in Britain is a *reservation;* a *booking office* and a *booking clerk* (railroad terms) appear in America as *ticket office* and *ticket agent. Fully booked* means 'all seats reserved.'
2. When something is *booked to an account* in Britain, the equivalent in America would be *charged.* See also **put down, 2.**

book of words   **libretto**

book seller   **bookstore**
In Britain, book advertisements generally advise you that the indispensable volume can be obtained at your *book seller* (or *book shop*) rather than at your *bookstore.*

bookstall, *n.*   **newsstand**
Synonymous with **newsagent; kiosk.**

boot, *n.*   **1. trunk (of an automobile)**
                                        2. shoe
                                        3. SEE COMMENT
                                        4. a bad-tempered old woman
1. See **Appendix II.E.**

2. The British use *boot* to include all leather footwear; but *shoe,* as in America, normally excludes that which comes above the ankle. If a farmhand or a countryman generally wanted to talk about his *rubber boots,* he would refer to his *Wellingtons,* standard country footwear even in dry weather. A British *boot* reaching barely above the ankle would be called a *shoe* in America. An American who would never refer to his *shoes* as his *boots* or to the process of *shining* them as *blacking* them nonetheless usually refers to the person who *shines* his *shoes* as a *bootblack,* although he sometimes calls him a *shoeshine boy.* A *shoe clerk* in America is a *bootmaker's assistant* in Britain even if the *boots* are not made in that shop.
3. *Boot* is used in a variety of British expressions: See **another pair of shoes (boots); (the) boot is on the other leg (foot); like old boots; put the boot in.**
4. *Slang, derog.* Usually prefaced by 'old.' *The old boot wouldn't stop complaining about my cats going in her garden.*

(the) boot is on the other leg (foot)   **the shoe is on the other foot**

Bootlace, *n.*   **shoelace**

boots, *n.*   **hotel bootblack**
He formerly was employed to gather shoes put just outside hotel-room doors at night, to be returned, polished, during the night. In military slang, *boots* means a 'rookie officer' in a regiment or other organization.

boot sale   SEE COMMENT
An automobile *boot sale* offers for sale all those things one has no further use for. It is called a *boot sale* because you fill the **boot** of your car with articles to dispose of, drive to an appointed place where others are engaging in the same operation, open the boot, strew some of the things around your car, leave some stuff in the boot, and hope to pick up a few pounds while ridding yourself of the stuff you can't stand having around any longer. Also called *car boot sale.*

booze cruise, *n.*   *Slang.* SEE COMMENT
A round-trip voyage (usually by ferry but also by Eurotunnel) from the UK to the **Continent** to buy liquor, tobacco, and other products that are normally cheaper in mainland Europe than in the UK.

boozer, n.   *Slang.* **1. a pub**
                                            2. someone who drinks too much alcohol
Jocular in sense 1, pejorative in sense 2.

(the) Border, *n.*   SEE COMMENT
The one between Scotland and England, which is what is meant when Britons or Scots use the expression *south of the Border. North of the Border* is heard as well.

bore, *n.*   **gauge**
In describing the internal diameter of a gun barrel: small *bore,* large *bore,* etc.

borough, *n.*   SEE COMMENT
(Pronounced BURRA (*u* as in *butter*). Basic unit of local government. See also **rotten borough.**

borstal, *n.*   **reformatory**
Inf. Borstal is the name of a town in Kent where Britain's original juvenile prison is located. It used to be called Borstal Prison but is now referred to as Borstal

Institution, reflecting the modern trend toward rehabilitation of young offenders. The Borstal System introduced the indeterminate sentence in juvenile cases requiring observation and treatment. Informally, *borstal* (lower case) has come to mean that kind of essentially remedial and educational institution, wherever located. Also called *remand home* or *remand center*.

boss-eyed   squinty
Slang. 'Cockeyed' or *one-eyed*.

bother, *n., interj.*   1. *Slang.* **trouble;**
                                                              row (dispute)
                                                              2. damn! rats!
1. *Inf.* A spot of bother in Britain is a *bit of trouble* in America, although serious trouble can also be referred to as a *spot of bother*.
2. *Slang.* Seen in mild exclamations, as in *Bother the boat train!* after learning that the planes are full. Somewhat milder than *blast!*

bothered, *adj.*   *Inf.* **concerned; interested**
People often say, if asked which option they prefer (e.g. tea or coffee to drink), *I'm not bothered.* The expression is really a synonym for *I don't care.*

bothy, *n.*   **hut; one-room cottage**
(Pronounced BOH-thee, rhyming with three.) Used by farm hands.

bottle, *n.*   *Inf.* **courage**
Informally speaking, *nerve* or *guts* might be more accurate translations.

bottom, *n.*   **1. foot (far end)**
                                                        2. staying power
1. In such phrases as *bottom of the garden; bottom of the street,* etc., in the same way that a British street has a *top* rather than a *head.*
2. *Slang.* Occasionally affected, perhaps half-jocularly and certainly self-consciously, in the expression *a lot of bottom,* indicating a good deal of courage and persistence.

bottom drawer   hope chest

bottom gear   low gear
Logically enough, **top gear** means *high gear.*

boundary, *n.*   1. SEE COMMENT
                                                        2. limits
1. A cricket term meaning a hit that sends the ball rolling all the way to the white line around the field that marks the boundary and counts as four runs. The ball doesn't have to land outside the line. If it does that, it scores six runs (see **six**). See also **Appendix II.K.**
2. See **city boundary; town boundary.**

bounder, *n.*   boor
A person, most often a man, guilty of unacceptable social behavior; an ill-bred person. The term does not necessarily imply low moral character, but it can.

bovver, *n.*   *Slang.* **trouble**

Bow Bells   SEE COMMENT
(Pronounced BOH BELLS.) Literally, the *bells of Bow Church*, also called St. Mary-le-Bow Church, in the **City** of London. The church got its name from the bows (arches) of its steeple or from the arches of stone upon which the church was built—those still to be seen in the Norman crypt. The most frequent use of *Bow Bells* is in the expression *within the sound of Bow Bells*, which means 'in the City of London' (see **City**). One is said to be a true cockney if born within the sound of Bow Bells.
　　See also **cockney; East End.** The ecclesiastical court of the Archbishop of Canterbury is held in the crypt of Bow Church, and its head is therefore called the *Dean of the Arches*.

bowler, *n.*   **1. derby (hat)**
                                                           2. SEE COMMENT
1. Also called in Britain a *billycock*. Designed in 1850 with felt supplied by a Mr. Bowler for (the story goes) Mr. William Coke, who somehow became Mr. Billy Cock.
2. *Bowler* has an entirely distinct meaning in cricket. The *bowler* (from the verb *bowl*) has approximately the same relationship to cricket as the *pitcher* has to baseball. He *bowls*, over-arm, rather than *pitches*, side-arm.

bowler-hatted, *adj.*   **back in civies**
Slang. To be *bowler-hatted* is to *be retired early* from military service with a bonus for retiring. A **bowler**, of course, is a hallmark of civilian attire. See also **demob.**

bowls, *n. pl.*   **lawn bowling**
A *bowl* (in the singular) in sports is a wooden ball not exactly spherical, or eccentrically weighted if spherical, so that it can be made to curve when rolling. Related to *boccie, boules, pelanca* (or *pétanque*), etc., but the bowling-greens of Britain are as meticulously maintained as the putting greens at the best American golf clubs.

box, *n.*   **1. intersection area**
                                                       2. *Slang.* **idiot box**
                                                              3. jock strap
1. *Box*, or *junction box*, is a British traffic term denoting the grid marked out at a street intersection **(crossroads).** One sees traffic signs reading DO NOT ENTER BOX UNTIL YOUR EXIT IS CLEAR—don't start crossing at an intersection and get stuck in the middle, thus blocking traffic coming at right angles.
2. Short for *goggle-box*, comparable to American *boob tube*.
3. The protective cup in the UK jock strap is sometimes made of hard material, hence the name *box*.

Boxing Day   SEE COMMENT
First weekday after Christmas, December 26, a legal holiday in Britain, unless Christmas falls on a Saturday, in which event December 27 is Boxing Day. This is the day on which Christmas gifts of money are traditionally given to the milkman, **postman** (mailman), **dustman** (garbage man), and others.

box-room, *n.*   **storage room**
The room in your house for suitcases and trunks. See also **lumber-room.**

box-spanner. See **spanner.**

box-up, *n.*   *Inf.* **mix-up**
Slang. Like occupying the wrong seats at the theater and being compelled to move. See **balls.**

boy. See **head boy; old boy; pot-boy; wide boy.**

braces, *n.*   **suspenders**
The American equivalent, *suspenders,* is used in Britain as the equivalent of American *garters.*

bracken, *n.*   **large fern**
Also, an area covered with ferns and undergrowth.

bracket, *n.*   SEE COMMENT
American *brackets* are square enclosing marks, thus: [ ]. In Britain, the term is generic for enclosing marks, and includes parentheses, thus: ( ). To differentiate while dictating in Britain, one must specify square brackets or round brackets.

bradbury, *n. Inf.*   *approx.* **a buck**
Sir John Bradbury, who became Secretary of the Treasury in 1914, signed the paper money issued by the Treasury, and his name, often shortened to *brad,* became the colloquial term for the bills themselves, particularly the one-pound note (see **note, 1.**). In 1919 Sir Warren Fisher succeeded Bradbury as the signer of the Treasury notes and the term *bradbury* gave way to *fisher,* until October 1, 1933, after which date all paper money was issued by the Bank of England, and Treasury notes ceased to be legal tender.

Bradshaw, *n.*   *approx.* **national passenger train timetable**
Short for *Bradshaw's Railway Guide,* originally published by George Bradshaw in 1839. Ceased publication *circa* 1965.

brakesman, *n.*   **brakeman**

brake-van, *n.*   **caboose**
Railroad term, more commonly called *guard's van.* The American equivalent (*caboose*) was used in Britain to mean 'galley on the deck of a ship,' now obsolete as a ship design feature. *Brake-van* relates to freight trains (**goods** trains), as opposed to *guard's van,* which applies to passenger trains. *Brake-vans* are cars that enable brakemen to reach and operate a train's brakes.

bramble, *n., v.i.*   **blackberry**
To go *brambling* is to go *blackberry picking.*

Bramley apple, n.   SEE COMMENT
A variety of large, tart apple, indigenous to the UK, used solely for cooking.

branch, *n.*   **local**
Specialized use in trade union circles: *Branch 101* would be *Local 101* in American union terminology.

brandy-butter, *n.*   **hard sauce**
Butter and brandy creamed together. Served with plum pudding, Christmas pudding, and mince pie. See also **rum-butter,** which it resembles. Also called *Senior Wrangler Sauce.* See **wrangler.**

brandy snap   SEE COMMENT
A type of cookie made according to a special recipe containing a good deal of corn (golden) syrup. Flat and thin or rolled with a cream filler. Delicious and fattening.

Branston pickle, *TM.*   SEE COMMENT
A popular sweet pickle named after a village in Staffordshire and launched in 1922.

brash, *n.*   **hedge clippings**
Or *dry twigs,* or both. A rustic term.

brass, *n.*   *Slang.* **dough (money)**
Slang. The more common British slang terms are **lolly** and **dosh.**

brassed off   *Slang.* **teed off**
Slang. Synonymous with **cheesed off** and *fed up.*

brass plate, *n.*   **shingle**
To *put up your brass plate* in Britain is to *hang out your shingle* and the like in America.

brawn, *n.*   **head cheese**

brazing lamp   **blowtorch**
Synonymous with **blowlamp.**

bread and butter pudding, *n.*   SEE COMMENT
A traditional dessert made with bread, butter, sugar, dried fruit, and milk and/or cream.

bread bin   **bread box**
Or bread basket, in American slang, one's stomach.

bread roll   **dinner roll**
See also **bap.**

break, *n.*   **recess**
School term. *Break* is used in both countries to mean a 'temporary suspension of activities' generally, for example, to use the bathroom. *Recess* usually refers to Parliament in Britain, and the term is not used to refer to the daily pause at school.

break a journey at . . .   **stop off at . . .**

breakdown gang   **wrecking crew**

breakdown van or lorry   **tow truck**

breaktime. See **playtime.**

breast-pin, *n.*   **stick-pin**
Worn in necktie.

breve, *n.*   **double whole note**
See **Appendix II.F.**

brew up   **1. make tea**
                                                               2. burn
1. *Inf.* Also a noun, *brew-up,* for which there is no equivalent American expression, since the institution of tea and tea-making in general is not a vital function of daily life. A *brew-up* is any making of tea, whether in a priceless China pot or a billycan, at any time of day or night. See also **be mum.**
2. This meaning was originally applied to an army tank that had been hit by enemy fire, but has also been used to describe an auto accident that has caused a fire.

brickie or **bricky,** *n., Slang.*   **bricklayer**

brick wall   *Inf.* **stone wall**
Inf. Any impenetrable barrier.

bridewell, *n.*   **jail**
An archaic term, from *St. Bride's Well,* in London, where there stood an early prison.

bridge coat   *approx.* **velvet jacket**
An old-fashioned garment no longer in common use. A long-sleeved velvet jacket, usually black, worn formerly by women for bridge in the evening. Perhaps the feminine equivalent of another vanishing garment—the *smoking jacket* (also of velvet, most often maroon).

bridlepath, *n.*   SEE COMMENT
An ancient right-of-way for horse riders and horse-drawn vehicles.

brief, *n.*   **1. instructions to trial lawyer**
                                                      2. *Inf.* **lawyer**
In America a *brief* is a written outline submitted to the court in the course of litigation. In Britain it is the **solicitor's** instructions to the **barrister.** A *briefless barrister* is an *unemployed* one. See also **solicitor; barrister.** A *dock brief* is one that bypasses the solicitor, consisting as it does of instructions given at the trial by the accused in a criminal case directly to the barrister who is going to defend him, without benefit of solicitor. For the origin of this term, see **dock,** 2.

briefs, *n., pl.*   **jockey shorts**

brigadier, *n.*   **brigadier general**
British military rank between colonel and major general.

bright, *adj.*   **1. well**
                                                                  2. pleasant
1. *Inf.* When asked how he feels, a Briton might say, *I'm not too bright,* where an American would use the expressions *not too well,* or *not up to snuff.*
2. *Inf.* When a Briton says, *It's not very bright, is it?* looking up at the sky, he means that the weather isn't very *pleasant.* See also **bright periods.**

Brighton, *n.*   SEE COMMENT
A seaside resort in the Southeast, the archetypical equivalent of Atlantic City of an earlier time. Imposing Edwardian hotels and fascinating lanes (known as *The Lanes*) lined with antique shops full of every description of furniture and a bric-a-brac, much of it quite good, characterize Brighton at its best.

Brighton Rock, *n.*   SEE COMMENT
A type of hard candy, often with lettering or a design formed by different colorings, originally sold in Brighton.

bright periods   **fair with occasional showers**
Synonymous with **sunny intervals.** A more accurate translation might be *rain with brief intermissions.* See also **bright.**

brill. See **Appendix II.H.**

brill, *adj.*   *Inf.* **terrific**
Slang. Brills! is used as an interjection meaning 'Great!' Said to be a shortening of *brilliant.*

bring off a touch, *Slang.*   *Slang.* **make a touch**
Succeed in borrowing desired funds.

Bristol fashion   **everything's A-OK**
Inf. Usually, *all shipshape and Bristol fashion.* The port of Bristol was traditionally efficient in years gone by. Nautical slang, taken into informal general usage, and still heard.

Bristols, *n. pl.*   *Slang.* **tits**
Slang. From London rhyming slang, formerly *Bristol city,* to rhyme with *titty.* There is only one Bristol City, but titties come in pairs, so the rhymesters pluralized City, then dropped it in the way they normally eliminated the rhyming word, and then proceeded to pluralize Bristol. Another word for this part of the anatomy is **charlies,** also spelled *charleys,* of uncertain etymology.

British Board of Film Classification, *n.*   SEE COMMENT
An independent non-governmental body that has exercised censorship and rating responsibilities over movies since 1913 and over videos since 1985.

broad, *n.*   **dame**
An offensive American term picked up in England.

broad arrow   SEE COMMENT
Symbol marking government property, formerly including convicts' uniforms.

broad bean   *approx.* **lima bean**
Similar, but larger, darker and with a coarser skin. The British variety is the seed
of a vetch known as *Vicia faba;* the American, that of the plant known as *Phaseolus
limensis.*

broadcloth, *n.*   **black woolen cloth**
In America, *broadcloth* is the equivalent of what the British and Americans term
poplin. British *broadcloth* is the kind of suiting material used for one's Sunday
best.

Broadmoor   SEE COMMENT
A hospital in Crowthorne, Devon, for the criminally insane. Patients are admitted
if a psychiatrist considers them mentally ill and dangerous.

broadsheet, *n.*   **1. handbill**
                                            2. large-sized newspaper
1. Also called *throwaway* in America and, picturesquely, *broadside. Handbill* used
to be the common term, but the British more often now use *leaflet.*
2. The size of *The New York Times,* as opposed to a tabloid.

Brock's benefit   **fireworks display**
Inf. Named for a noted manufacturer of fireworks. By extension, any great excite-
ment, air raid, Guy Fawkes Night (see **guy**), etc.

broken ranges   **broken sizes**
Odd sizes, offered in a sale.

broking firm   **brokerage firm**

brolly, *n.*   *Inf.* **bumbershoot**
Inf. The English term for umbrella is used quite seriously; the American word is
humorous. See **gamp.**

brothel-creepers, *n. pl., Slang.*   **crepe-soled shoes**

brown, *n.*   **1.** SEE COMMENT
                                            2. covey of game birds
1. *Slang.* A copper penny.
2. *Inf. Rare. The brown* means a *flying covey of game birds,* and *firing into the brown*
means, literally, 'aiming at the covey instead of choosing a particular bird,' and
by extension, firing into any crowd of people.

brown bread   **whole wheat bread**
The American term is now common in Britain.

Brownite, *adj.*   SEE COMMENT
A supporter of Gordon Brown, the **Chancellor of the Exchequer**

Brum, *n.*   SEE COMMENT
Slang. Short for *Brummagem,* an old slang name for *Birmingham,* said to approximate the local pronunciation of that name, but the *g* is pronounced soft. *Brummagem* came to be used as an adjective meaning 'shoddy,' a sense derived from the
counterfeiting of coins there in the 17th century. A *Brummie* is a native of that city.

brush up   *Inf.* **brush up on**
Inf. The British *brush up* their knowledge of a subject, while the Americans *brush up on* it.

B.S.T.   SEE COMMENT
British Standard Time, now obsolete. It was a system of all-year-round daylight saving time (called **summer time** in Britain), tried for a year or two in order to line up with European Standard Time, but abandoned in 1971.

Bt. See **Baronet.**

bubble, *v.*   **1. inform**
Rhyming slang. From rhyming slang for **bubble and squeak.**

bubble and squeak   SEE COMMENT
Leftover greens and potatoes—sometimes with meat—mixed together and fried; name derived from the sounds they make while cooking in the pan.

bubbly, *n.*   **champagne**
Slang. The term is also applied to sparkling wines from places other than Champagne.

buck, *n.*   **eel trap**
A basket used to trap eels.

bucket down   **rain cats and dogs**
Inf. Synonymous with pour with rain, tip down, and **rain stair-rods.** (A stair-rod is used to secure carpeting to staircase steps.)

bucket shop   *Inf.* **travel agency**
Especially one specializing in low-priced air tickets.

Buck House, *slang.*   **Buckingham Palace**

Buck's fizz   **mimosa**
In other words, orange juice and sparkling wine.

buckshee, *adj., adv.*   *Inf.* **for free (gratis)**
Slang. A corruption of *baksheesh,* used in the Near East to mean 'alms' or 'tip.' Also used in expressions like a *buckshee day,* describing a day unexpectedly free as a result of the cancellation of scheduled events or appointments.

buck up   **improve; check up**
Inf. Examples: *The railways had better buck up their ideas of service! Her idea of* encouraging *me was to say,* "Buck up!"

budget, *n.*   SEE COMMENT
The annual statement of projected national income and expenditures, made by the Chancellor of the Exchequer (counterpart of the Secretary of the Treasury) in the House of Commons. *A mini-budget* is an interim partial statement of the same sort. But in the popular mind, *budget* means 'tax bill,' because the new tax proposals included in the *budget* are the part that most immediately affects all of us.

budgie, *n.*   **small parakeet**
Inf. The common household abbreviation for *budgerigar,* a miniature Australian parrot with a long tapered tail, bred in greens, blues, and yellows.

buffer, *n.*   **1. bumper**
                                                                        2. *Slang.* fogy
1. Railroad term; but an American automobile *bumper* is a *fender* in Britain.
2. *Slang.* A silly person. Usually preceded by *old.*

buffet, *n.*   **snack bar**
Both countries use *buffet* to mean 'sideboard' or 'cupboard,' and the terms *buffet supper* and *buffet dinner* to describe meals where the guests serve themselves from a buffet. In all these senses Americans approximate the French pronunciation: BOO-FAY'. When it denotes a piece of furniture, the British sometimes pronounce it BUFF'-IT. It is the common British name for a *lunch counter* or *snack bar* at a railroad station, and in that case the British use a quasi-Frenchified pronunciation, educated people saying BOO'-FAY, the others BUFFY.

bug, *n.*   **bedbug**
Generic in America for 'insect' or 'infection' which is the generic British term. The word formerly meant 'bedbug,' except in the context of the microorganisms which cause flu and related epidemics: *He couldn't come; he's got a bug* or, *I must have caught a bug: I feel awful!*

bugger, *v.t.*   ***Slang.* foul up**
Slang. But as an expletive *bugger* has many different American equivalents: *I'll be buggered!* means: 'I'll be damned!' *Bugger you!* means 'Go to the devil!' *Bugger off!* means anything from 'Get the hell out of here!' to 'Fuck off!' depending on the circumstances. To *bugger off* is to *get the hell out* of somewhere, to *leave* in more or less of a hurry. Be aware, however, that *buggery* is a word meaning *sodomy,* and *bugger* means *commit sodomy* with. See also **bugger all.**

bugger all   ***Slang.* nothing**
Slang. A coarse intensification of **damn all,** not to be confused with exotic acts of intercourse.

Buggin's (Buggins') turn   SEE COMMENT
Promotion based on seniority (sometimes rotation) rather than merit. *Buggins* is an arbitrary name.

builder's merchant   **building supply firm**

building society   **savings and loan association**

building surveyor. See **surveyor.**

bulldog clip, *n.*   **binder clip**

buller, *n.*   **monitor**
Slang. Buller is short for *bulldog,* which is slang for **proctor**'s assistant. *A* proctor at Oxford or Cambridge is attended by two *bulldogs,* or *bullers,* who do the dirty work of disciplining.

bullock. See **jolly.**

bully beef. See **salt beef.**

bum, *n.*   *Slang.* **buttocks; can**
Slang. For obvious reasons, *Hallelujah I'm a Bum* would be modified to *Hallelujah I'm a Tramp* for Britain. See **arse.**

bumbag, *n.*   **fanny pack**

bumble, *n.*   **pompous bureaucrat**
Inf. Literally, a *bumble* is a mace-bearing ceremonial official at British universities or churches (also known as a *beadle*), who gets all decked out but really serves little purpose. Figuratively, he has given his name to any minor official puffed up with his own importance. The British use the word pejoratively, as Americans often use *bureaucrat*, to describe pompous officials (often lowly clerks) in love with red tape who delight in obstructing the expedition of what should be simple procedures. Now rare.

bumf (bumph), *n.*   **1. toilet paper**
                                                                               2. worthless paper
                                                                                        3. rubbish
Slang. An abbreviation of *bum-fodder* (see **bum**), this slang term for *toilet paper* has, apparently in ignorance of its inelegant origin, been extended as a pejorative for *dull paper work, dreary documents, worthless paper* of the kind generally associated with red tape and bureaucratic memoranda, and more recently, to mean 'rubbish,' in a phrase like *Look here, this may be a lot of bumf, but my theory is. . .*

bum-freezer, *n.*   *Slang.* **ass-freezer**
Slang. Especially a short jacket worn by schoolboys or tarts.

bummaree, *n.*   SEE COMMENT
(Accent on the last syllable.) Dealer or porter at Billingsgate or other licensed market. See **billingsgate.**

bumping-race. See **May Week.**

bump-start, *v.t.*   SEE COMMENT
Inf. To start a car by getting it to roll and suddenly throwing it into gear.

bump-supper. See **May Week.**

bun, *n., Inf.*   **squirrel**

bunce, *n.*   *Inf.* **windfall**
Inf. Originally, just any *money* or *profit* but later an unexpected profit, a *windfall*. It has now gained some currency as a verb, especially in the gerund, *buncing,* to describe the practice, in retail stores, of sticking new higher-price tags over the original lower-price labels on articles for sale.

bunches, *n. pl.*　　　　　　　　　　　　　　　**clearance items**
In periodic sales at clothing shops.

bun fight, *n.*　　　　　　　　　　　*approx.* **very large tea party**
Inf. Sometimes *bun feast.* There is no equivalent jocular American colloquialism.
Can also apply to a cocktail party or similar get-together.

bung, *v.t., n.*　　　　　　　　　　　　　　*Slang.* **1. give, pass**
　　　　　　　　　　　　　　　　　　　　　　　　2. bribe

1. *Bung me that monkey wrench, will you?*
2. *He wouldn't have gotten that contract without giving a bung to the client.*

bungalow, *n.*　　　　　　　　　　　　　　　**one-story house**
An American *bungalow* is the equivalent of a British *cottage.* Both modest structures.

bung-ho!, *interj.*　　　　　　　　　　　　　　**1.** *Inf.* **so long!**
　　　　　　　　　　　　　　　　　　　　　　2. *Inf.* **cheers!**

1. *Inf. Rare.* Synonymous with **cheerio!**
2. *Inf.* Synonymous with such words as *Santé, Salute, Skol, Prosit,* etc.

bun in the oven　　　　　　　　　　　　　　　*Inf.* **pregnant**
Looks like she's got a bun in the oven.

bunk, *n., v.i.*　　　　　　　　*Slang.* **take it on the lam; light out**
Slang. Alone, as a verb; or as a noun in *do a bunk.*

bunker, *v.i.*　　　　　　　　　　　　　　　　　　**refuel**

bunkered, *adj.*　　　　　　　　　　　　　　　　*Inf.* **messed up**
Slang. In Britain one gets *bunkered* in troublesome situations in which Americans
would describe themselves as *messed up* in the sense of 'entangled'.

bureau, *n.*　　　　　　　　　　　　　　　　　　　**secretary**
A writing desk with drawers. An American *bureau* is the equivalent of a British
chest of drawers.

burke, also burk, v.t.　　　　　　　　　　　　　**murder; suppress**
Slang. An honest man will not *burke* a fact merely to support a thesis. Sometimes
spelled *burk,* though derived from the name of a Scottish murderer, W. Burke
(hanged in 1829), who smothered people to sell their bodies for dissection. The
original slang meaning was to 'kill without leaving marks of violence.' *To burke a
question* is to suppress it as soon as it rears its head.

burn one's boats, *Inf.*　　　　　　　　　　*Inf.* **burn one's bridges**

Burns Night, *n.*　　　　　　　　　　　　　　　SEE COMMENT
The annual celebration of the life and work of the Scottish poet Robert Burns.
It usually takes the form of suppers, held on or around January 25th, the poet's
birthday.

bursar, *n.*   **treasurer; scholarship student**
A *bursar* is a *college treasurer* in Britain, as well as in America. It has an additional meaning in Britain, 'scholarship student,' which is synonymous with another British word unfamiliar to Americans, *exhibitioner.*

busby, *n.*   **tall fur hat**
Worn by Royal Horse Artillery and Hussars. See also **bearskin; Guards.**

busies, *n. pl.*   *Slang.* **dicks**
Slang. As everyone knows who enjoys reading detective stories.

busker, *n.*   **street entertainer**
From an old word, *busk,* meaning 'improvise.'

butcher, *n.*   *Inf.* **brutal killer**
Inf. Any person who kills wantonly, even for pay, can be called a *butcher* in America as well as Britain.

butchery, *n.*   **meat department**
Butchery would not generally be applied to a butcher shop (*butcher's* shop, in Britain), but rather to a *meat department.* American dictionary definitions include the meaning 'butcher business,' but the use of the term *butchery* is normally restricted to signify carnage.

Butlin's, *n.*   SEE COMMENT
Inf. William Butlin established a type of family holiday camp with everything **laid on:** separate **chalet**-bungalows around a central community building where those who wished to mingle participated in fun and games (movies, dancing, cards, etc.) under the somewhat authoritarian direction of the director of social activities, while nurses took care of the children, leaving the parents free for their revelry. The camps have proliferated, and, at moderate prices, are a boon to families of modest means.

butter bean   **white lima bean**

buttered eggs   **scrambled eggs**
The American term has gained precedence, but the British method of whipping eggs in a buttered saucepan is superior.

butter-muslin, *n.*   **cheesecloth**
Also called *muslin.* The references to different dairy products indicate that the material in question originated in both countries in dairy farm use. However, in each country the name is used without any conscious reference to happy days at the farm. What the Americans call *muslin* would be called *calico* in Britain; but *calico* in America means what the British would call a *cheap cotton print.*

butters, *adj.*   *Slang.* **ugly; undesirable**

buttery, *n.*   **larder**
Where wines and food are kept. A special British use: room in a **college,** especially at Oxford and Cambridge, for sale of food and drink to students.

buttons, *n., Inf.*   **bellhop**
See also **page.**

butty, *n.*   **1.** *Inf.* **buddy**
                                                                            2. *Inf.* **sandwich**
1. *Inf.* Pal, friend, chum, especially fellow-soldier. The British consider the usual
American term *buddy* a variant of *butty,* and a corruption of *brother.* The Americans consider *buddy* a development from baby talk for *brother.*
2. Served on a buttered roll or bread. The term is northern in origin but is used
elsewhere, usually preceded by the contents of the sandwich: *bacon butty, chip
butty,* etc.

buzz off, *v.i.*   *Slang.* **scram**
Slang. Synonymous with **cheese off; cut away; get stuffed; push off.**

by all means   *Inf.* **perfectly okay**
Inf. Means 'there is no objection whatever.' The British would not ordinarily use it
in the American hortatory sense, as in *By all means visit the Prado.*

By Appointment   SEE COMMENT
One may see on merchandise labels, shop signs or commercial stationery: *By
Appointment to . . .* naming some royal personage—the monarch, a prince, a duke.
This means that the purveyor has received a warrant of supplying that person-
age with the commodity or service in question. In the public toilets of the British
Museum, for example, each sheet of toilet paper was stamped in recent years
with the legend *'By Appointment to her Majesty.'*

by-blow, *n.*   **bastard**
A particularly uncharming word.

(obtaining money) by deception   **(obtaining money) under false pretenses**
The American usage is also heard in Britain, with *by* rather than *under.*

by-election, also bye-election, *n.*   **special election**
Of a **Member,** to fill a vacancy in the House of Commons.

by-law, also bye-law *n.*   **ordinance**
Used in municipal government. *By-laws* in America usually mean 'corporate
by-laws,' i.e., the procedural rules and regulations governing a corporation.

by the way, *pred. adj.*   **incidental**
By the way is used in both countries adverbially as the equivalent of *inciden-
tally.* Its use as a predicate adjectival phrase is fairly common in Britain, rare in
America.

C

cabbage-looking, *adj.*   *Inf.* **stupid**
Slang. Rare. I'm not so green as I'm cabbage-looking, i.e., 'I'm not as dumb as I look.'

caboose, *n.*   **galley**
In America, the last car on a freight train, used by the train crew. In Britain a kitchen on the deck of a ship.

cab-rank, *n.*   **taxi stand**

cack-handed, *adj.*   **clumsy**
Inf. Literally, *left-handed.*

cadge, *v.t.*   *Inf.* **scrounge**
To get something (money, cigarettes, etc.) by sponging or begging, from a friend or a stranger.

Caesar, *n.*   **Caesarean**
Inf. In both countries *operation* or *section* is understood; but the British sometimes use the name of the great Roman while the Americans always use the adjective derived from his name. In either case, a baby is delivered by cutting a section of the mother's abdomen.

café   SEE COMMENT
The term may be applied to several types of establishment, including those serving coffee and cakes. The most common usage, however, is for simple, modest restaurants serving breakfast and simple luncheon dishes to a predominantly working-class clientele. Many Britons deliberately mispronounce *café* as KAIF or KAFF.

caff, *n.*   **café**

cakehole, *n.*   *Slang.* **trap**
Slang. Mouth. *Put that in your cakehole.*

calendar, *n.*   **catalogue**
In the sense of a 'list of courses' offered by a university, together with appropriate regulations and descriptions of the courses, terms, and examination dates.

calendar, station. See **station calendar.**

calico, *n.*   **white cotton cloth; muslin**
Calico as used in America would be called a *cheap cotton print* in Britain. See also **butter muslin.**

call, *n., v.t., v.i.*   **1.** *vi.,* **visit**
                                           2. *n., vt., v.i.,* **bid**

1. Mr. Jones *called,* in America, means that Mr. Jones 'telephoned.' In Britain, it means that Mr. Jones 'dropped in,' 'came by.' Britons say *rang up* in the case of a telephone call.
2. Bridge term: *Let's see, you called two hearts, didn't you? A call* is a 'bid.'

call after   **name for**
The British *call* their babies *after* favored relatives and national heroes. Americans may name a child *for* someone or merely *call* a boy *Thomas* or the like.

call at   **stop at**
Both countries speak of vessels as *calling at* ports. The British occasionally apply the same term to trains. Thus one sees signs in the Charing Cross Railway Station at the gate (**barrier**) describing a particular train as *Not calling at London Bridge.*

call-box, *n.*   **telephone booth**
Also called *kiosk or telephone box.*

called to the bar   **admitted to the bar**
This British phrase applies only to **barristers** and refers to persons who have received a license to practice as barristers. See also **Inns of Court; barrister.**

caller, *n.*   **calling party**
A person making a telephone call is referred to as *caller* and is addressed by the operator as *caller.* In America the *caller* would be referred to as the *calling party* and would be addressed by the operator as *sir* or *madam.* See also **pay for the call; personal call.**

call 999   **call 911**
Young British children know they must dial or punch this number to get immediate attention from emergency services. If anything, 999 is easier to ring up than 911, but we can be sure no one will declare 911 obsolete.

call-out charge   **house call charge**
What the repair man charges when he visits your home because something's gone wrong.

call to order   **rebuke**
When a person violates the rules of parliamentary procedure or otherwise offends decorum at any meeting, the presiding officer *calls him to order.* In America it is the meeting that is *called to order.*

call-up, *n.*   **draft**
Military service term. A *call-up* card is a *draft* card.

Calor gas   **propane gas**
Proprietary name, but used generically for liquefied butane gas in pressurized containers in homes, on boats, etc.

camber, *n.*   **bank**
A British road sign proclaiming REVERSE CAMBER means 'road banked wrong way.'

camiknickers, *n. pl*   SEE COMMENT
All-in-one ladies' undergarment with camisole and **knickers.**

camp bed   folding cot
The British also use the word *cot*, but to them it means what the Americans call a *crib*. Also, *safari bed*, once proprietary.

CAMRA   SEE COMMENT
Acronym. Acronym that stands for Campaign for Real Ale, an organization founded in 1971 to improve the quality and choice of traditional beers, especially in pubs. Their primary concern is with maintaining the integrity of Real Ale.

candidature, *n.*   candidacy

candlestick telephone   upright telephone
The old-fashioned kind.

candy-floss, *n.*   1. cotton candy
2. SEE COMMENT
2. Used metaphorically for 'vapid thoughts.'

cane, *n., v.t.*   whip; switch
What Americans call a *cane*, the British prefer to call a *walking-stick*.

cane it, *v.*   *Slang.* 1. to travel at great speed
                                     2. to take alcohol or drugs in excess

cannon, *n.*   carom
Term in billiards.

cans, *n., pl.*   *Slang.* headphones

Cantabrigian, *n., adj.*   SEE COMMENT
Of Cambridge, from *Cantabrigia*, the Latin name for Cambridge. In a narrower sense, a Cantabrigian is a student or graduate of Cambridge University. Informally abbreviated to *Cantab.*, which is the usual form, and applies in America to Cambridge, Mass., and particularly Harvard.

canteen of cutlery, *n.*   silver set
Contained in a case, usually a fitted one. The metal, nowadays, is more likely to be stainless steel than silver.

canterbury, *n.*   magazine rack
Properly speaking, this word means a 'low stand with light partitions, built to hold music portfolios.' This original meaning is borne out by the fact that the genuine old ones are usually decorated with woodwork carved in the form of a lyre. People use them, lyre or no lyre, most often to hold magazines, newspapers, and the like.

Cantuarian, *n. adj.*   SEE COMMENT
This is the name of the official magazine of The King's School, Canterbury, a **public school** reputed to be the oldest functioning school in the world. The name

is derived from *Cantuaria,* the medieval Latin name for Canterbury, which in Roman times bore the name of *Durovernum.* Neither a King's School **old boy,** nor a member of the **staff** (*faculty*), nor a resident of Canterbury would be called a *Cantuarian,* in the way in which *Cantabrigian, Oxonian,* etc. are used with reference to Cambridge, Oxford, and other university cities. However, this rule does apply to Archbishops of Canterbury, who sign by given name followed by *Cantuar:. Cantuar* is an abbreviation of *Cantuariensis,* the Latin adjective formed from *Cantuaria.*

cap, *n.*   **1. letter (in athletics)**
                                                      2. diaphragm
1. Sports term, usually in the expression *win one's cap.* It generally indicates that one has played for one's county or one's country. To *be capped* is to *have won one's cap; uncapped,* generally, refers to players who have yet to win their *caps;* but an uncapped county player is one who has not yet been selected to play for England in a **Test Match.**
2. *Slang.* For contraceptive use.

(to) cap it all   **(to) make matters worse**
In other words, to complete the tale of woe.

caravan, *n.*   **house trailer**
As an automobile term. It is also used in the more original romantic sense. A *caravan park* is a *trailer court.*

car boot sale   SEE COMMENT
An informal gathering held in open rural space where individuals bring goods for sale. So named because they transport the goods in their car **boot** and unpack them for display to prospective buyers.

car breaker   **car wrecker**

cardan shaft   **drive shaft**
Automobile term. See **Appendix II.E.**

cardie, *n.*   *Inf., abbrev.* **cardigan**

cardigan. See under **Balaclava.**

cards. See **give (someone) his cards.**

care a pin   *Slang.* **give a hoot**
Slang. Almost always used, like its American equivalent, in the negative.

caretaker, *n.*   **janitor**
Caretaker, in America, implies the owner's absence. *Gardener* would be the term used by a Briton owning country property.

(in) Carey Street   *Slang.* **flat broke**
Inf. The High Court of Justice in Bankruptcy (commonly known as the Bankruptcy Court) used to be located on Carey Street in London. (It is now located around the corner at Victory House, Kingsway.) That is the origin of the peculiar phrase *to be in Carey Street,* which is usually used to describe the condition of being flat broke rather than in technical bankruptcy.

cargo boat   **freighter**

Carnaby Street   SEE COMMENT
A street in the Soho section of London, studded with apparel shops catering
to the young. In the 60s the name was used allusively to refer to youthful used
clothing; sometimes shortened to *Carnaby*, as in *Carnaby styling or attire*. Its heyday as the center of youthful fashion has gone, and it is now becoming identified
with tourist attractions.

carousel, *n.*   **rotating conveyor belt**
Like those conveying suitcases at airports. Spelled with one *r* in Britain.

car park   **parking lot**

carpet, *n.*   SEE COMMENT
British purists distinguish between *carpet* and *rug* on the basis of size: forty sq.
ft. or over is a *carpet*; under that size is a *rug*. The American distinction is based
on type of manufacture: a *carpet* is machine made; a *rug* handmade. Incidentally,
indolent Americans usually sweep things *under the rug*.

carpet area   **floor space**

carriage, *n.*   **1. car; coach**
                                                        2. freight
1. In Britain a railroad *car* or *coach* is called a *carriage; car* means 'automobile' and
coach also means 'bus'.
2. *Carriage* means 'freight' in the sense of *cost of shipping. Carriage forward* means
'freight extra'; *carriage paid* means 'freight prepaid.' See also **forward; freight.**

carriage rug   **lap robe**
Has given way to *travelling rug*. All terms have given way to effective car heaters.

carrier-bag, *n.*   **shopping bag**
While the hyphen is beginning to disappear from many Briticisms such as this
one, the meaning of *carrier-bag* remains constant, even though *shopping bag*
also is heard frequently—especially at grander clothing stores and department
stores.

carry-cot, *n.*   **portable bassinet**

carry on, *v.i., n.*   **1.** *v.i.,* **keep going**
                                                        2. *v.i.,* **flirt**
                                                        3. *v.i., n.,* **fuss**
                                                        4. *military command,* **as you were**
1. In road directions, *carry on* means 'keep going straight ahead.' It is the equivalent of *You first* when one is offering to hold a door or otherwise step aside for
someone. At times it seems to mean little more than 'O.K.' and once in a while it
replaces *so long*.
2. An old-fashioned way to conduct an amorous affair.
3. A slang noun meaning 'fuss': *This has been a most trying carry-on* (situation,
affair).

carry one's bat   *Inf.* **stick it out**
Inf. To *carry, carry out,* or *bring out one's bat* is to 'outlast the others,' *to stick it out* and finally *put it over* or *bring it off.* Stems from cricket as it used to be played: the batsman who was not put out left at the end of his **innings** carrying his bat out with him instead of leaving it for the next batsman.

carry the can   *Slang.* **be the fall guy**
Slang. The phrase is often lengthened to *carry the can back.* The *can* in question is said to be the one containing dynamite used in blasting operations. See also **hold the baby.**

cartridge, *n.*   **shell**
Shotgun ammunition. Used in both countries as well to mean the ammunition used in a rifle or revolver.

carve up   **swindle**
Slang. Especially, to cut a partner-in-crime out of his share of the loot. The noun *carve-up* has acquired the more general meaning of any swindle. It has been used in a quite different sense to mean a 'melon' in the sense of 'bonanza,' which may be the result of the legitimate splitting of a windfall, but somehow the impression lingers that the windfall may not have been all that legitimate.

case, *n.*   **box**
For example, a British shop advertises a *case* of dessert spoons where an American store would speak of a *set* or a *box.*

cashier, *n.*   **teller**
Banking term, used interchangeably with *teller* in Britain. In most American banks, the title *cashier* is reserved for the officer who is the equivalent of the *secretary* in non-banking corporations.

cash point   SEE COMMENT
Sign occasionally seen in supermarkets and other shops, indicating the place where one pays. The equivalent American sign would be CASHIER or PAY HERE.

casket, *n.*   **small box**
A *casket* in America means a 'coffin.' It never has this meaning in Britain.

cast, *v.t.*   **discard**
Special military term applied to superannuated cavalry horses. Unhappily they are usually slaughtered for horsemeat at a **knacker's** yard rather than sent to pasture.

caster sugar, *n.*   **finely granulated sugar**
Caster sugar is more finely grained than American *granulated sugar* but not powdery like American powdered or confectioner's sugar, which is called **icing sugar** in Britain.

casual labourer   **temp or occasional worker**
This term refers principally to workers like stevedores who show up for work but may or may not get any work that day. See also **casual ward.**

casualty ward   **emergency room**
In a hospital. The person in charge may be a **charge-nurse.** The term is often
shortened to *casualty,* just as the American equivalent becomes *emergency* ("Dr.
Kildare wanted in *emergency!*")

casual ward   **flophouse**
A place for temporary housing of the homeless. Synonymous with **doss-house;**
derived from the extension of **casual labourer** to mean 'pauper' or 'vagrant.'

cat, *n.*   **whipping**
Inf. Undoubtedly a reference to *cat-o'-nine-tails;* rarer as a practice than a word,
but there are still those who advocate "bring back the *cat,*" i.e., 'reintroduce cor-
poral punishment.' Incidentally, in the expression *room enough to swing a cat,* the
cat is not a screaming feline, but a *cat-o'-nine-tails,* a nine-knotted rope used for
flogging offenders.

catalogue company   **mail order house**

cat among the pigeons   *Inf.* **match in a tinderbox**
Inf. To *put the cat among the pigeons is* to *start a fuss* by introducing a highly inflam-
matory topic into a conversation.

catapult, *n. v.i.*   **slingshot**
The British use this word as the Americans do, as both noun and verb.

cat burglar, *Inf.*   *Inf.* **second-story man**

catch flies, *v.*   *Slang.* SEE COMMENT
To have one's mouth open in a **gormless** expression.

catch hold of the wrong end of the stick   *Inf.* **miss the point**
Inf. Sometimes *get* instead of *catch.*

catchment area, *n.*   SEE COMMENT
The official area from which users of a particular service are drawn. Most often
used for a school's students or a doctor's patients. *We live just outside the catchment area for Camden School for Girls.*

catch out, *v.t.*   **catch (in a mistake); detect**
A Briton will *catch you out* if you commit an error. He will also *catch out* the error.
The Americans usually omit the *out.* See **Appendix I.A.1.**

catch (someone) up, *v.t.*   **catch up with (someone)**
The British *catch you up* or *catch up with you.*

caterer, *n.*   **food supplier**
The term *caterer* is broad in Britain, including the more restricted American sense,
and can be understood as 'restaurateur.' In America, the term *catering* is confined
to the preparation and bringing of food to a home or other establishment and
serving it there for a special occasion.

cat-lap, *n.*   *Slang.* **soda water**
Slang. Dull people, novels, or movies would never be likened to *cat-lap:* the term
is reserved for weak tea and similar outrages on the deserving public.

catmint, *n.*   **catnip**

cat's-eyes, *n. pl.*   **road reflectors**
Reflector studs, set at close intervals into road surfaces along the white lines marking the lanes. Enormously helpful on unlighted roads and foggy nights, they are mounted in depressible rubber frames so that they can be driven over without harm.

cat's-meat, *n.*   **cat food**

cattery, *n.*   **cat-boarding kennel**
Also *cat-breeding establishment. Cattery* is heard in America.

cattle grid, *n.*   **cattle guard**

cattleman, *n.*   **cowhand**
A *cattleman* in America is a *rancher* or *cattle owner.* In Britain he works for somebody else.

caucus, *n.*   **political party committee**
A political organization that formulates party policy, election strategy, and the like. In Britain, the word is somewhat derogatory, implying the smoke-filled atmosphere of a powerful unofficial cabal. A *caucus* in America is an *ad hoc* political meeting of party regulars.

caught on the hop, *Slang.*   *Inf.* **caught napping**

caught on the wrong foot   *Inf.* **caught napping**
Slang. A term borrowed from **cricket.** A **batsman** *(batter)* put in this position by the **bowler** *(approx.* pitcher) is in difficulties.

cause-list, *n.*   **trial calendar**
Legal term.

cave!, *interj.*   *Slang.* **cheezit!**
Schoolboy slang. Rare. (Pronounced CAVEY.) This is the singular imperative of the Latin verb *caveo.* This imperative form may be familiar from reproductions of the well-preserved Pompeian floor mosaic showing the picture of a dog and bearing the legend *Cave canem* (beware of the dog). To *keep cave* is to *keep watch, act as lookout.*

ceased to exist   **been disconnected**
Gloomy intelligence imparted by the telephone operator: *Sorry sir, that line has ceased to exist.* A *ceaseline* is a *disconnected number.* Obsolete.

censure motion, *n.*   SEE COMMENT
A vote of no confidence in the government and its policies called by the opposition. Important bills are sometimes treated as matters of confidence, with a three-line whip, meaning that all members of the governing party are ordered to vote with the government.

centenary, *n.*   **centennial**
Both terms are used in both countries. Both pronounce *centennial* the same way; but *centenary* is usually accented on the first syllable and has a short *e* in the second syllable in America, whereas in Britain it is usually accented on the second syllable, with a long *e*, though it is permissible there to shorten the *e*, or even to accent the first syllable.

centillion. See **Appendix II.D.**

central reserve. See **centre strip.**

centreplate. See **sliding keel.**

centre strip   **median divider**
Called *central reserve* in the official Highway Code, an appellation as pompous as *median divider.* See also **dual carriageway.**

century, *n.*   **100 runs**
In a cricket match, the **batsman** who makes 100 runs is said to score a *century.* See **batsman.**

certified, *adj.*   **insane**
Inf. A past participle used as an adjective, both literally and hyperbolically, like its American equivalent. *Certified* is now heard in both countries. See synonyms under **bonkers** and **sectioned.**

C.H. See **Birthday Honours.**

chain, *n.*   SEE COMMENT
A person buying or selling a house may be caught in a series of transactions with several interdependent sales and purchases. This is a chain, and anyone selling or buying property is eager to avoid it.

chair, *n.*   **track socket**
Metal socket holding railroad track in place on a tie.

chairman (of a company), *n.*   **president (of a corporation)**
The Americans do not speak of the *chairman* of a company or corporation. They speak of the *chairman of the board,* meaning the 'chairman of the board of directors.' Such a *chairman* is not, strictly speaking, a corporate officer. He runs meetings of the board of directors but has only one vote on the board, and often the term implies more honor than power. Thus, an American corporate *president* or *chief executive officer (CEO)* is often said to have been kicked upstairs when he becomes chairman of the board. In a British company, the *chairman* is the equivalent of the *president* of an American corporation. See also **managing director.**

chalet, *n.*   SEE COMMENT
A small suburban house, far removed from the Swiss mountain cottage from which the name was stolen.

chalk and cheese   **night and day**
Worlds apart. As different as chalk from cheese is the usual phrase, the equivalent of *as different as night and day.* This is sometimes shortened to *chalk and cheese: Why, they're simply chalk and cheese.*

chambermaid, *n.*   **hotel maid**
Not a household servant as in America. See also **char; daily woman.**

chambers, *n. pl.*   **lawyer's office**
The **solicitor** will invite you to his or her *office;* a **barrister** more often to *chambers.*
An American lawyer would never speak of *chambers,* but that term is applied to
a judge's private office (usually adjoining the courtroom). See also **Inns of Court.**

champers, *n.*   **champagne**
Slang. Americans may be more familiar with the other British slang for this patri-
cian beverage: **bubbly.** As in *champagne,* the CH- is pronounced SH-. [Also spelled
shampers.] See **Harry** . . .

champion, *adj.*   **fine**
Slang. Champion is used adjectivally in America in sports terminology as, for
instance, *champion boxer, champion golfer.* In Britain it is occasionally used as the
equivalent of *fine* or *great.* Thus: *Alf is a champion lad!*

chance, *n.*   SEE COMMENT
A cricket player who misses a catch off a **batsman**'s bat, or a **football** (soccer)
player who misses a possible goal, is said to have had a *chance.* See **misfield.**

chance-child, *n.*   *Inf.* **love child**
Inf. Rare. The British term seems harsh beside the romantic American term. Both
countries use the unfeeling term *illegitimate child.* The British sometimes use the
term *come-by-chance* to mean the same thing.

chance-come, *adj.*   **fortuitous**
Describing anything that happens by chance.

chancellor, *n.*   **honorary university head**
University term. See also **vice-chancellor.**

Chancellor of the Exchequer   **Secretary of the Treasury**
See **Exchequer.**

chance-met, *adj.*   **met by chance**

chance one's arm, *Inf.*   *Inf.* **try one's luck**

chancer, *n.*   **risk-taker**
Usually used as a pejorative: *Mark is a good businessman, but he's a bit of a chancer.*

change. See **get much change out of.**

change down   **down shift**
Inf. An automobile term. The British also use the term *change up,* where the Americans would say *shift,* a term which in America is always understood to refer to
shifting up, i.e., shifting into higher gear. See **Appendix II.E.**

change the bowling. See **open the bowling.**

changing-room, *n.*   **1. dressing-room**
                                                             2. locker-room
1. In a clothing store.
2. In a gym or at a stadium, swimming pool, tennis court, and the like.

chap, *n.*   *Inf.* **guy; fellow**
The use of the word *chap* by Britons may seem affected to most Americans. Its
commonest equivalent in America is *guy,* which is colloquial. Americans also
use *fellow,* which is less inelegant than *guy* (as opposed to *person,* for instance),
but still seems to come off as somewhat deprecatory. *Guy* is common in Britain
now, though still less common than *bloke.*

chapel, *adj.*   **non-Anglican**
Used to describe a person adhering to a Protestant sect other than the established
church, i.e., the Church of England (also known as the Anglican Church). It is a
shortening of *chapelfolk* or *chapelgoer,* both of which are informal labels for members of such sects. The standard British nouns for such a person are **dissenter**
and **nonconformist,** which are interchangeable and sometimes capitalized. *Free
Church* is another synonym.

chap-fallen, *adj.*   **dejected**
Chap is an archaic variant of *chop,* meaning 'jaw' (as in, e.g., *lick one's chops*). *Chap-
fallen* describes a person whose jaws are hanging, i.e., who is in low spirits.

chapman, *n.*   **peddler**
Like the itinerant merchant it describes, the word is rarely met with nowadays.
Synonymous with *peddler,* which the British spell *pedlar.* They hawked *chap-
books,* little pamphlets containing street cries, short tales, tracts, and ballads.

char, *n.*   **1. cleaning lady**
                                                             2. tea
1. *Inf.* This word is displeasing to the ladies whom it describes. It is also used in
the combinations *charwoman* and *charlady.* The latter is minimally acceptable to
these ladies, who generally prefer to be called *daily help, daily woman,* or just *daily.*
Cleaner and cleaning lady are also common.
2. *Inf.* The British love their tea and some of the most cultured of them will affectionately offer it to you in the mildly humorous phrase *a cuppa char.* Sometimes
the *char* is omitted in this connection and *cuppa* is used alone. No slang American
counterpart.

charabanc, *n.*   **excursion bus**
A term formerly heard. When used, it is pronounced SHARABANG. Now referred
to as a *coach.*

charge-hand, *n.*   **foreman**
The workman *in charge* of a job.

charge-nurse, *n.*   **head nurse**
In *charge* of a ward. See also **casualty ward; sister.**

charge-sheet, *n.*   **police blotter**
To *take* a person *in charge* is to *arrest* him.

charge (something) to tax   impose tax on (something)

charity. See **as cold as charity.**

Charles's Wain   **Ursa Major; Big Dipper**
Other British names for the Big Dipper: **the Plough;** *the Great Bear; the Wagon.*

charley, *n., Slang.*   *Slang.* **botch job; mess**

Charley's dead. See **slate.**

charlie, *n.*   *Slang.* **jerk**
Slang. Some charlie has broken my vase! Or, *I felt a proper charlie* (i.e., *a real idiot*)! On occasion, *charlie* can take on the connotation of *patsy; fall guy.*

charlies (charleys), *n., pl.*   *Slang.* **tits**
Slang. Synonymous with **Bristols,** but apparently not rhyming slang (see **Appendix II.G.3**); etymology unknown.

charmer, *n.*   SEE COMMENT
Inf. This word now applies to either sex, to mean an attractive person, but in old-fashioned circles the connotation is still feminine. Used of men, it can imply a studied approach to the art of charming.

chartered accountant   **certified public accountant**
Almost always referred to in America as *C.P.A.*

chartered surveyor   **licensed architect**

chat show   **talk show**
Television term.

chattering classes   *Inf.* SEE COMMENT
A term applied derogatively to intellectuals, usually of left-wing or liberal bent, who discuss politics and social affairs but do not play an active role in either area.

chattermag, *n., v.i.*   *n.* **chatterbox** *v.i.* **babble**
Inf. A 'chattering magpie, a much-talking person,' given to gossiping.

chat up   *Slang.* **hand (someone) a line**
Slang. In Britain you *chat up* a person in the attempt to *win him* or *her over.* When the *chatting up* is directed by a male to a female, there is generally an implication of a sexual objective. *Sweet-talk* is another American equivalent. *Chat* (without the *up*), as in *chat the girls,* means 'flirt with.' Britons also *chat to* a person.

chav, *n.*   *Slang.* SEE COMMENT
A derogatory term for a working-class person, often dressed in expensive branded sportswear and excessive jewelry.

chaw-bacon, *n.*   **rube; hayseed**
Slang. Jaw-bacon is a variant.

cheap, *adj.*   **inexpensive; reduced (in price)**
In America a lady would express pride in her successful shopping expedition by saying, *The dress was cheap,* or *I bought it cheap.* However, she would not want to refer to the object of her shopping triumph as a *cheap dress.* If she wanted a new dress when the sales were on, she would never ask the saleslady to show her a *cheap* dress. She would ask for a *reduced* dress. Thus, it can be said that, except as a predicate adjective, *cheap* would be avoided in America as a synonym for *inexpensive* because of a reduction. As an attributive adjective, *cheap* in America connotes *tawdriness* in referring to things and persons and has a special slang connotation of *stinginess* when referring to persons, especially in the expression *cheapskate.* These meanings are secondary in the British usage of *cheap.* Thus *cheap tickets,* as advertised on railroad posters, may be *excursion fares,* and a *cheap* frock may be a very nice dress indeed, though inexpensive. See **on the cheap.**

cheapjack, *n., adj.*   **hawker**
At fairs, etc. Sometimes it means 'peddler.' *Cheapjack goods* are poor quality stuff, *shoddy,* the sort usually offered by this class of merchant. See **chapman.**

cheddar, hard. *See* **Hard cheese!**

cheek, *v.t.*   *Inf.* **to sass; be fresh to**
Slang. To *cheek* someone is to be impudent or rude to him. Not used as a verb in America.

cheeky, *adj.*   *Inf.* SEE COMMENT
Very impudent and disrespectful in speech or behavior.

cheerio! *interj.*   *Inf.* **so long!**

cheers! *interj.*   **1. here's how!**
                                                2. *Exclaim., inf.* **goodbye!**
                                                3. *Exclaim., inf.* **thank you!**
1. *Down the hatch! Here's mud in your eye! Chin chin! Salute! A votre santé! Skol! Prosit!* The British form was originally non-U (see **Appendix I.C.6**) and was frowned on in some U-circles where *Your health!* or *Good luck!* was preferred. It was gradually taken over, perhaps at first facetiously, and is now established practically everywhere.

cheesed off   *Slang.* **teed off**
Slang. Synonymous with **brassed off.**

cheese it!   *Slang.* **pipe down!**
Slang. Rather than *Look out! Somebody's coming!* or *Make yourself scarce!*

cheese off!   **get lost!**
Slang. Synonymous with **buzz off.**

cheese-paring, *adj., n.*   **penny-pinching**
A *cheese-paring* chap is a *stingy* one, and the noun *cheese-paring* describes this sorry attitude toward life. As a plural noun *cheese-parings* means 'junk,' odds and ends that ought to be thrown away. In this connection, see also **lumber.**

cheesy, *adj.*   *Slang.* **swanky**
Slang. In the sense of 'stylish' or 'chic,' the British and American meanings are directly opposite. This British use is going out; some say that it is already obsolete, but it is still heard occasionally in the countryside, among old folk. Along with the passing of its use in the first sense, the word has now acquired the American meaning in Britain.

Chelsea bun   *approx.* **Danish**
A rolled currant bun, usually with icing.

chemist, dispensing. See **dispenser.**

chemist's shop   **drugstore; pharmacy**
The *shop* can be omitted. See also **dispenser.**

cheque, *n.*   **check**
A matter of spelling. But isn't it peculiar that a *check* (or *cheque*) is a form of *draft*, that *draft* is sometimes spelled *draught*, and that *draughts* is the British form of *checkers?* In Britain, a *checking account* is a *cheque account*, a **current account**, or a **running account**.

Chequers, *n.*   SEE COMMENT
Official country residence of the Prime Minister, in Buckinghamshire.

chesterfield, *n.*   **sofa**
In America a *chesterfield* is a dark overcoat, usually with a velvet collar. The British *chesterfield* is a large overstuffed sofa, with a back and upholstered arms. In Canada, the term is applied to any large sofa or couch.

chest of drawers   **bureau; dresser**
In Britain a **bureau** is a writing desk with drawers of the sort Americans refer to as a *secretary,* and a **dresser** is a *kitchen sideboard with shelves.*

Chevy, *n.*   **face**
Rhyming slang. From *Chevy Chase.*

chewing gum   **gum**
In Britain **gum** by itself would be taken to mean 'mucilage.' The British are rapidly moving toward full acceptance of chewing gum.

chib, also **chub**   SEE COMMENT
Slang. **1.** A knife. **2.** To slash or cut off. **3.** To hit someone in the face with a broken bottle.

chicken, *n.*   **young chicken**
Chicken in America covers any size or age. An old one in Britain might be called a *fowl, hen,* or *boiler,* and *chicken yard* in American would be *fowl-run* in Britain.

chicken-flesh, *n.*   *Inf.* **goose pimples**
Inf. Usually *goose-flesh* in Britain. *Goose pimples* is considered an Americanism in Britain.

chicory, *n.*   **endive**
In a British **greengrocer's,** ask for *chicory* if you want *endive*—and vice versa!

chief bridesmaid   **maid of honor**

chief editor   **editor in chief**

Chief Whip, *n.*   SEE COMMENT
The Chief Whip maintains party discipline and looks after the day-to-day management of the government's business in Parliament. The official title is Parliamentary Secretary to the Treasury, and the Chief Whip is always a **cabinet member.**

child-battering   **child beating**
Battering is used for *beating* also in the expression *wife-battering*. But note that the American term *child abuse* may also imply sexual abuse in Britain.

child-minder, *n.*   SEE COMMENT
A person who looks after one or more children whose parents are working. A child-minder is distinguished from nannies by looking after the children in his or (usually) her own home, and by being legally required to register with the local authority. The term *babysitter* is becoming common in Britain. Also called a **sitter-in.**

chilled distribution   **(delivery by) refrigerated truck**

Chiltern Hundreds   SEE COMMENT
This name is derived from the term *hundred,* a now obsolete subdivision of a county, with its own court and other administrative features. These courts were abolished over a century ago. Three of these English hundreds in the County of Buckinghamshire, named Stoke, Burnham, and Desborough, came to be known as the *Chiltern Hundreds* because of their situation in the Chiltern Hills. The *Stewardship of the Chiltern Hundreds* is a nominal office under the Chancellor of the Exchequer, an "office of honour and profit under the crown," the holding of which has been considered, since 1701, incompatible with membership in the House of Commons. Since the middle of the 18th century a Member who held the office was required to vacate his seat in the Commons. Hence, to *apply for* or *accept the Chiltern Hundreds* (i.e., the stewardship thereof) means to 'resign one's seat' in the House of Commons. Since a Member is not allowed to resign his seat before the expiration of his term of office, the only way he can vacate the seat is to *apply for the Chiltern Hundreds.*

chimney-piece, *n.*   **mantelpiece**
Mantelpiece is now just as common in Britain.

chimney-pot, *n.*   SEE COMMENT
A metal or earthenware pipe added to the top of a chimney; ubiquitous in Britain (and much of Europe). Its function is to improve the draft and disperse the smoke. A *chimney-pot hat* is a *stovepipe*. This is sometimes shortened to *chimney-pot*, omitting the *hat*, like *stovepipe*.

chin, *v.t.*   *Slang.* **to hit someone on the chin**

chine, *n.*   SEE COMMENT

Apart from its meanings shared with American English (backbone, part of the backbone of an animal cut for cooking, ridge, crest, intersection of sides and bottom of a ship), a *chine* is also a deep ravine, but only on the Isle of Wight and in Dorset.

chinless wonder, *n.*   *Derog.* SEE COMMENT
An upper-class male with no distinction of intellect or character. See **Hooray Henry.**

chip, *n.*   **1. wood sliver**
                                                                 2. fruit basket
1. The thin material from which fruit and vegetable baskets are made. See **punnet.**
2. The basket itself.

chip, *v.t., Inf.*   **tease; kid**
As in, *They chipped me about my boy-friend.*

chip in   *Inf.* **butt in; break in**
Inf. In the sense of interrupting somebody else's conversation, a meaning not used in America, where it means to 'contribute,' in the way children make up a fund to buy their teacher a gift. The British use it that way too, and also have another phrase for that: to *pay one's whack.*

chipolata, *n.*   **small pork sausage**
(Pronounced CHIPPO-LAH'-TA.) The spicy meat is mixed with meal. The best are those ground, blended, and stuffed by your own butcher.

chippings, loose. See **loose chippings.**

chippy, *n.*   *Inf.* **1. fish and chip shop**
                                                                 2. carpenter

chips, *n. pl.*   **French fried potatoes**
Inf. One sees *French fried potatoes* on some British menus nowadays. See also **crisps** and **fish 'n' chips.**

chit, *n.*   **memo**
The British use it as well in its American meaning of an 'I.O.U.,' usually for drink or food in a club or military mess, or at a bar or pub. See **on the slate.**

chivvy, *v.t.*   *Inf.* **keep after; pursue**
Inf. Also *chevy.* To *put pressure* on someone; to *hurry* him *up,* in the sense of 'chase' him. Probably there is some connection with *Chevy Chase,* an old ballad, and a place on the Scottish border.

chock-a-block   **crammed together**
Inf. Rarely heard in America. Synonymous with *completely full.* See also **packed out with.**

chocker   *Inf.* **disgusted; fed up**
Slang. From **chock-a-block.**

chocolate vermicelli   **chocolate sprinkles**
See also **hundreds and thousands.** Britain and America know and use *vermicelli* as forms of spaghetti.

choked, *adj.*   **disgruntled**
Slang. Synonymous with **chuffed, 2;** *disappointed.*

choose how   *Inf.* **like it or not**
Inf. A north of England term.

chop, *n., v.t., v.i.*   *approx.* **change**
A special use of *chop* in the expression *chop and change,* which, used transitively,
means to 'keep changing' (e.g., to keep trading in your car for a new one). To *chop
and change,* used intransitively, means to 'shilly-shally.' To *chop in* (a variant of
chip in) is to 'break into a conversation, to 'put in your two cents' worth.' To *chop
logic* is to 'argue for argument's sake.'

chophouse, *n.*   **a restaurant specialising in steaks, cutlets, etc.**

chopper, *n.*   *Slang.* **penis**

choppers, *n., pl.*   *Slang.* **teeth**

chops of the Channel   SEE COMMENT
Inf. Passage from the Atlantic Ocean into the English Channel, so-called because
of the short, broken waves of the sea there.

chough, *n.*   **red-legged crow**
(Pronounced CHUFF.) A fairly common crow in some parts of Britain, notable for
its plaintive cry like a kitten's. Once believed to have swallowed the soul of King
Arthur. This name is included here because of the West Country expression *as the
chough flies,* a variant of *as the crow flies.*

Christian name   **first name**
Americans also say *Christian name* and *given name* but *first name* is much more
common. See also **middle name.**

Christmas club   SEE COMMENT
Different from the American scheme of the same name; a special sort of layaway
plan. In Britain one can join a Christmas club usually during the summer at a
neighborhood butcher shop or grocery store, accumulating modest periodic
deposits there to lessen the impact of the holiday bills for the turkey or roast beef
and its trappings.

chubby-chops   *Inf.* **a plump person**
Used in a jocular way, and not usually with the intention of offending.

chucker-out, *n., Slang.*   *Slang.* **bouncer**

chuffed, *adj.*   **1. delighted**
                                                                2. disgruntled
Slang. This curious bit of antiquated army slang has two diametrically opposite
meanings, depending on the context. One can say *chuffed pink* (tickled pink) to
mean 'pleased,' or *dead chuffed* to mean 'displeased.' In the second sense, *chuffed*
is synonymous with **choked.**

chump, *n.*   *Inf.* **nut (head)**

Slang. Chump, like *loaf, nod,* and other words, is a slang term for *head,* like *bean* in America. *Use your chump* is commonly heard, inviting the party addressed to stop being a fool. To be *off one's chump* is to be *off one's nut.*

chump chop   SEE COMMENT
Type of lamb chop, coming from the section between the thick end of the loin and the leg. A chump chop is mostly meat surrounding a little bit of bone. See **Appendix II.H.**

chunder, *v., n.*   *Slang.* **1. to vomit**
                                                                      2. vomit

Chunnel, *n.*   SEE COMMENT
Inf. English Channel tunnel.

chunter, *v.i.*   *Inf.* **blab on and on**
Inf. Like **rabbit on.**

C.I.D.   SEE COMMENT
The initials stand for *Criminal Investigation Department.* A *C.I.D. man* is a plain-clothes detective, a *Cop In Disguise.*

cider, *n.*   **hard cider**
Cider, in Britain, is always fermented and alcoholic. Americans distinguish between *cider* (which the British call *apple juice,* as do many Americans) and *hard cider,* which is simply *cider* to the British. See also **scrump.**

cinecamera, *n.*   **movie camera**

cinema, *n.*   **movie house**
In America, its connotation is technical rather than popular. See also **film; flicks; pictures.**

Cinque Ports   SEE COMMENT
(Pronounced SINK PORTS.) Literally (from Old French via Middle English) 'Five Ports' on the southeast coast of Britain. The five ports are actually seven plus *Tenterden: Hastings, Romney, Hythe, Dover, Sandwich, Winchelsea,* and *Rye.* They were instructed to protect England from possible invasion from the south.

cipher. See **nought.**

circs., *n. pl.*   **circumstances**
Inf. One of those abbreviations the British like, not only written *circs.,* but pronounced SERKS. See **Appendix I.D.9.**

circular road   **belt highway**
See **ring-road; orbital.**

circular saw   **buzz saw**

circumbendibus, *n.*   1. roundabout route or method
                                        2. long-winded story
                                        3. circumlocution
Inf. An old-fashioned jocularity involving mock Latin. Cf. **omnium gatherum.**

Circus, *n.*   **Circle**
Used in cities where Americans would normally use *Circle;* thus Piccadilly *Circus,*
Oxford *Circus,* etc., as compared with, e.g., *Columbus Circle* in New York.

(the) City, *n.*   *Inf.* **Wall Street; financial district**
Inf. The *City* of London is a precise geographical section of London and is chief
among several *Cities* (e.g., the *City* of Westminster) which are incorporated in
London. The *City* of London includes the financial district, and *the City,* as an
abbreviation of the *City of London,* is used in Britain exactly as *Wall Street* is used
in America. Geographically the *City* is larger than the London financial district
which it includes, whereas *Wall Street* is only a part of the New York financial
district in which it is included. The *City* measures one square mile and has 5,000
residents; and the sovereign of Great Britain and Northern Ireland cannot enter
it without the Lord Mayor's permission. The *City editor* of a London newspaper
is what would be called the *financial editor* in America (but *city editor,* in America,
means the person in charge of local news). See also **Throgmorton Street.**

city boundary   **city limits**

City editor   **financial editor**
See under **City.**

civilities, *n. pl.* See **amenities.**

Civil List   SEE COMMENT
The expenses granted by Parliament for support of the royal household and certain members of the royal family.

civil servant   **government employee**
The *civil service* is a term familiar to Americans, but Americans in the civil service
have expressed resentment at being referred to as *civil servants* and prefer to be
known as *government employees.*

(the) Civil War   SEE COMMENT
War between Charles I and Parliament. This war was fought in the 17th century
between the Royalists supporting King Charles I and the Roundheads led by Oliver Cromwell, ending with the beheading of Charles (or "Charles the Martyr," as
true blue Royalists called him).

Civvy Street, *Slang.*   **civilian life**

claim against tax   **take as a deduction**
Tax terminology.

clap, *v.t.*   **applaud**
Clap, in the sense of 'applaud,' is used intransitively in America. In Britain, one
claps a performer; in America, one *applauds* that performer.

clap eyes on, *Slang.*   *Inf.* **set eyes on**

clapped out   *Slang.* **tuckered out**
Slang. Frazzled; beat. See **fag; knock up; cooked; creased; flake out; jiggered; spun.**

clapper bridge   SEE COMMENT
A primitive type of bridge found in the West Country, consisting of large stones (five or six feet long by two or three feet wide, and about one foot thick) laid flat on boulders spaced about four feet apart across small streams.

clapper-claw, *v.t.*   **beat up**
Slang. Clapper-claw is often used intransitively in a figurative sense to mean 'claw one's way', e.g. to the top in a toughly competitive industry, or in politics.

claret, *n.*   *Slang.* **blood**
From the common word for red wine from Bordeaux, an Anglicized form of the French word *clairet*.

class, *n.*   **grade**
University term. In America, one's *college class* is the *year of graduation.* In Britain one's *class at university* is the place in the honours examinations, e.g., a *first,* an *upper* or *good second* or *lower second* (sometimes called a 2.1 or 2.2), or a *third. Class* is understood.

classic races. See under **guinea.**

clawback, *n.*   **ass-kisser** *Slang.*
Slang.

clean, *v.t.*   **shine**
Referring to shoes. See also **blanco.**

clear majority   **majority**
In British voting terminology, *majority* means what in America is called a *plurality.* To indicate an arithmetical majority, i.e., more than 50 percent, the British use the term *clear* or *absolute majority.*

clear up   **clean up**
A room, etc. Weary British parents tell their offspring to *clear up* rather than *clean up* their rooms.

clear-up rate   SEE COMMENT
Clearance rate, i.e. percentage of crime solved by the police. In the UK, where local police forces are all part of a national police service, comparison of *clear-up rates* in different areas is an important statistical exercise—and a field day for politicians and the press.

clearway, *n.*   **no-stopping thoroughfare**

cleg. *n.*   **horsefly**

clerk, *n.*
1. lawyer's assistant
2. church officer
3. town officer
4. office or store worker

(Pronounced CLARK.) This word originally meant 'clergyman' in Britain, but that meaning is now archaic.
1. It is commonly used by British lawyers to describe their assistants, and *law clerk* is a term not unknown in America.
2. The job of a lay person who renders miscellaneous services to a parish church.
3. An official, usually a lawyer, in charge of town records, who acts generally as the business representative of a town.
4. *Bank clerks, shop clerks,* and the like, are *general office workers* who keep books, do filing, and take care of miscellaneous office functions.

clerk of the works   **supply man; maintenance man**
This title denotes a person who acts as overseer of supplies and building materials for a contractor on a particular construction site, and acts as a kind of progress reporter, on site, among customer, contractor, and architect. This term also covers the position of one in charge of repairs and maintenance, such as outside painting and sidewalk repair, for instance, of a municipal housing unit (**council house** *estate*).

clever Dick, *Slang.*   *Slang.* **wise guy**

cling film, *n.*   **plastic wrap**

clinking, *adj.*   *Slang.* **damned good**
Slang. Thus, a *clinking* game, a *clinking* race, etc. It can also be used adverbially modifying *good:* a *clinking good game,* a *clinking good race.* See also **rattling; thundering.**

clippie, *n.*   **bus conductress**
Inf. In Britain there are bus conductors of both sexes. A male conductor is simply a *conductor;* a female *conductor* is a *clippie.* Both male and female bus conductors used to *clip* your ticket, i.e., *punch* your ticket, but only the lady conductors were called *clippies.* The word came into being during wartime when they replaced the men. It is going out of fashion now—as are buses with conductors. Most have just a driver, who takes money and issues tickets.

cloakroom, *n.*   **washroom**
Both terms are euphemisms for *toilet,* but beware: Following a *cloakroom* sign in a public place in Britain may lead you to another destination, because it is also used literally in that country. The British term *cloakroom ticket* means 'baggage check' or 'hat check.' See **loo.**

cloakroom attendant   **hat check girl**

clobber, *n.*   **1.** *Inf.* **get-up**
                                        2. *Inf.* **gear**
1. *Slang.* This word means 'attire' and is generally used when there is something peculiar about the attire, as for example, *He appeared in the strangest clobber,* or *He had borrowed somebody else's clobber.* See **rig-out.**

2. *Slang.* The word acquired the further meaning of 'gear,' 'junk,' 'one's full equipment' in World War I.

close, *n.*   **dead-end residential area**
(Pronounced CLOCE.) A *close* is a kind of *cul-de-sac* broadened out at its end. The term is used also to describe the enclosed land around a cathedral.

close crop, *n.*   **crew cut**
See also **short back and sides.**

close season   **closed season**
Referring to hunting, fishing, etc. Here, the British omit the *d*. It's turned the other way around in the legal phrase *closed company* (British) for *close corporation.* See **Appendix I.A.3.**

closet, *n.*   **toilet bowl**
A euphemism. *Water closet* is old-fashioned British for *lavatory. Closet* (see **pedestal**) is the polite term occasionally seen in house-furnishing catalogues for the bowl itself. A *clothes closet* in Britain is a *cupboard* or *wardrobe.*

close the doors, please!   **all aboard!**
Heard in railroad stations and often followed by "Train is about to depart!"

closing-down sale   **liquidation sale**
Although sometimes it seems to mean only a 'closeout' of a particular item or line of merchandise.

closing time. See **during hours.**

closure, *n.*   **cloture**
The British form for 'cutting off debate' is not generally used in America, and vice versa.

clot, *n.*   *Slang.* **jerk**
Slang. A strong pejorative. "She is suffering from marital thrombosis," quipped the doctor's wife. "She's got a *clot* for a husband."

cloth, washing-up. *See* **tea-towel; washing-up cloth.**

cloth-cap, *adj.*   *Inf.* **blue-collar**

cloth-eared, *adj., inf.*   **deaf**
Characterizing someone who either purposely or through lack of attention misunderstands what is said to him.

clothes-peg, *n.*   **clothespin**

clothes-prop, *n.*   **clothespole**

clotted cream.   SEE COMMENT
Clotted cream is made by scalding milk and skimming off what rises to the top. For one of its delicious applications, see **cream tea.** Incidentally, *clotted* is derived

from the *clot* or *clout* (cloth) with which the cream is covered during the process, and does not refer to the consistency of the cream. See **Devonshire cream.**

clubland, *n.*   SEE COMMENT
St. James's, an area of London including the palace of that name. It is bounded on the north by Jermyn Street, on the west by St. James's Street, on the south by Pall Mall (pronounced *Pal Mal*), and on the east by Lower Regent Street, and is called 'clubland' because it houses many of London's famous clubs. St. James's palace was once the royal residence, and although it has not been so used since the time of Queen Victoria, the British court is still designated as 'the Court of St. James's.'

club together, *v.i.*   **join up; pool**
Britons, as well as Americans, *club together* to buy a going-away gift for a friend or a memento for a retiring colleague.

clue, *n.*   **notion**
I haven't a clue is a common expression in Britain, meaning 'I haven't the slightest idea.' It is interchangeable with another British expression: *I haven't the foggiest. He hasn't a clue,* however, means 'he is hopelessly ignorant or stupid.' If the pronoun is third person, of either gender or number, the expression is pejorative. See next entry.

clued up, *adj.*   *Inf.* **well-informed or briefed**

clueless, *adj.*   *Inf.* **hopeless**
Inf. Describing someone who doesn't know what it's all about or which end is up. See also **clue.**

clutch, *n.*   SEE COMMENT
Inf. Clutch, in addition to its other uses as noun and verb, means a 'set of eggs,' or a 'brood of chickens.' *Clutch* is also used in *a clutch of friends* to indicate a swarm of followers that might surround a movie star or other celebrity.

clutter, *n.*   **junk**
Clutter literally means *litter* or any untidy miscellany in both countries. But whereas an American might say, *Our weekend guests arrived with an awful lot of junk,* a Briton would probably describe them as having brought along a great deal of *clutter.* See also **lumber.**

C.M.G. See under **V.C.**

coach, *n.*   **inter-city bus**
See also **carriage** and **motor coach.**

coarse, *adj.*   **common**
A special meaning applied to fresh water fish: *coarse* would exclude salmon and trout and other sporting fish caught with a fly. *Coarse* fish are run-of-the-mill types.

coatee, *n.*   **short coat**
Worn by women and infants. In American, a *coatee* historically has been a short coat with tails.

cob, *n.*   **wall material**
A mixture of clay, gravel, and straw.

cobble, *n.*   SEE COMMENT
Lump coal the size of smallish cobblestones.

cobble, *v.t.*   **run up; put together roughly**
To *cobble* something, or to *cobble* something *together,* is to put it together roughly.
A professor in a hurry will *cobble* a lecture together. This verb is used also to mean
'mend' or 'patch,' especially of shoes, indicating its back formation from *cobbler,*
which in Britain means not only 'shoemaker,' but also 'clumsy workman,' a sense
archaic in American usage.

cobblers, *n. pl., interj.*   SEE COMMENT
Cockney rhyming slang (see **Appendix II.G.3**) omitting, as usual, the rhyming word; short for *cobblers' awls,* rhyming with *balls,* so that its meaning as an
interjection is 'balls!' particularly in the sense of 'forget it!' said in response to
a preposterous proposal. As a noun, it is used to describe anything considered
rubbish or nonsense, as in *That's a lot of cobblers!*

cock, *n.*   *Slang.* **bull**
Slang. Stuff and nonsense. We've all heard of *cock and bull* stories. The British have
chosen the *cock,* the Americans the *bull.* Americans are squeamish about using
cock. Britons have mocked such delicacy by referring to *roostertails* for prepran-
dial drinks, *pet roosters* for *petcocks, roostered hat, go off half-roostered,* and similar
constructions. However, *cock* is generally taboo in mixed company, except when
it clearly refers to the male bird, or in **that cock won't fight.**

cock-a-hoop, *adj., Slang.*   *Inf.* **on top of the world**
Exultant and boastful, as in *His cock-a-hoop chortling could be heard everywhere.*

cock a snook   *Slang.* **thumb one's nose**
Slang. (*Snook* rhymes with COOK.) Sometimes *cock snooks.*

cockchafer, *n.*   **June bug**
The noisy beetle that usually arrives in May. The British are amused by the American name because **bug,** to them, normally means 'bedbug.'

Cocker. See **according to Cocker.**

cockerel, *n.*   **1. young rooster**
                                                                    2. young tough
1. Americans, too, occasionally use this word to mean a 'young rooster.'
2. Metaphorical extension. But not heard in America in this sense.

cockney, *n., adj.*   SEE COMMENT
Inf. Also used adjectivally meaning, literally, 'characteristic of a born **East Ender.**'
A *cockney* accent is not deemed one of the more socially acceptable ways to pro-
nounce English. But those possessing such an accent are often very proud of it
and during the 60s it became a fashionable accent to attempt to imitate. See also
Bow Bells.

cockshy. See **coconut shy.**

cock-up, *n.*   *Inf.* **mess; muddle**
Slang. You've never seen such a cock-up in your life! (The bank robbers got away
and the police arrested the bank manager by mistake.) See also discussion under
balls, 2.

coconut shy   SEE COMMENT
A game in fairs, in which the contestant throws balls at a heap of coconuts
(pronounced COKER-NUTS) for prizes. More or less interchangeable with *cockshy,*
which is somewhat more general, in that it includes any game in which balls or
sticks are thrown at a variety of targets. A *cockshy* may be the target itself, and the
word is also used figuratively to mean a 'butt.' *Cockshy* is also used to mean 'trial
balloon': *I put up a cockshy memorandum* (to test opinion).

cod, *n., v.t., v.i.*   **1.** *n.,* **joke; parody; take-off**
                                                  2. *v.t., v.i.,* **tease; spoof**
                                                  3. *Slang. v.i.,* **horse around**
Slang. In the first meaning, *cod* is used attributively in expressions like a *cod version of "Hamlet"* or a *cod cockney accent.*

codswallop, *n.*   *Slang.* **baloney**
Slang. (Pronounced and sometimes spelled COD's WALLOP.) *Hot air.* Origin
unknown. See also **gammon; rot; balls; rubbish; all my eye and Betty Martin!**
and **cobblers.**

C. of E.   **Church of England**
The established church. See **chapel; dissenter; nonconformist.**

coffee-stall, *n.*   **street coffee stand**
Similar to the hot dog wagon and pretzel stand seen on the streets of some American cities.

coffee sugar   SEE COMMENT
Sugar in large crystals, usually brown or honey-colored; occasionally varicolored. Americans tend to approach it cautiously, and it makes for table talk. The
usual name for it in shops is *sugar crystals.* See also **demerara.**

coiner, *n., inf.*   **counterfeiter**
Of counterfeit coins, that is.

coin it, *v.i.*   *Inf.* **to make a lot of money**
Americans would speak of someone *minting it.*

collar stud   **collar button**
Used when shirts had detachable collars.

collar-work. See **against the collar.**

collections, *n. pl.*   **mid-years**
Term-end examinations at Oxford and elsewhere. See **college.**

college, *n.*   **school; house (dormitory)**
This word, which in American educational terminology always denotes an institution of higher learning and is roughly synonymous with *university,* does not
necessarily mean the same thing in Britain. Eton College and Lancing College are
what are known as **public schools,** roughly equivalent to what Americans call
prep schools, and City of London College is a secretarial school. On the other hand,
the colleges of Oxford and Cambridge (about twenty-five at each) are more or
less autonomous institutions each with its own buildings, including hall of residence (see **hall**)—*house,* in the American 'college dormitory' sense—dining-halls,
chapel, principal's residence (see under **Fellow**), bedrooms and studies for Fellows (see also **don**), tutors (advisers) and undergraduates (students), senior and
junior common-rooms, and campus (**quad** at Oxford, **court** at Cambridge). Some
colleges, like All Souls and St Antony's, Oxford, are for graduates only. Most are
now coeducational. The phrase *college graduate* would not be used in Britain. The
person would be called a *university graduate. College* is also applied to learned or
professional institutions, such as the Royal College of Physicians.

college grounds   **campus**
Campus is used increasingly in Britain, especially at the newer **(redbrick)** universities.

college of further education   *approx.* **extension school**
For persons who have left school and wish to continue their general education or
learn a trade.

colleger, *n.*   SEE COMMENT
One of the 70 (out of 1,100) Eton students who live *in college* (i.e., *on campus;* see
college). The others are called **oppidans.**

collier, *n.*   **coal freighter**
It means 'coal miner' in Britain as well, but not in America.

Collins, *n.*   *Inf.* **bread-and-butter letter**
Inf. Synonymous with **roofer.** Now obsolescent.

collywobbles, *n., pl.*   *Inf.* **butterflies in the stomach**
She had a bad case of the collywobbles before her audition.

coloured, *adj., n.*   *approx.* **non-white**
Colored in America signifies black, whether of African or West Indian origin. In
Britain the term includes Indians, Pakistanis, and persons of mixed parentage.
Unfortunately, it has also become a noun in Britain, often in the plural. As both
adjective and noun it is offensive.

colt, *n.*   1. *Slang.* **rookie**
                                                     2. *approx.* **junior varsity player**
1. *Inf.* In professional cricket, a player in his first season.
2. *Inf.* At school it can refer to a boy who is a member of any junior team, not
necessarily cricket.
In America, neither sense is heard.

combination-room, *n.*   **common-room**

Meeting-room at Cambridge University. There is a junior *combination-room* for undergraduates. The senior combination-room is for **Fellows.**

combinations, *n. pl.*   **union suit**
Referring to underwear. *Union suits* are on the way out in America. *Combinations* are dying out more slowly in Britain. **Combs** (short *o;* the *b* is silent) is an informal abbreviation.

comb-out, *n.*   **intensive search**
Inf. Sometimes the Americans also use *comb* or *combing* for this process.

combs. See **combinations.**

come, *v.t.*   **act**
Slang. To *come* the hero or the bereaved spouse is to *act* the part, to *put it on.*

come a cropper   *Inf.* **take a tumble**
Inf. Fail in an endeavor.

come a mucker. See **under mucker.**

come a purler   *Slang.* **fall on one's face**
Slang. Rare. Like the American equivalent, used both literally and figuratively. Thus, it might apply not only to the physical act of stumbling, but also to a business or theatrical fiasco, or the messing up of plans for a picnic.

comeback, *n.*   *Slang.* **oomph**
Inf. A person who does not have much *comeback* is one who does not have much *on the ball,* i.e., is dull and not very good company.

come-by-chance, *n.*   **love child**
Inf. See **chance-child.**

come-day-go-day, *adj.*   **shiftless**
Too easygoing, apathetic; a drifter. It sometimes has the additional connotation of carelessness about money—*easy come, easy go.*

come down   **1. graduate**
                                                         2. SEE COMMENT
1. *Inf.* This is a university term. To *come down* is to *graduate.*
2. *Inf.* To leave university finally or to commence vacation. A vacation from work, generally, is called a **holiday** in Britain; but in university life, holidays at Christmas, Easter, and the summer hiatus are known as *vacations,* and the same is true of the Law Court calendar. The long university summer vacation is known as the *long vac. Come down* means the same thing as *go down,* and the choice of phrase depends on the vantage point of the speaker: if you are at the university you talk of *going down;* the student's parents, however, would talk to their friends and relations about Sam's *coming down.* It depends on the position of the speaker in relation to the university. *Come down* and *go down* are not to be confused with **send down,** also a university term, meaning 'expel.' No colloquial American counterpart.

come expensive   *Inf.* **come to a lot**
Inf. To *cost too much.*

come home trumps. See **come up trumps.**

come it strong   *Inf.* **lay it on thick**
Inf. To *overdo it.* Applies, e.g., to excessive demands. It has been used about an ostentatious party: *That's coming it strong, isn't it?*

come on   **menstruate**
Inf. One of many euphemisms.

come on to   **begin**
Thus: *It came on to snow last night.*

come over, *v.i.*   *Inf.* **go (become)**
Inf. As in *I was so astounded I came over numb.*

come the acid   *Slang.* **be a wise guy**
Slang. Usually in the negative imperative: *Don't come the acid with me!* as a reproof given to a smart alec who has given a snide answer to a question. Has other shades of meaning as well, depending on context: 'exaggerate,' 'be too big for one's breeches,' 'try to burden someone else with one's own job,' generally, to 'make oneself objectionable.'

come top   *Inf.* **come out on top**
Inf. To **win.**

come to the horses, *Slang.*   *Slang.* **get down to brass tacks**

come to the wrong shop. See **shop.**

come up trumps   *Inf.* **come up roses**
Inf. Also *turn up trumps* and *come home trumps.* In context, it means 'not fail or disappoint,' to 'be there when you're needed': *He came up trumps when the going was bad.*

comforter, *n.*   **1. baby pacifier**
                                                             2. woolen scarf
Two distinct meanings, as opposed to the American meaning of *comforter,* which is 'quilt.' See also **duvet; eiderdown.**

comic, *n.*   **humorous comic**
Americans use the term *comics* to designate all narrative newspaper strips, whether horror, macabre, tales of adventure, or funny. In Britain, the term tends to mean 'funny comics,' unless otherwise specified, e.g., as in *horror comic.*

coming, *adv.*   **going on**
Used adverbially in expressions of age: *Mary is coming seventeen.*

command paper. See **Paper.**

commem, *n.*   SEE COMMENT
Inf. Abbreviation of *commemoration,* an annual celebration at Oxford in commemoration of founders and benefactors.

commercial traveller   **traveling salesman**
In the proper context, *traveller* by itself is understood in this sense.

commission agent   **bookmaker**
A lofty euphemism. See also **turf accountant.**

commissionaire, *n.*   **uniformed doorman and the like**
In Britain, *commissionaires,* usually doormen but sometimes also messengers and
other types of clerk, are normally pensioned military men. More specifically, they
are members of the *Corps of Commissionaires,* an organization formed many years
ago to provide decent employment for ex-regular army men, and run on military
lines. A more common British term is **porter.**

Commissioner for Oaths   **notary public**

commode, *n.*   **chamber pot**
Commode in America usually means a 'chest of drawers.' It has the secondary
meaning there, rarely used, of a chest or box holding the chamber pot. In Britain,
it signifies this homely commodity, usually in the form of a chest or chair.

common as muck/brass, *adj.*   *Derog.* **very low-class.**
Usually applied to someone considered coarse or uncouth.

Common Entrance Examinations   SEE COMMENT
Prep school entrance exams. *Prep school,* in the American sense, is what the British call **public school.** *Common Entrance Examinations,* though national in scope,
are prepared by a private body organized by the public schools of Britain. The
same entrance examinations are given to all candidates for the schools, but each
public school has its own requirements as to the grades achieved in these examinations. See also **council school.**

commoner, *n.*   SEE COMMENT
Anyone below the rank of **peer.**

common lodging-house. See **Rowton House.**

common-or-garden, *adj.*   **unexceptional**

(the) Commons, *n.*   SEE COMMENT
Shortening of *House of Commons,* the lower legislative chamber. The upper one,
the **House of Lords,** is a respected debating chamber but has little power in normal times except to delay or amend non-financial measures.

company, *n.*   **corporation**
A business term; sometimes called *limited company* or *limited liability company,* the
essence of this form of business organization in either country being the *limitation*
of its liability to the value of its net worth, thus insulating from risk other assets
of the individual(s) involved. *Ltd.* is the British equivalent of *Inc. Company* does

not necessarily connote incorporation in either country. It may denote a partnership or even a sole proprietorship. See **corporation.**

company director. See **director.**

compensation, *n.*   **damages**
In America, *compensation* includes not only *damages* but also more generally, *emolument* or *payment,* whether salary or fee. In Britain *compensation* is not used except to indicate *restitution* or *damages* after suffering physical injury or any other kind of loss.

compère, *n.*   **master of ceremonies; emcee**
(Pronounced COM'-PARE.)

completion, *n.*   **title closing**
Term used in real estate transactions.

compliments slip   SEE COMMENT
A transmittal slip, usually printed, that is sent with enclosures by professionals and tradesmen, and sometimes accompanies their bills. The slip contains the phrase *With compliments,* followed by the name and address of the sender. The phrase does not mean that the sender is giving anything away, as it might suggest in America, where *With so-and-so's compliments* indicates a gift.

compositor, *n.*   **typesetter**

comprehensive school. See **eleven plus.**

compulsory purchase   **condemnation**
A legal term, meaning the forcible sale to a public authority of property for public use, pursuant to the right of eminent domain.

concession, *n.*   **discount**

conchy, *n., Slang.*   **conscientious objector**

confab, *n.*   *Slang.* **a chat or talk**
Abbrev. of confabulation.

confectioner's, *n.*   **candy store**
Synonymous with **sweet-shop.**

confidence trick   **confidence game**

confined to barracks   *Inf.* **confined to quarters**
Int. An ambulatory but slowly convalescing invalid might say: *I'd love to come, but I'm afraid I'm confined to barracks.*

confinement theatre. See **theatre.**

conjurer, conjuror, *n.*   **magician**
All three terms are used in both countries.

conk, *n.*   1. *Slang.* **beak (nose)**
                                                           2. *Slang.* **noodle (head)**
Slang. In meaning **2.**, it is used in the expression *off one's conk,* i.e., *nuts.* Synonymous with **loaf.**

conker, *n.*   1. **horse chestnut**
                                                             2. **rubber**
Slang. No American slang equivalent. Meaning **2.** applies exclusively to the game of darts, which is standard equipment at every proper British pub. When the game score is one-all, if there's time someone says, *Let's play the conker,* meaning the *rubber.* See also the next entry.

conkers, *n. pl.*   **horse chestnut game**
Every child has a string with a horse chestnut (called a **conker**) tied to the end, and, in turn, tries to break the other children's chestnuts.

conservancy, *n.*   **river or port commission**
For example, the Thames Conservancy.

conservatoire, *n.*   **conservatory (music school)**
Conservatory, in Britain, would usually mean 'greenhouse,' but it can also be used to mean a 'music school.'

consignment note   **bill of lading**
Railroad term.

consols, *n. pl.*   SEE COMMENT
Abbreviation of *consolidated annuities,* government securities of Great Britain which were consolidated in 1751 into 3 percent bonds, which in Britain are known as stocks. They have no maturity, but are part of the national debt. There are now both $2^1/_2$ percent and 4 percent *consols* which sell at heavy discounts that vary with fluctuations in prevailing interest rates. Accent on either syllable.

constable, *n.*   **policeman; patrolman**
A *constable* is a *policeman* and is the usual form of address to a policeman below the rank of sergeant. A *chief constable* would be known in America as a *chief of police.* See also **bobby** for slang synonyms, and **P.C.**

constituency, *n.*   **district**
A *Parliamentary constituency* is roughly equivalent, in British politics, to a *Congressional district* in America. See also **Member.**

construe, *n.*   **construction**
Used as a noun, it means an 'exercise in syntactical analysis,' as in the teacher's warning: *Next Tuesday, we'll have a construe of an* **unseen** (a passage for sight translation).

consultant, *n.*   1. **specialist (medical)**
                                                         2. **counsel (legal)**
These are special meanings in the respective professions, but the word has the same general meaning as in America. For those unfamiliar with the American term *counsel* as used in definition **2.**, it applies to a lawyer sharing quarters and loosely connected with a law firm but not acting as a partner.

content, *n., adv.*   **aye**
House of Lords voting terminology. *Not content* means 'nay'. The *contents* are the
ayevoters. (Accent on the second syllable.) Cf. **placet.**

Continent, the   **mainland Europe**

continental quilt. See **duvet.**

contract hire   **lease**
For instance, rental of office equipment or farm machinery, for a specified period
after which it must go back to the owner, as opposed to *lease,* in the British usage,
implying (in this connection) that after the initial hiring period, the item may be
kept under an agreed extension of the original term.

convener, also convenor. See under **works.**

convenience, *n.*   **rest room**
A masterpiece of understatement for a public lavatory, one of life's necessities!
A *public convenience* is often called a *comfort station* in both countries—a battle of
euphemisms. See **cloakroom; loo.**

convoy, *n.*   **caravan**

coo!, *interj.*   *Slang.* **gee! gosh!**
Slang. See also **cor!**

cooee, coo-ee, cooey. See **within cooee (coo-ee) of**

cook, *v.t.*   *Slang.* **juggle**
Slang. To *cook* records or accounts is to *tamper with* them. In Britain people *cook the
books.* In America this reprehensible practice is known as *juggling the books* as well
as *cooking the books.* Synonymous with **fiddle.**

cooked, *adj., Slang.*   1. *Slang.* **baked**
                                                                   2. *Slang.* **tuckered out**
1. Especially after sitting in the sun.
2. Or *beat,* like an exhausted runner. See **clapped out; fag; knock up, 2.**

cooker, *n.*   **stove**
Cooker is the normal British word for *stove.* A Briton would hardly ever say *electric
stove,* but *gas stove* is heard. See **hob.**

cookery book   **cook book**
See **Appendix I.A.3.**

cool box, *n.*   **cooler**

cop. See **not much cop.**

coper, *n.*   **horse trader**
Also seen as *horse-coper* and *horse-dealer.*

copper, *n.*   **1. laundry boiler**
                                                                    2. a coin of low value
1. Neither the word (in this sense) nor the appliance is much used nowadays; but they exist and persist. The word also has a slang meaning: 'cop' (see **bobby**).
2. In Britain there are two brown coins, the penny and the two-pence coin. Both are coppers. The term is also used figuratively to refer to a small amount of money, as in *They don't have a copper between them.*

copper-bottomed, *adj.*   *Inf.* **cast-iron; sound**
Inf. Often *one hundred percent copper-bottomed,* and most frequently applied to financial matters. The usage arises from the image of a ship so treated, so that its bottom tends to resist the onset of barnacles. This is reinforced by the belief that copper-bottomed pans are more solid and last longer than those not so equipped. In another context, modifying the noun *excuse,* it is the equivalent of *airtight.*

copperplate printing   **engraving**
As on stationery, calling cards, and so on.

copse, *n., v.t.*   **small wood (wooded area)**
This is a shortening of *coppice,* a noun shared with America. As a verb it means to 'cover (an area) with woods.'

cor! *interj.*   *Slang.* **gee! gosh!**
Slang. A corruption of *God.* See **blimey; coo.**

coracle, *n.*   **basket-shaped boat**
Welsh and Irish inland waterways wicker boat, formerly made by craftspersons.

cor anglais   **English horn**
The British call it by the French name. *Cor* by itself refers to the *tenor oboe.*

co-respondent shoes   **two-toned shoes**
Jocular. The flashy, disreputable type, usually brown and white. In easy no-fault divorce, there is no need for co-respondents.

corf, *n.*   **creel**
After one catches a fish in Britain, is kept it alive in a *corf* or a creel submerged in water. Plural *corves.*

coriander, *n.*   **cilantro**

corker, *n.*   *Inf.* **humdinger**
Of a thing or a person.

corking, *adj.*   *Inf.* **outstanding**
Something that is corking could also be called a **corker.**

corn, *n.*   **grain**
The American term *corn* has its equivalent in the British word *maize,* but more and more the British use the term *sweet corn,* though it is hard to grow in Britain and is not nearly as commonly found there as in America. The British use the noun *corn* as a synonym for the American term *grain.* See **Indian meal.**

corned beef   **canned pressed beef**
What the Americans call *corned beef* is known as *salt beef* in Britain.

(The) Corner, *n.*   *Slang.* **bookie's joint**
Slang. Rare. The Corner is slang for the betting establishment known as Tattersall's (betting rooms), which was originally located in London near Hyde Park Corner.

corner-boy, *n. Slang.*   *Slang.* **tough; loafer**

corner shop, *n.*   SEE COMMENT
A small independent shop in a town or city, selling newspapers and basic groceries and provisions.

cornet, *n.*   **cone**
Brass musical instrument and a conical wafer to hold ice cream.

cornflour   **corn starch**

corporation, *n.*   **municipality**
The American *corporation* has its equivalent in the British *company*. The British *corporation* is generally understood to be a *municipal corporation*. Thus, a *corporation swimming-bath* would be a *municipal* or *public swimming pool* in America, a *corporation car park* would be a *municipal parking lot*, etc. Of late, the British have begun to use *corporation* in the American sense, especially in tax terminology.

corrector, *n.*   **proofreader**
Short for *corrector of the press.*

corridor, *n.*   **aisle**
Referring to railroad cars etc. See **aisle.**

corrie, *n.*   **mountainside hollow**
Scottish.

Corry   **Coronation Street**
Slang. Coronation Street is a television soap opera first televised in 1960 and popular throughout its history.

cosh, *n., v.t.*   **blackjack**
Slang. A cosh is a *blackjack.* To be *coshed* is to be *hit on the head,* whether with a blackjack or some other unpleasant weapon. *Coshed* would find its American equivalent in *mugged.*

cos lettuce, *n.*   **romaine**
See also **web lettuce.**

costermonger, *n.*   **fruit and vegetable pushcart vendor**
Sometimes shortened to *coster.* His pushcart is known in Britain as a **trolley** or **barrow.** See also **pearly; fruiterer; greengrocer's.**

costings, *n. pl.*   **costs**
A business term used in arriving at the price to be charged for a product.

cost the earth. See **pay the earth; come expensive.**

costume, *n.*   **lady's suit**
This is somewhat old-fashioned and non-U, but still frequently heard, especially in dry cleaning establishments. With most Britons, *suit* applies to both sexes.

costume, bathing. See **bathing costume; swimming costume.**

cot, *n.*   **crib**
See also **camp bed.**

cotch, *v.i.*   *Slang.* **relax, hang out**

cottage, *v.i., n.*   *Slang.* SEE COMMENT
The word refers to the solicitation by male homosexuals of sex with strangers. As a verb it means *the practice,* as a noun *the place* (often a public restroom) where solicitation takes place.

cottage pie   SEE COMMENT
A cottage pie is made with chopped beef or the remains of a roast ground up (minced), topped by a layer of mashed potatoes and baked in the oven. Compare with **shepherd's pie.**

cotton, *n.*   **thread**
In the sense of 'sewing thread.' And cotton is not wound on *spools* in Britain but on *reels.*

cotton bud, *n.*   **cotton swab/Q-Tip**

cotton wool   **absorbent cotton**
For metaphorical uses, see **live in cotton wool; wrap in cotton wool.**

council, *n.*   *approx.* **town**
Literally, a local administrative body of a village, town, borough, city, county, etc. But the word is used, particularly in the country, exactly as Americans use *town,* in the sense that it is the *council* to which you apply where there is a problem about schools, sewage, roads, and the like.

council house   **municipal or public housing unit**
So-called because the government agency regulating housing is known as a *council,* whether *district council, county council,* or other. The rent in *council houses* is extremely low. A multi-family unit of this sort in America is called, generically, a *public housing project.* The equivalent in Britain would be a *council house estate* or *council housing estate.*

councillor, *n.*   **councilman**
A member of a *council* (e.g., a district council, county council, local administrative bodies) is a *councillor.*

council school   **public school**
See **State School.**

council tax, *n.*   **property tax**

Set by a local council to help pay for services such as policing and garbage collection. Council tax replaced the old **rates** system of local taxation, which it closely resembles. It is a property tax in all but name, being based on the value of the property.

counsel. See **barrister.**

counterfoil, *n.*   **stub**
Referring to checks and checkbooks; also to the part of a bill one detaches and keeps.

counter-jumper, *n.*   **salesperson**
Slang. No American slang for this contemptuous (and now rare) term. A counter-jumper presumably had to jump over a counter to go to other parts of his crowded shop.

count out the house   **adjourn Parliament**
When fewer than a quorum of forty **Members** are present in the House of **Commons.**

country round   **day's route**
Referring to a delivery route (see **roundsman**) or round of professional visits.

county, *adj., n.*   *approx.* **quality**
Inf. This word has no exact equivalent in America. It has the connotation of good breeding and activity in local affairs like riding to hounds and opening flower shows. Such a person is *county,* i.e., a member of the local gentry, and it is hard to say whether *county* in such cases is an adjective or a noun. Never applied to a city dweller.

courgette, *n.*   **zucchini**
Courge is French for *gourd* or *squash. Courgette* is the diminutive. See also **marrow.**

court, *n.*   *approx.* **campus**
Cambridge University term, also given as *courtyard,* for an area bounded by college buildings. The Oxford equivalent is **quad** (for *quadrangle*).

court-card   **king, queen, or jack**
Referring to playing cards.

court of inquiry   **fact-finding board**
A military term.

court shoe   **pump**
Woman's light shoe with a low-cut upper.

cove, *n.*   *Slang.* **guy; fellow**
Slang. See also **chap.**

Coventry, send to. See **send to Coventry.**

cover, *n.*   **coverage**
An insurance term, indicating the aggregate risks covered by a particular policy.

cow, *n.*   *Inf., derog.* **woman**

Often preceded by *silly*; always offensive, though sometimes couched in jocular terms.

cowboy, *n.*   SEE COMMENT
Slang. Term applied to an itinerant self-employed workman (e.g., builder, roofer, electrician) who undercuts a skilled man and does a job of awe-inspiring incompetence. *Don't let him anywhere near your roof—he's just a cowboy!* In America, the term *cowboy* is applied to a reckless driver.

cow gum, *n.*   rubber cement

cow pat, *n.*   cow pie

cracker, *n.*   snapper
The kind served at children's parties. The use of the word in the American sense is creeping in, but the British generally call *crackers* **biscuits.** See under **biscuits.**

crackers, *adj.*   *Slang.* **cracked; nuts**
Slang. Predicate adjective only: *I think they all are going crackers.* See synonyms under **bonkers.**

cracking, *adj. & adv.*   *Slang.* **1. full of pep**
                                                            2. *Inf.* **very good**
1. *Slang. Get cracking!* means *Get busy! Get going! Get moving! Get to work!*
2. *Adj., adv. That was a cracking speech.* Also used as an intensifier, as in *That was a cracking great meal.*

crackling, *n.*   SEE COMMENT
In the UK, unlike the USA (and most of the rest of the world), pork is usually cooked with the skin (rind) left on rather than being removed beforehand. When cooked properly, the skin becomes crisp and crunchy—like pork scratchings. In most households, the crunchy skin is just as highly prized—if not more highly prized—as the meat itself.

crack on (with)   *Inf.* **get working, make progress with**
May be used on its own, as in *We didn't start till late, but we're cracking on now,* or with *with,* as in *We're cracking on with it now.*

crammer's, *n.*   cram school

cram on   step on
Slang. To *cram on* the brakes is to step hard on them.

cramp, *n.*   clamp
A portable tool for pressing things like planks together, or a metal bar to hold masonry together. The British use *clamp* as well.

cranky, *adj.*   eccentric
The usual meaning in America is 'irritable,' 'ill-tempered.' The British usage reflects the noun *crank* in the sense of 'eccentric person,' a meaning common to both countries.

crash, *n.*   **1. collision**
                                                         2. wreck
The British tend to use *crash* to describe both cause and result. *Crash repairs* means automobile 'body work.' *Crash barrier* is the *center guard rail* on express highways, synonymous with **centre strip, central reserve,** etc.

crawl, *v.i.*   *Inf.* **cruise**
Inf. Of taxis. See also **gutter crawl.**

crazy pavement. See **pavement.**

cream, clotted. See **Devonshire cream.**

cream cracker   **soda cracker**

creamed potatoes   **mashed potatoes**

cream off   **take the best (people) out of**
Inf. Skim the top talent off a group. For example, the police complained it was official policy to *cream off* the best talent on the force and put them into administrative jobs, rather than keep them on the regular force to train and set examples for new recruits.

cream tea   SEE COMMENT
Afternoon tea with **clotted cream,** which is rich, sweet, delicious, thicker than American whipped cream, and is meant to be piled on top of the jam on top of the scones, creating in all likelihood a dish with more calories than any other substance known to man. See also **high tea.**

crease, *n.*   *approx.* **foul line**
As a sports term, the crease is the line behind which a player must stand in the game of *bowls,* as well as the line which defines the position of both bowler and batsman in cricket. In American *ice hockey* the crease has a comparable function.

creased, *adj.*   *Slang.* **tuckered out**
Slang. See also **clapped out.**

crease up   *Inf.* **laugh uncontrollably**

crèche, *n.*   **day nursery**
(First *e* sounds like AY or EH.) Used occasionally in America to describe the traditional nativity scene.

credit slip   **deposit slip**
A banking term.

creek, *n.*   **inlet**
In Britain a *creek* usually means an 'inlet on a seacoast' or a 'small harbor.' Its secondary British meaning is the same as its principal American meaning: a 'small stream,' or 'minor tributary of a river.'

creepy-crawly, *n.*   **insect**
Slang. Most often, a spider; but used the way Americans use *slug,* to describe a disgusting person, the kind that seems to have *crawled* out from under a rock, and gives you the *creeps.*

CREST   SEE COMMENT
Acronym. The Central Securities Depository for the UK stock exchange, the system in which agreed trades (buying and selling) are settled.

crib, *n.*   *Slang.* **pony; trot**
Slang. A verbatim translation used by students in violation of school rules. This word is also used in America. *Pony* and *trot* do not appear in this connotation in Britain. The verb *crib* is heard in British and American schools.

cricket, *n.*   SEE COMMENT
Britain's national sport, with vital social overtones and symbolism. Thus, *not cricket* means 'unfair' or 'ungentlemanly,' and *It isn't cricket* must be familiar to millions outside Britain who haven't the slightest acquaintance with the game, so that the very word *cricket* has built into it the strongest implication of fair play.

Crikey!, *interj., Slang.*   *Slang.* **Good heavens!**

Cringe-making, *adj.*   *Inf.* **painfully embarrassing**
Literally: enough to make you cringe. Used especially of the behavior of another: *His singing was so bad it was cringe-making.*

crinkle-crankle, *adj.*   **winding**
Inf. A rare adjective used to describe serpentine red brick garden walls, full of twists and turns.

crisps, *n. pl.*   **potato chips**
Crisps (short for *potato crisps*) are called *potato chips* in America. The British shorten *potato crisps* to *crisps*. British *chips* are *French fried potatoes* in America. The Americans often shorten *French fried potatoes* to *French fries*. See also **chips; fish 'n' chips.**

crit, *n.*   **review**
Inf. For *criticism.*

crock, *n.*   *Inf.* **wreck**
Inf. Often used in the expression a *bit of a crock,* meaning a 'chronically ailing person,' not necessarily a hypochondriac. To *crock up* is British slang for 'break down' and *crocked* means 'broken down,' i.e., 'disabled,' rather than *drunk,* which is its special American slang meaning.

crocodile, *n.*   **line of schoolchildren**
Inf. Always led or followed (or both) by a teacher or teachers.

croft, *n.*   **small landholding**
A *crofter* is one who rents a *croft.* (The term is used almost exclusively in Scotland.)

cross bench, *n.*   SEE COMMENT

A *bench,* in Parliament, for independent members who vote with neither the government nor the opposition. See also **front bench; back bench.**

cross bencher, *n.*   **an independent or neutral MP**
That is, one who has allegiance to no particular party. As rare in Britain as it is in the United States.

crossing the floor   SEE COMMENT
To permanently change allegiance from one party to another. The phrase has a concrete meaning in Britain, since the House of Commons is a long room in which members of the government party sits across from the **Opposition** parties.

crossroads, *n.*   **intersection**
This word is used in America to mean the *intersection* of roads, but is more apt to be used figuratively in the sense of a 'dilemma urgently requiring decisions.' It would not be used in America referring to a street *intersection* in a city, and in the country Americans would use *crossroad* or *intersection,* or, in deep rural areas, *four corners.*

cross-talk comedians   **comedy team**
One meaning of *cross-talk* is *repartee.*

crotchet, *n.*   **quarter note**
Musical term. See **Appendix II.F.**

crown, *n.*   SEE COMMENT
Five **shillings,** but there was no crown coin or bill in general circulation even before the decimalization of the currency.

Crown Prosecutor   SEE COMMENT
The Crown Prosecution Service is a nationwide organization, part of the central government, which is responsible for all official prosecutions of criminal cases. It is headed by the Director of Public Prosecutions and is divided into approximately 40 areas, each with its own Chief Crown Prosecutor. While U.S. prosecutors may work under state or local as well as federal law, all prosecutors in the UK work under a single criminal code. Their job is sometimes referred to as public prosecutor. See also **private prosecution; district attorney**

crown stroller, *Slang*   *Slang.* **road hog**
The crown being the high center of a road.

crow to pick   *Inf.* **bone to pick**
Inf. A disagreeable subject to bring up. Also a fault to find. The British *pick bones* as well.

crumb, *n.*   **inside of loaf**
The part of a loaf of bread that is not crust; the soft inner part.

crumpet, *n.*   **1.** SEE COMMENT
          2. *Slang.* **nut (head)**
          3. *Slang.* **dish (desirable woman)**
1. There are no *English muffins* in Britain, toasted or otherwise. In Britain the *muffin* is a light, flat, round, spongy cake which is toasted and buttered. In America a *muffin* is a quick bread made of batter, baked in a cup-shaped pan, which does

not have to be toasted. The nearest thing to a British *crumpet* is what Americans call an *English muffin*.

2. *Slang*. A *crumpet* means a 'head,' for which American slang supplies *nut*, *bean*, *noodle*, etc. It is used in Britain especially in *barmy on the crumpet*, meaning 'crazy in the head.' See also **loaf**. This use may be obsolete.

3. A *nice bit of crumpet* is the usual phrase. See **bit of fluff**. This usage is vulgar. In a sentence like *Getting any crumpet?* crumpet is a euphemism. The equivalent American question normally omits the object of the verb: *Getting much lately?*

crutch, *n.*   **crotch**

cry off   **call off**
In the sense of 'discontinue' or 'bow out'.

cry stinking fish   **deprecate oneself**
Slang. The verb *to cry* has the little used meaning, in both Britain and America, of "announce for sale," and in both countries, to *cry* (something) *up* is to *praise* or *extol* it. To *cry up one's wares*, then, is to *boast about one's products*. To *cry stinking fish* is to call attention to one's failures (literally, to *condemn one's own products*), which would appear to be a study in masochism, like sucking on a sore tooth.

C3   *approx. Inf.* **4-F; unfit**
Inf. A term of population classification, designating the class composed of the mentally or physically deficient. The technical term has developed the connotation of *unfit* or even *worthless*. Perhaps the closest equivalent is the former American Selective Service (draft) classification 4-F.

cubby, *n.*   **cubbyhole**
Often expanded to *cubby-hole* (in America a general term for any little nook where one stuffs odds and ends), but not much heard any more except among quite senior citizens and among pre-school children, who keep their belongings in *cubbies*. The American term is heard as well in Britain.

cuckoopint, *n., Inf.*   *Inf.* **jack-in-the-pulpit**
A wild flower.

cufuffle, *n.* See **kerfuffle.**

cul-de-sac, *n.*   **dead-end street**
Cul-de-sac and *blind road* are British terms for what in America would be called a *dead-end street*, at the entrance of which there is often placed a sign saying DEAD-END STREET or NO THROUGH ROAD. See also **close**.

cully, *n. Slang*.   *Inf.* **pal**
Companion.

cupboard, *n.*   **1. closet**
                                                                 2. kitchen cabinet

1. See **closet** for British meaning.
2. The term is now used in Britain as well.

cupboard love   *Slang*. **sucking up**

Inf. Describes the activity of a person trying to curry favor, with the strong implication of insincerity and self gain. The term refers to the behavior of pets when they think their owner is opening the cupboard to get food for them. The word 'love' is ironic.

Cup Final   SEE COMMENT
Generally, the final match in any competition awarding a cup. It is usually understood to refer to **football** (*soccer*). See **up for the Cup.**

cuppa, *n.*   **cup of tea**
Slang. No American slang equivalent. Often used in expressions like *He's not my cuppa,* meaning 'He's not my kind of person.' See also **char, 2.**

curate, *n.*   **vicar's assistant**

curate's assistant, *Inf.*   **muffin stand**

curate's egg   SEE COMMENT
Inf. Something both good and bad. This curious phrase originated from a *Punch* cartoon that appeared in 1895. A humble curate is breakfasting with his bishop, overawed by the very presence of that dignitary, and the caption reads:

"I'm afraid you've got a bad egg, Mr. Jones."
"Oh, no, my Lord, I assure you! Parts of it are excellent."

curlies, *n. pl.*   *Vulgar.* **short hairs**
Vulgar. To have someone by the *short and curlies* is to have him at a considerable disadvantage, as for example by the pubic hairs.

curling tongs   **curling iron**

curly, *adj.*   **gruesome**
Slang. A brutal murder might be spoken of as *curly.* A reflection of this use may be found in the following American usage: *It would make your hair curl.*

current account   **checking account**
Synonymous with **running account.** Cf. **deposit account.**

curriculum vitae, *n.*   **résumé**
Almost always abbreviated as *CV.*

curse of Scotland   **nine of diamonds**
Inf. Various apocryphal derivations have been suggested, all of them fun.

cushy, *adj.*   *Inf.* **easy, undemanding**
Used especially of a job or another task. A legacy of the British Empire, deriving from the Hindi word *khush* (pleasant).

custard, *n.*   **custard sauce**
A word of explanation: In America, *custard* is a sweetened mixture of milk and beaten eggs, baked until set, and served as a dessert (**pudding;** see also **dessert;**

sweet; afters), with or without a sauce of one sort or another. In Britain, it can mean that too, but normally refers to the same mixture in running liquid form, thicker or thinner, done in a double boiler (**double saucepan**), served as a sauce over pies, compote, and the like.

custom, *n.*   **business**
Commonly used in Britain where Americans would say *business* or *customers,* as in: *An attractive shop-front* (see **shop**) *will bring in custom.* See also **trade.**

cut, *adj. Slang*   *Slang.* **tipsy**

cut along, *Inf.*   *Inf.* **run along**

cut a long story short, *Inf.*   *Inf.* **make a long story short**

cut away!   *Slang.* **beat it!**
Slang. See synonyms under **buzz off.**

cute, *adj.*   **shrewd**
In America, *cute* is generally applied to children, especially babies, or things like little girls' dresses, and means 'pretty, dainty, attractive.' In Britain, one speaks of a *cute* maneuver, or describes a lawyer or businessman as *cute,* in the sense of 'shrewd, clever, ingenious.' The American sense is not used in Britain, but one does hear in America of a clever move or tactic described as 'cute,' often 'pretty cute,' usually with a note of admiration or even rueful envy.

cutlet, *n.*   **chop**
Butcher's term applied especially to lamb, and meaning the seven or eight rib chops closest to the neck.

cut one's lucky, *Slang.*   *Slang.* **take a powder**

cut-throat, *n., Inf.*   **straight razor**

cutting, *n.*   **clipping**
Meaning 'newspaper clipping.' One employs a *cutting service* in Britain, in America a *clipping bureau.* Sometimes the sense is clarified by amplifying the term to *press cutting,* and *press cutting agency* is synonymous with *cutting service.*

cut up, *adj.*   **upset**
Slang. Wrought up, broken up, agitated, disturbed. Sometimes *all cut up.*

cut up for   **leave (as an estate)**
Slang. How much did he cut up for? is indelicate slang for 'How much of an estate did he leave?' This usage refers to a decedent's estate.

cut up rough *Slang.*   **make a fuss (row)**

CV   *abbrev.* **curriculum vitae**

D

dab, *n.*   *Inf.* **whiz**
Inf. Used in the expression to *be a dab at,* sometimes lengthened to *be a dab hand at,* meaning to 'be especially adept at.'

dabbly, *adj.*   **wet**
Slang. A *dabbly* summer is one with frequent rain. Most people think that *dabble* is used only in the expression *to dabble in,* i.e., 'engage in superficially,' as to *dabble* in the market or in a hobby. But its primary meaning is to 'moisten intermittently'—hence a *dabbly* summer.

dab in the hand, *Slang.*   **bribe**

dabs, *n. pl., Inf.*   **fingerprints**
And the singular **dab** means 'fingerprint.'

daddy-longlegs, *n.*   **crane fly**
In Britain, a *daddy-longlegs* is a *crane fly,* an insect of the family *Tipulidae* of the order *Diptera,* resembling an enormous mosquito and popularly called the *mosquito hawk.* In America called also *harvestman,* but not identical with the British insect.

daft as a brush   *Inf.* **very silly**

daggerplate. See **sliding keel.**

daily woman   **cleaning woman**
Inf. Often shortened to just *daily.* Sometimes *daily help.* See also **char, 1.**

dainty, *adj.*   *Inf.* **picky; finicky**
Inf. About food; a term applied to young children who are hard to please at mealtime. See also **faddy.**

dambusters   *Inf.* SEE COMMENT
In May 1943, Lancaster bombers from an elite RAF squadron audaciously attacked dams on the Ruhr River of Germany. Using specially designed 'bouncing bombs' designed to be launched from a low height, they aimed to breach the dams and flood the industrial areas lying below them. The raid had limited success, but tremendous propaganda value; it went into the language as a synonym for any brave and successful enterprise. *The job went like dambusters.*

Dame, *n.*   SEE COMMENT
A woman who is knighted becomes a *Dame.* A *Dame* should not be confused with a **Lady.** See also **Lord** for other titles.

damn all   *Slang.* **nothing at all**
Slang. This expression is in fairly wide use and would not be considered improper in normal company, even mixed. Americans might hesitate for a moment before

saying, I can't find *a damned thing*. The British would say, "I've got damn all," or more commonly, "bugger all" or "fuck all."

damp course   **insulating layer**
A *damp course* or *damp-proof course* is a layer of tarred felt, slate, etc., placed above the house foundation to prevent deterioration in the walls of a building caused by *rising damp*, a troublesome phenomenon in Britain.

dampers, *n. pl.*   **flat cakes**
Slang. Made of flour and water, usually by Boy Scouts, and not recommended for gourmets. *Damper* is used as well in the various senses in which it is used in America in connection with fireplaces, pianos, etc., and figuratively in the sense of a 'wet blanket.'

damp squib   *Slang.* **bust; dud; lead balloon**
Inf. One of those things, like a Church Bazaar or a Charity Ball that was going to be a howling success, but. . . . A squib literally is a firework, giving us all we need to understand 'damp squib.'

damson, *n.*   **a small blue-black plum**

darbies, *n. pl.*   *Slang.* **bracelets**
Slang. Handcuffs. The British term is said to be derived from the expression *Father Darby's bands* or *bonds*, a particularly rigid form of debtor's bond invoked by usurers in the good old days.

Darby and Joan   SEE COMMENT
Inf. This sentimental nickname for any loving couple of advanced years is supposed to have originated from an allusion in a ballad that appeared in 1735 in a publication called *Gentleman's Magazine*. The poem, entitled "The Joys of Love Never Forgot," went:

> Old Darby, with Joan by his side,
> You've often regarded with wonder.
> He's dropsical, she's sore-eyed,
> Yet they're never happy asunder.

Membership in Darby and Joan Clubs all over Britain is open to those whom Americans so tactfully call *Senior Citizens* and *Golden Agers* and the British *Old Age Pensioners*, usually shortened to *O.A.P.s.*

dashed, *adv.*   *Slang.* **damned**
Slang. Milder than *damned* in expressions like *dashed good, dashed bad*, and the like. Also heard in *Well, I'm dashed*, where Americans would say, *Well, I'll be damned! Dashed* may be on the way out as language becomes freer in a more permissive society.

daughter concern   **subsidiary**
A company owned by another company. The family relationship of the subsidiary is recognized in the American expression *parent company*, but the Americans keep the sex of the subsidiary a secret.

davenport, *n.*   **writing table; escritoire**
In America this word means 'large sofa.'

daylight robbery   *Inf.* **highway robbery**
Inf. Figure of speech, like *holdup*, meaning 'unashamed swindling,' an 'exorbitant price or fee.'

day return. See return.

day sister. See sister.

day tripper. See tripper.

dead-alive, *adj.*   *Inf.* **dead; more dead than alive**
Inf. Sometimes *dead-and-alive*. Of a person, 'unspirited'; of work or a place, 'monotonous, boring.'

dead cert   *Inf.* **sure thing**
Slang. Cert is short for *certainty*.

dead keen on. See keen on; mad on.

dead man's shoes   SEE COMMENT
This rather grim phrase describes something that somebody is waiting to inherit or succeed to, for example, his boss's job.

dead on   *Slang.* **on the nose**
Inf. Exactly right. See **bang on** for synonyms.

dead set at. See make a dead set at.

dead slow   **extremely slow**
Often seen on traffic signs meaning *as slow as possible*. In both countries, ship-board signal from bridge to engine room.

dead stock   **farm machinery**
The term *dead stock* is occasionally used to mean 'unemployed capital' or 'unsalable merchandise.' However, it has a special use in connection with the sale of country property. One sees signs advertising an auction of such and such a farm property, sometimes with *livestock* and sometimes including *dead stock*. Undoubtedly, an echo of the common term *livestock*.

dead to the wide. See to the wide.

deaf-aid   **hearing aid**

deals, *n. pl.*   **lumber**
For British meaning of *lumber*, see **lumber,** *n.*

dean, *n.*   **cathedral head**
See under **head, 1.**

death duties   **inheritance tax**
The estate tax levied on property after the owner's death.

debag, *v.t.*   *Inf.* **cut down to size**
Slang. Literally, *debag* means to 'pull somebody's pants off,' **bags** being slang for 'pants,' or as the British say, *trousers*. Figuratively, it means to 'deflate' a person.

debus, *v.t., v.i.*   **get out of an automobile**
(Accent on second syllable: DEE-BUS, EM-BUS.) *Embus* is to *get in.* See *detrain* and *entrain.* Military terms. Also applied to unloading ammunition etc. from a vehicle.

decasualization   SEE COMMENT
Increasing the number of so-called permanent jobs in a nation's economy, perhaps by abolishing casual labor. See **casual labourer.**

decillion. See **Appendix II.D.**

decoke, *v.t.*   **decarbonize**
To *do a ring job* on a car.

decorate, *v.t.*   **paint**
In context, *decorating* a room or a house means 'painting' it, and *house painters* are sometimes referred to as *decorators.* The word has nothing to do with *decoration* in its general sense, nor with interior decorating.

deed-poll, *n.*   **unilateral deed**
A legal term describing a document signed by a single party. *Poll* is an old verb meaning to 'cut evenly,' as for instance, the edge of a sheet. A *deed-poll* is written on a *polled* sheet, one that is cut evenly and not indented. The common use of a *deed-poll* nowadays is as a document by virtue of which one changes one's name.

degree day   **commencement**
This is a university term and has nothing to do with weather measurements, as in America.

degree of frost   **degree below 32°F**
In America, $20°F$ is $20°$ *above zero,* or simply *20 above,* or even more simply, *20.* In Britain, $20°F$ is announced as $12°$ *of frost.* Formula: $X°$ of frost in Britain $= (32 - X)°$ above 0 in America.

dekko, *n., Slang.*   *Slang.* **gander (glance)**
A look: *She asked to have a quick dekko.*

demarcation dispute   **jurisdictional dispute**
Between unions, or between different departments in a company. At risk is the work available.

demerara, *n.*   SEE COMMENT
(Rhymes with SAHARA.) Raw cane sugar, light brown, frequently served with coffee. Imported from Demerara, in Guyana. See also **coffee sugar.**

demisemiquaver, *n.*   **thirty-second note**
Musical term. See **Appendix II.F.**

demister, *n.*   **defroster**
Automotive term. See **Appendix II.E.**

demo, *n.*   **demonstration**
Inf. A *street demonstration,* or a *demonstration* of something the demonstrator wants you to buy. In the U.S., a sample recording by a musician.

demob, *v.t.*   discharge
Inf. (Accent on the second syllable.) Short for *demobilize* and *demobilization.* A military term. See **bowler-hatted.**

demonstrator, *n.*   laboratory assistant
At an academic institution.

dene, *n.*   **1. sandy stretch by the sea**
2. dune
3. wooded vale

denominational school   **parochial school**

denture, *n.*   **removable bridge**
A denture, in America, is usually understood to denote a set of upper or lower false teeth. It is used that way in Britain, too, but the term is also used for any removable bridge, whether one or more teeth are involved. *Bridge* means 'fixed bridge' only. Dentures, in the American sense, are occasionally referred to in Britain, especially by older people, as *dentacles* or *dentals.*

departmental store   **department store**

deposit account   **savings account**
Cf. **current account, running account.**

Derby, *n.*   SEE COMMENT
(Pronounced 'Darby'). The famous annual horse race held at Epsom Downs every June. It is a flat race for three-year-old horses, run over a distance of one-and-a-half miles.

de-restricted road   **road without speed limit**
For many years there were no speed limits on British country roads. Now the government has imposed an overall speed limit of 70 m.p.h. However, as one approaches a city, town, or village there are signs reading "30" or "40" restricting the driver to those limits while passing through those areas. Once beyond the geographical limits, you find a de-restriction sign, which means that you are back on the overall speed limit of 70 m.p.h.

Desert Island Discs   SEE COMMENT
A popular, long-running radio program on BBC Radio 4 in which a guest chooses eight pieces of music that he or she would like to have if stranded, alone, on an island. The guest talks about his or her life, both generally and with reference to the music, and an excerpt from each piece is played on air. The phrase 'Desert Island …' has entered common usage as describing any favorite in any category: *Desert Island dish, Desert Island book,* etc.

desiccated coconut   **shredded coconut**

Des. res., *n.*   *abbrev.* **desirable residence**

dessert, *n.*   **fruit course at end of meal**
In Britain *dessert* is a fresh fruit course (sometimes also nuts and/or trifling sweetmeats) served at the end of a meal either after, or in place of, what the British call a *sweet*. British *dessert* can be any fresh fruit. *Dessert* in America is a generic term for the last course of the meal whether it consists of fruit, pudding, ice cream, or whatever. In spite of the aforementioned restricted use of *dessert* in Britain, the British use *dessert plates, dessert knives, dessert forks,* and *dessert spoons.*

destructor, *n.*   **incinerator**

detached house. See **semi-detached; terrace.**

detain, *v.t.*   **1. arrest**
                                              2. keep
1. Often used in this sense in America. *Three men were detained in connection with the shooting of a policeman. A man was detained after a* **raid** *on a bank.* See also **assisting the police.**
2. Used commonly about people *kept* in the hospital after an accident, as opposed to those whose injuries were superficial. In American you would be *kept in the hospital;* in Britain you would be *detained in hospital* (no article). See also **Appendix I.A.2.**

detained during the Queen's (King's) pleasure   **sentenced to an**
                                              indeterminate term
Sometimes, *during His/Her Majesty's pleasure.* Predictably, there is the story of the woman so sentenced during the reign of a male monarch: "I thought I was too old for that sort of thing."

developer, *n.*   **real-estate developer**
Used by itself, in Britain and in America, the term describes a person engaged in the purchase of land and the erection of buildings on it. It sometimes appears in the phrase *property developer.* In both countries *developer* also means 'photographic developing solution.'

development area   SEE COMMENT
An area suffering from temporary or intermittent severe unemployment.

devil, *n., v.i.*   **1. law apprentice**
                                              2. literary hack
Americans may be familiar with the old-fashioned term *printer's devil* meaning 'printer's errand boy' or 'junior apprentice.' In Britain *devil* has two additional meanings.
1. Assistant to junior legal counsel in the **chambers** of a **leader.**
2. *Hack,* or *ghostwriter.* To *devil* is to act in either of these lowly capacities, often underpaid in the literary field, and not only unpaid, but a privilege usually paid for, in the legal field.

devil on horseback   **prune wrapped in bacon**
One of many different types of **savoury,** served on a small piece of toast. Sometimes an oyster replaces the prune. See also **angel on horseback.**

devilry, *n*   **black magic**
The British say *deviltry* as well to refer to this diabolical art.

devolution, *n.*   **home rule**
(The *e* is long in British English, short in American.) Governmental decentralization. A term that has lately come into vogue in political discussion. A devolution-
ist is one who urges decentralization of government.

Devonshire cream (clotted cream) See **clotted cream.**

dewar   **thermos bottle**
Sir James Dewar was a British physicist who invented the 'dewar' or 'Dewar ves-
sel,' a double-walled glass container with the air between the walls exhausted to
prevent conduction of heat in either direction. Rarely heard nowadays.

dhobied, *adj.*   **washed**
Inf. From *dhobi,* meaning 'washing.' Usage restricted to retired India hands.

diabolical, *adj.*   *Inf.* **1. extremely bad**
                                                                                    2. SEE COMMENT
In sense 2, as an intensifier meaning lamentable. *It's a diabolical shame that she
didn't get into Oxford.*

dialling tone   **dial tone**

diamante, *n.*   **rhinestone**

diamond jubilee   SEE COMMENT
The usual meaning in Britain is 'sixtieth anniversary,' though it occasionally
means 'seventy-fifth,' as in America.

dibs, *n., Slang.*   *Slang.* **dough (money)**
Lolly is more usual. See **brass.**

dicey, *adj.*   **touch and go**
Slang. A term based on the figurative aspect of the throw of the dice. Applied to
the weather in the perennial British problem of whether or not to plan a picnic
and similar games of chance. A somewhat less common British slang equivalent
is **dodgy.**

dickey, *n.*   **rumble seat**
Slang. Also given as *dicky.* This was the familiar name in the old days for the servant's seat in the rear of a carriage.

dicky, *adj., Slang.*   *Inf.* **shaky**

dicky-bird, *n.*   *Rhyming slang.* **word**

diddle, *v.t.*   *Slang.* **screw**
Slang. In the sense of 'fleece' or 'gouge,' i.e., to 'do somebody out of something.'

digestive biscuits   SEE COMMENT
Somewhat close to Graham crackers, and very tasty. Sometimes shortened to
digestives. See also **Bath Oliver.**

digs, *n. pl.* place **(rooms; lodging)**
Inf. Short for *diggings*. A Briton speaks of his *digs* in the way an American speaks of his *place,* or his *pad*. Mostly actors' and students' terminology. See **drum.**

dim, *adj.* *Slang.* **thick; thickheaded**
Slang. Short for *dim-witted*. See also **as dim as a Toc H lamp.**

ding-dong, *n., Slang.* **1. heated argument**
2. noisy party

ding dong, *n.* *Inf.* **a noisy argument**

dingle, *n.* **dell**
Sometimes combined as *dingle-dell*. Usually a deep hollow, shaded with trees.

dinky, *adj.* **pretty; dainty**
Inf. This word is the equivalent of the American term *cute* or *cunning* in the sense of 'sweet' or 'adorable,' not in the sense of 'sly.' The word *dinky* in America has the pejorative meaning of 'ramshackle' and is more or less synonymous with the American slang term *cheesy* which, however, in Britain can mean 'swanky.'

dinner-jacket, *n.* **tuxedo**
Americans say *dinner jacket* too, but *tuxedo* is never used in British English. Commonly shortened to D.J.

dinner lady, *n.* SEE COMMENT
A woman employed to prepare and serve school lunches.

diplomatist, *n.* **diplomat**
The shorter form is almost universal nowadays.

directly, *conj.* **as soon as**
Immediately after: Directly he left the room, she began to talk freely.

director, *n.* *approx.* **executive**
To the British layman *director* means about the same thing in the context of business epithets as *executive* would mean to an American layman. Directorships in British companies and American corporations (see **chairman; company; managing director**) amount roughly to the same thing, although their duties and prerogatives (as a matter of law) and their functions differ in some respects in the two systems. In both countries important personages are frequently elected to membership on boards of directors as window-dressing and don't participate actively in the affairs of the company. But the general connotation of *director* in Britain is that of an 'operating executive' whose American opposite would be the company's *vice-president-in-charge-of-something-or-other*.

directory enquiries. See **enquiries.**

dirty week-end **illicit weekend**
Inf. A few days spent with one's lover, with the implications of all those circumspect arrangements.

dish, *n.*   **serving dish; platter**
Although both countries use *dishes* generically, *dish* in Britain usually has the narrower meaning of 'serving dish' and *platter* is considered archaic.

dished, *v.t.*   *Inf.* **cheated**
Inf. Often carrying the meaning of 'defeated through illicit means.'

dish-washer. See **wash up.**

dishy, *adj.*   *Slang.* **very attractive**
Slang. Usually applied to people, but also to inanimate objects, such as sports cars.

dismal Jimmy, *Slang.*   *Slang.* **gloomy Gus**
A person eager always to see the negative side of anything, no matter how positive.

dismiss, *v.t.*   **put (someone) out; get (someone) out**
Cricket term. One doesn't *get* or *put* the **batsman** *(batter)* out. He (and when he is last in the batting order, his side) is said to be *dismissed* when he is run out, caught, etc.

dismissal with disgrace   **dishonorable discharge**
A term applied to noncommissioned soldiers and sailors alike. A naval officer would be *dismissed with ignominy,* an army officer *cashiered.*

dispatch, *n.*   **mailing and handling**
As in *Price £1 + 40p. for dispatch.* See also **posting (postage) and packing.**

dispensary. See **dispenser.**

dispenser, *n.*   SEE COMMENT
In America a *dispenser* usually means a container that feeds out some substance in convenient units, or a *vending machine.* The British use the word *dispenser* that way, too, but primarily it means in Britain what Americans would call a *pharmacist,* a person in the profession of making up medical prescriptions. *Dispensing Chemist* is a sign commonly seen on the store front of a British drugstore **(chemist's shop).** The related word *dispensary* means the 'drug department' of a drugstore, hospital or doctor's office **(surgery).**

dissenter, *n.*   SEE COMMENT
A member of a Protestant sect that has split off from the established church, i.e., the Church of England. See also **chapel.**

distemper, *n.*   **canine distemper**
A common and fatal infectious disease of cats and dogs.

district, *n.*   **precinct**

div, *n.*   *Slang.* **a pitiable person**

divan, *n.*   **sofa; couch**
Divan is not nearly so frequent in America as in Britain: *couch* is rarely used in this connection by the British.

diversion, *n.* **detour**
A traffic term. All too frequently one sees a road sign reading DIVERSION leading one away from the main road and only sometimes back onto it.

divi; divvy, *n.* **dividend**
Slang. Short for *dividend,* especially that distributed periodically. As used in Britain, *dividend,* which in America applies only to shares of stock, can refer as well to bond interest.

division, *n.* **1.** SEE COMMENT
2. SEE COMMENT
1. Area represented by a Member of Parliament: corresponds to *Congressional District* (see **constituency; Member**).
2. A term used in sentencing convicted criminals. Preceded by *first, second,* or *third,* it means 'lenient,' 'medium,' or 'severe' treatment in prison, as prescribed by the sentencing judge.

divvy. See **divi.**

divvy up *Slang.* **divide up, share out**
When we've finished trick-or-treating, we'll divvy up the sweets.

DIY *abbrev.* **Do It Yourself**
The abbreviation is used for an approach to home improvements and, more generally, for any job you do yourself rather than paying someone else to do it. Building-supply stores aimed at the domestic market are sometimes called DIY stores.

D-notice *approx.* **press publication restriction**
Notice given by the *D-notices Committee,* representatives of government and press, to newspapers, ordering them to omit mention of material that might endanger national defense. The *D* stands for *defence.* A wartime institution, now rare.

do, *n.* **1. deal**
2. swindle
3. ruckus
1. *Quite a do*—a wedding, for instance—would more likely be *quite a deal,* or *a big deal,* in America.
2. The nasty transaction by which one is *done.*
3. Americans would be likely to say *ruckus* or *hoax.*

do, *v.t.* **offer**
In America a shop does or doesn't *have, sell, keep, stock,* or *make* a particular item. The British often substitute *do* in those cases. A stationer may *do* daily newspapers but not the Sunday edition. An upholsterer may *do* hangings but not slipcovers (which he would call **loose covers**). A certain restaurant will be recommended because, though their soups are indifferent, they *do* a good mixed grill.

do a runner. See **runner.**

do bird *Slang.* **serve time**
Slang. In prison. *Bird* here is short for *birdlime* (the sticky stuff people spread on twigs to catch birds) which is cockney rhyming slang for *time.* See **Appendix II.G.3.**

do (someone) brown   *Slang.* **take (someone) in**
Slang. To *fool* someone, to *pull the wool over his eyes.*

dock, *n.*   **1. basin**
                                                            2. SEE COMMENT
1. The British use *dock* to denote the water between what Americans call *docks*
and the British call *wharves.* But note the expression *dry dock* which means the
same thing in both countries.
2. A *prisoners' detention area* in the courtroom. *In the dock* means 'on trial.'

dock brief. See **brief; dock.**

docker, *n.*   **longshoreman**

docket, *n.*   **judgment roll**
In British legal parlance a *docket* is a register in which judgments are entered, but
the term can be narrowed to mean an 'entry' in such a register. In America, also
meaning a list of causes for trial or persons having causes pending.

dockyard, *n.*   **navy yard or shipyard**

doctor, *v.t.*   **castrate or spay**
Applied to animals of both sexes. Not in America. Both countries also use the
verb *neuter,* which is now more common in Britain.

doddle, *n., Slang*   **cinch**
Anything easily accomplished. In a narrower sense, *doddle* can mean 'money
easily obtained.'

dodge, *n.*   *Slang.* **racket**
Slang. That's my dodge, meaning 'That's my racket,' can be used, somewhat impu-
dently, to mean nothing more than 'That's the business I'm in.' More generally, a
dodge is any *shrewd device* or *sly expedient.*

Dodgem cars, *TM.*   **bumper cars**

dodge the column   *Slang.* **goof off**
Slang. To *shirk one's duty.* The British expression, taken from the military, may be
thought to have a somewhat more elegant sound.

dodgy, *adj.*   **tricky**
Risky; doubtful; uncertain. See **dicey.**

do (someone) down   *Slang.* **do (someone) dirt**
Synonymous with **do (someone) in the eye.**

do for   **SEE COMMENT**
Inf. No precise American colloquial equivalent. When a British housewife tells
you that Mrs. Harris *does for* her, she means that Mrs. Harris is *acting as her house-
keeper,* or is what the British call her *daily help* (see **char; daily woman**): *I will be
sure to do for my son.* Can be applied also to one's children and to outside helpers,
like gardeners, handymen, and others performing similar functions.

dog-end, *n.*   **cigarette butt**
Slang. Vagrants' cant. See also **end; stump.**

doggo. See **lie doggo.**

dog's body, *n.*   *Slang,* **gofer**
Slang. This quaint term was originally British nautical slang. *Dog's body,* in that
idiom, means a 'dish of dried peas boiled in a cloth.' For reasons apparently lost
in history, it also means 'junior naval officer.' As a matter of obvious practical
extension, it came to mean 'drudge,' hence an *errand boy* (in the slang sense)
or in an even slangier sense a *prat boy,* or *gofer.* Also spelled *dog's-body* and
dogsbody.

dog's bollocks *Slang, vulgar.*   *Slang.* **the bee's knees**

dog's breakfast   **unholy mess**
Inf. Unlike a *dog's dinner* (see **like a dog's dinner**).

dog's dinner. See **like a dog's dinner.**

do (one's) head in   *Inf.* **drive to distraction**
Said of an annoying problem or behavior. That loud music from next door is
doing my head in. His constant complaining does my head in.

do (someone) in the eye   *Slang.* **do (someone) dirt**
Slang. To play (someone) a dirty trick. Synonymous with **do (someone) down.**

(the) dole, *n.*   **unemployment benefits**
Inf. Common term, somewhat pejorative, for *unemployment compensation.* The
equivalent of welfare and/or unemployment compensation under the British
system, with its own rules, regulations, arithmetic, and heartbreaks.

dollop, *v.t.*   **1. serve in large quantities**
                                               2. cover with a large quantity
Inf. From the noun *dollop,* meaning a *blob* of something. In meaning 1, it is usually
found in the expression *dollop out.* In meaning 2, it is usually seen in the passive
voice, as in *dolloped in mud.*

domestic science   **home economics**
The arts of cooking and sewing—the study of household management—are
euphemized by the educational terminology of both countries. In the UK, however, both are now taught (along with other practical subjects) under the heading
of Design and Technology.

domiciliary, *n.*   **house call**
Adjective used as a noun; short for *domiciliary visit.* Used especially by doctors to
designate what has become a practically obsolete practice.

don, *n.*   *approx.* **college teacher**
A *don* (contraction of *dominus,* Latin for 'lord') is a *teacher,* whether a **Head**
(*dean*), a **Fellow** (*assistant*), or tutor (*adviser*) at a **college,** primarily at Oxford
and Cambridge, but also at other old universities like Edinburgh and Durham.

The derivation from *dominus* is clearly seen in *dominie,* which is Scottish for 'schoolmaster.'

done, *Inf.*   **1. arrested**
                                                                   2. prosecuted
Almost always seen in a phrase like *he was done for theft.*

(be) done   *Slang.* **(be) had**
Slang. In the sense of taken advantage of, or even *cheated.* See **do, 2.**

done and dusted, *adj.*   **finished**
That project is done and dusted now.

done to the wide. See **to the wide.**

donkey jacket, *n.*   SEE COMMENT
A woolen three-quarter-length coat, usually dark blue, with a waterproof panel across the shoulders.

donkey's years   *Inf.* **a dog's age**
Inf. Both expressions mean 'a very long time,' although donkeys usually live longer than dogs. See also **moons.**

donkey-work, *n.*   **drudgery**
Slang. Like clearing the weeds under the hedges.

Donnybrook, *n.*   *Inf.* **free-for-all**
See under **Kilkenny cats.**

doodle-bug, *n.*   **flying bomb**
Slang. Hitler's V-1 rocket, the 'flying bomb' sent over southern England in World War II.

doolally, *adj.*   *Slang.* **nuts**
Slang. Deolali was a sanitorium in Bombay to which British soldiers were sent when their time of service expired, and where time hung heavily on their hands while waiting for a troopship to take them home. The boredom in the camp produced all sorts of peculiar behavior, for which the expression *the Doolally tap* was coined, *tap* being East Indian for 'fever.' See synonyms under **bonkers.**

doom, *n.*   **painting of the Last Judgment**
A *doom* may also be a sculptural group depicting the Final Day.

do one's nut, *Slang.*   *Slang.* **1. work like mad**
                                                              2. blow one's top

doorstep salesman   **door-to-door salesman**
Synonymous with **knocker.**

do porridge   *Slang.* **serve time**
Slang. In jail. Synonymous with **do bird.** See also **porridge.**

DORA, *n.*   SEE COMMENT
Acronym for *Defence of the Realm Acts,* passed in August 1914, giving the government wide powers during wartime. Between the wars, chiefly associated with
pub opening hours. See **during hours.**

dormitory, *n.*   **commuting town**
Used by itself, but more commonly in the phrase *commuters' dormitory town.* The
term *bedroom community* means the same thing, in America.

Dorothy bag   **tote bag**

dosh, *n.*   *Slang.* **money**

doss, have a. See **have a doss.**

dosser. See **doss-house.**

doss-house, *n.*   *Slang.* **flophouse**
Doss is British slang for a 'bed' in what Americans call a *flophouse. Doss house* is
common to both languages, but it is hardly ever used in America. In British slang,
the word *doss* is also a verb meaning to 'sleep in a flophouse' but, less specifically,
to *doss down* is to 'go to bed,' usually in rough, makeshift circumstances. See also
casual ward; have a doss.

dot, off his. See **off one's dot.**

dot and go one   *Inf.* **gimpy**
Inf. A lame person who walks with a limp or drags a leg, based on the supposed
rhythm of one walking with a wooden leg.

do the dirty on   *Inf.* **betray, cheat**
He wouldn't share the loot, so I did the dirty on him.

dotty, *adj.*   *Slang.* **loony**
Slang. See synonyms under **bonkers.**

double, *adj., n.*   1. SEE COMMENT
                                                                           2. SEE COMMENT
                                                                        3. **double portion**
                                                                           4. **heavy; thick**
1. *Double* and *treble* are used in giving telephone numbers in Britain. Thus, Belgravia 2211 was Belgravia *double two double one;* Grosvenor 3111 was Grosvenor
three one double one or *three treble one.*
2. In oral spelling, one always says *double* the letter (*double-b* for b-b, etc.) rather
than repeat it.
3. A use of *double* is heard in the pub. If you ask for a whiskey you get what Americans would consider a smallish quantity. When you want a decent drink of whiskey
you ask for a *double.* A common synonym of *double* in this sense is *large.* A *large* or
double drink is twice a single portion, which for many years was by law, in England,
one-sixth of a gill, and a gill is one-fourth of a pint, which meant that a single was
one-twenty-fourth of a pint! (See **Appendix II.C.2.**) Since the introduction of metric
measurement, a single has been 25ml and a double 50ml.
4. And then there are *double (heavy)* and *single (light)* cream. See **double cream.**

double-barrelled, *adj.*   hyphenated
Inf. Referring to surnames, like Sackville-West.

double-bedded, *adj.*   with a double bed
When you reserve **(book)** a hotel room for two in Britain the clerk usually asks
you whether you want a *double-bedded room* or a *twin-bedded room. Single-bedded
room* is used to describe what is called a *single room* in America.

double bend. See **bend.**

double blue. See **blue,** *n.*

double cream   heavy cream
Very heavy cream, much thicker and richer than American heavy cream, which is
called just plain *cream* in Britain.

double Dutch   *Inf.* **Greek**
Inf. Unintelligible gobbledygook, as in *It's all double Dutch to me!* In addition, *Double
Dutch* is the name given to a complex form of jump rope, seen primarily in Amer-
ican city playgrounds.

double figures   **double digits (ten or more)**
Inf. But not over ninety-nine, where one gets into *treble figures. Double figures* is
used commonly to indicate the attainment of a new plateau, as in *He's gone into
double figures,* about a **batsman** *(batter)* in cricket who has broken nine, i.e., made
his tenth run, or, *We've gone into double figures,* by someone who has just increased
the staff from eight to eleven.

double saucepan   **double boiler**
Double boiler is also used in Britain.

(jam) doughnut, *n.*   **jelly doughnut**

do (someone) up   **do (someone) in**
To *exhaust, wear out: The long walk did us up.*

do (someone) well, *v.t.*   *Inf.* **treat (someone) right**
Inf. In the British phrase *they do you well,* referring, for example, to one's enjoy-
ment of hospitality at a hotel, the *do* is equivalent to *treat* in America, but an
American would be more likely to say *they treat you right,* or *they do all right by
you,* or *they take good care of you.* To *do yourself well* means to 'live comfortably.'

dowlas, *n.*   **heavy linen or muslin**

down, *adv.*   SEE COMMENT
Inf. From London; **up** means *to London.* A person living outside London might ask a
friend, "How often do you go up?" and the meaning would be quite clear: "How
often do you go to London?" *Come up* would be used if they were talking in London. *Go down* and *come down* would be used, depending on the vantage point of the
speaker, to mean 'go' or 'come to the country,' i.e., to somewhere outside of London.
But people living in Scotland or in the north of England may talk of *going down* (i.e.,
south) to London—to the confusion of southerners, the despair of geographers, and
the discomfiture of certain northerners. See also **down train.**

down, *n.*   **dislike**
Inf. To *have a down on* someone means to 'be prejudiced' against him.

down at heel   *Inf.* **down at the heels**
Inf. Note singular of *heel.* See **Appendix I.A.2.**

down-market, *adj.*   **lower class**
Inf. But sometimes it means only 'lower priced.'

downs, *n. pl.*   **uplands**
An American asked a Briton what the *downs* were and the Briton answered: "The *downs* are the ups." They are, and the South Downs are the open rolling hills of southern England, which are usually dotted with cattle and sheep. *Downs* can be *ups* because the word is etymologically related to *dune* and has nothing to do with the direction *down.*

down tools   *Inf.* **to stop work/go on strike**

down train   SEE COMMENT
Train from London. A train in Britain goes *up* to London even if it has to travel south (or east or west) to get there; and it goes *down* from London no matter what direction it has to take to leave that fine city. Since there can be no more important end to a British railway trip than arrival in London, London must be the *up* end, and one therefore takes the *up train* to London no matter where one starts the journey.

downy, *adj.*   *Inf.* **sharp**
Slang. A *downy card* is a *smart cookie.*

doyen, *n.*   **dean**
(Pronounced DOY'-EN, or as in French.) Indicating the senior member of the group, like the *doyen* of the diplomatic corps, the *doyen* of the London Bar. *Doyen* is rarely used in America; *dean* is sometimes used in Britain.

dozy; dozey, *adj.*   *Inf.* **dopey**
Inf. Slow witted, lazy.

drain, *n.*   *Slang.* **nip**
Slang. An undersized drink of something.

drain, laugh like a. See **laugh like a drain.**

drains, *n. pl.*   **plumbing; sewerage system**
The *drains* of the house are its *drain pipes,* or *plumbing and sewerage system.* When a real estate advertisement in Britain uses the term *main drainage,* the house is connected to a public sewer system.

dram, *n.*   **a small alcoholic drink**
Usually used in Scotland, for Scotch whisky.

draper's shop   **dry goods store; haberdashery**
The *shop* can be omitted, and the *draper's* can also mean a 'haberdashery,' in the American sense of 'men's shop.' But a British **haberdashery** would be called a *notions store* in America. See also **Manchester; fancy goods; haberdashery; soft furnishings.**

draught excluder   **weather stripping**

draughts, *n. pl.*   **checkers**
The famous board game.

draw (*in game or sport*)**,** *n.*   **tie**

drawing office   **drafting room**

drawing-pin, *n.*   **thumbtack**
Synonymous with **push-pin.**

drawing-room, *n.*   **living room**
Living-room and **sitting-room** are also used in Britain, with sitting-room the most common term. Use of drawing-room usually implies that the house is a grand one. **Lounge** is heard in hotels, on board ships, or in the expression *lounge bar.*

draw it mild!   **don't exaggerate!**
Term derived from *drawing* of beer, now widely applied as an expression encouraging conservatism.

draw stumps. See **up stumps.**

draw the long bow   *approx.* **lay it on thick**
Inf. Usually found in the expression *I'm not drawing the long bow*, where Americans might say, *I'm not kidding* or *I am not exaggerating.*

dreadful warning, *Inf.*   **coming attractions**
Rare.

dress circle   **first balcony**
Of a theater; also heard in America. *Balcony* is not used in this context in Britain, where the *dress circle* would be described as the 'first gallery' of a theater. The term *gallery,* in theater parlance, is restricted to the topmost balcony housing the cheapest seats, called the **gods** in Britain.

dressed to the nines   *Slang.* **all dolled up; dressed to kill**
Inf. Sometimes *dressed up to the nines.* Synonymous with *(got up)* **like a dog's dinner.** *To the nines* means 'to perfection.'

dresser, *n.*   SEE COMMENT
Kitchen sideboard with shelves. Americans use *dresser* principally to mean a 'bureau' or 'dressing table.'

dressing gown   **bathrobe; wrapper**
In America *dressing gown* refers to something a little fancier than *bathrobe. Bathrobe* is not used in Britain, where men and women have *dressing gowns.*

dress show   **fashion show**

drill. See **what's the drill?**

drinking-up time, *n.*   SEE COMMENT
The short period in a pub for finishing drinks between last orders and closing time.

dripping, *n.*   **the fat produced by meat during cooking**
Used mainly in reference to the fat produced by cooking beef.

drive, *n.*   **driveway**

drive a coach and horses through   *Inf.* **knock holes in; flout**
Inf. Generally applied to Acts of Parliament that are ignored and made to appear
useless.

driver, *n.*   **motorman**
British **trams** (tramways) and American trolleys (trolley cars) are both practically
obsolete, but when they were in common use the man who operated them was
known as a *driver* in Britain and a *motorman* in America. The same distinction
exists today with respect to the **underground** or **tube** (*subway*). On a bus, however, he is the *driver* in both countries. On a British train, he is the **engine driver;**
on an American train, the *engineer.*

drive (someone) up the wall   *Slang.* **drive (someone) crazy**
Slang. He (she) drives me up the wall is commonly used in Britain and America.

driving licence   **driver's license**

driving seat   **driver's seat**

drop a brick   *Slang.* **make a booboo**
Slang. In the special sense of committing an indiscretion.

drop a clanger   **make a gaffe**
Slang. See also **put up a black; howler.**

drop down dead   **drop dead**
Makes an already final phenomenon even more final.

drop-head, *adj., n.*   **convertible top**
Referring to automobiles. See also **Appendix II.E.**

drop off the hooks, *Slang.*   *Slang.* **kick the bucket**

drop-scene, *n.*   **backdrop**
Sometimes *drop-curtain.* Theater talk. The British term covers not only an entire
painted scene, but occasional scenery.

dropsy, *n.*   **tip; bribe**
Slang. Often with the implication of hush-money.

dross, *n.*   **scrap coal**
A mining term. A Scottish family will buy *dross* to use with household coal as
an economy measure. The word is also used informally to describe anything of
inferior quality.

drug in the market   **drug on the market**
Something nobody wants.

drum, *n.*   SEE COMMENT
Slang. Living quarter, brothel, night club.

dry martini. See **martini.**

D.S.O. See **V.C.**

dual carriageway   **divided highway**
See also **centre strip.**

dubbin, *n.*   **leather dressing**
A greasy preparation for softening leather and making it waterproof. Sometimes
spelled *dubbing.* Popular with British and American soldiers.

duck, *n.*   1. *approx. Inf.* **goose egg**
                                                      2. *approx.* **honey**
1. As a cricket term, to *get a duck* is to *be bowled* (*put out,* approximately) without
scoring a single run. If this happens on the first ball bowled (first pitch, approximately), you get a *golden duck.* This type of *duck* is short for *duck's egg.* The victim
is *out for a duck.*
2. *Inf. Duck* is used as a form of address traditionally by barmaids and frequently by purveyors of other types of merchandise, especially the older ladies
of that group. It is used by females to persons of both sexes, but by males only to
females. It is a term of extremely casual endearment, and in this use is synonymous with *love, lovey, dear, deary,* and *darling* as forms of address.

ducking and diving   *Inf.* **evading the question**

dud cheque, *Slang.*   *Slang.* **bum check; rubber check**

dues, *n. pl.*   **fee(s)**
Dues, generally associated in America with the cost of membership in an organization, has the general meaning in Britain of *fee* or *charge* as in *postal dues (postage),
university dues (tuition),* etc. Agents' commissions are also called *dues* in Britain.

duff, *v.t.*   **fake**
Slang. To *duff* merchandise is to make old stuff look new in order to fool the customer.

duffer, *n.*   **peddler of faked merchandise**
A *duffer* in Britain is a con man who, selling shoddy goods, claims them to be of
great value because they were stolen or smuggled. It is sometimes used in Britain
generically, to mean any *peddler* (spelled *pedlar* in Britain). In both countries it also
commonly means a 'person inept at games.'

duff gen. See **gen.**

duff (someone) up, *v.*   *Inf.* **beat (someone) up**

dug-out, *n.*   *Slang.* **old retread**
Slang. More specifically, retired officer taken back into military service.

dull, *adj.*   **gloomy**
A term used all too frequently in describing overcast weather.

dumb-waiter, *n.*   **lazy Susan**
An American *dumbwaiter,* a small elevator, is in Britain a **service lift.**

dummy, *n.*   **baby pacifier**

dungarees, *n. pl.*   overalls

dunnage, *n.*   *Inf.* **duds; personal baggage**
Inf. More generally, *personal belongings;* one's *stuff. Dunnage,* in standard English, means the 'loose material packed around cargo' to prevent damage.

during hours. See **opening hours.**

dust, *n.*   household refuse
In addition to its more usual meaning in both countries.

dustbin, *n.*   garbage can

dustcart, *n.*   garbage truck

dustman, *n.*   garbage man

dust road. See **metalled road.**

dust-up, *n.*   brawl
Slang. Kick-up and *punch-up* are synonyms.

dutch, *n.*   wife
Slang. Especially in *my old dutch,* a term of endearment, like *my old girl, my dear old better half.* Perhaps an abbreviation of *duchess,* with the *t* thrown in by reference to *Dutch.*

duvet, *n.*   eiderdown quilt
(Usually pronounced DEW'-VAY, but DOO-VAY' and DOO'-VET are also heard.) It differs from an **eiderdown** in that it has a removable washable cover, hangs over the sides of the bed, and is used as a complete bed covering without top sheet or blankets. It is also called *continental quilt* in Britain.

D.V., W.P.   *approx.* **God willing**
These initials stand for *Deo volente, weather permitting.* This is an old-fashioned British joke and reflects the Briton's firm belief that British weather is so uncertain that, when plans are being discussed, appeal should be made not only to the Almighty but to the elements as well. *Deo volente* is Latin for *God willing.*

dye stamp   engrave
Stationery, for example. A term used in printing.

dynamo, *n.*   generator
See **Appendix II.E.**
In the U.S., *dynamo,* formerly much used, especially to describe a D.C. generator, is now rarely heard; an A.C. generator is now usually called an *alternator,* especially as an automotive part; a *generator* can be A.C. or D.C.

E

each way   SEE COMMENT
Inf. At an American track, you can bet to win, place, or show, or any combination
of the two, or all three. Betting on all three in America is called *betting across the
board.* In American horse racing, to *place* means to 'come in second,' to *show* to
'come in third.' In British betting, *place* describes any of the first three to come in
(or in a race with very few horses entered, either of the first two). At a track in
Britain (a **race-course**), if you *have a quid each way* and your horse wins, you win
two bets: the odds on the winner, plus a proportion of those odds. If your horse
merely places, you win only the quid (one pound) you bet on the place bet. In
America if you *bet across the board* and have picked the winner, you win three bets,
at descending odds, for win, place, and show, respectively.

eagre, eager, *n.*   **tidal flood**

ear-bashing, *n.*   *Inf.* **a good talking-to**
Curiously, one never *ear-bashes*; one only gets the bashing in question.

early closing   SEE COMMENT
At one time, most British villages and towns had an *early closing day.* This custom
is observed in a few parts of America, but even in those towns there are often
nonconforming individual holdouts, a practice rare in Britain. In the smaller
British villages and towns, all the shops closed for lunch, usually from 1:00 P.M. to
2:00 P.M. or 2:15 P.M. every day, but on *early closing day* they shut at 1:00. for good.
This is now rarer in Britain than it once was, but early closing can still catch out
passing tourists.

Early Day Motion (EDM)   SEE COMMENT
An EDM is a motion tabled on the order paper by Members of Parliament when
they want a debate on a particular matter. EDMs can only be debated if they gain
support of over half the MPs in Parliament, and this rarely happens.

early days   **too soon;** *Slang.* **jumping the gun**
Inf. This phrase means *prematureness.* Thus: *It's early days to reach that conclusion.*

early on   **early in the picture**
This expression, meaning 'at an early stage,' is becoming stylish in America.

earner, *n.*   *Inf.* **a profitable enterprise**
Made popular by a character in *Minder,* a hugely popular television series of the
1970s.

earth, *n., v.t.*   **1. ground**
                                                         2. cover with soil
                                                          3. run to ground
1. Term used in electricity. The Americans *ground* a wire; the British *earth* it. The
same distinction occurs in the noun use of this electrical term.

2. To *earth* the roots of a plant is to *cover* them *with soil.*
3. *To earth* a fox is *to run* it *to earth.*

earth floor or earthen floor   **dirt floor**

earthly, *adj.*   **chance; hope**
Inf. Often used elliptically, always in the negative, to mean '(not a) chance;' '(not a) hope.' A slang American equivalent in some contexts is *no way.* For example, *Do you think he'll succeed?* might be answered, *Not an earthly!* in Britain, and *No way!* in America.

East, *n.*   **Orient**
The British usually speak of the *East* rather than the *Orient.*

East End   SEE COMMENT
The Eastern part of London, which, like its Manhattan parallel, the Lower East Side, was the area in which immigrants settled during the first half of the century. Much of it is still essentially a working-class area.

east end of a westbound cow   **south end of a northbound horse**
All this to avoid saying or hearing *ass.*

easy about it. See **I'm easy (about it).**

easy as kiss your hand. See **as easy as kiss your hand.**

easy meat   1. *Slang.* **a cinch**
                                                                2. *Slang.* **sucker**
1. *Slang.* Something or someone easily obtained, attained, or mastered, as in, *It was easy meat getting it right,* or *getting the tickets.*
2. *Slang.* Originally the phrase was applied mainly to people, connoting passivity or gullibility, as in, *The immigrants were easy meat for the politicians. Pushover* and *easy pickin's* are other American equivalents. It is still used of a susceptible woman.

easy-peasy, *adj.*   *Slang.* **very easy**

eat one's terms   **study for the bar**
To *study for the bar* is a less general term in Britain than in America. It refers only to preparation to become a **barrister.** An aspiring barrister *eats his terms* or his *dinners* (three dinners in the Hall of his **Inn of Court** each of four Terms per year) in order to *keep his terms* in compliance with British bar admission requirements. This phrase is a pleasant survival from the days when the Inns of Court more or less constituted residential universities where, naturally, the students took their meals.

eddy forth   **sally forth**
Both used by the British and by the Americans.

eejit, *n.*   *Inf.* **idiot**
From an Irish pronunciation.

effing, *adj.*   SEE COMMENT
Euphemism for *fucking. It was effing awful.*

effing and blinding, *v.*   *Slang.* **to use obscenities freely**
He was effing and blinding in front of the children.

eiderdown, *n.*   **quilt; comforter**
Used generically for all quilts, not necessarily those filled with the soft feathers of
the female eider. See also **duvet.**

Eights Week. See May Week.

Elastoplast, *n.*   **Band-Aid**
The proprietary name for adhesive bandage.

electric fire   **electric heater**
See under **fire.**

electricity pylon, *n.*   **transmission tower**

elementary school   **grade school**
Or *primary school* in America.

elephant's, *adj.*   *Slang.* **drunk**
Slang. Drunk. Short for *elephant's trunk.* Cockney rhyming slang; see **Appendix
II.G.3.**

elevator, *n.*   **lift**
An *elevator* in Britain is not a device for vertical conveyance of people or things.
Its generic meaning is 'anything that lifts,' but its common meaning is 'shoe lift.'
(This use is seen in America, too, in the term *elevator shoes.*) Conversely, a British
lift is an American *elevator.*

eleven, *n.*   **cricket team; soccer team**
Inf. In American sports terminology, an *eleven* would mean a 'football team'
(using *football* in the American sense; see **football**). An *eleven* in Britain refers to
cricket or soccer and means a 'side.' Roman numerals are often used: first XI (the
first team), second XI (the reserve team). Similarly, a rugby team is a XV, but note
that a rowing crew is an *eight*, not an VIII, though in listing their order, crews
might be designated *1st VIII, 2nd VIII,* etc.

eleven plus   SEE COMMENT
An examination, in the nature of an aptitude and achievement test. Meant to be
taken at the end of primary school, it determined what type of secondary education was most suitable for the child, with the most academically gifted going
to *grammar schools,* those exhibiting a practical bent to technical or vocational
schools, and the remainder, a majority, to *secondary modern schools.* In practice, the
examination was looked upon by parents as a pass/fail exam for the prestigious
grammar schools. Formerly widespread but now eliminated except for scattered
pockets of resistance in Britain, this system has been largely replaced by nonse-
lective *comprehensive schools,* which aim to provide for all aptitudes and levels of
ability. Public education (called *state education* in Britain) is free. Parents may opt
out of the state system by sending their children to fee-paying private schools.
Those catering to children aged 8–12 are called **prep schools;** those for 13–18 year
olds are called **public schools.** The entrance examination for public schools is
called the **Common Entrance Examination.**

elevenses, *n. pl.*   *approx.* **morning coffee break**
Inf. Also called *elevens* and *elevensies.* The light refreshments consumed in this British morning exercise consist usually of a cup of tea or coffee and a **biscuit** or two. *Morning coffee* is another term used by the British to describe this social practice, which takes place at home, in hotels, and in tearooms.

embus. See **debus.**

Employment Secretary   *approx.* **Secretary of Labor**

encash, *v.t.*   **cash**
One *encashes* (accent on the second syllable) a **cheque** (*check*). Now rarer than *cash.*

end, *n.*   **butt**
Patrons of London theaters and other public places are usually provided with wall receptacles, partly filled with sand, bearing the legend "*Cigarette Ends.*" See also **stump; dog-end.**

endive, *n.*   **chicory**
In a British vegetable store (**greengrocer's**), if you want *chicory* ask for *endive,* and vice versa.

endorse, *v.t.*   **record on license**
Under a point system similar to that used in America, a British operator's license is said to be *endorsed* with a record of the offense.

engage, *v.t.*   **hire; employ**
A Briton *engages* a chauffeur and *hires* a car; an American *hires* a chauffeur and *rents* a car. In America, one *rents* a house to or from another. In Britain, you *rent* a house *from* the owner and *let* your own *to* a tenant. However, the sign TO LET is seen in both countries.

engaged, *adj.*   **busy**
It is as frustrating to be told by a British telephone operator that the line is *engaged* or to hear the *engaged tone* as it is to hear the word *busy* or the *busy signal* in America. *He's engaged,* used by a British **telephonist,** is just as irritating in Britain as the dreary American equivalents *He's busy talking* or *He's on the wire.*

engine driver   **engineer**
Railroad term.

enquiries, *n. pl.*   **information**
(Stressed on the second syllable.) *Directory Enquiries* is the term you use in Britain when you want *Information* to look up a telephone number for you. *Enquiries* also appears on signs in offices, railway stations, etc., where the American sign would read "Information." *Trunk enquiries* formerly meant 'long-distance information.' See **national call.**

enquiry, *n.*   **investigation**
(Stressed on the second syllable.) This word is often used where *investigation* would be used in America, e.g., in discussing an attempt to ferret out

wrongdoing in a government department. A similar sense is found in the British term *enquiry agent,* which would be *private investigator* or *private detective* in America. It is also used as the equivalent of the American term *hearing,* e.g., *planning enquiry,* which is the British equivalent of *zoning hearing.* An *enquiry office* is an *information bureau.*

ENSA, *n.*   *approx.* **USO**
An acronym for *Entertainments National Service Association.* Like the American *USO* (stands for *United Service Organizations*) it supplied entertainment to the armed forces. ENSA gave its final show on August 18, 1946, the last of two and a half million performances.

ensure, *v.t.*   **make sure**
Instructions from a travel agency: "Please *ensure* your baggage is correctly labelled." (See **Appendix I.E.** for the third *l* in *labelled.*) This usage of *ensure* would be found in commercial, government or other 'official' communications, rarely, if ever, in ordinary writing or speech.

entrance fee   **initiation fee**
This is the term used by the British to describe the initial fee paid on joining a club.

entry, *n.*   **entrance**
Sign over a door in a public building. See **No Entry.** The American term **no entrance** is used as well.

erk, *n.*   *Slang.* **rookie**
Slang. Formerly *airk,* which meant aircraft mechanic and technician. After it became *erk,* it was taken as 'beginner, rookie.'

Ernie, *n.*   SEE COMMENT
Used in selecting **Premium Bond** winning numbers; an acronym for *electronic random number indicator equipment.*

escape lane (road)   SEE COMMENT
A means of egress off a main highway for a vehicle in difficulties; usually in the U.S. called *emergency exit* or *egress.*

Esq., *n.*   **Mr.**
Short, of course, for *Esquire.* In addressing letters, *Esq.* follows the name, and is simply the equivalent of *Mr.* preceding the name. American convention calls for addressing lawyers as *Esq. Esq.* is not used where the name is preceded by a title (e.g., Prof. C.E. Jones, Sir Charles Smith). See **Appendix I.D.7.**

Essex girl   *Inf., derog.* SEE COMMENT
A derogatory term for someone of working-class origins and supposedly low intellect, low moral standards, and crassly acquisitive values. Essex is the county on London's eastern border, and the term is mostly one of metropolitan snobbery. There is no precise American equivalent, but many areas have a comparable form of prejudice.

(the) Establishment   SEE COMMENT
The Establishment describes those British institutions (and their representatives) that symbolize tradition and conformity and wield considerable social, finan-

cial, and political influence: the upper classes, the Church of England, *The Times*, **Whitehall,** and the Marylebone Cricket Club. *The Establishment* is used roughly the same way in America, but its components are quite different. According to Leonard and Mark Silk (*The American Establishment*, Basic, 1980), the Establishment, American style, is a "bringing together of intellectuals, under the benevolent governance of (big) business, rather than that of the state."

estate, *n.*   **real estate development**
Usually found in the terms *housing estate,* meaning a 'residential development,' or *industrial estate,* signifying an area designated for industry, workshops and offices. British housing officials and other experts use *estate* or *housing estate* as the exact equivalent of the American term *housing project,* to denote any development of one or more buildings comprising a number of households.

estate agent   **real estate broker**
Synonymous with **land agent.**

estate car   **station wagon**
It also used to be called *estate wagon,* but that term is rarely heard nowadays. Often shortened to *estate.*

Eurosceptic, *n.*   SEE COMMENT
Someone who is sceptical about the European Union and its aims, and therefore critical of Britain's involvement. Such people may be of any of the political parties, but are more likely to be Conservative than Labour. See also **Little Englander.**

evens, *n. pl.*   *Inf.* **even money**
Inf. The odds: *Evens on . . .* means 'I will lay you *even money* on . . .'

ever so   **very**
He's ever so handsome. She was ever so kind. Non-U. See **Appendix I.C.6.**

everything in the garden's lovely   *Inf.* **everything's hunky-dory**
Inf. An old-fashioned catch phrase.

everything that opens and shuts   *Inf.* **everything but the kitchen sink**
Inf. The price of my new car includes everything that opens and shuts. The expression could apply as well to a hand at cards full of trumps and honors.

except for access   *approx.* **no through trucks**
Preceded by numerals indicating width or weight (e.g., 6′ 6″, or 3 **tons**) on a sign at the ingress of a back road, forbidding entrance (**entry**) to a vehicle over the specified width or weight, unless it is in fact headed for a destination on that road. See **access,** for a different usage of that word by itself. See **pinch-point.**

Exchequer, *n.*   **Treasury Department**
The *Chancellor of the Exchequer* is the British equivalent of the *Secretary of the Treasury.* But the Chancellor has more power than his or her American counterpart to set economic policy.

exclamation mark   **exclamation point**

exclusive line   **private line**
Telephone term, the opposite of **shared lines** or *party lines*. Rarely used nowadays.

ex-directory, *adj.*   **unlisted**
Referring to telephone numbers.

exeat, *n.*   **temporary school leave**
(Pronounced EX'EE-AT.) Term used in schools and colleges. Like the more familiar word *exit*, it is a form of the Latin verb *exire*, 'to go forth'; here literally meaning *let him go out*.

(the) Executive, *n.*   **(the) Executive Committee**
Used the way Americans use *the Management* at the end of notices posted in public places, like railroad stations and post offices.

exercise book   **notebook**
Sometimes referred to as a **jotter.**

exhibition; exhibitioner. See under **bursar.**

export carriage   **overseas shipping**
Seen as an extra charge item on bills for goods sent overseas, like tea bought in England and shipped to America.

express, *adj., adv.*   **special delivery**
Post office term. The American designation has now been adopted by the Post Office. See **recorded delivery.** The U.S. Post Office now has 'Express Mail,' a premium overnight service available at a price.

ex-service man   **veteran**

external painting   **outdoor painting**
Builders' and contractors' term.

extractor fan   **exhaust fan**

extra-mural studies   **extension courses**

Extraordinary General Meeting. See under **Annual General Meeting.**

Eye-tie, *n.*   *Slang, offens.* **Italian**

 **F**

fab, *adj.* *Slang.* **cool**
Slang. A teenage truncation of *fabulous,* largely out of fashion now, though it can be used as a jocular exaggeration.

facecloth, *n.* SEE COMMENT
The British call an ordinary washrag or *facecloth* a **flannel.**

facer, *n.* *Inf.* **obstacle**
Inf. Facer is rarely heard in either country in its literal meaning of 'blow in the face.' In Britain it has the special meaning of a difficulty you suddenly come up against.

faculty, *n.* **college department**
In America, the *faculty* of a college is its entire teaching body. In Britain, this is called **staff,** and *faculty* is confined to groups of academically related subjects, i.e., departments, as in *Faculty of Medicine, Law,* etc.

faddy, *adj.* *Inf.* **picky**
Inf. Often used to describe persons who are fussy about their food and difficult to please. See also **dainty.**

fadge, *v.i.* **suit**
Slang. Especially in the expression *It won't fadge,* meaning 'It won't suit' (or 'do' or 'fit'). "How will this *fadge*?" asks the sleuth, "No good, it won't *fadge*."

faff, *v.* *Inf.* **dither, fuss**
Often used in combination with *about: If you don't stop faffing about, we'll miss the train.*

fag, *n., v.t., v.i.* **1.** *v.i.,* **toil**
2. *v.i.,* **exhaust**
3. *n., Slang.* **drag**
4. *n., Slang.* **cigarette**
5. SEE COMMENT
1. *v.i., Slang.* To *toil painfully.*
2. *v.t., Slang.* To *tire* or *wear (someone) out.*
3. *n., Slang.* In the sense of 'drudgery'; a painfully boring job.
4. *Slang. Cigarette* in Britain.
5. *Slang.* In **public school** slang, when seniors *fag,* it means that they are using the services of juniors; when juniors *fag,* it means that they are rendering services to seniors and the junior so serving is known as a *fag.*

faggot, *n.* **1. crone**
2. spiced meatball
1. *Inf.* Chiefly a country term, summoning the image of a battered old slut.

2. Made of chopped pig innards (see **offal**) and fairly heavily spiced. The common American slang use of *faggot* to mean 'male homosexual' has caught on in Britain.

fains I!   SEE COMMENT
Slang. Also *fain I! vains I!* and other regional variants like *fainites! vainites!* and even *cribs! scribs! crosses! keys!* and goodness knows what else, usually accompanied by conspicuously crossed fingers. All these are truce words meaning that the crier wants his pals to wait a minute—calling for a halt, for example, in a fast children's game. Only an unscrupulous bully would take advantage of a call for truce. See a special use of *fains* under **Quis? Bags I!** is the opposite of *fains I!* Exceedingly rare.

fair, *adv.*   *Inf.* **surely**
Inf. That sermon fair set us thinking! Substandard; mostly rustic.

fair cop   *Inf.* **justified arrest**
Always used in the expression *It's a fair cop.* Criminal slang that has found its way into common usage as a way of expressing acceptance of wrongdoing, justified punishment, etc.

fair do's   *Inf.* **fair enough**
Implying acceptance of a less-than-perfect outcome or decision.

fair-light, *n.*   **transom**

fair old . . . , *adj.*   *Inf.* **quite a . . .**
Inf. A fair old job means 'quite a job' (*a major chore); a fair old mix-up* means 'quite a mix-up' (a snafu of major proportions).

fair's on   *Inf.* **what's fair is fair**
Inf. To the friend who paid for a round of drinks, a Briton might say: "*Fair's on . . . ,* this one's on me."

fairy cake   **cupcake**

fall about laughing   *Slang.* **die laughing**
Slang. Sometimes shortened to *fall about,* with *laughing* understood, especially in the **cockney** idiom.

fallen off the back of a lorry   *Slang.* **hot**
Slang. A **lorry** is a *truck.* A thief or black marketeer, seeking to dispose of ill-gotten wares, approaches a pedestrian and assures him that the fur coat or wristwatch or whatever *fell off the back of a lorry* and went unclaimed by police.

fall over backwards   *Inf.* **bend over backwards**
Do one's darndest to accomplish something worthwhile.

family butcher   **butcher shop**
Often *first-class family butcher,* typically one that does not serve institutions. See also **butchery.**

fancy, *v.t.* SEE COMMENT
To find (someone or something) attractive. The usual object of fancy is a person, but may just as easily be an article of clothing or a particular dish or meal.

fancy goods notions
See also **draper's shop; haberdashery.**

fancy one's chances *Inf.* **have high hopes**
Inf. The hopeful swain *fancies his chances* with the girl; the team with a comfortable margin *fancy their chances* for the cup. One may fancy one's own or another's chances, but when the expression applies to a third party, it is often found in the negative. After attending a disappointing first night: *I don't fancy its chances,* or, about a friend about to enter a tournament: *I don't fancy his chances.*

fanny, *n.* **1.** *Slang.* **backside**
2. *vulgar.* **cunt**
1. *Slang.* Originally, this word meant the female pudenda, but the American sense—'backside,' 'behind,' 'derrière'—appears to have become its primary meaning now in Britain, as a result of importation from America, where it has never had the second meaning. Yet it might be just as well to avoid its use in Britain, because there are those, among the elderly at least, and perhaps the not-so-elderly in less chic circles, who might be shocked, and certainly puzzled, if it were applied to a male.
2. *Vulgar Slang.* This is the original British meaning, and the word is still understood or may be understood that way in some circles.

Fanny Adams. See sweet Fanny Adams.

fare stage **bus fare zone limit**
In both countries *stage* appears in the phrase *stage of a journey,* and as part of *stage-coach,* especially in American movies about the Wild West. In Britain, *fare stages* are the *zone limits* for purposes of computing bus fares.

farthing *n.* SEE COMMENT
One fourth of an old penny, a coin long since demonetized; but the term is still used figuratively to mean a 'bit' in expressions like *It doesn't matter a farthing.* See **Appendix II.A.** and, for idiomatic use, **halfpenny.**

fart in a colander, *Slang* **restless soul**
One who jumps around from one chore to the next, unable to make up his mind what to start first. This indelicate expression suggests an anal wind emission unable to decide which hole in the colander to pass through. Synonymous with **tit in a trance.** Little used.

fashionista, *n.* *Inf.,* SEE COMMENT
A person who is unusually interested in clothing and fashion; usually used ironically or derogatorily.

fast, *adj.* **express**
Applied to trains and to roads (express or limited highways). A local train is called a **stopping train,** or **slow train.**

Father Christmas **Santa Claus**
The British also use *Santa Claus.*

Father of the House, *n.*   SEE COMMENT
The MP with the longest continuous service in the House of Commons. If that person is a woman, the term will be **Mother of the House.**

fat rascal , *Inf.*   soft bun
Stuffed with black currants.

faults and service difficulties   telephone repair department
This was the department you asked for on your neighbor's telephone when yours wasn't working. A *faulty* telephone is one that is out of order. Now obsolete.

feed, *n.*   1. feeding
                                                                2. straight man
1. Usually in the context of formula feeding. To *go onto feeds* is to *go onto formula,* e.g., *My little one is on six feeds a day.* Technically, a *feed* can be any variety—breast, formula, or cereal.
2. The member of the comedy duo who *feeds* cues to the gag man.

feeder, *n.*   child's bib

feel, *v.i.*   feel like
For example, *I feel a perfect fool!*

feeling not quite the thing, *Inf.*   *Inf.* feel below par

felicitate, *v.t.*   congratulate

Fellow, *n.*   member of college governing body
In Oxford and some other universities, also called **don.** The chairman of the governing body is called the *Master* in most **Oxbridge** colleges, but in addition to the eight Masters, there are seven Wardens, five Principals, three Provosts and two Rectors. At Cambridge, *Master* is the title with only four exceptions: one each of Provost, President, Mistress and Principal. At Oxford and Cambridge *Fellow* can best be defined as 'senior teaching or administrative member' of a college. There are all sorts and varieties of *Fellow: Research Fellows, Junior Research Fellows, Honorary Fellows, Emeritus Fellows, Quondam* (or *ex-*) *Fellows.*

fender, *n.*   bumper
Old automobile term; but American *fender* is British **wing.** *Bumper* is now universal. (See also **Appendix II.E.**)

(the) Fens, *n. pl.*   SEE COMMENT
Name given to the marshy district of the eastern part of the country, west and south of *the Wash,* a shallow bay in that section of England.

fetch, *v.t.*   bring
As in, to *fetch* a price in an auction. The British use *make* in the same way.

fête, *n.*   fair
(Pronounced FATE.) An important part of British life. Most organizations, as well as every village in Britain, down to the smallest, organize a fête. The village fête is annual and is a small-scale country fair, sometimes preceded by a parade with floats.

fiddle, *n., v.t., v.i.*   **swindle**
To *fiddle* is to *cheat,* and to *fiddle the books* is to *engage in shady dealings.* A *fiddle* is usually a minor cheat. To *be on the fiddle* is to engage in minor swindling. When the offense is of major proportions, the British use *swindle.* See also **diddle; do; carve up; ramp; sell a pup; swizz; take down; cook.**

fiddling, *adj.*   **petty; futile; contemptible**

field, *v.t.*   **put up**
Speaking of political candidates. Americans and Britons alike *field* teams or armies, i.e., put them in the field, but only the British *field* candidates.

fieldsman, *n.*   **fielder**
Cricket vs. baseball (See also **batsman**). *Fielder* is commonly used in Britain, but *fieldsman* is unknown in America.

fifty-fifty sale   **split even**
You collect all those things you want to get rid of, take them to a scheduled charity sale, and split the proceeds *fifty-fifty* with the charity.

file, *n.*   **loose-leaf binder**
A British schoolboy or university student will keep his notes in a *file.*

filibuster, *n., v.i.*   **buccaneer**
Filibuster originally meant the same thing in both countries: as a verb, 'engage in unauthorized warfare against a foreign power,' as a noun, a 'buccaneer' or 'pirate' engaged in that activity. In Britain, it does not have the specialized American sense of an endless speech, especially in the Senate and the House of Representatives, designed to obstruct proceedings and prevent a vote on unwanted legislation.

fillet, *n.*   **1. tenderloin**
                                                                         2. filet
(Rhymes with MILLET, not MILLAY.) On an American restaurant menu the equivalent would be *tenderloin steak,* or perhaps *filet mignon.* The term may also be applied to pork, lamb, etc.
2. A piece of fish served without the bones.

fill in   **fill out**
The British fill *in* or fill *up* a form; the Americans fill *in* or fill *out* a form. See **Appendix I.A.1.** *Fill out* is creeping into Britain.

film, *n.*   **movie**
A *film* is a *movie* (i.e., a motion picture). A **cinema** is the theater that shows it. In old-fashioned slang, one went to the **flicks** to see a *flick.*

filthy, *adj.*   *Inf.* **lousy**
Inf. As in *Filthy weather we're having; She's had a filthy time of it; He has a filthy temper.*

financial, *adj.*   *Inf.* **well-heeled**
Inf. Mainly Australian and New Zealand, but used jocularly in Britain on occasion. *Let me buy the drinks; I'm financial tonight* or, *I'm feeling financial.*

financial year   **fiscal year**
An accounting term.

find, *v.t.*   **like**
When the manager of the inn asks you as you are leaving, "How did you *find* us?" he is asking you how you *liked* his inn.

fine down   *Inf.* **thin down; clear up**
Inf. To *fine* (something) *down, away* or *off* is to make it thinner. Transitively, referring to the brewing of beer, it means to 'clear up'. Intransitively, referring to any liquid, it means to 'become clear,' as in the case of a wine whose sediment has settled.

finger   **shot of booze**
Slang. An alcoholic drink one finger-thickness in the glass.

fingerling, *n.*   **young salmon**
In America, more broadly, it means anything small and specifically any fish no longer than your finger.

fire, *n.*   **heater**
As in *electric fire; gas fire;* but also used eliptically meaning either. See also **-fired.**

fire brigade   **fire department**

-fired   SEE COMMENT
The British speak of *oil-fired, gas-fired,* etc., *central heating.* This is shortened to *oil heat, gas heat,* etc., in America. See also **fire.**

fire-flair *n.*   **stingray**

firefly, *n.*   **lightning bug**

fire-guard, *n.*   **fire screen**

fire-irons, *n. pl.*   **fireplace implements**

fire lighter, *n.*   **fire starter**

fire office   **fire insurance company office**

fire-pan, *n.*   **metal grate**

fire-raising, *n.*   **arson**
A *fire-raiser* is an arsonist.

fire station, *n.*   **firehouse**

firewood, *n.*   **kindling**
Firewood, in America, is any wood for burning, usually in a fireplace for heat, but also outdoors for cooking. The American term includes *kindling.* In Britain where many fireplaces contain grates for the burning of coal, *firewood* denotes merely

wood to start the fire with, and is either gathered outdoors or is bought at the **ironmonger's** (*hardware store*) in small wire-bound bundles of thin, short sticks.

first, *n.*   *Inf.* **summa**
Inf. First is a university term which is short for *first-class honours* and is roughly equivalent to *summa* in America, which is short for *summa cum laude*. There are *seconds* and *thirds* as well. See **class.** One says, *He got a first in physics.*

first class   *approx.* **major league**
Sports terminology. This pairing is as approximate as the respective national games; *first-class* cricket, *major league* baseball. There is also *second-class* cricket, very roughly analogous to *minor league* baseball, involving the second **elevens** of first class counties and the first **elevens** of second class counties, each category with its own championship.

First Division   SEE COMMENT
The old term for the premier league in the football standings, now called **Premiership.** The term is still used, informally, for any grouping that is considered to be preeminent in its field, and is also the name of the trade union for top civil servants.

first floor   **second floor**
Americans use *first floor* and *ground floor* interchangeably to describe an apartment on the ground level, and *main floor* or *street floor* to describe the ground level of a shop or office building. The British use *ground floor* to describe all of those things, but when they say *first floor,* they mean the next floor up, i.e., the floor above the ground floor, or what Americans call the *second floor.* This difference continues all the way to the top, of course. Though Americans call the floor above the ground floor the *second floor,* inhabitants of that floor are also heard to say that they live *one flight up.*

first knock. See **take first knock.**

fish, *n.*   **fish and seafood**
In Britain *fish* usually includes *seafood,* edible salt water shellfish.

fish, wet. See **wet fish.**

fisher. See **bradbury.**

fish fingers   **fish sticks**

fishing story, *n.*   **fish story**

fishmonger's   **fish store**

fish 'n' chips   SEE COMMENT
Fish fried in batter and served with French fried potatoes (see **chips**). This fish used to be cod, most of the time, in the cheaper places, and plaice, a European flatfish, in the better places, and here and there other varieties of fish. As a result of overfishing the price of cod has rocketed, and haddock and hake are the normal fare in the usual fish 'n' chips place. In the more casual type of establishment,

this dish used to be served wrapped in a piece of newspaper (a practice made illegal), and some gourmets insist that the newspaper ink lent an incomparable flavor that cannot be duplicated. The normal procedure is to douse this dish in malt vinegar, Brown Sauce, or Daddy's Sauce, and/or ketchup.

fish-slice,   SEE COMMENT
Inf. Literally, a cook's implement for serving and for turning fish while it is cooking, and for removing it from the pan.

fit?, *adj.*   *Inf.* **all set?**
Inf. Usually asked in the form, *Are you fit?*

fitments, *n. pl.*   **fixtures**
Of a shop or factory.

fits. *See* **give (someone) fits.**

fitted, *adj.*   **wall-to-wall**
Used of carpeting. Another phrase, though less common, is *edge-to-edge. Wall-to-wall* is beginning to be used frequently, especially in its extended senses.

fitter, *n.*   **plumber; mechanic**
Americans use the phrase *steam fitter* to refer to a mechanic who installs or repairs steam pipe systems but do not use *fitter,* as the British do loosely, to mean a 'repairman' or 'plumber.' In Britain you send for the *fitter* whether your home radiator or your boat engine, as just two examples, is out of order.

fittings, *n. pl.*   **fixtures**
Shop fittings in Britain are called *store fixtures* in America.

fit-up, *adj.*   1. *Slang.* **pick-up**
                                                                              2. **frame-up**
1. *Slang.* Theatrical slang, to describe a temporary touring company, assembled from hither and yon and provided with portable stage scenery. The term can be applied to other types of organization.
2. Also used in phrases such as *The cops fitted me up.*

five honours. See **four honours.**

fiver, *n.*   *approx.* **five**
A *fiver* is a *five-pound note* (see **note**), worth about $8. A *fiver* (more commonly a *five*) in America is, of course, a *five-dollar bill.*

fives, *n.*   **handball**
The games are roughly similar.

five-star. See **four-star.**

fixings, *n. pl.*   **hardware**
What Americans call the *hardware* on a window, swinging gate, or other such equipment, is called the *fixings* in Britain.

fixture, *n.*   **scheduled sporting event**
In the British sports world what the Americans call an *event* is called a *fixture*.

fizz, *n.*   *Inf.* **sparkling wine**
Including Champagne, though not confined to it.

Flag Day   **Tag Day**
The day on which people solicit you for contributions to a cause and give you
something to put on your lapel to prove you've come through. In Britain you get
little flags; in America you may get paper poppies on the end of a pin. Obsolete,
but see **Poppy Day.**

flake out   *Inf.* **pass out**
Inf. Faint, collapse from exhaustion.

flaming, *adj., adv.*   *Slang.* **damned**
Inf. Synonymous with **flipping, ruddy, bloody.**

flan, *n.*   SEE COMMENT
Sponge cake or pastry with fruit filling, usually with a layer of whipped cream as
well. *Flan* in America is caramel custard.

flannel, *n.*   **face cloth**
Also known in America as *washcloth* or *washrag*. But when the British talk of a
wash-cloth they mean what is known in America as a *dishcloth*.

flannel, *n., v.t., v.i., Slang.*   1. *n., Slang.* **soft soap; flattery**
                                              2. *v.t., Slang.* **soft-soap; flatter**
                                              3. *v.i., Slang.* **talk one's way out**
                                              4. *n., Slang.* **nonsense**

flapjack, *n.*   1. SEE COMMENT
                                                      2. **lady's flat compact**
1. Type of cookie. *Flapjack* now also means 'pancake' in Britain.
2. A portable container for face powder.

flares, *n.,pl.*   **bell-bottoms**

flash, *adj.*   **flashy**

flash Harry   SEE COMMENT
Someone who is **flash** in his manner or habits, i.e. ostentatiously and obnox-
iously displaying the evidence of his wealth.

flat, *n.*   **apartment**
A block of flats is an *apartment house*. See **block; apartment.**

flat, *adj.*   **dead**
Describing batteries that have come to the end of their useful lives.

flatmate, *n.*   **roommate**
More precisely: someone with whom one shares an apartment without sharing
a bed.

flat out   **at full speed**
Inf. Flat out to a Briton suggests a race, particularly a horse race, with the winner (by a nose) going *all out,* using every ounce of power. In Britain, it does not have the sense of 'plainly' or 'directly,' as in (American) *I told him flat-out what I thought of him.*

flat spin. See **in a flat spin.**

fleck, *n.*   **lint**
Inf. The bits that cling annoyingly to dark woolen clothing. **Fluff** and *lint* are the usual terms in Britain and America.

fleet, *n., adj.*   **1. creek**
                                                                      2. shallow

Heard from time to time.

Fleet Street   **the press**
Inf. See **Throgmorton Street, Wardour Street,** and other street names used synec-dochically, to indicate various businesses and professions. Fleet Street, EC1 and EC2, once housed nearly all of Britain's national press and major news agencies. Even though the last moved out in 2005, the term is still used.

flex, *n.*   **electric cord; extension**
Abbreviation of *flexible,* used as a noun.

flexible (table) lamp   **gooseneck lamp**

flexitime, *n.*   **flextime**
A system in Britain and America whereunder an employee works a fixed number of hours but at times partly as the worker chooses.

flick-knife, *n.*   **switchblade**

flicks, *n. pl.*   **movies**
Slang. Still heard. See **film.**

flies, *n. pl.*   **fly**
The *fly* of a man's trousers is commonly heard as *flies* in Britain.

flimsy, *n.*   **thin copy paper**
Inf. Particularly the type favored by Her Majesty's ministries. The word can also mean a carbon copy of something typed on such paper. Now rare.

flipping, *adj., adv.*   **damned**
Slang. More or less equivalent to **bloody** but thought to be more polite. Pejorative and intensive. See synonyms under **bloody.**

flit, *v.i.,n.*   **move on, depart**
Especially from one abode to another, with the intention of escaping from some-thing undesirable. *He'll probably flit to escape his debts.* As a noun, used in the phrase *to do a flit.*

float, *n.*   **petty cash fund**

flog, *v.t.*   **1.** *Slang.* **push**
                                                  2. *Slang.* **sell illegally**
                                                  3. *Slang.* **lick (vanquish)**
                                                  4. *Slang.* **swipe**
1. *Slang.* In Britain *flog* describes the hard sell, whether the insistent effort to *dispose of goods* or to *press an idea.*
2. *Slang.* Applies to stolen or smuggled goods *flogged* on the black market, for example. See also **fallen off the back of a lorry.**
3. *Slang.* To *flog* one's competitors, whether in sports or competitive examinations, is to *trounce* them, to *beat them all hollow.*
4. *Slang.* To borrow without the owner's permission, with only the vaguest intention of returning.

flog it   **plod**
Military slang. To *flog it* is to *walk* or *plod.* See also **foot-slog.**

floor, *v.t.*   SEE COMMENT
Inf. When a British schoolboy stands up to recite and isn't prepared, the teacher (**master**) *floors* him, i.e., tells him to sit down. *Floor* shares the general American colloquial meaning 'overcome' or 'shatter' someone with a devastating riposte. Now rare.

Floral Dance. See **Furry Dance.**

fluff, *n.*   **lint**
A *bit of fluff* was British slang for *chick* in the sense of *gal.* It might have referred to the relative youth of the female companion of an older man, but no real harm was meant by it. See **fleck; bit of.**

fluff, *v.t., v.i.*   **1.** *Slang.* **juggle**
                                                             2. lie; bluff
1. *Slang.* As in *fluff the books* (accounts).
2. *Slang.* As in *Don't take him seriously; he's fluffing.*

fluffy, *adj.*   *Inf.* **unserious**
A pejorative term, often just a sign of unthinking snobbery.

flutter, *n., v.i.*   **gamble**
Slang. A *flutter* is a small *bet.* The usual expression is *Have a flutter.*

fly, *adj.*   **wide awake**
Slang. Ingenious, crafty, clever. The current American term *street-wise* is a close equivalent.

fly a kite, *Inf.*   *Inf.* **send up a trial balloon**

fly on the wall   **invisible onlooker**
Inf. Someone who would give anything to be a *fly on the wall* means he would love to witness a meeting, confrontation, etc. unobserved.

fly-over, *n.*   **overpass**
A bridge or viaduct for carrying one road over another.

fly-post, *v.i.*   SEE COMMENT
To put up notices or advertising rapidly and surreptitiously on unauthorized walls.

fly-tip, *v.i.*   SEE COMMENT
To dump garbage illegally, especially for profit as a service to other businesses or as way of cutting costs within a legitimate business. Businesses in the UK are usually charged by the local council for the disposal of large quantities of waste, and fly-tipping lets them avoid that charge.

fobbed off (with)   *Slang.* **stuck (with)**
Slang. Both countries use *fob off* in the sense of palming off inferior merchandise, but only the British use the past passive participle this way to indicate the resulting situation of the victim.

fob pocket   **watch pocket**
Tailor's term.

fogged, *adj., Slang.*   **befuddled**

foggiest, *adj.*   *Inf.* **faintest**
Inf. Usually met with in the negative expression *I haven't the foggiest,* meaning 'I haven't the slightest (idea)'. In this expression, *foggiest* is used as a substantive, like *slightest* or *faintest* when the modified noun (*idea* or *notion*) is omitted.

folding, *n.*   *Inf.* **paper money**
Also called **notes** in Britain, and referring particularly to the higher-denomination notes (£20 and £50).

Follow?, *v.i.*   **See?**
Often heard in Britain and America in the question *Do you follow?* meaning 'Do you see?' or 'Are you with me?'

folly, *n.*   **whimsical structure**
A peculiar, nonfunctional structure built for no apparent reason other than the whim of an estate owner with too much leisure and money and lots of whimsy; usually found on 18th-century English estates.

fool, *n.*   SEE COMMENT
A dessert of stewed fruit, crushed and mixed with custard or cream and served cold.

football, *n.*   **soccer**
As the name of a game, *football,* in Britain, is short for *Association football,* the game that Americans call *soccer.* The nearest equivalent in Britain to American football is the game called *Rugby football,* or simply *Rugby,* but most commonly called *rugger.* This game is played in uniforms like the ones used in *soccer,* without helmets, padding, nose guards, etc.

footer, *n.*   **soccer**
Schoolboy slang. See **football.**

footpath, *n.*   SEE COMMENT
An ancient right of way for walkers only. Landowners are legally obliged to keep
footpaths clear and open to the public. See also **footway.**

footplate, *n.*   **engineer's and fireman's platform**
Railroading. The engineer (**engine driver,** in Britain) and fireman are known
collectively as *footplatemen.* Loosely used to designate the whole locomotive cab.

foot-slog, *v.i.*   **trudge**
Slang. A *foot-slogger* is a *hiker;* the word is sometimes taken to mean 'infantryman.'
See also **flog it.**

footway, *n.*   **sidewalk**
An old-fashioned term, still seen on street signs threatening pedestrians with
fines if they permit their dogs to "foul the *footway.*" Also *footpath.* In the countryside, where there aren't any sidewalks, both words refer to any path for walkers.
Pavement is the common British term.

footy, *n.*   *Inf.* **football**
The game, that is; not the ball itself. Sometimes spelled *footie.*

(the) forces, *n. pl.*   **(the) service**
In the sense of the *armed forces.* A Briton would speak of 'leaving the forces.' An
American would most likely say something like 'When I get out of the army.'

forecourt, *n.*   **front yard**
Applied in Britain to a service station, *forecourt* means the 'area where gas (**petrol**) is pumped.' Thus one sees help-wanted ads for a *forecourt attendant,* i.e.,
somebody to man the gas pumps. Also, in Britain and America, a tennis term
meaning the area near the net.

Foreign Office   *approx.* **State Department**
Now called the Foreign and Commonwealth Office (FCO).

Foreign Secretary   SEE COMMENT
Cabinet Minister in charge of the **Foreign Office.**

forerib, *n.*   SEE COMMENT
What Americans call the *rib*—the four to six ribs from which rib-eye steak and rib
roast are obtained—Britons almost always call *forerib.*

forged, *adj.*   **counterfeit**
The British speak of a forged **note,** the Americans of a *counterfeit* bill.

for it   *Inf.* **in for it**
Inf. In deep trouble. *Oh, he's for it now!* See also **for the high jump.**

fork supper   **buffet**
Inf. This term is applied to a meal that can be eaten without a knife. *Fork lunch*
is also used. Roughly speaking, the American equivalent of *fork* in this context
might be thought to be *buffet,* as in a well-planned *buffet lunch* or *buffet dinner,*

at which a knife is not needed. A *fork meal* in Britain is definitely one in which a knife is superfluous. For the converse of this situation, see **knife-and-fork tea.**

form, *n.*   **1. grade**
                                                                   2. class
1. A school usage. Used in America, but rarely.
2. As in, He *was punished for sleeping in form.*

for the high jump   *Slang.* **in for it**
Slang. A grim echo of a hanging (the *high jump*). The phrase is now used to refer to any threatened or imminent punishment; especially drastic punishment.

for the matter of that   **for that matter**
The American form is used in Britain as well.

fortnight, *n.*   **two weeks**
This is a common word in Britain, somewhat archaic or formal in America. *Today fortnight, Monday fortnight,* etc., mean 'two weeks from today, two weeks from Monday,' etc. *Week* is used in the same way in Britain: *today week, Friday week,* etc. *This day fortnight* (or *week*) is still heard, too. *I'd rather keep him a week than a fortnight* is a quaint, if mildly callous, way of saying, *He's a big eater.* See also **Appendix I.D.5.**

for toffee. See **toffee.**

forward, *v.t.*   **ship**
By land, sea, or air.

fossick, *v.i.*   *Slang.* **mess around**
Slang. With no clear purpose. To *fossick after* something is to *rummage about* for it. The word derives from an Australian term for those who picked over abandoned gold workings. In some British dialects *fussock* means 'bustle about,' and that may be reflected here as well. See also **frig about.**

found, all (*or* **fully.**) See **fully found.**

foundation member   **charter member**

foundation-stone, *n.*   **cornerstone**

fourball, *n.*   **foursome**
Golf term. When the British say *foursome,* they mean a 'Scotch foursome,' a two ball match, in which the partners on each side stroke alternately at one ball. An American foursome has two players on each of two teams, all playing their own balls.

four honours   **100 honors**
A term used in bridge, meaning any four of the top five cards in the trump suit. *Five honours,* as you might expect, means 150 honors.

fourpenny one, *Inf.*   *Slang.* **sock on the jaw**

four-star   **premium**
Designation of gasoline (**petrol**) high-octane rating. *Two-star* is *regular.* In America
four stars are the domain of generals and admirals.

four up. See **make a four up.**

Four Wents   **Four Corners**
This is not only a general term meaning 'intersection' but a very common place
name in the British countryside. The *Four Wents,* or the *Four Went Ways,* is always
a place name designating a specific intersection. The *Four Corners* is a classic
bucolic general term rather than a specific place name in the American countryside. The *Went* in the British expression is derived from the word *wend,* in the
sense of 'turn' or 'direct.'

fowl, *n.* See under **chicken.**

fowl-run, *n.* See under **chicken.**

foyer, *n.*   **lobby**

fraternity *n.*   **religious organization**
Never has the sense of 'male college society' (*frat*), an institution unknown in
Britain.

frazzled, *adj.*   *Inf.* **worn out**
Slang. Applied to a person who has looked after obstreperous children for far too
long, put in too much overtime, etc.

Fred Karno's army   *approx. Inf.* **Coxey's army**
Inf. Fred Karno was a **music-hall** (*vaudeville*) comedian during World War I
and did an act involving a joke army. Jacob Sechler Coxey was a U.S. political
reformer who led a civilian march on Washington in 1894 to petition Congress
for unemployment relief. (He died in 1951 at the age of 97.) Old-fashioned
Americans use the phrase *Coxey's army* to describe any motley throng. Among
old-fashioned Britons, *Fred Karno's army* is a term usually applied to any sort of
chaotic organization.

Free Church. See **chapel.**

freefone, *n.*   **toll-free number**
Also given as freephone.

freehold, *n.*   *approx.* **title**
This term, as opposed to *leasehold,* means 'title to real estate,' whether outright or
for life. It implies *ownership* as opposed to *tenancy.* A person enjoying such ownership is a *freeholder.* In 1430, Parliament limited the right to vote in the election of
Members of Parliament to *forty-shilling freedholders,* i.e., those owning real property whose rental value was at least forty shillings per annum, a respectable sum
in those days. Today, nearly all British subjects have the vote.

free house   SEE COMMENT
Most pubs are tied in with a particular brewery, at least in the beer and ale
department, serving only that brewery's brand. The brewery owns the premises

and leases the pub to the operator, who is known as the **landlord** (though he is, legally speaking, the tenant), or **publican.** The pub has its own historic name and a standing or hanging decorative pub sign, sometimes beautifully painted and occasionally ancient, but the effect is somehow a little marred by the appearance of another sign, the name of the brewery, which has the effect of depersonalizing the management. A *free house* is a pub not affiliated with a brewery. It serves whatever brands of ale and beer it chooses. See **tied; pub.**

free issue of new shares   **stock dividend**

free line   **line**
When most calls were connected by a switchboard operator (**telephonist**), you would ask for a *free line* when you wanted to dial the number yourself. In Britain and America, you may request a *line.*

free of   **entitled to the use of**
To make someone *free of* something is to give him the right to use it. A person *free of* a company or a city is one entitled to share in the privileges of membership in the company or citizenship in the community. To make someone *free* of your house, car, library, etc. is to allow him the free use of it, to make free of it.

free-range eggs   **eggs from uncooped hens**
As opposed to *battery* eggs. This usage is increasingly common in the U.S.

freight, *n.*   **cargo**
In Britain, *freight,* by itself, is applied to transportation by water or air, though railroads use the terms *freight rates, freight sheds,* etc. In America the term is applied to transportation by land or by air, and *cargo* is the marine term. See also **forward; goods.**

French beans   **string beans**

French toast   SEE COMMENT
A delicious morsel of bread buttered on one side and toasted on the other. Simple enough to concoct, but never met with in America, where *French toast* is bread soaked in a mixture of eggs and milk, fried, and eaten with syrup or molasses or sprinkled with cinnamon and sugar.

fresh butter   **sweet butter**
Unaugmented by salt, that is. And more often called *unsalted butter.*

fresher, *n.*   *approx.* **freshman**
Slang. A British university term and a little more restricted than *freshman. Freshman* applies to the entire first year; *fresher* normally covers only the first term. *Freshman* (despite its second syllable) and *fresher* apply to both sexes.

fret, *n.*   *Slang.* **tizzy**
Inf. People, when agitated, *fret* in both countries. The word is used as a noun in Britain in the expression *in a fret* in situations where Americans would be apt to say *in a tizzy.*

fridge, *n.*   **refrigerator**
Inf. Also occasionally spelled *frig,* but always pronounced *fridge,* the universal term in Britain for *refrigerator* or *icebox.*

fried bread   SEE COMMENT
A uniquely British preparation: a slice of white bread fried in (usually) vegetable oil or (occasionally) butter. Served as part of a **fry-up,** more often than not in a **café.** Very bad for you, and very tasty.

friendly, *n.*   *approx. Inf.* **exhibition game**
Inf. Adjective used as a substantive with *match* understood. It means a game the result of which is not reflected in any official record and has no effect on championships.

friendly action   **action for a declaratory judgment**
A legal term, meaning a lawsuit brought to get a point decided, rather than for money damages or other relief.

friendly society   **mutual insurance group**
A common and extremely useful type of organization, even in an advanced welfare society. Its members are pledged to provide assistance to one another in old age, in illness, and in similar situations.

Friendship Town. See twin with . . .

frig about   *Slang.* **mess around**
Slang. The British use *frig* also in the sense *waste time* common in America. See also **fossick.**

frightfully, *adv.*   *Inf.* **awfully; very**
Inf. A word of the privileged but it hangs on tenaciously, and not only among the genteel.

frillies, *n. pl.*   *Inf.* **undies**
Inf. Out of fashion—the word, that is.

fringe, *n.*   **bangs**
Coiffure term.

Fringe Theatre. See under West End.

frock, *n.*   **dress**
Among some people in Britain the everyday word for a *woman's dress.* Common among people of all ages for little girls' dresses. Note that misbehaving clergymen may be *unfrocked*, while misbehaving ladies get themselves *undressed.*

frock-coat, *n.*   **Prince Albert**
A long, double-breasted frock coat.

from the off   **from the word go**
Somewhat old-fashioned, but still used jocularly.

front, *n.*   **seaside promenade**
Referring to seaside places, and also called *sea front.* A *front* or *sea front* is like an American *boardwalk*, except that the walking surface is not made of wood. People in Britain do not talk about going to the *beach* or *shore;* they go to the *sea-side.*

front bench   SEE COMMENT
Describes the benches in the House of Commons and the House of Lords occupied by **ministers** (*cabinet members*) and other members of the government and
members of the opposition **shadow** cabinet. Those who occupy them are *front-
benchers*. See also **back bench.**

frontier, *n.*   **border**
The word means *border between nations* in both countries, but in Britain it does
not have the special meaning of the part of the country that forms the outer limit
of its populated area. In view of Britain's history, it is understandable that the
connotation, having had no application for so long a period, would now be lost.

frost, *n.*   *Slang.* **bust**
Slang. If an American went to a party that he would later describe as a *bust* (or
a *dud*), his English counterpart would have characterized it as a *frost.* Now rare.

frosted food   **frozen food**
Sign in Harrods, the great store in London: FROSTED FOODS. A refrigerator salesman (**shop assistant** in a **fridge shop**) would point with pride to a large *frosted
foods compartment,* which Americans would call a *freezer.* And so, nowadays,
would most Britons.

frowsty, *adj.*   **stuffy**
Inf. Frowst is a British colloquialism meaning the 'fusty stale heat in a room.'
From this colloquial word we get *frowsty,* which describes the way the unfortunate room smells. *Frowsty* is related to the adjective *frowzy,* also spelled *frouzy* in
America, which means 'close,' in the sense of 'musty,' 'fusty,' and 'smelly,' and by
association 'dingy.' But nowadays in either country it is also commonly used in
the sense of 'unkempt.'

frowzy. See **frowsty.**

fruiterer, *n.*   **fruit-seller**
Either wholesale or retail, and often selling vegetables as well. See also **costermonger; greengrocer.**

fruit machine   *Slang.* **slot machine**
Slang. A one-armed bandit, typically paying out small sums even when you hit
the jackpot. What you get out of a fruit machine in Britain is either exhilaration or
despair. *Slot machine* is a British term for what Americans call a *vending machine.*

fruity, *adj. Inf.*   *Inf.* **spicy; sexy**

fry-up, *n.*   *approx.* **fry**
A *fry* in America is any fried dish, or more generally a social function involving
the eating of a fried dish (e.g., *fish-fry;* cf. *clambake*). In Britain it is a concoction
of eggs, bacon or sausage, black pudding, mushrooms, tomatoes, **fried bread,** or
any selection of these items.

fubsy, *adj.*   **fat and squat**

fug, *n.*   **stuffiness (room)**
Inf. In addition to this noun meaning, *fug* sometimes appears as a verb. To *fug* is to like to have it stuffy, in a room, a car, or any other enclosure.

(in) full fig   *Slang.* **all decked out**
In full dress.

full marks   **full approval**
Inf. I give him full marks for that! or *Full marks to him!* expresses the appreciation of a performance beyond criticism.

full-on, *adj.*   *Inf.,* SEE COMMENT
Total, direct, no-holds-barred. *It was a full-on attack.* The term can also be used adverbially, e.g. *We partied full-on.*

full out   **complete**
In both countries *full out* can also indicate *at full power* and maximum speed, *full throttle.*

(a) full plate. See **have enough on one's plate.**

full stop   **period**
The British never use *period* for the dot at the end of a sentence, though they generally understand this American usage. Americans avoid *stop* except in dictating telegram and cable messages. *Full stop* is peculiarly British except that Americans do sometimes use it when reading printed proof aloud.

full to bursting   *Inf.,* **sated, stuffed**
I couldn't eat another bite. I'm full to bursting.

fully booked. See **book.**

fully found   **all expenses paid**
Salary £15, fully found means that you get £15 per week, and all expenses, like transportation, board and lodging, and so on. *All found* is also used. Both terms are now rare.

funeral furnisher   **undertaker**
Americans have their euphemisms too. Consider *mortician.*

funfair, *n.*   **amusement park, fairground**

funky, *adj.*   *Slang.* **chicken**
Slang. This word is used much more commonly in Britain than in America. The noun *funk* has one meaning in Britain which it does not have in America: 'coward.' *You're a funk* would be *you're chicken* in America. The adjective *funky* is not commonly used in America in this sense. It is also now rare in Britain.

funniosity, *n.*   **a gag**
In Britain a jocular term for anything that makes one laugh.

funny bone   **crazy bone**

fun of the fair. See **all the fun of the fair.**

furnishings, soft. See **soft furnishings.**

Furry Dance   SEE COMMENT
An ancient ritualistic folk dance, seen these days only at Helston in Cornwall on certain days of the year; also called the **Floral Dance,** and pronounced as though it rhymed with HURRY (U as in BUT).

fuss, *v.t., Inf.*   agitate

fuzz. See **in a fuzz.**

gadzookery. See **Wardour Street.**

gaff, *n.* *Slang,* **honky-tonk**

Slang. Sometimes *penny gaff.* An entirely different British use is seen in the slang expression *blow the gaff,* which means 'spill the beans.' An American slang use is found in *stand the gaff,* where *gaff* means 'strain' or 'rough treatment.' None of these *gaffs* has anything to do with *gaffe,* from the French, meaning *faux pas.* The term is also used jocularly to refer to one's home.

gaffer, *n.* **1. old duffer**
2. boss

1. With the implication of the countryside, and humorously affectionate rather than in any sense pejorative.
2. When used by a gang of unskilled laborers, *the gaffer* means the 'man in charge,' the 'boss' of the gang, the 'foreman,' and, if anything, is mildly pejorative, without the slightest trace of humor or affection. But the expression *good gaffer* has been used to describe a *good boss.* And *gaffer* is sometimes used as schoolboy slang for 'headmaster,' a special kind of boss. In the U.S., the gaffer is the senior electrician on a film unit.

gagging for it *Inf.* **desperate for sex**

gain on swings, lose on roundabouts *Inf.* **you win some, you lose some**

Inf. Or, *gain on roundabouts, lose on swings.* The *roundabouts* in question are *merry-go-rounds* (see **roundabout, 2.**) and the expression is taken from the playground scene. It expresses resignation to the approximate effect that *you can't win 'em all;* there are pros and cons to most of life's decisions. Perhaps *six of one and a half a dozen of the other.*

gall, *n.* **rancor**

In Britain *gall* (apart from its medical implications) is also slang for *impudence* or *effrontery,* as it is in America.

gallon, *n.* See **Appendix II.C.2.a.**

gallop, *n.* **bridle trail**

gallows, *n. pl.* **gallows tree**

galoshes, *n. pl.* **rubbers**

In America *galoshes* are *overshoes,* waterproof boots that are worn over shoes and reach to about the ankle. They would be called *snowboots* in Britain, though *galoshes* is sometimes used by Britons in the American sense. See also **Wellingtons; boot; gumboots; snowboots.**

game, *n.*   **kind of thing**
Inf. Game is much used in Britain in a variety of phrases and a variety of ways.
A man says to his much-divorced friend who is contemplating another plunge,
I should think you'd have enough of that game! A mug's game (see **mug**) is *something
for the birds*, an activity that only a fool would engage in. *I wonder what her game is*
means *I wonder what she's up to* i.e., *what's her angle? Play the game* means 'do the
right thing.' *On the game* means 'living as a prostitute.' *She's on the game* means
'She's a whore.' See also **Stuff that for a game of soldiers!**

game, *v.i.*   **gamble**
Americans speak jocularly of the *gaming table*, but rarely if ever use the verb *game*.
The verb is still heard in Britain, where *gaming* is the preferred euphemism for
gambling, as in America.

gammon, *n.*   **ham**

gammon, *n., v.t., v.i.*   **humbug**
Inf. Nonsense intended to deceive. The verb, used intransitively, means to 'engage
in talking humbug'; transitively, to *gammon* someone is to *pull his leg, put him on*.
Slang of a bygone day. But see **humbug**, which has nothing to do with any of this.

gammy, *adj.*   **lame; game**
Slang. Usually in the expression *gammy leg*, meaning 'game leg.' An arm may be
gammy as well.

gamp, *n.*   **umbrella**
Inf. A big one, named after Sarah Gamp, in *Martin Chuzzlewit*, a bibulous lady
who carried a large cotton umbrella. The common slang term in Britain is **brolly**.

G&T, *n.*   *abbrev.* **gin and tonic**

gang. See **breakdown gang; navvy.**

ganger, *n.*   **gang foreman**
In charge of a gang of workers. Often applies to a foreman in charge of men
working on the railroad.

gangmaster, *n.*   SEE COMMENT
Someone who provides workers (often migrants, and sometimes illegally) to do
work for another person, particularly for seasonal agricultural work and the like.

gangway, *n.*   **aisle**
In theaters, ships, stores and in the **House of Commons.** Americans, of course,
have gangways here and there, but have aisles everywhere you look. See also
aisle for an especially British sense of the word.

garden *n.*   *approx.* **yard**
Garden is used, in its literal sense, the same way in both countries. But the British
use *garden* to refer to one's property outside his house, the way Americans use
yard. Also, the British often use *garden* as a synonym for *lawn; How nice your garden looks!* may be said of your *lawn* even when there isn't a single flower showing.

garibaldi, *n.*   **currant cookie**
Inf. The popular name of this hard rectangular cookie (**biscuit**) is *squashed fly* (jocular, if just the least bit unappetizing). The old **public school** name for them was *fly cemeteries.* Garibaldi was a 19th century Italian patriot. The *garibaldi,* otherwise, used to be the name for a sort of loose blouse worn in the mid 1800s by women and children in imitation of the garb worn by Garibaldi's soldiers.

gash, *n., adj.*   **1.** *n.* **waste; garbage**
                                                              2. *adj.* **superfluous; extra**
                                                                      3. *adj.* **free**

gasper, *n.*   **cheap cigarette**
Slang. The preferred slang term is **fag.**

gastropub, *n.*   SEE COMMENT
A pub that specializes in providing high-quality meals.

gate, *v.t.*   **confine to quarters**
Inf. That is, to punish by confinement. To be *gated* is to be *confined to college* (see **college**) during certain hours, or in some cases entirely, for a certain period, varying with the severity of the offense committed. The principal aspect of the punishment is the interruption of one's evening social life.

gaudy, *n.*   SEE COMMENT
Oxford college alumni dinner and celebration. From *gaudium,* Latin for 'joy' and *gaudeo,* 'rejoice,' whence *Gaudeamus igitur, juvenes dum sumus* "Let us therefore rejoice while we are young." Literally, *gaudy* means any feast, but it is usually understood in the narrower sense.

Gawdelpus, *n.*   *Slang.* **pain in the ass**
Slang. An exasperating person; intentional mispronunciation of *God-help-us.* Synonymous with **Gawdf'bid,** which was originally cockney rhyming slang (see **Appendix III.G.3**) for *kid,* i.e., *child,* the kind known as a *little terror.*

Gawdf'bid. See **Gawdelpus.**

gazette, *v.t.*   SEE COMMENT
There are three official journals for the publication of official notices in the United Kingdom: the *Belfast Gazette, Edinburgh Gazette,* and *London Gazette.* They come out twice a week with official public notices of such things as government appointments, bankruptcies, etc. To *gazette* something is to have it published in one of these publications.

gazump, *v.t.*   *Inf.* **jack up**
Slang. The accent is on the second syllable. To *jack up* the price of a piece of real estate after the asking price has actually been met, just before the contract is signed. This current usage to describe such unworthy methods appeared first in the spelling *gazoomph,* and was derived from the more general meaning of the term *gazumph* (*gezumph*) which covers the various kinds of swindling that go on at dishonest auctions.

GBH, *n.*   *acronym,* **Grievous Bodily Harm**

GCHQ, *n.*   SEE COMMENT
Acronym. Government Communications Headquarters. The "centre for Her Majesty's Government's Signal Intelligence (SIGINT) activities," i.e. electronic intelligence-gathering, located in Cheltenham, Gloucestershire. Do not drop in for a visit without making an appointment.

GCSE, *n.*   SEE COMMENT
Stands for *General Certificate of Secondary Education.* Subject-based standardized tests taken by students 14 to 16 years of age.

gear, *n.*   *Slang.* **cool**
Slang. A teenage term.

gearbox, *n.*   **transmission**
Automotive term. See also **Appendix II.E.**

gearing, *n.*   **leverage**

gear-lever, *n.*   **gearshift**
See also **Appendix II.E.**

gee, *interj.*   *Inf.* **horsie**
Inf. Gee! and *gee-up!* are used in both countries to urge a horse on. In Britain *gee-ho!,* and *gee-wo!* are heard, too, and *gee-gee* was originated by children as a juvenile colloquialism equivalent to *horsie. The gee-gees* is used jocularly in the way the Americans say *the ponies,* i.e., *the horses,* as in the expression *play the ponies.*

gefuffle. See **kerfuffle.**

gen, *n.*   *Slang.* **inside dope**
Slang. (Pronounced JEN.) *Gen* is short for *general information,* and like so many slang expressions, started in the armed forces. *Duff gen* means 'bum dope,' 'misleading information.' See **gen up; griff.**

general election, *n.*   SEE COMMENT
A British Parliament serves a maximum of five years. At any point within that period, the government can dissolve Parliament and set the date for another general election, when all members of Parliament have to **stand** for re-election. In normal circumstances, the date of the general election will be close to the five-year deadline. If there is a crisis of some kind, however, the date can come well before it.

general meeting. See **Annual General Meeting.**

general post   *approx.* **circulation**
A mass changing of places, as at a party where the guests are just sitting around. The hostess suggests a *General Post!* meaning that the guests should start moving around, circulating. Appears to be derived from the children's game of Post

Office, which involved complex rules determining who kissed whom. The expectation is that under *general post* everybody kisses everybody else.

General Post Office. See **G. P. O.**

general servant   **maid of all work**
Inf. Sometimes informally shortened to *general.*

gentle, *n.*   **maggot**
As used for fishing bait.

gentry, *n. pl.*   SEE COMMENT
In position and birth, the class just below the nobility. See **landed,** 3.

gen up   **1.** *Inf.* **fill in**
                                                                   2. *Slang.* **bone up**
1. *Slang.* To *fill (someone) in,* in the sense of 'putting (him) in the know.'
2. *Slang.* To *acquire the necessary information* about someone or something before taking a step. See also **gen.**

geography of the house   **location of the john**
Inf. A considerate host in an expansive mood may ask a guest, under appropriate circumstances, *"Do you know the geography of the house?"* A guest unfamiliar with the layout might elicit the same information through the use of the same euphemism. See also *have a wash,* under **wash,** and **wash up.** Said to be **non-U.** For a discussion of *non-U* see **Appendix I.C.6.**

Geordie, *n., adj.*   SEE COMMENT
Native of Tyneside. Also the dialect they speak in that part of northeastern England. In Scotland especially, the term can be applied to any coal miner.

George, *n.*   **automatic airplane pilot**
Slang. Believed by some to have been derived from the old saying *Let George do it.*

get. See **git.**

get across (someone)   *Inf.* **get (someone) riled up**
Inf. The British as well as the Americans also speak of *getting a person's goat.*

get a duck. See **duck, 1.**

get a rocket. See **rocket.**

get knotted!, *Slang.*   *Slang.* **stop bugging me!**

get much change out of   *Inf.* **get anywhere with**
Inf. These expressions (in their respective countries) are almost always in the negative. When a Briton says, "He didn't get much change out of me," he is saying, in the American idiom. "He didn't get anywhere (or very far) with me." Like **wash** in *That won't wash* or **wear** in *The boss won't wear that for a minute, get much change out of* is rarely encountered in the affirmative.

get off with   SEE COMMENT
Slang. To make progress with a member of the opposite sex, stopping short, however, of what grandmother used to call 'going the limit.' Cf. **have it off, 4,** which includes the attainment of the limit.

get one's bowler. See **bowler-hatted.**

get one's cards. See **give (someone) his cards.**

get one's colours   SEE COMMENT
Be made a member of a team, in sports. More specifically, establish one's competence in a sport and earn the right to wear the team colors. To *give (someone) his colours* is to include him or her in a team, usually as a permanent or regular member rather than as a temporary substitute. The Oxford color is dark blue, Cambridge light blue.

get one's eye in   SEE COMMENT
Inf. The **batsman** in **cricket** must initially 'feel out' his adversary, the **bowler,** before changing his stance from defensive to aggressive and beginning to make runs. This initial period is known as *getting his eye in* and is more fully explained under **play oneself in.**

get one's feet under the table   SEE COMMENT
To get settled in, especially in a relationship.

get one's head down. See **put one's head down.**

get one's head in one's hand   *Slang.* **catch hell**
Slang. In other words, get your head chopped off and handed to you.

get one's kit off   **to undress**
Kit means clothing, and to take it off is to disrobe. But this phrase has specific connotations: (a) undressing as a spectacle (*The leering men shouted, 'Get your kit off!'*) and (b) undressing in preparation for sex.

get one's own back on   *Inf.* **get back on**
Inf. That is, *get even with, avenge oneself.* Also, *get something back on.*

get one's skates on   *Inf.* **get going**
Slang. Start moving, hurry. In the armed forces, it means 'desert.'

get on (someone's) wick   *Inf.* **bug (someone)**
Slang. Or, *get on someone's nerves.*

get on with   **get along with**
A different sense from that in which one *gets on with* one's work. It applies to human relations. Also not to be confused with **get on with it!**

get on with it! *Inf.*   *Inf.* **get going!**

get-out, *n.*   *Inf.* **out**
Inf. In the sense of evasion, an *avenue of escape,* one's *way out* of a jam.

get out of it!   *Slang.* **come on!**
Slang. Meaning 'quit your kidding!' Synonymous with **give over!**

get stuck in   *Inf.* **get going**
Slang. To *get stuck in again* means to 'resume an interrupted task.' Thus, plotting
our next year's vacation together, a friend writes: *I can get stuck in again when the
new year's schedules are to hand. Get stuck in!* or *get stuck into it!* means 'get going!'
or 'quit stalling!' when spectators are exhorting their team, which appears to
have slowed up. In a more general sense, *getting stuck in* simply means engaging
seriously with the task at hand.

get stuffed. See **stuff.**

get the better of   **get the best of**
You *get the better of (triumph over)* somebody in Britain but the Americans use the
superlative. Lest you think Americans always resort to superlatives, the reverse
is true in the following sense: an American says, *I'd better leave now,* while his
British friend will sometimes say, *I'd best leave now.*

get the bird. See **give (someone) his cards.**

get the chop, *Slang.*   **1.** *Slang.* **be bumped off (get killed)**
                                      2. *Slang.* **get the gate (be fired)**

get the push. See **push.**

get the stick   *Slang.* **catch hell**
Slang. When a person has been severely criticized, the British might say he *got the
stick, got a lot of stick* or *got a bit of stick.* Derived, presumably, from the vanishing
custom of caning schoolchildren for misbehavior. One hears *take the stick* as well.

get the wind up   *Inf.* **be jumpy**
Inf. In a situation where an American is nervous about something, the Briton *gets
the wind up* about it. To *have the wind up* is to be 'scared' rather than merely 'nervous.' To *put the wind up* somebody is to 'scare him.' Strangely enough, to *raise the
wind* is to *raise the money. Windy,* by itself, means 'nervous' or 'jumpy.'

getting on for   **well nigh**
Inf. Thus: *Getting on for thirty years before, Elsie had married happily.* Or, *It's getting
on for one o'clock.*

get up (someone's) nose, *Slang.*   *Slang.* **get in (someone's) hair**

get upsides with   *Inf.* **get even with**
Inf. To *turn the tables* on someone, or to *avenge oneself.*

get weaving, *Inf.*   *Inf.* **get going**

get your knickers in a twist. See **knickers.**

geyser, *n.*   **water heater**
Geyser is a geological term in both countries denoting a hot spring which shoots
up a column of steaming water at fixed intervals. The most famous of these is

Old Faithful in Yellowstone National Park. But to a Briton the primary meaning of *geyser* is 'water heater,' and the word evokes the image of a smallish white cylindrical tank with a swiveling faucet underneath, located on the wall next to the kitchen sink or in the bathroom. In this specialized meaning, the word is pronounced as though spelled GEEZER. See also **immersion heater.**

ghastly show. See **bad show!**

giddy fit, *Inf.*   dizzy spell

giddy-go-round, *n.*   merry-go-round
More commonly **roundabout.** See also **carousel.**

giggle, *n.*   *Inf.*, SEE COMMENT
To have a giggle with someone is to have an enjoyable, lighthearted time with them. *We went to the pub for a drink and a giggle.*

gig-lamps, *n., pl.*   *Inf.* **specs**
Slang. Meaning 'eyeglasses.' *Pebble gig-lamps* are thick ones, *pebble* in this sense being old English for 'natural rock crystal.'

gill, *n.*   **1. ravine; torrent**
                                                2. See Appendix II.C.2.b.
1. The *g* is hard. Usually a *deep ravine* and wooded. When it means *torrent,* it refers to a *narrow mountain torrent.*

gilts   **government bonds**
Short for gilt-edged securities. See also **shares.**

gin and it   SEE COMMENT
A cocktail made from gin and Italian sweet vermouth. Distinguished from a martini by the choice of vermouth and the high proportion of vermouth to gin.

gin and Jaguar belt   **expensive suburb**
Inf. Of London, synonymous with **stockbroker belt.**

ginger-beer   **homosexual**
Slang. Rhyming slang for *queer.*

ginger biscuit, also ginger-nut, *n.*   **gingersnap**

ginger group   *Inf.* **young Turks**
Inf. Any activist group that thinks its own political party or organization is moving too slowly and wants to push it forward or to move ahead on its own.

ginger-up, *n., Inf.*   *Inf.* **pep talk**
Inf. Without the hyphen, to **ginger up** means 'give a pep talk to.'

gin-stop, *n., Inf.*   *Inf.* **gin mill**

gippo, *n., Slang.*   **army stew**
And a more tasteful dish is easy to find.

gippy tummy   **diarrhea**
Slang. Also spelled *gippie, gyppy, gyppie. Gippy* was common British slang for an Egyptian soldier or cigarette. *Gippy tummy* describes what happens to many travelers who visit tropical countries.

girdle, *n.*   **griddle**
Thus giving rise to *girdle-cakes,* with Vermont maple syrup.

Girl Guide   **Girl Scout**
Boy Scouts are Boy Scouts in both countries, but *Girl Scouts* become *Girl Guides* in Britain.

Giro, *n.*   SEE COMMENT
A system of credit transfer between banks, widely used by the **G.P.O.** (*Post Office*). From *giro,* Italian for *circulation* (of money).

git, *n.*   *Slang.* **jerk**
Slang. Very occasionally *get,* and often coupled with a deprecatory adjective, as in *you silly git . . . !* Synonyms: **poon; swab; twit; jobbernowl; juggins; muggins.** Of these, only *twit* is used commonly.

give (someone *or* **something) a miss**   *Inf.* **pass (something) up**
Inf. One *gives a miss* to a play that has had bad notices or a restaurant where one's friends have had a poor experience. One might do the same thing in the case of the fifth wedding of a dear pal: here Americans might say, *I'll sit this one out!* But to *give someone (or something) a miss* doesn't necessarily imply distaste. One can have seen the Tower of London once too often and decide this time to *give it a miss,* despite past happy experiences there. Or, if you've borrowed too often from your friend Tim and have lost again at poker, while you are wondering where to get it this time, you might reflect, *This time I'll give Tim a miss.*

give (someone) a shout   *Inf.* **call out**
Inf. A Briton will promise to *give you a shout* when he is ready, where an American would promise to *let you know.*

give (someone) best   *Inf.* **bow to (someone)**
Inf. To *give* somebody *best* is to *admit his superiority,* and in that sense to *bow to him.*

give (someone) fits, *Slang.*   *Slang.* **give (someone) hell**

give (someone) gyp *Inf.*   *Inf.* **beat**

give her one   *Slang.* SEE COMMENT
Exceedingly vulgar. When a man says he would like to do this to a woman, he is saying—in the crudest terms imaginable—that he would like to have sexual intercourse with her. There is no comparable phrase for women to express this particular form of sexual desire.

give (someone) his cards   *Slang.* **give (someone) his pink slip or**
                                                          his walking papers
Slang. To *fire (someone).* Synonyms: **give (someone) the bird;** *give (someone) the chop,* which can have the far more sinister meaning of 'bump off' (see **get the chop**). Conversely, to *get one's cards, the bird,* or *the chop* is to *be fired* (unless *chop* is

being used in the more drastic sense). One can also be said, somewhat wryly, to *collect one's cards*. To *ask for one's cards* is to *give up one's job,* to *resign.*

give (someone) his colours. See **get one's colours.**

give (someone) in   **turn (someone) in**
To *turn a person over to the police.*

give in part exchange   **trade in; turn in**
In Britain you *give* your old car *in part exchange* when you buy a new one, in the same way in which you *trade it in* in America.

give (someone) out   **call (someone) out**
A cricket term. The American term is not used. The *someone* in the cricket term is the player who is (in the American term) called out by the umpire after an appeal (see **How's that?**) by the other side. *Give* is thus used in cricket where *call* would be used in baseball.

give over!   **come on!**
Slang. Synonymous with **get out of it!** Can also mean 'stop it!'

give (someone) stick   *Slang.* **give (someone) hell**
Slang. A severe dressing-down. You may also hear *give (someone) some stick.*

give (someone) the bird   *Slang.* **give (someone) the hook**
Slang. See synonyms under **give someone his cards.**

Give Way   **Yield**
Road sign in Britain, meaning 'Yield right of way.' In many parts of America there are road signs to the same effect, reading YIELD.

glass, *n.*   **1. crystal, lens**
                                                                  2. SEE COMMENT
1. *n.* Referring to watches and clocks. The term *crystal* is used in Britain, too, but only in the trade.
2. *v.t. Slang.* To hit (someone) with a glass.

glass fibre   **fiberglass**

glasshouse, *n.*   **1. greenhouse**
                                                                  2. stockade
                                                                  3. lock-up
1. The standard meaning.
2. *Military slang. Army prison.* The naval equivalent in both countries is *brig.*
3. The term has been extended to mean any sort of detention center, such as those proposed for the confinement and treatment of young offenders.

glasspaper, *n.*   **sandpaper**

Glaswegian, *n., adj.*   SEE COMMENT
Of Glasgow. As noun, a native or inhabitant of Glasgow. As adjective, referring to the language, customs, etc. of that city.

G.M.T.   Greenwich mean time

go, *n.*   turn; try
If a child is demonstrating his new tricycle to his British friend, the friend will, after a certain interval, ask, *May I have a go?* In America, he would ask if he might *try* it or *take a turn. Go* is used in Britain also in the sense of 'taking a shot' at something, like a stuck window or something in your eye. When used in America, always accompanied by *at it: Have another go at it.*

go, *v.t.*   bid, declare
Inf. Bridge term. *We went two, partner* means 'we bid two.'

go a mucker. See mucker.

goat, *n.*   fool
Inf. To act the *goat* or to play the *goat,* or the *giddy goat,* is to play the *fool.*

gob, *n.*   *Slang.* **trap**
Slang. Mouth; thus; *Shut your gob!*

gob, *v.i.*   spit
Slang. Vulgar.

gobsmacked, *adj.*   *Inf.* **astonished**

gobstopper, *n.*   SEE COMMENT
A large, hard, long-lasting sucking candy, so big that it **stops** (*fills*) one's **gob.**

go down. See come down.

gods, *n.*   *Inf.* **(peanut) heaven; peanut gallery**
Inf. The *gallery* of a theater, the part nearest heaven. The gods are the cheapest seats in the theater, and to sit there is to evince deep enthusiasm combined with shallow pockets.

go for six   get smashed
Slang. Describes the accidental destruction of breakable ornaments around the house, like porcelain objets d'art, as the result of careless dusting and the like.

goggle-box, *n.*   *Slang.* **boob tube; idiot box**
Slang. In both countries affectionately pejorative terms have been invented for the television set.

going spare   *Slang.* **on the loose**
Slang. Referring to girls who are available, easy to get. But see **go spare.**

golden duck. See duck, 1.

golden handshake   dismissal with bonus
Payment to executives who are let go with a generous severance allowance, often undeserved.

goloshes. See **galoshes.**

go missing, *Inf.*   disappear

go nap. See **nap.**

gone, *v.i.*   *approx.* **become; turned**
Used in expressions of time, like *It had gone four o'clock by the time Frank arrived.*
Americans would say *It was after four when Frank arrived.* More generally, in
expressions other than those of time, the American equivalent would be *turned,*
for example, in an expression of this sort: *The Dead Sea Scrolls had gone all black
(had all turned black).* See also **just going.**

gone for a burton   *Slang.* **kicked the bucket**
Slang. Originally Royal Air Force slang perhaps referring to Burton ale, describing the men who failed to return from the mission. Now applied to less serious
situations, like a broken glass. See **go for six.**

gong, *n.*   *Inf.,* SEE COMMENT
An award given in **Birthday Honours.** Use of the term would usually imply disapproval or at least scepticism about the recipient's worthiness: *Dr. Connell finally
got his gong after all those years of sitting on government committees.* More informally,
any award or honor.

gongs, *n. pl.*   *Slang.* **medals**
Slang. Humorous service terms for *medals;* jocular, affectionate military slang,
with the accent on understatement and self-depreciation.

good egg   a decent person

good innings   long run
Inf. One who has had a *good innings* (**innings** is treated as singular in Britain) has
had a *good long life,* or a *good spell* of something, like a term of office.

good in parts   good and bad
For origin see **curate's egg.**

good job   *Inf.* **good thing**
Inf. As in *Good job it didn't rain during the picnic.*

good party?   *Inf.* **how'd it go?**
Slang. Asked of someone returning from a mission.

goods, *n. pl.*   freight
A railroad term. A *goods-waggon* is a *freight car.* See also **freight; forward.**

good show! *Inf.*   *Inf.* **nice work!**

good value   *Inf.* **good stuff**
Inf. Thus: *That lad is very good value.* See also **value for money.**

go off, *v.t.*   SEE COMMENT
1. Of food, to become rotten. *This meat stinks. It's gone off.*

2. To cease to like someone or something. *I used to like Jenny but I've gone off her now.*

go off the boil   **quiet down**
Inf. Said, for instance, of an official inquiry that starts off like a house afire but turns out to be only a nine-day wonder.

goolies, *n. pl.*   *Slang.* **balls**
Slang. Also spelled *ghoulies.*

gooseberry, *n.*   *approx. Inf.* **fifth wheel**
Inf. The superfluous third party who sticks like glue to the (un)happy couple who are aching to be alone. To *play gooseberry* is to *act as chaperon.* All this has nothing to do with *gooseberry,* the fruit, or *gooseberry fool,* the dessert.

goosebumps, *n.*   **goose pimples**

goosegog, *n.*   **gooseberry**
Inf. A common jocular corruption of the fruit *gooseberry. Goosegog eyes* are watery eyes, reminding one of gooseberries.

go pear-shaped, *v.*   *Inf.* **go wrong**

go racing   **go to the races**

gormless, *adj. Inf.*   **lacking sense, stupid**

go spare, *Slang.*   **1.** *Slang.* **get sore (angry)**
                                                        2. be baffled
                                                    3. *Slang.* **go AWOL**
But see **going spare;** and see **send (someone) spare.**

Go to Bath! *Slang.*   *Slang.* **don't talk nonsense**
Insane people formerly were sent to Bath to be cured by its mineral waters.

go to bed   **have sexual intercourse**

go to ground   *Inf.* **lie low**
Inf. Hide out; from fox hunting, when the pursued beast takes to its lair.

go to the bad, *Inf.*   *Inf.* **go to the dogs**

go to the country   **have a general election**
General elections (for **Members** of Parliament) are held every five years. The Government, however, can resort to a general election short of that time in order to test public opinion, usually in case of a crisis, and must do so if it loses its majority in the **Commons.**

goulash, *n.*
Slang. Bridge term: dealing the next hand without shuffling, so as to produce extraordinary hands.

go up   *Inf.* **enter university**

government, *n.*   **administration**
The British talk about the *Blair government,* the Americans about the *Bush adminis-tration.* Each phrase refers to the people ruling the country at the moment.

Government Communications Headquarters. See GCHQ.

governor, *n.*   **1. warden**
                                                          2. *Slang.* **boss; mister; dad**
1. Head person at a prison.
2. *Slang.* A British worker might speak of his *boss* as his *governor* and would address the person that way. A cab driver in Britain might well address a passenger as *guv'nor,* equivalent to the American *doc* or *mister.* Old-fashioned Britons may still use *guv'nor* in the sense of *dad.*

gownsman. See town and gown.

G.P.O.   SEE COMMENT
Stands for *General Post Office,* the old name of the organization that handles the mail, telegrams, old age pension payments, as well as maintaining savings accounts and a credit transfer system known as **Giro.** The company is now known simply as the Post Office. Nothing to do with **general post.**

grace and favour   SEE COMMENT
Describing a residence occupied rent-free by permission of the royal family, like a cottage within the area of Kensington Palace grounds, or the residence of the person in charge of the **race-course** at Ascot, which was established by the sov-ereign in 1711.

gradient, *n.*   **grade (hill)**
Gradient can mean 'grade' or 'slope' in America, too, but it is not as commonly used. *Gradient* would be the more common term in Britain as, for instance, in an automobile instruction book advising which gear to use when starting up a hill.

graduate   **college graduate**
The British make a fuss about one's having graduated from college, or university as it is called. The British are notoriously prone to putting lots of initials after people's names, particularly on business letterheads. These initials may refer to **Birthday Honours,** membership in a trade or professional association, or just college degrees. On an ordinary business letterhead it would not be uncommon to see listed *John Jones, B.A. (Oxon.), George Smith, B.Sc. (Cantab.),* etc. (*Oxon. and Cantab.* are abbreviations reflecting the Latin spellings of Oxford and Cam-bridge.) A particularly old-fashioned male might use the term *university man* to mean *graduate.*

graft, *v.i. Slang.*   **knock oneself out**

grammar school, n.   SEE COMMENT
A state-maintained school that selects its students by an academic exam at the age of 11. See also **eleven plus.**

gramophone, *n.*   **phonograph**

granary bread   SEE COMMENT
A delicious dark bread. They remove most of the roughage, refine some of it, and
put the refined part and some of the unrefined part back into the dough.

Grand National, *n.*   SEE COMMENT
A famous annual steeplechase run at Aintree, Liverpool.

granny waggon, *Slang.*   *Slang.* **jalopy**

grasp the nettle, *Inf.*   *Inf.* **take the bull by the horns**
Grab a nettle sometime and see what courage is required to do so.

grass, *v., n.*   *Slang.* **squeal (inform)**
Slang. This word is derived from cockney rhyming slang (see **Appendix II.G.3**)
grasshopper, meaning 'copper,' i.e., *policeman. Grass* sometimes appears as a noun,
meaning both 'informer' or 'stool pigeon' and the 'act of informing' itself. It may
also appear as an intransitive verb (*The lousy so-and-so grassed*) or a transitive
verb, usually in a phrase including *up*: *He grassed me up.* See also **supergrass.**

gratuity, *n.*   **veteran's bonus**
Government bonus to war veterans; a special British usage, in addition to meanings shared with America.

Grauniad, *n.*   SEE COMMENT
An affectionate nickname, coined by Private Eye, for the *Guardian* newspaper,
renowned in the past for its typographical errors.

grease-proof paper   *approx.* **waxed paper**
Not quite the same but generally serving the same functions. The British variety
comes not in rolls but in sheets, is more nearly opaque, heavier, and stiffer.

greasy, *adj.*   **slippery**
Slippery generally, not only because of the presence of grease. A wet road or a
lawn tennis court after a sudden shower would be described as *greasy.* The same
distinction exists in the figurative sense; be just as careful of dealing with a *greasy*
Briton as with a *slippery* American. Americans also use *oily* in the same uncomplimentary sense.

Great Bear   **Big Dipper**
Other British names for the *Big Dipper: Charles's Wain,* the *Plough.*

Greats, *n. pl.*   SEE COMMENT
Inf. Oxford *classics finals. Greats* refer to the B.A. course of study as well as to the
exams, and the course includes philosophy in addition to classical literature and
history. See also **moderations; responsions; smalls.**

Great War   **World War I**
Not heard much any more because of World War II. Britons now often call it
'World War I.'

greedy, *adj.*   *Inf.* **gluttonous**
Possessing an unrestrained appetite, especially for rich (and usually unhealthy)
foods.

green belt   *approx.* **no-building zone**
The *green belt* is the area around a British municipality that is kept green, i.e.,
where building and development are not allowed, lest the overpopulated Britain
develop into one megalopolis.

green card   SEE COMMENT
Insurance card covering British motorists in foreign countries.

green fingers, *Inf.*   *Inf.* **green thumb**
Skill in raising plants.

greengage, *n.*   **an edible green plum like fruit**

greengrocer's, *n.*   **fruit and vegetable store**
See also **fruiterer; costermonger.**

Green Paper. See under **Paper.**

green pepper, *n.*   **bell pepper**

green pound   SEE COMMENT
A unit of value applicable to British transactions in connection with the Common
Agricultural Policy of the European Economic Community, commonly known as
the Common Market. The use of the *green pound* may make food imports from
Common Market countries cheaper for the British consumer, and conversely,
British food exports to those countries harder to sell.

greens, spring. See **spring greens.**

Gretna Green   SEE COMMENT
A small village in Dumfriesshire, Scotland, near the border with England, where
runaway young couples from England could be married according to Scottish
law by a simple declaration before witnesses, made to a **landlord,** toll-keeper,
blacksmith, etc. When the blacksmith officiated, the couple were said to be 'married over the anvil.' In 1856, a law was enacted that impeded impulsive couples
by requiring residence in Scotland of one of the parties for a minimum of 21 days
before the ceremony. In 1940, marriage by declaration was abolished by Scottish
law, but the place still attracts young couples because minors may marry there
without parental consent.

grid, *n.*   **map reference system**
The *National Grid,* a metric system of vertical and horizontal lines superimposed
on the map of Britain, divides it into lettered squares with numbered subdivi-
sions, providing a reference system for all regional maps. See also **National Grid.**

Grievous Bodily Harm   SEE COMMENT
A criminal charge arising from an assault resulting in serious injury to the victim.
The lesser offense is Actual Bodily Harm. See also **GBH.**

griff, *n.*   *Slang.* **inside dope; info**
Slang. Synonymous with **gen:** originally navy slang, and thought to be derived
from *griffin* (meaning 'tip on the horses,' or, more generally, 'hint'), which became
World War II slang for 'warning,' in the phrase *give the griffin.*

griffin. See **griff.**

grig, *n.*   **small eel**
The other meanings, 'grasshopper' or 'cricket,' and figuratively a 'lively person,'
are American as well as British. *Merry* (or *happy*) *as a grig* is a common phrase
equivalent to *gay and lively, bright and merry, happy as a lark.*

grill, *v.t.*   **1.** *v.t.* **broil**
                                                                                                 2. *n.* **broiler**
                                                                                          3. SEE COMMENT
3. A dish based on grilled (broiled) meat. "Grills" is a common British restaurant
sign and is the equivalent of *steaks and chops.* This usage is found in both countries in the term *mixed grill.*

grind, *n.*   **1.** *Slang.* **drag**
                                                                                                 2. *Slang.* **lay**
1. *Slang.* In the sense of a boring *task,* not *person;* usually in the expression *a bit of
a grind. Grind,* in America, implies *tough going*
2. *Slang.* A crude word usually used pejoratively in the British phrase *not much of
a grind,* i.e., an unsatisfactory sexual partner.

grinder, *n.*   **crammer**
To *grind,* in the sense of 'study hard,' is common to both countries; also to *cram,* in
the sense of 'preparing intensively for a particular examination.' But where Americans would describe as a *crammer* one who waits until the last moment to *bone up*
(**mug** or *mug up* in Britain), the British call him a *grinder.* See **crammer's** for British
use of the word.

grip, hair. See **hair grip.**

grip, kirby. See **kirby grip.**

griskin, *n.*   **lean bacon**
More particularly, the *lean part of the loin.*

grit, *n.*   **fine gravel**
A *gritting truck* or **lorry** is a *sanding truck.* GRIT FOR ICE, a roadside sign, offers
sand to motorists in need of traction. *Gritting truck* or *lorry* is sometimes shortened to *gritter.*

grizzle, *v.i., Slang.*   **whimper**
Or, more informally, express dissatisfaction. *The baby's grizzling; he may be hungry.*

grotty, *adj.*   *approx. Slang.* **cruddy**
Slang. A grotty little schoolboy pinched her **knickers.** *This is a grotty little restaurant—
look at the stains on the table-cloths.* From *grotesque.* See also **ropy; tatty; tinpot.**

ground, *n.*   **field**
A sports area: a cricket *ground,* a **football** *ground* (or **pitch**), etc.

ground, spare. See **spare ground.**

ground floor. See **first floor.**

ground-nut, *n.*   **peanut**
Synonymous with **monkey-nut.**

group of companies   **conglomerate**
The term *(So-and-So) Group of Companies* (seen on signs, letterheads, etc.) indicates a *conglomerate.*

Grub Street   SEE COMMENT
Grub Street is the former name of a London street, changed to *Milton Street* in 1830. Samuel Johnson described it as "Much inhabited by writers of small histories, dictionaries, and temporary poems; whence any mean production is called *grubstreet.*" The term is now used metaphorically for starving writers, literary hacks, and their output.

Grundyism. See under **wowser.**

guard, *n.*   **1. conductor; brakeman**
                                                                   2. stopper
1. A railroad term. *Conductor* is used in Britain to mean the official in charge of passengers on a bus.
2. Term used in contract bridge.

guard dog   **watchdog**

Guards, *n. pl.*   SEE COMMENT
Also known as *household troops* (comprising the regiments of Foot Guards, Horse Guards and Life Guards), part of whose duty is to attend the sovereign ceremonially. A member of any of these regiments is known as a *guardsman.* See **Life Guard.**

guardsman. See **Guards.**

guard's van   **caboose**
See under **brake-van.**

gubbins, *n. pl.*   **1. innards**
                                                    2. *Slang.* **thingamajigs**
1. *Slang.* The *insides* of something: the *gubbins* of a car—all the bits and pieces mechanics have to get at.
2. *Slang.* Also used as a vague reference to any old junk, equivalent to *thingamagigs* or *whatchamacallits.*

guffy. See **jolly.**

guggle, *v.i.*   **gurgle**
The British use *gurgle,* too. *Guggle* appears to be pejorative, as applied to a person in a state of impotent rage or hysterics.

guide dog   **Seeing Eye dog**

guildhall, *n.* **town hall; city hall**
The *Guildhall* in the **City** of London is what Americans would call the *City Hall* if London were an American city. In other municipalities, whether town or city, the British use the expression *town hall* rather than *city hall* to refer to the municipal office building.

guillotine, *n., v.t.* **1. cloture**
2. limit by cloture
1. *Inf.* Limitation of debate in Parliament by fixing the times at which specific parts of a bill must be voted on.
2. *Inf.* The act of thus limiting debate.

guinea, *n* SEE COMMENT
Formerly a coin worth one pound, one shilling. The *guinea* was originally a gold coin created for use in the African trade. It was theoretically pegged at twenty shillings (the same as the pound) but after a certain degree of fluctuation was fixed at twenty-one shillings. *The Guineas* is the familiar name of two of the five classic British horse races, all for three-year-olds, consisting of the *One Thousand Guineas* and the *Two Thousand Guineas,* both run at Newmarket in Suffolk each April. The other three are the Derby (pronounced DARBY), run at Epsom Downs in Surrey on the first Wednesday of June, the Oaks, also at Epsom the following Friday, and the St. Leger at Doncaster in Yorkshire each September.

(a) guinea to a gooseberry *Inf.* **ten to one**
Inf. Long odds.

gum, *n.* **mucilage**
A stickum. If you want something to chew, ask for *chewing gum.*

gumboots, *n. pl.* **rubber boots**
See also **snowboots; Wellingtons; boot; galoshes.**

gump, *n.* *Slang.* **horse sense**
Inf. Short for *gumption,* common sense.

gum tree. See up a gum tree.

gun, *n.* **hunter**
A *member of a shooting party* in Britain where they **shoot,** rather than *hunt,* game birds. See **shoot.**

Gunpowder Plot SEE COMMENT
In 1605, a small group of Catholics, led by Guy Fawkes, attempted to blow up King James I and the Houses of Parliament with barrels of gunpowder in the basement. The plotters were caught, and the foiling of the plot is celebrated at the annual **Bonfire Night.**

gut, *n.* **river bend**
At Oxford and Cambridge, referring especially to narrow passages in the boat-race course.

gutted, *adj.* *Inf.* **very disappointed**

gutter-crawl, *v.i.*   **cruise for a pickup**

guy, *n., v.t., v.i.*   **1.** *n., Slang.* **fright; sight**
2. *n., Slang.* **slip (vanishing act)**
3. *v.t.* **ridicule**

1. *n., Slang.* As a noun it means a 'grotesquely dressed person' in such a weird getup that American or British onlookers would call him a *fright*, a *sight*, a *scarecrow*, or something of that sort. Literally, a *guy* is a *scarecrow* of a special sort: a limp, shapeless bundle of rags often propped up against walls, wearing frightful masks and caps, surrounded by children begging *a penny for the old guy*. The word is derived from Guy Fawkes and his famous, thwarted gunpowder plot to blow up King James I, the Prince of Wales, and all the Members of Parliament on November 5, 1605. See **Bonfire Night.**
2. *n., v.t., v.i., Slang.* In the British slang expression *give the guy* to someone, *guy* means 'slip' and to *do a guy* is to 'perform a vanishing act.' As an intransitive verb *(slang)*, to *guy* means to 'take it on the lam,' i.e., to 'decamp.'
3. *v.t., Slang.* As a transitive verb, to *guy* is to *exhibit in effigy* and by extension, to *make a monkey of,* i.e., to *ridicule.*

Guy Fawkes Night. See **Gunpowder Plot** and **Bonfire Night.**

gymkhana, *n.*   **horse show**
This peculiar word is occasionally used in America to mean a 'sports car meet.' Technically, it refers to any public sports field or sports meet.

gym shoes   **sneakers**
See also **plimsolls.**

gym slip (gym tunic)   **gym suit**

gym vest   **T-shirt**
Old-fashioned. *T-shirt* is far more common now. See also **singlet.**

gyp, *n.*   **college servant**
This is a special term restricted to the universities of Cambridge and Durham. The same functionary is called a *skip* at Trinity College, Dublin, and a *scout* at Oxford.

gyp, gives me. See **gives (someone) gyp.**

gyppo, gyp, *n.*   *offens.* **a gypsy**

haar, *n.*   **sea mist**
Cold sea fog on the east coast of England and Scotland.

haberdashery, *n.*   **notions store**
In America a *haberdashery* is a men's outfitter. In Britain it is one of those shops that sell pins, needles, thread, tapes, and a little of this and a little of that. Nowadays the term is used mainly to describe the merchandise sold in such establishments, and, increasingly, in the *haberdashery* departments of department stores. See also **draper's shop; fancy goods.**

had for a mug. See **mug, 1.**

haggis, *n.*   SEE COMMENT
A popular English dish until the 18th century, now considered specially Scottish; made of the heart, liver, and **lights** of a sheep, minced and mixed with oatmeal, suet, and seasoning, and then boiled in the sheep's stomach. It may be boiled, steamed, baked, fried in slices, or even microwaved; and it tastes much better than it sounds.

hairdresser's, *n.*   **1. barber shop**
      2. beauty parlor
The British term is used for both types of establishment, but nowadays the British male usually talks of going to the *barber;* the female, to the *hairdresser.*

hair grip   **hairpin; bobby pin**
Also *hair-slide* and **kirby grip.**

hairpin bend, *n.*   **switchback**

half, *adv.*   **half past**
Inf. In expressions of time, e.g., *half twelve,* meaning 'half past twelve.' *Half eleven* means 'half past eleven.' Note that *half after* is American, as is *quarter of,* which in Britain is always *quarter to.*

(a) half, *n.*   SEE COMMENT
A half pint of beer. Form of address to a **publican.** See also **(the) other half.**

half, not. See **not half.**

half, the other. See **(the) other half.**

half-and-half, *n.*   **ale and stout mixed**
But some **publicans** say it can mean 'mild and bitter' mixed, so that when a customer who is not a regular asks for one, it is wise to request a fuller description. Not as commonly drunk as it was in years gone by.

half a tick, *Slang.*   **half a minute (right away)**

half-cock. See **at half-cock.**

half-day, *n.*   SEE COMMENT
Day of the week on which shops close for the day at 1:00 P.M. See **early closing.**

half hunter. See under **hunter.**

halfpenny, *n.*   SEE COMMENT
(Pronounced HAYP'-NY.) The old one was discontinued on August 1, 1969, as a
step in the decimalization of the British currency system. (See **Appendix II.A.**)
A *halfpenny* or *halfpenny's worth* is what a halfpenny will buy; hence, a very small
amount.

half-term, *n.*   SEE COMMENT
Brief **school** vacation. See under **term.**

half-yearly, *adj., adv.*   **semiannual; semiannually**

hall, *n.*   **large public room**
In the context of country **gentry,** *hall* refers to the ample residence of a **landed**
proprietor in Britain. In British universities a *hall* is a building for student living
or teaching, and in British **colleges** a common *dining-room.* When it is equivalent
to *passage* as used in America, it means only an 'entrance passage.' In its general
sense, *hall* finds its equivalent in the British word **passage.** *Hall* is used in both
countries in the names of concert halls, as in Carnegie Hall (New York) and
Albert Hall (London).

hall of residence   **dormitory**

Halt, *v.i.*   **Stop**
The equivalent of an American *Stop* sign used to be and sometimes still is a British road sign reading HALT, but STOP is now coming into general use. Once in a
while *Halt* appears coupled with a place name to indicate a railroad stop in the
middle of nowhere, but near the designated place.

hammer, *v.t.*   **declare insolvent**
Inf. And suspend from trading. An informal expression in financial circles, to
describe the suspension of a brokerage firm unable to meet its commitments. The
verb is derived from the London Stock Exchange practice of declaring a person or
firm bankrupt with three taps of a gavel or hammer on the rostrum.

hammered, *adj.*   *Inf.* **1. exhausted**
                                                                       Inf. **2. drunk**

hampton, *n.*   *Slang. vulgar.* **prick**
Slang. The male member. Shortening of *Hampton Wick;* cockney rhyming slang.
See **Appendix II.G.3.** *Wick* is an archaic word meaning 'town' or 'district,' still
found in place names like *Hampton Wick, Warwick,* etc., and in the word *bailiwick,*
the sphere of operations of a bailie (a Scottish magistrate) or a bailiff (a sheriff's
officer).

hand, *n.*   **handwriting**
As in *His hand is impossible to decipher; She writes a fine italic hand.*

hanger, *n.*   **hillside woods**
This special British meaning is used to describe a wooded area on the side of a
steep hill or mountain.

hanging matter   SEE COMMENT
Inf. Literally, a capital crime for which hanging was the penalty. Used after a
negative, usually in the expression *It's not a hanging matter,* meaning 'It's not all
that serious.'

hang up one's hat   *Inf.* **settle down**
Inf. The context is matrimonial.

Hansard, *n.*   SEE COMMENT
The printed reports of Parliamentary debates. Comparable to the Congressional
Record.

ha'p'orth, *n.*   **trifle**
Inf. (Pronounced HAY'-P'TH.) Contraction of *halfpenny worth,* as much as one could
buy for a halfpenny in the old days (before August 1, 1969, when the old halfpenny was demonetized). Note the old adage: *Don't spoil the ship for a ha'p'orth of
tar,* i.e., 'Don't be penny-wise and pound-foolish.' See also **halfpenny; Appendix
II.A.**

happy as a sandboy   *Inf.* **happy as a clam**
Inf. The words *at high tide* are often added, and always implied, in the American
version. A sandboy sold sand.

happy as Larry, *adj.*   **perfectly content**
The American equivalent would be *happy as a clam.*

harass   SEE COMMENT
Usually pronounced 'Harris,' with the noun pronounced *harris*ment.

hard, *n.*   **hard labor**
Slang. In prison, doing hard time.

hardbake, *n.*   **almond taffy**

hard-baked, *adj.*   **hard-boiled**
The British use both terms interchangeably. Also, *hard-cooked* and *hard-bitten.*

Hard cheese!   *Inf.* **Tough luck!**
Slang. meaning *bad luck.* Occasionally, *Hard cheddar!; hard lines!*

hard-cooked, *adj.*   **hard boiled**
Of eggs, not of people.

hard done by   *Inf.* **done dirt**
Inf. Ill-used.

Hard lines! See **Hard cheese!**

hare, put up the. See **put up the hare.**

hare, start a. See **start a hare.**

hare off, *Inf.*   *Slang.* **vamoose**

Harley Street   SEE COMMENT
Used synecdochically to denote the British medical profession at its most specialized and most expensive. On this street the fashionable private doctors flourish,
but note: most of them also work in the **National Health Service.**

Harrovian, *n., adj.*   SEE COMMENT
Of Harrow; a *Harrovian* is either an *inhabitant of Harrow* (the town where the
famous school is located) or a *member of Harrow,* the **public school** which takes its
name from the town, whether student or graduate **(old boy).** Its playing-fields,
together with those of Eton, are said to supply the future leaders of Britain.

harrow, under the. See under **the harrow.**

Harry . . .   SEE COMMENT
This is a word used in conjunction with another word in slang expressions. Why
Harry? The only answer obtainable was, Why not? The second word in the combination is usually a corrupt form of a standard word. Thus: *Harry spaggers* is
spaghetti; Harry champers (see **champers**) is *champagne; Harry Roughers* is a *rough
sea* and *Harry Flatters* a *calm (flat) sea. Harry Blissington* is *quite marvelous, absolutely
glorious.*

hash mark, *n.*   **number sign**

Hatton Garden   **the diamond industry**
Inf. The name of the London street where most of the diamond merchants are
located is applied colloquially to designate the industry generally.

hat trick   **triple achievement**
Slang. Any triple achievement, the bringing off of any series of three successes,
like three company acquisitions or a lawyer's winning three cases in a row. In
cricket, a bowler took three wickets with three balls, the triumphant bowler
was presented with a new *hat.* Americans use *hat trick* when speaking of ice
hockey.

haulm, also halm, *n.*   SEE COMMENT
(Rhymes with HAWM.) A collective noun, meaning the stalks or stems of growing
things generally, and especially thatching material. It can be used in a singular
sense, too, meaning 'one stem' or 'stalk.'

have a bash at   *Slang.* **take a shot at**
Slang. To *have a bash at* something is to *give it a try.* Synonymous with **have a go
at.** See **go.**

have a doss, *Slang.*   *Slang.* **get forty winks**

have a down on, *Inf.*   *Inf.* **be down on**

have a go at. See **have a bash at.**

have a mind to. See **minded to**

have an early night, *Inf.*   **go to bed early**

have a quid each way. See under **each way**

have a read   **be reading**
Inf. To *have a read* is settling in a comfortable armchair, and the common expression is *have a good read,* i.e., be wholly absorbed in that activity. *The book is a good read* connotes that the book is substantial, entertaining and not too demanding—a phrase now creeping into American reviewers' jargon.

have a rod in pickle for   *Inf.* **be laying for**
To *have a rod in pickle for* someone is to be *nursing a grudge and aching to punish him, and waiting to pounce on him at the first opportunity.* Presumably, the pickling solution will keep the rod pliable until it is used.

have a slate loose, *Slang.*   *Slang.* **have a screw loose**
The slates, of course, are on one's roof.

have a time of it
Synonymous with *have a rare time of it.* See under **rare.**

have a word with   **speak to**
About a particular matter, with the object of accomplishing something. *I'll have a word with him* implies that the speaker is about to try to get something done about something, with a degree of assurance about the outcome.

have enough on one's plate   **have plenty to do**
Inf. Often in the expanded form *enough on one's plate as it is. A full plate* means the same thing. A form sometimes used is *a lot on one's plate,* which connotes the state of being busy rather than overworked.

have everything in the shop window. See under **shop.**

have (someone's) guts for garters   *Inf.* **to give (someone) hell**
Slang. The figurative meaning is of a savage dressing down, perhaps accompanied by punishment of some kind (demotion or the like). The literal meaning is even more savage: removing the visceral organs and using them as an article of clothing. Happily, the act is illegal.

(to) have had one's chips   *Inf.* **(to) have had it**
Slang. To *be beaten; licked.* You've *had your chips, little man.*

have (something) in one's eye   *Inf.* **have (something) lined up**
Slang. Referring, for instance, to a better paying job than the one you have now.

have it off   1. *Slang.* **pull (bring) it off**
                                                   2. **win a bet**
                                                   3. *Slang.* **make it**
                                                   4. **have an affair**
1. *Slang.* Referring to any achievement.
2. *Slang.* At the track, usually.
3. *Slang.* With a sexual partner. Sometimes *have it away.* Both expressions indicate consummation.
4. *Slang.* Intransitive use, referring to either sex.

have jam on it   *Inf.* **have it easy**
Inf. To *be in clover, be feeling no pain,* etc. To *want jam on it* is to *want egg in your beer.*

have no mind to   *Inf.* **not care a rap about**
Inf. For example, *He is so old that he has no mind to basketball.*

have no time for   *Inf.* **have no use for; not think much of**
Inf. Americans commonly use the expression: *I don't think much of him,* or *I have no use for him,* where the British might say *I have no time for him.* Predictably, to *have a lot of time for* someone is to *have a high opinion of* him.

have (someone) on, *Inf.*   *Inf.* **kid (someone)**

have (something) on, *Inf.*   *Inf.* **have (something) going**

have one over the eight   *Inf.* **get somewhat tight**
Inf. When somebody has *had one over the eight,* he is not terribly drunk but is certainly under the influence. The inference may be that one ought to be able to put away eight pints of beer without effect—no mean feat for the inexperienced beer drinker!

have (someone) on toast, *Slang.*   **have (someone) at one's mercy**
A marvelous metaphor.

have (something) put in hand   *Inf.* **get (something) under way**
Inf. If a Briton needed a secretary, he would mention it to friends, apply to agencies, and the like, and would thus *have* the operation *put in hand;* while an American would *get* it *under way.*

haver, *v.i.*   **talk nonsense**
(Pronounced HAY′-VER.) Like **blather,** with which it is synonymous, it is mainly Scottish, and with an -s added becomes a plural noun meaning *nonsense.*

have square eyes   **be a television addict**

have the penny and the bun, *Inf.*   *Inf.* **have your cake and eat it, too**

have the pull of. See **pull.**

have the wind up. See **get the wind up.**

have (someone) up   **bring charges against (someone)**
To bring someone before a court of justice or a government agency.

Have you been served?   **Is someone helping you?**
Question asked by a salesperson (shop *assistant,* or simply **assistant**). Sometimes,
Are you being served?

head, *n.*   **1. principal; dean**
                                                     2. top of the bottle
1. *Head* is a shortening of *head teacher, headmaster,* or *headmistress,* all of which
terms are used in America where, however, *principal* is the common term in secondary schools and *dean* in colleges. **Dean,** in Britain, usually denotes a church
official, although it is sometimes used there in the American sense of a *college*
faculty head or department head. *Principal* is seldom seen in Britain in this connection, where its definitions include, only incidentally, *headmaster* (of a **college**).
2. In Britain, the cream still rises to the top of the container and is called the *head.*
As in America, the same word also describes the *froth on beer.*

head boy; head girl   *approx.* **top boy; top girl**
In British schools generally, below the university level, the headmaster *(principal),*
with the recommendations of the **staff** *(faculty),* designates one student as the
head boy or *head girl,* as the case may be. This fortunate student is the one who has
made the best all-round contribution to school life. The title is an honorable one
and involves the burden of exemplary conduct with no special privileges except
that of leading the cheers on the occasion of the visit of a notable personage.

headlamp, *n.*   **headlight**
See also **Appendix II.E.**

headmaster. See **head.**

headship, *n.*   **office of school principal or college dean**

head teacher, *n.*   **school principal**

health visitor   *approx.* **health inspector**
An official of the local **council** or the **National Health Service** who visits homes
after childbirths, children's clinics, schools, and elderly people to check up and
advise on matters of health.

heaped, *adj.*   **heaping**
Teaspoonful, tablespoon, etc.

hearty, *n.*   *Slang.* **jock**
Inf. A university term for an athlete or sportsman; the opposite of an **aesthete.**

heath, *n.*   **wild open land**
Usually covered with shrubs. *The Heath* in London refers to *Hampstead Heath,* a
beautiful, very large park in northwest London.

Heath Robinson   **Rube Goldberg**
Applicable to a mechanical contrivance of amusingly superfluous complexity.

heavy gang   **third-degree squad**
Slang. Tough police interrogators. The *heavy gang* or *heavy mob* are the rough boys
in the force.

he bought the farm   **his plane was shot down**
Slang. A very sad bit of R.A.F. argot, for which there would appear to be no
American slang equivalent. The expression alludes to the many pilots who were
"going to settle down and buy a farm" when the war was all over. In some cases
it was all over too soon. *He's bought it* has apparently superseded the longer
phrase, and it can now refer to a premature death as a result of any disaster, like
that of a racing driver in flames.

hedge, *n.*   **stone wall**
Inf. A special usage. In some cases the wall is level and wide enough to walk on
cross-country. Stone walls may take the place of green hedges.

hedgerow, *n.*   **a hedge of shrubs bordering a field**

heel bar   **while-U-wait shoe repair shop**

Heinz hound   **mongrel**
Slang. Alluding to the 57 varieties of breeds found among its forebears.

helter-skelter, *n.*   **carnival slide**
Inf. Upon payment of a small fee, one sits on a mat and travels down a dizzying
spiral slide.

hemidemisemiquaver, *n.*   **sixty-fourth note**
Musical term. See **Appendix II.F.**

hemlock, *n.*   *approx.* **poison**
A fatal potion made from a poisonous herb, *Conium maculatum* (*maculatum* means
'spotted' and the stems of the plant have spots). To a scholar it calls to mind Soc-
rates, whom the Athenian court sentenced to die by drinking a cup of hemlock
in 399 B.C.

hempen fever   SEE COMMENT
Death on the gallows, on a *hempen* rope.

**Her Majesty's
Stationery Office**   **Government Printing Office**
Often shortened to *HMSO.*

hessian, *n.*   **burlap**

HGV   *Acronym.* **heavy goods vehicle**

hi!, *interj.*   *approx. Inf.* **hey! hello!**
Inf. Designed to call attention; often a remonstrance. Can be a greeting, as in America.

hiccup, *n.*   **hitch**
Slang. A snarl, any sudden obstruction that interferes with one's plans.

hide, *n.*   **hiding place**
Of a specialized type—for the observation of wild life. It is sometimes used also
to mean 'hunting blind.'

hidey-hole, *n. Inf.*   hideaway

hiding to nothing. See **(be) on a hiding to nothing**

High Court, *n.*   SEE COMMENT
Also known as the High Court of Justice. The supreme court dealing with civil
law cases.

Highlands, *n., pl.*   SEE COMMENT
A mountainous region in northern Scotland.

highly-strung   high-strung
See **Appendix I.A.3.**

High Street   Main Street
The British commonly name the principal thoroughfare of their villages and towns
The High Street, and in referring to it, they still retain the definite article (see **Appendix I.A.2**). British *High Streets* are about as common as American *Main Streets.*

high table, *n.*   SEE COMMENT
The table in the dining room of an academic institution at which the teaching
staff sit. The term is used mostly in the colleges of Oxford and Cambridge, where
staff and students take meals together.

high tea   light supper
High tea includes something cooked: eggs or sausages or Welsh rarebit or any
combination of these. It is the equivalent of a *light supper,* and is eaten early in the
evening.

Hilary. See under **term.**

hip, *n.*   *Inf.* **the blues**
Inf. Also used as a transitive verb meaning to 'give the blues' to someone, i.e.,
to 'depress' him. As a noun, it is sometimes spelled *hyp,* revealing its derivation
(hypochondria). Now often called the *pip.* See also **(the) hump.**

hire. See under **engage.**

hire-and-drive, *n.*   rent-a-car

hire-purchase, *n.*   installment plan
Also known colloquially as the **never-never,** suggesting that the final payments
are never made. Also, that which is repossessed is known as *hire-purchase snatch-back.*

hissy fit, *n.*   *Inf.* **tantrum**

hit (someone) all over the shop, *Inf.*   *Inf.* **run rings around (someone)**

hit for six. See under **six.**

Hitler's War   World War II
Inf. See also **Great War.**

hit off, *Inf.*   mimic accurately

hive off   split off
Inf. Used of a group that splits off from the main organization, like a swarm of bees deserting the hive or a group of employees leaving their jobs in a company to start their own company.

HMSO. See **Her Majesty's Stationery Office.**

hoarding, *n.*   billboard
The primary meaning of this word (apart from its use as present participle of *hoard*) is 'construction site fence,' the roughly built temporary type, on which people are fond of posting notices despite the customary advice to the contrary, and through the holes or chinks of which people are fond of peering. *No Hoarding* is not an injunction in times of shortages of commodities; it means *Post No Bills*, which sometimes appears as *Stick No Bills.*

hob, *n.*   range
In other words, the kitchen appliance used for stove-top cooking. See also **cooker.**

hockey, *n.*   field hockey
To a Briton *hockey* means 'field hockey'; to an American, 'ice hockey.' If a Briton wants to talk about the type played on ice, he calls it *ice hockey.* If the American means the game played on the ground, he says *field hockey.*

hogget, *n.*   yearling sheep
In certain British country dialects the name *hogget* is applied to a *young sheep* before the first shearing of its coat.

hoick, *v.t.*   jerk
Slang. Particularly, to *raise* or *hoist* with a jerk. The noun *hoick* comes from rowing slang: a *jerk* at the end of a poorly executed stroke.

hoist, *n.*   freight elevator
See also **lift; elevator.**

holdall, *n.*   carryall

hold a watching brief. See under **watching brief.**

hold on!   just a minute!
In Britain, an interjection, without the sense of 'wait!' or 'be patient!' or 'hold your horses!', though it has these meanings as well.

hold the baby   *Slang.* **hold the bag**
Slang. Usually in the phrase *be left holding the baby.*

hold the ring   stay out of it
Inf. To *hold the ring*, or *keep the ring*, is to *stay out of a situation* or to *remain on the sideline.* The expression is also used in the context of keeping third parties from interfering in a fight. The ropes forming the prize ring in the old days were not attached to posts but were held by the spectators, thus forming the ring.

hold-up, *n.*   **traffic jam; delay**
Inf. Any delay, whether as a result of heavy traffic, fog, road construction, etc.

hole-and-corner, *adj.*   **underhand**
Inf. A *hole-and-corner man* is a *shady character* or *operator*, and *hole-and-corner work* is *shadiness* generally.

hole-in-the-corner, *adj., Inf.*   **played down**
Imparting a slight connotation of shabbiness. *The wedding had a hole-in-the-corner air.*

holiday, *n.*   **vacation**
An employee in Britain looks forward to his or her *holiday,* and while on vacation is a *holidaymaker.* But the university student in Britain speaks of *vacations,* and the summer recess is the *long vacation,* often shortened to *long vac* or simply *long.* See also **come down.**

hols, *n.pl.*   **vacation time**
Inf. Short for *holidays.*

home and dry   *Inf.* **having achieved one's goal**
Inf. Or *over the hump,* or *home free,* i.e., *doing all right.* Sometimes *home and dried,* and even extended occasionally to *home and dried on the pig's back.*

Home Counties   SEE COMMENT
Counties nearest London, especially Buckinghamshire, Berkshire, Hertfordshire, and Sussex.

home-farm, *n.*   **residence farm**
The farm lived on by a farmer who works several farms that he rents.

home from home   **home away from home**

homely, *adj.*   *Inf.* **homey**
Homely is used in Britain to mean 'simple,' 'unpretentious,' 'nothing fancy.' A *homely* woman in Britain is a friendly, unassuming, domestic type. It is quite possible to be attractive and homely in Britain. *Homely,* in America, is uncomplimentary and means *not good looking* or even *ugly.*

homeminder, *n.*   **house-sitter**
Cf. **child-minder.**

Home Office   SEE COMMENT
There is no precise equivalent in the U.S. government for the UK *Home Office.* Its areas of responsibility include immigration, policies on crime, the police, the issuing of passports for UK citizens, and community and race relations among other things.

Honourable, *adj.*   SEE COMMENT
Usually abbreviated to *Hon.* For the use of this term in the system of British titles, see **Lord.**

Honours   SEE COMMENT
A term applied to undergraduate degrees awarded to students achieving exceptional academic distinction. The standards needed to achieve an Honours degree were once laid down by individual universities; now they are overseen, at most universities, by the Quality Assurance Agency for Higher Education (QAA). A degree qualifying for the term is often listed (on **CVs** and the like) as *BA Hons.* or *B.Sc Hons.* See also **Birthday Honours.**

honours, four. See **four honours.**

honours even   *Slang.* **even Stephen**
Inf. Synonymous with **level pegging.**

Honours List, *n.*   SEE COMMENT
A list of people who receive a title and praise from the monarch as a reward for their work, for instance, service to the community or country. Two lists are announced each year.

Hons. See **Honours.**

hon. sec.   SEE COMMENT
Abbreviation for *honorary secretary,* a noble term bestowed upon long-suffering, unpaid, general factotums of nonprofit organizations. There are *hon. treas.* as well, who handle the money.

hood, *n.*   **convertible top**
Automobile term. See also **Appendix II.E.**

hood rat   *Inf.* **hoodlum**
The term is applied pejoratively (and often unfairly) to teenagers who wear hooded sweatshirts with the hoods up, the implication being that they wear their hoods to hide their faces during the commission of a crime.

hoo-ha, *n.*   **uproar; row**
Inf. Trouble, a *to-do.* See also: **shemozzle; scrum; dust-up; slang; Kilkenny cats; barney.**

hook it   *Slang.* **beat it**
Slang. The Americans *make off, take a powder, get out of town, take it on the lam,* and do lots of other picturesque things to get away from the police, their wives, and other troublesome people. Synonymous with **leg it.**

hook off   **uncouple**
Railroad term.

hooligan, *n.*   **hoodlum**

hoop, *n.*   **wicket**
In croquet. See **wicket** for British uses of that term, both literal and figurative.

Hooray Henry   SEE COMMENT
A pejorative term for a young upper-class man. Often shortened to *Hooray.* In both cases the accent is on the first syllable, and *hoo* rhymes with *too.*

hooter, *n.*
         1. *Slang.* **schnozzle**
         2. automobile horn
         3. factory whistle

hoover, *n., v.t., v.i.*
         1. *n.,* **vacuum cleaner**
         2. *v.t., v.i.,* **vacuum (clean)**
Originally *Hoover* was a trademark, but the word has now become generic, like aspirin, thermos, etc. It is also used as a verb: one hurries home to *hoover* the carpet because guests are coming. The trademark was derived from the name of the pioneer in the field, William Henry Hoover (1849-1932). Mr. Hoover was an American—the first mayor of North Canton, Ohio.

hop; hopper. See under **oast.**

horses. See **come to the horses.**

hospital job   **made work**
Inf. The term *hospital job* has acquired a dishonorable connotation and now commonly signifies an unscrupulous worker's conversion of a straightforward assignment into a "career." He came to fix a shutter in May and is somehow still around in August. Now rare.

hospital nurse   **registered nurse**
Still addressed and referred to in Britain as **sister,** whether or not the hospital or the nurse in question is connected with a religious order. The order of rank in Britain is *nurse, sister, matron;* and *sister* is applied properly only to a nurse of sister rank, but it is often loosely used to describe or address any nurse.

hostelry, *n.*   **inn**
The shorter form *hostel* in both countries indicates a specialized type of *inn* for young people or for others with special requirements.

hotel page   **bellhop**
Often shortened to *page.* An informal term is *buttons.*

hot ice   **dry ice**
Dry ice is the more usual term in Britain.

hot on
         1. *Inf.* **tough on**
         2. good at
1. *Inf.* Thus: *The boss was hot on latecomers.*
2. *Inf. He's hot on gardening,* i.e., *expert at it.* Synonymous with **dab.**

house, *n.*
         1. building
         2. show
1. As part of the title of an office building, with a capital *H.* For instance, the British speak of *Esso House,* the Americans of the *Empire State Building.*
2. If there are two shows a night, the British talk of going to the first *house* or the second *house,* whereas Americans go to see the first *show* or the last *show.* See also **House Full.**

House Full   *approx.* **Sold Out**
Sign seen outside Covent Garden and certain theaters, imparting the intelligence that there isn't even any standing-room. The *Standing Room Only* sign goes up first, succeeded, when appropriate, by *House Full.* See **house, 2.**

household troops. See **Guards.**

housemaid, *n.*   chambermaid
A **chambermaid** in Britain is a *hotel maid.*

houseman, *n.*   intern
A hospital term.

House of Commons   SEE COMMENT
1. Britain's most important political institution, the elected legislative body. It is
where the government sits and where the elected members of Parliament debate
and pass all legislation.
2. The building where the Commons sit.

House of Lords   SEE COMMENT
The upper house of Parliament, with little real political power. The House of
Lords comprises the peers of the realm.

housewife, *n.*   sewing gear kit
Pronounced HUZZIF in this meaning.

housing estate   residential development

howler, *n., Inf.*   *Inf.* **boner**
An error so great, one howls in anguish at the sight of it.

How's that? *interj.*   SEE COMMENT
The cry, called an *appeal,* to the umpire in a cricket game by one or more of the
team (**side**) in the field demanding a ruling that the batter (**batsman**) is out on
one technicality or another.

How's your father   sexual intercourse
They were having a bit of how's your father on the sofa.

hoy, *Interj.*   drive
Hoy! is used in herding or driving cattle. To *hoy* a herd is to *drive* it by gestures
and shouts of *hoy!* or whatever else comes to mind.

huggery, *n.*   drumming up trade
Inf. Activities of **barristers** wooing **solicitors.** Rhymes with SKULDUGGERY.

hullo! *Interj.*   hey! (what's going on?)
(Accent on the first syllable.) It is not only a simple greeting; it can also be an
expression of surprise—*what's happening here?*

hum and ha, *Inf.*   *Inf.* **hem and haw**
Sound of hesitation.

humane society   lifesaving service
A *humane society* man would be called a *lifeguard* in America. A *humane society* in
America is a benevolent organization for the care and shelter of pet animals.

humble pie   crow
People eat *crow* in America, and, rarely, *humble pie;* in Britain it is never *crow,*
always *humble pie.* Both terms signify *humiliation,* especially that of *eating one's*

words, i.e., having to retract a previous categorical assertion. The *humble* in *humble pie* is a corruption of *umbles,* a word now obsolete in both countries, and a variant of *numbles,* an archaic English word for the entrails of a deer. *Umble pie,* long ago, was a pie of the inferior parts of a deer served to huntsmen and other servants. The inferior parts included the heart, the liver, and the **lights.**

humbug, *n.*   **mint candy**
Hard, with white and brown stripes, and very tasty.

(the) hump, *n.*   *Slang.* **(the) dumps**
Slang. You can wake up with *the hump,* or get it or have it. People and things that give you *the hump* would be said to *get you down. The hump* would seem to imply a certain amount of irritation combined with depression, like *the sulks. I've got the hump* means 'I'm fed up.' If you're *humpy,* you're *down in the mouth, in the dumps.* See also **hip.**

hump, *v.t*   *Inf.* **lug; schlepp**
Inf. The image is that of one wearily carrying a heavy burden. *Schlepp* is heard increasingly in Britain.

hundred, *n.*   SEE COMMENT
Subdivision of a county in the old days. See **Chiltern Hundreds.**

hundreds and thousands   *approx.* **multicolored sprinkles**
Tiny candies spread on top of cookies, cakes, or ice cream. See also **chocolate vermicelli.**

hundredweight, *n.*   SEE COMMENT
112 pounds in Britain; 100 pounds in America.

hunt, *v.i.*   **skip; miss**
Inf. If your motor is *hunting* in Britain, it is alternately racing and stalling.

hunt, in the. See **in the hunt.**

hunt, out of the. See **in the hunt.**

hunter, *n.*   **watch with hinged covers**
If it has hinged covers front and back, it is a *hunter;* if only a front cover, a *half hunter.* These names derive from the function of the cover(s): to protect the watch on the hunting field.

huss.   SEE COMMENT
A kind of fish. See also **Appendix II.H.**

hustings, *n. pl.*   SEE COMMENT
In Parliamentary and other major elections, candidates gather for prearranged assemblies where those from all the parties can present their platforms and debate the issues. These assemblies are *hustings,* from an Old English word meaning 'house of assembly.'

hyp. See **hip.**

hyper-market, *n.*   **giant supermarket**

I

ice, *n.*   **ice cream**
In some British restaurants, *ices* means *ice cream*. The British use *sorbet* for *sherbet*, but *sherbet* in Britain means 'powdered candy,' a sweet sugar-like substance that children eat through licorice sticks or by dipping lollipops into it. *Water ice,* meaning 'sherbet' in the American sense, is sometimes seen on British menus instead of *sorbet.*

icing sugar   **powdered sugar**
See also **castor sugar.**

identification parade   **police lineup**

identity disc   *Slang.* **dog tag**
The Americans prefer the slang expression, for which there is no British slang equivalent.

I have to say that . . .   **I beg to say that . . .**
Have here does not express necessity, any more than the *am* in *I am to say,* in officialese, expresses futurity, or the *beg* in the corresponding American phrase implies a request for permission. The entire phrase, in each country, should be omitted.

ilk. See **of that ilk.**

ill, *adj.*   SEE COMMENT
The British use *ill* in the usual American senses, but also in ways in which it would not appear in America. Thus, one often hears a television announcer describe the victim of an accident or a shooting as 'seriously ill,' where an American would have been likely to use a phrase like 'in critical condition.' Note that **sick** is generally not used as a synonym for *ill,* but much more narrowly, to mean *nauseous,* and to *be sick* is to *throw up.*

I'll be blowed   *Interj.* **I'm amazed!**

I'll be bound   *Inf.* **I bet**
Inf. This expression comes only at the end of a sentence so that it never takes a dependent clause.

I'm easy (about it)   **It's all the same to me**
Inf. I'm easy (about it), in answer to a question posing a dilemma or an alternative, e.g., *Would you rather I came at 10:00 or 11:00?* means *I don't care,* or *It's all the same to me. I'm easy about it* has a British equivalent in *I don't mind.* Usually shortened to *I'm easy.* See also **mind, 2.**

immersion heater   **hot water heater**
An *immersion heater* heater heats water for the whole house, as opposed to a **geyser,** which provides a supply of hot water in a particular room, usually the kitchen. Often referred to as the *immersion.* Now a somewhat old-fashioned term.

immigrant, *n.*   **non-white**
Inf. Used by some as a pejorative synonym for **coloured,** which in Britain includes Asians and persons of mixed ancestry as well as of African descent. Properly speaking, in either country, any person entering another country to settle there permanently is an *immigrant.* See also **asylum seeker.**

I'm not bothered   **I don't care**

imperial, *adj.*   *Inf.* **unsurpassable**
Inf. As in, an *imperial balls-up* (see **balls**) which is *one lousy mess.*

importune, *v.t.*   **solicit**
In America, *importune,* in addition to its primary meaning of 'beset, ply, dun,' can mean 'to make improper advances toward' someone. In England, *importune* is used in the special sense of 'solicit for immoral purposes,' and is commonly used to describe the activities of active prostitutes.

impost, *n.*   **punishment task**
Schoolboy slang. Rare. An informal shortening of *imposition,* sometimes written *impo,* referring to an unpleasant task assigned as a punishment at school, like having to write, *I shall not pass notes during Scripture* 500 times.

impression, *n.*   **printing**
Thus: First published January 1968
   Second *impression* February 1968 . . .
In a book printed in America the *second impression* would be called the *second printing.*

imprest, *n.*   SEE COMMENT
Funds advanced to a government employee for use in official business. Formerly, it meant an advance payment to a soldier or sailor on enlistment.

in a cleft stick   *Slang.* **in a pickle**
Inf. The two branches of a *cleft stick* are like the *horns of a dilemma.*

in a flap, *Inf.*   *Inf.* **het up**

in a flat spin   *Slang.* **rattled**
Slang. Usually in the expression *going into a flat spin,* meaning agitated or panic-stricken.

in a fuzz, *Slang.*   *Slang.* **in a tizzy**

in aid of   **for (used for)**
What's that in aid of? 'What's that for?'—asked by someone pointing to an object whose function is unclear. Can also be asked about intangibles like a shout or a trip.

in a state   *Inf.* **worried, anxious**
Similar to **in a tizzy.**

in a tizzy   *Inf.* **upset, flustered**
She was in a tizzy because she couldn't find her train ticket.

in a way; in a great way. See **way.**

in (someone's) bad books   *Inf.* **in dutch with (someone)**
Inf. Variant: *in (someone's) black books.* Synonymous with **in the cart.**

in baulk, balk   *Inf.* **in a spot**
Inf. Meaning 'in difficulties.'

in care   **in a foster home**

incident room   *(approx.)* **situation room**
A term beloved of English detective story writers; temporary headquarters set
up during the investigation of the crime; a control room where the hero-detective
and staff meet and discuss things.

indent, *n., v.t.*   **requisition**

indexed. *See* **index-linked.**

index-linked, *adj.*   **adjusted for inflation**
Describes savings programs, investments, etc. where the income and/or capital are geared to the British cost-of-living index (the *UK General Index of Retail
Prices—RPI* for short). *Index-linked* is sometimes shortened to *indexed,* and the
process has been dubbed *indexation,* which can be applied to wages and salaries
as well.

Indian. See **red Indian.**

Indian meal   **corn meal**
An old-fashioned term, little used nowadays, just as Indian corn is little used to
mean what Americans call *corn* and Britons **sweetcorn.**

indicators, *n. pl.*   **car signals**
And to signal that you're turning, you *indicate.*

indoors   **at home**

industrial action   **union protest activity**
Anything from a slow down to a full-fledged strike.

industrial estate. See under **estate.**

ingle-nook, *n.*   **chimney corner**
A word that summons up an irresistibly cozy, even stirring, image of the quint-
essential Briton by his or her hearth. Rooms in old houses sometimes have fireplaces as much as eight or ten feet wide, with a grate or stove in the center from
which the smoke runs into a narrow flue. Comfortable chairs can be placed on
either side, within the fireplace.

ingrowing, *adj.*   **ingrown**
Referring to toenails or facial hair. The Americans seem resigned to a *fait accompli.*

in hand

1. at one's disposal
2. under control

1. As in, *Aberdeen still has two games in hand,* and though trailing at the moment, might yet win the Scottish first division **football** (soccer) championship. In this sense, *in hand* would be *to go* in America: ... *two games to go.*
2. *Being attended to:* **Not to worry;** *the matter is in hand.*

inland, *adj.*   **domestic; internal**
The British speak of *inland* postage rates and *inland* revenue. The opposite number of an American *internal revenue agent* is the British *inland revenue inspector.* But see **internal.**

in low water

1. *Inf.* **hard up**
2. *Slang.* **in hot water**

1. *Inf.* Financial stress is the usual connotation.
2. *Inf. Difficult straits* or a *depressed state* generally (e.g., the weak position of a political party out of favor) is the broader implication, and in this sense its American equivalent would be *in hot water. Low in the water* is a variant, meaning 'up against it.'

innings, *n. sing.*   **inning**
Note the *-s,* which does not make *innings* plural. An American *inning* is a British *innings.* The standard British plural is the same as the singular; informally, it is *inningses.* The technical term is used only in cricket, but has found its way from there into general, figurative use, especially in the phrase **good innings.**

Inns of Court   SEE COMMENT
These are the four legal societies which alone may admit persons to the bar in the sense of allowing them to practice as **barristers** as distinguished from **solicitors.** These societies are the Inner Temple, Middle Temple, Lincoln's Inn, and Gray's Inn. The term *Inns of Court* denotes not only those societies but also their buildings in London.

in one's gift   **at one's disposal**
With particular reference to a **living,** but also to an appointed job.

in pod   *Slang.* **knocked up**
Slang. Both countries use inelegant terms for "pregnant." See also **preggers** and **pudding club.** See **knock up** for its various British meanings.

inquiry. See **enquiry.**

insect, *n.*   **bug**
Americans use *insect* and *bug* more or less interchangeably. In Britain *bug* means 'bedbug.' *Bug* has slang meanings in both countries.

inside (of a bus)   **bottom**
And the *outside* of a bus is its *top.* These terms refer to double-deckers and are reminiscent of the days when the top was uncovered, and therefore the *outside.* Nowadays it's all inside, literally speaking, but *outside* is still often heard from conductors.

inspectorate, *n.*   SEE COMMENT
Governmental body for inspection of schools, prisons, and a few other public institutions. Performs some of the functions of a Board of Education.

in store. See under **store.**

instruct, *v.t*   **retain**
Term used in the legal profession. In Britain a client instructs a **solicitor,** that is, **engages** him. In America a client *retains,* engages, or hires a lawyer. The term is also used in accountancy and with **estate agents.**

insulating tape, *n.*   **electrician's tape**

intake, *n.*   **entrants**
Inf. Those recently *taken in.* Covers entrants into a university, the ministry, the armed forces, etc. The slang American equivalent in military and sports usage would be *rookies.*

interfere with   **molest**
To *rape, sodomize,* or otherwise sexually attack (e.g., a child). The British circumlocution is even more euphemistic than the American.

interior-sprung, *adj.*   **inner-spring**
Type of mattress.

internal, *adj.*   **domestic**
Term applied to air travel. But see **inland.**

international, *n.*   SEE COMMENT
Also *internationalist.* An athlete who has represented his or her country abroad, especially at soccer, rugby, or cricket, although for cricket the proper term is *test player* (see **Test Match**).

interval, *n.*   **intermission**
The short period of time between acts at the theater or between the halves of a concert. *Tea in the interval?* (at the matinee) or *Coffee in the interval?* (at an evening performance) used to be the courteous and comforting question addressed to members of the audience by British ushers in most theaters, and if the question was answered in the affirmative, you were served at your seat. The practice no longer exists, sadly. Stronger beverages may be procured at the bar in every British theater.

in the basket   *Slang.* **no soap; no dice**
Slang. When a proposed project is *in the basket,* it's *no soap (rejected, discarded, nothing doing).*

in the cart, *Slang.*   *Slang.* **in the soup**

in the club. See **pudding club.**

in the dock. See **dock, 2.**

in the driving seat, *Inf.*   *Inf.* **in the driver's seat**

in the event   **as it turned out**
Thus: *In the event, the vote was much closer than expected.* The phrase does not connote futurity, as does an expression like *In the event of rain . . . ,* but refers to something that actually came to pass despite predictions or expectations to the contrary.

in the hunt   *Inf.* **in the running**
Inf. And *out of the hunt* is *not in the running.*

in the picture   **fully informed**

in the same case   **in the same situation**
Used when comparing one person's situation with another's.

in trade. See **trade.**

in train   **coming along**
Sometimes *on train.* These expressions are not often heard in America. In Britain
the phrases are heard quite frequently, as the normal response of merchants or
contractors to whom one is complaining about delay: *It is in train,* meaning he has
done all he can, and you must be patient.

in tray, *n.*   **in box**
Both receptacles provide efficient means for letting papers pile up on one's desk
and serve as visible reminders of our dilatory natures. The British by now surely
have filled their *in trays* to overflowing and we also hear them saying they have
in boxes that need attention.

in two shakes of a duck's tail, *Inf.*   *Inf.* **in two shakes of a lamb's tail**
Inf. Lamb's tail, as well, in Britain. *Shake,* by itself, can mean 'moment' in either
country, *of a duck's* or *lamb's tail* being understood. *In a brace of shakes* is synonymous in Britain with *in two shakes of a lamb's* or *duck's tail.*

inty, *n.*   **(school) recess**
Schoolboy slang. Rare. The *interval* of freedom.

invalid carriage   **electric tricycle**
Formerly issued by the Ministry of Health, in some cases to working people who
could not otherwise get around. Now replaced by electric buggies.

invalid's chair   **wheelchair**
Also called **bath chair** and **wheeled chair.** Now obsolete.

inverted commas   **quotation marks**

invigilator *n.*   **proctor at school examinations**
To *invigilate* is to *keep vigil,* i.e., watch over students during examinations.

ironmonger *n.*   **hardware dealer**

I say!   **gosh, wow!**
Old-fashioned but often heard. It might be paraphrased in certain situations as
That's amazing!

-ish, *adv.*   **somewhat; sort of; rather; about**
Inf. Tacked on to an adjective or adverb, this suffix adds an attenuating nuance,
with the same force as placing *somewhat, fairly,* or *sort of* before the word, or *about*
or *around* in expressions of quantity or time. Americans are familiar with *-ish* after

adjectives of color: *reddish, greenish,* or of general age: *youngish, oldish.* But the British are prone to add *-ish* to almost anything: *tallish, fattish, poorish;* to numerals in expressions of quantity: *How many people were at the party? Oh, fiftyish;* in general or specific expressions of time: *earlyish, latish; I'll get there elevenish* ('around eleven o'clock'); and with adverbs: *The play began slowish* ('got off to a rather slow start'), but **smartish** is used instead of *quickish.* There are British uses that do not occur in American speech: After a name, meaning *characteristic of,* as in *That's a Maryish gesture* ('one characteristic or reminiscent of Mary'); *That's a Teddyish reaction* ('the way Teddy would react'). By itself, as an answer or reaction, meaning 'well, sort of,' or 'if you say so,' or 'somewhat,' to someone else's statement or question: *She's pretty. Well, -ish. I found the food in that restaurant quite good. How about you? -Ish,* or, *Only -ish.*

I shall be glad if you will . . .   Please . . .
Officialese, properly objected to.

I spy strangers!   SEE COMMENT
A term used in the **House of Commons** for anyone who is not a member of Parliament. Strangers are allowed to watch parliamentary debates from the Strangers' Gallery but Parliament maintains its right to debate in private. If an M.P. cries, *I spy strangers!,* the speaker must put forward a motion that all strangers leave the Strangers Gallery forthwith. If the motion is passed, the debate continues in private.

issue, *v.t*   furnish
Used as follows: *There is no charge for issuing you with our credit card.* The British might also have said: *. . . for issuing our credit card to you.* The Americans might say *furnishing you with* or *supplying you with* but would not use *issue* in the British construction.

it. See gin and it.

item, *n.*   plank
An *item* in a political *program* in Britain is what Americans would call a *plank* in a political *platform.*

It isn't true!   That's (or It's) incredible!

izzard, *n.*   (letter) z
Archaic.

jack, *v.t.* *Inf.* **steal**
Abbr. of 'highjack.'

jacket potato, *Inf.* **baked potato**

Jack the lad, *n.* *Slang.* SEE COMMENT
A man who is independent and sly, and who looks out for himself. There might
be an implication of impropriety, but rarely enough to call for outright moral condemnation. *Operator* is an approximate American equivalent.

Jag, *n.* *Inf.* **Jaguar car**

jakes, *n.* *Slang.* **can (privy)**
Slang. Archaic word for outhouse, toilet.

jam, *n.* **treat**
Slang. A real *jam* is British slang for a *real treat.* A *jam sandwich* in Britain can mean
what it does in America, but it is also a term used to mean the kind of layer cake
that has preserves between the layers. See also **jam sandwich.**

jam, money for. See **money for jam.**

jam on it. See **have jam on it.**

jam sandwich **police car**
Slang. So named because the vehicles have been white with a red stripe along the
middle, suggesting jam between two slices of white bread. Cf. **panda car; Z-car.**

jam tomorrow, *Inf.* *Inf.* **pie in the sky**
Easy enough to promise jam, harder to provide it.

Janeite, *n.* **Jane Austen fan**
Sometimes spelled *Janite.* Not an American word, since Jane Austen is not a
national craze.

jankers, *n., pl.* *Slang.* **jug**
Slang. In the special sense of *military jail. Jankers* has other meanings in military
slang: 'defaulters'; their 'penalty' or 'punishment'; the 'cells' themselves. To get
ten days' *jankers* is to be confined to the *stockade* for that period.

jaunty, *n.* **master-at-arms**
Naut. Slang. Head policeman on a naval vessel. The official title in both the Royal
Navy and the United States Navy is *master-at-arms*, often abbreviated to *M.A.A.*

jaw, *n.*   **talking to**
Slang. A contemptuous term. A *pi-jaw (pi-* is short for *pious)* is one of those lectures or sermons delivered by a schoolteacher or a scout leader on a man-to-man basis to prepare the nervous youngster for life's pitfalls. More generally, a conversation or a meeting.

jaw-bacon. See **chaw-bacon.**

jaw-jaw, *n., v.i.*   **1. endless discussion**
                                                 2. drone on and on
Slang. See also **jaw.**

jellied eel   SEE COMMENT
A traditional Cockney dish, pieces of eel simmered till soft and served cold with their cooking liquid (liquor). The liquor sets to a jelly, hence the name. Less popular now than it once was.

jelly, *n.*   **gelatin-type dessert**
Jelly is used in Britain as in America, but in a British restaurant if you wanted Jell-O or its equivalent for dessert, you would ask for *jelly.*

jelly-bag cap   **stocking cap**
Inf. Jelly-bags are used for straining jelly and are made of the kind of stretchable material associated with what Americans call *stocking caps.*

jemmy,   **jimmy**
British burglars use *jemmies;* their American colleagues use *jimmies. Jemmy* is also used as the British name for a dish made from sheep's head.

Jeremiah, *n.*   *Inf.* **gloomy Gus**
Inf. Everybody knows (or should know) that Jeremiah was a doleful prophet.

jerry, *n.*   *Inf.* **potty**
Slang. Also called *jerrycan* or *jerrican,* a 5-gallon *chamber pot.* With a capital *J* it is British slang for a *German,* or *Germans* collectively.

jersey, *n.*   **pullover; sweater**
See also **jumper; woolly.**

jib, *v.i.*   **hesitate, buck**
Inf. Normally applied to balking horses and in Britain, informally, to cars as well or even to stubborn persons.

jiggered, *adj.*   **1.** *Slang.* **pooped**
                                                 2. *Slang.* **up the creek**
                                                 3. *Slang.* **damned!**
1. *Slang.* After a long day's work, you're *jiggered.*
2. *Slang.* In a tough situation, like running out of gas in the middle of the night, you'd feel *jiggered.*
3. *Slang.* The exclamation *I'm jiggered* means 'I'll be damned' as in *Well, I'm jiggered—fancy meeting you here!*

jiggery-pokery, *n., Inf.*   *Inf.* **hanky-panky**

jim-jams, *n. pl. Slang.*   *Slang.* **willies**
A fit of nervousness or depression.

Jimmy, dismal. See **dismal Jimmy.**

jink, *v.t., v.i.*   **dodge**
To *dodge about* jerkily, to avoid being hit. Said of game birds and extended to
warplanes.

job, *v.t.*   **1. rent (horse and carriage)**
                                                                          2. prod
1. The British used to *job* horses and carriages in the old days, the verb being
applied to both supplier and user (the way Americans use *rent*). *Jobbing,* in this
sense, described an arrangement for a specified period of time, and the supplier
was called a *jobmaster.*
2. Also meaning *stab,* though this is little used.

jobber, *n.*   SEE COMMENT
On the London Stock Exchange, there are a dozen firms that act as wholesalers
and are analogous to oddlot firms on the New York Stock Exchange, in that they
are principals, acting for their own account, rather than brokers acting only as
agents for buyer or seller.

jobbernowl, *n., Inf.*   *Slang.* **dope; jerk**

job centre, *n.*   SEE COMMENT
A government-run employment agency.

job of work   **job**
Inf. In the sense of *work to be done.*

job seeker's allowance, *n.*   SEE COMMENT
A payment made to someone who is looking for work. It may be income-based
(depending on income and savings) or contribution-based (depending on
National Insurance contributions made while working).

jobsworth, *n.*   *Inf.* SEE COMMENT
A particularly bureaucratic person who would never break the rules. Derives
from the saying, *It's more than my job's worth to do that for you.*

Joe Bloggs   **Joe Doakes**
Mr. What's-his-name; anybody who isn't anybody; Tom, Dick, or Harry; the man
in the street. Sometimes given as Fred Bloggs.

John Dory
See **Appendix II.H.**

johnny, *n.*   *Inf.* **guy**
Slang. Usually pejorative. For the British meaning of *guy,* see **guy.**

John O'Groats   SEE COMMENT
A small town on the northeasternmost tip of Scotland. Though a tourist destination of some note, its most famous feature is the expression *From Land's End
to John O'Groats*, a short way of saying: *From one end of the British Isles to the other.*

join, *v.t.*   **board**
To *join* a train, ship, plane, etc. is to *board* it.

joiner, *n.*   **carpenter**
Technically speaking, *joiners* in both countries, as distinct from *carpenters*, engage
especially in interior light carpentry (doors, shelves, etc.) and cabinet making.
The British appear often to use the terms interchangeably, but *joiner* is rarely
heard in ordinary American speech.

joint, *n.*   **roast**
In Britain that tasty leg of lamb or roast of beef or loin of pork is known as a *joint*.
Popular for Sunday lunch, hence the *Sunday joint*.

jokes, *adj.*   *Slang.* **funny**

jollop, *n.*   *Inf.* **guck**
Slang. Any witches' brew you take for whatever ails you, like patent medicines
and home remedies.

jolly, *n.*   *Slang.* **leatherneck**
Slang. A *Royal Marine*. Synonymous with *guffy* and *bullock*.

jolly, *adv., Inf.*   *approx.* **mighty (very)**

joskin, *n.*   **bumpkin**
Slang. Sailors use this term to describe any lubberly hand. The exact meaning of *joskin*
is a man from the Norfolk area who works as a farmhand during the summer and on
trawlers in wintertime, and is therefore, presumably, a green hand on board.

josser, *n., Slang.*   *Slang.* **geezer**

jotter, *n., Inf.*   **1. steno pad**
                                                                     2. notebook

2. Also **exercise book.**

judder, *v.i.*   **shake**
Violently and noisily. A bit of onomatopoeia, also influenced by *shudder*. It can
apply to anything from a jalopy to an opera singer, and is also used as a noun to
denote the phenomenon.

Judy, *n.*   *Slang.* **broad**
Slang. An uncomplimentary word for *woman*, suggesting that she's no beauty.

jug, *n.*   **pitcher**
In Britain it is the milk *jug* or water *jug* which is placed on the table. *Jug* is also a
slang word for 'poison' in both countries.

juggernaut, *n.*   **large truck**
Inf. Very large; short for *juggernaut lorry*. (See **lorry**.) Usually refers to an enormous trailer truck (see **articulated lorry**). The word is related to *Jagannath*, an

idol of the Hindu god Krishna that was drawn in processions on vast carts and under whose wheels fanatics threw themselves in their ecstasy, to be crushed to death.

juggins, *n.*   *Slang.* **dope; fool**
Slang. Synonymous with **muggins.** See also **git.**

jumble, *n.*   SEE COMMENT
Goods sold at a *jumble sale* or unwanted things in the house allocated to the local *jumble sale.* Can also be used loosely to mean 'junk.'

jumble sale, *n.*   **rummage sale**

jumper, *n.*   **pullover**
This term is used to describe a woman's *pullover sweater.* See also **jersey; woolly.**

jump jockey, *Inf.*   **steeplechase rider**

jump leads   **jumper cables**

jump to it, *Inf.*   *Inf.* **hop to it**

junction box. See **box.**

junk   **worn-out rope**
Old, worthless stuff, rubbish, which is called *junk* in America, is generally referred to as *rubbish* or **lumber** in Britain, where *junk,* though now extended to mean 'rubbish' generally, was long more especially a nautical term meaning 'worn-out hawsers' or 'cables' which are either discarded or picked apart for use as caulking material or in making swabs.

just, *adv.*   *adv.* **right**
Where an American would say, "I can't find it now, but it was *right* over there," i.e., no farther than that, a Briton would say " . . . *just* over there." Were the Briton to say, " . . . *right* over there," he would mean ' . . . way over there,' i.e., no nearer than that. If he said, "Drink it *right* up," he would mean 'drink it all,' whereas an American would mean "drink it at once, *right* now."

just a tick!   *Inf.* **right with you!**
Inf. See also **hold on!**

just going   **just about**
Used in expressions of time of day: *it's just going twelve* means *it's just about twelve,* or, *practically twelve.* The expressions *just on* and *going on for* are used by the British in the same way: *it's just on nine o'clock,* or *it's going on for nine,* i.e., *it's not quite* or *it's just about nine.* See also **gone.**

just here   **right here**

just on. See **just going.**

K

K., *n.* SEE COMMENT
Inf. To *get one's K.* is to *be knighted* (see **Birthday Honours**).

K.C. See under **take silk.**

kedgeree, *n.* SEE COMMENT
(Accent on the first or third syllable.) Composed of fish, usually smoked haddock, cooked with rice and eggs, and other variable ingredients. The word is derived from the Hindi word *khichri.* It is normally a breakfast dish, and not very common.

keel, *n.* **1. barge**
2. 21 tons 4 cwt.
1. Type of boat used, usually to carry coal, on the Rivers Tyne, Humber, etc. Still seen, but going out of use.
2. Weight of coal that can be carried on a *keel,* and still used as a wholesale coal measure. Since a British *ton* is 2240 lbs. and a British cwt. (**hundredweight**) is 112 lbs., a *keel* is, in American terms, 47,488 lbs., or a sliver under $23^3/_4$ tons. See also **Appendix II.C.1.**

keelie, *n.* *Inf.* **tough**
Slang. A Scottish term, derived from the Keelie Gang, a band of hoodlums that terrorized the streets of Edinburgh in the early 19th century. It is applied particularly to street ruffians from Glasgow and environs.

keenest prices **biggest bargains**
Inf. Often seen in advertisements: *For keenest prices shop at So-and-So's.*

keen on *Inf.* **enthusiastic about**
The object of the enthusiasm is most likely to be sexual in nature (*I'm really keen on him*), but it may be a composer, a hair style, an article of clothing, etc. *Dead keen on* and *mad keen on* indicate mounting degrees of enthusiasm.

keep, *v.t.* **raise**
A Briton who *keeps* pigs is not simply having them as pets; he is in business and in America would be said to be *raising* them.

keep a straight bat *Inf.* **play fair**
Inf. One of many expressions borrowed from **cricket,** which is itself synonymous with *fair play* in the mind and idiom of a Briton.

keep cave. See **cave.**

keeper, *n.* **custodian; guard**
Keeper is the usual British term for a *museum guard* or *zoo employee.* To a Briton, **guard** would normally invoke the image of a railroad conductor or a sentry.

keep obbo on   *Inf.* **keep an eye on**
Slang. An *obbo* was an observation balloon in World War I. *Keeping obbo* is policemen's slang for *surveillance*.

keep one's terms. See **eat one's terms; Inns of Court.**

keep shtoom, *v.*   *Inf.* **keep quiet**
Also spelled *shtum*. From the Yiddish word meaning *silent* or *dumb*. Direct borrowings from Yiddish are rarer in the UK than in the United States, but this is one that has found its way into common speech.

keep the ring. *See* **hold the ring.**

keep your eyes skinned. *Inf.*   *Inf.* **keep your eyes peeled**

Keep your pecker up!   *Inf.* **Chin up!**
Inf. In this expression, *pecker* means 'spirits' or 'courage.' This connotation of *pecker* is probably derived from its original meaning of a 'bird that pecks' (e.g., *woodpecker*), and by extension that with which it pecks, i.e., its beak, which became slang for 'nose.'

Kendal green   **green woolen cloth**
Coarse in texture. Takes its name from Kendal, a town in England where the cloth was originally made.

Kentish-fire, *n.*   SEE COMMENT
Prolonged rhythmic applause to express disapproval. The expression is attributed to anti-Catholic demonstrations in Kent in the early 1800s.

Kentish man   SEE COMMENT
Native of the County of Kent, England, born west of the River Medway. If born east of it, he is a *man of Kent.*

kerbside-crawl.   SEE COMMENT
Slang. **Crawl** is used by the British the way Americans use *cruise* to indicate the slow driving of a car. *Kerb-crawl* describes the nasty conduct of a motorist on the prowl for women foolish enough to accept an invitation to hop in. **Gutter-crawl** is synonymous. (*Kerb* is spelled *curb* in America.)

kerfuffle, *n.*   **fuss; commotion; dither**
Slang. Found also in the spellings *cufuffle* and *gefuffle,* and probably in others as well. It is sometimes used as synonymous with **shemozzle.**

kettle-boy, *n.*   **tea maker**
Formerly, boy employed on a construction site to keep the tea kettle going all day long.

kettle-holder, *n.*   **pot-holder**

keyless watch   **stem-winder**

kibble, *n., v.t.*   **1.** *n.,* **mine bucket**
                                                        2. *v.t.,* **grind**

Kibbled wheat is *cracked wheat.*

kick the beam   **lose out**

kick-up. See **dust-up.**

Kilkenny cats   **squabblers**
Inf. Based on an old Irish legend about two cats who fought each other so long
and so murderously that finally there was nothing left but their tails. The figurative meaning of the phrase retains reference to the audible squabbling of the cats,
rather than to their gruesome end.

King's (Queen's) evidence   **state's evidence**
In Britain, the accused cooperates with the prosecution by *turning King's* or
Queen's evidence, the phrase being determined by the sex of the sovereign at the
time. In America, the phrase is *state's evidence.*

kinky, *adj.*   **1. sexually unconventional**
                                                        2. twisted; odd
                                                        3. sophisticatedly off-beat
                                                        4. *Inf.* **cool**

1. *Slang.* Or appealing to such tastes.
2. *Slang. Peculiar; kooky.*
3. *Slang.* As of clothes, for instance.
4. *Teenage slang.* Synonymous with **gear** and **fab.**

kiosk, *n.*   **1. newsstand**
                                                        2. telephone booth

kip, *n., v.i.*   **1. rooming-house**
                                                        2. room in a rooming-house
                                                        3. bed
                                                        4. sleep
Slang. The *house,* the *room* in the house, the *bed* in the room, the *sleep* in the bed;
sometimes seen in the expressions *go to kip, have a kip, take a kip, or kip down,* meaning to 'turn in for a night's sleep or a nap.'

kipper, *n.*   *Inf.* **kid; tot**
Slang. Synonymous with a like-sounding British slang word—**nipper.**

kirby grip *n.*   **bobby pin**
Also known in Britain as *hair-slide* and *hair grip.*

kissing gate   *Approx.* **cattle gate**
Kissing gates found in rural Britain are gates hung with the side away from the
hinge swinging within a V-shaped or U-shaped enclosure in such a way that people can get through but cattle can't. You push the gate away from the nearside of
the V or U, step into the latter, slide over to the other side, and push the gate back.
This quaint device may have acquired its romantic name because it was the place
where a swain said goodnight to his lady love, and a certain amount of lingering
was in order.

kiss of life   **1. mouth-to-mouth resuscitation**
                                                          2. boost
1. The life-saving procedure.
2. *Inf.* Probably modeled on the phrase *kiss of death,* it has acquired the meaning
of something that revitalizes or provides new hope for an ailing project, situation,
etc.

kiss your hand. See **as easy as kiss your hand.**

kit, *n., v.t.*   **outfit**
As a noun, *outfit* in the sense of special dress, like *skiing kit, camping kit,* etc. As a
verb, *outfit* in the sense of *equip.* Sometimes lengthened to *kit up.*

kitchen garden   **family fruit and vegetable garden**

kitchen towel   **paper towel**

kith and kin   **friends and relations**
One's own people.

knacker, *n.*   SEE COMMENT
One who purchases animal carcasses and slaughters superannuated livestock
for rendering into various products. The plant in which this is done is called a
knackery or *knacker's yard.*

knackered, *adj.*   *Slang.* **tuckered out**
Slang A grim image, derived from the previous entry.

knave, *n.*   **jack**
In playing cards. *Jack* is another name for this card in Britain.

knees-up, *n.*   *Inf.* **a party with dancing**

knickers, *n. pl.*   *Inf.* **panties**
Inf. In America *knickers* would be understood as short for *knickerbockers,* which is
the British term for *plus fours,* an article of wearing apparel still seen there. See
also **camiknickers.** To *get your knickers in a twist* is to *get all het up* about something or to *make a muddle* of things.

knife-and-fork tea   *Approx.* **light supper**
Inf. A **high tea** at which meat or fish is served and a knife is required. See also
high tea; cream tea.

Knight. See **K.**

knighthood, *n.*   **the rank of knight**

knob, *n., Slang.*   *Slang.* **scab (strikebreaker)**
Scab is now more common.

knob, *n.*   **lump**
Of butter, sugar, etc.

knobble. See **nobble.**

knobs. See **with knobs on!**

knock, *n.*   *Slang.* **hit (success)**
Slang. Synonymous with the British sense of **bomb.** But see **bit of a knock.**

knock, *v.i.*   *Slang.* **wow (impress)**
Slang. To *knock* someone in American slang is to *disparage* him, but in British slang
it means to *impress* him greatly, i.e., *to knock him dead,* and is probably short for
knock for six (see **six**).

knock acock   *Inf.* **bowl over**
Inf. To *astonish,* to present with the unexpected.

knocked off, *adj.*   *Inf.* **confused, dazed**
She's been a bit knocked off since her stroke.

knocker. See **up to the knocker.**

knocker, *n.*   **door to door salesman**
Slang. To *work on the knocker* is to *work from door to door.* Synonymous with **doorstep salesman.**

knocker-up, *n.*   **1. arouser**
                                                                  2. SEE COMMENT
1. *Inf.* A person whose job is to summon sleeping railroad workers or miners to
their jobs.
2. *Inf.* The term is used also in political circles, to describe a party worker charged
with the function of getting out the vote.

knock for six. See **six.**

knocking-house, *n., Slang.*   **whorehouse**

knocking shop, *n.*   *Slang.* **brothel**

knock on   *Inf.* **turn up**
Inf. To *knock on* for work is to *turn up for work;* generally applied to **casual labour-
ers;** an echo of the more common *knock off* (work), used in both countries.

knock-on effect   **side effect**
The concomitant result, incidental consequence.

knock oneself up   **knock oneself out**
To *overdo it.*

knock-out, *n.*   **1. warm-up**
                                                                  2. elimination contest
1. A tennis term, synonymous with **knock-up.**
2. A competition involving the elimination of losers, on the way to the finals.

knock up   **1. wake up by knocking**
                                                                  2. exhaust; wear out
                                                                  3. *Inf.* **throw together**
                                                                  4. earn

1. *Inf.* A respectable American male will go to great pains to avoid *knocking up* a lady friend, as he understands the term, because in his country it is an indelicate expression for getting a lady into a delicate condition. In Britain, *knocking* people *up* means waking them up by knocking on their door.
2. *Inf.* Another common British usage to be avoided in America: *I'm quite knocked up*, or *He does knock me up*. This refers merely to exhaustion, physical or emotional.
3. *Inf.* An unrelated British meaning is 'throw together,' as in, *Don't stand on ceremony, come along, we can always knock something up*, referring to the preparation of an impromptu meal. This usage was originally American, but is now exclusively British.
4. *Inf. Rare.* As in, *He knocks up twenty thousand* **quid** *a year*, **I'll be bound.**

knock-up, *n.*   **warm-up**
Tennis term, synonymous with **knock-out, 1.**

know the form, *Inf.*   *Inf.* **have the inside dope**

knuckle duster   **brass knuckles**

K.O.   **kickoff**
Inf. A British football abbreviation. Thus, on a poster advertising a football game, "*K.O.* 3:00 P.M." It also means 'knockout,' a boxing term, as in America.

L

label, *n.*   sticker; tag

labourer. See **agricultural labourer; casual labourer.**

labour exchange   *approx.* **state employment office**
In this meaning, the words are often capitalized: *Labour Exchange.* In lower case, the term can denote any union building which houses its headquarters, meeting rooms, etc.

lacquer, *n.*   **hair spray**

lad   SEE COMMENT
Americans are familiar with this word in the sense of 'boy' or 'youth,' but do not use it commonly as the British do. Examples: 'He's a good lad' (about a dependable, or a generous, or an honest *man*). 'Good lad!' (said to a mature man who has come through with a good deed or a nice gesture). 'Get your lads out' (spoken in a TV drama by a police captain to a subordinate as instructions to get his men out on the street to hunt for the villain). Americans might use *boy* in some of these cases. *The lads* is the term in which British labor leaders refer to their members, rather than 'the men' or 'the members.' Used that way, the term suggests loyalty, solidarity, and affection. The word may also have a connotation of mild moral disapproval, especially in the sentence 'He's a bit of a lad.' See also **Jack the lad.**

ladder, *n.*   **run**
This term applies to ladies' stockings and pantyhose **(tights).** *Ladder-proof* hose, etc., are advertised in Britain just as *run-proof* articles are advertised in America, but the ladies remain skeptical on both sides of the Atlantic.

Lady, *n.* **(in titles)**   SEE COMMENT
The daughter of a duke, marquess, or earl (in which case *Lady* is used with the forename, e.g., *Lady Jane Smith*); *or* the wife of a *peer* (except a duke), a *baronet,* or *knight* (in which case *Lady,* without the forename, is followed by the name of the peerage or surname as the case may be, e.g., *Lady Bloomsbury, Lady Smith*). (Coincidentally, Lady Bloomsbury may also be a peeress in her own right.) If Lady Jane Smith marries Mr. Bloggs, she becomes *Lady Jane Bloggs.* See also **Lord; Dame; K.; baronet; peer.**

ladybird, *n.*   **ladybug**
Also called a *golden-knop.*

Lady Day   SEE COMMENT
March 25, so called because that is the day of the Feast of the Annunciation. See **quarter-day.**

ladyfy (ladify), *v.t.*   SEE COMMENT
To *ladyfy* or *ladify* a woman is to make a lady of her, though it can mean merely to lend dignity to a woman by calling her a lady. *Ladified* describes a woman exhibiting the airs of a refined lady.

Lady of Threadneedle Street. See Old Lady of Threadneedle Street.

lag, *n., v.t.*   **1.** *Slang.* **jailbird**
                                                          2. *Slang.* **send up; pinch**
Slang. A *lag* is a *jailbird* and the word is usually found in the expression *old lag.* To be *lagged* is to be *sent up,* although *lagged* sometimes means merely 'pinched,' 'arrested,' whether or not the unfortunate is eventually *sent up.* A *lagging* is a *stretch.* There exists an organization called the *Old Lags Brigade,* which consists of hardened criminals placed on last-chance probation before they are imprisoned.

lager lout, *n.*   *Inf.* SEE COMMENT
A person (usually male) who gets drunk and behaves in a rowdy, abusive, and sometimes violent manner in public. The intoxicating beverage could, of course, be anything; lager is specified because that was the drink supposedly favored by the young men whose behavior gave rise to the expression in the 1980s. Their fathers would have drunk **ale,** and would not (so it is thought) have behaved like hooligans.

laid on. See lay on.

lambs' tails   **catkins**
Inf. Lambs' tails in Britain, in addition to making good soup, also refer to *catkins* hanging from certain trees such as the hazel and willow, and *catkins* in both countries are *downy flowerings* or *inflorescences.* The word *catkin* is a rather cloying diminutive of *cat* (formed like *manikin, pannikin,* etc.) and was invented because of the resemblance of those inflorescences to cats' tails.

lame duck   **1.** *Slang.* **hard-luck guy**
                                                          2. stock exchange defaulter
1. *Slang.* A *person in difficulties, unable to cope.* The narrow American usage, describing an incumbent political official or body still in office after losing an election but only because the winner has not yet been seated, is a highly restricted application of this British meaning. This narrow American usage, however, appears to have been adopted by some British political pundits. The term can also be applied to a firm in financial difficulties, or a troubled industry.
2. *Slang.* This term also describes a person unable to meet his obligations on the London Stock Exchange. Also a *lossmaking company.*

Lancashire hotpot, *n.*   SEE COMMENT
A traditional stew of meat, potatoes, and onions.

land agent   **real estate broker**
Synonymous with **estate agent.**

landed, *adj.*   **1.** *Inf.* **O.K.; in good shape**
                                                          2. *Inf.* **out of luck; lost**
                                                          3. SEE COMMENT
Depending on the context, this participial adjective can have two exactly opposite meanings, even if used in identical sentences.

1. *Inf.* If one were waiting for the last available table in a restaurant which was being held until 8 o'clock for someone else, one could say, *If he doesn't show up by eight, we're landed,* meaning *we're okay.*
2. *Inf.* If one's friend who had the tickets to a show or match were alarmingly late, the same sentence could be expressed, and . . . *we're landed* would mean 'we're out of luck'; 'we've had it.'
3. *Landed gentry* describes those of the **gentry** who own land.

landlord, *n.*   **innkeeper; pub keeper**
In addition to its wider general meaning in both countries, *landlord* has the special British meaning and flavor of 'inn-keeper.' Many **pubs** were once real *inns* and a few still have rooms for rent, but even at those that no longer let rooms, the keeper is still called *landlord* and is so addressed by clients not familiars of the establishment who don't feel privileged to address him by name. **Publican** is synonymous with *landlord* in this sense and comes from *public house,* a term still in use but far less common than *pub.* See **free house** for a discussion of the landlord's business arrangements. See also **pub; during hours.**

Land of the Leal   **heaven**
Leal is a Scots form of *loyal.*

Land's End   SEE COMMENT
The southwesternmost area of Cornwall. See also **John O' Groats.**

landslip, *n.*   **landslide**

land (someone) with   **saddle (someone) with**
Often used in the passive form, *landed with.* Synonymous with **lumbered with,** though the latter invokes an added dimension of inconvenience.

larder, *n.*   **pantry**

lardy cake, *n.*   SEE COMMENT
A sweet flat cake made of bread dough, sugar, lard, and dry fruit.

large, *adj.*   **double**
As used in ordering a drink at the pub or restaurant. A *large* whiskey (*whisky* in Britain for Scotch; Irish *whiskey* has the *e*), gin, vodka, etc. is a *double* portion. See under **double, 3.**

lark, *n.*   **job; type of activity**
Inf. "It's too hot for this *lark*," says a sweating laborer doffing his jacket, using *lark,* specifically a *sport,* as a sardonic synonym for *job* or *task*—the same type of British humor as found in "Are you happy in your work?" addressed to one who is palpably miserable as he plugs away at an unwanted task.

lasher, *n.*   **pool**
Particularly, one formed by water spilling over a **weir.**

lashings, *n. pl., Slang.*   *Slang.* **scads**

lash out, *v.i.*   *Inf.* **throw money around**
Slang. To *lash out* on something is to spend money on it recklessly and without stint.

lash-up, *n. Slang.*   **1. fiasco**
                                                        2. improvisation

last orders   SEE COMMENT
The last orders for drinks allowed before closing time in a pub. *Last orders, please!*

last post   **taps**
Virtually the same as *taps*—not the tune, but the function. There are two British
posts, called *first post* and *last post.* The first one comes about ten minutes before
the other, as a sort of ready signal.

laugh like a drain, *Slang.*   *Slang.* **horselaugh**

lavatory paper   **toilet paper**
Delicacy, like the American use of *tissue.*

lawk(s)!   *Inf.* **lordy!**
Vulgar. Used jocularly by the upper classes. *Lawks-a-mussy* is the fuller expression.

Law Lords, *n. pl.*   SEE COMMENT
Members of the **House of Lords** who sit in the highest court of appeal. Roughly
equivalent to the U.S. Supreme Court, though rulings by the Law Lords are subject to review by the European Court of Justice.

Law Society   *approx.* **Bar Association**
There is a national *Law Society* and there are also many local ones in Britain just as
there are a nationwide *Bar Association* and many local ones in America. In certain
matters such as the setting of ethical standards of conduct, the furtherance of
legal education, and so on, the functions of the British and American bodies coin-
cide. Membership in *law societies* is confined to **solicitors** only. **Barristers** have
their own group, which is known as the General Council of the Bar.

lay, *v.t.*   **1. set**
                                                                   2. impose
1. The table.
2. A tax, as in a tax laid on wealth by certain governments.

layabout, *n.*   **loafer; hobo**

lay-by, *n.*   **driver's rest area**
Roadside parking space. When you see a road sign reading LAY-BY as you drive
along in Britain, you know that up ahead on your left, there will be a turn-out
which broadens into a parking area. People use it for short-term parking, e.g., to
take a nap, to look at the view, or as a picnic area.

lay (someone) by the heels   **track (someone) down**

lay on   **provide; arrange for**
Very commonly seen in the participial form *laid on* meaning 'provided for in advance.' Thus, office quarters can be rented in Britain with or without a secretary *laid on.*

lay on the table. See **table.**

lay (oneself) out to   **put (oneself) out to**

laystall, *n.*   **rubbish heap**

lea. See **ley.**

leader, *n.*   **1. newspaper editorial**
                                                              2. chief counsel
                                                              3. concert master
This word has three distinct British meanings that are not found in America:
1. It means 'newspaper editorial,' especially the principal one. There is a related (and rather unattractive) word *leaderette,* which has nothing to do with female leaders but means a 'short editorial paragraph' following the main one. The expression *fourth leader* is a British inside joke, originated by *The Times* (London). It denotes a humorous discursive essay.
2. Another meaning is 'leading counsel,' the senior barrister on a team of lawyers trying a case.
3. Finally, it means the 'concert master' of an orchestra, i.e., the first violinist who sits to the conductor's left and is his right-hand man, acting as his liaison with the rest of the players.

Leader of the House, *n.*   SEE COMMENT
A member of the government who is mainly responsible for the arrangement of government business in the Commons.

Leader of the Opposition   SEE COMMENT
The leader of the main party not in power, and the counterpart to the prime minister in the **Shadow Cabinet.**

lead for the Crown   **act as chief prosecuting attorney**
See also **leader, 2.**

league table   **teams' performance records**
Originally applied to tables ranking the records of teams or clubs constituting an athletic league, it has been extended to refer to tabulated comparisons of performances in any field of endeavor.

lean, *adj.*   *Inf.* **drunk**

leasehold. See **freehold.**

leat, *n.*   **open watercourse**
Enabling a mill etc. to operate.

leather, *n.*   **chamois**
For wiping or polishing automobiles etc.

leave, *v.t.*   **graduate from**
In the expression *leave school,* which in America connotes dropping out, but in
Britain means simply that the student is graduating. See also **leaver; school-
leaver.**

leave alone   **not deal with**
In the sense of 'leave undisturbed.' *Leave me alone!* for *Let me alone!* formerly was
nonstandard in America; not so in Britain.

leave in the lurch   **abandon, desert**
Inf. As in *He went off to America, leaving his family in the lurch.* See **shoot the moon.**

leaver, *n.*   *Inf.* **short-timer**
In America, such a person is known as a graduating senior. One about to complete the curriculum at a **prep school** or **public school** at the end of that term is
known as a *leaver.* On the completion of the term the *leaver* becomes an **old boy** or
old girl. See **school-leaver; leave.**

leave well alone   **leave well enough alone**

leaving gift   **retirement present**

lecturer, *n.*   **instructor**
In a British university. See also **reader.**

left-arm, *adj.*   **left-handed**
To describe a left-handed **bowler** (*approx.* cricket counterpart of a pitcher); but a
left-handed **batsman** (*batter*) is called *left-hand.*

left luggage office   **checkroom**

lefty, *n.*   *Slang.* **leftist**
Inf. The American usage meaning 'left-handed person' is often heard in Britain.

legal aid   SEE COMMENT
In Britain, *legal aid* is supplied from Government funds made available to liti-
gants who otherwise could not afford to pay for legal services. In America, there
are Legal Aid Societies supported by private contributions.

legal figment   **legal fiction**
A proposition accepted as fact for the sake of argument or convenience, though
without foundation in fact. *Legal fiction* is used in Britain also.

leg it   *Slang.* **beat it**
Walk hard, run hard.

legitimate drama   **stage plays**
This phrase means very different things in the two countries. In Britain it refers to
dramatic works of established merit as opposed to melodrama or farce, no matter
how well known, e.g., *Hamlet* vs. *East Lynne,* or *The Rivals* vs. *Charley's Aunt.* In
America the *legitimate theater* means the 'stage' as opposed to any other form of dramatic representation, and *legitimate drama* includes any play produced on the stage.

leg-pull, *n.*   **hoax**
Inf. Joking attempt to deceive someone.

lemon curd   **lemon cheese**

lengthman, lengthsman, *n.*   **road maintenance man**
A *lengthman* is a laborer charged with the duty of keeping a certain *length* of road
in good condition. The word developed in the old days before the creation of a
countrywide system of hard-surfaced roads requiring the services of teams of
road workers equipped with all kinds of heavy machinery. It evokes the image of
the solitary worker equipped with only a spade, a high degree of independence,
and a noble sense of responsibility.

let. See **engage.**

let alone   **not to mention**
She does not have a time of her own, *let alone* an independent income.

let-out, *n.*   *Inf.* **loophole**
Inf. Often used attributively, as in the phrase *let-out clause* meaning 'escape
clause.'

letter-box   **mailbox**
See also **pillar-box; post-box.**

letter post   **first-class mail**
The terms *first-class mail* and *second-class mail* are now current in Britain to indicate priorities for delivery.

let the shooting. See under **shoot.**

let the side down. See under, *v.t.* **side.**

levant, *v.i.*   **skip town**
Slang. Commonly after welshing, or welching, on a gambling loss.

level, *adj.*   **1. even**
                                                        2. close
1. When players are *level* in a game, it means that they are *even* in winnings.
2. However, a *level* race is not a *tie* but only a *close* race.

level crossing   **grade crossing**
Of a railway and road.

level par   **par**
Golf term used by sports announcers to mean 'par,' in describing the performances of tournament contestants.

level pegging   **even Stephen**
A term borrowed from cribbage, in which the score is kept by advancing *pegs*
along a series of holes in a board. It applies to equal scores in games or mutual
obligations between friends or businessmen which wash each other out.

levels (A-levels; O-levels). See **A-levels.**

ley, *n.*   **temporary pasture**
(Pronounced LAY.) *Ley-farming* is the system of putting a given area into grazing
pasture for a few years, then *catching the fertility,* as they say, and using that area
for a particular crop. A *ley* is a *rotating pasture;* variant of *lea.*

Liberal Democratic Party   SEE COMMENT
A political party formed in 1988 when the Liberals merged with the short-lived
Social Democratic Party. Usually shortened to Lib Dem.

Liberal Jew   **Reform Jew**
In America, the three branches of Judaism are Orthodox, Conservative, and
Reform; in Britain, Orthodox, Reform and Liberal.

Lib-Lab, *adj.*   SEE COMMENT
Inf. Anything involving both Liberal and Labour party supporters. Originally
it applied to members of the Liberal party in the beginning of the century who
supported the new Labour party. *Lib-Labbery* was coined to describe an alliance
between the two parties and is now usually used to denote shady political dealings.

licenced, *adj.*   **having a liquor license**
Sign seen on most British hotels and restaurants. See also **off licence.**

lich- (lych-) gate, *n.*   SEE COMMENT
A roofed churchyard gate, under which the coffin is placed while awaiting the
arrival of the officiating minister. Also called *resurrection gate. Lich* is an obsolete
English word for 'body.'

lick and a promise   *Inf.* **quick job**
Inf. Term meaning a *light wash,* useful in describing a boy's morning wash.

lido, *n.*   **public open-air swimming pool**
The *Lido* is Venice's famous bathing resort. A *lido,* in Britain, is a public swimming
pool. One sees the term **corporation** *swimming-bath,* meaning 'public swimming-bath.' *Corporation* in that phrase is the equivalent of the American term
municipal. Pronounced LIE'-DOUGH.

lie doggo   *Inf.* **lie low**
Slang. Literally, to *lie doggo* is to *lie motionless,* the way a dog does; to *play dead.*
Figuratively it means to 'bide one's time.'

lie-down, *n.*   *Inf.* **rest**
Taken horizontally, on the sofa or the bed, and more often than not resulting in
a nap.

lie down under   *Inf.* **buckle under**
Inf. To *give way* to the other party, to accept without protest.

lie in   **sleep late**
Inf. In the morning. One can *lie-in* or *have a lie-in.* Synonymous with **sleep in.**

lie up   *Inf.* **take to one's bed**
Inf. With the connotation of not feeling well.

life-belt, *n.*   **life preserver**

Life Guard   SEE COMMENT
Member of the senior of the two regiments of Household Troops–all six feet tall or
more. (The other regiment is called the *Blues and Royals*.) The household involved
is the royal household. Properly speaking, a member of this elite cavalry regiment is called a *Life Guardsman. Lifeguards* in the American sense of people who
save other people from drowning were sometimes called **humane society men,**
but the American term is more common in Britain.

life vest   **life jacket**
The British say *jacket,* too, but British Airways' pamphlets and signs remind passengers that there is a *life vest* under each seat.

lift, *n.*   **elevator**
To go higher in a building without walking, the British use *lifts,* the Americans
elevators. To stand up higher, the British put **elevators** into their shoes, the Americans *lifts.*

lighting-up time   SEE COMMENT
Time of day when lights must be lit by vehicles on the road.

lights, *n. pl.*   **sheep's lungs**
Used as food, either on their own or as an ingredient in other dishes. Suitable for
humans or dogs.

like a dog's dinner   *Inf.* **all dolled up**
Inf. To be *got up like a dog's dinner* is to be *dressed to kill.* Somewhat pejorative; not
quite synonymous with **dressed to the nines.** See also **dog's breakfast.**

like old boots, *Inf.*   *Inf.* **like a house afire**

like one o'clock   **1. promptly; quick and lively**
                                                             2. *Inf.* **to a T**
(Main stress on *one.*)
1. *Inf.* Sometimes it has the sense of 'vigorously.'
2. *Inf. Does that suit you, sir? Like one o'clock!*

limb, *n.*   *Inf.* **little devil**
Inf. Limb is a shortening of the phrase *limb of the devil* or *limb of Satan* and is used
to mean 'mischief-making youngster,' the way *little devil* is used in America. See
also **kipper; basket.**

limb of the law   **arm of the law**
Referring to lawyers, policemen, and the like.

limited company   **corporation**
Also called *limited liability company,* more usually just *company.* See **company;**
corporation.

line, *n.*   **track**
In Britain it is the railway *line* one mustn't cross, according to the signs, whereas
Americans use the word *line* to mean a whole railroad company, rather than the
track itself. Passengers in America are warned not to cross the *track.*

line of country   **one's business or occupation**
Inf. Very often in the negative, to indicate that something is beyond one's capabilities: *I'm afraid that's not my line of country.* Alternatively, *That's not up my street.* An American equivalent would be *not in my line.* Used in the affirmative, in a sentence like, *I'd take it to Jones; that's just his line of country,* the American version would be *That's just up his alley.*

liners, *n.*   **underpants**
Inf. Worn under **knickers.**

lining, *n.*   **striping**
Term used in painting, e.g., the painting of automobiles.

link, *v.t.*   **link arms with**
To hook one's arm through another's.

linked signals   **staggered lights**
Traffic lights graduated so that you always have a green light if you drive within the proper speed limit.

linkman   **1. anchorman; moderator**
                                            2. go-between
1. In radio and television.
2. Originally described a position in soccer **(football);** now extended to mean any go-between.

lino, *n.*   **linoleum**
Inf. (Pronounced LIE'-NO.) The British almost always use the informal shortening. *Linoed* means 'covered with *linoleum.'* A *linoed* floor is a *linoleum* floor.

lint, *n.*   **surgical dressing**
For the British equivalent of American *lint* see **fleck.**

lip salve   **lip balm**
Also means "flattery."

liquidizer, *n.*   **blender**

listed building   SEE COMMENT
A building recognized by law as having historical or architectural value and therefore protected from demolition or unauthorized alteration.

listening room   **control room**
Where the engineer of a television or radio station sits.

literal error   **misprint**
Typographical error, usually shortened to *literal* or called *typo* as it is in the USA.

litter bin   **trash basket**

little basket. See under **basket.**

Little Englander, *n.*   SEE COMMENT
Originally coined during the Boer War to mean someone who believed that the British Empire should not extend beyond the shores of the UK. Now it usually

means someone who is geographically inward-looking and ignorant or contemptuous of other countries. Such people are likely to be **Eurosceptics.**

little-go, *n.*   SEE COMMENT
Inf. Former term for the first examination for the B.A. degree at Cambridge or Oxford; now archaic.

little Mary, *Inf.*   **stomach**
A colloquial euphemism for the stomach.

live in cotton wool   **live a sheltered life**
Inf. **Cotton wool** is *absorbent cotton,* used here as a metaphor for careful packing to provide insulation from the traumata of life in this harsh world. See also **wrap in cotton wool.**

live like a fighting cock   **eat high off the hog**
Inf. To insist on the best of fare; a *fighting cock* always gets the best.

liverish, *adj.*   **glum, bad-tempered**

Liverpudlian, *n., adj.*   SEE COMMENT
Native or inhabitant of Liverpool, England. Of Liverpool. Their dialect is called **Scouse.**

liver sausage   **liverwurst**

livery, *n.*   **costume**
Livery is used generically in Britain and America to describe certain types of uniform, such as those worn by chauffeurs. In Britain it is now also applied to characteristic *color schemes* like those of the various divisions of the British railway system.

living, *n.*   **benefice**
Ecclesiastical term for the position of rector, vicar, etc. with income and property.

loaf, *n.*   *Slang.* **bean (head)**
Slang. Short for *loaf of bread,* cockney rhyming slang for 'head' but now adopted as general slang as in such expressions as *Use your loaf!* See **Appendix II.G.3.**

loan share; loan stock   **bond**

lobbyist, *n.*   **political journalist**
One frequenting the hall of the **House of Commons** to pick up political news. Sometimes called *lobby correspondent.* By now the term has acquired the common American meaning as well, though perhaps with a little less suggestion of impropriety.

local, *n.*   **1. neighborhood bar**
                                                         2. native
1. *Inf.* Britons often talk of nipping down to the *local (local pub).*
2. *Inf.* Usually heard in the plural, the *locals* is an affectionate term meaning the *natives,* the people in a particular community who look as though they haven't

just moved out from the city, have been around a while, really belong there, and are going to be around for some time to come. Compare **tripper.**

loch; lough, *n.*   **1. lake**
                                                                         2. sea inlet
1. In Scotland. Americans usually pronounce it LOK. The Scots pronounce *loch* like the Germans. *Lough* is the Irish form of *loch,* pronounced the Scottish way. 2. *Loch* can also mean 'narrow inlet,' known then correctly as *sea loch.* See also **lough.**

locum, *n,*   **doctor covering for another**
Inf. The term is also applied to a clergyman's temporary replacement. *Locum* is an informal shortening of *locum tenens.* A literal translation of *locum tenens* would be 'one holding a place,' and by inference, a 'person taking somebody else's place,' i.e., a 'replacement.'

lodger. See under **boarder.**

loft, *n.*   **attic**

lofty catch   *approx.* **pop fly**
A cricket term.

loiter with intent   SEE COMMENT
Short for *loiter with intent to commit a crime;* more specific than *vagrancy.*

lollipop man (woman; lady)   *approx.* **children's traffic guide**
Inf. Employed to assist children across the street. The *lollipop* label is derived from the form of the stick carried, which is surmounted by a disk reading: STOP. CHILDREN CROSSING.

lolly, *n.*   **dough (money)**
A piece of the lolly, the lollipop, has its American slang equivalent in *some of the gravy.* See also **brass; dibs.** A *lolly* in Britain (reminiscent of *lollipop*) is also ice cream or water ice on a stick.

Lombard Street   *approx.* **Wall Street; money market**
Inf. London's money market, named after its function as principal street for banking and finance; analogous to *Wall Street* when used that way. But *the* **City** is the more usual expression for the financial community generally. *It's all Lombard Street to a China orange* means *the odds are a hundred to one* (or *a thousand to one*). Variations are: *all Lombard Street to a Brummagem sixpence* (see **Brum**): . . . *to ninepence,* . . . *to an egg-shell.*

long, *adj.*   *Slang.* **boring; tedious**
Largely an adolescent usage.

long chalk. See **not by a long chalk.**

long firm, *Inf.*   *Inf.* **set of deadbeats**

long-head, *n,*   *Slang.* **shrewd cookie**
Inf. The adjective is *long-headed.*

long odds on   **heavy favorite**
This is a sports term, used as a phrasal noun.

long pull   **extra measure**
Inf. In a **pub,** the *long pull* is a measure of beer or other liquid refreshment over and above the quantity asked for; in other words, a drink with a built-in dividend. Sometimes the *long* is omitted, so that a *pull* means the same thing as a *long pull.*

long sea outfall   **remote sewage disposal pipe**
This awkward phrase describes a sewage pipe that sticks way out into the ocean in order to dispose of the effluent of a seaside town without (supposedly) polluting the beaches.

long-sighted, *adj.*   **farsighted**
In Britain *far-sighted* is hardly ever used literally to describe corporeal optical capacity. It is almost always used in the figurative sense of *looking ahead,* a figurative use shared with America. The British term for *nearsighted* is *short-sighted,* which is always used figuratively in America to describe a person who doesn't plan ahead, and this figurative use, too, is shared with Britain. In other words, the British use *long-sighted* and *short-sighted* literally where the Americans would say *farsighted* and *nearsighted.* The British use *far-sighted* figuratively, as the Americans do; and the Americans use *shortsighted* figuratively, as the British do.

long-stay, *adj.*   **long-term**
Applied, e.g., to hospital patients.

long stop   **1.** SEE COMMENT
                                        2. backstop; reinforcement
1. In **cricket,** the fielder back of the wicket-keeper, who is there to stop the balls that get away from the wicket-keeper.
2. *Inf.* Extended to describe any person or thing that serves to prevent or check an undesirable result in case the person primarily in charge is wanting.

long vac. See under **come down; holiday.**

loo, *n, Inf.*   *Inf.* **john**
Bathroom, lavatory, washroom, rest room, convenience, boys' room, little boys' room, girls' room; little girls' room, gents', gents' room, ladies', ladies' room, privy, water-closet, W.C., powder-room—the euphemisms have proliferated like mushrooms after a shower. The word *toilet* is sometimes avoided as too euphemistic, while to most Americans it seems indelicate. In public notices in Britain, *toilet* is the usual term, perhaps because *toilet* or a recognizably similar term (*toilette, toiletta, toilet-ten*) is thus used in many foreign countries whose nationals often come to Britain. In Britain at one time the educated and literary said *lavatory* or *W.C.*; others said *loo* or *toilet.* The common American euphemism is *bathroom.*

looby, *n. Slang.*   **simpleton**
Also a lazy person.

look like . . .   **look as if . . .**
Look like, plus a gerund, is used as the equivalent of *look as if* followed by a subject and a subjunctive: *Next week looks like being crucial for the Labour Party (looks as if it*

were going to be). This practice seems nonstandard to Americans, but is acceptable in British informal speech.

look out   1. pack
                                                                       2. select
Look out has a good many British uses shared with America, but there are two not so shared:
1. While watching you pack for a trip, your British friend might say, "*Look out* your **woollies;** it's cold where you're going." *Look out,* in that sense means 'pack,' and your friend is advising you to *take along* a few sweaters. Better follow the advice.
2. One can also *look out* facts in reference works while engaged in a research project. Here, *looking out* means 'looking up,' and then 'selecting' the data you find for use as authority to prove whatever it is you're trying to prove.

look-out, *n.*   outlook
Inf. Prospect, as in stock market forecasting: *The look-out for that group of companies is bleak.* It also has the connotation of *lot* or *fate* when it refers to something then future, now past: *To die at 18—that had been a poor look-out,* i.e., *a sad fate. Look-out* has the ordinary American informal meaning as well ('responsibility,' 'concern'), as in: *Keeping petrol in the car is your look-out.* Conversely, the standard American meaning of *lookout* (no hyphen), a *point* from which one gets a wide view of the landscape, is often **viewpoint** in Britain, which of course may refer to things abstract rather than concrete in America.

look-out window   picture window

look round   look
As a noun phrase: a *good look,* an *inspection.* See also **recce; shufty.**

look slippy! *Slang.*   be quick

look smart! *Slang.*   get a move on

loopy, *adj., Slang.*   *Slang.* **loony**

loose-box, *n.*   horse stall

loose chippings   loose gravel

loose covers   slipcovers

loose waterproof   slicker

Lord, *n.* **(in titles)**   SEE COMMENT
A marquess, earl, viscount, or baron (i.e., any peer except a duke) is referred to socially not by these full titles but as *Lord So-and-so* (without forename); his wife is *Lady So-and-so* (see **Lady**). The eldest son of a duke, marquess, or earl takes a spare title of his father's (known as a *courtesy title*) and is therefore *Lord Somebody-or-other.* Other sons of dukes and marquesses have names of the form *Lord John Smith,* and their sisters are *Lady Jane Smith* and so on. The other children of earls, and all the children of viscounts and barons, are merely *Honourable,* which means

that in conversation they are plain *Mr* or *Miss;* but in addressing an envelope to them one should write "The Hon. John Smith," and "The Hon. Mrs John Smith" to their wives. In addition to members of the peerage, the title *Lord* also belongs to certain dignitaries such as the Lord Chancellor, the Lord Chief Justice, etc., and judges in court are addressed as *My Lord,* pronounced M'LUD or M'LORD. A Lord's signature consists of his title without a forename, e.g., Lord Smith will sign simply "Smith." Bishops are *Lords Spiritual.* For their signatures see **Cantuarian.**

A **commoner** raised to the peerage may take a title different from his surname. Thus Benjamin Disraeli became the earl of Beaconsfield (Lord Beaconsfield). Nowadays, however, it is increasingly the practice to keep the surname (to avoid the risk of one's identity being eclipsed). Thus Mr or Sir R. Grey may become Lord Grey. The Labour statesman Mr George Brown elected to become Lord George-Brown, and the ex-diplomat Sir Gladwyn Jebb became Lord Gladwyn (thus, intentionally or not, putting back to square one anybody who was in the habit of addressing him by his first name). See also **House of Lords.**

Lord Chamberlain   SEE COMMENT
Head of management of the Royal Household; formerly the authority who granted play licenses, a censorship office now happily abolished.

Lord Chancellor, *n.*   SEE COMMENT
The government cabinet minister who is head of the judiciary.

lords and ladies   jack-in-the-pulpit
The name of a wild plant, also called *cuckoo pint.*

lorry, *n.*   truck.
To *lorry-hop* or *lorry-jump* is to *hitchhike.* An **articulated lorry** is a *trailer truck.* See also **bender; juggernaut.**

lost property office   lost and found
Also, **baggage service.**

lot, *n.*   1. *Slang.* the works
                                                                                        2. group
                                                                                3. *Slang.* bunch
1. *Inf. The lot* means 'the whole lot,' 'the whole kit and caboodle,' 'the works.' Thus, *They gave me a beautiful room, marvellous food, wonderful service . . . the lot! The gift was all wrapped up in fancy paper, gold string, the lot. The lot* also means 'all' of something. At a sale, there are three dresses hard to choose from. You ponder and ponder and finally say (recklessly), "I'll take *the lot,*" i.e., 'all' of them.
2. *Inf.* It also has the meaning of 'group.' In an American Chinese restaurant, they are fond of arranging dishes into Group A, Group B, etc. They do it in Britain too, and there you might say, "We'll have two from the first *lot,* three from the second *lot,*" etc. From directions written by a friend: "At the first traffic lights you turn right, at the second *lot,* left."
3. *Inf. Lot* means 'group' in another sense, too, the sense in which Americans use the slang term *bunch.* Thus, if a Briton saw a group of unsavory-looking characters on a street corner, he might think, *I don't like the looks of that lot,* where an American would refer to them as *that bunch. You lot* means 'the lot of you,' i.e., 'all of you,' in addressing a group of people, and might come out in America as *Hey, you guys.*

(a) lot on one's plate. See **have enough on one's plate.**

loud hailer	**bullhorn**

lough, *n.*   **tidal stream**
Particularly in the **Fens.**

lounge, *n.*   **living room**
Also meaning 'waiting-room.'

lounge bar   SEE COMMENT
Synonymous with *saloon bar*. *Lounge bar* is sometimes used instead of *saloon bar* to indicate the fancier and more exclusive part of a **pub.** But, like so many other things in Britain, it isn't quite that simple, because some bars boast *saloon bars* as well as *lounge bars*, and even *saloon lounges*.

lounge suit   **business suit**

love, *n.*   *approx.* **honey**
Inf. Often spelled *luv* in allusion to its Northern (North of England) origin and pronounced LOOV (-OO- as in LOOK) for the same reason. Widely used as a very informal term of address in the North of England: by men only to women, but by women without distinction as to sex, a primarily working-class vocative (when applied to strangers). The nearest American equivalent would be *honey*, which used to have a particularly Southern flavor, but by now has spread all over the country. It is also used between couples, and by parents to children.

lovely!, *interj.*   **great! fine!**
Lovely! is heard all the time in Britain and is by no means the exclusive property of the cultured. *Lovely!* covers a multitude of expletives: *fine! great! wonderful! marvelous! terrific! that's it!* and even *wow!* It can also be used in place of *thanks*.

lovely and . . .   **nice and . . .**
Where Americans would say a refreshing drink is *nice and cold*, Britons are more likely to say *lovely and cold*.

low in the water. See **in low water.**

(Her Majesty's) Loyal Opposition   **party not in power**
Loyal to the monarch; *opposed* to the party in power. Almost always shortened to *the opposition*.

(the) Loyal Toast   SEE COMMENT
As the coffee is served at a meal which is part of the proceedings at a regular meeting of an organization like a guild, Rotary Club, and that sort of thing, the chairman stands up and announces, in stentorian tones: *"The Loyal Toast!"* Thereupon all stand, raise their glasses, and say in unison: *"The Queen!"* They take a swallow and sit down, and thereafter—and only then—is smoking permitted.

L plate   *approx.* **Student Driver**
A large red *L* (standing for *learner*) on a square white plate attached to the rear of an automobile gives fair warning to all. An *L-driver* is one who has not yet passed his driving test, and is allowed to drive only with another person in the car and with the L plate as a warning to other drivers.

£ s.d.   **dough (money)**
(Pronounced ELL-ESS-DEE.) Spelled £ *s.d.* (or *L.S.D.*) it means 'pounds, shillings, pence.' These three letters are the initials of the Latin ancestors of those three words: *librae, solidi,* and *denarii.* The Roman occupation of Britain, of course, occurred a good many years ago, but the symbols remained until February 15, 1971, when Britain put its money on the decimal system (see **Appendix II.A**), shillings were abolished, and the abbreviation of *pence* changed from *d* to *p*.

lucerne (lucern), *n.*   **alfalfa**

lucky-dip, *n., Inf.*   *Inf.* **grab bag**
Enduringly popular at school fairs, village **fêtes,** and the like.

lud, *n.*   **Lord**
Old-fashioned pronunciation of *Lord* in addressing a judge; see **Lord.**

Luddites   SEE COMMENT
Workers who grouped together in the 18th century to destroy machinery that caused loss of jobs. Now used for anyone deemed to be irrationally opposed to new technology.

luge, *n.*   **toboggan**

luggage, *n.*   **baggage**
Britons *register luggage,* Americans *check baggage.* On a British train, bags go into the *luggage* **van;** on an American train, into the *baggage car.*

Luke's Little Summer   *Inf.* **Indian summer**
Inf. Other British names: *St. Luke's Summer; St. Martin's Summer.*

lumber, *n., v.t.*   **1. junk**
                                                                2. clutter
Lumber is old furniture, stuff, doodads, and general junk around the house not good enough to use or be seen by your guests, not bad enough to throw away; you never really want to see it again but you can't bear to part with it. So you put it into your **lumber-room** or **box-room,** the way Americans stuff their attics, and wish with all your heart that you had never been *lumbered* with it. The British use *lumber,* especially *lumber up,* also as a verb. To *lumber up* a room is to *clutter it up.*

lumbered with   *Inf.* **saddled with**
Slang. See **landed with.**

lumber-room, *n.*   **storage room**
See also **box-room.**

lumme! *interj.*   *Slang.* **whew!**
Slang. Corruption of *love me!*

(the) lump, *n.*   *approx.* **independent contracting**
Slang. Originally, laborers and artisans who were willing to work by the day. Now the practice of workers in various phases of the construction business who decline to be hired as employees on a wage basis and instead, subcontract on their own as independent contractors, paid by the main contractor without

deduction for income tax, health insurance, or anything else. The name of this practice derives from the giving of a *lump* sum to the group, regardless of the time involved or any other factor. The **lumper** is the middleman who handles the arrangements.

lumper, *n.*   contractor
Slang. See under **lump.**

luncheon voucher   lunch coupon
A fringe benefit granted employees by some employers. Vouchers are redeemable at certain restaurants up to a certain value. Often abbreviated to *L.V.* on the signs appearing in the windows of the establishments that honor them. Not as common now as they once were.

L.V. See **luncheon voucher.**

M

ma'am, *n.*   SEE COMMENT
This highly specialized form of contraction of *madam* is used as the proper form
of addressing the Queen and other senior **Royals,** and when it is so used it is pronounced M'M by servants and MAHM by all others. Also used in addressing other
ladies in the royal family, and as the equivalent of *sir* in the women's military
services.

mac, *n.*   raincoat
Slang. Short for *mackintosh* (sometimes *macintosh*), a waterproof material patented
in the early 19th century by Charles Macintosh, an amateur chemist. Macintosh was awarded the patent for waterproofing cloth by cementing two pieces
together with rubber dissolved in a chemical solvent, thus making it suitable for
a number of uses, including raincoats.

macadam, *n.*   blacktop
After J.C. McAdam, who late in the 18th century invented the building of roads
with layers of crushed stone. **Tarmac,** short for *tar macadam,* added tar to the
crushed stone layers. But since tar is almost universally added to the crushed
stones these days, *macadam road* is used in Britain the way Americans use *blacktop
road.* See also **metalled road.**

machinist, *n.*   machine operator
This term, used by itself in Britain, can mean any kind of machine operator, especially a sewing machine operator. The British also use the term *machine-minder*
where Americans would say *machine operator.*

mad on   *Inf.* **crazy about**
Inf. Americans also say *mad about* and the British also say *crazy about,* but only the
British say *mad on* to mean infatuated. When a Briton wants to be emphatic, he
says *mad keen on,* or sometimes *dead keen on,* or even **struck on.**

maffick, *v.i.*   exult riotously
Mafeking is a small town in Cape Province, South Africa. During the Boer War it
was besieged from October 13, 1899, to May 17, 1900, when the siege was raised.
The relief of Mafeking was cause for great rejoicing and the populace of London
and elsewhere celebrated the happy event with extravagance and exultation. The
-ing ending was mistakenly believed by the general public to indicate a gerund,
and *maffick* came to mean, to the many who had never heard of the place, 'celebrate hilariously' usually with the assistance of alcoholic stimulants.

magistrate, *n.*   *approx.* **justice of the peace**

magistrate's court   SEE COMMENT
A court that is held before two or more **justices of the peace** or a **Stipendiary
Magistrate,** and which deals with minor crimes and preliminary hearings.

216

maiden over   SEE COMMENT
In cricket there are two **bowlers.** Each bowler bowls to the opposing **batsman** six
times. This constitutes an *over.* If the batsman fails to make a single run during
the *over,* the result is called a *maiden over,* and the bowler is said to have *bowled a
maiden over.* Metaphorically *maiden over* can be used as an elegant and dramatic
way of describing any achievement of consistent skill, one in which the protagonist triumphs over the assaults of his opponent.

maiden speech   SEE COMMENT
The first speech made in Parliament by a newly elected M.P. On this occasion, it
is customary for the other M.P.s not to interrupt, and to praise the speech after-
wards. After the maiden speech the M.P. is fair game for the robust comments
that characterize parliamentary debate.

maid of honour   1. lady in waiting
                                                          2. cheesecake
1. An unmarried woman who attends a queen or princess.
2. The edible variety; a small round one.

mainland, *n.*   SEE COMMENT
This refers to the main island of Britain. Anyone living on a smaller island (e.g.
Northern Ireland, the Isle of Wight or the Isle of Skye), will talk of going to the
mainland.

mains, *n. pl.*   SEE COMMENT
The outside source of gas, electricity, or water. Thus, directions on an electric
appliance: *Disconnect mains before adjusting controls.* And if you want to replace a
faulty tap, you *switch the water off at the mains.*

maisonette, *n.*   SEE COMMENT
This term is sometimes applied to any small house or apartment, but generally
refers to a part of a house (usually on more than one floor) rented separately
from the rest of the dwelling. It is gaining some currency in the United States to
describe a luxury duplex with a separate entrance on the ground floor, embedded
in a high-rise apartment building.

maize, *n.*   corn
See discussion under **corn.**

major, *adj.*   (the) elder
Used after a surname. In a British **public school** the eldest or most senior of three
or more students then attending who have the same surname has *maximus* (the
superlative form of the Latin adjective *magnus,* meaning 'large' or 'great') placed
after his name; thus Smith *maximus,* i.e., Smith *the eldest,* to distinguish him from
the other Smiths then at the school. The youngest would be Smith *minimus* (*minimus* being the superlative form of *parvus,* Latin for 'small'). The corresponding
Latin comparatives, *major* and *minor,* are used when there are only two with the
same surname. At some public schools, *major* has been used to mean 'first to
enter,' even if an older Smith enters the school later, while the first Smith is still
attending; and at other schools *maximus* and *minimus* have been used to refer not
to age but to academic standing.

majority, *n.*   plurality
A voting term. When the British use the term *majority* in discussing an election
they mean what the Americans call a *plurality.* If they want to indicate an arithmetical majority (i.e., more than 50 percent), they use the term *clear majority.*

major road. See **arterial road.**

make, v.t.   bring
Bring a price in an auction sale. *Fetch* is used in the same way.

make a balls of   *Inf.* **mess up**
Vulgar Slang. See also **balls, 2.**

make a dead set at, *Inf.*   *Inf.* **make a play for**

make a (the) four up   **make a fourth**
For instance, at bridge or tennis doubles.

make all the running   *Slang.* **go the limit**
Slang. Refers to the degree of sexual intimacy permitted by the lady. Not to be
confused with **make the running.**

make a meal of. See **make heavy weather of**

make game of, *Inf.*   **make fun of**

make hay of   *Inf.* **overthrow**
Inf. Make short work of. Also *throw into confusion.*

make heavy weather of   SEE COMMENT
Inf. Applies to a situation where one finds something harder than anticipated. The
implication is that one finds a situation very trying, and is making it unnecessar-
ily difficult, and that one is making a big fuss over little or nothing; making a big
deal out of what should have been easy going; not getting on with a relatively
simple task, through bumbling stupidity. Also, **make a meal of.** See **hospital job.**

make off with   *Inf.* **run through (money); squander**
Inf. As in *I made off with my salary in one day.* In both countries the phrase is also
used to mean 'steal.'

make old bones   *Inf.* **live to a ripe old age**
Inf. Gloomily enough, seen almost exclusively in the negative: *He'll never make
old bones.*

make oneself scarce   **scram; skedaddle**
When someone realizes that he's in—or about to be in—trouble, he *makes himself
scarce.*

make one's number with   **contact**
Inf. The person you *make contact with* is often your opposite *number* (e.g., in another
department of the government, or perhaps someone a bit senior). The implication
is that of 'getting across' to someone whom it is important to be in touch with; to
'register,' as it were, to 'make your existence known.' When a naval ship spotted
another sail on the horizon, the Captain *made his number* to the other ship by means
of signal flags. As soon as the answering number was received, each Captain con-
sulted his Admiralty schedule to find out which ship was senior, and therefore
could take command with the right to give orders to the other.

make out a case for   **make a case for**

make the running   **take the lead**
Inf. In a competitive situation. For another kind of headway, see **make all the running.**

make up   **fill**
British **chemists** (druggists) *make up* prescriptions rather than *fill* them.

-making   SEE COMMENT
Hyphenated with such words as *shy-, shame-, sick-,* to create a series of mildly precious, jocularly expressive adjectives. See also the adjective *off-putting,* under **put (someone) off.** This construction is said to have been the invention of Evelyn Waugh.

malicious wounding   **crimes of violence**
Term from criminal law.

Malteser, *n.*   **a popular chocolate candy**
In informal usage, especially in London, also a slang term for the people of Malta. The candy itself resembles a Milk Dud.

man, *n.*   **valet**
As obsolescent as the institution itself. If a woman today speaks of *my man* she presumably means 'the man I am living with.' Of course, there is also the patronizing *my good man.*

manager, *n.*   **producer**
In speaking of the theater, *manager* is the equivalent of *producer* in America. See also **producer.**

managing director   *approx.* **executive vice president**
In a British company, the offices of **chairman** and *managing director* can be combined in one person. This is not common and the division of functions and authority, as between these two offices, will vary from company to company, as it does between *chairman of the board* and *president* in American corporations. Roughly speaking, the *chairman* makes policy, while the *managing director* runs the show day by day. See also **chairman.**

Manchester, *n.*   **dry goods**
Short for *Manchester goods,* denoting cotton textile wares such as draperies, curtain materials, bedspreads, and the like. Signs reading simply MANCHESTER used to appear in some department stores. See also **draper's shop.**

Mancunian, *n., adj.*   SEE COMMENT
Meaning a native or resident of Manchester. Also of Manchester. The Romans called the place *Mancunium.*

mange tout, *n.*   **snow pea**

manhandle, *v.t.*   **handle**
The British use this the way it is used in America to mean 'handle roughly,' 'deal roughly with,' but it has also the more literal meaning in Britain shown above.

manifesto. See **party manifesto.**

manky, *adj.*   **rotten**
Slang. A strong term for *quite inferior;* also spelled *mankey* and *mankie.*

man of Kent. See under **Kentish man.**

man of the match   *approx.* **most valuable player**
The title is conferred upon the player chosen by an outside authority, usually
a veteran player himself, as the best achiever in a particular match. This is the
common procedure in cricket matches of special significance. Imitated in modern
World Series. See **match.**

manor, *n.*   *Inf.* **beat, turf**
Inf. In the sense of 'domain, bailiwick.' As a police usage, it is synonymous with
patch used in this sense. It is also used by criminals to describe the 'official' terri-
tory of one gang or another.

mantelshelf, *n.*   **mantelpiece**
The terms are used interchangeably in Britain, though mantelpiece is now more
common.

marching papers   *Inf.* **walking papers**
Inf. Also *marching orders.*

marg(e), *n.*   **margarine**
Inf. Each country has its own way of abbreviating *oleomargarine.*

mark, *n.*   **type (sort)**
The phrase *of much this mark* means 'very much like this.' Thus a Briton might be
heard to say, *At school we slept in beds of much this mark.* This use of *mark* to mean
'type' has been extended to include 'model,' as used in the expressions Mark I,
Mark II, etc., especially in descriptions of new models of cars as brought out year
after year.

mark, *v.t.*   *Inf.* **cover**
Inf. A term used in **football.** In the British game, a player is said to stay close to,
to *mark,* an opposing player who may be receiving the ball; in the American game
that would be called *covering* the receiver. The player who marks is the *marker.*

market, *n.*   **weekly market**
Many British towns have a *weekly market day,* a particular day of the week on
which a market, usually open-air, is held for the sale of all kinds of wares,
arranged in stalls. As might be expected, these markets, which constitute normal
commerce among the natives, seem like fairs to the visitor for they crackle with
the festive air of a bazaar. Such a town is called a *market town.*

market garden   **truck farm**
A *market gardener* is a *truck farmer,* and *market garden* and *truck farm* are used in
both countries.

marking name   **street name**
The broker's name, in which securities are registered for trading convenience.
The true owner's name is posted in the broker's books and records.

Marks & Sparks   SEE COMMENT
Inf. A joke name for *Marks & Spencer,* a chain store (**multiple shop**) selling clothing, housewares, and food and drink. See also **Woollies.**

Mark Tapley   Pollyanna
One who sees only the bright side. See *Martin Chuzzlewit* by Dickens.

Marlburian, *n., adj.*   SEE COMMENT
Of Marlborough. Marlborough is the site of a famous **public school** in Wiltshire. An *old Marlburian* is a graduate of that school. Marlborough is pronounced MAWL-BRUH.

Marmite, *TM.*   SEE COMMENT
A yeast and vegetable extract used as a spread on buttered toast.

marquee, *n.*   large tent
In America *marquee* generally denotes a rigid canopy projecting over the entrance to a theater or other public hall, and the word evokes the image of large illuminated letters spelling out the names of stage and movie stars, double features, and smash hits. This significance is never attributed to the word in Britain, where it means a 'large tent' of the sort used on fair grounds and brings to mind Britain's agricultural fairs (see **agricultural show**), village **fêtes,** large private parties, and the Henley Regatta.

marriage lines   marriage certificate
The American term is now common in Britain.

marrow, *n.*   *approx.* **squash**
A kind of oversized *zucchini.* When the British say *squash,* unless they are using it as a sports term, they mean a 'soft drink,' usually lemon squash or orange squash (see **squash**).

martini, *n.*   vermouth
If you ask for a *martini* in a British pub, you will probably get a glass of *vermouth.* Whether it is dry or sweet will depend upon chance, but in either event it will be warm. If you ask for a *dry martini,* you will get a glass of *dry vermouth.* If you want a *dry martini* in the American sense, better ask for a *gin and French,* specify extremely little French, and that it be served very cold, by stirring the mixture over ice cubes (formerly, **blocks of ice**), but further specify that the ice be removed (unless you want it on the rocks); and furthermore, if it would grieve you terribly not to find an olive or a piece of lemon rind in it, you had better remain in America. A **gin and it**—*it* being an abbreviation of *Italian vermouth*—is still occasionally ordered, but not by Americans.

mash, *n.*   mashed potatoes
Inf. Occasionally, *creamed potatoes* in Britain. A pub used to present *sausages and mash* in the **public bar** at three shillings and *sausages and creamed potatoes* in the **saloon bar** at four shillings, sixpence. Same dish.

masses of, *Inf.*   *Inf.* **tons of**

master *or* mistress, *n.*   teacher
Below university level. For the meaning of *Master* at the university level, see **Fellow.** A *form-master* has about the same functions as a *home-room teacher.* In all these uses, *teacher* is gaining in popularity.

match, *n.*   **game**
Two **sides** (teams) play a *match,* rather than a *game,* in Britain.

match, test. See **Test Match.**

matchcard, *n.*   **scorecard**

mate, *n.*   *Inf.* **buddy**
Inf. Matey or *maty* is a slang adjective for *chummy.* A *penmate* is a *pen pal.*

mater, *n.*   **mother**
Slang. Old-fashioned upper-class slang. Pronounced to rhyme with *later.*

maths, *n.*   **math**

matinee coat   **baby coat**
Also found as *matinee jacket.*

matron. See under **sister.**

maximus. See under **major.**

may, *n.*   **hawthorn**

Mayfair, *n.*   SEE COMMENT
Used attributively, rather in the same way as *Park Avenue* in America, to describe
mannerisms, as in, *Her accent's terribly Mayfair.* Mayfair, lying directly east of
Hyde Park, is one of London's most expensive areas and synonymous with great
wealth.

May Week   SEE COMMENT
May Week is a Cambridge University function that lasts several days longer than
a week and is celebrated in June. It is a festive period after finals are over, the
principal festivities being a series of balls and *bumping-races. Bumping-races* are
boat races among eights representing the various colleges (see **college**) in which
a boat that catches up with and touches another (called *bumping*) scores a win. A
bump-supper is held to celebrate four wins.

maze, *v.t.*   **bewilder**

MB, *abbrev.*   **Bachelor of Medicine**
In Britain, the degree needed to practice medicine is a bachelor's degree, and may
be taken either as one's only university (college) degree or after taking a bachelor's degree in another subject. An MD is a post-graduate degree taken only by a
small percentage of physicians.

M.B.E. See under **Birthday Honours.**

M.C. See **V.C.**

M.D.   **retarded**
Inf. Stands for *mentally deficient.*

mean, *adj.*   **stingy; petty**
In America *mean* is most commonly understood as 'cruel' and 'ill-tempered.'
In Britain it means 'stingy' or 'petty,' 'ignoble.' *Mean* has an additional slang
use in America, especially in jazz circles and among the youth: *He blows a mean
horn.* Here, *mean* has the implication of *punishing:* something that makes a deep
impression, that you won't soon forget—something that almost hurts. Curiously,
the British, to express the same reaction, would say, *He blows no mean horn,* introducing a negative, and here *mean* probably signifies 'average' or 'mediocre,' its
original meaning.

means test   SEE COMMENT
A test establishing the financial means of disabled or unemployed people in
order to determine their eligibility for welfare or housing benefits. *Means-test* is
used as a transitive verb meaning to 'apply a means test' to someone, and *means-
tested* as an adjective describing a benefit thus determined.

meant to   **supposed to**
A Briton asks, for instance, *Are we meant to throw rubbish in that* **bin?** Or he might
say, *The Russians are meant to be good chess players,* i.e., *reputed* to be.

mear. See **mere.**

meat and drink   *Inf.* **just what the doctor ordered**
Inf. Or *made to order,* i.e., just the opportunity one was waiting for, particularly in
a competitive situation like sports, a court trial, an election, etc.; a source of great
pleasure to the protagonist, when the adversary plays into his hands, and he can
pounce.

meat-safe   **food cupboard**
Built of wire mesh and fast becoming obsolete, giving way to the refrigerator.
Although it is called a *meat-safe,* it can be used to preserve any food.

mediatize, *v.t.*   **annex**
This historical term means to 'annex a smaller country, usually a principality, to a
larger one.' The former ruler retains his title and may be permitted to keep some
governing rights. Hence, the expression *mediatized prince.*

medic, *n.*   *Inf.* **a doctor or a nurse**

Medium wave (radio)   **AM radio**

megger, *n.*   SEE COMMENT
Device for the measurement of insulation resistance; from *megohm,* meaning
'1,000,000 ohms.'

Melton Mowbray pie. See **pork pie.**

Member, *n.*   SEE COMMENT
The British opposite number of a *congressman* is a *Member of Parliament,* colloquially abbreviated to *M.P.* and commonly shortened to *Member.* The area represented by *M.P.* is known as a **constituency.**

memorandum and articles of association   **corporate charter**

mend, *v.t.* **repair**
You may hear Britons talking about having their shoes, flat tires (**punctures**), and chairs *mended,* but their cars, plumbing, and television sets *repaired.* The distinction appears to be on the way out. Nowadays the upper classes tend to have most things *repaired* rather than *mended,* though really old-fashioned types still tend to have many things *mended.* Thus in the villages, you often hear references to the *shoe mender, the watch mender,* and so on. One word the British rarely use as the equivalent of *mend* or *repair* is *fix,* an Americanism.

mental, *adj.* **crazy**
Inf. An American will speak of a disturbed person as a *mental case.* The British content themselves, informally, with the adjective alone.

mentioned in dispatches **cited for bravery**
A military term. To be *mentioned in dispatches* is to be honored by being mentioned by name in a military report for bravery or other commendable acts of service.

MEP, *acronym.* **Member of the European Parliament**

mercer, *n.* **textile dealer**
Usually designates an exclusive shop, dealing in expensive high-style fabrics, with the emphasis on silk.

merchant, *n.* **wholesaler**
The usual implication is that he deals principally in international trade.

merchant bank *approx.* **investment bank**
Specializing in the acceptance of bills of exchange in international commerce and investment in new issues.

mere; mear, *n.* **lake**
Or *pond;* almost never used in America. A poetic term.

metalled road **paved road**
The British speak of *unmetalled, unpaved, unmade,* and *dust roads,* all synonymous. *Road-metal* is a British term for the crushed stone that forms constitutes the layers of macadam roads (see **macadam**).

metals, *n. pl.* **rails**
When a train *leaves the metals* in Britain it has been *derailed.*

meteorological office **weather bureau**
And the much reviled official whom the Americans call the *weatherman* is the *clerk of the weather* in Britain.

meths. See **methylated spirit.**

methylated spirit **denatured alcohol**
Usually shortened to *meths,* which is also used to refer to the unhappy derelicts who drink it.

(the) Met(s) **(the) London Police**
Inf. Short for *the Metropolitan Police,* the London police force.

met office, *abbrev.*   **meteorological office**
This informal name is almost always used, even in newspaper reports and the like. See **meteorological office.**

metricate. See **metrification.**

metrification, metrication, *n.*   **adoption of metric system**
Giving rise to the verbs *metrify* and *metricate.* This change, required by Britain's entry into the European Community, caused something of an upheaval in British society. Though fiercely resisted for decades, its progress has been steady and its eventual triumph over traditional British weights and measures (see **Appendix 2C**) is inevitable.

metrify. See **metrification.**

metropolitan district   SEE COMMENT
A phrase used to express the concept of incorporation of surrounding areas into a city unit, creating a governmental subdivision larger than the old city. Americans express the same concept by the use of *Greater* as in *Greater New York, Greater Chicago,* etc., as do the British.

Michaelmas   SEE COMMENT
(Pronounced MICKLE-M's.) September 29, the feast of St. Michael.

midden, *n.*   **garbage heap**
Or *dunghill. Kitchen midden* is used in both countries to describe a heap of seafood shells or other refuse marking the site of a prehistoric settlement.

Middle England, *n.*   SEE COMMENT
A standard term for the people who supposedly represent traditional views and values, or for the views and values themselves. *Middle England would not approve.*

middle name   *approx.* Inf. **nick**
Inf. In America John Henry Smith has a *first* name, a *middle* name, and a *last* name. Sometimes in Britain he would commonly be said to have two *Christian* or *given* names or *forenames* and a *surname.* John Henry Samuel Smith would be said to have two *middle* names in America, three *Christian* or *given* names in Britain. The term *middle name* itself may also be used either jocularly or bitterly in both countries but usually in somewhat different ways. In America (rarely in Britain) a wife speaking of her husband's favorite dish (or sport) might say about him, *Apple pie* (or *hockey*) *is his middle name!* In Britain a person complaining of another's hypocritical conduct might say, *His middle name is Heep!* (after the knavish Uriah in *David Copperfield*). The corresponding expression in America would be: *He's a regular Uriah Heep!*

mike, *v.i.*   *Slang.* **goof off**
Slang. To *idle;* also expressed by *be on the mike.*

mild, *n.*   SEE COMMENT
A low-alcohol ale.

mileometer, *n.*   **odometer**

milk float   **milk truck**
Light low vehicle of stately gait, required to prevent churning. Electric-powered.

milliard, *n.*   **billion**
See **Appendix II.D.**

mince, *n.*   **chopped meat**
The common name by which a Briton orders from the butcher what an American
would call *chopped meat* or *hamburger.* Sometimes the British use the term *minced
meat* instead. *Mincemeat* generally means, in both countries, the mixture of chopped
apples, raisins, candied orange rind, suet, etc., which goes into mince pie.

mincemeat tart   **mince pie**
Mince pie would be understood in Britain to mean a small individual one. See
also **pie.**

mincer, *n.*   **meat grinder**

Mincing Lane   SEE COMMENT
Inf. An actual street in London, which has given its name to the *tea business,* just
as other London streets have become symbols and nicknames for other lines of
endeavor.

mind, *v.t., v.i.*   **1. watch out for**
                                                                 2. care
                                                              3. mind you
1. When a train stops at a curved platform at a British railroad station, there are
attendants who say, or signs that read, *Mind the gap!* Where there is an unexpected step, you will be enjoined to *Mind the step,* i.e., *to watch out for* it. In *Mind
you do! mind* means 'make sure.'
2. In America, *I don't mind* means 'I don't object.' In Britain it also means 'I don't
care,' in the sense of indifference when an alternative is offered. Thus, if asked,
Would you rather stay or go? or *Do you want chocolate or vanilla?,* a Briton who
would be happy either way says, "I don't mind." See also **have no mind to.**
3. In the imperative, *mind* often omits the *you* in Britain: *I don't believe a word of
it, mind!* The British do not use *mind* in the sense of *obey.* British and American
parents *mind* (*look after*) their children. American children *mind* (or should mind,
i.e., *obey*) their parents.

minded to   SEE COMMENT
When a Briton says that he or she is 'minded to' do something, he is (rather
formally) expressing the likelihood that he will follow that course of action. A
common variant is 'have a mind to.'

minder, *n.*   **bodyguard**
A *minder* is a *personal bodyguard;* in underworld slang, a *lookout.* Nothing to do
with **child-minder.**

mineral, *n.*   **soft drink**
One sees MINERALS on signs in British restaurants, tea rooms, etc. They are offering *soft drinks.* This use of the term is related to the term *mineral water* which one
still hears in America. See also **squash.**

minge, *n.*   *Inf.* **female pubic hair**

mingy, *adj.*   *Inf.* **tight (stingy)**
Inf. A **portmanteau** word: combination of *mean* and *stingy.* It applies not only to
persons but also to things, like a *mingy* portion of something. See also **mean.**

mini, *n.*   **Mini Minor**
The *Mini Minor,* a small car formerly produced by the British, was the origin
of the popularization of the prefix *mini* to describe anything small. When used
alone, as a noun, it refers to any of the various miniature skirts worn by British
and American females.

mini-budget. See under **budget.**

minim, *n.*   **halfnote**
See **Appendix II.F.**

minimus. See under **major.**

minister, *n.*   **cabinet member**
A term relating to government officials. The officials whom Americans describe
as *cabinet members* are known as *ministers* in Britain. But not all *ministers* (in the
political sense) are in the British cabinet, only the most senior ones. See also
Member.

minor. See under **major.**

misfield, *n., v.i.*   *approx.* **commit an error**
A cricket term, for a fielding blunder, rather than an official ruling or statistic that
goes into the imperishable archives. To *misfield* is to be guilty of the blunder. See
chance.

missing. See **go missing.**

mission, *n.*   *Inf.* **a tedious task**
Adolescent slang.

miss out on   **miss**
Also, *skip.* If you don't like artichokes, for instance, you *miss them out* at the dinner table. Often lengthened to *miss out on* with the same meaning: 'interntional
passing up,' rather than 'missing something to one's regret.' Also, in automobile
engines, meaning 'misfire.'

mistress. See under **master.**

mithered, *adj.*   **hot and bothered**
Inf. Of Lancashire origin. See also **moider.** *Moithered* is heard as well.

mixed, *adj.*   **coed(ucational)**
Applies to secondary schools, many of which are still for girls or boys only.

mixed bag   **assortment**
Inf. Of persons or things, implying a considerable variation in type or quality.
In the U.S., commonly refers to a situation with both good and bad features. See
curate's egg.

mixer, *n.*   SEE COMMENT
A soft drink (e.g., tonic, club soda, lemonade, or the like) intended for mixing with
a measure of **spirits.** Coca-Cola is always Coca-Cola, but only when intended for
serving with rum is it a mixer. Pubs might advertise *Large spirits + mixer–£3.50.*

mixture as before   **same old story**
Inf. When you have a medical prescription renewed in Britain, the label often bears the expression *"The mixture as before."* The phrase is jocularly applied to situations which amount to the *same old story,* as when delegates to labor negotiations or peace conferences return after an interval and present each other with nothing new.

mizzle, *n., v.i.*   **drizzle**
Apparently a **portmanteau** concoction of *mist* and *drizzle.*

mobile police   **patrol cars**

mobile production   **traveling show**

mobility unit   SEE COMMENT
Public housing adapted to meet the needs of handicapped persons.

mock exam   **practice examination**
Given and taken in both **public** and **state** schools so that students can get a taste of what they'll find in **GCSEs, A-Levels,** and other national tests.

mod. cons. See all mod cons.

moderations, *n. pl.*   SEE COMMENT
First exams for B.A. degree especially in classics at Oxford. Often abbreviated to *mods.* The examiner is called a *moderator.* See also **Greats; responsions; smalls.**

moderator, *n.*   SEE COMMENT
1. Officer presiding over math tripos. See **tripos.**
2. Examiner for moderations. See **moderations.**
3. Presbyterian minister presiding over church group.

modernizer, *n.*   SEE COMMENT
In politics, public administration, business, etc., one who wants to change long-established policies and/or working methods to bring them up to date. As always, what one person views as modernizing another will view as useless tinkering—or even worse.

mog, moggy, moggie, *n.*   **cat**
Inf. A *kittycat,* especially one without a pedigree. If one were distinguishing between a Burmese of venerable ancestry and a garden variety pussycat, one might be tempted to characterize the latter as 'just a moggy,' but it would be preferable to eliminate the 'just' in all other cases. *Mog, moggy,* etc. are highly respectable designations, even if they are corruptions of *mongrel.*

moider, *v.t.*   **bother**
Inf. Moidered is north of England dialect for *hot and bothered.* See also **mithered.**

molehill, *n.*   **little hill**
Small hill thrown up by a burrowing mole.

Mondayish, *adj.*   SEE COMMENT
Describing the feelings of one facing the prospect of the week's work ahead, after the festivities or relaxation of the weekend. Applies as well to a clergyman weary as a result of his Sabbath labors.

money for jam   *Inf.* **easy pickings**
Inf. Like taking candy from a baby. Description of a task embarrassingly easy. See
also **easy meat; piece of cake; as easy as kiss your hand; snip.** Sometimes *money
for jam* appears to mean 'something for nothing,' in the sense of a good return for
negligible effort. Synonymous, in this sense, with *money for old rope.*

money for old rope. See **money for jam.**

money-spinning, *n., adj.*   **1. money raising**
                                                        2. moneymaking
1. A *money-spinning* event is one that enriches the treasury of a do-good organization.
2. A *money-spinning* play is simply a hit that is raking it in. A *money spinner*
is a *money maker,* anything that makes money, a financial success. See also
word-spinning.

monger, *n.*   **dealer**
This word is almost always used in combination with the word that denotes
the particular trade involved. Examples: *cheesemonger, fishmonger, ironmonger*
(for hardware merchant). The usual practice is to put an apostrophe *s* after the
combination word: *I'm going to the fishmonger's; I have to get my lamp repaired at the
ironmonger's. Monger* fits into other combinations of a derogatory nature: *scandal-
monger, warmonger,* and the new pejorative term *peacemonger,* for a *dove.*

monkey, *n., Slang.*   **$500; £500**

monkey-freezing, *adj.*   *Inf.* **biting cold**
Slang. Euphemistic ellipsis of *cold enough to freeze the balls off a brass monkey.* See
also **as cold as charity.**

monkey-nut, *n.*   **peanut**
Synonymous with **ground-nut** and thought by some to be slang or at least mildly
jocular.

monomark, *n.*   **registered identification mark**
An arbitrary symbol, consisting of letters, numbers, or both, for purposes of
identification.

mooch. See **mouch.**

moonlight flit   **skipping town**
Inf. To *do a moonlight flit* (or **shoot the moon**) in Britain is to *blow town at night*
with your belongings, with no forwarding address, in order to get away without
paying the rent or settling with your creditors. It is like *doing a bunk* (see **bunk**),
but at night.

moonraker, *n.*   *Slang.* **yokel**
Inf. The legend is that certain Wiltshire hayseeds pretended to rake the moon out
of a pond, mistaking the moon's reflection for a piece of cheese. In fact, they were
trying to gather in their kegs of brandy.

moons, *n., pl.*   *Inf.* **ages**
Slang. I haven't seen him in moons. See also **donkey's years.**

moonshine, *n.*   *Inf.* **castles in the air**
Inf. Visionary ideas. These can result from imbibing *moonshine* in the American sense.

moor, *n.*   **wasteland**
Open and overgrown, often with heather. See also **heath.**

mop up   **sop up**
That which Frenchmen do in public, and most other nationalities do in private, in order to gather up that irresistible last bit of gravy on the plate.

morally certain   **quite sure**
About 90 percent certain: almost convinced, much stronger than *reasonably sure.*

moreish, *adj.*   **makes one want more**
Inf. Used of food. See **-ish.**

more power to your elbow, *Inf.*   *Inf.* **more power to you**
A jocular toast of encouragement to a boozer.

morning coffee. See **elevenses.**

morning dress, *n.*   SEE COMMENT
Formal day clothing for men. Usually worn at weddings, it comprises a frock coat, grey **trousers,** and top hat.

morning tea   SEE COMMENT
In British country hotels, one is asked, "Will you be wanting morning tea?" Before you go down to breakfast, the **chambermaid** will bring you a cup.

morris dance   SEE COMMENT
A ritual folk dance performed all over England, usually during May Day ceremonies, by persons in costumes representing set characters said to refer back to the legend of Robin Hood. The term *morris* is a corruption of *Moorish.*

mortarboard. See **academicals.**

most secret   **top secret**

MOT, *acronym*   SEE COMMENT
Every car over three years old must have an annual safety check carried out on behalf of the Ministry of Transport (MOT). The check is conducted by a licensed garage, and the certificate resulting is called an MOT certificate. It is the equivalent of the annual car inspections mandated under state law in the United States.

Mothering Sunday   **Mid-Lent Sunday**
Fourth Sunday in Lent, called *Laetare Sunday* because on that Sunday the *introit* in the Latin Mass began *Laetare Jerusalem* ('Rejoice, Jerusalem'). The British name was derived from the custom of children bringing small gifts to their mothers on that day—the original Mother's Day.

mother-in-law, *n.*   SEE COMMENT
Inf. An old joke; a way of asking for an *old and bitter* (*ale* understood). Not current.

Mother of the House. See **Father of the House.**

mother's ruin   **gin**
Inf. An old nickname for *gin.*

motion, *n.*   **bowel movement**

motor, *v.i.*   **drive**
The British also use *drive,* but no American other than William Buckley would ever say, "We *motored* across the country."

motor-bike, *n.*   **motorcycle**
Inf. Now usually shortened to *bike,* which also means 'bicycle.'

motor coach   **intercity bus**
Usually shortened to *coach.*

motorway, *n.*   **turnpike**

mouch; mooch, *v.i.*   *Inf.* **hang around**
Slang. Both forms rhyme with HOOCH. To *mouch round* or *mouch about* a place is to *hang around* it or just *hang.*

mount, *n., v.t.*   **mat**
Term used in framing, *mount* a picture.

mousetrap cheese   *approx. Slang.* **rat cheese**
Slang. Describes any humble type of hard cheese, like Cheddar and Lancashire (as opposed, for example, to Stilton and the fancier numbers). Usually the word implies a left-over bit, going somewhat stale, but edible; something you'd be willing to offer an old friend who dropped in, but not the vicar.

move house   **move**
The British occasionally use the shorter American form for *change residence;* but see **Appendix I.A.3.**

moving stairway   **escalator**
Interchangeable with *moving staircase.* The British are now more familiar with *escalator.*

M.P. See **Member.**

Mrs Grundy. See **wowser.**

Mrs Mop or Mopp   **cleaning woman**
Inf. Mrs Mopp (two *ps*) was a character in the interminable radio program *It's That Man Again* (familiarly known as *ITMA*) during World War II. Her oft-repeated line was, *Can I do you now, sir?*

much of this mark. See under **mark.**

muck, *n., v.i.*   **mess**
Slang. The British government makes a *muck* of things, in about the same way the American government makes a *mess* of things, and in the same way in which all the other governments seem to be making whatever-it-is-they-call-it these days. Whereas Americans *mess around,* Britons *muck about.* To *muck in* is to *pitch in,* with

the connotation that the task in question is a menial one. To be *in a muck sweat* about something is to be *upset* about it, deeply concerned and worried.

mucker, *n.,*   **1.** *Slang.* **spill**
                                                      2. spending spree
1. *Slang. To come a mucker* is to *take a spill.*
2. *Slang. To go a mucker* is to *go on a spending spree* or *throw your money around.*

muddle (in a)   **confused**

mudlark, *n.*   *approx.* **scavenger**
Of a special sort: a person—usually a child—who searches the mudflats between high and low tide for whatever may be found in the way of flotsam or jetsam.

muff, *n.*   **oaf**
Inf. Muff is used in both countries as a verb meaning 'miss.' One can *muff* any kind of opportunity, in life generally. In sports, one *muffs* a catch. From this the British developed the noun *muff,* meaning 'awkward, rather silly person.' Apparently, however, in context, it can be used almost as a term of endearment, as in, *What a silly little muff you are!*

muffetee, *n.*   **knitted wrist cuff**

muffin, *n.*   **small spongy cake**
This has nothing whatever in common with what Americans call *English muffins,* which are unknown in Britain. Instead, it is a light, flat, round, spongy cake, served toasted and buttered.

mug, *n., v.i.*   **1.** *Slang.* **gullible person**
                                              2. *Slang.* **grind; bookworm**
                                                              3. face
1. *Slang.* To be *had for a mug* is to be *taken in,* i.e., taken for a *dope.* A *mug's game* is *something for the birds; my idea of nothing at all; a profitless endeavor.*
2. *Slang.* The British also use *mug* and *mug up* verbally, meaning 'bone up,' e.g., for an examination (see also **sap; swot**).
3. *Slang.* Anybody's face.

muggins, *n.*   *Slang.* **simpleton; fool**

mull, *n., v.t., v.i.*   **mess; mess up**
To *mull* (or *mull over*) in America is to *ponder* or *cogitate,* an activity that often winds up in a *mull* in the British sense.

multiple shops   **chain store**
Often shortened to *multiples.* The American term is now just as common.

multi-storey, *adj.*   **high rise**
Note the *e* in storey. See **Appendix I.E.**

mummy, mum, *n.*   **mama; mommy**
Mummy and *mama* start in childhood, but *mummy* lingers on longer in Britain than *mama* does in America, where it usually becomes *mother.* The Queen Mother is facetiously called the *Queen Mum* and sometimes, affectionately, *Queenie Mum.*

mump, *v.t.*   *Slang.* **cadge**
Slang. Archaic. To *mump* something is to get it by begging, to *cadge* or *wheedle* it out of someone. *Mumping* is a British police term for accepting minor gifts from people on the beat.

munch, *n.*   **a snack**
Slang. Also used generally of food. A happy teenager might express her approval of a meal by calling it a *good munch.*

muniment room   SEE COMMENT
The storage and/or display room of a castle or church or other ancient monument where historical records and treasures are kept. A *muniment* is a document listing items in archive.

mushy peas, *n. pl.*   SEE COMMENT
Cooked, soft marrowfat (large) peas. Found in working-class **cafes** and **eel and pie shops.**

music centre   SEE COMMENT
Combination CD-player, cassette player, and radio. See also **radiogram.**

music-hall, *n.*   **vaudeville theater**
A *music-hall* **turn** is a *vaudeville act.* **Variety** is a usual British term for *vaudeville.*

muslin, *n.*   **cheesecloth**
See also **butter-muslin; calico.**

mustard-keen, *adj.*   **enthusiastic**
Inf. Also, *keen as mustard.* This phrase involves a pun on Keen's Mustard, a once-popular product.

mutton, *n.*   SEE COMMENT
The flesh of a sheep over two years old used as food.

muzz, *v.t., Slang.* See **muzzy.**

muzzy, *adj.*   *Slang.* **woozy**
Slang. The implication in *muzzy* is that the unfortunate condition it describes is the result of too much drink. The slang British verb *muzz,* used transitively, means to 'put somebody *hors de combat,*' not in one fell swoop by slipping him a mickey, but in nice, easy stages.

My dear . . .   **Dear . . .**
In America, the addition of *My* in the salutation of a letter makes it more formal; in Britain, more intimate.

my learned friend   SEE COMMENT
A courtesy title used by lawyers in court to refer to each other. They may also say, 'My friend,' with no slight intended.

my old dutch. See **dutch.**

N

N/A   **not applicable**
Abbreviation used in filling out forms; for instance, the blank space for *maiden name*, in a form being completed by a male.

NAAFI, *n.*   SEE COMMENT
(Pronounced NAFFY or NAHFY.) Standing for *Navy, Army, and Air Force Institutes,* an organization that operates canteens and service centers for members of the British armed forces, similar to an American PX.

naff, *v.i., adj.*   SEE COMMENT
Slang. Anything *naff* is shabby or cheap, or *tatty. Naff off!* is the equivalent of *Bugger off!* (see **bugger**), or in America, *Fuck off!*

nailed on, *Slang.*   *Slang.* **nailed down; all set**

nail varnish   **nail polish**
Also given as *nail polish* and *nail enamel.*

nancy boy, *n.*   *Inf., derog.* **an effeminate or homosexual male**
Also seen as *nancy,* and sometimes used as an adjective.

nanny, *n.*   **full-time babysitter**

nanny state   SEE COMMENT
A pejorative term applied to public policies by people who think that the government is being overly protective of its citizens, at the expense of civil liberties and/or common sense.

nap, *n.*   *Inf.* **tip (on the races)**
Inf. To *go nap* is to *bet your stack.* A *nap selection* is a racing expert's list of betting recommendations. *Nap* is an abbreviation of *napoleon* (lower case *n*), a card game in which players bid for the right to name the trump, declaring the number of tricks they propose to win. A *nap* or *napoleon* in this game is a bid to take all five tricks, the maximum. *Nap hand* has acquired the figurative meaning of being in the position where one is practically sure of winning big if willing to take the risk. See also **pot, 1.**

napper, *n., Slang.*   *Slang.* **noodle (head)**
Synonymous with **loaf; noddle.**

nappy, *n.*   **diaper**
Inf. A diminutive of *napkin,* and the everyday word for *diaper,* which is also heard in Britain.

nark, *n.* *Slang.* **stool pigeon**
Slang. Originally *copper's nark,* i.e., *informer.* Jocularly and pejoratively extended to the publishing business, where a *publisher's nark* means a 'publicity man.' *Nark* is not related to the American term *nark* or *narc* meaning 'federal narcotics agent.' The British term came from the Romany word *nak* (pronounced NAHK) meaning 'nose.'

narked, *adj.* *Slang.* **sore**
Slang. In the sense of 'angry.'

narky, *adj. Slang.* *Slang.* **bitchy**

nasty, *adj.* **disagreeable**
In Britain, *nasty* means disgustingly dirty; obscene; unpalatable. *Nasty* (usually in the plural) has been used to mean 'gremlin' or 'bug' in the sense of 'defect' in computer programs. *Nasties* was a facetious name for *Nazis* in the thirties and forties.

nasty piece (bit) of work *Slang.* **louse**
Inf. A contemptible person.

National Assistance. See National Insurance.

national call SEE COMMENT
This is the modern term for **trunk call.** The new charging system is not necessarily based on distance, however, as a national call may be to a special number at a call center just a mile or two from the person making the call.

National Curriculum, *n.* SEE COMMENT
The compulsory set of subjects that schools must teach children aged five to 16.

national enquiries **long-distance information**
England is a small country and when you want to ascertain an out-of-town telephone number, you dial a three-digit number to get the desired number anywhere in the United Kingdom and all of Ireland, whether long distance or local. See also **enquiries.**

National Grid SEE COMMENT
The nationwide systems supplying gas and electricity. While local companies sell both products to consumers, the maintenance of the energy infrastructure is the responsibility of two heavily regulated utility companies.

National Health Service SEE COMMENT
In Britain, free medical care is available to everyone, and funded out of general taxation. The organization responsible for medical care is the National Health Service, usually referred to by the acronym NHS. See also **health visitor.**

National Insurance **Government Insurance System**
State-regulated compensation to the sick, aged, and unemployed based on a system of compulsory contributions from workers and employers, including certain supplementary benefits formerly known as *National Assistance.*

national insurance number **social security number**

nation of shopkeepers. See under **shop.**

natter, *n., v.i.*   **chatter**
Inf. As a verb, it can mean 'grumble,' but this sense appears to be increasingly less common. *Nattering* on the High Street as one meets neighbors is what makes shopping such a pleasure and wastes so much time. Don't be misled by *natterjack,* which is not a male gossip but rather a *Buto calamita,* a *yellow striped toad* indigenous to Britain.

naturist, *n.*   **nudist**
And *naturism* is *nudism.*

naught. See **nought.**

naughty, *adj.*   **wicked**
In both countries, *naughty* is a word usually associated with children. It is also heard in Britain in adult contexts, but usually as an exercise in jocular understatement which seems somewhat affected, thus (referring to a particularly bloodthirsty murder): *That was a naughty thing to do.* Obscene words are rather coyly called *naughty words* in both countries, but in Britain the usual term would be *rude.* See **rude, 3.**

navvy, *n.*   **construction worker**
Especially a road, railway, or canal worker. A *gang of navvies* is a *construction crew.* This term is unknown in America, where it would more likely be given as *hard-hat.* See also **lengthman.**

N.B.G.   **no damned good**
Inf. The jocular abbreviation of *no bloody good.*

nearly, *adv.*   **almost**
Where Americans tend to say *almost,* Britons tend to say *nearly. We're nearly there, the chicken is nearly done,* etc.

near-side lane   **slow lane**
Since traffic keeps to the left in Britain, and the *near* refers to the edge of the road, the *near-side lane* refers to the leftmost one for regular driving. The one nearest the center is called the *off-side lane,* and is used for passing. The terms *near-side* and *off-side* can also refer to the sides of a vehicle: e.g., the *off-side front wheel.*

near the bone. See **near the knuckle.**

near the knuckle   *Inf.* **off color**
Inf. Bordering on the indecent. Synonymous with **near the bone.**

neat, *adj.*   **straight**
Referring to undiluted alcoholic beverages. Some Americans say *neat;* some Britons say *straight.*

neck, *n., v.t.*   **1.** *Inf.* **nerve**
                                                                                2. *Inf.* **drink (a beer, etc.)**
1. *Inf.* In the sense of 'cheek' or 'gall' or 'impudence.' Often found in the expression *brass neck.*

2. *Inf.* Used especially by young people, for whom the aim is to get a drink *down their neck* as fast as possible.

neck and crop **headfirst**
Inf. Headlong, bodily. The way people get thrown out of barrooms in western movies.

(the) needle, *n.* **pins and needles**
Slang. The kind of nervousness one gets when kept in suspense.

needle match **grudge match**
A game or match that is hotly contested, with a background involving a certain amount of acrimony. A county cricket match between arch-rivals is said to *have a lot of needle.*

neeps, *n. pl.* *abbrev.* **parsnips**
Scottish in origin, but used elsewhere.

nervous nineties, *Inf.* SEE COMMENT
In cricket, it is a signal accomplishment for a **batsman** to make 100 runs, known as a **century.** As he approaches this desideratum, a batsman sometimes tightens up, and when he makes his 90th run, becomes understandably nervous, or, as the British say, **nervy.** At this point, he is said to be *in the nervous nineties.* The term has been extended to other sports, as in the case of a **football** (soccer) team leading its league towards the end of the season or to any situation where the protagonist is close to triumph, but with pitfalls looming.

nervy *Slang.* **jumpy**
Slang. Britons express themselves as feeling *nervy* or describe someone as looking *nervy.* In each case, the American equivalent would be *jumpy.* In other words, a *nervy* person in Britain can be *jumpy* or *wearing,* depending on the context.

net curtains, *n. pl.* **sheers/under-drapes**

(the) never-never, *n.* **installment plan**
Slang. The serious British equivalent for *installment plan* is **hire-purchase.** *The never-never* is popular, wistful, jocular slang.

New Labour SEE COMMENT
Beginning in the 1980s, some politicians in the Labour Party sought to bring their policies toward the center of the political spectrum and away from traditional socialist views on matters such as taxation, trade union rights, and public ownership of essential industries. They came to call their movement New Labour, to distinguish it from the "Old Labour" policies that had failed to win an election since the 1979 Conservative victory under Margaret Thatcher's leadership. Under the leadership of Tony Blair, elected prime minister in 1997, New Labour continued its move to the political center.

Newmarket, *n.* SEE COMMENT
Newmarket is a horseracing town. It is also the name of a card game. A *Newmarket* or *Newmarket coat* is a *tightfitting overcoat* for men or women.

new penny. See **Appendix II.A.**

newsagent, *n.*   **newsdealer**
See also **kiosk, 1.**

news editor, *n.*   **city editor**
For British use of *city editor,* see under **City.**

newsreader, *n.*   **newscaster**
Often shortened to *reader* on radio and TV.

news-room, *n.*   **periodical room**
The reading room in a library where newspapers and magazines are kept. *News-room* in America, *news-room* in Britain, are newspaper terms referring to the news section of a newspaper office or a radio or television station.

New Town. See under **overspill.**

New Year Honours. See under **Birthday Honours**

next turning. See under **block.**

nice bit of work   *Slang.* **quite a dish**
Slang. Other complimentary slang in the same vein: *nice bit of crumpet* (see **crumpet**); *nice bit of stuff; nice bit of skirt.* Apparently, *a nice bit of* almost anything would do. *Nice bit* is often *nice piece* in these expressions. See also **bit of . . . ; nasty piece (bit) of work.**

nice to hear you   **nice to hear your voice**
A common telephone phrase. Americans say, *How nice to hear your voice,* or *How good to hear from you.*

nick, *n.*   **1. station house**
                                                                      2. *Inf.* **shape**
1. *Slang. Police station,* also *prison.*
2. In the sense of 'physical condition.' Usually in the phrase *in good nick,* meaning 'in the pink.' The term may be used for both people and machines, cars, etc.

nick, *v.t.*   *Slang.* **pinch**
Slang. In both senses: to *steal* something, or to *arrest* someone.

nicker, *n.*   **a pound**
Slang. Unit of currency, not weight. Low-class, petty criminals' cant. The common slang term is **quid.** See also **knickers.**

nide, *n.*   **brood of pheasants**

night-cellar, *n., Slang.*   *Slang.* **dive**

night on the tiles   *Slang.* **night on the town**
Slang. This phrase is derived from the custom among cats of having fun at night on rooftops, which in Britain are often made of tiles.

night sister. See **sister.**

night watchman   SEE COMMENT
Inf. Cricket term. If a player is out just before close of play on a given day, a weak
batsman is put in at that point, out of batting order, to preserve the stronger
batsman. The poor chap who probably will be out early the next day is called the
night watchman.

nil, *n.*   **nothing**
Used in game scores where Americans would use *nothing*, e.g., *six goals to nil,*
except in cricket, where *nought* is the term.

nineteen to the dozen   *Slang.* **a blue streak**
Inf. Usually seen in the expression *talk nineteen to the dozen*, talk incessantly. See
also **talk the hind leg off a donkey.**

1922 Committee, *n.*   SEE COMMENT
A committee made up of all backbench Conservative **Members.**

nipper, *n.*   *Inf.* **kid, tot**
Slang. See also **limb.**

nippy, *adj., n.*   1. *adj., Slang.* **snappy**
                                                         2. *n.* **waitress**
1. *adj. Slang. Look nippy!* means *Make it snappy!*
2. *n., Slang.* As a noun, *nippy* is slang for *waitress*. The term was confined originally
to the nimble girls at Lyons Corner Houses (a restaurant chain), but then became
generic. *Nippy* is just about on its way out except in the sense of 'chillingly cold.'

nip round   *Inf.* **pop over**
Inf. One *nips round* to the pub for a quick **pint.** One can nip *up* as well as *round*. To
nip up somewhere is to make a hurried trip there and back.

nit, *n.*   *Slang.* **dope; jerk**
Slang. Short for *nitwit*. Also in America and Britain, meaning the egg of a louse or
other parasitic insect.

nix!, *interj.*   *Slang.* **cheese it!**
Slang. Nix! is an interjection used in Britain to warn one's colleagues that the boss
is snooping around. As in America, it is used also to signify a strong *No!*, i.e.,
Nothing doing! Cheese it! (or *Cheezit!*) has become rather old-fashioned in America.
There would seem to be no modern equivalent, perhaps because people are so
much less afraid of the boss these days. *Look busy!* or *look smart!* is probably the
closest equivalent.

nob, *n., Slang.*   *Slang.* **a swell**
He sure plays the *nob*, don't he.

nobble, *v.t.*   1. **tamper with**
                                                           2. *Slang.* **fix**
                                                           3. **scrounge**
                                                           4. *Slang.* **nab**
                                                           5. *Slang.* **rat on**
Slang. Sometimes spelled *knobble*. In any of its meanings, an unpleasant bit of
British slang:

1. One *nobbles* a racehorse to prevent its winning.
2. One *nobbles* a jury to get the desired verdict.
3. *Nobble* also means "scrounge," with the implication of getting something away from somebody through sly, dishonest maneuvering.
4,5. To *nobble* a criminal is to *nab* him, or get him *nabbed* by *ratting on* him.

nob's pronoun   SEE COMMENT
Grammatically-deficient anglophones everywhere might sometimes say *John gave it to he and I* rather than *him and me*. In Britain, that particular mistake is identified with **nobs,** who appear to think that saying *he and I* sounds more genteel or perhaps **posh** than *him and me*. Thus, it is their pronoun—even if others make the same mistake.

noddle, *n.*   *Slang.* **noodle (head)**
Slang. Often shortened to *nod*. Synonymous with **loaf; napper.**

no effects   **insufficient funds**
Banking term; for the more up-to-date term, see **refer to drawer.**

No Entry   **Do Not Enter**
Road sign indicating one-way street.

nog, *n.*   SEE COMMENT
Strong ale, once brewed in East Anglia; sometimes spelled *nogg*. In America *nog* is used as short for *eggnog* and refers to any alcoholic drink into which an egg is beaten.

no hoarding. See hoarding.

no joy   *Inf.* **no luck**
Inf. Words announcing *no success* in any of life's small endeavors, when you vainly try to reach someone by dialing one number after another, or when you call a box office and find tickets are sold out.

nonce, *n.*   *Inf., derog.* SEE COMMENT
A sex offender, especially one who abuses children.

nonconformist, *n., adj.*   **non-Anglican**
As a noun, synonymous with **dissenter.** See also **chapel.**

non-content, *n.*   *approx.* **nay-voter**
One who votes against a motion in the House of Lords.

nonillion. See Appendix II.D.

non-resident, *n.*   *approx.* **transient**
One may see a sign in front of a British hotel reading MEALS SERVED TO NON-RESIDENTS, or words to that effect. In that use, *non-resident* is used in the sense of a 'person not living at the hotel,' and has nothing to do with national domicile.

(a) nonsense, *n.*   **(a) muddle; fiasco**
Preceded by the indefinite article, especially in the expression *make a nonsense of*. In describing a military embarkation that went wrong and turned into a fiasco, a character may say, "It was all rather a *nonsense*."

non-U   See **Appendix I.C.6.**

no reply   **no answer**
A telephone term. In America one says *there's no answer*. In Britain the unhappy
formula is *There's no reply*. See also **ceased to exist.**

Norfolk capon   *Inf.* **red herring**
Inf. A false issue.

Norfolk dumpling   SEE COMMENT
Inf. Norfolk type, synonymous with *Norfolk turkey,* meaning a native of the country of Norfolk.

Norfolk sparrow   **pheasant**
Inf. So called because pheasant are plentiful in the area.

norland, *n.*   **north**
Norland is a common noun and is simply short for *northland.*

North Country. See under **West Country.**

nose to tail, *Inf.*   *Inf.* **bumper to bumper**

nosey-parker, *n., v.i.*   *Inf.* **busybody**
Inf. When used as a verb, it means to 'be a rubberneck' or 'be a busybody' and
take much too great an interest in other people's affairs. This term is said to have
alluded to Dr. Matthew Parker, a 16th-century archbishop of Canterbury who
was once chaplain to Anne Boleyn and Henry VIII. A religious fanatic, he stuck
his nose into every aspect of church affairs.

(is) not a patch on   *Inf.* **doesn't hold a candle to**
Inf. Doesn't come anywhere near; isn't in the same league with.

not a sausage   *Slang.* **not a damned thing**
Slang. Usually refers to money.

not at all   **you're welcome**
The American term used to sound peculiar to British ears. *You're welcome* is now
heard increasingly, undoubtedly as a result of its constant use by American visitors. In small matters, the British often say nothing at all (to the surprise of most
Americans, some of whom mistakenly consider the silence somewhat rude) in
response to *Thank you*. In more important matters, they say *Not at all!* or *That's
all right!* A warmer response is *Pleasure! Thank you,* incidentally, is heard all the
time from persons serving you, like waiters and waitresses, salespersons, tailors
taking your measurements, and the like. It is sometimes so often repeated that
it seems more like a nervous tic than a spoken phrase. *Thank you!* from a porter
pushing a baggage cart (**trolley,** in Britain) is the equivalent of *Gangway!* See
Pleasure! Americans are told *ad nauseam* to *have a good day.*

not best pleased   **not too happy**

not by a long chalk, *Inf.*   *Inf.* **not by a long shot**
Britons waste their time playing various pool and billiard games, while Americans profit from shooting baskets and clay pigeons.

note, *n.*   **1. bill**
                                                                                                        2. tone
1. Referring to paper money: a 5-pound *note,* a 10-pound *note,* and so forth.
2. In musical terminology, the English use the term *note* in instances where Americans would use *tone.* Examples: 3 *notes* lower; 5-*note* scale. When an Englishman uses *tone* in such expressions, he means what the Americans would call a *whole tone.*

notecase, *n.*   **billfold**
See also **pocketbook.**

not-for-profit   **nonprofit**
Applied to organizations with no commercial aims.

not half   **1. not nearly**
                                                                                               2. not at all
                                                                                               3. terrifically
One must be extremely careful in interpreting the expression *not half:*
1. *Inf.* When a Briton says to a departing guest, "You haven't stayed *half long enough,*" he means *not nearly long enough.*
2. *Inf.* When a Briton gives his opinion of his friend's new necktie by describing it as *not half* bad, he means 'not at all bad,' i.e., 'quite satisfactory,' 'pretty good.'
3. *Slang. Not half* has a peculiar slang use as well. Thus, in describing the boss's reaction when he came in and found everybody out to lunch, a British porter might say, "He didn't half blow up," meaning that he did blow up about as completely as possible. In other words, *not half* is used ironically, meaning 'not half—but totally.' As an expletive, by itself, *not half!* might find its American equivalent in *not much!* meaning, of course, the exact opposite: 'very much!' 'and how!' as in, *Would you like a free trip to California? Not half!*

nothing (else) for it   **unmistakably**
There's no choice, no other way out or *nothing else to do about it.*

nothing starchy   *Inf.* **no fuss or feathers**
Slang. See **starchy.**

nothing to make a song about, *Inf.*   *Inf.* **nothing to write home about**

notice, *v.t.*   **review**
In Britain a book can be spoken of as *reviewed* or *noticed. Noticed* implies that the review was brief.

notice board   **bulletin board**
For instance, the one at offices listing vacant posts, company news, and so forth.

not much cop   *Slang.* **no great catch**
Slang. Not worth much; referring to persons or objects of little or no value.

not on   **1. impracticable**
                                                                                            2. *Inf.* **bad form**
1. *Inf.* An employee asks to have his salary doubled. Answer: "It simply isn't on."
2. *Inf.* Denoting impropriety.

not on your nelly   *Slang.* **not on your life**
Slang. From rhyming slang (see **Appendix II.G.3.**), *not on your Nelly Duff* (who-
ever she was), the rhyme being with *puff,* old slang for 'life.'

not so dusty   *Inf.* **not so bad**
Inf. In answer to the question *How are you?*

Not to worry!, *Inf.*   *Inf.* **Don't let it bother you! No problem!**

nought (naught), *n.*   **zero**
It is used in scoring—*ten to nought.* In that sense Americans would probably use
nothing instead of *zero.* As a term in arithmetic, a British synonym is **cipher,** also
spelled *cypher.*

Noughties, *n. pl.*   SEE COMMENT
The decade at the beginning of the century. Nought is a synonym for zero; hence
the name.

noughts and crosses   **tick-tack-toe**

nous, *n.*   **savvy**
It looks French, but is the Greek word for 'mind' or 'intellect' and rhymes with
HOUSE. It can also mean 'gumption.'

nowt. See **nought.**

nr.   **near**
A term used on envelopes in addressing letters: thus, Sandhurst, *nr.* Hawkhurst,
to differentiate that Sandhurst from the Sandhurst in Surrey. See also **Appendix
I.D.9.**

nullity, *n.*   **annulment**
Term in matrimonial law. If an American can't stand his or her spouse but has
no grounds for divorce, a lawyer can look into the chances of obtaining an *annulment.* A British lawyer would determine whether there are grounds for a *nullity
suit.* But they are doing the same thing.

number. See **make one's number.**

number plate   **license plate**

Number 10 Downing Street   SEE COMMENT
Usually shortened to *No. 10.* The seat of executive power and residence of the
prime minister. Like *the White House,* it is not only an address but is also used
figuratively to refer to the chief executive's office.

nurse, *v.t.*   **fondle**
A use not met with in America: to hold a baby on one's lap caressingly. The verb
is also used to describe the attentions of a politician to his constituency to con-
vince the voters of his devotion to their interests.

nursing home   **private hospital**
Also *convalescent home. Nursing home* is heard more and more in America.

nut, do one's. See **do one's nut.**

nut-case, *n.*   *Slang.* **nut**
Slang. The Americans refer to a crazy person as a *case* or a *nut.*

nutter, *n.*   *Slang.* **nut**
Slang. A crazy character: synonymous with **nut-case.**

O.A.P. *approx.* **senior citizen; retiree**
Inf. Stands for *old age pensioner,* and refers to those entitled to draw old age pensions from the government; in addition they are granted reductions in certain public conveyance fares, prices of admission to some entertainments, sports events, and the like, a practice not unknown in America. The British are now replacing *O.A.P.* with *pensioner,* and occasionally with the unattractive euphemism *Senior Citizen.*

oast, *n.* **hops kiln**
The *oast* (the hop-drying *kiln* itself) is housed in an *oast-house,* a red brick tower almost always cylindrical like a silo. The oast-house is topped by a cone-shaped vented cap, painted white, which is rotated by the action of the wind pushing against a protruding vane. The part of southeastern England known as the *Weald,* particularly the hilly Kent and Sussex countryside, is dotted with hundreds of these structures, usually single but often in pairs or clusters of several, lending a special character to the landscape.

oats, *n. pl.* **oatmeal (uncooked)**
The proper term when you shop at the grocery. Cooked and on the breakfast table, it is **porridge.** *Oatmeal* is becoming increasingly common.

obbo. See **keep obbo on.**

O.B.E. See under **Birthday Honours.**

oblique, *n.* **slash**
Sometimes called *oblique stroke* or simply *stroke* in Britain, and many names in America, including *virgule, diagonal, slant,* and even *solidus,* the latter being the Latin ancestor of *shilling,* a reference to the *shilling stroke,* as it was sometimes called in Britain in the old days before the monetary system was changed, when the *stroke* meant 'shilling(s).' Thus: 15/- meant '15 shillings.' See **Appendix II.A.**

O.C. **Officer Commanding**
Subordinate to the C.O., who commands an established group such as an infantry battalion, while an O.C. commands an *ad hoc* unit such as a demolition training center, a rations dump, an intelligence group, etc.

occupier, *n.* **occupant**
In Britain one who occupies a house is its *occupier.* One occupying a room, railroad compartment, etc., is an *occupant* in both countries. *Occupier* always refers to a dwelling. When the occupier owns the house, he is called *owner-occupier.*

octillion. See **Appendix II.D.**

odd, *adj.*   **1. peculiar**
                                                   2. occasional
1. *Odd* is used much more in Britain than in America to describe an eccentric person. The British, generally speaking, like to regard themselves as *odd* in that sense.
2. *The odd* is the equivalent of *an occasional,* in sentences like *He makes the odd trip to town,* or, *I work mainly in my office, but do have the odd meeting with a client elsewhere,* or, *The odd novice will chance swimming in these dangerous waters.*

odd man, *n.*   **handyman**

oddments, *n. pl.*   **odds and ends**
Especially applied to broken sets of merchandise for sale. Used in America not with the British meaning, but two others: *oddities,* strange people or things; and *eccentricities.*

odds and sods, *n. pl.*   **bits and pieces**

odd sizes   **broken sizes**
Not all sizes available, referring to merchandise for sale.

off, *n.*   **start**
Inf. Especially, the start of a horse race. *It was ten minutes before the off.*

off, *adj.*   **1. bad form**
                                                     2. spoiled
1. *Inf.* Thus: *It was a bit off to be doing her nails at the restaurant table.* Synonymous with **not on, 2.**
2. *Inf.* In the sense of 'rancid' or 'rotten,' referring to spoiled food. Thus: *The butter's gone off.*

offal, *n.*   **viscera**
A butcher's term covering liver, kidneys, tongue, etc., or animal insides generally.

off cut   **remnant**
Store sign: RETAIL OFF CUT CENTRE would read REMNANTS in America as applied to textiles, and probably ODD LENGTHS referring to lumber, etc. *Off cut* refers primarily to lumber, but can apply to textiles, carpeting, pipe, etc.

offer for sale   **secondary issue**
Of stock.

offer for subscription   **public issue**
Of stock. Today commonly called I.P.O., initial public offering. See also **offer for sale.**

offer-up, *v.t.*   **put in place**
In instructions for a plastic substance for making screw fixings in masonry: After inserting the material into the masonry opening, one is to " . . . *offer-up* the fixture and drive home the screw."

office block. See **block.**

offices, *n. pl.*   conveniences
Synonymous with another British word which has a meaning unknown in America—**amenities** in the sense of *conveniences,* as applied to a house. A real-estate agents' term: *All the usual offices,* i.e., electricity, hot and cold running water, kitchen, lavatory, etc. See discussion under **amenities.** Less common nowadays than it once was.

official, *n.*   officer
For example, *bank official.*

off licence   1. license to sell alcoholic beverages
                                     for consumption off the premises
                                                        2. package store
1. Sign on shop indicating it possesses such a license. See under **during hours.**
2. The shop itself.

off-load, *v.t.*   1. *Slang.* **bump**
                                                          2. *Inf.* **saddle**
1. *Inf.* To *displace* an ordinary airplane passenger in favor of a VIP, a very important person.
2. In the sense of 'passing the buck,' i.e., *saddling* someone with an undesirable burden.

off one's chump; off one's dot; off one's onion, *Slang.*   *Slang.* **off one's rocker**

off one's own bat   on one's own
Inf. Used in expressions indicating doing things without the help of anybody else. A term derived from cricket. See also **on one's pat, on one's tod,** both meaning 'being alone.'

off-putting. See **put (someone) off.**

off-side lane   passing lane
See under **near-side lane.**

off-side mirror   wing mirror

off the boil   past the crisis
Inf. When a situation is *off the boil,* it is coming under control, calming down, past the crisis stage.

off the mark   having made a start
Technically, a cricket term. To be *off the mark* is to have made your first run after coming to bat. In general language, it means 'off to a start,' signifying at least initial success. See also **slow off the mark.**

off-the-peg, *adj., Inf.*   *Inf.* **off the rack; ready-to-wear**

of that ilk   SEE COMMENT
This curious phrase, as used in Scotland, has an extremely restricted sense. It applies to persons whose last names are the same as the name of the place they come from; historically they were chiefs of clans. From a misunderstanding of this usage, *ilk* has acquired the meaning 'sort,' or 'kind'; used generally in a pejorative sense: *Al Capone, and people of that ilk,* or even *Freudians and their ilk.*

. . . of the best   **1. strokes**
                                                                      2. pound note(s)
1. *Inf.* To give a schoolboy *five of the best* is to give him *five strokes of the cane.*
2. *Inf.* A much pleasanter meaning: *A thousand of the best* is £1,000. The context will cure any possible ambiguity.

oik, *n.*   *Slang, derog.* SEE COMMENT
A person with little formal education whose opinions merit scant respect. Always used pejoratively.

old, *adj.*   SEE COMMENT
Inf. Used especially in addressing intimates, coupled with a variety of nouns, thus: *old man, old chap, old bean, old thing, old fruit, old egg, old top,* but *old boy* (not as a form of address) has the special meaning of 'alumnus' (see **old boy**). All old-fashioned.

(the) Old Bill   *Slang.* **(the) cops**
Slang. Underworld usage. *Watch it! Here comes the Old Bill!*

old boy; old girl   **alumnus; alumna**
Inf. In the frame of reference of secondary education, *old boy* would be *alumnus* or *graduate* in America. When you get to the university level, *old boy* no longer applies. At **Oxbridge,** the British would refer to a graduate as an *Oxford (Cambridge) man (woman)* or *graduate,* or say, simply, "He (she) was at Oxford (Cambridge)." It would remain *alumnus* or *graduate* in America in formal terms, but *old grad* colloquially. The *old-boy net* or *network* refers to the bonds established among the boys at **public school,** which are supposed to operate throughout life in social and, particularly, in business and professional life. Related, of course, to the *old school tie,* in which the *tie* appears to be an accidental pun referring to both the necktie displaying the school colors and the connections establishing the upper-class kinship characteristic of British public school boys.

old cock   **old man**
Slang. Used vocatively, with *cock* being a synonym for rooster: 'Look here, *old cock,* maybe I can help you.' See also **old.**

old dutch. See under **dutch.**

Old Lady of Threadneedle Street   SEE COMMENT
Inf. Bank of England; the expression is derived from its address.

old man of the sea   SEE COMMENT
A person one cannot shake off. From the legend of *Sinbad the Sailor.*

old mossyface, *adj.*   **the ace of spades**

old party   *Inf.* **old-timer**
Inf. In the sense of an *old person,* not doddering but almost. The term is jocular, and usually slightly pejorative, but without malice. "How did the accident happen?" "Well, this *old party* came along in a 1965 Austin, and . . . " *Party,* generally, means 'person' in colloquial conversation, derived in this usage from *party* in legal parlance, as in *party of the first part, guilty party,* etc.

old school tie. See under **old boy.**

old soldier   *Inf.* **old hand**
Inf. Implying that he's a crafty fellow. *Don't come the old soldier over me,* means 'Don't try to put one over on me.' A variant is *old stager.*

old stager, *Inf.* See under **old soldier.**

old sweat, *Inf.*   **old soldier**

O-levels. See under **GLSE.**

omnium gatherum   **1. mixture**
                                                                    2. open house
Slang. Mock Latin. *Omnium* is the genitive plural of *omnis,* Latin for 'all'; *gatherum* is a fake Latinization of 'gather.' Applied to:
1. Any motley collection of persons or things.
2. A party open to all comers.

on, *prep.*   **1. over**
                                                                    2. SEE COMMENT
1. A poker term used in the description of a full house. Thus, aces *on* **knaves,** which in America would be aces *over* jacks. See **Appendix I.A.1.**
2. The British use this preposition in two ways unknown in America. When telling you someone's salary, they will say, *He's on £25,000.* And when relaying news of the current results in a contest of some kind, e.g. an election, they would use *on* before the relevant number: *Labour are on 198 to the Conservatives' 124 and the Liberal Democrats' 28.*

(be) on a hiding to nothing   **face annihilation**
Or, less dramatically, *face insuperable odds, be without a prayer,* i.e., *with no hope of success. Hiding,* in this expression, is synonymous with *thrashing,* and *a hiding to nothing* means 'a thrashing to bits.'

on a lobby basis   **off the record**
Describing the condition on which politicians supply information to newspaper reporters. See **lobbyist.**

on a piece of string   *Inf.* **in a tight spot**
Inf. A bad place to be on either continent. Usually in the phrase to *have someone on a piece of string,* describing someone being manipulated by someone else.

on a plate   **on a silver platter**

on appro   **on approval**
Inf. Describing merchandise taken but returnable at the customer's option. *Appro* is accented on the first syllable.

once in a way   **once in a while**
Rarely, that is.

one-eyed village   *Inf.* **one-horse town**
Inf. Also known in America as a *whistle stop.*

one hundred percent copper-bottomed   **absolutely sound**
Inf. Especially applied to financial matters. The usage arises from the belief that a copper-bottomed pan or broiler is much more solid and longer lasting than one

made of other metals; or it may have arisen from the image of a ship sheathed with copper. In another context, modifying the noun *excuse,* it is the equivalent of *airtight.*

one in the eye   *Slang.* **a crusher**
Inf. That's one in the eye for you means 'That'll hold you for a while.'

one-off, *n., adj.*   **one of a kind**
The *only one made,* or *run off,* referring to manufactured goods.

oner, *n., Slang.*   **1. outstanding person or thing**
                                                            2. K.O. blow
                                                            3. *Inf.* **big fib**
(Pronounced WUNNER, from *one* (as in *one of a kind*); possibly influenced by the careless pronunciation of *wonder.*)

on form, *adj.*   **in great shape**
As everybody knows who has spent any time at all wagering hard-earned funds on the outcome of a horse race, we rely on a *form* in making our bets. This is the information that ranks the horses in a race based on how fast each horse is said to be, the health of the horses, the success rates of the jockeys, and the like. A horse that runs up to expectations is said to be *on form.* A horse below par is said to be *off form.* Because horse racing is so popular, the phraseology of the sport of kings, as it is called, often spreads beyond the racetrack. Thus, a person who does his job well, or who excels at squash or any of the rest of life, is also said to be *on form,* but in America such a person is much more often said to be *in great shape.*

on heat   **in heat**
See **Appendix I.A.1.**

o.n.o.   **or near offer**
Usually seen in real estate advertisements and used car ads: 'xyz amount *o.n.o.*'

on offer   **on sale**
Indicating a special offer, thus: *Yardley's bath soap is on offer this week.* In America there would most likely be a sign on the counter or in the window reading SPE-CIAL or TODAY'S SPECIAL or SPECIAL THIS WEEK. Not to be confused with **under offer,** meaning 'for sale,' but only subject to rejection of a pending offer.

on one's pat   **on one's own**
Slang. From rhyming slang. *Pat Malone for alone.* Synonymous with **on one's tod.** See also **off one's own bat.**

on one's tod   **on one's own**
Slang. Rhyming slang from *Tod Sloan,* a famous jockey, for *alone.* Synonymous with **on one's pat.** See also **off one's own bat.**

on second thoughts   **on second thought**
How singular of the Americans! But they do have second thoughts.

on strike   **at bat**
A **cricket** term. Two batsmen are always "up" at the same time, one at either end
of the **pitch**. The one to whom the bowler is bowling at a given moment is said
to be *on strike.*

on the cards   **in the cards**
See **Appendix I.A.1.**

on the cheap   **cheaply**
Inf. Something bought *on the cheap* is a *bargain.* The phrase can mean 'on a shoe-
string' in certain contexts, thus: *We started the business on the cheap; We were getting
along on the cheap.* See also **cheap.**

on the day   **when the time comes**
Thus: *On the day, the people will see the light and vote the other way.* A favorite usage
of politicians. Also *on the night:* famous last words of theatrical performers when
things aren't going well at rehearsal: *It'll be all right on the night,* i.e., when the
curtain really goes up.

(be) on the game   **(be) a prostitute**
Slang. Synonymous with **(be) on the knock.**

on the hob, *Slang.*   *Slang.* **on the wagon**

on the hop. See **caught on the hop.**

(be) on the knock   **(be) a prostitute**
Slang. Not to be confused with *be on the knock-off,* which is underworld jargon for
living by thievery. Synonymous with **(be) on the game.**

on the loose   **on a spree**
Inf. Rather than merely *fancy-free,* which the expression connotes in America.

on the right lines   **on the right track**

on the side   **on the kitchen counter**
Curiously, the term *counter* is commonly used, yet many Britons still persist in
saying that the thing you're looking for is *on the side* rather than *on the counter.*

on the slate   *Inf.* **on the cuff**
Inf. Synonymous with **on tick.** Usually heard in pubs, in the expression *Put it on
the slate,* said to the **landlord** by a **local** out of funds. In the old days, the reluctant
landlord actually had a slate on which such transactions on credit were recorded.

on the spot   **alert**
Inf. Right there when he's needed. There is a flavor of this British usage in the
old-fashioned expression familiar to Americans, *Johnny-on-the-spot.*

on the stocks   *Inf.* **in the works**
Inf. Already started, describing any project on which work has already begun. Borrowed from shipbuilding, where stocks hold back a ship while it is building and
must be released when building is complete.

on the strength   **on the payroll**
The strength is the working force of an organization. The use of *strength* in this connection is related to the use of *strong* in an expression like *twenty strong,* to describe the size of a group. See **strong.**

on the teapot, *Inf.*   *Inf.* **on the wagon**

on the telephone   **having a telephone**
In America *on the telephone* means 'speaking on the telephone.' In Britain if you want to get in touch with someone and want to know whether or not he has a phone, you ask him, *Are you on the telephone?* In America you would ask, *Do you have a phone?* The term is little used now that telephone usage is nearly universal.

on the tiles. See **night on the tiles.**

on the up and up   *Slang.* **going places**
Slang. Quite a different meaning in Britain! Describes a person or company moving ahead satisfactorily.

on thorns, *Inf.*   *Inf.* **on tenterhooks**

on tick   **on the cuff**
Inf. See also **on the slate.**

on train. See **in train.**

On your bike! *Slang.*   *Slang.* **Get lost!**

oof   *Slang.* **dough**
In the sense of 'money.' This word is at the least old-fashioned; it may now be obsolete. It is short for *ooftisch,* a Yiddish corruption of *auf dem Tisch,* which is German for 'on the table.' In other words, *money on the table,* also known as *cash on the barrelhead.* The current slang term is **lolly** or **dosh.**

open-cast mining   **strip mining**

open goods-waggon   **gondola car**
See **truck.**

opening hours   SEE COMMENT
Inf. Pubs used to be open more or less at all hours, but during World War I they were forced to close during certain hours. This provision was included in **DORA.** The establishment of pub closing hours was deemed necessary to prevent workers from stopping at a pub for a quick one in the morning on the way to the munitions factory and somehow never getting there. *Time gentlemen, please!* means that the legal closing hour is at hand—or, more often, past.

opening time. See **during hours.**

open the bowling, *Inf.*   **set the ball rolling; get things started**
A term borrowed from **cricket.** One starts the game by bowling (over-arm) the first ball, which 'opens the bowling,' and thus gets things under way. See **bowler,**

2. To *change the bowling* (literally, to put in a new bowler) is to *make a change* generally, as when a firm has to replace an executive or any employee, a technique, its
image, the advertising, etc.

Open University   SEE COMMENT
Correspondence courses in Britain involving written materials and reading lists,
supplemented by live tutorial sessions and television and radio lectures, and in
some courses some attendance at a regular university. These courses are govern-
ment-funded and open to anyone without regard to scholastic qualifications. There
are examinations and an A.B. degree can be earned in a minimum of three years.

operating-theatre, *n.*   **operating room**

oppidan, *n.*   SEE COMMENT
An Etonian living off campus. At Eton there are seventy *collegers,* also known
there as **scholars** or *foundation scholars,* and 1,030 (or thereabouts) *oppidans* (from
oppidum, Latin for 'town'). The *collegers,* or *scholars,* are the privileged few who
live in *college.* The *oppidans* attend the same courses but live in school boarding-
houses in town.

opposite prompt   **stage right**
Short for *opposite prompter* and often abbreviated to *o.p.* This archaic circumlocution was based on the position of the prompter's box in the old days. *Prompt*
(short for *prompt side,* often abbreviated to *p.s.*) naturally means 'stage left.' These
terms sometimes mean the exact reverse, particularly in old theaters, where the
prompter's box was located on the other side of the stage.

(the) opposition, *n.*   **1. (the) competition**
                                                                               2. SEE COMMENT
1. *The opposition* is the *competing firm* in one's profession or business.
2. *The Official Opposition* is the largest party not in power in the **House of Commons.**

ops room   **operations planning room**
Inf. A military expression. A *tour of ops* is an R.A.F. term meaning the number of
missions to be completed in order to earn a rest period.

optic   SEE COMMENT
Measuring device fastened to the neck of liquor bottles in pubs. The device is
called an *optic* because the liquor flows out of the upside-down bottle into a
transparent vessel and is thus visible to the naked eye. In this fashion, not a
micron over the legal minimum escapes into the waiting glass, whereas American bartenders tend to be more liberal, on the whole, in dispensing their shots.
See **double, 3; Appendix II.C.2.b.**

orbital, *n.*   SEE COMMENT
Another name, from 'orbital road,' for what is also called a *circular road* or **ring-
road,** to describe a bypass encircling a town. The adjective is used as a noun.

orderly bin   **street litterbox**

order paper   **legislative calendar**
An *order paper* is the Parliamentary equivalent of an American Congressional
calendar.

order to view   **appointment to look at**
Term used in house hunting. A written order issued by the real estate agent.

ordinary, *adj.*   **regular**
Regular mail, to a Briton, sounds like *mail at regular intervals* rather than *normal* mail (i.e., not special delivery or registered, etc.).

ordinary call   **station-to-station call**
Telephone call. In Britain a *person-to-person* call is known as a *personal* call. Both terms are now rare.

ordinary shares   **common stock**

ordnance datum   **sea level**
Above sea level is commonly seen in Britain; *above ordnance datum* is never seen in America.

Ordnance Survey   SEE COMMENT
A government department created in the 19th century for the purpose of creating detailed maps of all of the UK. Though privatized in recent years, the organization still updates its maps, which are marvels of cartography and still essential documents for **ramblers** and other tourists.

organize, *v.t.*   *Inf.* **round up, arrange**
Inf. As in, *It's too late to organize a baby sitter,* when you get a last-minute invitation to play dinner or to bridge. To *organize* somebody or something is to 'get hold of,' to 'arrange for,' the person or thing that fills the need.

(the) other half   **another drink**
Inf. When your kind friend notices that you've finished your drink—the first one, anyway—he asks solicitously, "How about the other half?" And when you've done with that one, the kind friend is known to repeat the delightful question, in the same words.

other place. See **another place.**

other ranks   **enlisted men**
Non-officers. Frequently referred to as *ORs.*

OTT. See **over the top.**

outdoor relief   SEE COMMENT
Aid given by a poorhouse to an outsider. Also known in Britain as *out*-relief; now obsolete.

outgoings, *n. pl.*   **expenses**
This British word is used to cover not only *household expenses* but also *business overhead.* Note that *overhead is overheads* in Britain, a real plural taking a plural verb. In America usually called *outlay.*

outhouse, *n.*   SEE COMMENT
Any building incidental to and built near or against the main house; not an outdoor privy, as in America.

out of bounds   **off limits**
Applies principally to military personnel.

out of the hunt. See **in the hunt.**

outwith, *prep.*   **outside**
A Scottish usage, as in, *This pay-rise* (raise in pay) *cannot be allowed as it is outwith the pay code* (wage ceiling).

oven glove   **pot-holder**

over, *n.*   SEE COMMENT
Cricket term; explained under **maiden over.**

overall, *n.*   **1. coverall**
                                                               2. smock
The British use *overall,* or **boiler suit,** in the sense of a 'one-piece work garment' and also to describe what Americans would call a *smock.*

overbalance, *v.i.*   **lose one's balance**
The British sometimes use the verb transitively as well, meaning to 'make (someone) lose his balance.' The usual American meaning is 'outweigh.'

overdraft, *n.*   **bank loan**
The universal British term for having an overdrawn bank account. This may happen by prior arrangement (having an overdraft facility) or through imprudent spending. This type of overdraft is arranged in advance (a banking practice now spreading in America). The inadvertent type, or an intentional overdraft not previously arranged for, results in a letter from the bank.

overleaf, *adv.*   **on the reverse side**
Of a page or printed notice. See also **P.T.O.**

overspill, *n., adj.*   **surplus population**
An *overspill* city is a new British sociopolitical phenomenon. It is a made-to-order city designed in accordance with blueprints drawn up under the New Towns Act to take care of surplus urban population. Thus, there exist the New Towns of Crawley, Stevenage and Basildon.

overtake, *v.t., v.i.*   **pass**
A traffic term. *Do Not Overtake* is the British road sign equivalent of *No Passing.*

over the eight. See **have one over the eight.**

over the moon   **in raptures**

over the odds   **above market value**
To *ask* or *pay over the odds* for something is to demand or pay a price in excess of the generally accepted price for the item in question.

over the road   **across the street**

over the top   **going too far**
Inf. Excessive, as in *Calling him a thief was over the top.* To *go over the top* is to *overact,*
especially in the theater, in which context it would mean to 'ham it up.'

owner-occupier. See under **occupier.**

Oxbridge, *n. adj.*   SEE COMMENT
Oxford and Cambridge; a **portmanteau** concoction. Used when contrasting
Oxford and Cambridge with 19th-century universities such as Birmingham,
Manchester, and Sheffield, which were referred to as the **redbrick universities,**
originally a pejorative term. The image of these universities, however, has been
greatly enhanced. No comparable term is yet current to describe a third group
of universities established in the 20th century. Of several terms heard, the most
pleasant is the *Shakespearean universities,* so-called because their names (Essex,
Sussex, Warwick, Kent, Lancaster, York) suggest the dramatis personae of his
historical plays. *Oxbridge* is used as an adjective in such expressions as *Oxbridge
type, Oxbridge accent,* etc., implying a perceived superiority to others. See also
redbrick university.

Oxford bags. See **bags.**

Oxonian, *n. adj.*   SEE COMMENT
Of Oxford. From the Latinized name of the city, *Oxonia.* In a narrower sense, an
Oxonian is a student or graduate of Oxford University. Abbreviation: *Oxon.*

oxter, *n.*   **armpit**
Mostly North of England and Scottish, but used occasionally in other parts by
obscurantists.

P

p., *n.*   SEE COMMENT
Abbreviation of *penny* or *pence,* and pronounced as P. See **Appendix II.A.**

P.A.   secretary
Abbreviation of *personal assistant.*

pack, *n.*   deck
In the expression *pack of cards. Deck* is also used in Britain.

package deal   turnkey deal
Package deal is used interchangeably with *turnkey deal* in Britain in the oil industry
to indicate a fixed price for the drilling of an exploratory well to an agreed depth.
It is not so used in America, where *turnkey* is the correct term.

package holiday   package tour
A trip for which the customer pays a fixed sum, which covers costs for travel,
accommodation, and often meals at the destination.

packed lunch, *n.*   sack lunch

packed out   *Inf.* **packed full**
Inf. For instance, a popular restaurant in London may be *packed out with* people at
lunch time. See also **chock-a-block.**

packet, *n.*   package
The delivery man in Britain leaves a *packet* at the door; in America this would be
a *package.* Applied to cigarettes, the American term is *pack. Pay packet* is the British equivalent of *pay envelope. Packet* has a number of slang uses as well. To *pay a
packet* is to *pay a fortune* (or *an arm and a leg*); synonymous with **pay the earth;** and
things that cost a lot are said to *cost a packet.* If you win a lot of money at a British
track or on the London Stock Exchange, you *make a packet.* The American equivalent of this would be a *pile.* See also **twenty.**

pack it in   desist; finish
Slang. Synonymous with **pack up** as that term applies to persons. *I used to garden, but because of my bad back, I packed it in.* Sometimes, *pack it up.* Also means to
'leave,' 'depart,' or 'quit' (e.g., for the day).

pack it up. See **pack it in.**

pack up   *Slang.* **quit; conk out**
Slang. Applies to both persons and things. Of persons, it means to 'retire,' 'throw
in one's hand.' Also, to 'leave,' 'depart'; see under **pack it in.** Of machines, for
example, to *conk out,* or *break down,* usually for good.

paddle, *v.i.*   **wade**
To go wading in shallow water. The British use *wade* in the sense of walking
through water, mud, snow, or any obstructive material, rather than engaging in a
pleasant aquatic pastime.

paddy, *n.*   **tantrum**
Inf. Paddywhack is a variant.

page, *n.*   **bellhop**
Sometimes *hotel page* or *page-boy*. Occasionally called *buttons*.

pair, *n.*   **floor**
Pair was formerly used on building directories to indicate what *floor* a tenant
occupies. A person on the *third pair* means a person 'three flights up.' Old-fashioned building directories usually put the number of the pair first, followed by
the name of the occupants.

pair of tongs. See under **barge-pole.**

Paki, *n. adj.*   **Pakistani**
Slang. (Rhymes with WACKY.) An abbreviated form with offensive racist connotations. *Paki-bashing* is an unpleasant word for the unpleasant activities of roaming
gangs looking for people of South-Asian descent to beat up.

palaver   **affair; business**
Slang. A *palaver*, literally, in both countries, is a *powwow*, a prolonged parley,
usually between parties of different levels of culture. In both Britain and America, it has acquired the significance of *idle talk* or *chatter*, but in Britain alone it is
common slang for *affair* or *business* in the sense of 'big deal' or 'fuss'; anything
complicated by red tape or confusion. The word almost always appears in the
expression *such a palaver. I'd love to go to the opera but getting tickets is such a palaver!*

palette-knife, *n.*   **spatula**
It can also mean what it does in America: a metal blade with a handle, used for
mixing and sometimes applying artists' colors.

palliasse, *n.*   **straw mattress**

panache, *n.*   **flair; swagger**
Panache has the literal meaning of 'plume,' as on a helmet. It is found in Britain in
phrases such as *professional panache*, describing, for instance, a doctor or lawyer
who acts very sure of himself; in America, too, for *flamboyance*.

Pancake Day, *n.*   **Shrove Tuesday**
Shrove Tuesday is the day before Ash Wednesday, the first day of Lent. Pancakes (a
thinner, lighter version than those eaten in America) are commonly eaten on that
day even by people who do not pay much attention to Lent.

pancake roll   **egg roll**
Now rare; the more common term is **spring roll.**

panda car   **police car**
A familiar sight on residential beats is the small police car, usually light blue with
white doors and a large POLICE sign on top. They are all blue in London. See also
jam sandwich; Z-car.

panel, *n.*   SEE COMMENT
List of **National Health Service** doctors for a given district. A *panel doctor* is one
on such a list; a *panel practice* is one consisting of National Health patients. Less
common now than it once was.

pannage, *n.*   **pig food**

pantechnicon, *n.*   **moving van**
Also *pantechnicon van*. *Pantechnicon van* is the equivalent of *moving van*, but *van* is
dropped so that *pantechnicon* has come to designate the van. This strange word
was the name of a London building known as *The Pantechnicon* (an obsolete word
for 'bazaar' or 'exhibition of arts and crafts'), which over a century ago housed a
collection of the wonders of the Victorian age. It failed as a commercial venture
and the building was turned into a furniture warehouse while keeping the name,
which was inevitably transferred to the vehicles used. See also **removals.**

pantomime, *n.*   SEE COMMENT
Often *panto* for short. This is a British form of show, produced during the Christmas season, based on fairy tales or legends, involving singing, dancing, clown-
ing, topical humor, and almost anything but the silence which is associated with
the word in its ordinary sense. Adults are admitted if accompanied by children.

pants   **1. underpants**
                                                                  2. *Slang.* **rubbish**
1. *n. pl.* The British equivalent of American *pants* is *trousers*. In Britain *pants* are
underwear, usually men's shorts; but *pants* in Britain can also include ladies' *panties*. See also **shorts; frillies; knickers; liners; smalls.**
2. *adj.*

Paper, *n.*   *approx.* **government publication**
There are White, Blue, and Green *Papers*. White and Blue Papers are official documents laid before Parliament by command of one of the Secretaries of State and
are known as *command papers*. The short ones are bound in a white cover, the long
ones in a blue cover. *White* and *Blue* are simply a matter of binding. *Green Papers,*
issued in green bindings, a later development, cover government plans to be
placed before the public as a basis for discussion in advance of decision.
  Black Paper is a relatively new term, meaning a 'pamphlet' (unofficial, non-
governmental) issued by an *ad hoc* group on any given subject, expressing a
view contrary to that of the government or analyzing what they consider to be a
scandal.

paper knife   **letter opener**

paper round   **paper route**

paraffin, *n.*   **kerosene**
The British equivalent of American *paraffin* is **white wax** or *paraffin wax*.

paralytic, *adj.*   *Slang.* **very drunk**
Also used as an intensifier for drunk: *He was paralytically drunk.*

parish, *n.*   *approx.* **town**
The parish was formerly the subdivision of a county constituting the smallest
unit of local government, and was regulated by what was known as a *parish council.* Originally, the term had the familiar religious connotation; but when used
alone, it was, in proper context, understood to mean 'civil parish.' The American
approximation of *parish* in that sense would have been *town,* in rural areas. *Parish*
is now obsolete as a unit of government.

park. See under **car park; caravan.**

parking bay   **parking space**
The space covered by a parking meter, or an outdoor parking space for rent.

parky, *adj.*   **chilly; brisk**
Slang. Meteorological slang: *A parky day, isn't it?*

parson's nose   *Inf.* **pope's nose**
Inf. That part of a fowl that goes over the fence last.

part brass rags   *Inf.* **break things off**
Slang. Originally a naval expression, based on buddies' sharing their brass-
cleaning rags. When the friendship ceased, they *parted brass rags.* Now applied to
any severance of a pair, persons who have worked together.

part exchange. See **give in part exchange.**

parting, *n.*   **part**
Both British and Americans *part* their hair, but the result is known as a *parting* in
Britain and a *part* in America. See also **turning** for *turn.* See **Appendix I.A.3.**

party candidate   SEE COMMENT
When Americans go to the polls they vote for all sorts of offices, from president
down, and they either vote the *straight ticket* or *split their ticket.* A Briton votes
only for his *M.P.* (**Member** *of Parliament*), and if his vote is based on party rather
than choice of individual, he votes for his *party candidate.*

party manifesto   **political platform**
Also, **programme.**

pass, *n.*   **passing grade**
Referring to school examinations: thus, *O-level pass, A-level pass,* etc. See **A-levels.**
A *pass degree* is a lesser level of academic distinction than an *honours degree.* See
also **class; first.**

pass, *v.t.*   **1. leave (a message)**
                                                              2. refer

1. As in, *He isn't in now. Would you care to pass a message?*
2. As in, *I'll pass you to the person who handles your account.*

passage, *n.*   **corridor**

passbook, *n.*   SEE COMMENT
In addition to its meaning shared with America ('savings bankbook'), this word
has two further meanings in Britain: 1. A book supplied by a bank for the recording of deposits and withdrawals in a checking account (**current account**) as well
as in a savings account (**deposit account**). 2. The document formerly issued to
non-white persons by the South African government, which they had to carry at
all times; a type of identity card.

passing, *n.*   **passage**
Referring to a bill in Parliament.

passman   SEE COMMENT
A person who takes a degree at a university without distinction—the recipient of
what Americans call a Gentleman's C.

pass out   **graduate**
Usage confined to the military, meaning to 'complete military training.' The act
itself is not called *passing out,* but rather *passage out.* In this sense, nothing to do
with the curse of drink, though *pass out* is used (and happens) in Britain that way
as well.

past a joke   *Inf.* **not funny**
Slang. Intolerable. Describes a situation that can no longer be laughed off or toler-
ated. *His drinking is past a joke.*

past praying for   **in desperate straits**
Inf. Beyond hope; up the creek without a paddle.

pasty, *n.*   SEE COMMENT
The only one-word American approximation is *knish.* The most famous *pasty* of
all is the *Cornish pasty,* which originated in the Duchy of Cornwall but is now
ubiquitous in Britain and is usually filled with seasoned meat mixed with vegetables. *Pasties* can be filled with almost anything—there are *jam pasties* and *fruit
pasties* as well as *meat pasties.* See also **pie; tart.** Rhymes with *nasty.*

patch, *n.*   *Inf.* **police beat**
Inf. A special usage, as where a policeman says of a particularly unpleasant homi-
cide case, *I'm glad it isn't on my patch.* Synonymous with **manor** used in this sense.
More generally, it can be used as a synonym for turf. *I don't know any place to eat
around here—it isn't my patch.* For other idiomatic uses of *patch,* see **bad patch** and
not a patch on.

pater, *n.*   **father**
Slang. Old usage; **public school** style.

Paternoster Row   SEE COMMENT
Inf. Formerly, the *publishing industry.* Paternoster Row in London was for cen-
turies the street where booksellers and publishers had their home. Destroyed in
World War II. The phrase is rarely used today.

patience, *n.*   **solitaire**
Name for the endless varieties of card game played by a lone player. *Patience*
is the British name and *solitaire* the usual American name, although *patience* is

occasionally heard among older people in America. The game *solitaire* in Britain describes a game played by a lone player with marbles on a board containing little holes into which the marbles fit.

patrial, *n.*   SEE COMMENT
One having the right of abode and exemption from control in the U.K. under the Immigration Act 1971. The important innovation was to confer such rights on Commonwealth citizens who have a parent born in the U.K. Descendants of patrials have the right of free admission to the U.K.

Patrol, *n.*   *approx.* **School Zone**
Signs reading PATROL 150 YARDS, PATROL 125 yards, etc., often with a picture of a child, are the equivalent of SCHOOL ZONE signs in America. The implication is that a **lollipop man** or **woman** may be on duty.

pavement, *n.*   sidewalk
Sidewalk is not used by the British. *Crazy pavement* (more often *crazy paving*) denotes irregularly shaped, sometimes varicolored flat stones used in the building of garden paths, patios, etc. *Pavement artists* make very elaborate colored chalk drawings in London and other cities on sidewalks and hope for tips from passersby.

pawky, *adj.*   sly

pay bed   **paid hospital bed**
As opposed to a free bed under the **National Health Service.**

pay-box, *n.*   **box office**

pay code   **wage ceiling**

P.A.Y.E.   **pay as you go**
These dreary initials stand for *pay as you earn,* which is the British name for the income-tax system which provides for the withholding of income tax by employers.

pay for the call   **accept the charge**
This is the term used by the operator in the process of putting through a collect call (**reverse-charge call,** in Britain). The American operator asks the person at the other end of the line, *Will you accept the charge?* The British operator asks, *Will you pay for the call?*

paying-in slip   **deposit slip**
Banking term.

pay one's shot   **chip in**
Inf. Synonymous with **pay one's whack.** See **whack, 3.**

pay one's whack. See **whack, 3.**

pay on the nail, *Slang.*   *Slang.* **pay spot cash**

pay packet. See **packet.**

pay policy   **wage control**
In Britain, an arrangement between the government and the trade unions, as opposed to formal legislative control. Also referred to as *wage restraint*. See also **social contract; wage restraint.**

pay (someone) in washers   *Slang.* **pay (someone) peanuts**
Slang. A contemptuous idiom used by people connected with engineering, *washers* being of negligible value.

pay the earth   *Inf.* **pay a fortune**
The British also say *cost a fortune*, as well as *cost the earth.*

pay up, *v.i.*   **pay**
For any debt, e.g. in a restaurant or bar.

P.C.   **1. Privy Councillor**
2. Police Constable
3. postcard
4. politically correct
1. See under **Birthday Honours.**
2. If your daughter's going out with a *P.C.,* you may hope for 1. but must be prepared for 2. See **constable.** *P.C.* is the official title, as in *P.C. Smith.*
3. Usually in lower case, **p.c.**

peak viewing time   **prime time**

pearly, *n.*   *Inf.* **fruit and vegetable pushcart vendor**
Called a *pearly* when dressed in *pearlies,* a holiday costume richly adorned with mother-of-pearl buttons. When so attired, pearlies and their wives are sometimes called *Pearly Kings* and *Pearly Queens.* The prosaic name for these flamboyant street vendors is **costermonger,** and their costumes date back more than a century.

pea-stick *n.*   **bean pole**

pebble-dash, *n.*   **pebble-coated stucco**
A frequent building surfacing in Britain. It gets dirty rather quickly and appears to be totally unwashable because of the rough texture.

peckish, *adj.*   *approx. Inf.* **empty**
Inf. Peckish means 'hungry,' 'wanting a snack,' hankering after a little something to fill the void. Undoubtedly, *peckish* is derived from *peck* as in *pecking* at food, a little of this and a little of that, the way a chicken eats.

pedestal, *n.*   **toilet bowl**
Sometimes *w.c. pedestal,* a euphemism for *toilet bowl,* seen, for example, in lavatory signs on certain British railroad cars requesting passengers not to throw various objects into the *w.c. pedestal.*

pedestrian crossing, *n.*   **crosswalk**

pedlar, *n.*   *Slang.* **blabbermouth**
Inf. Pedlar is usually spelled *peddler* in America. Its literal meaning is the same in both countries, evoking the image of a *pack-carrying* or *wagon-driving hawker*

of small and extremely miscellaneous merchandise. In Britain it has a figurative meaning: 'gossip' as indeed most *pedlars* must have been, since they saw everything that was going on.

pee, *n., v.i.*   **1. urination**
                                                                     2. urinate
Inf. Surprisingly, to Americans at least, this word has become acceptable in familiar speech, even in mixed company, while Americans go to great lengths to dream up euphemisms.

peeler. See **bobby.**

peep-behind-the-curtain. See **Tom Tiddler's ground.**

peep-toes, *n. pl., Slang.*   **open-toed shoes**

peer, *n.*   SEE COMMENT
A member of the titled nobility. A peer's wife or a female peer in her own right is a *peeress*. See also **Lord; Lady; Dame; K.**

peg away   *Inf.* **plug along**
Inf. To *stay with* a job, no matter how tired you get. See also **soldier on.**

peg out, *Slang.*   *Slang.* **kick the bucket**
See also **drop off the hooks; turn up one's toes.**

pelican crossing   **pedestrian crossing**
Pe(destrian) li(ght) con(trolled) crossing: it ought to be spelled *pelicon,* but close enough. See also **zebra.**

pelmet, *n.*   **valance**

pen knife, *n.*   **pocketknife**

penny, *n.* See **Appendix II.A.**

penny dreadful   *Inf.* **dime novel**
Inf. Sometimes called a *penny blood* or a *shilling shocker.* All these terms may have an old-fashioned ring, but are still in use, often jocularly.

(the) penny dropped   *Slang.* **I (he, etc.) got the message**
Slang. Something clicked. Used to describe the situation where the protagonist is at first unaware of the significance of what is going on, can't take a hint or two, and then—finally—the veil lifts: *it dawns on him; he gets the point; it clicks.* Metaphor from a vending-machine (which the British call **slot-machine**). See also **penny in the slot.**

penny-farthing, *n.*   **high-wheeler**
Inf. Primitive bicycle.

penny gaff. See **gaff.**

penny in the slot   *approx. Inf.* **took the bait**
Inf. Said when one succeeds in evoking a predictable reaction from someone, by baiting him.

penny reading   SEE COMMENT
An old-time show consisting of a series of short skits and sketches, usually comic.
The price of admission was a penny. The practice is kept alive at some of the
public schools.

pennyworth, *n.*   SEE COMMENT
Sometimes *penn'orth.* A *pennyworth* is, literally, as much as can be bought for a
penny. The expression *not a pennyworth* means 'not the least bit.' *Pennyworth,* in
the expression *a good* or *bad pennyworth,* means a 'bargain.'

pension cover   **pension benefits**

pensioner, *n.*   **senior citizen**
See **O.A.P.** Also, in Cambridge, an undergraduate without financial assistance
from the university.

pepper-castor (-caster), *n.*   **pepper shaker**

pepper-pot, *n.*   **pepper shaker**

perambulator, *n.*   **baby carriage**
But practically always shortened to *pram.*

pergola, *n.*   **trellis**
Pergola, in America, evokes the image of a rustic garden house to escape into
out of the rain or for children to play house in or adolescents to daydream in.
Technically it means an 'arbor' or 'bower.' But in Britain, especially in the country, it is the name for a *trellis* running in a straight line and usually constructed
of slim tree trunks as uprights and branches as crosspieces and Y-shaped supports, all still wearing their bark, and forming a frame for the training of climbing roses. *Trellis* is now just as common.

period return. See **return.**

perish, *v.t.*   **destroy**
Perish is, of course, in both countries an intransitive verb. The transitive use
is very rare in America and is now heard only in dialect. In Britain one still is
perished by (or with) cold, thirst, etc. This does not mean one has died of it but
merely been distressed or at least made seriously uncomfortable. When heat or
cold *perishes* vegetation, it does mean 'destroy.' *Perishing* can be used in Britain
as an adverb, as in *perishing cold.* It's *perishing cold,* which means 'terribly cold,' is
another British way of saying **bloody** *cold.*

perks, *n. pl.*   **fringe benefits**
Inf. Shortening of *perquisites.* Gaining currency in America.

permanent way   **roadbed**
Railroad term. It means the 'roadbed' or the 'rails' themselves. The epithet *permanent* derives from the earliest days of railroad construction, when the gangs laid
temporary trackage, and then later put in the *permanent* tracks, after the right of
way had consolidated.

perry, *n.*   **pear cider**
A fermented pear juice drink in Britain. See also **cider; scrump.**

personal allowance
Income tax term.

personal exemption

personal call
See also **pay for the call; caller.**

person-to-person call

Perspex, perspex, *n.*

plexiglass

perv, *n., abbrev.*

Slang. **pervert**

peterman, *n. Slang*
Also in America called a 'peteman.'

safe cracker

petrol, *n.*
A *petrol station* is a *filling station.*

gasoline

petrol bomb

Inf. **Molotov cocktail**

petty, *n.*
Slang. A lavatory. Heard mostly in the North of England.

Slang. **john**

pewter, *n.*
Slang. Used in this context *pewter* means only 'prize' (money or any object), the kind of *loot* you bring home from a church bazaar. This use was derived from the fact that the prize was often a tankard, usually of pewter.

Slang. **booty**

PFI, *acronym*   SEE COMMENT
Private Finance Initiative. A type of financing of public projects (e.g. hospitals) in which government funding and private funding are combined.

P45   SEE COMMENT
An employment-leaving certificate given by an employer on the termination of someone's employment. It provides information on gross earnings and tax paid. To be handed one's P45 is to be fired, or **sacked.**

P.G.   **boarder**
Inf. Stands for *paying guest,* a euphemism for what Americans would call a *boarder* and Britons call a **lodger.** *Paying guest* would seem to be close to a contradiction in terms. Can be used as a verb: to *p.g.* (or *PG*) with someone is to *board* with him.

picotee, *n.*   SEE COMMENT
A variety of carnation having a border of a color different from the main color of its petals. The border is usually darker.

pictures, *n. pl., Inf.*
See also **film; cinema.**

movies

pie, *n.*   **meat-pie; deep-dish pie**
An ordinary American pie would often be called a *tart* in Britain (see **tart**). In Britain, unless otherwise specified, *pie* means 'meat pie' (see **pasty**), rather than anything involving fruit, and a request for a fruit-pie (*apple pie, cherry pie, etc.*) would produce the equivalent of an American *deep-dish pie.*

pie and mash   SEE COMMENT
A popular meal served in cafés and pubs of a meat or fish pie and mashed potatoes.

pie and pint man   SEE COMMENT
Slang. A person of extremely modest means. The *pie* in question is a *meat pie* (see **pie**); the *pint* is a *pint of bitter* (see **bitter; pint**). A meat pie and a pint of bitter (*beer*) would make the meal, presumably at a **pub,** of one living on a low budget. By contrast, a *pieman* is a vendor of *pies.*

pie-hole, *n.*   *Inf.* **mouth**

pie shell   **pie crust**
Especially the prepared type for sale at the grocer's.

piggy-in-the-middle, *n. Inf.*   SEE COMMENT
The *innocent victim* of a situation; one caught in a difficult situation not of his own making, like a dispute between good friends both of whom appeal to him for support. From the children's game *piggy-in-the-middle,* in which a child is caught in a circle of his peers and must struggle to get out. *Monkey-in-the-middle* is the American counterpart.

pig it   **1. live like a pig**
                                                               2. eat like a pig
Slang. Becoming current in America. To *pig it* with someone is to share his quarters, with the connotation of having to squeeze in and live untidily for the time being.

pigs might fly, and. See **and pigs might fly.**

pi-jaw. See **jaw.**

pikelet, *n.*   SEE COMMENT
A small, round, crumpet-like cake, originating in Wales. In many families, served mainly at Christmas.

pile, *n.*   **Inf.** SEE COMMENT
A large country house. *He'll never have to worry about money—he's got that huge pile in Wiltshire.*

pile on the agony   *Inf.* **lay it on thick**
Inf. To intensify the painful narrative, sparing no detail; but it may also be used to indicate any excessive or exaggerated action or display, such as, e.g., a painfully lavish entertainment or feast. See also **come it strong.**

pillar-box   **mailbox**
In the form of a high, hollow, red pillar. See also **letter-box; post-box.**

pillock, *n.*   *Slang.* **a stupid or foolish person**

pinch, *v.t.*   *Inf.* **swipe**
Slang. Pinch and *swipe* meaning 'steal,' and *pinch* meaning 'arrest' are used in both countries; but in the meaning 'steal,' *pinch* is favored in Britain and *swipe* in America, where *pinch* more commonly means 'arrest.' In America you're *pinched* if you are caught *swiping;* in Britain, you're *nabbed* if you are caught *pinching.*

pinch-point, *n.*   SEE COMMENT
Restriction on vehicles beyond a certain width. See **except for access.**

pink, *v.i.*   *Inf.* **ping; knock**
Inf. Describing the sound made by an automobile engine when the ignition is over-advanced.

pink gin   SEE COMMENT
Gin and angostura bitters, with water added.

pinny, *n.*   **apron**
Inf. Child's abbreviation of *pinafore.*

pint, *n.*   *approx.* **beer**
If a Briton asks for a *pint* he means a 'pint of **bitter,**' an Imperial pint of 20 ounces. If his thirst or budget is of more modest proportions, he will ask for a **half,** or *half of bitter,* which means 'half a pint,' i.e., 10 oz. Since *bitter* is usually of two grades, *ordinary bitter* and *best bitter,* the regular client, whose taste in the matter is a known quantity, need not specify. Otherwise he will volunteer the grade, or the person behind the counter will ask. Standing by itself, in this context, a *pint* in Britain means about the same thing as a *beer* means in America. At one of the meetings of the E.E.C. in 1976, the British were formally allowed to hang on to *pints* in beer, so long as they went metric in everything else. At the time of writing, the exemption was scheduled for termination. But it has a way of surviving all manner of attacks. See also **pub; during hours.**

pinta, *n.*   **pint of milk**
Inf. (The *i* is long as in *ice.*) Originated in the National Dairy Council's advertisement *Drinka pinta milka day!* Never to be confused with **pint.** Probably a corruption of *pint of.*

pip, *n.*   *Slang.* **beep**
Slang. When you make a call from a telephone booth, as your party answers, you hear a series of rapid *pips* and must promptly insert your coin in order to be heard. Short *pips,* called *beeps,* are the sounds you are supposed to hear, in America, every 15 seconds, if your call is being recorded.

pip, *v.t.*   1. *Slang.* **blackball**
                                                                   2. *Slang.* **wing (wound)**
                                                                   3. *Slang.* **pull rank on**
                                                                   4. *Slang.* **nose out**
Slang. For use 4. see **pip at the post.**

pip at the post, *v.t.*   *Inf.* **nose out**
Inf. The post referred to is the winning post in a horse race. *Pip at the post* means 'defeat at the last moment.'

pissed, *adj.*   *Inf.* **blind drunk**
Slang. Usually reserved for instances of advanced inebriation. A vulgarism like **pee,** which is heard widely. See also **sloshed; squiffy; to the wide; well away.**

pisser, *n.*   *Slang.* **the toilet**

piss off   1. *Slang.* **leave**
                                                                   2. *interj.* **get lost!**
1. *We pissed off to the pub after dinner.*
2. *Piss off!*

piss-up, *n.* *Slang.* **a riotous party**
The implication is that drunkenness will be the norm. One of the commonest terms of abuse for a supposedly stupid or incompetent person is to say that he *couldn't organize a piss-up in a brewery.*

pit *n.* **rear of orchestra**
What is called the *orchestra* in America turns up in Britain as the **stalls.** The *pit* used to be the name for the rear of that part of the theater.

pitch, *n.* SEE COMMENT
A technical term in **cricket:** the narrow rectangular strip between the **wickets** along (or parallel to) which the **batsmen** run; often confusingly to neophytes, itself called the *wicket.* In **football** (*soccer*), however, the whole field is called the *pitch. Pitch* is sometimes used colloquially, like *wicket,* to mean *situation:* to be *on a* good pitch (or *wicket*) is to be *in a good spot.* It is also slang for *hangout* or *spot,* to describe the established location of a beggar, peddler, prostitute, pimp, tout, or other street person whose living strongly involves the territorial imperative, and in this use is synonymous with **turf.**

pitch upon **select by chance**
Inf. The police pitched upon him as the likeliest suspect.

placeman, *n.* **public office holder**
With the strong implication that the appointment was motivated by self-interest.

placet, *n.* **aye**
An affirmative vote in an ecclesiastical or university body. *Placet* is the impersonal third person singular of the Latin verb *placere* (to *please, be acceptable*). Cf. **content.**

plaice, *n.* SEE COMMENT
A small flat fish, cheaper than sole, **brill,** and **turbot,** very popular for frying and broiling.

plain, *adj.* **homely**
See under **homely.**

plain as a pikestaff, *Inf.* *Inf.* **plain as the nose on your face**
A pikestaff is a wooden stick with a pointed tip.

planning permission **building permit**
Short for *town and country planning permission.* A *town and country planning committee* is the British opposite number to an American *zoning board.*

plantation, *n.* **planted grove**
Of trees or shrubs.

plaster, *n.* **Band-aid**

Plastercine, *TM.* **modeling clay**

platelayer, *n.* **tracklayer**
A man hired to inspect and repair railway rails.

plates (of meat), *Rhyming slang.*   **feet**

play a straight bat   **play fair**
Inf. Act correctly; do the right thing. A term from **cricket** that is applied widely.

play for safety   **play safe**

play for (someone's) side, *Inf.*   **be on (someone's) side; side with (someone)**

play oneself in   **settle down**
Inf. The cricket batsman initially feels out the bowler in order to 'get his eye in,'
and thus settle down before he feels that it is now safe to start to attempt runs.
This initial period of settling down is known as *playing oneself in*—one of the
many cricket terms lent to the general language. Thus, a detective interviewing
a nervous witness gives him time to *play himself in* before serious, pointed questioning begins. He talks about the weather, the curse of heavy traffic on the roads,
the current political crisis, and then—wham!—goes into the active phase: "You
knew the deceased for many years, didn't you, Mr. Wiggins?" and "Where were
you on the night of . . . ?" and so on and so on. If he's successful, the detective has
given the witness an opportunity to *play himself in.*

play-pit, *n.*   **sandbox**

play the game. See **game,** *n.*

playtime, *n.*   **recess**
School term, applicable especially to kindergarten and first grade, children four
to six years old. In **prep school** (ages eight to 13) the term is more often *breaktime.*

play (something) to leg   **brush (something) off**
Inf. A term borrowed from **cricket.** When the **batsman plays** a ball **to leg,** he turns
or sweeps it away with his bat, rather than attempt to hit it hard and try to make
runs. Thus, to **play** a ball **to leg** is a defensive tactic; and to **play** an embarrassing
question **to leg** is to brush it off somehow and evade the issue.

play truant   **play hooky**
The American term is almost unknown in Britain.

play up!, *interj.*   *Inf.* **come on!**
Inf. Yelled by sports fans to urge on their team, as in, *Play up, United!*

play (someone) up   **1. play up on (someone)**
                                                              2. pester
1. In Britain your trick knee or your hi-fi *plays you up;* in America it *plays up on you.*
2. Pupils who deliberately annoy their teachers are said to *play them up.*

PLC/Plc/plc   SEE COMMENT
Stands for *public limited company,* one whose shares (under the Companies Act
of 1980) can be traded on the Stock Exchange. The three letters follow the name
of such a **company,** as opposed to *Ltd.* following the name of a private limited
company. In America, *Inc.* is used whether or not the corporation's stock can be
traded on an exchange.

Pleasure!   **Don't mention it!**
A somewhat warmer response than the usual *Not at all, Pleasure* is a contraction
of *It's a pleasure* or *My pleasure*. *Don't mention it* is heard, and sometimes *Think
nothing of it*. *You're welcome*, which until recently was never heard and immediately marked the user as American, is now uttered more and more frequently by
Britons. See also **Not at all.**

plimsolls, *n.*   **sneakers**
Another British term is **gym shoes.** *Plimsolls* is the common British word for
sneakers, so named after Samuel Plimsoll, who also lent his name to the expression *Plimsoll's Mark* (or *Plimsoll Line*), which is the line showing how far a ship is
allowed by law to be submerged when loaded. In addition, he is known as one of
the moving forces behind the British Merchant Shipping Act of 1876.

plonk, *n.*   **cheap wine**
Slang. Plink-plonk was a variation on *blink-blonk*, a jocular play on *vin blanc* by the
British Tommy in World War I. When the *plink* was dropped, the *plonk* that stayed
on should still have been reminiscent of *blanc,* but somehow came to apply to any
cheap wine.

plonker, *n.*   *Inf.* **fool**
A person of poor judgment and few talents. Dork would be an approximate
American equivalent.

plot (of land), *n.*   **lot**

Plough, *n.*   **Big Dipper**
Other British names for the *Big Dipper* are *Charles's Wain* and *Great Bear.* But see
big dipper.

plough, *v.t.*   *Slang.* **flunk**
Slang. That is, to *flunk* a pupil, not an exam. Undoubtedly short for *plough under.*
Sometimes used intransitively, in which case it does mean 'flunk an exam,' but
exam is understood.

ploughman's lunch   *approx.* **bread and cheese**
Inf. A large piece of French bread, an enormous slab of Cheddar cheese, a vast
chunk of butter, and a couple of sour pickled onions. A favorite at **pubs.** The dish
may nowadays feature other cheeses or even a slice of paté.

plough the sand(s), *Inf.*   **work in vain**

ploy, *n.*   **1. job**
                                                            2. toy
Inf. The meaning *toy* refers to *educational toys,* and looks like a **portmanteau**
formation of *play* and *toy*. In other words, a *toy* that keeps the kids busy with a
job, like fitting things together. *Ploy* is now anything calculated to get results by
outwitting or upsetting the other fellow.

PLR. See **Public Lending Right.**

plumber's bum, *n.*   SEE COMMENT
Bum is the posterior, and *plumber's bum* is that portion of the posterior that becomes visible when the workman bends low to inspect a drain. Commonly used for any inadvertent exposure of the anal cleft.

plum duff   **plum pudding**
(The *duff* is *dough* pronounced like ROUGH.)

plummy, *adj.*   SEE COMMENT
Used to describe the speech, and especially the accent, of the high-born.

plump, *v.i.*   **vote wholeheartedly**

plus fours, *n.*   **knickers**

po, *n.*   *Inf.* **pottie**
Slang. Short for the *pot* in *chamber pot,* and pronounced like the POT in the French *pot de chambre.* The French pronunciation is supposed to make it less clinical.

pocketbook, *n.*   **1. pocket notebook**
                                                       2. billfold
In Britain a lady's handbag is always called a *bag* or a *handbag,* never a *pocketbook.* That term is reserved there for a *pocket notebook* or a *folding wallet,* which the British also call a *notecase* or *billfold.*

podge, *n.*   *Inf.* **fatty**
Inf. Podge gives rise to the adjective *podgy,* which has its American equivalent in *pudgy.* See also **fubsy.**

po-faced, *adj.*   *approx.* **impassive**
Slang. A *po-faced* person is one who exhibits a deliberately blank expression, a poker face, to his audience. There is more than a hint of hauteur in this epithet. See **po.**

pogged, *adj.*   *Slang.* **stuffed**
Slang. After too much food: *I'm pogged!*

point, *n.*   **1. electrical socket**
                                                   2. railroad switch
1. *Point* often appears as *electrical point* or *power point.* Sometimes it is used in combination with another word, as in *razor point,* thus indicating an electrical outlet to be used for a particular purpose.

point duty. See **pointsman, 1.**

pointsman, *n.*   **1. traffic policeman**
                                                   2. switchman
1. *Point duty* is the *traffic detail* and a *policeman on point duty* is a *traffic cop.*
2. The railroad man in charge of switches.

poker school   **poker session**

policy, *n.*   **landscaped ground**
The landscaped area around a country house. Usually in the plural, the *policies*, and more common in Scotland than in England.

politician, *n.*   **1.** *approx.* **government official**
                                              2. political scientist
Going back a few years, a *politician* was one, whether or not in power at the moment, skilled in the science of government and politics generally. The term had little, if any, pejorative implication as in America, where it brings to mind the scheming and manipulation characteristic of party politics: unenlightened self-interest, the smoke-filled room. Until recently in Britain, a *statesman* was merely a higher order of *politician* in the British sense, the recognition of whose service, experience, wisdom, and resulting power entitled him to the more eminent label. Until recently, *politicians* in Britain were still *statesmen,* whereas in America, *politicians* were *politicians!*

polling-day, *n.*   **election day**
The British also use the term *voting-day,* as well as the American term. Signs reading POLLING STATION appear where VOTE HERE signs would be posted in America.

pollywog, *n.*   **tadpole**

polo neck   **turtleneck**
Applied to sweaters with high collars which are folded down, so that there is a close-fitting double layer around the neck. See also **turtle-neck; roll-neck.**

ponce, *n., v.i.*   **pimp**
Slang. A much fancier British synonym is *souteneur,* taken over from the French, in which language its literal meaning is 'protector,' indicating something about certain French attitudes. To *ponce about* is to *swagger,* apparently on the assumption that ponces make a very good living and have the wherewithal to live it up.

pond, *n.*   **pool**
Artificial or natural. In America, *pond* usually describes a body of water smaller than a lake. In Britain, it means a 'pool made by hollowing or embanking.' The British also use it as a verb. Transitively, it means to 'dam up' (e.g., a stream); intransitively, of water, to 'form a pool.'

pong, *n., v.i.*   **stink**
Slang. Reek would be the American equivalent. *Pongy* is the adjectival form.

pontoon, *n.*   **blackjack**
A card game. *Pontoon* is a corruption of the French name for the game, *vingt-et-un.* The game is also known as *twenty-one.* A *pontoon,* of course, is a flat-bottomed boat serving as a bridge or ferry.

pony, *n., Inf.*   **£25**

poodle   **puppet**
Slang. Pejorative used in political circles.

poodle-faker, *n.*   SEE COMMENT
Slang. A quite specialized word, describing a naval officer who paid social visits ashore to curry favor in certain quarters.

poof, *n.*   *Slang.* **pansy**
Slang. Derogatory term for male homosexual or an effeminate man. Sometimes spelled *pouf; pouffe; poove; puff.*

poon, *n.*   *Slang.* **jerk**
Slang. **Public school** slang, describing a *middle-class jerk* (**twit**)—one of those hopelessly middle-class types frowned upon by those superior *public school* chaps. The adjective *poonish* is applied to genteel middle-class activities and functions. See synonyms under **git.**

poop, *n.*   *Slang.* **dope**
Slang. Short for *nincompoop.*

poor show. See **bad show.**

poor tool   *Inf.* **total loss**
Inf. To be a *poor tool* at an activity is to be a *total loss* at it, a *bust.*

poove. See **poof.**

pop, *n., v.t.*   **1.** *n., v.t., Inf.* **hock (pawn)**
                                                    2. *v.t.* **fasten**
1. *Slang. Popshop* means 'pawnshop.'
2. *Slang.* To fasten with **poppers.** Also, *pop up.*

poplin, *n.*   **broadcloth**
In Britain, *broadcloth* describes a special kind of woolen material. See **broadcloth.**

popper, *n.*   **snap**
Used to fasten articles of apparel. See also **snapper; pop, 2.**

poppet, *n.*   *Inf.* **sweetie**
Inf. A term of endearment used especially in describing or addressing little ones and pets.

popsie, *n.*   *Slang.* **cutie**
Slang. Originally the epithet for an *old man's darling,* but now extended to include anybody's *cutie.*

porch, *n.*   **covered approach to doorway**

pork pie   SEE COMMENT
A dish made from chopped pork and seasonings baked in a sealed pastry crust. The pie may be small, to serve one, or large enough to serve four or more. It is often served cold but is traditionally heated briefly in the oven.

pork scratchings, *n. pl.*   **pork rinds**

porridge, *n.*   **1. (cooked) oatmeal**
                                                               2. SEE COMMENT
1. To *keep your breath to cool your porridge* is to 'keep your advice for your own use,' i.e., to practice what you preach.
2. *Slang.* To *do porridge* is to 'serve time.' Synonymous with **do bird.** A popular television comedy series about life in prison is entitled "Porridge."

porter, *n.*   **doorman**
The British often use *hall porter* to distinguish a *doorman* from a *railway porter. Porterage* is used to describe the services of a doorman. Where an American would say that his apartment house has a *doorman,* the Briton would say that there is a *porter* at his **block of flats** or *porterage* is **laid on** *with his flat.* See also **commissionaire.**

portmanteau, *n.*   **blend word**
The figurative meaning is that of a made-up word combining the sounds and meanings of parts of two other words, like *squarson,* combination of *squire* and *parson; mingy,* combination of *mean* and *stingy; smog,* combination of *smoke* and *fog,* etc.

posh, *adj.*   **smart, stylish**
The literal meaning does not convey all the connotations of this word in British English. A *posh person* has a great deal of money and an effortless mastery of the ways of genteel society, and his or her clothing, behavior, etc., reflect those things. But such a person who has fallen on hard times will still possess *a posh accent* and, for a time, even *a posh car;* one may be poor but still posh. On the other hand, a *parvenu* can have both posh car and (through practice) a posh accent, but still not be considered posh by those for whom posh is about breeding and upbringing. If there is a single American word that most closely approximates the meaning of posh, it is *classy.*

position, *n.*   **situation**
Position has two British uses which one almost never hears in America: it means 'situation,' in the sense of 'location,' of a house or other building. The other British meaning is also 'situation' but in the figurative sense of the 'way things stand.' For instance: *The position is that the company is insolvent,* or, *Do you understand the position?*

positive discrimination   **affirmative action**
The promotion and encouragement of increased employment of members of minority groups and women.

post, *n., v.t.*   **mail**
See also **G.P.O.; letter post; recorded delivery.**

postage (posting) and packing   **shipping and handling**
As used in mail order advertising, where the 'handling' charge often appears to ring in a wee bit of extra profit. Almost always shortened to P&P. See also **dispatch.**

postal course   **correspondence course**

postal shopping   **mail order buying**

postal van   **mail car**
Railroad term.

postal vote   **absentee ballot**

post-box   **mailbox**
The smallish red iron boxes in rural areas bear the initials of the sovereign in
whose reign they were erected. A Briton will announce with pride that the box
near his home is a V.R. box! Occasionally called *posting box* or *letter box.* See also
pillar-box.

post-code, *n.*   **zip code**
In Britain, a combination of numbers and letters. Example: NW5. The full post-
code would have another three characters, always beginning with a number, e.g.
2XB.

poste restante   **general delivery**
Permanently borrowed from the French. Literally it means 'mail remaining'
('waiting to be picked up').

post-free   **postpaid**

post-graduate, *adj.*   **graduate**
As in *post-graduate student, degree,* etc.

postman, *n.*   **mailman**

postman's knock man   **unskilled hunter**
Inf. Rare. The phrase means an 'unskillful hunter' (*shooter,* in Britain—see **shoot**)
who fires two barrels at almost everything he spies on the wing and rarely hits
anything.

post-mortem   **autopsy**
More commonly used in Britain.

Post Office   SEE COMMENT
Usual name for the **G.P.O.** Americans think of their post office as a place to mail
letters and parcels and buy stamps and money orders. The *Post Office* in Britain
has a much wider scope; see **G.P.O.**

pot, *n.*   **1.** *Slang.* **boodle**
                                              2. *Slang.* **favorite (horse racing)**
                                                              3. SEE COMMENT
1. *Slang.* Used alone or in the expression *pots of money.* To *put the pot* on a horse at a
British **race-course** is to *shoot your wad* or *bet your stack* at an American track. The British also use the expression to *go nap* on a horse to describe the same vice (see **nap**).
2. *Slang.* The *pot* is also British slang for the *favorite* in a horse race.
3. *Slang.* A British slang usage sometimes heard (occasionally lengthened to *pot-
hunter*) is to describe a person who enters a contest not for the sport of it but only
for the prize. Another British slang use is in the expression to *put* someone's *pot
on,* which means to 'squeal on' him, or 'spill the beans,' for which the British also
use the expression *blow the gaff. A big pot,* however, means something entirely
different: *VIP.*

pot, *v.t.*   *Inf.* **potty**
Inf. To attend to a very young child's need.

potato, *n.*   **hole in one's sock**
Slang. **Wellingtons** are said to cause *potatoes.*

pot-boy, *n.*   **bartender's assistant**
Potman means the same thing. Literally, someone who helps out in a pub, but
sometimes used figuratively in the sense of *prat boy* as a pejorative term meaning
somebody at anybody's beck and call. See also **dog's body.**

pot-house, *n., Slang.*   *Inf.* **pub**
More formally known as a *public house.*

potted lecture   *Slang.* **canned spiel**
Inf. A pre-set brief spiel, usually in the nature of a demonstration, often with
slides. The author's dentist asked his hygienist to deliver her *potted lecture* on a
new method of brushing teeth.

potty, *adj.*   *Slang.* **nutty**
Inf. The implication is eccentricity rather than outright lunacy, for example, **dotty**
or **bonkers.**

pouf, also pouffe. See **poof.**

poulterer, *n.*   **poultry dealer**
Sometimes, POULTER appears on store signs. Increasingly rare as butchers and
supermarkets sell poultry.

pour with rain   **pour**
Raining cats and dogs would be the American equivalent. See also **bucket down;
rain stair rods.**

power point. See **point.**

poxing, *adj.*   **plaguing**
Slang. Annoying, irritating. Derives from the archaic *a pox on . . .!*

poxy, *adj.*   *Slang.* **worthless, pitiful**
Applicable to people, possessions, or the performance of a task.

practical, *n.*   **lab test**
Inf. Short for practical examination, like being given a frog to dissect in a biology
exam.

praeposter, preposter. See **prefect.**

pram, *n.*   **baby carriage**
Inf. Short for *perambulator.*

prang, *v.t.*   **1. crash land (an aircraft)
                                                          2. bomb (a target)**
Slang. From meanings 1. and 2. the use of the word has been extended to cover
non-aeronautical accidents as well, and even minor ones. One can *prang* a car in

a collision, or merely one's knee or arm while working around the house. *Bump* would be the equivalent here.

prat, *n.*   **an unpleasant person**

praties, *n. pl. Inf.*   *Slang.* **spuds**

prawn, *n.*   **shrimp**
Small in American terms, because *shrimps* in Britain are generally tiny things compared to what Americans mean by the term. A Briton would consider a *prawn* a large, rather than a small, shrimp. What Americans think of as shrimps are generally called *scampi* in Britain, a term usually confined in America to cooked shrimps in restaurants with continental cuisine.

preemie, *n.*   *Inf., abbrev.* **premature baby**

prefect, *n.*   *approx.* **monitor**
A school boy or girl who attains a quasi-official position to help keep order. In some **public schools,** called *praepostor* or *prepostor.* See also **head boy** or **girl.**

preference shares   **preferred stock**

preggers, *adj.*   *Slang.* **knocked up**
Slang. Great with child.

Premiership   SEE COMMENT
Also called the *Premier League,* this comprises the top 20 **football** clubs in the standings. Teams may be promoted into the Premiership if their performance is exceptional, and Premiership teams may be relegated to a lower division if they perform poorly. Formerly called the **First Division.**

Premium Bond   **government lottery bond**
Monthly lottery drawings are held with cash prizes going to the holders of the bonds with lucky serial numbers. They bear no interest. In America the same phrase describes regular interest-bearing corporate bonds callable before maturity, on short notice, for redemption at a premium.

prentice, *adj.*   **amateurish**
Inf. As in, *It's only a prentice job,* or, *The novel is a prentice piece of work.* A *prentice hand* is an *inexperienced worker.*

prep, *n.*   **1.** *approx.* **homework**
                                                                2. study hall
Inf. Short for *preparation. Prep* is the name for both the work the student does to prepare for the next day's classes and for the session at boarding school at which he does it. *Prep* is usually supervised by a **prefect** or **master** who not only keeps order but is available to help the struggling student. Work to be done at home is called *homework* in Britain as well as in America.

prep school   **pre-preparatory school**
In this phrase, *prep* is an abbreviation of *preparatory.* A *prep school* is a private school for boys or girls who enter at the age of five or seven. It is called a *prep*

school because it *prepares* the children for **secondary school,** which they enter at 13 (boys) or 11 (girls).

presenter, *n.*   newscaster
See also **newsreader.**

preservation order, *n.*   SEE COMMENT
A legal order forbidding unauthorized alteration of property, which may be in public or private ownership. The order may apply to a building or even a whole village, and also to natural features such as trees or hedgerows.

press-up, *n.*   push-up

pressure, *n.*   voltage
So used by the Royal Navy in World War II.

pressurize, *v.t.*   press
Britons often say that someone pressurized someone else to do something. Proof that the Queen's English is not always grammatically correct.

prezzy, *n. Inf.*   present (gift)

pricey (pricy), *adj., Inf.*   expensive

primary school   elementary school

Prime Minister's Questions   SEE COMMENT
Every Wednesday afternoon the prime minister must come to the House of Commons and answer oral questions for half an hour. The sessions begin with 'friendly' questions from the prime minister's own party, but often turn into heated exchanges with the Opposition parties. Sometimes abbreviated as *Pam's.*

principal boy   *approx.* **star**
A special designation pertaining to **pantomimes,** usually called *pantos.* The *principal boy* is always played by a girl, or should be. There is a *principal girl,* too; also a star; also a girl.

printed paper rates   third-class mail

prison van   police wagon
See **van.**

private, *adj.*   personal
On envelopes, meaning that nobody but the addressee is to open.

private bar. See under **pub.**

Private Member's Bill   SEE COMMENT
The legislative agenda for Parliament is set almost entirely by the government, but in every session a small amount of parliamentary time is set aside for bills proposed by ordinary members from all parties. There is a limited number of those bills, which are allocated to members in a lottery, and they rarely become law.

Private Prosecution   SEE COMMENT
In exceptional cases where the Crown Prosecutor decides that there is insufficient evidence for the state to try someone for a crime, interested parties (e.g. the victim's family) may ask permission to prosecute the accused using their own funds. The applications are rarely allowed, and such prosecutions are extremely rare.

private school   SEE COMMENT
A *private school* is a school supported solely by fees paid by parents. See **prep school; public school.**

private treaty   contract
In advertisements of real estate for sale, one often sees the phrase *for sale by private treaty,* which means that the common British practice of putting up real estate for sale at auction is not being followed in that case. Agreement between buyer and seller establishes the sale price.

Privy Council, *n.*   SEE COMMENT
Originally the monarch's council of advisers, it consists nowadays of all past and present members of the cabinet.

privy purse   SEE COMMENT
Funds supplied by the British Government for the private expenses of the sovereign.

prize, also prise, *v.t.*   pry open
Prize is known in America but *pry* is more common; vice versa in Britain. In Britain one usually *prizes* open a lid etc.

Prize Day. See **Speech Day.**

proctor, *n.*   *approx.* **college monitor**
A *senior proctor* and a *junior proctor* are selected each year at Oxford and Cambridge as officials charged mainly with disciplinary matters. To *proctorize* is to exercise that function. The word is used in somewhat the same sense in some American colleges, with the emphasis on dormitory and examination discipline, but the American verb is *proctor,* same as the noun. *Prog* is the slang form, and can be used as a transitive verb, as in *He was progged,* university slang for 'reported by the proctor.'

producer, *n.*   1. director
                                                                       2. producer
1. In the British theater, *producer* and *director* are both used to mean 'director' in the American sense, and *theatrical manager* means 'producer' in the American sense.
2. In the film industry *producer* and *director* are used as in America.

prog. See **proctor.**

programme, *n.*   platform
What Americans call the *platform* of a political party is called its *programme* in Britain. Also, *party manifesto.*

prompt, *n.*   stage left
See **opposite prompt.**

(the) Proms, *n. pl.*   SEE COMMENT
Inf. Short for *Promenade Concerts,* a series started by Sir Henry Wood in 1895, held annually during the summer at the Royal Albert Hall in London.

propeller shaft   drive shaft
Automobile term. See also **Appendix II.E.**

propelling pencil   mechanical pencil
Scarcely seen today, having given way to the ballpoint pen.

proper, *adj., adv.*   *Inf.* **regular; real**
Inf. Used by the British as an intensive. If a friend should see you sipping lemonade in a pub, he might ask why you're not having a *proper* drink, i.e., a *real* drink, an *honest to goodness* drink. A *proper pushing lad* is a *real go-getter.* Less complimentary is an expression such as a *proper fool,* where the adjective emphasizes the degree of folly. *Good and proper* is an adverbial phrase in a sentence like, *I told him off good and proper!*

property, *n.*   real estate
A *property dealer* would be called a *real-estate operator* in America.

provinces. See under **regions.**

proxy bomb   dummy bomb

P.T.   *Inf.* **physical education**
Inf. Stands for *physical training;* usually abbreviated like its American counter-part. Physical Education (PE) is now the more common term.

P.T.O.   over
Placed at the bottom of the page and indicating *please turn over.* See also **overleaf.**

pub, *n.*   SEE COMMENT
Inf. An approximate equivalent is *bar. Pub* is short for *public house.* A synonym for *pub* is the **local,** which is short for the *local pub* (note that *local* can also mean 'native'; see **local**). Traditionally, every pub had at least two bars: the *public bar* and the *saloon,* or *private bar,* which is appreciably more elegant; and drinks served in that room cost a little bit more. One is apt to find a carpet on the floor of the *saloon bar,* but the darts board, the bar-billiards table, and the shove-half-penny board would normally be found in the *public bar.* See also **free house; tied; opening hours; bitter; pint; landlord; pot-house; shebeen.**

pub-crawl, *n., v.i.*   **make the rounds (of pubs)**
Inf. To *pub-crawl* is to visit and give one's custom to one pub after another, and *pub-crawl* is also the noun describing this function.

publican, *n.*   *approx.* **saloon keeper**
The *publican,* also known as the *landlord* or *pubkeeper,* is the *proprietor* of a **pub.** See also **landlord.**

public bar; public house. See **pub.**

public convenience   **comfort station**
A battle of euphemisms, both meaning 'public toilet'; a municipal institution
which still flourishes in some British towns and villages but seems to be disappearing in America.

Public Lending Right   SEE COMMENT
A scheme that pays writers from government funds for the borrowing of their
books from public libraries in the UK.

public prosecutor. See **crown prosecuter.**

public school   SEE COMMENT
Until the Middle Ages, children fortunate enough to receive any education were
taught privately and locally: at home, in local churches, monasteries, etc. The
term *public school* appeared in the 14th century to describe a new phenomenon:
a school open to children from all over the country. The oldest of those schools
still functioning are, by tradition, called public schools. Some date from the Middle Ages, others from the 19th century. The most famous are Eton and Harrow.
Winchester, Westminster, and Charterhouse are just three examples of equal or
greater antiquity. Other schools where students pay tuition (and often boarding)
fees are called private or independent schools.

public transport   **mass transit**

pudding, *n.*   **dessert**
Pudding is often shortened to *(Inf.) pud,* rhyming with GOOD. But see **dessert;** see
also **sweet; afters.**

pudding club   **pregnancy**
Slang. In the pudding club (or simply *in the club*) means 'pregnant.' See also **preggers** and **in pod.**

pudsy, *adj.*   **plump**
See also **podgy; fubsy.**

puff, *n.* See **poof.**

pukka, *adj.*   **genuine**
Of Hindi origin, meaning permanent, occasionally spelled *pucka* or *pukkah;* sometimes wrongly used to mean 'super' and 'smashing.' A *pukka sahib* is a real *gentleman.*

pull, *n.*   **1. extra measure**
                                                                        2. advantage
1. When you get more beer (or other liquid refreshment) than you ask for in a
pub, you get a *pull,* also known as a *long pull.* To dispense **real beer** at a pub, a
handle must be pulled. See also **long pull.**
2. To have a *pull* over someone is to have an *advantage* over him.

pull down   **tear down**
House-wrecking term.

pulled down, *Inf.*   *Inf.* **under the weather**

pull one's socks up   *Inf.* **shape up; get going**
Inf. To *start moving,* to *show more stuff: He'd better pull his socks up if he wants to keep his job.* Americans might say *pull himself together.* See also **buck up.**

pull-up, *n.*   **diner**
Diners in America can be anything from shabby to magnificent. *Pull-ups* are usually quite shabby, shacklike establishments. See also **café; transport café.**

pull up   *Slang.* **bowl over**
In the sense of 'make a deep impression on.' Thus: *It was a good play, but what really pulled me up was Derek's performance.*

pull up sticks   *Inf.* **pull up stakes**
Inf. Fold one's tent and move on. See also **up-stick.**

pumpship, *n. v.i.*   **(take a) pee**
Inf. (Stressed on the first syllable.) Sometimes two words: *pump ship.* Originally nautical, for *pump out the bilge,* it was extended to the general language to mean *urinate.*

pun, *v.t.*   **tamp**
Pun appears to be a variant of *pound.* A *punner* is a *tamper,* i.e., a tool with which one tamps the earth, rubble, etc.

punch-bag, *n.*   **punching bag**
Also given as *punching-bag.*

punch-up. See **dust-up.**

puncture, *n.*   **flat**
Puncture would sound old-fashioned or at least pedantic in America. *Flat* is slowly being adopted by the British.

punka(h), *n.*   **ceiling electric fan**
An Anglo-Indian term for a large fan, usually of cloth in a rectangular frame, hanging from the ceiling and operated by a rope pulled by a servant known as a *punka(h)-walla(h).* By extension applied to ceiling electric fans, the kind one sees mostly in period movies. See **walla(h).**

punner. See **pun.**

punnet, *n.*   **small fruit basket**
A *small basket* for vegetables or fruit, traditionally woven of thin pieces of wood that are known in Britain as **chip** but now more commonly made of plastic. Strawberries and raspberries are sold in Britain by the *punnet,* which allegedly comes in one-pound and half-pound sizes, but the boxes may have crumpled paper at the bottom and thus contain as little fruit as possible.

punter, *n.*   **bettor**
Technically, to *punt* is to *bet against the house* in a card game; but informally it means to 'bet on a horse race' or 'speculate on the stock market,' and the usual meaning is 'bettor' or 'speculator' as the case may be. See **Appendix II.G.5** for

British betting terms. *Punter* can also mean 'John' or 'trick' in the sense of 'prostitute's client.' More informally, it can mean any customer, especially one of a retail business.

purchase, hire. See **hire-purchase; never-never.**

purchase tax   *approx.* **excise tax**
Now replaced by the *Value Added Tax*, usually abbreviated to *V.A.T.* or *VAT*, pronounced either way.

purler. See **come a purler.**

purpose-built, *adj.*   **built to order**
Especially built for a given purpose, according to specifications, like a movie theater built as such instead of having been converted from an opera house.

purse, *n.*   **money pouch**
Not used in Britain to mean 'lady's handbag.' See also **pocketbook.**

push, *n.*   *Slang.* **gate**
Slang. To *get the push* is to *get the gate, be fired.* See **sack.**

push along, *Inf.*   *Inf.* **get moving**

push-bike   *Inf.* **bike**
Inf. As distinguished from *motor-bike* and *moped.* Also called *push-bicycle* and *push-cycle.*

pushcart, *n.*   **baby carriage**
An occasional use; *pushcart* usually means 'handcart,' and the usual term for *baby carriage* is **pram.** *Pushcart* in the American sense is **barrow** in Britain.

push-chair   **stroller**
Child's folding chair on wheels.

pushed for   *Inf.* **pressed for**
Inf. In Britain, one is *pushed*, rather than *pressed*, for time, money, etc. *Pushed*, used alone, generally means 'pressed for time.' *Pushed for* suggests scarcely able to find enough *time, money, facilities*, etc.

push off!   *Slang.* **scram!**
Slang. Synonyms under **buzz off.**

push-pin, *n.*   **thumbtack**
Synonymous with **drawing-pin.**

push the boat out   1. *Inf.* **outdo oneself**
                                                              2. *Inf.* **treat**
1. *Inf.* To act more generously than the occasion requires; to be lavish, but not ostentatious. Often used in commenting on splendid entertainment one has enjoyed, particularly as a dinner guest: *They didn't half push the boat out!* See **half, 3.**

2. *Inf.* Often heard in the expression *(so-and-so's) turn to push the boat out,* meaning that it's his turn to pay for the next round of drinks, today's trip to the movies, and that sort of thing.

put about   1. *Inf.* **put out (be a nuisance)**
                                                 2. *Inf.* **plant (a rumor)**
1. *Inf.* As in: *I hate to put you about, but I really need the shipment by tomorrow.*
2. *Inf.* As in: *It was put about that they were almost bankrupt.*

put a bung in it!   *Slang.* **shut up!**
Slang. An alternative to **put a sock in it!** *Bung* is easier to visualize than *sock,* somehow.

put a foot wrong   *Inf.* **slip up**
Inf. Seen almost exclusively in the negative: *He'll never put a foot wrong,* indicating a meticulous person. Sometimes one sees *put a foot right,* also in the negative: *I can't put a foot right today* means 'I shouda stayed in bed.'

put a sock in it!   *Slang.* **stow it!**
Slang. Or a *bung* if you prefer. The equivalent of *Belt up!* or *Pack up!* in Britain or *Shut up!* in America.

put (someone's) back up   *Inf.* **get (someone's) back up**
Inf. The American form is occasionally used as well.

put by   **brush aside**
As in: *The difficulties facing us cannot be put by indefinitely,* meaning *permanently deferred.*

put down   1. **put to sleep**
                                                                2. **charge**
                                                                3. *Inf.* **fold**
Three wholly unrelated meanings:
1. Euthanasia of pets. The British expression has now become common among dog breeders in America.
2. *Put it down, please,* is the way the customer asks the shop to charge it. Alternatively he might say, *Please book it to me,* or, *Book it to my account.* See also **on the slate; on tick.**
3. What a wise person does in a poker game when he senses that his chances are slim.

put in hand. See **have (something) put in hand.**

put (someone) in the picture   **explain the situation to (someone);**
                                                 bring (someone) up to date

put it across (someone)   *Inf.* **let (someone) have it**
Inf. To *punish.* The teacher became angry at the obstreperous pupil and really *put it across him.* To *put (something) across* also has the usual American meaning of 'put it over,' i.e., *accomplish the objective.*

put (someone) off   **disturb**
Inf. To *put* one *off* one's balance, or *off* one's stride. *Off-putting* is an adjective describing the person or thing that has that effect. It seems just the least bit precious, perhaps jocularly, like other hyphenated adjectives ending in the participial *-ing*, like *shame-making*. It has the special flavor, sometimes, of *appetite-spoiling*, both literally and figuratively; it always connotes enthusiasm-dampening.

put one's arse to anchor, *Slang.*   **sit down**

put one's back into   *Slang.* **knock oneself out at**
Slang. Expressing the idea of arduous devotion to a task at hand. See also **do one's nut, 1.**

put one's feet up   **relax**
Inf. A dinner hostess might say to a tired friend: *Come earlier and put your feet up.* Putting one's feet up connotes easy chairs, possibly a brief nap, freshening up, and in the case of a really kind hostess, even a drink.

put one's head down   *Inf.* **get some shuteye**
Inf. Also *get one's head down, snooze.*

put one's hoof in   *Inf.* **get a word in edgewise**

put one's shirt on   *Inf.* **bet one's bottom dollar on**

put on side   *Slang.* **put on the dog**
Slang. See also **side, 2.**

put paid to   *Inf.* **finish**
Inf. In the sense of 'put an end to.' Thus: *The rain put paid to our picnic.* Derived from the image of stamping 'paid' on a bill, thus putting an end to that transaction.

put (someone's) pot on   *Slang.* **squeal on (someone)**
Slang. To *put* Harry's *pot on* is to *squeal on* Harry.

put the boot in   *Inf.* **1. kick hard**
                                                              2. take a decisive step
In sense 2, usually used for a move designed to conclude some difficult situation; *When his grades didn't improve, the head teacher decided he had to put the boot in.*

put the 'phone down   **hang up**
Not as in America, where it means putting it down for a moment, as when interrupted by a knock on the door.

put the pot. See **pot, 1.**

put the shutters up   *Inf.* **fold**
Slang. To *go broke* and, if necessary, into bankruptcy.

put the wind up. See under **get the wind up.**

put through (on telephone), *v.t.*   **connect**

put-to, *n.*   *Slang.* **brass tacks; crunch**
Slang. The Prime Minister makes brave speeches and fine promises, but when you get down to the put-to . . .

putty, *n.*   **muddy bottom**
Nautical slang. The kind of stuff you should be careful not to get your keel stuck in.

put up   **1.** *v.t.,* **raise**
                                              2. *v.i.,* **run for office**

1. The rent is *put up* in Britain, *raised* in America.
2. Short for *put up the deposit* required of candidates.

put up a black   *Inf.* **fall on one's face**
Inf. To *get a black mark;* close to **blot one's copybook.**

put up the hare, *Inf.*   *Inf.* **get something going**

pye-dog, *n.*   **mongrel**
Also *pie-dog* and *pi-dog.* Term used in India for an *ownerless mongrel,* running wild.

pylon, *n.*   **high tension tower**

QAA. See **Honours (2).**

Q.C. See **take silk.**

quad, *n.* *approx.* **campus**
Inf. Oxford University term, short for *quadrangle*. It denotes a square bounded by
college buildings rather than the whole campus. Some American colleges also
use the term *quad*. The Cambridge equivalent is **court.**

quadrillion. See **Appendix II.D.**

Quango, *acronym.* SEE COMMENT
Acronym for 'quasi-autonomous non-governmental organization.' These are
public bodies receiving government funding, and reporting/advising on official
matters, but independent (in theory) of central government.

quant, *n., v.t., vi.* **boat pole**
A *quant* is a punting pole with a flange near the tip to prevent its sinking into mud,
used to propel the boat along. As a verb, to *quant* is to pole the boat, or to punt.

quantity, bill of. See **bill of quantity.**

quantity surveyor **materials appraiser**
Particularly in the contracting business, with expert knowledge of specifications
and prices.

quarrel with one's bread and butter *Inf.* **bite the hand that feeds one**
Inf. Generally, like its American equivalent, restricted to negative statements, e.g.,
One shouldn't quarrel with one's bread and butter. So don't quit your job until you
have lined up a new one.

quart, *n.* See **Appendix II.C.2.**

quarter, *n.* **quarter of a pound**
Inf. One asks for a *quarter* of those chocolates (pointing) at the **sweet-shop.** *Quarter of a pound* would sound ponderous in Britain. This would apply equally, of
course, to mushrooms at the **greengrocer's,** nails at the **ironmonger's,** etc. The
usage has become steadily rarer as **metrification** has taken hold.

quarter-day, *n.* *approx.* **due date**
Quarter-days are the four days in the year when quarterly payments traditionally
fall due in Britain and are the common dates for tenancy terms. They are: **Lady**

Day (March 25); Midsummer Day (June 25); Michaelmas Day (September 29); Christmas Day (December 25).

quartern, *n.*   SEE COMMENT
Four-pound loaf of bread, but now archaic.

quaver, *n.*   **eighth note**
Musical term. See **Appendix II.F.**

quay, *n.*   **wharf/pier**
Pronounced key.

(the) Queen   **1.** SEE COMMENT
                                                                      2. SEE COMMENT
1. *Inf.* To stay at a dance through *the Queen* is to stay to the very end. The term dates from the days when it was usual to play *God Save the Queen* to close the proceedings, and *the Queen* in this context is simply short for the title of the national anthem.
2. *Inf.* The toast to the Queen, known as the **Loyal Toast.**

Queen Mother   SEE COMMENT
The mother of the reigning monarch. Informally, *Queen Mum.*

Queen's Speech, *n.*   SEE COMMENT
A speech written by the government, and delivered by the **Queen,** outlining the government's agenda for the year at the beginning of a new parliamentary session. The Queen sits in the **House of Lords,** and **Black Rod** summons the Commons to listen.

queer, *adj.*   *Inf.* **queasy**
Inf. Unwell or *indisposed,* not really ill. *I went queer* has no homosexual connotations whatsoever. See also **sick.**

queer card, *Inf.*   *Slang.* **oddball**

(in) Queer Street   *Inf.* **hard up**
When the British talk of somebody's being *in Queer Street,* they mean that he or she is in bad trouble, in a bad way, in bad odor. The expression originates in the custom of writing *Quaere* ('enquire') against a person's account when it was considered advisable to make enquiries about him before trusting him.

queer the pitch   **stymie; thwart**
To *queer someone's pitch* is to *thwart him,* to *spoil his chances* before he begins. A *pitch* is part of a **cricket ground** *(field)*; in **football** *(soccer) pitch* is used to describe the entire playing field. To *queer someone's pitch,* then, is to *mess up his game,* not literally, but figuratively in the sense of 'spoiling his chances.' There are some however, who claim that this term is not derived from cricket, but from **pitch** in the sense of the territorial prerogative of bookmakers and outdoor entertainers on the streets of London and other cities.

quench, *v.t.*   **squelch**
To *shut* (somebody) *up.*

query, *n., adv.*   **1.** *n.* **complaint**
                                                                     2. *adv.* **approximately**
1. *n.* This connotation of *query* is not met with in America. It appears most frequently in the phrase *query department* of an organization.
2. *adv. Query,* after an adjective, indicates that the adjective is only approximate,
and the quality or quantity expressed is somewhat doubtful or questionable. A
teacher might characterize a student's performance (the British often use **alpha,**
beta, gamma, rather than *A, B, C* in marking) as *beta-alpha query,* or *beta, query
alpha,* i.e., *somewhere between A and B but I don't know exactly where,* or *beta, query
minus (B, but perhaps* a bit closer to B minus).

question in the House   SEE COMMENT
There'll be a question in the House means, 'This is going to be brought up in Parliament at 'question time' (the period when **Members** may question **ministers**). The
nearest American equivalent would be: *This is going to be brought up in Congress,*
but more likely before a House or Senate committee. Legislators in the United
States do not, of course, have regular opportunities to question directly the executive branch of the government.

queue, *n., v.i.*   **line; line up**
(Pronounced CUE.) The verb sometimes takes the form *queue up.* Foreigners
are often surprised at the self-imposed discipline that leads the British to form
queues. Queue-jumping leads to very positive remonstrations. Americans stand
either *in* or *on* a line; but Britons stand only *in* a queue. See **Appendix I.A.1.**

quick as thought, *Inf.*   *Inf.* **quick as a wink**

quid, *n.*   SEE COMMENT
Slang. One pound (£), referring to British money, not weight. No American slang
equivalent except *buck* for *dollar.* In general use, unlike many other slang currency
terms. See also **have a quid each way.**

quid each way. See **each way.**

quieten, *v.t., v.i.*   **quiet down**

quintillion. See **Appendix II.D.**

Quis?   **Who wants this?**
Inf. Public school and upper-middle-class cant, pronounced *quiz,* addressed by
an individual amid a group of his or her peers. The 'this' can be anything from
the remains of something being eaten to a comic book or any old bit of anything
found while cleaning out a desk. The affirmative answer is *Ego* (a suitable Latin
answer to a question in Latin); the negative response is *fains.* Very rare. See **fains I!**

quite, *adj.*   *Inf. approx.* **up to snuff**
Inf. Quite used as an adjective—not as an adverb modifying an adjective or an
adverb—is found in negative expressions only, such as: *He isn't quite,* meaning,
'He isn't quite acceptable socially.' An example of **posh** language.

quite, *adv.*   **absolutely**
Used alone, as a response, expressing more or less emphatic agreement; roughly
equivalent to *That goes without saying.* 'Are you sorry the holiday's over?' 'Quite.'

quiz, *v.t.*   *Inf.* **poke fun at**
Quiz originally meant to 'make fun of' and also to 'look curiously at,' but because of the popularity of American television quiz programs, the more common meaning of the word in Britain now is the American one, i.e., to 'interrogate.'

quod, *n.*   *Slang.* **pokey**
Slang. Clink, a slang term in both countries, is derived from an actual prison of that name in Southwark (London) where there is still a *Clink Street.* The old prison is long gone. See also **porridge, 2.**

R

rabbit, *n.*   *Inf.* **dub**
Inf. In sports, a beginner or a player of little skill; a *duffer.*

rabbit on   **jabber away**
Slang. On and on and on. Originates from rhyming slang (see **Appendix II.G.3.**) *rabbit and pork* (shortened to *rabbit*) for *talk.*

R.A.C.
Abbreviation for Royal Automobile Club.

race-course, *n.*   **racetrack**
The British never use *race-track* for horse racing but do use the term for auto racing and use *dog-track* for greyhound racing.

Rachmanism, *n.*   SEE COMMENT
Inf. The practice of taking over lower-class residential property and deliberately creating intolerable living conditions in order to force the poor tenants to get out, so that the landlord can then turn the property to more profitable commercial uses. The term is derived from a man named Rachman, who in the 1960s pioneered in this type of manipulation.

racialist, *n., adj.*   **racist**
And *racialism* is *racism.*

rackety, *adj., Slang.*   *Slang.* **harum scarum**

rack-rent, *n.,*   **extortionate rent**
Rack-renting is the wicked practice of exacting excessive rent from tenants.

R.A.D.A.   **Royal Academy of Dramatic Art**
(Pronounciation rhymes with 'Prada' as an acronym.)

radiogram, *n.*   **radio-phonograph**
Radiogram is no longer heard much in Britain or in America.

R.A.F.   **Royal Air Force**
This doughty band, who fought the Battle of Britain, are almost invariably referred to by their initials.

rag, *v.t., v.i., n.*   **1.** *v.i., v.t., Inf.* **fool around; tease**
                                                                                2. *n., Inf.* **stunt; gag**
1. *Inf. Rag* is used intransitively to mean 'fool around' or 'kid around,' in a manner involving a little mild horseplay. Transitively it means to 'tease' or to 'pull someone's leg.'
2. *Inf.* A *rag* is a *stunt* or *gag* and from this use we get *rag-week,* which is a week at the university during which students put on *stunts* in aid of charity, especially dressing up and riding around on weird and grotesque floats.

rag-and-bone man, *Inf.*   *Inf.* **junkman**
A peddler who deals in old clothes etc.

raglan. See **Balaclava.**

raid, *n.*   **burglary**
In America *raid* brings up the image of a group assault of one sort or another,
particularly military or police. One reads in British newspapers of a *raid* made
last night on a house or shop. All it means is a 'burglary,' the work of one or more
persons called *raiders.* A *dawn raid* in the stock market is something different:
an attempt to gain control of a corporation by swiftly buying up shares of stock
through tempting offers to shareholders, a takeover attempt.

railway, scenic. See **scenic railway; switchback.**

railway carriage. See **carriage.**

rain stair-rods   *Inf.* **rain cats and dogs**
Inf. Synonymous with **bucket** or **tip down; pour with rain.** Very old-fashioned,
and exceedingly rare.

raise the wind. See **get the wind up.**

rake up   *Inf.* **dig up**
Inf. In the sense of 'procure with difficulty.' Also used in Britain in the usual
American sense of 'bring up an old sore subject,' like a complaint or a scandal.

rally, *v.t., Inf.*   *Inf.* **pull (someone's) leg; kid**
A good-natured act.

rambler, *n.*   SEE COMMENT
A person who regularly takes walks in the country for recreation and exercise.

Ramblers' Association   SEE COMMENT
A large private organization aiming to promote the interests of ramblers, especially as regards right of access to private land.

ramp, *n.*   **1. bump**
                                                            2. *Slang.* **racket**
                                                                 3. talk up
1. A special use, to denote a bump deliberately built into a private or restricted
road to encourage people to drive slowly; synonymous with **rumble strip.** The
term is used as well to denote the point at which the true and the temporary
surfaces join where road repairs are going on. The road signs say BEWARE RAMP.
The *bump* in question is occasioned by the fact that the temporary surface is at a
somewhat higher level.
2. *Slang. Ramp* is also sometimes used as transitive or intransitive verb meaning
'swindle.'
3. Especially a product or a company whose prospects one seeks to enhance.

random, *adj.*   *Inf.* **surprising, unexpected**

randy, *adj., Slang.*   *Slang.* **horny**

ranker, *n.*   **1. soldier in the ranks**
2. officer risen from the ranks

rape, *n.*   SEE COMMENT
Don't be alarmed if you see one *rape* after another when you look at an old map of the County of Sussex, England. That is what the six old divisions of the county used to be called.

rare, *adj.*   *approx. Inf.* **great**
Inf. Rare is an informal intensive. A *rare* lot of something is a *helluva* lot of it. *Rare* also implies *excellence*. A *rare* something is a *splendid* something. A *rare* time is a *swell* time; a *rare old* time is even sweller. But watch out, because in the expression have a *rare time of it*, *rare time* means quite the opposite: a 'tough time.'

rasher, *n.*   **slice or strip of bacon**

rate, *n.*   **local tax**
Usually in the plural, meaning 'local real estate taxes.' A *ratepayer* is a local *tax-payer*.

rate, *v.t.*   *Inf.* **hold in high esteem**
My friends don't like the new teacher, but I really rate her.

Rather!, *interj., Inf.*   *Inf.* **And how!**
Also translatable as 'without doubt!'

rating, *n.*   **able seaman**
Low rank of British sailor, just above *ordinary seaman*.

rats!   *Slang.* **baloney!**
Slang. Also 'Nonsense' or 'I can't believe it.'

rattling, *adj., adv.*   **1. brisk**
2. *Slang.* **damned**
1. *Inf.* A *rattling* pace is a *brisk* one.
2. *Inf.* A *rattling* good story is an *unusually* good one or more likely a *damned* good one. In the adverbial use, *rattling* has about the same meaning as **ripping.**

raver, *n.*   *Slang.* **knockout**
Slang. In the sense of *raving beauty*. Synonymous with the old-fashioned Briticisms *stunner, smasher,* etc.

ravers. See **stark ravers.**

(have a) rave-up, *n.*   *Slang.* **(have a) ball**
Slang. A helluva good time.

razzle, *n.*   *Slang.* **spree; binge; toot**
Slang. Americans go on a *spree*; happy Britons go on *the razzle*. They also go on *the spree* (note the definite article). See **Appendix I.A.2.**

R.D.   **insufficient funds**
These letters are an abbreviation of **refer to drawer,** a bank indication of incipient penury.

R.D.C.   SEE COMMENT
These letters are short for *Rural District Council,* the governing body of a *rural district,* once an area comprising a group of parishes, now become obsolete since the creation of *district councils.* See **council; parish.**

reach-me-down, *adj.*   *Inf.* **ready-made**
Slang. As a plural noun *reach-me-downs* became slang for *ready-made clothes.* It may have come from the image of a salesperson *reaching* to get a stock garment *down* off a shelf. Not heard now: *off-the-peg* is the common term, and *ready-made* is creeping in. Unrelated to American *hand-me-down.*

read, *v.t.*   **major in**
One *reads* philosophy at Oxford, for example, or law, or chemistry. An American *majors* in a subject.

read, *n.*   SEE COMMENT
A *read* is a spell of reading, time spent in reading, an opportunity to read: 'The reviewer said my novel was a good *read.*'

reader, *n.*   *approx.* **associate professor**
In a British university, the order of academic hierarchy is assistant lecturer, lecturer, senior lecturer, *reader,* and professor. The term *professor* is more exclusive than in America, where it covers the grades of assistant professor and associate professor, as well as (full) professor. See also **don; Fellow; master.**

Reading (of Parliamentary Bill), *n.*   SEE COMMENT
Every **bill** is formally put before Parliament in three successive readings (First, Second, and Third Readings), when it is discussed and reported on by a committee.

reading glass   **magnifying glass**

read (someone; something) up   **read up on (someone; something)**
For example, *I read him up before interviewing him,* or, *I read the subject up before lecturing on it.*

(the) ready, *n.*   *Slang.* **dough**
Inf. Ready is colloquially short for *ready cash.* Often, *the readies.* Synonymous with **brass; dibs; lolly.**

ready for off, *Inf.*   **ready to go**

reafforest, *v.t., v.i.*   **reforest**
The noun is *reafforestation.* Both countries use *afforest* to describe the planting of land with trees, but they differ in describing the renewal of forest cover.

real jam. See **jam.**

rebate, *n.*   **rabbet**
Term used in carpentry. But American carpenters (**joiners**) say *rabbet.*

recce, *n.*   *Inf.* **gander (look-see)**
Inf. An abbreviation of *reconnaissance* which became the official term among the military from World War I days, when one *went out on a recce.* It is pronounced RECKY and is in the general language. *Shall we try that pub? Let's have* (or *do*) *a recce first.* See also **shufty.**

Received Pronunciation   SEE COMMENT
Commonly called *R.P.* An accent confined virtually to English people and those educated at English **public schools.** R.P. speakers believe their speech has no indication of where they were born or live.

reception, *n.*   **1. office**
                                                                       2. front desk
1. A sign on a place of business reading *Reception* would read *Office* in America.
2. *Reception* at a hotel would be known as the *desk* or *front desk* in America; and the *reception clerk* or *receptionist* at a hotel is called *room clerk* in America.

reception-room   **waiting room**
A room available for receiving visitors or company.

record card   **index card**

recorded delivery   *Approx.* **certified mail**
The post office (**G.P.O.**) gives one a *certificate of posting (mailing)* but holds on to the *certificate of delivery. Registered post* is the approximate equivalent of *special handling,* and allows insurance up to a certain sum. An *A.R.* (*advice of receipt,* also known as *advice of delivery*) is the approximate equivalent of a *return receipt* in America.

recorder, *n.*   **criminal court judge**

recovery van   **tow car**
Also called *wrecker* in America.

red as a turkey-cock, *Inf.*   *Inf.* **red as a beet**

red biddy   **cheap red wine**
Slang. Any cheap red wine or a shot of whisky in a glass of such wine. Very rare, having been replaced by **plonk.**

redbrick university   SEE COMMENT
A now somewhat dated term for a British university other than Oxford and Cambridge. The name is derived from the use of red brick in the building of the first universities established after the original old ones, which were constructed of gray stone. Now, *redbrick universities* are built of whatever pleases the architect. Used alone, as an adjective, *redbrick* may still connote a "self-made" image as opposed to the privileged, upper-class image of Oxford. See also **Oxbridge.**

redcap   **military policeman**

red card, *n.*   SEE COMMENT
In **football,** a piece of red card is held up by the referee in a game to indicate that a player has to be sent off for foul play. It is also used generally to mean fired for a misdemeanor.

redemption fee   **prepayment penalty**
A term used in mortgage financing; the fee charged for paying off before maturity.

Red Indian   **Native American**
When a Briton says *Indian* he means a 'native of India.' If he has in mind an *American Indian,* he says *Red Indian.*

redirect, *v.t.*   **forward**
Directions to post office on envelope: *Redirect to* . . . . Americans would write *Forward to* . . . .

red rag   *Inf.* **red flag**
Inf. Usually in the phrase *a red rag to a bull,* meaning something that enrages a bull.

redundant, *adj.*   **(made or become) unemployed**
This harsh word normally used in Britain describes a person who has lost his or her job because of automation, reorganization, or deterioration of economic conditions generally, and not through poor job performance. *Redundancy* is the equally oppressive noun for the condition. To *make someone redundant* is to terminate his employment, or fire him, or let him go. In the plural, *redundancies* means *unemployment generally,* in a sentence like: *There has been a considerable increase in redundancies in that area. Redundant* is met with occasionally, in British usage, in the sense of *superfluous,* as in *Home computers will make newspapers redundant,* or *Improved widespread electronic communications systems will make daily trips to the office redundant.* The word is not used that way in America. It is used, commonly in Britain and exclusively in America, in its grammatical application, to indicate tautology (as in *free gift*).

reel, *n.*   **spool**
Reel of cotton is *spool of thread.* See also **cotton.**

referee   **reference**
A *referee* is *one who gives someone a reference* for employment, admission to a club, etc. *Referee* has many of the other meanings intended in America.

refer to drawer   **insufficient funds**
Refer to drawer, discreetly written in red on the upper left-hand corner of the face of the check (**cheque**) explains that the check writer's bank doesn't trust him, and returns the check to the payee's bank, which then debits the payee's account. If the check writer's bank trusts its depositor, the legend (still in red ink) is lengthened to: *Refer to drawer; please re-present* (note hyphen). See also **overdraft,** which is quite another matter in Britain. See also **Queer Street.**

Reform Jew   **Conservative Jew**
See also **Liberal Jew.**

refuse tip   **garbage dump**
See also **tip.**

(the) regions, *n. pl.*   SEE COMMENT
The country outside London and the **Home Counties.** This is a relatively new
term for what used to be called *the provinces.* It has implications of **devolution**
(home rule) and local identity.

register, *v.t.*   **check**
At one time, the British *registered* their *luggage* and Americans *checked* their *baggage.* Now the British, too, say *check.*

registered post. See **recorded delivery.**

Register Office   **marriage clerk's office**
Often incorrectly called *Registry Office* by the British. A *registry* is something quite
different, as shown below.

registrar, *n.*   **resident doctor**
Hospital term describing a doctor on call who is an assistant to a specialist.

registry, *n.*   **domestic employment agency**
An old-fashioned term for those seeking to employ domestic servants.

relief, *n.*   **deduction; exemption**
Income-tax terminology. On your British income tax return you get *relief* for business expenses and *relief* for dependents. The analogous American terms would be
deductions and *exemptions. Tax relief,* as a general term, would be called *tax benefit*
in America.

relief, out- or outdoor. See **outdoor relief.**

remand home   **reformatory**
Reform school is used in both countries. See also **borstal.**

Remembrance Sunday   **Veterans' Day**
Formerly *Remembrance Day.* The Sunday nearest November 11, originally called
Armistice Day in both countries, a day for honoring the memory of those who fell
in World War I (the **Great War** in Britain). After World War II the concept was
enlarged to embrace the additional victims, and the names were correspondingly
modified.

remembrancer, *n.*   SEE COMMENT
Still seen in the official titles *Queen's* (or *King's*) *Remembrancer,* an officer charged
with the collection of debts due the monarch, and *City Remembrancer* (usually
shortened to *Remembrancer*), who represents the City of London (see **City**) before
committees of Parliament. With a lower-case *r* it has the same meaning in both
countries: 'reminder,' 'memento.'

remission, *n.*   **time off**
For good behavior; a term in penology.

remould, *n., v.t.*   **retread**
The British *remould their tyres;* the Americans *retread their tires.*

removals, *n. pl.*   **moving**
Thus, on a business sign: J. SMITH & COMPANY, REMOVALS. On large moving vans
it is common to see the phrase REMOVAL SPECIALISTS. See also **pantechnicon.**

remove, *n.*   **1. degree removed**
                                                          2. partial school promotion
1. This meaning is shared with America, where it is seen much less frequently
than in Britain. The British speak of something which is one *remove* from the **dustbin,** which means 'one step removed' from the garbage can, i.e., just about ready
to be thrown out; or something may be based at *several removes* from something
else, thus constituting a thinly disguised plagiarism in the arts, for instance.
2. A *partial promotion* at school, moving the student up a half-grade. It has nothing whatever to do with being removed from school. In some schools a *remove*
does not mean the *promotion* but rather the *intermediate grade* itself to which the
student is promoted if he is not poor enough to stay back but not good enough to
go up a whole grade.

renter, *n.*   **exhibitor**
In the special sense of 'film distributor.'

rent-protected, *adj.*   **rent controlled**
Referring to government protection of tenants.

repairing lease   **net lease**
Under which the tenant pays all the maintenance expenses, including real estate
taxes (**rates**) and a net rental to the landlord. The complete technical label is *full
repairing and insuring lease.*

reserve, *n.*   **1. surplus**
                                                                     2. reservation
1. Term used in corporate finance.
2. As in *game reserve; Indian reserve. Reservation* in this sense is strictly American.

reserve price   **upset price**
At auctions, the lowest price at which an item will be sold.

reset, *v.t., v.i.*   **receive (stolen goods)**

resident, *n.*   **person registered at a hotel**
Nothing to do with domicile. See **non-resident.**

residual estate   **residuary estate**
A term relating to the administration of estates denoting what's left after
expenses, debts, taxes, and specific and cash legacies.

responsions, *n. pl.*   SEE COMMENT
Oxford entrance examination, originally the first of three examinations for an Oxford
B.A. and colloquially called **smalls.** The name was later applied to the entrance
examination, which was abolished in 1960. There are now two examinations: **moderations** (called *mods*) and *final schools* (called **Greats** when the subject is classics).

restaurant car   **dining car**
Another British name for this luxury, which is beginning to disappear in Britain,
is *buffet car* (see **buffet**). The menu in a buffet car is much more restricted, and
there is no table service.

resurrection gate. See **lich-gate.**

resurrection pie, *Slang.*   **dish made of leftovers**

retrospective, *adj.*   **retroactive**
Describing the effect, e.g., of a statute applicable to past actions or events.

return, *n.*   **round-trip ticket**
In Britain one might ask for a *return* to London on the train or bus, meaning a
'round-trip ticket.' A *day return* is valid only that day on certain trains; one can
also purchase a *period return* where the return journey must be completed by a
specific date. A one-way ticket is called a *single.*

return, *v.t.*   **elect**
The electorate *returns* a candidate. There is an echo of this usage in *election returns.*

return post   **return mail**

(the) Revenue, *n.*   **Treasury; I.R.S.**
The technical names of the central taxing authorities are *Inland Revenue Department* (Britain) and *Internal Revenue Service* (United States). The British often
shorten their name to *the Revenue;* the common names in America are *the I.R.S.*
and *the Treasury. Revenue,* as the subject of a sentence written by a Briton, would
be followed by a plural verb: *Revenue have expressed the opinion* . . . . See **Appendix
I.A.4.** Also **inland.**

reverse camber. See under **camber.**

reverse-charge call. See **transferred charge call.**

reversionary interest   **remainder (interest)**
In British law, a *reversionary interest* is an interest in property that vests after an
intervening interest like a life estate or the right to income for a stated period. In
American law, a *reversionary interest* or *reversion* is an interest retained by the cre-
ator of a trust, which takes effect after the termination of the trust.

revise. See **revision.**

revision, *n.*   **review**
A school term for reviewing past work in preparation for examinations. Also, as a
transitive verb, *revise* meaning *review.* Thus, *We are now revising all our Latin verbs.*
See also **prep.**

rhino, *n.*   *Slang.* **dough**
Slang. The wherewithal. See also **ready; lolly; brass.**

rhubarb, *n.*   **stage mob noise**
Inf. English actors murmur or shout 'rhubarb' to one another to simulate crowd
noises.

ribbon development   **linear suburban expansion**
Building development parallel to a highway, between villages or towns, containing residences, shops, necessary services, etc., instead of circular expansion, thus

(theoretically) tending to preserve more of the green belt, but not looked upon with favor.

rick, *n., v.t.*   haystack
A 'loose pile' of anything, like hay or brush. As a verb it means 'stack.'

ride, *n.*   forest riding-path
There is an uncommon American use of *ride* as a noun denoting a road built especially for riding. As used in Britain, *ride* implies that the road in question runs through the woods. Such roads anywhere help reduce the risk of forest fires. In Britain, there are some country lanes called 'Ride,' rather than 'Lane' or 'Street.'

riding, *n.*   SEE COMMENT
Subdivision of a county. Not used except with respect to Yorkshire, which is understood in the names the *North Riding*, the *East Riding*, and the *West Riding*. There are only three, because *riding* was originally *thriding*, meaning a 'one-third part.' *Thriding* lost its *th* because it was hard to pronounce after Nor*th*, Eas*t*, and Wes*t*.

right, *adj.*   *Inf.* **real**
Inf. Used like *complete*, as in *He's a right hero*, or *I felt a right idiot*. Usually humorous; sometimes ironical, as in the case of a friend who turned out to be of the fair weather variety. See also **proper.**

right, *interj.*   *Inf.* **sure! O.K.!**
Inf. A term of assent to an order or proposal, not to a statement.

Right Honourable Friend   SEE COMMENT
The formal term used by **Members of Parliament** when referring to another Member in debate in the **House of Commons.**

rights issue   SEE COMMENT
A sale of **shares** by a company to existing shareholders. Rights to shares are determined by the size of any investor's holding, and the shares are usually sold at a substantial discount to the current share price. Rights issues are a way for companies to raise money without going to the bank for fresh funding.

right to buy   SEE COMMENT
The right is of a local authority (council) tenant to buy his or her home at a heavy discount to its market value. The policy was introduced in the Housing Act 1980, the year after Margaret Thatcher became prime minister, as part of her government's plans to increase home ownership. Controversial at the time, the right to buy was electorally popular and has indeed increased home ownership, but it has also contributed to a shortage of housing available for people with limited incomes. See **social housing.**

rig-out, *n.*   *Inf.* **getup**
Inf. A person's unusual outfit or attire.

ring book   **loose-leaf notebook, ring notebook**

ring doughnut   **doughnut**
An old-fashioned term for an ordinary doughnut, i.e. one with a hole in the middle.

ring-road; ringway, *n.*   **beltway; by-pass**
A single route around a town; a *bypass*. In a big city like London, it can consist of a succession of streets constituting a route arranged to avoid congested points. See also **orbital.**

rip, *n.*   *Inf.* **hell-raiser**
Inf. Literally, a *lecher,* a man of lax morals, but more commonly much less pejorative, with the emphasis on mischief and usually applied to youngsters.

ripping, *adj.*   *Inf.* **great**
Slang. Ripping is also used as an adverb with *good:* one can have a *ripping* time or a *ripping good* time. Once in a while one hears the adverb *rippingly,* as in *Things went rippingly.* Practically out of the language now. See also **rattling.**

rise, *n.*   **1. raise**
                                                                        2. gain
1. In salary.
2. On the stock market. And a *fall* is a *loss.* Some newspaper stock market reports list the number of *rises* and *falls,* rather than *gains* and *losses.*

rise, *v.i.*   **adjourn**
The House (of Commons) *rises* for the summer recess or at the end of a session.

rising, *adv.*   *Inf.* **going on**
Inf. Used only in expressions of age, as in *she is sixteen, rising seventeen.* Synonymous with **coming.**

rising damp. See **damp course.**

rising powder   **baking powder**
Both terms are used in Britain, though *baking powder* is now far more common.

risk, at. See **at risk.**

riveting, *adj.*   **fascinating; absorbing**
A participial adjective to describe something that attracts and holds one's attention, to the exclusion of whatever else is happening; that glues one to his chair or keeps one on the edge of it. *Too riveting* means 'terribly exciting.' *Positively riveting* means 'utterly fascinating.'

roach, *n.*   **small carplike fish**
Caught for sport only in streams and an occasional moat. Eaten very rarely, if at all, nowadays.

road-metal. See **metalled road.**

road, *n.*   **way**
Inf. The British use *road* in a number of instances where Americans use *way. In someone's road* means 'in someone's way,' and to *get out of someone's road* is to *get out of his way.* But rail*road* is the common term in America, rail*way* in Britain.

road-sweeper, *n.*   **street cleaner**

Road Up   **Road Under Repair**
Roadside warning sign.

roadway, *n.*   **pavement**
Pavement in Britain means 'sidewalk.'

Road Works   **Men Working**
Roadside warning sign.

Robert. See **bobby.**

rocket, *n.*   **1.** *Slang.* **hell**
                                                              2. *n.,* **arugula**
Slang. A severe reprimand. To *get a rocket* is to *catch hell.*

rod in pickle for. See **have a rod in pickle for.**

roger, *n., v.t.*   *Slang.* **screw**
Slang. Vulgar slang for sexual intercourse. Also used as a verb: *roger someone.*

Roller, *n.*   *Inf.* **Rolls-Royce**

rollie, also rolley. See **roll-up.**

rollmop, *n.*   **pickled herring**
Pickled after rolling the filet and skewering it. The correct term is actually *roll-mops,* which is the singular in the Scandinavian languages where the word originates.

roll-neck, *adj.*   SEE COMMENT
Applied to sweaters with a loose, rolled down collar. See also **polo neck; turtleneck.**

roll-on, *n.*   **girdle**
A lady's undergarment.

roll-up   SEE COMMENT
A hand-rolled cigarette. More common in Britain than in America. Also, *rollie; rolley.* See also **skin.**

roly-poly pudding   SEE COMMENT
Suet pudding wrapped in a cloth and steamed. Covered in jam. Called **spotted dog** when improved with currants or raisins.

roneo, *n., v.t.*   **duplicate**
Inf. On a roneo machine, a sort of mimeographing apparatus. Proprietary name *Roneo.* Obsolete word, obsolete technology.

roof, *n.*   **top**
In automobile context, a *roof* in Britain is a *hard top.* A soft one, i.e., a *convertible top,* is called a *hood* in Britain. See **Appendix II.E.**

roofer, *n.*   *Inf.* **bread-and-butter letter**
Inf. Synonymous with **Collins.**

roof-rack, *n.*   **luggage rack**
See **Appendix II.E.**

roopy, *adj., Slang.*   **hoarse**

ropy, *adj.*   *Slang.* SEE COMMENT
Shabby, coming apart at the seams, like threadbare clothes or a nearly extinct
jalopy. It is occasionally used about oneself, as in *I'm feeling ropy as hell.* The usual
circumstance is a hangover. See also **grotty.**

rose, *n.*   *Inf.* **frog**
Inf. In the sense of a 'flower holder,' i.e., the article on the bottom of a shallow
vase into which you stick the stems.

rot, *v.t., v.i.*   **1. spoil**
                                                                        2. *Inf.* **kid**

1. *Slang.* To *rot* a plan is to *spoil* it.
2. *Slang.* Intransitively, to *rot* is to *kid* or *kid around.*

rot, *n. Slang.*   **1. nonsense**
                                                                    2. SEE COMMENT
1. Common to both countries, but much oftener heard in Britain.
2. A term expressing a sudden series of failures in an endeavor (business, sport,
etc.) Thus, *A rot set in.*

rota, *n.*   **roster**
List of persons acting in turn. *By rota* means 'in turn': *Saturday morning* **surgery** *is
taken by rota, by the three doctors in group practice.*

rotten borough   SEE COMMENT
In olden days, **Members** (of Parliament) represented *boroughs* (towns; *borough*
comes from old English *burg*). A *rotten borough* was one which had degenerated in
size, or even ceased to exist as a town, but continued to be represented in Parliament despite lack of a constituency.

rotter, *n.*   *Slang.* **cad, scoundrel**

rough, *n.*   **1. heavy work**
                                                                    2. *Slang.* **tough**
1. *Slang.* The *rough* is used to indicate the *heavy work* around the house. Thus,
there might be a companion type of servant who did the cooking but somebody
else in the household to do the *rough.*
2. *Slang.* Street rowdy; tough guy.

round, *n., prep., adv.*   **1. sandwich**
                                                                        2. route
                                                                        3. around
1. The British use the word *sandwich* the way the Americans do. After all, it was
said to be the Earl of Sandwich who ate meat between slices of bread during a
twenty-four-hour gambling bout. But in a British pub you may well hear the cus-

tomers ask for a *round* of ham or a *round* of beef instead of for a *sandwich*. This is to distinguish a complete square from a diagonal half.
2. *Round* also means 'route,' in the sense of 'delivery route.' See also **country round; roundsman.**
3. In Britain, *round* is used in almost every case where *around* would be used in America. See also **about** for another British equivalent of the American *around*.

roundabout, *n.*   **1. traffic circle**
                                                    2. merry-go-round
2. See also **carousel.**

rounders, *n. pl.*   SEE COMMENT
Children's game resembling baseball.

round on   **1.** *Inf.* **turn on**
                                                    2. *Slang.* **squeal on**
1. *Inf.* To make some kind of unexpected answer to someone, implying an angry retort; to *let him have it*.
2. *Inf.* To *peach* on him.

roundsman, *n.*   **delivery man**
With a regular route; thus, the baker's *roundsman*, the milk *roundsman*. See **country round.**

round the bend   *Slang.* **crazy**
Slang. Usually in the expression *drive round the bend,* meaning 'drive crazy.' Also, **round the twist.**

round the twist. See **round the bend.**

row-de-dow, *n.*   **uproar**
Inf. Obsolescent.

rowlock *n.*   **oarlock**
(Pronounced ROLLOCK or RULLOCK).

Rowton house   SEE COMMENT
A type of lodging for poor men, with better conditions than what the British call a *common lodging-house,* one usually fitted out with a dormitory with beds that can be rented for the night. *Rowton houses* were named after Lord Rowton, an English social reformer (1838–1903) who became interested in London housing conditions and devised a plan for a hotel for poor men. Uncommon nowadays.

royal, *n.*   **member of the royal family**
Inf. Can also apply to foreign royalty.

Royal Commission   SEE COMMENT
A body of persons appointed by the Crown to look into and file a report on some matter. Cf. **working party.** It would appear that, unlike a working party, a *Royal Commission* is all too often a device created to give a burial to a nagging question.

rozzer, *n.*   *Slang.* **cop**
Slang. An outmoded term. The British share *fuzz* with the Americans. See **bobby** for synonyms.

R.P. See **Received Pronunciation.**

RSPCA, *acronym*   SEE COMMENT
Royal Society for the Prevention of Cruelty to Animals. The British equivalent of
the ASPCA.

R.S.M.   **1.** SEE COMMENT
                                                                     2. SEE COMMENT
1. The initials stand for *regimental sergeant-major,* which in certain contexts has
become a more or less generic bit of symbolism of the strict disiplinarian.
2. Royal Society of Medicine.

rub along   *Inf.* **get by**
Inf. As in *How do you manage without a steady job? Oh, we rub along.*

rubber, *n.*   **eraser**
It does not mean 'contraceptive' in Britain.

rubbish!   *Interj.* **nonsense!**
Interj. Or *tommyrot!* The British term is rarely used as an interjection in America.

rub up the wrong way   *Inf.* **rub the wrong way**
Inf. See **Appendix I.A.3.**

ruby wedding   40th **wedding anniversary**
Marriages seem not to be made in heaven anymore, so today's Americans and
Britons do not encounter many *ruby weddings.* Wedding observers in both countries use the same customs in designating what today are considered marathon
anniversaries to be celebrated with gifts made of various materials and gems:
silver for 25th, ruby for 40th, golden for 50th, and diamond for 75th.

ruck, *n.*   **1. common herd**
                                                                  2. *Slang.* **also-rans**
                                                                  3. rugby scrum
1. *Slang.* Usually seen in the phrase *common ruck,* or the phrase *ruck and truck.*
2. *Slang.* In a more limited sense, it refers to the main body of competition left out
of the running.
3. *Slang.* A specialized meaning. See **scrum.**

rucksack, *n.*   **backpack**

ruddy, *adj.*   *Slang.* **damnable**
Slang. Ruddy came into use as a euphemism for **bloody.**

rude, *adj.*   **1. inconsiderate**
                                                               2. frank
                                                               3. *Inf.* **dirty (indecent)**
                                                               4. robust
Apart from its several common meanings shared with America, this adjective has
several uses in Britain not found in America:
1. *Inconsiderate,* as in: *It is rude of me not to let you know my plans sooner.*
2. *Frank, outspoken, indiscreet,* as in: *May I be rude and tell you that I don't like your
new hat?* Or, with a slightly different nuance, *May I be rude and ask you how much
you paid for that car?*

3. *Indecent, improper,* as applied, e.g., to a joke, or a picture or statue.
4. As used in the expression *rude health.*

rude boy/girl   *Slang.* SEE COMMENT
An impudent, antisocial child, usually a teenager of a lower socioeconomic status
than the person using the phrase.

rudery, *n., Inf.*   **piece of rudeness**

rug. See under **carpet.**

rugger. See **football.**

rum, *adj.*   *Inf.* **funny (peculiar)**
Slang. The usual meaning of *rum* is 'funny' in the sense of 'peculiar' or 'strange.'
For example: *What a rum way to dress!* But in combination with certain nouns, *rum*
has other meanings: a *rum customer* is a *dangerous customer,* a person not safe to
meddle with; a *rum go* is a *tough break;* a *rum start* is a *funny thing* of the sort that
so often happens on the way to the theater if one can believe comedians' patter; a
rum old do is a *funny situation,* a *bizarre happening;* a *mixed-up affair.* (*We started out,
it began to rain, we ran inside, the sun came out, we went out again, it began to pour with
rain, we rushed back inside—it was a rum old do!*) All three words in this idiom are
Briticisms. See **do** in this connection.

rumble, *v.t.*   *Inf.* **see through**
Slang. To see the real character of a person; to get to the bottom of a situation.

rumble strip   **speed bumps**
Raised bumps placed across a road to slow down motorists—a sensible precau-
tion in both countries. See also **ramp, 1.**

rumbustious, *adj.*   **rambunctious**
Inf. Obstreperous; unruly.

rum-butter, *n.*   **hard sauce**
More or less interchangeable with **brandy-butter,** containing at least soft brown
sugar, grated orange and lemon rind, butter, and rum. Served with rich fruit pudding, baked apple, baked banana, mince pie.

rump steak, *n.*   **sirloin**
The British use *sirloin,* but it refers to what the Americans call *porterhouse.* See
Appendix II.H, and comment under **sirloin.**

rumpy, *n., Inf.*   **Manx cat**
A tailless creature.

rumpy pumpy, *n.*   *Slang.* **sexual intercourse**
A coy, archaic phrase. It connotes an old-fashioned, slightly leering attitude to
sex, and is still used ironically by people who don't agree with the view of human
sexuality implied in the term itself.

run-away, *n.*   **drain**
Something to let the water through.

run in   *Inf.* **break in**
Inf. What one does to new automobiles. The British *break in* wild horses but *run in* new cars.

runner, *n.*   **1. stringer**
                                                                              2. winner
1. In the sense of part-time local newspaper correspondent.
2. Even if a few people do believe that the race is not always to the swift, we all have our ways of referring to outstanding ideas, painters, athletes, proposals, and all the rest. In America we wish to know the feasibility of something, the quality of someone, and the like—in short, will it fly? The British put it differently. They want to know whether someone or something will ever be good enough to get into a race—will it be a *runner?*

runner, do a   *Inf.* **disappear**
Underworld slang now commonly used. *He ate his meal, and then did a runner without paying.*

runner beans   **string beans**
But usually long and flat, not the round-sectioned **French bean.** Often shortened to *runners.*

running account   **checking account**
Synonymous with **current account.**

running shed   **roundhouse**

run out   **put out**
A **cricket** term. One of the ways a player is put out in this game.

run the rule over   **take a look at**
Inf. To *go over* something *cursorily;* examine it for correctness or adequacy. *This is my summary; would you be good enough to run the rule over it?*

run-up, *n.*   SEE COMMENT
In British politics, the *run-up* to election is the period of the campaign approaching the vote. The term can be used to cover the period of approach to any event, e.g. the *run-up* to the Prime Minister's speech on a certain topic, referring to the period of feverish preparation. *Run-up* is borrowed from cricket, where the **bowler** acquires momentum by *running up* to the point at which he releases the ball.

rush, *v.t.*   *Slang.* **soak**
Slang. For instance: *How much did they rush you for that sherry?* To *rush* is to *charge,* with the distinct implication that the price was too high.

rush one's fences   *Slang.* **jump the gun**
Slang. To *go off half-cocked;* to act or react with undue haste.

rusticate, *v.t.*   **expel temporarily from university**
To be *permanently expelled* is, in Britain, to be **sent down.** *Rustication* occurs in the case of less serious offenses.

S

sack, *n., v.t.*

1. *n.* **dismissal**
2. *v.t.* **fire**
3. *v.t.* **expel**

1. *Inf.* As in, *get* or *give the sack.*
2. *Inf.* From a job. See synonyms under **give (someone) his cards.**
3. *Inf.* From a secondary school. From a university, the term for *expel* is *send down.*

safari bed. See **camp bed.**

safe storage **safekeeping**

saffron bun SEE COMMENT
Also called *saffron cake.* A delicacy of Cornish origin, bright yellow in color. If you should happen to look into a 15th-century British cookbook (or *cokeryboke,* as they were called) you would find that virtually all cakes and many breads were heavily "strewn forth" with saffron.

St. Luke's summer **Indian summer**
Also called *Luke's little summer* and *St. Martin's summer.*

St. Martin's summer **Indian summer**
Also called *St. Luke's summer* and *Luke's little summer.*

saithe. See **Appendix II.H.**

. . . salad, *n.* **. . . and salad**
Chicken (ham, beef, etc.) *salad* on British menus means *chicken* (etc.) *and salad:* not the chopped up variety familiar to Americans. In Britain you get a serving of chicken or other meat *and* a portion of salad.

Sally Army, *abbrev.* **Salvation Army**

saloon, *n.*

1. **sedan**
2. **parlor**

1. A *saloon motorcar,* which can be shortened to *saloon* in proper context, is what Americans call a *sedan.*
2. *Saloon* is commercialese in Britain, except on a ship (and see *saloon bar* and **saloon-car**). In the commercial idiom the British use the terms *hair-dressing, billiards,* etc., *saloon* where the American term would be *parlor;* but in ordinary speech, a man would simply refer to his barber, a woman to her hairdresser.

saloon bar. See **pub.**

saloon-car **parlor car**
Also *saloon-carriage,* in a railroad car.

saloon car, *n.*   **sedan**

salt beef   **corned beef**
No matter where served in all of Britain, scarcely resembling New York City's
kosher corned beef. Once a diet staple of the British army in the field, its army
nickname is *bully beef*. See also **corned beef.**

salting, *n.*   **1. salt marsh**
                                                                                  2. tide-flat

1. Usually found in the plural.
2. Land periodically flooded by ocean or inlet tides.

sand, *n.*   **grit**
Inf. In the sense of *determination, courage,* steadfastness of purpose.

sandboy. See **happy as a sandboy.**

sanitary towel, *n.*   **sanitary napkin**

sanitation officer. See under **refuse tip.**

sap, *n., v.i.*   **1. *v.i., Slang.* cram**
                                                                        2. *n., Slang.* grind
1. *Slang.* To *sap* is to *cram,* See also **mug; swot.**
2. *Slang.* A *sap* is a *grind,* in the two distinct senses of 'zealous student' and 'tough
job.' (The American slang meaning 'fool' is shared with Britain.)
    One wonders whether this latter meaning reflects the anti-intellectual atmo-
sphere that gave rise to the term *egghead. Verbum sap,* or as we usually say, *A word
to the wise is sufficient.*

sapper, *n.*   **army engineer**
Especially a private, engaged in the building of fortifications in the field, etc.

sarky, *adj.*   *abbrev.* **sarcastic**

sarnie, *n.*   *Inf.* **sandwich**

Sassenach, *n., adj.*   SEE COMMENT
A derogatory term for English (man), from the Gaelic for *Saxon* noun and adjective.

sauce, *n.*   *Inf.* **cheek**
Inf. In the sense of 'impudence' or 'impertinence.' Often heard in the phrase
bloody sauce.

sauce-boat, *n.*   **gravy boat**

sausage, *n.*   *approx.* **weather stripping**
Inf. Sausage-shaped form, velvet stuffed with sawdust, used to keep out under-
the-door drafts.

sausage roll   SEE COMMENT
1. Baked sausage meat in pastry. See also **pie; pasty; stargazey.**
2. *Inf.* Anything sausage-shaped, including people.

saveloy, *n.*   SEE COMMENT
A smoked pork sausage, usually sold only in fish and chips shops.

save one's bacon, *Slang.*   *Inf.* **save one's skin**

save the mark!   **God help us!**
Sometimes *God save the mark!* A sarcastic or scornful interjection. *He calls himself an impressionist—God save the mark!*

savoury, *n., adj.*   **1. tidbit**
                                                                2. SEE COMMENT
1. A *canapé* or sometimes something larger served usually at the end of dinner, after dessert; but the term also covers an *hors d'oeuvre* or *appetizer.* Examples might be a sardine or anchovy on toast, a modest welsh rarebit, and so on. When served after dessert, it is always served hot.
2. Any dish that is not sweet. As an adjective, used to describe such as dish; *I prefer savoury dishes to sweet.*

say boo to a goose   *Inf.* **open one's mouth**
Inf. Have the courage to express disapproval. Usually in the negative: *He wouldn't say boo to a goose,* meaning 'He was afraid to open his mouth (to say a word).' Describes a milquetoast.

scarper, *v.i., Slang.*   *Slang.* **scram**
Escape, run away.

scatty, *adj.*   *Slang.* **whacky, absentminded**
Slang. Americans are more apt to say *scatterbrained* or *feebleminded.*

scene-shifter, *n.*   **stagehand**

scenic railway   **miniature railway**
Child's railroad train in an amusement park or tourist attraction.

scent, *n.*   **perfume**
A *scent spray* is an *atomizer.*

scheduled building. See **listed building.**

scheme, *n.*   **plan**
In Britain the noun does not always have the American connotation of 'slyness' or 'sharp practice' (in fact one may talk of government or private housing *schemes*), but the noun *schemer* and the verb to *scheme* do have that connotation.

scheme of arrangement   **reorganization plan**
Of a corporation in financial difficulties.

schemozzle. See **shemozzle.**

scholar, *n.*   **scholarship student**
Learned persons are called *scholars* in both countries, but the word is not used in America, as it commonly is in Britain, to denote a *student on a scholarship.* In the

North of England the term applies to any schoolboy, as it can in America, and once did all over England.

school, *n.*   SEE COMMENT
An American may speak of Harvard as his *school;* no Briton would apply that term to his university. The word is confined in Britain to the grades below college level (*college* in the American sense; *university* in the British). For the distinction in Britain between *college* and *university,* see **college.**

schoolboy cake   cheap fruit cake
Inf. Made with a minimum of fruit, and that consisting almost entirely of currants; the type commonly served at boarding-schools and sold at railroad stations, cheap cafés, etc. In earlier times, it was called *shouting cake,* and it is still so referred to jocularly by older folk: the currants were so far apart they had to shout at one another—unlike *whispering cake,* the ubiquitous fruit-laden British wedding cake, so richly laden that the components were close enough to whisper to one another. Now rare.

school dance, *n.*   school prom

school-leaver, *n.*   *approx.* **high-school graduate**
A student who has completed formal education at a secondary school level, is not going on to college, and is now ready to go to work for a living. The shorter term **leaver** is occasionally used in **prep school** and **public school** circles to describe a student about to complete the curriculum there.

school treat, *n.*   school party
Usually away from school, on private grounds thrown open for the occasion.

schooner, *n.*   large sherry (port) glass
An American *schooner* is a *tall beer glass.* In Britain, where beer is usually drunk in very large glasses as a matter of course (see **pint**), a *schooner* is a glass reserved for a more than usually generous portion of sherry, or sometimes port.

scoff, *n., v.t.*   1. *n., Slang.* **good eats**
                                                        2. *v.t., Slang.* **wolf**

1. *n., Slang.* A schoolboy term.
2. *v.t., Inf.* To *gobble* or *knock back* food.

sconce, *n., v.t.*   *approx.* **fine**
Slang. A highly specialized Oxford term, applicable only to undergraduates dining in **hall** (i.e., in the college dining-room). To *sconce* a fellow student is to *fine* him a tankard of ale, or the like, for a breach of table etiquette. *Sconce,* as a noun, means the 'forfeit' so imposed. The table of offenses varies with the college.

scone, *n.*   *approx.* **baking powder biscuit**
(Should rhyme with JOHN though the long o is also heard in some circles. See **Appendix I.C.6.**) Usually served at room temperature, while the approximate American equivalent is served warm. The usual fare for *tea.*

scoop the pool   *Slang.* **make a killing**
Slang. Originally a stock exchange term.

score off, *v.*   **get the better of**
Inf. In an argument or in repartee.

Scotch egg   SEE COMMENT
This is a pub delicacy consisting of a hard-boiled egg, coated with a blanket of
pork sausage meat, which is then breaded and deep-fried.

Scotch foursome. See **fourball.**

Scotch woodcock   SEE COMMENT
Scrambled eggs (the British sometimes call them *buttered eggs*) on toast first spread
with anchovy paste. The recipe for Scotch woodcook in *Mrs. Beeton's Household
Management* follows:

> *Scotch Woodcock (Anchois à l'Écossaise)*
> *Ingredients.*—The yolks of two eggs, one gill of cream (or cream and milk in
> equal parts), anchovy paste, toast, butter, cayenne, salt.
> *Method.*—Cut the toast into two-inch squares, butter well, and spread them with
> anchovy paste. Season the eggs with a little cayenne and salt; when slightly beaten
> add them to the hot cream, stir over the fire until they thicken sufficiently, then
> pour the preparation over the toast, and serve as hot as possible.
> *Time.*—Ten minutes. Sufficient for six to eight persons.

Scouse, *n.*   SEE COMMENT
Inf. (Rhymes with MOUSE.) Denotes a native of Liverpool and the Liverpool dialect. A native of Liverpool is also called a *Liverpudlian.*

scout. See **gyp.**

scrag, *n.*   **neck of lamb**
A cheap cut used for stewing, and consisting mostly of bone and gristle.

scraggy, *adj.*   **scrawny**
Lean and skinny.

scrap, *n.*   **junk**

scrapyard, *n.*   **junkyard**

scray, *n.*   **tern**
A seabird.

screaming abdabs, *n.*   *Inf.* **nerves**
She's had the screaming abdabs ever since that road accident.

scree, *n.*   **mountain slope**
But *scree* (or *screes*) can also be used to denote the pebbles or small stones and
rocks that dribble or slide down when people walk up a steep slope covered with
loose gravel.

screw, *n.*   1. *approx. Slang.* **take**
                                                                        2. **nag**
                                                                        3. *approx.* **twist; bit**
                                                                        4. *n.* **prison guard**

1. *Slang.* In the sense of 'salary.' It is hard to find an exact American slang equivalent. *Take* may do, but it is broader than *screw* because it would cover the concept of *profit* as well as that of *regular wages.*
2. *Slang.* An old and shaky horse.
3. *Slang.* It is occasionally used to mean a 'rumpled-up ball of paper'—the sort thrown into a wastebasket; at other times a 'bit of salt or tobacco,' or anything of that sort contained in a piece of twisted paper.

screwed, *adj.*   *Slang.* **tight**
Slang. Loaded, pickled, stinko, etc.

scribbling-block, *n.*   **scratch pad**
Also *scribbling-pad.*

scrimmage. See **scrum.**

scrimshank, *v.i.*   *Slang.* **goldbrick**
Military slang. To *shirk.* Originally a nautical slang expression alluding to the man who idly swung the lead he was supposed to be taking soundings with. Medical humor: a doctor fed up with signing excuses so that lazy employees could attend *soccer* matches attested that a patient was suffering from *plumbum pendularum,* mock Latin for *lead swinging.* See also: **skive; dodge the column; swing the lead; swing it; skulk; slack; soldier; mike.**

scrip, *n.*   **1. temporary stock certificate**
                                                     2. *Inf., n.* **prescription**
In Britain a *scrip* is a *temporary certificate* issued to one entitled eventually to receive a formal stock certificate. In America *scrip* is applied to a formal certificate representing a fraction of a share. In the bad old days of U.S. company towns (mining towns were a prime example), one company would pay a *scrip* which could only be used in company-owned stores—now an illegal practice.

scrotty, *adj.*   **crummy**
Anything far from first quality can be said in England to be *scrotty,* thought of in American to be *cheesy.*

scrubber, *n.*   **loose woman**
Slang. A pejorative term for one who gives that impression.

scruffy, *adj.*   **untidy, shabby**

scrum, *n.*   **scrimmage; melee**
Inf. Short for *scrummage,* which is a variant of *scrimmage. Scrimmage* has the general meaning of 'confused struggle' or 'melee' in both countries. In British Rugby football, the *scrummage* is the mass of all the forwards surrounding the ball, which has been thrown on the ground between them. As a sports term, the British usually use the shortened form *scrum.*

scrummage. See **scrum.**

scrump, *v.t., v.i.*   **steal fruit**
Also *scrimp, skrump.* Particularly apples. *Scrumpy* is a rough, usually very strong cider. The name implies that it has been made from all old apples lying around. See also **cider.**

scrumpy. See under **scrump.**

scrutineer, *n.*   **ballot counter and inspector**

scug, *n.*   **fink**
School slang. Extremely derogatory in the cruel way peculiar to children. It means
a person with bad manners, unfriendly, a bad sport, and generally one to be
shunned.

scullery, *n.*   **back kitchen**
Room for washing dishes etc.

scunner. See **take a scunner at.**

scupper, *v.t.*   *Slang.* **do (someone) in**
Slang. Scupper is a noun in both countries, meaning a 'drain in a ship' designed to
carry water off a deck. As a British verb, *scupper* means 'ambush and wipe out.'
In nautical circles, to *scupper* is to *sink a ship,* with the implication of finishing off
the crew as well.

scurf, *n.*   **dandruff**
Both terms used in both countries.

scutter, *v.i., Inf.*   **scurry**

scuttle, *n.*   SEE COMMENT
A *scuttle* is a *coal pail,* usually called a *coal scuttle* in both countries. The word,
however, has an exclusively British additional meaning: a 'wide shallow
basket.'

S.E. See **Standard English.**

sea, *n.*   **beach**
Sea and *seaside* are used in Britain where Americans would usually say *beach,* or
less commonly, *shore,* to mean a 'seaside resort,' like Brighton in Britain or Atlantic City in America. See **beach** for British use of the word. See also **front; bathe.**

sea fret   **sea fog**
Nautical jargon.

sea front. See **front.**

season ticket   **commutation ticket**
In America one thinks of a *season ticket* as something entitling one to see all the
games at a given ball park. In Britain it usually refers to train travel and can be
valid for anything from a month to a year. In this sense, it is occasionally shortened to *season,* as in railroad station signs reading PLEASE SHOW YOUR SEASON. A
season ticket holder is a *commuter. Season ticket* can also apply to a series of performances, in which sense it would be synonymous with *subscription.*

secateurs, *n. pl.*   **pruning shears**
(Accent on the first syllable, which rhymes with DECK.) Such shears are operated
with one hand.

second, *n.*   **magna**
A university term. *Second* is short for *second-class honours* just as *magna* in the U.S. is short for *magna cum laude.* In some universities a second-class degree is further divided into an *upper* or (informally) *good second* and a *lower second.* See also **first; class.**

second, *v.t.*   **transfer temporarily; detail**
Denotes a temporary transfer of an employee to another department of the company, or of a soldier to another unit.

secondary modern. See **eleven plus.**

secondary subject   **minor**
At college. In American colleges, students choose a *major* (in which they *specialize*) and usually a *minor.* In Britain, the student **reads** his main subject, and elects a *secondary subject.*

second class. See **first class.**

second eleven   **second rank**
Inf. Or *Grade B*—a term borrowed from **cricket.** See **eleven.**

sectioned   SEE COMMENT
Compulsorily detained under a section of the Mental Health Act 1983. This may come about because a person is considered a danger to himself or others, and unable to consent to vital medical treatment.

see a man about a dog   SEE COMMENT
A term used in answer to the question *Where are you going?* when the respondent doesn't want to answer honestly. It is almost always used when the destination is the bathroom (**loo, lavatory**), and is sometimes offered pre-emptively as one rises from the table at the pub: *I've got to go see a man about a dog.*

see (someone) far enough   *Inf.* **see one in hell**
Inf. As in *I'll see him far enough before I invite him to dinner again.* Sometimes given as to *see one further.*

Seeing-to, *n.*   **1.** *Inf.* **act of sexual intercourse**
                                          2. *Inf.* **beating**
A curious and unpleasant pairing of usages. In sense 1, the term may be jocular or insulting. In sense 2, of course, it is always a euphemism for cruel violence.

see (someone) off, *Slang.*   *Slang.* **polish (someone) off**
Nothing to do with fond good-byes.

see (someone) out   **last for the rest of (someone) life**
Inf. This coat will see me out, says the elderly person who feels guilty about an expenditure at a sale. *It'll outlive me,* he or she might have said.

see the back of   *Inf.* **see the last of**
Inf. Almost always after *I'll be glad to* . . .

select committee   SEE COMMENT
A small committee of **MPs** set up to investigate and report on a particular subject. Subcommittees in the House and Senate are the U.S. equivalents.

self-selection, *n., adj.*   **self-service**
Applying to retail stores.

sell (someone) a dummy   *Inf.* **put it over on (someone)**
Inf. A term borrowed from rugby.

sell (someone) a pup   *Slang.* **stick (someone)**
Inf. To *sell someone a pup* is to *stick him,* i.e., to cheat him, especially by getting a high price for inferior merchandise.

Sellotape, *n., TM*   **adhesive tape**
Proprietary names. In Britain also given as *sellotape.*

sell the pass   **betray a cause or trust**
Inf. To cede the advantage to one's adversaries. Term borrowed from the language of mountain warfare.

sell up   *Inf.* **sell out**
Inf. If a Briton were to sell his residence and also wanted to liquidate the furnishings he would speak of *selling up* everything, i.e., *selling out* lock, stock, and barrel. It means 'sell out' also in the sense of 'sell out a debtor's property' in a forced sale.

semibreve, *n.*   **whole note**
Musical term. See **Appendix II.F.**

semi-detached, *adj.*   **two-family**
In America a *two-family house* may be divided horizontally or vertically. In Britain a *semi-detached residence* is a one-family house joined to another by a common or party wall. The two halves are often painted different colors. When more than two residences are joined together, the series is called a *terrace.*

semiquaver, *n.*   **sixteenth note**
Musical term. See **Appendix II.F.**

semolina, *n.*   **milled durum wheat**

S.E.N.   **practical nurse**
Stands for *State Enrolled Nurse.* See also **sister.**

send down   **expel**
A term from university life. In referring to school, the British slang term is *sack.* See also **rusticate.**

send (someone) spare   *Slang.* **drive (someone) nuts**
Slang. See also **go spare.**

send to Coventry   *Inf.* **turn one's back on**
Inf. To *ignore socially; give the cold shoulder to.* The primary factor of this punishment is that nobody is to speak to the poor chap.

send-up, *n.*   *Inf.* **take-off**
Inf. Or *put-on.* A *send-up of* a music hall song in America would be a *take-off on* it. To *send* someone *up* is to *make fun of* him. Incidentally, in both countries one can be *sent up* (to jail or gaol).

send up rotten   **pan**
Slang. To 'deprecate, to get bad reviews.'

senior lecturer   **assistant professor**
Approximate equivalent in the teaching hierarchy. See **reader.**

Senior Service   **Royal Navy**
Senior Service does not mean the Army.

Senior Wrangler. See **wrangler.**

Senior Wrangler sauce. See **brandy-butter.**

septillion. See **Appendix II.D.**

sergeant-major   **top sergeant**
See also **R.S.M.**

serve, *v.t., v.i.*   **wait on**
In a shop, to *serve* someone is to *wait on* a customer. *Are you being served?* (sometimes shortened to *Are you served?*) would usually come out as, *Is someone helping
you?* in an American store.

servery, *n.*   *approx.* **service counter**
Generally a room from which meals are served. Thus, at a pub one might find
a sign pointing to the GARDEN AND BAR SERVERY, indicating the room to which
one must go in order to obtain food and drink to be consumed in the garden or
the bar.

service engineer   **skilled mechanic**
An epithet applied to one experienced in refrigerators, dishwashers, etc.

service flat, *n.*   **hotel apartment**
In the plural, *service flats* is seen in the expression *block of service flats,* which
would correspond to an American *apartment hotel* or *residential hotel.* See also
apartment; flat.

service lift   **dumbwaiter**
A **dumb-waiter** in Britain is also what is known in America and in Britain as a
lazy Susan.

service occupancy. See under **vacant possession.**

serviette, *n.*   **napkin**
Still used occasionally but *table-napkin* is widely used.

servitor. See **sizar.**

set, *n.*   1. *approx.* **group**
                                                        2. **apartment; suite**
                                                            3. **paving block**
                                                         4. **badger's burrow**

1. A school term; thus the *A set,* the *B set,* etc., meaning 'group' (within a given grade or form) based on the ability of the students. In this sense, the word is giving way to a newer term, **stream.**
2. In this use, restricted to apartments in such exclusive and historic addresses as the residence known as *Albany* in London, with its sixty-nine *sets,* or to groups of rooms at the various **Inns of Court,** where *sets* is short for *sets of chambers.* See **chambers.**
3. Variant of *sett.*
4. Variant of *sett,* which can also mean badger's debris outside the burrow.

set about   *Slang.* **lay into**
Slang. An expression that one gang member would be apt to use to encourage his mates when about to take on a rival gang. *Let's set about that* **lot!**

set book, *n.*   **required reading**
Specific reading assignment for an examination.

set down   **let off**
A term used in transportation: passengers are *set down* in Britain and *let off* or *dropped off* in America. Signs seen in Britain: At a railroad station: PICK UP AND SET DOWN. NO PARKING. At bus stops: SETTING DOWN POINT ONLY (interchangeable with ALIGHTING POINT).

set fair   **put up**
Stable term: to *set a horse fair* is to *put it up,* i.e., *get it all set* for the night.

set lunch   **table d'hôte; prix fixe**
See also **set tea.**

set out one's stall, *Inf.*   **display one's credentials**

sett. See **set, 3. and 4.**

set tea   **afternoon tea**
Tea with little sandwiches and cakes, obtainable at hotels and restaurants; a complete tea at a fixed price. See also **tea.**

settee, *n.*   **couch**

set the Thames on fire   *Inf.* **set the world on fire**
He will never set the Thames on fire is said about a person who shows no sign of great achievement in his life.

sexillion, sextillion. See **Appendix II.D.**

Shadow Cabinet, *n.*   SEE COMMENT
Members of the main opposition party who direct their party's policy in a particular area—health, defense, and so forth. The members of the Shadow Cabinet are their party's **front bench,** and would hold ministerial positions if their party were in power.

shag   *Slang.* **fuck**
This vulgar Briticism and its American counterpart can be thought of as the verb to engage in sexual intercourse. But as in American explicit vulgarisms, phrases

borrowed from Latin seem to represent the dignifying of an act that is better expressed in the language of the barnyard.

shake. See **in two shakes of a duck's tail.**

shake down   *Inf.* **put up (for the night)**
Slang. In Britain it is very hospitable of you to *shake* somebody *down,* especially if that person lacks a place to sleep. In America, apart from its slang meaning of 'extortion,' a *shake-down* is an *improvised bed.* This use is reflected in the British use of *shake down.* None of this, of course, has anything to do with a *shakedown cruise,* which is a phrase used in both countries meaning a 'new ship's initial trip' made in order to break in both engine and crew.

Shakespearean university. See under **Oxbridge.**

shambolic, *adj.*   **chaotic**
Inf. From *shambles.* Used occasionally to describe situations or places that are in a state of extreme disorder.

shammy. See **wash leather.**

shandrydan, *n.*   **rickety vehicle**
Originally a chaise or shay, a light open two-wheeled horse-drawn carriage for two, usually with a hood; later applied to any ancient dilapidated vehicle. This term is hardly ever met with these days.

shandy, *n.*   SEE COMMENT
A drink consisting of beer and lemonade or ginger beer in equal parts, which some British children drink in their early teens in preparation for the eventual **pint.** Short for *shandygaff.*

shank's pony   **shank's mare**

shape, *n.*   SEE COMMENT
An old-fashioned word for any dessert like gelatin, blancmange, mousse, etc. shaped in a mold.

shared line   **party line**
The more fortunate have **exclusive lines.** Also called *shared service.*

share-pushing   **stock touting**
Not necessarily fraudulent but with the implication of sharp practice.

share raid. See **raid.**

shares, *n. pl.*   **stocks**
Usual name for corporate equities. *Stock,* or *stocks,* in British financial circles, usually means 'government bonds,' but can mean 'corporate stock' as well, as in America; and *stockholder* can refer to either type of security. *Tap stocks* are those that are always available. The term is applied also to government bonds sold by the government departments holding them when they reach a certain

market price. They may be short-term or long-term. *Taplets* are small issues of this kind.

sharpen, *v.t.* sharp
Musical term, make or become *sharp*. See **Appendix I.A.3.**

sharpish, *adv.* soon, promptly
Get there at 9 sharpish!

shave hook scraper
Used to prepare metal for soldering.

shaw, *n.* 1. thicket
2. stalks and leaves
1. Mainly poetic.
2. Mainly Scottish, and referring particularly to turnip and potato crops.

sheaf, *n.* *Inf.* **wad; bankroll**
Inf. Referring to paper money: *sheaf of* **notes** would be a *bankroll* or a *wad* in America. *Sheaf* is usually used for a tied-up armful of wheat.

shebeen, *n.* *approx.* **speakeasy**
(Accent on the second syllable.) An unlicensed pub in Ireland. See **licensed.**

shelf company SEE COMMENT
A corporation formed by a lawyer (**solicitor**) or an accountant, held available for the use of a client needing to organize a company.

sheltered accommodation assisted living
The tenants may be the elderly or the disabled. Also known as *sheltered housing.*

sheltered trade domestic monopoly
Describing a business that gets no competition from abroad, for example, a railroad.

shemozzle, *n.* *Inf.* **mix-up; row**
Slang. A *mix-up*, a *mess*, a *confused situation* generally; in a narrower use, a *row*, in the sense of 'dispute,' a *rhubarb*, a *melee*. The British spell this word variously; a sampling of variants: *schemozzle, shemozzl, shimozzel, chimozzle, shlemozzl, shlemozzle, schlemozzle, schlemazel*. Its origin is in London racetrack cant. The first *l*, and certainly the spelling *schlemazel*, crept in out of confusion with the totally unrelated Yiddish term *schlemaz(e)l*, meaning 'hard-luck guy.'

shepherd's pie SEE COMMENT
A *shepherd's pie* is usually made of chopped meat or the remains of a lamb roast, ground up (**minced**), topped by a layer of mashed potatoes and baked in the oven. See **cottage pie.**

sherbet. See under **ice.**

shilling. See **Appendix II.A.**

shilling shocker   **dime novel**
Also known in Britain as a **penny dreadful** or a **penny blood.** All of these terms
are old fashioned.

shingle, *n.*   **beach pebbles**
A beach so covered would be known as a *shingle beach* (as opposed to a *sandy
beach*). In America it would be called a *pebble beach* or *pebbly beach*.

shipping order   **large order**
Inf. One of those interminable orders being given by the customer just ahead of
you.

shipshape and Bristol fashion. See **Bristol fashion.**

shire, *n.*   SEE COMMENT
(Pronounced SHER, sometimes SHEER, when used as a suffix.) Old word for
county, now rarely used except in the plural (the *Shires*) meaning the 'hunting
country.' It is found mainly as a suffix in the names of most of the counties, as, for
example, in *Hampshire, Yorkshire*.

shirty, *adj.*   *Slang.* **visibly irritated, annoyed**
Don't get shirty with me!

shoal, *n.*   *Inf.* **crowd**
Inf. A *multitude,* like a *shoal* (or *shoals*) *of correspondence* to attend to.

shock, *n.*   **sensation**
Inf. Common usage in journalism, especially on the daily posters at newsstands
purporting to inform the public what today's big story is, but really only acting
as a teaser. Thus: SHARES DROP SHOCK (Stock Market Collapse Sensation!); OLD
BAILEY CONFESSION SHOCK (Murder Trial Confession—Wow!); BUDGET SHOCK
(Terrible New Tax Bill!!), etc. A *shock result* in sports is an *upset*. In jocular usage,
one says *shock horror*—a parodic adaptation of the journalistic phrase.

shocker, *n.*   1. *Inf.* **stinker**
                                                         2. **cheap novel**
1. *Inf. Shocker* is used to describe a bad case of almost anything; a stretch of
wretched weather, a new tax, an embarrassing utterance by a public figure, a
dress in very bad taste, overcooked Brussels sprouts, boring dinner party. Sometimes it is used in a rather exaggerated way, as in: *Isn't letter-writing a shocker!* See
also **shocking.**
2. Short for **shilling shocker.** It can also mean a 'sensational novel' as opposed
to a *thriller.*

shocking, *adj.*   *Inf.* **awful**
Inf. As in *Isn't it shocking?* (about the weather, etc.). *Shocking* is used in much the
same way as **shocker, 1.**

shoe mender   **shoemaker**
See also **mend.**

shoot, *v.t.*   **hunt**
A Briton *hunts* foxes and deer but *shoots* game birds and rabbits. Americans *hunt* quail, for instance. To *let the shooting* is to lease the right to hunt birds on your property.

shoot, *n.*   **1. shooting party**
      2. shooting expedition
      3. shooting practice
      4. shooting area

shoot a robin   *Inf.* **run into a streak of bad luck**
Slang. He must have shot a robin would be said of one suffering the lot of Job: one piece of bad luck after another. The Ancient Mariner was concerned with the albatross; a robin suffices in this quaint British expression. It's much worse than spilling salt, walking under a ladder, being crossed by a black cat; more like breaking a mirror.

shooting!, *interj.*   *Inf.* **good shot!**
Inf. A complimentary observation in certain sports like tennis, basketball, etc.

shooting-box, *n.*   **hunting-lodge**
The lodge would be modest in size.

shoot the cat   *Slang.* **toss one's cookies**
Slang. To *throw up;* the common expression is **be sick.** See also **sick up; queer.**

shoot the crow   *Inf.* **decamp**
Slang. Normally used to describe the sudden departure of someone else, rather than oneself. *Where's Jones these days? Shot the crow, it looks like.* See also **shoot the moon.**

shoot the moon   *Slang.* **skip town by night**
Slang. See also **moonlight flit; shoot the crow; hook it; leave in the lurch.**

shop, *n.*   **store**
A matter of usage. *Shop* is used in a few British informal expressions that one does not hear in America. *You have come to the wrong shop,* means 'I can't help you' (because you are applying to the wrong person). To *sink the shop* is to *keep mum* generally and more specifically to *keep your activities under wraps. All over the shop* means 'in wild disorder.' *A nation of shopkeepers* refers to Britain itself. *Shop-soiled* is *shop-worn* in America. To *have everything in the shop window* is to *play the big shot,* without having anything to back it up.

shop, *v.t.*   **1. jail**
      2. squeal on
Slang. In the British underword to be *shopped* is to go to *jail,* and by extension to be *squealed on* by your accomplice so that you wind up in jail (spelled *gaol* in Britain, but pronounced like *jail*).

shop assistant. See **assistant; clerk, 4.**

shopping-bag, *n.*   *Inf.* **pack; bunch; bagful**
Slang. A *whole bunch* of something; a *miscellany.* The subject-matter itself may be omitted if the context is clear. 'She arrived with a shopping-bag,' says a doctor,

meaning that the troublesome patient barged in with a plethora of ailments, a bagful of ills, all kinds of complaints.

shop-walker, *n.*   **floorwalker**
Attendant in a department who directs customers to merchandise of interest to them.

short, *n.*   **straight drink**
Inf. A modest serving of hard liquor, sherry, vermouth, etc., as opposed to a mixed drink (e.g., gin and tonic) or beer. This is pub terminology. Note that *straight*, in this context, is **neat** in Britain, and *hard liquor* is **spirits.** See also **double.**

short and curlies   *Slang.* **pubic hair**
Almost always used in the phrase *to have someone by the short and curlies,* meaning to have the person completely in one's power. *With all the money I owed him, he had me by the short and curlies.*

short back and sides   **close haircut**
Not a crew cut (which is called a **close crop** in Britain); rather, the normal British gentleman's style until World War II, and still, more or less, the Army private's, although that is changing in many parts of the world.

short commons   **short rations**
Originally a university term denoting the daily fare supplied to students at a fixed charge. The phrase has become somewhat pejorative with the connotation of *subsistence living, meager pickings,* so that the person said to be *on short commons* might also be described as *on his uppers.*

shorthand typist   **stenographer**
This term is now somewhat old-fashioned and is being supplanted by *secretary* even if the person involved is not properly speaking a *secretary* but only a *stenographer.* This is an example of the British tendency to pay honor to the dignity of labor—illustrated also by *shop* **assistant** for *salesperson, automotive engineer* for *garage mechanic,* etc. See also **P.A.**

shorthand writer   **court stenographer**

shortlist, *n.*   **group of final candidates**
From whom the winner of a job, an award, etc. will be chosen.

shorts, *n. pl.*   **(outdoor) shorts**
Shorts, in Britain, are not underwear. In America the word can refer to either underwear or outdoor apparel, depending on the context. The British term for *underwear shorts* is **pants,** sometimes *underpants,* though the *under* would seem to be superfluous because the word *pants* alone implies that. *Pants,* in the American sense of 'outdoor wear,' are *trousers* in Britain.

short-sighted. See under **long-sighted.**

short time   **part time**
As in, *Many workers are on short time . . . ,* i.e., are still employed, but not full time. Does not apply to a regular part-time worker.

shot, *n.*   *Slang.* SEE COMMENT
Formerly a measure of upper cylinder lubricant. Thus, as you drive up to a gas
pump (**petrol** *station*) in Britain, you may ask for *two and two shots,* meaning 'two
gallons of gas and two shots of lubricant' which is mixed into the gas.

shot about   *Slang.* **beat**
Slang. In the sense of *exhausted; knocked out.*

shot of   **rid of**
Inf. Said to be a cockney version of *shut of,* but the variant appears to be in more
general use than the original. *Shut of* would seem to be used when referring to
a person who is a nuisance to be got rid of, while *shot of* can refer to persons or
things one would rather do without. *Shed of* would appear to be an Americanism
derived from *shut of.*

shout, *n., v.i.*   **treat**
As a noun, one's *turn* to buy the drinks. *It's my shout this time* means 'This one's
on me.' As a verb, to *shout* is to *stand drinks.*

shouting cake. See **schoolboy cake.**

shove-halfpenny   SEE COMMENT
Common pub game. Played by shoving well-polished old halfpennies (pronounced HAY' PNEEZ) or token disks with the flat of the hand along a board
separated into horizontal sections having numerical values. Possibly the most
frustrating game in the world.

show, *n.*   **1. chance**
                                                                     2. affair
1. *Inf.* To say of someone that he had no *show* at all is to say that he had no *opportu-*
nity of proving or defending himself. One might plead, *At least give him a fair show!*
2. *Inf.* Speaking of his new, up-and-coming partner, the older man might say,
Jones is doing well, but it's still my show, i.e., *I'm still in charge around here.* See also
bad show!; good show!

show a leg   *Inf.* **rise and shine**
Slang. Term used in the Royal Navy to rouse the sleeping sailor.

shower, *n.*   *Slang.* **washout**
Slang. When someone is referred to as a *shower,* or *a perfect shower,* he is a *total loss,*
a *washout.* See also **wet.**

show friendly to (someone)   **act in a friendly manner towards (someone)**
Make a friendly gesture toward (someone). But see **friendly action.**

show-house, *n.*   **model home**
And *show-flat* is *model apartment.*

showing favour   SEE COMMENT
A term used in criminal law to describe the offense of giving aid and comfort to
the criminal element, applied especially to police officers who accept bribes for
helping them in their unlawful pursuits, e.g., by tipping them off about impend-
ing police raids.

show one's colours, *Inf.*   stand up and be counted; reveal
                                                    one's character or party

Shreddies, *n. pl.*   *Inf.* **Shredded Wheat**

shrewd, *adj.*   **1. sharp; biting**
                                                          2. severe; hard
1. Describing a wind, cold weather, pain, etc. A literary use; archaic in common
speech.
2. Applying to a blow or a thrust. These meanings are in addition to the shared
meaning of 'astute' or 'wise'.

shrimp. See under **prawn.**

shtoom. See **keep shtoom.**

shufty, *n.*   *Slang.* **gander; look-see**
Slang. (The *u* is pronounced like the oo in BOOK.) This word, of Arabic origin, with
its variant *shufti,* is often used as a verb in the imperative: *Shufty!* meaning, 'Look!'
Originally military stuff, but soldiers often take their special slang with them
when they reenter civilian life, and it passes into general speech. See also **recce.**

shunting yard   **switchyard**

shut, *v.t.*   **close**
Where Americans say *close,* Britons often say *shut. Shut the door* is the most prominent example.

sick, *adv.*   **sick to one's stomach**
When a Briton says *sick* he means 'queasy,' not sick all over or sick generally. If
that were the case he'd say **ill.** To *be sick* means to 'throw up.' See also **sick up;
queer.** However, he uses *sick* in compounds with *bed, benefit, call, leave, list, pay,
room,* etc. *Sickmaking* (see **-making**) is slang for *sickening, disgusting.* See also **ill.**

sick as a cat   **sick as a dog**

sickener, *n.*   *Slang.* **bellyful**
Slang. After a long unpleasant experience: *I have had a sickener of that!*

sicker, *n.*   **sick bay**
Schoolboy slang. Infirmary. Very old, and not much heard any more.

sickie, *n.*   *Inf.* **sick leave**

sick up   **throw up**
Inf. A vulgar expression for *vomit.* The usual expression is *be sick; throw up* is
hardly used. See also **sick; queer.**

side, *n.*   **1. team**
                                                                    2. airs
                                                                 3. English
                                                               4. TV channel

1. To *let the side down* is to *be found wanting* at the crucial moment, in the clutch, so as to frustrate the good work of one's colleagues. The term originated in sports, but can be applied to any situation.
2. *Inf.* To *put on side* is to *put on airs, put on the dog.*
3. A billiards term, synonymous with **spin.** In this usage, to *put on side* means to *put English* on the ball. This appears to be the earlier meaning of *put on side* and there are those who believe that meaning **2.** evolved from meaning **3.**
4. Britons might ask *what side is it on?,* though *channel* is increasingly used.

sideboard, *n.*   **buffet**

sideboards, *n. pl.*   **sideburns**
Inf. The British say *sideburns,* too.

sidesman, *n.*   **deputy churchwarden**
Especially, one who passes the collection plate.

signal-box, *n.*   **switch tower**

sign off   **1. initial**
                                                                 2. SEE COMMENT
1. In the sense of initialing a document signifying having read and disposed of it.
2. For a TV or radio station, to *sign off* is to cease broadcasting for the day.

sign-posted, *adj.*   SEE COMMENT
Applied to road directions, meaning that the route is clearly marked by road signs at all intersections where one must turn. "Not to worry, it's all sign-posted" is reassuring.

sign the poisons book   SEE COMMENT
When you buy certain medicines in Britain, the druggist (**chemist** or **dispenser**) has you *sign the poisons book* where appropriate. This is a handy arrangement, presumably, in connection with autopsies and other situations. In America, a comparable record is maintained by the druggist himself.

silencer, *n.*   **car muffler**

silk, take. See **take silk.**

silverside, *n.*   **top round**
Butcher's term.

Silver Streak, *Inf.*   **English Channel**

simnel cake   SEE COMMENT
This is a fancy ornamental cake with a thick layer of marzipan and various kinds of decorations, served at Easter.

simple, *adj.*   *Inf.* **not all there**
Inf. A term meaning something between 'silly' and downright 'feebleminded.' *Simpleton* and *simple-minded* are related; but *simple* used by itself means something a little stronger. One thus afflicted might be said in both countries to *have*

a screw loose, rocks in his head, bats in his belfry, or to be *without the benefit of certain of his marbles.*

single, *n.*   **one-way ticket**
See also **return,** which is a *round-trip ticket.*

single cream. See under **double, 4.**

single cuff/double cuff   **barrel cuff/French cuff**
Said of men's shirts and their sleeves.

singlet, *n.*   **undershirt; T-shirt**
Singlet is being replaced by *T-shirt,* and the common word for *undershirt* is *vest.*

single-track, *adj.*   **one-lane**
Road term.

sink, *n.*   **kitchen sink**
A *sink,* in Britain, is a *kitchen sink,* not a bathroom sink, which is called a **basin.**

sink differences, *Inf.*   *Inf.* **bury the hatchet**

sink the shop. See under **shop.**

sippet, *n.*   **crouton**

sister, *n.*   **nurse**
The term *sister* is not applied to nurses in America except to nuns who nurse in Catholic hospitals. Until a recent attempt at reorganizing the terminology, a *sister* was the head nurse of a ward and there were *day sisters* and *night sisters. Theatre sisters* (the theatre in question being an *operating-theatre*), were those who handed scalpels and things to surgeons. The head nurse of a hospital was called *matron.* Except in the context of medical practice, *nurse,* in Britain, would connote *children's nurse* (whence *nursery*) rather than *hospital nurse.* See also **theatre; casualty ward; health visitor.**

sister company   SEE COMMENT
One of a number of subsidiaries of a parent company, in relation to the other subsidiaries. See **company.**

sit an examination   **take an examination**
Also **sit for an examination.**

sit-down, *n.*   *Inf.* **rest, break**
Usually accompanied by a **cuppa,** and implying a respite from chores or other work.

sit down under   *Inf.* **stand for**
Inf. To *put up with.* What the British won't *sit down under,* the Americans won't *stand for.* The British use *stand for* as well.

site, *v.t.*   **locate**
Large-scale industry is *sited* in the Midlands. Americans would have said *located* or *situated.*

sitrep, *n.*   SEE COMMENT
Report on current situation; a military abbreviation.

sitter-in, *n.*   **baby-sitter**
An archaic term. See also **child-minder.**

sitting, *n.*   *approx.* **serving**
Some London restaurants have several *sittings* a night; that is why it's so important to **book** (reserve) in advance. Nobody rings up a restaurant and asks for this or that *sitting* (which is simply a restaurateur's term) as one used to on large ships.

sitting, *adj.*   **incumbent**
In discussing American presidential elections, British television commentators and newspaper columnists invariably refer to the 'sitting president.' Americans call the president the *incumbent,* using the adjective as a substantive to describe the one in office.

sitting-room, *n.*   **living-room**
Sitting-room sounds old-fashioned in America. *Living-room* is coming into use as a synonym for **sitting-room.** See also **lounge; reception-room; drawing-room.**

sitting tenant   **statutory tenant**
A tenant *in situ,* who is legally entitled to remain so despite the expiration of his or her lease.

situations vacant   **help wanted**
Advertisement page heading. Synonymous with **vacancies.**

situpon, *n.*   *Inf.* **backside**
This is a particularly coy word, usually applied to the female genitals by a health-worker who is uneasy about referring to the anatomical parts by their proper name. *And how is your situpon feeling?*

six, *n.*   SEE COMMENT
In cricket, a fly ball that lands beyond the **boundary** (the white line marking the outer limits of the playing field, or **ground**) scores six runs, as compared with a *boundary,* which scores only four. A *six* is the supreme achievement of a batsman, and rarely happens. It is far rarer than a home run in baseball. To *hit* (sometimes *knock*) a person *for six* is to *knock him for a loop, knock the daylights out of him,* in the sense of demolishing an opponent in an argument. One can *hit something* (as well as *someone*) *for six:* a weak argument from an adversary, for example. See also **batsman; cricket.**

sixpence, *n.*
See **Appendix II.A.**

sixth form   SEE COMMENT
The normal curriculum at a secondary school (usually ages 13–18) consists of five
forms (*grades*). Some pupils go into a higher form, called the *sixth form*, to prepare
for university. A pupil in this form is called a *sixth-former.* See also **A-levels** and
AS-Levels.

sizar, *n.*   SEE COMMENT
Student at Cambridge, and at Trinity College, Dublin, on part or full scholarship.
Originally, a *sizar* had to perform certain duties for other students that are now
taken care of by paid employees of the College. *Servitor,* now obsolete, was the
approximate equivalent at some Oxford colleges. See also **bursar.**

skew-whiff, *adj., adv., Inf.*   crooked(ly); askew

skier. See **sky ball.**

skilly, *n.*   SEE COMMENT
Broth made of oatmeal and water, usually flavored with meat. A very thin type
of gruel. Also known as *skilligalee,* and *skilligolee,* accented on the final syllable.

skimble-scamble, skimble-skamble, *adj.*   confused, rambling, incoherent
This lively adjective might describe a narration of a frightening experience, or
an attempt to explain something beyond the speaker's power of comprehension.

skin, *n.*   cigarette paper
Slang. See also **skin up, roll-up.**

skin up, *v.i.*   *Slang.* to roll a cigarette
Using a **skin,** and either with tobacco or with something illegal.

skinful, *n.*   *Slang.* load on
Slang. An awful lot to drink. To *have got a skinful* or *one's skinful* is to *be stinkin'*
drunk.

skinhead, *n.*   *approx. Inf.* young tough
Slang. A special breed of hoodlum characterized by very closely cropped hair. See
also **rough.**

skint, *adj., Slang.*   *Slang.* dead broke

skip, *n.*   1. Dumpster
                                                                  2. refuse container
                                                                  3. college servant
1. Large refuse container used by building contractors at the site. Cf. **skivvy-bin.**
2. See **gyp.**

skipper   captain
Inf. Of a cricket **side.**

skipping-rope, *n.*   jump rope
And to *skip* is to *jump rope. See* **Appendix I.A.3.**

skirt, *n.* **flank**
Butcher's term; a *skirt* of beef.

skirting, skirting-board, *n.* **baseboard**

skive, *v.i.* *Slang.* **goldbrick**
Slang. Military slang, synonymous with **scrimshank** and **dodge the column;** to *goof off, shirk, get out of working.* The term is now used throughout society. *A skiver* is a practitioner of this type of evasion. See also **swing it; swing the lead.**

skivvy, *n., v.i.* SEE COMMENT
Inf. A term of derogation for a female domestic doing menial work. No American slang equivalent.

skivvy-bin, *n.* **dumpster; public rubbish receptacle**
Inf. About ten ton capacity; strategically placed by local authorities for dumping refuse that the regular **dustman** won't take away.

skulk, *v.i.* **shirk**
As an intransitive verb *skulk* means to 'hide' or 'slink about' in both countries. A third meaning, to 'shirk,' is exclusively British.

sky ball *approx.* **pop fly**
A cricket term, often written *skier* (pronounced SKY' ER).

slack, *v.i., Slang.* *Slang.* **goof off**

slag, *n.* **1. waste from coal mining**
2. *Slang.* SEE COMMENT
2. A pejorative term for a woman, especially one whom the speaker considers promiscuous or physically unattractive.

slag heap, *n.* SEE COMMENT
A hill comprising the waste from a mine. Old slag heaps are often planted with grass to disguise their origin.

slag off, *v.t., Slang.* SEE COMMENT
To *criticize, mock,* or *deride.* To *slag someone off* is to *give him hell, let him have it,* or criticize him severely when he is not present.

slang, *v.t.* **abuse; revile**
Inf. A *slanging-match* is an *altercation,* a *helluva row,* in which everybody washes everybody else's dirty linen but nobody's gets clean.

slang, back. See **back slang.**

slant-tailed, *adj.* **fastback**
Automotive term. See also **Appendix II.E.**

slap, *adv.* *Inf.* **right**
Inf. Examples: *slap through* is *right through; slap into* is *right into.* To walk *slap* into someone is to *bump* into him. Now rare.

slap-down, *adv.* *Inf.* **one hundred percent**
Inf. As in: *I am slap-down on his side,* referring to a disagreement between two persons. An American would be likely to say: *I am one hundred percent with* (or *against*) *him.*

slap-head, *n.* *Slang.* **bald man**

slapper, *n., Slang.* SEE COMMENT
A derogatory term for a sexually promiscuous woman.

slap-up, *adj.* *Inf.* **bang-up**
Inf. First rate, great, terrific, up to date. The British once used both *slap-up* and *bang-up* commonly; both would be considered old-fashioned now. A *slap-up do* meant a 'bang-up job,' a first-rate piece of work, and especially a splendid party with no expense spared.

slash, *n., v.i., Vulgar.* **(to) piss**

slate, on the. See **on the slate.**

slate, *v.t.* *Inf.* **pan**
Inf. To express a harsh criticism. Thus: *The reviewers slated the book unmercifully.* Synonymous with **send up rotten.** But when a Lancashire girl says *I am slated,* she means her petticoat is showing. Slate roofs are common in that county; the slabs are affixed in layers, like shingles, and sometimes a slab hangs over the edge when it is not supposed to. Another quaint expression on the subject of slips showing is "Charley's dead!" which, when said to a woman, means 'Your slip is showing.'

slate club **lodge**
In the sense of 'mutual aid society.' The members pay modest weekly dues, called **subscriptions** in Britain.

slaughtered, *adj.* *Inf.* **very drunk**

slavey, *n.* SEE COMMENT
Slang. A maid of all work. Usually connotes one employed to do more work than one should. No American slang equivalent.

sledge, *n., v.t.* **sled**
Children go *sledging* in Britain, but *sledding,* or more commonly *coasting,* in America, where a *sledge* is a heavy vehicle used in pulling loads, usually over snow or ice.

sleeper, *n.* **railroad tie**

sleep in **sleep late**
Not used in the American sense of domestic servants who live with the family they work for.

sleeping partner   silent partner

sleeping policeman. See **ramp; rumble strip.**

sleep rough   sleep in the open
Inf. Out of doors, the way the youngsters do it for fun on the road, and the homeless do it because they're homeless.

sleepy, *adj.*   overripe
Of fruit, especially pears.

sleepy sickness   sleeping sickness
Encephalitis lethargica in both countries.

sleeve link, *n.*   cuff link

slice, *n.*   bracket
A term used in connection with British taxation. The rates go up as the *slices* go up. American rates follow a similar type of pattern, but the *slices* are known as *brackets.* Synonyms are **band** and **tranche** (the latter borrowed from the French).

slide, *n., v.i.*   1. fall; drop
                                                       2. barrette
1. Used of stock exchange prices when the news is bad.

sliding keel   centerboard
The British use *sliding keel* to refer to a hinged centerboard, and *centreboard* and *centreplate* for the kind that pull up vertically without pivots. Both countries used *daggerplate* for small *centerboards* that can be pulled up and out and stored when not in use.

slim, *v.i.*   diet
As in, *I mustn't have any butter on my toast; I'm slimming.* An American would say: *I am dieting,* or more commonly, *I am on a diet.* See also **bant.**

slime, *v.i., Slang.*   *Inf.* **get away with it**

slinger, *n.*   sausage
Army slang. Can also mean *dumpling.* A more common slang term for an English sausage is **banger.**

slip, *n.*   extreme side seat
Theater term. There are *upper slips* and *lower slips* (depending on which gallery), too near the side walls to afford satisfactory vision.

slip-on shoes   loafers
More usually called *slip-ons.*

slipover, *n.*   sleeveless sweater

slipper bath   SEE COMMENT
A bathtub in the shape of a slipper, with one covered end. Did they ever exist in America? Just about obsolete in Britain.

slippy. See **look slippy!**

slip road   access road
The road by which one enters or leaves a parkway or turnpike.

slip seat   jump seat

Sloane Rangers   SEE COMMENT
The sardonic name given young upper class or upper-middle class persons living
in the vicinity of Sloane Square. They dress expensively and conservatively (silk
scarves tied under their chins), and spend weekends in the country hunting.
Often shortened as Sloaney, and not used as much as it once was.

slop, *n.*   cop
Slang. Slop developed as a shortened form of *ecilop,* which is *police* spelled backwards. This is an example of **back slang.** For synonyms see **bobby.**

slope off, *Slang.*   *Inf.* **sneak off**

slop out   SEE COMMENT
Slang. To *slop out* is to carry out one's chamber pot, slops-pail, or whatever vessel
is provided in unsanitary, overcrowded prisons for the inmates. This is a hateful
practice imposed on prisoners in antiquated quarters lacking proper toilet facilities, much protested by the inmates.

slops, *n. pl., Slang.*   **1. sailors' clothes and bedding**
                                                         2. sloppy clothes
1. Issued by the navy.
2. Ready-made, and uncared for.

slosh, *v.t.*   smack
Inf. In the sense of 'hit.'

sloshed, *adj.*   *Slang.* **smashed**
Slang. Tipsy, *tight, squiffed,* i.e., *intoxicated.* See also **have one over the eight; skinful; squiffy; pissed.**

slot machine   vending machine
Not for gambling. A distinction worth remembering, as the British phrase may
well raise unfounded hopes in an American's breast. See also **fruit machine,** and
expressions derived from *slot machine:* **penny in the slot; (the) penny dropped.**

slowcoach *n., Inf.*   *Inf.* **slowpoke**

slow off the mark,   *Inf.* **slow on the uptake**
Inf. See also **off the mark.**

slow train   local
And **fast** *train* is the term for *express.* See also **stopping train.**

slut, *n.*   SEE COMMENT
In Britain, a slut can be a woman with poor housekeeping habits as well as a
woman of loose morals.

slut's wool   **dust balls**
Inf. The stuff that collects under the bed, behind the bureau, and other hard-to-reach places.

sly fox. See **Tom Tiddler's ground.**

smack, *v.t.*   **spank**
A euphemism applied solely to the hitting of (usually) a child, for purposes of chastisement. Whereas spanking is usually taken to mean the application of palm to backside, smack can mean any type of slap. Used also as a noun. *I gave her a smack.*

smacker, *n.*   SEE COMMENT
Slang. Pound (currency). *Smacker* is also old-fashioned American slang for *dollar,* in this sense competing with *simoleon, bone,* and *buck.* Also meaning a loud kiss in Britain as well as in America.

small ad   **classified ad**

small beer   *Inf.* **small-time**
Inf. Matters or persons of little importance are *small beer.*

smallholding, *n.*   SEE COMMENT
An agricultural unit smaller than a commercially-run farm. *Smallholdings* will produce one or more of the products of farming—crops or animals—but their owners, who are called smallholders, do not normally derive their sole income from them. They are often a kind of hobby for the wealthy.

small hours   **wee hours**
Anytime from 1 A.M. to 3 A.M. Surely you and I are not up at those hours. Or are we missing something?

smalls, *n. pl.*   **1.** *Inf.* **undies**
                                                            2. SEE COMMENT
1. Thus called whatever their size—or the size of the wearer.
2. *Smalls* was the informal term for **responsions,** once an Oxford examination procedure, now abolished.

smarmy, *adj.*   *Slang.* **oily**
Slang. In the sense of 'toadying,' or fulsomely flattering.

smartish, *adv.*   *Slang.* **on the double**
Slang. Tell the doctor to get here smartish! To walk *smartish* or *smartly* is to be going at a rapid pace. For a different and more common use of -ish, see **-ish.**

smash, *n.*   *Slang.* **smashup**
Slang. Traffic accident.

smashing, *adj.*   *Inf.* **terrific**
Inf. And a *smasher,* meaning 'something terrific,' usually refers to a girl, sometimes to a car. Adopted in America.

smooth in   **get settled**
Inf. "I haven't smoothed in yet"—said by a man in a village antique shop when
asked where the nearest **post-box** was. He'd been in the village only a week or so
and hadn't settled in yet, found his way about, got to know the place, etc.

snaffle, *v.t.*   **grab, take**
Especially with a connotation of taking more than one's due. *The gingerbread men
smelled so good, I snaffled the lot.*

snag, *n.*   *Inf.* **trouble; catch**
Inf. When a Briton wants to explain what is holding something up, he very often
starts the sentence with the phrase, *The snag is . . . .* Americans tell you what the
catch is, or the *hitch,* or the *problem,* or the *trouble.*

snapper, *n.*   **snap**
Fastener used in dressmaking. An American *snapper,* the kind served at children's
parties, is called a **cracker** in Britain. See also **popper.**

snap-tin, *n., Inf.*   **sandwich box**

snick, *n.*   SEE COMMENT
Inf. A cricket term for a ball not hit squarely but caught by the edge of the bat. See
also **cricket; batsman.**

snicket, *n.*   **alley**
Synonymous with **twitten.**

sniggle *v.i.*   **fish for small eels**
Term used in both countries.

snip, *n.*   **1. a bargain**
                                                             2. *Inf.* **sure thing**
                                                                  3. *Inf.* **cinch**
                                                                  4. *Inf.* **steal**
1. *Inf.* An advantageous purchase.
2. *Inf.* In the sense of a 'cinch,' a 'certainty.' This usage originated in racing slang;
sometimes *dead snip.*
3. *Inf.* In the sense of 'anything easily done.'
4. *Inf.* In the sense of 'bargain.'

snob, *n.*   SEE COMMENT
Slang. A shoemaker or *cobbler,* for which there appears to be no slang American
equivalent. This usage is pretty well confined to oldtimers in the countryside.

snog, *v.i., v.t. Slang.*   **neck**
Kiss and caress, that is. May also be used as a noun; *we had a quick snog.*

snookered, *adj.*   *Slang.* **up the creek; in a tight spot.**
Slang. (The oo is long, as in ROOF.) The British borrow their adjective describing
this unhappy condition from the game of *snooker,* a variety of pocket billiards.

snorter, *n.*   **1.** *Slang.* **humdinger**
    2. punch in the nose
1. *Slang.* Anything outstanding.
2. *Slang.* But it can be used metaphorically, as in *I wrote him a snorter* (i.e., an angry letter).

snorting, *adj.*   **fabulous**
Slang. Rarely heard nowadays.

snotty, *n.*   **1. midshipman**
    2. *Slang.* **short-tempered**
    3. *Inf.* **snooty**
Slang. Sometimes *snottie*. Midshipmen wear buttons on their sleeves. A naval joke is that they are there to prevent the young sailors from wiping their noses on their sleeves.

snout, *n., Slang.*   **1.** *Slang.* **stoolie**
    2. *Slang.* **butt**
1. A police informer.
2. A *cigarette,* especially in prison argot.

snowboots, *n. pl.*   **galoshes**
Slang. In Britain **galoshes** are what the Americans call *rubbers,* or *overshoes.* See also **gumboots; Wellingtons; boots.**

snowed up   **snowed in**
See **Appendix I.A.1.**

snuff it   *Slang.* **croak**
Slang. Synonymous with **drop off the hooks,** i.e., *kick the bucket.*

snug, *n.*   SEE COMMENT
At some **pubs,** the bar-parlor, a room offering more privacy than the rest of the establishment. Often called the **snuggery.**

snuggery, *n.*   **den**
Slang. One's particular hideaway at home. Also applied to a bar-parlor in a **pub.** See **snug.**

sociable, *n.*   **S-shaped couch**
Designed for two occupants partly facing each other.

social contract   SEE COMMENT
Historically, this phrase has meant a presumed voluntary agreement among individuals pursuant to which an organized society is brought into existence, or an agreement between the community and the governing authority defining the rights and obligations of each party. In Britain after 1974, it long signified an unwritten arrangement between the Labour Government and the trade unions, whereunder, in consideration of **wage restraint** by the unions, the government carried out certain policies, such as price control, limitation of corporate dividends, maintenance of welfare benefits, etc., in favor of the unions. Used less nowadays than in days gone by. See also **pay policy.**

social housing   SEE COMMENT
Living quarters provided as a public service for those who cannot afford
free-market rents or property prices. Social housing can take many forms and be
provided by different funding bodies: local councils, public-service employers
(e.g. hospitals), private charities and sometimes private companies. Often different sources will work together on a single scheme. The importance of social
housing has increased since the **right to buy** led to a depletion of local councils'
housing stock.

sock drawer   SEE COMMENT
Inf. To put something into one's *sock drawer* is to secrete it in safekeeping. For
example, a confidential document, not intended for another's eyes. The closest
American expression might be the *cookie jar,* a place to secrete money taken from
the household budget.

socket, *n.*   **electrical outlet**

sod, *n.*   *Slang.* **bastard**
Slang. This vulgar term of abuse should really not be used in mixed company.
Technically, it cannot be applied to a woman. The reason is that it is short for *sod-
omite.* However, British people of both sexes, unaware of its origin, are now heard
to hurl it at persons of either sex. *Sod all* is an intensification of *bugger all,* which is,
in turn, an intensification of **damn all,** and means 'not a goddamned thing.' *Sod*
means 'goddamn' in the expression *sod him (her, it, them).* *Sodding* is another way
of saying *goddamned,* as in *sodding little bastard.*

sod all. See under **sod.**

sodding. See under **sod.**

Sod's Law   **Murphy's Law**
Inf. If anything can possibly go wrong with a test or experiment, it will. Originally applied to the natural sciences, the use of this law has been extended to
cover day to day living and reads simply, *If anything can possibly go wrong it will,*
to which has been added, *and it will happen at the worst possible moment.*

soft furnishings   **curtain material**
In a British department store, if you wanted the drapery department, you would
ask for *soft furnishings;* if you asked for the *drapery department* you would find
yourself looking at dress materials. See also **draper's shop.**

soft goods   **textiles**

soldier on   *Slang.* **stick with it**
Inf. To *soldier,* often *soldier on the job,* means to 'loaf on the job' in both countries,
to 'shirk.' To *soldier on,* by itself, means to 'persevere doggedly,' to 'stay with it,'
'keep plugging' or whatever else one who resembles John Bull does in the face of
hopeless odds.

soldiers, *n. pl.*   **bread strips**
Inf. Bread cut into strips, to be dipped into soft-boiled eggs; term used mostly by
children. Grown-ups sometimes call them *fingers.*

solicitor, *n.*   **lawyer**
But it is not that simple; *lawyer* in the sense of 'general practitioner.' See also **bar-rister.** In America the use of *solicitor* in the British sense is restricted to the office of solicitor general of the United States and of certain individual states.

solitaire. See under **patience.**

sonic bang   **sonic boom**

soon as say knife. See **as soon as say knife.**

SOP   **Senior Officer Present**
Inf. Not, as one might think from American usage, an abbreviation of *standard operating procedure.* This term originated as a response to the military *Who's in charge here?* It has come to be used by non-military personnel as well.

soppy, *adj., Slang.*   **mushy**

sorbet. See **ice.**

sorbo rubber   **sponge rubber**
Used in the manufacture of children's bouncing balls, dog's toy bones, as well as the interior of cricket balls.

sorted, *adj.*   SEE COMMENT
You will often hear people say that a problem has been *sorted,* where Americans might say *solved.*

sort of thing   *Inf.* **kind of; like**
Inf. Appended to a statement, this phrase muddies or attenuates it somewhat, pulls its teeth a little, lessening its impact *ex post facto,* like *so to speak, more or less, practically,* and inelegantly, *kind of,* or (in the mouths of so many youths) *like,* both of which, however, more often come first. Thus: *He's a clever chap, but apt to get confused, sort of thing,* or, *The poor man is reduced to begging, sort of thing.* An ungrammatical and tiresome usage. To make matters worse, latterly, *sort of style* has raised its silly head.

sort out   **1. work out**
                                                                          2. take care of
1. Very frequently used by the British in the best tradition of muddling through. Things are always going to be *sorted out* later, or will *sort themselves out.* There is a lurking suggestion of *mañana* in this amiable expression.
2. Another meaning altogether is to 'straighten (someone) out,' to 'let him have it,' to 'give him a going over.' Junior has taken the car without permission and Senior suddenly needs it: *Just wait till he gets back, I'll sort him out!* An irate American daddy might say, *I'll straighten him out!* or, *I'll tell him a thing or two!*

souteneur. See **ponce.**

south of the Border. See **(the) Border.**

spadger, *n., Slang.*   **sparrow**

spaghetti junction   **cloverleaf**
Inf. Jocular, semi-pejorative for any cloverleaf, but particularly for a complex one. The epithet was first applied to an especially complicated one in Birmingham, which evoked the image of a mess of cooked spaghetti.

spanner, *n.*   **wrench**
A *spanner in the works* is a *monkey wrench in the machinery.* A *box spanner* is a *lug wrench.*

spare, bit of. See **bit of spare.**

spare, go. See **go spare.**

spare, going. See **going spare.**

spare, send (someone). See **send (someone) spare.**

spare ground   **vacant lot**

spare line   **allocated line**
But not yet connected. Telephone term.

spare room   **guest room**

sparking-plug   **spark plug**
See **Appendix II.E.**

spark out   *Slang.* **pass out cold**
Slang. Usually, to *pass spark out,* meaning to 'pass out,' whether from booze, fright, or exhaustion. In an extreme case, it can even mean to 'pass out for once and for all time; to die.' But see **pass out.**

spatchcock, *v.t.*   **interpolate**
Inf. A *spatchcock* is a fowl hurriedly cooked after being killed. This curious word appears to be a shortening of *dispatchcock*—one quickly *dispatched* by being disposed of in a hurry. (Are there distant echoes of poaching in this?) Somehow *spatchcock* became a verb, meaning to 'insert' or 'interpolate,' with a hint that the insertion was the hurried result of an afterthought; and there is the implication that the interpolation changed the force and meaning of the original message. *Spatchcock* is not under any circumstances to be confused with a *spitchcock,* an entirely different kettle of *eel* which has been *split and broiled.* One can also *spitchcock* ('split and broil') a fish or a bird or a fowl, and thus we somehow get back to *spatchcock!* Indeed, *spitchcock* is now the more common term for this type of dish.

spate, *n.*   **flood**
Used in America only metaphorically to mean an 'outpouring,' the word also refers to literal floodings in Britain.

speaking clock   SEE COMMENT
One dials a certain telephone number, and the 'speaking clock,' a usually very pleasant voice, answers with the correct time.

speak up!   **louder!**
An exhortation not to courage, not to candor, but simply to audibility.

speciality, *n.*   **specialty**

spectacles, *n., pl.*   **eye glasses**

spectators' terrace   **observation deck**
Airport term. See also **waving base.**

Speech Day   SEE COMMENT
Also *Prize Day.* An aspect of public, state, and prep school life. Prizes are given
out, speeches are made, parents mill about, and tea is drunk.

spencer, *n.*   **1. thin shirt or sweater worn under dress**
                                                  2. short tight-fitting jacket
1. An old-fashioned garment, still sometimes worn by elderly ladies.
2. Either a short, sometimes fur-trimmed close-fitting jacket worn by women and
children in the past two centuries, or a short, tight jacket with collar and lapels
once sported by men.

spend a penny   *Inf.* **use a bathroom**
Inf. This is a term pertaining principally to ladies and derives from the fact that
their arrangements, even in the simpler operations, in public places, once were
different from men's in that the little cabinets involved were locked and required
the insertion of a coin (it used to be a penny) in order to unlock them; just another
bit of evidence to prove that it is a man's world. The term is less often used by
men. Their euphemism is *have a* **wash.** The term is becoming old-fashioned and
is used rarely, nowadays, by the younger generation. The common euphemism
is *use the* **loo** or *go to the loo.* In a restaurant or other public place, one would not
inquire as to the whereabouts of the *loo;* the anxious patron would ask either for
the Gents' or the Ladies.' See also **pee.**

spif(f)licate, *v.t.*   *Slang.* **crush**
Slang. To *knock the hell out of,* to destroy.

spin, *n.*   **English**
Billiards term. Achieved by striking an object ball on a slant.

spinney, *n.*   **thicket**
A small wood, a thicket.

spirit level, *n.*   **carpenter's level**

spirits, *n. pl.*   **hard liquor**

Spithead nightingale   **bosun**
Inf. In the Royal Navy. *Spithead* is a naval anchorage near Portsmouth, the *nightingale* the sound of a bosun's whistle.

spiv, *n.*   *Inf.* **sharp operator**
Inf. A person who lives by his wits, managing to skirt the law. More specifically, a
petty criminal small-scale black market operator. Also applied to race-track touts.

spliff, *n.*   *Slang.* **joint; marijuana cigarette**

split-arse, *adv., Slang.*   *Slang.* **lickety-split**

split of a hurry, *Inf.*   *Inf.* **one hell of a hurry**

split on   *Inf.* **squeal on**
Inf. See also **put (someone's) pot on; round on; grass; snout.**

spoil, *n.*   **rubble**
Rare in America, this British term is used to describe the material that comes out
of a hole during excavation.

spondulicks, *n.*   *Slang.* **money**

sponge bag   **toilet kit**
A small, zippered, waterproof bag of toilet articles. The old ones were like miniature duffle bags with drawstrings.

sponge finger   **ladyfinger**
But *ladyfinger* is now used in Britain.

sport one's oak   SEE COMMENT
Inf. Originally and still mainly a university expression. An outside door would
usually be of *oak*—or used to be, at any rate. *Sport,* in this curious usage, means
'show ostentatiously,' as in *sport a new shirt.* Thus, when you *sport the oak,* i.e.,
make a point of showing the outside of your front door to the public, you are
telling the world to stay out; that you are busy and don't want to be disturbed, at
any cost. Perhaps a closer definition would be *hang out the* DO NOT DISTURB *sign.*
Very old-fashioned now.

Sports Day   SEE COMMENT
Sports Day is an annual function at most schools. On *Sports Day* the following
things happen:
1. The parents are invited to watch the students engage in athletic competitions.
2. Tea is served and platters of goodies are distributed by well-scrubbed students.
3. It rains.

spot, *n.*   **1.** *Inf.* **bit**
                                                             2. pimple
                                                             3. (decimal) point
1. *Inf.* For example, a *spot* of lunch. A *spot of tea* means something more than just
a cup of tea. It involves something solid as well, even if minuscule. A *spot to eat*
is a *bite.* See **tea.**
2. *Inf.* Usually found in the plural. *Spotty* means 'pimply' in a phrase like *a spotty
youth.*
3. Where an American would express the number 123.45 as '123 point 45,' a
Briton might say '123 *spot* 45.' Rarer now than it once was.

spot-on, *adv.*   *Inf.* **on the nose**
Inf. Meaning, 'in exactly the right place.' The British congratulated U.S. astronauts for landing *spot-on target.* Also **bang on; dead on.**

spotted dog   SEE COMMENT
Inf. Roly-poly pudding with raisins or currants. The image is that of a Dalmatian. Sometimes called *spotted Dick.* See **roly-poly pudding.**

spring-clean, *n.*   **spring cleaning**
For once, it's the Americans who add the *-ing;* usually it is the British. See **Appendix I.A.3.**

spring greens   **young cabbage**
With their heads still unformed. Very tender and tasty.

spring onion   **scallion**

spring roll   **egg roll**
See also **pancake roll.**

SPUC, *acronym*   **Society for the Protection of the Unborn Child**
A prominent anti-abortion organization.

spun, *adj.*   *Slang.* **fagged**
Slang. Done in; tuckered out. Past participle of *spin,* in its sense of 'whirling someone around,' perhaps by delivering a blow that sends him spinning.

spunk, *n.*   *Slang.* **semen**
But the meaning 'pluck' or 'courage' is the usual sense of *spunk.*

squab, *n.*   **back of car seat**
See **Appendix II.E.**

squails, *n. pl.*   SEE COMMENT
A game played with small wooden disks called *squails,* on a round table called a *squail board.*

square, *n.*   **1. paper napkin**
                                                             2. mortar-board
1. *Inf.* See also **serviette.**
2. *Slang.* University jargon.

square, *adj.*   **even**
Inf. As in *a square hundred* (*pounds,* e.g.), where an American would speak of *an even hundred.*

square-bashing, *n.*   **close order drill**
But in a more general sense, loosely applied to any type of marching about on a military parade ground or barrack square.

squareface, *n.*   **gin**
Inf. From the squarish shape of the bottles in which gin was originally sold in South Africa, and often still is in Britain (*Bombay, Gordon's, Boodles,* etc.)

(the) Square Mile   SEE COMMENT
The heart of the **City.**

squarson, *n.*   SEE COMMENT
Combination of squire and parson, a **portmanteau** word.

squash, *n.*   **soda pop**
A soft drink. A *lemon squash* is a *lemonade,* an *orange squash* an *orangeade,* and so on. The drink is commonly made from a concentrate to which water is added. See also **minerals.** *Squash* is also slang for a *crowded party* or *meeting.*

squashed fly biscuits. See **garibaldi.**

squib, damp. See **damp squib.**

squiffer, *n.*   *Slang.* **squeeze-box**
Slang. Usually refers to a concertina rather than an accordion.

squiffy, *adj.*   *Slang.* **tipsy**
Slang. Americans use *squiffed* which, however, indicates a somewhat more advanced stage of the curse of drink than *squiffy.*

squireen, *n.*   SEE COMMENT
A *small landowner;* more commonly used in Ireland than England.

squitters, *n. pl., Slang.*   *Slang.* **the runs**

S.R.N.   SEE COMMENT
Common abbreviation for *State Registered Nurse.*

staff, *n.*   **personnel**
The British use the word *staff* where the Americans would say *servants* or, in a business, *employees* or *personnel.* STAFF ONLY is a sign frequently seen on doors in business establishments visited by the public, particularly hotels, restaurants and the like. *Short-staffed* would be *short-handed* in America. *Staff finder* is occasionally seen as a heading in British newspapers where the American equivalent would be *help wanted. Staff vacancies* is another phrase meaning the same thing. *Staff bureau* and *staff agency* are somewhat more elegant terms for *employment agency.* In educational institutions, *staff* is used to denote the entire teaching body, as opposed to *faculty,* the equivalent American term. In Britain, **faculty** refers only to departments, like the *Faculty* of Medicine, of Law, of Engineering, etc.

staggerer, *n.*   *Inf.* **blow**
Inf. In the sense of a 'riposte,' 'retort,' or a 'bit of repartee' that knocks the other person off balance. Sometimes used to describe an event that knocks the stuffing out of you.

staging post   **stopover**
Inf. By extension, used to describe a major preparatory stage, e.g., *The talks may prove to be a staging post on the road to peace.* Often, a regular stopping place, especially on air travel.

stall, *n.*   **1. stand**
                                       2. orchestra seat
1. A *stall* generally is an *outdoor counter* or *stand* for the purveying of goods, particularly food (see **coffee-stall**). See also **set out one's stall.**
2. A *seat in the orchestra.*

stall, set out one's. See **set out one's stall.**

stalls, *n. pl.*   **orchestra**
The stalls are the equivalent of *the orchestra* as a description of that part of a theater, concert hall, etc.

stand, *v.i.*   **run**
A Briton *stands* for office; an American *runs* for it. One might wonder what the sociological implications are in this disparity of usage.

standard, *n.*   **grade**
Still used to indicate the year (first, second, etc.) at school, but rather old-fashioned now and restricted to primary school. **Form** is generally used of secondary and higher schools.

Standard English   SEE COMMENT
Commonly abbreviated to S.E. Considered by some to be the English used everywhere by educated people.

standard lamp, *n.*   **floor lamp**
Other American equivalents are *standing lamp* and *bridge lamp.*

stand down   **1. retire; withdraw**
                                                                2. postpone
1. To *retire* from a team, a job, the witness stand. Used both transitively and intransitively. In military circles, to *stand down* is to *go off duty:* in politics, to *withdraw one's candidacy.*
2. To *postpone,* to *discontinue temporarily,* as in *Rescue operations had to be stood down because of heavy seas.*

standing order   **money transfer order**
Written instructions filed with one's bank for the making of periodic payments to a third party, such as mortgage payments, alimony payments, and other obligations you had better not default on. This is common practice in Britain, rare in America. The American equivalent given above is not a term in common banking usage.

stand in (someone's) light, *Inf.*   **stand in (someone's) way**

stand off   **lay off**
To discharge temporarily employees who have become superfluous or, as they say in Britain, **redundant.**

stand one's own   **hold one's own**

stand-up (piano)   **upright (piano)**

stanley knife   **box cutter**

starchy, *adj.*   *Inf.* **stuffy**
Inf. As in the expression *nothing starchy about him!*

stargazey, *n.*   SEE COMMENT
Inf. A kind of pie made in Cornwall with small fish, usually with the heads looking out through the pastry crust and stargazing. Also *starrygazey.*

staring, *adj., adv.*   **1.** *Inf.* **loud**
                                                                     2. *Inf.* **raving**
1. *Inf. Unpleasantly conspicuous, eye-shattering,* as a *staring* pink tie or a weird
checked vest.
2. *Inf.* Only in the common phrase *stark staring mad.*

starkers, *adj.*   *Inf.* **stark naked**
Slang. Sometimes *starko.* See **Harry. . . .**

stark ravers   *Slang.* **nuts**
Slang. Raver by itself connotes homosexuality. As to the *-ers* in *ravers,* see **Harry** . . .
An old-fashioned term, giving way to **bonkers.**

start a hare   **raise an issue**
Inf. Often time-wasting. But related to rousing an animal from its lair.

starters, *n. pl.*   **appetizers**
Slang. As in, *What do you fancy for starters, love?* Chi-chi restaurants occasionally
use the terms *starters* and *afters* self-consciously in menus.

starting handle   **crank**
Automobile term, now rather archaic. See **wind,** *v.t., and* **Appendix II.E.**

star turn   *Inf.* **topnotch talent**
Inf. A **turn,** in vaudeville days, was an *act;* a *star turn* was a *headliner.* The term
was extended to include a *top performer* in any field: *the tops.* It is used to designate the chief or central figure in any situation. But *star turn* can at times be
used pejoratively, to describe a person who is a *star* in a way that doesn't do him
credit.

stately home   SEE COMMENT
A large old house, especially one open to the public

State Opening of Parliament   SEE COMMENT
Each parliamentary session is opened by the Queen who reads the speech prepared for her by the government **(Queen's Speech).** The Queen sits in the **House
of Lords,** to which all the members of the **House of Commons** are summoned
by **Black Rod.** Thus are the three constituents of Parliament—the Commons, the
Lords, and the Monarch—all in one place to hear what the government proposes
to do in that parliamentary session.

state school   **public school**
For the meaning of *public school* as used in Britain, see **public school.**
The *council school* in Britain is the government-operated facility that Americans
call *public school.* **Public schools** in Britain are what Americans call *prep schools* or
private schools.

station calendar   **bulletin board**
On the wall at major railroad stations.

station-manager, *n.*   **station agent**
Also *station-master.*

statutory business   **official business**
A basis for avoiding parking tickets for government vehicles in either country.

stay, *v.i.*   **live; reside**
Mainly Scottish: *I stay in Morningside, on the south side of Edinburgh,* or, *He comes from Aberdeen. Really? Whereabouts does he stay?*

STD   SEE COMMENT
Under the old telephone system, to be on *STD* meant to be hooked into the automatic long-distance dialing system. The letters stand for *Subscriber Trunk Dialling.* (See **trunk call.**) The letters are also used as an acronym for sexually transmitted disease.

steading, *n.*   **farmstead**
A farm with buildings.

steady on! *Interj.*   *Approx:* **easy does it!**

step out   *Inf.* **step on it**
In England, to *step out* is to *hurry* or *hurry up.* Informally, it can also mean 'lead a joyful social life.' In America, to *step out* is to go to a party or dance, or on a date; sometimes, to go out on the town.

stew, *n.*   **fish tank**
In addition to all the conventional verb and noun meanings of *stew.*

stick, *n., v.t.*   **1.** *n.,* **pole**
                                                 2. *n., Slang.* **guy**
                                                 3. *v.t.,* **stake up**
                                                 4. *v.t.,* **post**
                                                 5. *v.t.,* **stand**
1. *n., Inf.* Ski terminology.
2. *n., Inf.* Particularly in an expression like, *He's not a bad old stick.*
3. *v.t., Inf.* Term used in gardening, with special reference to peas.
4. *v.t., Inf.* Especially in the sign STICK NO BILLS. Sign alongside Hyde Park (London): BILL STICKERS WILL BE PROSECUTED. See **hoarding.**
5. *v.t., Inf.* In the sense of 'bear' or 'tolerate,' as in, *I can't stick it a minute longer!*

stick, get the. See **get the stick.**

stick, give (someone) some. See **give (someone) some stick.**

stick, wrong end of. See **(get hold of the) wrong end of the stick.**

stickjaw, *n.*   **chewy candy**
Slang. Life *taffy,* which is called **toffee** in Britain.

stick no bills! See **stick, 4.**

stick out, *v.i., Inf.*   *Slang.* **stick to one's guns**

stick up puzzle
Slang. British robbers, as well as American, *stick up* their victims. But a second British slang meaning has its approximate American equivalent in the verb to *stick,* meaning to 'stump,' or 'present someone with an unsolvable problem.' In this connotation *stuck-up,* in Britain, would mean 'completely at a loss,' the American equivalent being *stuck;* but it can also indicate unjustified superiority in Britain as well as in America. (The more usual term for this obnoxious attribute in Britain is **toffee-nosed.**)

sticky finish bad end
Inf. The highly unpleasant kind one should do his utmost not to come to.

sticky tape adhesive tape
See also **Sellotape.**

sticky wicket tough situation
Inf. A **wicket,** in **cricket,** is said to be *sticky* when it is drying out after rain. On such a wicket, the ball on its way to the **batsman,** after bouncing in front of him, behaves erratically, especially when bowled by a *spin-bowler* expert at imparting a twisting motion to the ball after it bounces. Obviously, a batsman batting on a *sticky wicket* is in a tough, tricky situation; and the term, like so many others from cricket, has been extended metaphorically to the general language. See **wicket.**

stiffie, *n.* *Slang.* **1. erect penis**
2. SEE COMMENT
2. A formal invitation printed on thick card, always assumed to be attended by someone of importance. In **posh** circles, the term a *stiffie from* **Buck House** means *an invitation to a party at Buckingham Palace.* The slang may be jocular, but you may be sure that the stiffie will be prominently displayed at the recipient's home.

sting, *v.t.* *Slang.* **soak**
Slang. To *sting* somebody such and such an amount for something is to 'soak' him, i.e., 'overcharge' him. Thus, in an antique shop, *What do you suppose he will sting us for that table?* Its use in America is normally confined to the passive participle *(stung)* in this context. In a sentence such as, *I'd love champagne but I don't want to sting you,* the considerate young lady is telling her escort that she doesn't want the dinner check to get too big.

stinging nettle, *n.* SEE COMMENT
A native plant that causes a rash on contact.

stirrer, *n.* SEE COMMENT
Someone who causes trouble between others, especially among friends, family, or colleagues. Their activity is called *stirring,* and it is no more popular in Britain than in the United States. **Mixer** is a synonym.

stock-breeder, *n.* cattleman

stockbroker belt suburb for nouveaux riches
In which the houses may be *stockbroker Tudor, phony Tudor* in the manner of Anne Hathaway's Cottage.

stock cube, *n.*   **bouillon cube**

stockholder, *n.*   **livestock farmer**
In this usage, synonymous with **stock-breeder** and nothing to do with corporations; but it can have the usual American meaning as well.

stockinet, *n.*   **elastic knit fabric**
Used especially for bandages.

stocking filler, *n.*   **stocking stuffer**

stockist, *n.*   **retailer**
A shopkeeper who stocks the articles in question. *Who are the stockists for that DVD player?*

stockjobber, *n.*   **dealer in stocks**
In America, this word is most frequently used as a contemptuous reference to a stock salesman, particularly one who promotes worthless securities. In Britain it has no such shady connotation, describing merely an agent who acts as go-between or intermediary between brokers, never dealing directly with the public.

stocks. See **shares.**

stodge, *n., v.t., v.i.*   **1.** *n.,* **heavy food**
                                                               2. *n.,* **glutton**
                                                         3. *v.t., v.i., Inf.* **stuff**
1. *n., Slang.* Used especially of old-fashioned puddings, which lie so heavily on the stomach.
2. *n., Slang.* Who overeats and feels *stodgy.*
3. *v.i., Slang.* In the sense of 'stuff oneself.' See also **pogged.**

stoker, *n.*   **locomotive fireman**
The British and American usages are identical in shipboard terminology, but in Britain the term applies equally to railroad train crew members.

stomach warmer   **hot-water bottle**
Usage is regional and the American term is commonly used.

stone, *n.* See **Appendix II.C.1.f.**

stone cladding   **stone facing**

stone the crows!   *Inf.* **good heavens!**
Inf. A gentle expletive, an expression of disgust or surprise.

stonewall, *v.i.*   *Inf.* **stall**
Inf. The unsportsmanlike practice of playing for time in cricket. The trick is for the **batsman** merely to defend his **wicket** rather than attempt to score runs, so that time will run out. Like *keeping possession* in American football and taking plenty of time to go into and out of the huddle with one's eye on the clock, or *freezing the ball* in basketball. As with many cricket terms, it has been

taken into the general language to describe *stalling for time,* which is close to, but not identical with the narrower American use of the term to mean 'obstruct discussion.'

stonk, *n.*   *Inf.* **going over**
Slang. Literally, a *heavy shelling,* a word based upon a World War II military term for a highly specialized artillery technique christened *Standard Regimental Concentration,* a mouthful quickly shortened to *Stonk,* and then erroneously applied to just about any artillery action in the way professional jargon is so often misapplied by amateurs. The term passed into civilian use to describe anything that is devastating, like being thoroughly chewed out by the boss, for instance.

stonker. See **stonking.**

stonking, *adj.*   *Inf.* **wonderful**
Usually used as an intensifier: *It was a stonking great party.* The term *stonker* may also be found as a noun, meaning something of merit. *That wine was a real stonker.*

stony, *adj.*   *Slang.* **broke**
Slang. Flat broke; stone broke, in fact.

stood out   **postponed**
Procedural term, in law.

stooge about   *Slang.* **kill time**
Slang. Somewhat more actively than, for example, playing solitaire; implies some activity, like a **pub-crawl,** or aimless driving around. See also **fossick; frig about.**

stook, *n.*   **shock of grain**
Stack of sheaves of grain stood on end in a field so that they remain upright.

stop, *v.t., v.i.*   **1. stay**
                                                                                2. fill
1. Thus: *He stops in bed till noon,* or, *Why don't you stop at my house instead of the inn?* To *stop away* is to *stay away.* Also, *I'm happy and I want to stop like this.* A good pal will *stop up* with you all night when you're in trouble. With a bad cold, you may want to *stop in* for a couple of days.
2. Dental terminology. Cavities are *stopped* or *filled* in Britain, and a *stopping* is a *filling.*

stoppage, *n.*   **deduction from wages**
For example, withholding tax.

stopping train   **local (train)**
An express is a **fast** train. A *stopping train* makes many stops at many intermediate stations.

store, *n.*   **warehouse**
It is also used to mean a 'shop,' usually a large one. *Stores (n. pl.)* means 'supplies,' like food provisions at home, or *stock* in the sense of the 'inventory of a business.'* A common sign on small shops in villages: POST OFFICE AND STORES, where *stores* means 'provisions and supplies.'* *In store* means 'in storage,' but also has the same figurative meaning as the American usage: "What has the future in store for me?" *Cold store* is *cold storage.* See also **shop.**

storekeeper, *n.*   **employee in charge of supplies**
Of supplies, parts, etc. There is a special use in American naval terminology, describing one handling naval stores and spare parts. The British equivalent of *storekeeper* in the usual American sense is *shopkeeper.* See **shop** and **store.**

stout, *n.*   **strong beer**
Dark brown; often asked for by the brand name "Guinness," among others less well known. See also **bitter.**

stove up, *v.t.*   **disinfect**
Slang. To disinfect generally, as to *stove up* clothing in a flop house; *delouse.* *Stove-up* is the noun describing the procedure.

straightened out   *Slang.* **fixed**
Slang. Describing an official 'on the take.'

straightforward, *adj.*   *Inf.* **cut-and-dried**
This word means 'frank' and 'honest' in both countries. A common additional British meaning is 'simple,' in the sense of 'presenting no complications.' Someone is presented with a contract to sign and after reading it through says that it seems perfectly *straightforward;* or a garage mechanic looks at some engine trouble and happily answers that the problem is perfectly *straightforward.*

straight on, *adv.*   **straight ahead**

streaky bacon   **bacon**
The kind commonly seen in America, less so in Britain; having alternate streaks of fat and lean.

stream, *n.*   **1. lane**
                                                          2. SEE COMMENT
1. Traffic usually flows in *streams* in Britain rather than in *lanes* as in America. It is customary in Britain to speak of the left *stream,* the right *stream,* and the wrong *stream.*
2. *For school usage, see* **set, 1.** *Stream* is also used as a verb in this connection meaning 'classify according to ability' and then divide into groups.

street, *n.*   **1.** *Inf.* **class**
                                                          2. *Inf.* **alley**
1. *Inf. She's not in the same street as her sister* would be *She's not in the same class,* in America. And to be *streets ahead* of or *streets better* than someone is to *outclass* him. *To win by a street* is to *win by a mile.* This term originated in horse-racing and is used metaphorically in other pursuits. *Win by a distance* is also said in racing.
2. *Inf.* If something's *up your street,* it's *up your alley.* Also *down your street.* See also **line of country.**

street rough, *Slang.*   *Slang.* **toughie**

streets ahead of. See **street, 1.**

strength. See **on the strength.**

'strewth!, *interj.*   *Inf.* **good God!**
Slang. A mild oath. It is a contraction of *God's truth.* Also spelled *'struth.*

strike off   **1. disbar**
                                                             2. revoke license
1. Short for *strike off the rolls,* applying to lawyers.
2. Short for *strike off the register,* applying to doctors. But a doctor who is *struck off*
in Britain may continue to practice, being deprived only of the right to prescribe
dangerous drugs or to sign a death certificate.

striking price   SEE COMMENT
When a new issue of stock is issued on a bid basis with a minimum price per
share stated, and the issue is oversubscribed, the issuing company allocates the
offered shares among the bidders on an equitable basis at a *striking price,* i.e., a
figure at which the bargain is *struck,* near the highest bid.

strimmer, *n.*   **weed wacker/weed eater**

Strine, *n., adj.*   SEE COMMENT
Inf. comic name for Australian speech, its sounds and idioms. This word, coined
by an Australian, represents the nasal and swallowed deformation of *Australian*
in the accents of that country.

strip lighting   **tubular fluorescent lighting**

strip-wash, *n.*
Not often heard. The common term is **bed bath.**

stroke. See **oblique.**

strong, *adv.*   SEE COMMENT
The British sometimes speak of a *four-strong family,* i.e., 'a family consisting of
four persons.' Americans would normally refer to a *family of four.* The phrase
one-strong family is also seen, meaning a 'family of one' or 'a person living *solo.*'
Americans use *strong* this way, too, but generally in the case of larger groups such
as military forces, and the noun usually precedes the number followed by *strong*
as in, *a detachment 200 strong; a working party 150 strong.*

strong flour   SEE COMMENT
Flour made from durum, or hard wheat. It is the kind used in the making of *pasta*
products.

stroppy, *adj.*   **bad-tempered**
Slang. To *get someone stroppy* is to *rile* him, *get his goat, get his dander up.* A *stroppy*
kid is one that is said to need licking into shape: aggressive and quarrelsome.

struck on, *Slang.*   *Slang.* **stuck on; nuts about**
See synonyms under **mad on.**

strung up   *Inf.* **het up; strung out**
Inf. On edge; high-strung. Strung is seen in the American expression *high-strung*
(**highly-strung** in Britain), but that describes a type of person, while *strung up*
describes the condition of the moment. *Strung out* is the current vernacular in
America, where it also means 'heavily addicted to drugs.'

stuck in. See **get stuck in.**

stuck up. See **stick up.**

stud. See **cat's-eyes.**

studentship, *n.*   **scholarship**
In the sense of an award of financial aid for a student. *Scholarship* is the common
term in both countries, but *studentship* is used at some British colleges. See also
bursar; sizar.

stuff, *v.t.*   *Slang.* **lay**
Slang. An unattractive word for copulation. To *get stuffed,* in this sense, would be
the passive voice (if one can speak of the *passive* in connection with this activity);
but used as an expletive, *Get stuffed!* is simply a vulgar way of saying *Get lost!* See
also **Stuff that for a game of soldiers!**

Stuff that for a game of soldiers!   **Screw that!**
This peculiar expletive sentence refers to any foolish or unprofitable enterprise
the speaker has finally decided to abandon. *How's that for a game of soldiers?*
means 'Whaddya think of that mess?' in angrily describing a foul-up or sorry
situation.

stumer, *n.*   *Slang.* **bum check**
Slang. By extension, a *counterfeit bill* or a *slug* (counterfeit coin); and by further
extension, *anything phoney.*

stump, *n.*   **butt**
Cigar *stump* (also *stub*); cigarette **end.**

stumps. See **up stumps; wicket.**

stump up, *Slang.*   *Slang.* **pay up; come across**

sub, *n., v.i.*   **1.** *n.,* **advance**
                                                   2. *v.i., Inf.* **make a touch**
1. *n., Inf.* An advance on future earnings or expectations, thus: *He had to take a £5
sub on next week's pay.*
2. *v.i., Inf.* To *sub* is to *make a touch. Touch* somehow evokes the image of a reluctant lender. With *on, sub* becomes transitive, taking as object the future earnings
or the lender. Thus, one can *sub on* next month's dividends, or *sub on* one's pal or
daddy.

subaltern, *n.*   SEE COMMENT
(Accented on the first syllable.) A military term, denoting a commissioned officer below the rank of captain.

sub-editor, *n.*   copy editor
A newspaper term.

subfusc, *n., adj.*   1. dull
                                                            2. SEE COMMENT
1. *adj.* Its common meaning is figurative: 'dull,' 'characterless.' *Subfusc* university clothes are not necessarily *drab;* in this sense the word may mean merely 'quiet' or 'modest.'
2. *n.* It also has the literal meaning of 'dusky' in both countries. It is rarely used in America in either sense. It is a shortening of *subfuscous*—meaning 'somber; dusky.' At some universities, including Oxford and Cambridge, *subfusc* is used as a noun meaning the 'uniform worn for formal occasions,' such as commencement and the taking of exams. For men it consists of dark suit, socks and shoes, white shirt and white bow tie, gown, and mortarboard, the last being carried under the arm; for women, dark skirt (long or short), black stockings and shoes, white shirt, black scarf or choker, gown, and a beret in the shape of a soft mortar-board, with four points, so worn that one of the points lies on or above the middle of the forehead.

subject, *n.*   citizen
A British *subject;* an American *citizen.* There is still enough loyalty to the British monarch to permit the use of a word that might be offensive to the American sense of independence, at least since the Yorktown surrender. When a Briton speaks of himself as a *citizen,* it is usually of a town or city. He would seldom be a *citizen* of Great Britain, except in formal language, though there is a category referred to as 'citizen of the United Kingdom and Colonies.'

subscription, *n.*   dues
A Briton pays his *subscription* to his club or other organization; never his *dues. Subscription* is an American euphemism for *price of admission* to a dance, political dinner, charitable affair, etc., in which use the British settle for *ticket.*

subscription library   lending library

subway, *n.*   pedestrian underpass
An American *subway* is called **underground** or **tube** in Britain. *Subways* in Britain are generally for getting to the other side of the street without peril to life and limb. *Subway* is beginning to be used in Britain in the American sense.

sucking pig   suckling pig

sucks, *n. pl.*   *Slang.* **washout (fiasco)**
Slang. Sucks! or *What a suck!* expresses derision at another's failure after a boast.

sucks to you!, *Slang.*   *Inf.* **so there!**

sugar crystals. See **coffee sugar.**

sultana, *n.*   **white raisin**
In Britain a *sultana* is a small seedless raisin, light yellow in color. *Sultanas* are used in puddings, cakes, buns, etc. (see **bath bun**). In America *sultanas* are a variety of grape, pale yellow in color, which when dried become what Americans call *white raisins.* They are also used as a source of white wine. With an initial capital *s*, *Sultana*, in America, is a trademark for a particular brand of seedless raisin, whether dark or white.

Summer Eights. See **Torpids.**

summer pudding   SEE COMMENT
Line pudding bowl with crustless bread; fill with mush of any summer fruit and large chunks of bread without crust; cover top with bread; cool or freeze; turn out when mass is soaked and congealed.

summer time   **daylight saving time**
The American term is also used in Britain but to British ears the familiar American phrase sounds rather old-fashioned. The British are on G.M.T. (Greenwich Mean Time), which is five hours later than Eastern Standard Time. See also **B.S.T.**

sump, *n.*   **crankcase**
Automobile term. See also **Appendix II.E.**

sun-blind, *n.*   **(shop) awning**

sunny intervals. See **bright periods.**

sun-trap, *n.*   **sunny, sheltered place**
A phrase much used in travel advertising. The picturesque noun is an allusion to the elusiveness of the British sun, which must be *trapped* and sheltered from the wind.

superannuation scheme   **pension plan**

superelevated, *adj.*   **banked**
Of roads and highways.

supergrass, *n.*   SEE COMMENT
In the 1980s, a controversial change in legal policy made it possible for members of criminal organizations (including the IRA) to escape prosecution or otherwise gain lenient treatment in return for extensive testimony against their partners in crime. To **grass** someone is to inform on him. The new high-level grass was informally dubbed a supergrass.

supplementary benefits. See **National Insurance.**

supply bill   **appropriation bill**
A *supply bill* in Parliament is what the U.S. Congress calls an *appropriation bill.*

supply teacher　　　　　　　　　　　　　　　**substitute teacher**

supporter, *n.*　　　　　　　　　　　　　　　**best man**
But only at a royal wedding. More commonly a fan of a sports team.

supremo, *n.*　　　　　　　　　　　　　**governor; overseer**
An official installed as supreme leader to take command over hierarchies previously established.

surgery, *n.*　　　　　　　　　**1. doctor's (dentist's) office**
2. doctor's (dentist's) office hours
3. day's schedule of doctor (dentist)
4. M.P.'s (lawyer's) session with constituents (clients)
5. M.P.'s (lawyer's) temporary outside quarters
1. A doctor's or dentist's office is always called his (her) *surgery* in Britain, never *office.*
2. *The period when he (she) is available at the office.*
3. *Doctor has a very large surgery today,* says the nurse through whom one is trying to get an appointment. She means he has a very heavy schedule, i.e., lots of patients that day.
4. *Inf.* When a Member of Parliament travels to his **constituency** *(district)* and holds a session at which he makes himself available to his constituents, he is colloquially said to *give a surgery.* The same usage applies to a lawyer who receives clients out of his office.
5. *Inf.* The place where this happens is also colloquially called a *surgery.*

surgical spirit　　　　　　　　　　　　　　　**rubbing alcohol**
More properly, **methylated spirit.**

surround, *n.*　　　　　　　　　　　　　　**area surrounding**
A border around something, like a gravel walk around (or nearly all the way around) a rose garden, or a floor covering between a carpet and walls.

surveyor, *n.*　　　　　　　　　*approx.* **building inspector**
The general meaning is the same in both countries, but a *chartered surveyor* is a *licensed architect* and is usually engaged by a careful British prospective purchaser to look over a building before the contract is signed. If things go wrong later, the purchaser can sue the surveyor, who has received a fee for his written report. In this sense *surveyor* describes a privately engaged expert building inspector. A *building surveyor* is something different: a specialist in all aspects of real estate development, from negotiating for the purchase of the land through completion of the construction, including all aspects of financing, packaging and sale. There are large firms as well as individuals engaged in this activity, hired by the property developer usually at a fee equal to 10 percent of the total development cost.

sus law　　　　　　　　　　　　　　　　SEE COMMENT
Inf. Sus, in this expression, is short for *suspect.* This troublesome law corresponded, to a certain degree, to the American vagrancy laws and was subtitled 'loitering with intent.' The law, now repealed, permitted the police to question and even detain 'suspects' at random if they believed that there was reason to suspect that those involved might have been planning a criminal act.

sus out   1. *Slang.* **case**
                                                                    2. *Inf.* **figure out**
1. *Slang.* As in *case the joint,* i.e., *reconnoiter.*
2. *Slang.* As in, *I'm trying to sus out what he means by it.*

suspenders, *n. pl.*   **garters**
Vertical ones, whether ladies' or men's; not the round kind like those worn by
Knights of the Garter. *Suspenders,* the American term for the apparatus that holds
up trousers, are called **braces** in Britain.

swab, *n., Slang.*   oaf; *Inf.* **jerk**
More formally, a contemptible person.

swacked, *adj.*   *Inf.* **loaded**
Slang. Drunk, from a Scottish verb *swack,* meaning 'drink heavily.'

swagger, *adj.*   *Inf.* **swell**
In the sense of 'fashionable' or 'smart,' but with the pejorative implication of
self-satisfaction.

swan, *n., v.i.*   *Slang.* **junket**
Slang. A trip of one sort or another whose ostensible purpose is official business, but whose primary motivation is pleasure. To *go swanning* is to take such
a trip.

swan upping, *v.*   SEE COMMENT
An annual function that goes back centuries: the taking up and marking of the
swans that inhabit the Thames. The purpose of the activity is to make an official
enumeration of the swans that live on the river.

swat. See **swot.**

swede, *n.*   **yellow turnip**

sweet, *n.*   **dessert**
Or *sweet course.* In America *dessert* is broad enough to include anything served as
the last course. In Britain *dessert* is generally a fruit course served at the end of
dinner. There is a good deal of Anglo-American confusion about this and a certain amount of internal British confusion.

sweetcorn, *n.*   **corn**
This is the word (sometimes given as *sweet corn*) that Britons usually use for the
food that Americans call corn—i.e., corn on the cob or the kernels either fresh,
canned or frozen. For the other uses, see **corn** and **Indian meal.**

sweet eff-all   *Slang.* **not a goddamned thing**
Slang. Seems to be a combination of **sweet Fanny Adams** and **damn all,** but the *eff*
is more likely the *f* in *fuck* than the *F* in *Fanny.* With those two idioms and this and
bugger all and **sod all,** the British appear to have gone to a good deal of trouble
to invent ways of saying *'nothing at all.'*

sweet Fanny Adams   **nothing at all**
Slang. Fanny Adams was a real live girl who was killed two years after the end of the American Civil War. Her murderer cut her into little pieces and threw them into a hop field. The legend of that obscene crime led to the coining of the name *Fanny Adams* as military slang for 'tinned mutton.' This seems to have nothing whatever to do with *sweet Fanny Adams* meaning 'nothing at all.' Sometimes abbreviated to *sweet F.A.*, and believed by some to be nothing more than the euphemism discussed in the preceding entry.

sweets, *n. pl.*   **candy**
Boiled sweets are *hard candy.*

sweet-shop, *n.*   **candy store**
Synonymous with **confectioner's.**

swept-out, *adj.*   **streamlined**

swimming-bath, *n.*   **swimming pool**
Originally an indoor *swimming pool.* The American term is taking over for outdoor as well as indoor pools.

swimming costume   **bathing suit**
Or **bathing costume** or *swimsuit* or *bathing suit.*

swing-door, *n.*   **swinging door**

swingeing, *adj., adv.*   *Inf.* **whopping**
Inf. Present participle of the archaic verb to *swinge,* meaning 'strike hard.' Now, as *swingeing,* meaning 'huge' or 'daunting.'

swing it   *Slang.* **goof off**
Slang. See **swing the lead.**

swing the lead, *Slang.*   *Slang.* **goof off**
More properly, *malinger* or *shirk duty.*

swipes, *n. pl., Slang.*   *Slang.* **lousy beer**
Also *weak beer.*

Swiss roll   **jelly roll**

switchback, *n.*   **roller coaster**
Now more commonly called **scenic railway.** But *switchback railway* is a term describing zigzag railways for climbing hills. Synonymous with **big dipper.**

switched on   *Slang.* **turned on**
Slang. Interested, excited, by art, marijuana, nature, anything. The American expression is also used.

switch on/off   **turn on/off**
Britons are still more likely to *switch on the TV* than to *turn it on,* though in some quarters the American usage is gaining in popularity.

swizz, *n., Slang.*   **swindle**
The longer form, *swizzle,* can be used as a transitive verb meaning to 'swindle.'
But a *swizzle stick* is the bartender's tool for frothing a mixed alcoholic drink.

swop, n., v.t., v.i.   **scythe**
A country term. The scythe in question is a small one also known in the country
as a **bagging-hook.**

swot, *n., v.t., v.i.*   *Slang.* **cram**
Slang. Swot (also *swat*) means 'cram.' A *swot* is a *grind,* synonymous with **sap.** *To
swot up* is to *cram* or *bone up* and is synonymous with *mug up* (see **mug, 2**).

T

ta   **thanks!**
Inf. Heard increasingly. Americans have no corresponding informal term. See also **ta-ta.**

table, *v.t.*   **submit for discussion**
This term means exactly the opposite of what it means in America, where to *table* an item is to *shelve* it or to postpone discussion of it, perhaps hoping it will never come up again. In Britain *lay on the table* means postpone indefinitely.

table money   **allowance**
Expense money issued to officials who must entertain clients.

tack, *n.*   *Slang.* **chow; grub**
Good tack is *good eating.* Synonymous with **tuck.**

Taffy, *n.*   **Welshman**
One of those objectionable nicknames (e.g., *Paddy, Paki*).

tail. See **top and tail**

tail after   **pursue**
Follow closely.

tailcoat, *n.*   **cutaway**

take a decision   **make a decision**

take against   **oppose**
Also, *begin to dislike.*

take (one) all (one's) time   **be all one can do**
Inf. It takes me all my time to pay for the food means *It's all I can do to pay for the food.* Thus, *He's so fat it takes him all his time to get up the stairs.*

take a rise out of, *Inf.*   *Inf.* **get a rise out of**

take a scunner at (against), *Slang.*   **take a dislike to**

take down, *Inf., Slang.*   **1.** *Inf.* **take (a letter)**
        2. *Slang.* **take (cheat)**

take first knock *Inf.*   **go first**
Inf. A term taken from cricket; synonymous with **bat first.**

take in charge   **arrest**
See under **charge-sheet.**

take into care   SEE COMMENT
When a child is taken from its parents who are deemed unfit, in America the
authorities are said to *take custody* of the child. In Britain, the child is *taken into
care.*

take it in turns to   **take turns**
The British form is followed by the infinitive of the verb, the American form by a
gerund. Thus in Britain two good friends of a sick man would *take it in turns to* sit
by his bedside, while in America they would *take turns* sitting there.

take no harm   **suffer no harm**

take on   *Inf.* **catch on**
Inf. Catch on is used in Britain as well.

take (someone's) point   **see (someone's) point**
I take your point rather than the American *I see your point* or *I get your point.*

take silk   SEE COMMENT
Become a Q.C., Queen's Counsel, or *K.C., King's Counsel,* both specially recognized
barristers. The title depends upon the sex of the sovereign. The word *silk,* by
itself in this context, denotes such a counsel, thus: *John Jones, a silk, accepted the*
brief (i.e., *took the case*). The *silk* is the robe worn to replace the ordinary robe
worn by other than a Q.C. or K.C.

take the biscuit   *Slang.* **take the cake**
Slang. As in *That takes the biscuit!* To surpass all others, especially in stupidity,
cheek, impudence, effrontery, and the like.

take the mickey out of   *Inf.* **act disrespectfully toward**
Aggressively undermine someone's self-confidence. Also, *take the mick out of; take*
the piss out of.

take the piss out of. See **take the mickey out of.**

take the rise out of, *Inf.*   *Inf.* **get a rise out of**

take the shilling   **enlist**
Inf. From the days when the Recruiting Sergeant gave the new recruit a shilling,
known as the *King's* (or *Queen's*) *shilling.*

take (make) up the running   **take the lead; set the pace**
A racing term, often used figuratively of, e.g., participants in a conversation who
seem to compete with one another in their exchange.

taking, *n.*   *Inf.* **state of agitation**
Inf. To be in a *taking* is to be *upset,* to be having a *fit* of anger or nerves. An
old-fashioned idiom.

takings, *n. pl.*   **revenue**

The term is applied mostly to small businesses, e.g. shops and market stalls, and most often to the money taken in a single day's business.

talent-spotter   **talent scout**
Both terms used in both countries.

talk the hind leg off a donkey   *Inf.* **talk a blue streak**
Inf. Or *off an iron pot.*

talk through (out of) the back of one's neck. *Inf.*   *Inf.* **talk through one's hat**
With never an end in sight.

tally plan   **installment plan**
A *tally plan* or *tally system* was the method by which a *tally shop,* owned or serviced by a *tallyman* or *tallywoman,* operated a retail business accommodating needy customers who could not pay cash, the accounts being recorded in a pair of matching books, one for each party, and usually paid weekly without billing. In depressed areas, the practice has given way to regular installment buying, called **hire-purchase,** or more popularly the **never-never,** in Britain.

Tannoy, *n.*   *Inf.* **P.A. system**
Inf. A proprietary name gone generic.

tap, *n.*   **faucet**
Tap (as a noun) is heard in America, *faucet* is also heard in Britain. But Americans speak of *tap*-water, never *faucet*-water.

taped, *adj.*   *Slang.* **nailed down**
Slang. One who *has it all taped* has thought of everything, and provided for all contingencies; he's got it *all worked out,* and *buttoned down.*

taplets. See **shares.**

tap stocks. See **shares.**

taradiddle, tarradiddle, *n., Inf.*   *Slang.* **fib**

tardy *adj.*   **sluggish**
Also has the American meaning of 'late.'

tariff, *n.*   **1. schedule of charges**
                                         2. minimum sentence
1. In Britain, this word used alone can mean 'hotel charges' or 'restaurant charges.'
2. Especially one imposed by the **Home Secretary** rather than a judge.

tarmac, *n.*   **1. blacktop**
                                           2. airfield
1. In America *tarmac* refers to the bituminous binder used in the making of tar roads. *Tarmac* started out as a trademark for a binder for road surfaces, but now generally refers to any bituminous road surface binder. It is a shortening of *tar macadam,* which in America describes a pavement built by pressing a tar binder over crushed stone, and in Britain a 'prepared tar concrete poured and shaped on

a roadway to construct a hard surface.' As a transitive verb, *tarmac* means to *tar* a road. See also **macadam**.
2. *Tarmac* has now acquired the specialized meaning of 'air-field,' especially the part made of this material.

tart, *n.*   **1. pie**
                                                                                    2. loose woman
1. What Americans think of when they recall Mom's apple pie or cherry pie would often be an apple *tart* or cherry *tart* in Britain. For the meanings of British *pie* see **pie.**
2. Favorite epithet of jealous wives on the way home from a party at which their husbands have looked longingly at another female.

tart up   *Slang.* **doll up**
Slang. Often applied to interior decoration, and almost invariably pejorative, indicating that the décor was gaudy, and possibly tawdry as well. *He had his digs tarted up by a Knightsbridge designer.* Also used in reference to writing style: *She writes a dreadfully tarted up prose. Overdone* is the adjective that comes to mind, but perhaps it is stronger than that.

ta-ta, *interj.*   *Inf.* **bye-bye**
Inf. (First *a* as in HAT, second as in HAH, stress more or less equal). Such baby-talk is heard among adult cockneys, as is **ta.**

tater, 'tatur, tatie, *n.*   *Slang.* **spud**
Slang. The lowly *potato,* always welcome at the dinner table.

tatt, *n., v.i.*   **1.** *n.* **frills**
                                                                    2. *v.i.* **fritter away one's time**
1. *n., Slang. The décor of the apartment was lovely and without tatt.*
2. *v.i., Slang.* Do more or less useless jobs just to pass the time.

tatties   *Inf.* **potatoes**
Especially in Scotland.

tatty, *adj., Inf.*   **shabby**
See **grotty.**

taws, *n.*   **lash**
A thong, cut into narrow strips at the end, used for chastising children. Also *tawse.* A Scottish word.

taxman, *n.*   *Inf.* **the Inland Revenue**
Or any of its employees, especially those whose job it is to deal directly with taxpayers.

tax point, *n.*   **effective date**
An example of this tax usage: **V.A.T.** (value added tax) on certain items went up from 8 percent to 25 percent May 1, 1975. An order for such an item is given April 25 for delivery May 2. You pay 25 percent, says the tax office: the *tax point* is the delivery date, not the date of the order.

tea, *n.*   SEE COMMENT
In Britain, one drinks afternoon tea at about 4:00 P.M., taken with **biscuits,** bread and jam, **scones,** and the like. But *tea* also covers an evening meal consisting of

a light supper. *Tea* in this sense is heard primarily among the working class and children, and is really short for **high tea.**

teach someone's grandmother to suck eggs   **instruct an expert**
Slang. To attempt to instruct or advise someone more experienced than oneself, or to try to educate an expert on a matter within his field—like telling Albert Einstein how to approach the matter of relativity.

tea lady   SEE COMMENT
The member of the staff at the office or shop who makes and brings around the tea at 11:00 A.M., and 4:00 P.M. There will be a **biscuit** or two as part of the offering. It is considered good practice to suspend business discussion during the ceremony. Occasionally tea gives way to coffee, but the functionary in question will never be called the *coffee lady*. This job, like the relaxed style of office life in which it plays a role, is increasingly rare.

tear a strip off (someone)   *Slang.* **bawl (someone) out**
Slang. The *strip* is a noncommissioned officer's stripe. The expression, in military circles, suggests demotion for a misdemeanor.

tearaway, *n.*   *Inf.* **hell-raiser**
Inf. The term does not necessarily imply a bad character. A *tearaway* is a wild youngster, a cut-up, who is probably going to straighten out in time.

tease, *n.*   *Inf.* **tricky job**
Inf. "It was quite a *tease*," said the Mr. Fixit, explaining why it took so long and cost so much for what had at first seemed the simple job of repairing the lawn mower.

teat, *n.*   **1. nipple**
                                                                    2. bulb
1. On a baby bottle.
2. The *rubber bulb* of a medicine dropper.

tea-towel, *n.*   **dish towel**
Mostly designed for drying dishes. Also referred to as a **washing-up cloth.**

teetotalist. See **TT.**

telegraph pole   **telephone pole**
Both functions are served in both countries, which somehow assign different priorities to the respective wires.

telephone box. See **call-box; kiosk.**

telephonist, *n.*   **switchboard operator**
(Accent on the second syllable.)

telly, *n., Inf.*   *Inf.* **TV**
Also, **goggle-box.** See also **have square eyes.**

temporary guest   **transient**
Hotel term.

ten. See under **twenty.**

tenner, *n.*   **sawbuck**
Inf. A *ten-pound* **note** (*bill*).

term, *n.*   **trimester**
Term, in the British system, and *semester* and *trimester* in the American, are the respective designations for fixed parts of the school year. To complicate matters still further, *terms* often have quite different names in different British institutions. As only one example, the three eight-week terms at Oxford are called Michaelmas, Hilary, and Trinity. At Cambridge they are Michaelmas, Lent, and Easter. *Half-term* is a brief vacation occurring about midway through the term in most British **schools.**

terminus, *n.*   **terminal**
A railroad or bus term. The British, however, use *terminal* to refer to the city center where one picks up the bus to the airport.

terrace, *n.*   **row of joined houses**
A specialized British use of the word. A *terrace house* is known as a *row house* in America. See **semi-detached.**

terraces, *n., pl.*   **standing room**
Used only of a sports arena. Sometimes *terracing.*

Test. See **Test Match.**

test bed, *n.*   **proving-ground**
Literally, an iron framework for resting machinery being tested.

Test Match   **international match**
This is principally a cricket term, now also applied to rugger. A *Test Match,* e.g., between England and Australia, has about the same importance in England as the *World Series* in America. The English team is always referred to as the *England side,* never the *English side;* but the Australians are always referred to as the *Australian side,* the West Indians as the *West Indian side,* etc. *Test Match* is often shortened to *Test:* thus, *What happened in the Melbourne Test?* See also **cricket.**

Thatcherite, *adj.*   SEE COMMENT
Describing the extreme free-marketeering policies of Margaret Thatcher, prime minister from 1979 to 1990, and of those who have followed her beliefs. The closest comparison in recent American politics would be Reaganite, and Lady Thatcher and President Reagan were close ideological allies.

that cock won't fight   **that excuse (plea, plan) won't work**

that's it!   **right!**

that's the job!   *Slang.* **that's the ticket!**
Slang. Often *that's just the job!*

that's torn it!   *Slang.* **that does it!**
Slang. Said in exasperation when things have gone wrong.

theatre, *n.*   **operating room**
Short for *operating-theatre*; a *theatre sister* is an *operating-room nurse*; a *confinement theatre* is a *labor room*. See comments under **lint** and **sister.**

then?   SEE COMMENT
A bit of friendly jocularity. *Then?* at the end of a sentence is little more than punctuation. "Been doing a bit of work, then?" says the gardener to the boss as he notes a weeding job done in his absence. "Off on a holiday, then?" says your rustic neighbor, as he strolls by and catches sight of you lugging a valise to your car.

theological college   **divinity school; seminary**

there's a . . .   **that's a . . .**
As in, *There's a good boy.*

there's no shifting it   *Inf.* **it's unshakable**
Inf. Once he's made up his mind, there's no shifting it. Seems to be used only in the negative.

thermic lance   **blowtorch**
Rarely heard nowadays.

thick, *adj.*   *Inf.* **dull and stupid**
And someone who is dull and stupid could be called a thicko or a thicky. *As thick as two short planks* is a standard insult.

thick ear, *Slang.*   **cauliflower ear**

thin on the ground   **few in number**
Inf. Often used to mean 'short of help,' 'understaffed.'

third party insurance   **liability insurance**

Third Programme   SEE COMMENT
The BBC (British Broadcasting Company) broadcasts four different radio programs, Radio 1, 2, 3, and 4, in addition to two television programs, BBC 1 and BBC 2. In the early days, there were only three radio programs, known as the First, Second and Third Programmes. The last-named maintained a higher intellectual and artistic level than the other two, so that to *be Third Programme* was to be something of an intellectual, or to have leanings in that direction, and to be interested and more or less versed in the arts. Now it's *Radio 3* for the highbrows.

threap, *n., v.t.*   1. *n.* **accusation.**
                                                                       2. *v.t.* **scold**
Heard in Scotland and the North of England.

three-star. See **four-star.**

threshold agreement   **union cost-of-living contract**

Throgmorton Street   *approx. Inf.* **Wall Street; the market**
Inf. A street in the City of London whose name is used as a nickname for the London Stock Exchange, and the securities fraternity and their activities generally, just
as nearby *Mincing Lane* is used for the wholesale tea business. The British often
use the term **the City** to denote the financial community as a whole. See **City.**

throstle, *n.*   **song-thrush**

through, *adj.*   **1. connected**
                                                                 2. still in contention
1. This meaning is restricted to telephone operator usage. Thus, *You're through!*
means 'Your party is on the line!' or 'You're connected!' When a British telephone
operator says *You're through!* it sounds about as grim to an American as *Your time
is up!* must sound to a Briton. In Britain the operator does not tell you when your
time is up; instead there are three short beeps on a long distance call or a series of
rapid pips on a local call from a pay station. No pips when you dial directly from
a private telephone.
2. This meaning relates to elimination competitions in sports, called **knock-outs**
in Britain. Thus (in cricket): *In the North, Yorkshire and Lancashire are through.* That
means that they are 'still alive' in American sports parlance. *Through,* in American English, would more likely be taken to mean the exact opposite: 'finished,'
'eliminated.'

throw a wobbly   *Inf.* SEE COMMENT
To *throw a wobbly* is to express anger or uncertainty about something. It is akin
to having a temper tantrum: *He threw a wobbly when he heard about the escalating
building costs.* But it may also connote anxiety about something: *When he learned
that he would have to ride bareback, he threw a wobbly.*

throw one's bonnet (cap) over the windmill   **throw caution to the winds**
Evokes the Victorian atmosphere of a young lady involved in an impetuous
elopement; but this expression is current usage.

throw out   **add on; build**
Referring to adding an extension to a structure: to *throw out* a wing, thus enlarg-
ing a building or a room. The British also talk of *throwing out* a pier, i.e., building
one out into the water.

throw up, *n. Inf.*   **throw in**
In both cases, it's *the sponge* or *the towel* that is thrown up signaling defeat.

thumping, *adj., adv.*   *Inf.* **enormously**
Inf. Rarely used by itself to mean 'enormous,' as in *a thumping lie;* usually in combination with *great* or *big; a thumping great feast. Thumping good* means the same
thing: a *thumping good* victory is an *overwhelming* one.

The Thunderer   *Inf.* **The Times**
The London newspaper, that is.

thundering, *adv.*   *Inf.* **mighty**
Inf. In the sense of 'extremely'—a *thundering* good actor; a *thundering* good piece
of mutton. An old-fashioned word.

thunder-mug, *n.*   **chamber pot**
Slang. The commode that may contain it used to be referred to as a *thunder-box.*
Like the commodities in question, the terms are not common but are heard now
and then.

thundery trough   **line squall**
A nautical term for a meteorological phenomenon to give one pause.

tick, *v.t., v.i.*   **check**
Please tick where appropriate, seen in instructions for filling out a form or on an
advertisement coupon. A *tick list* is a *check list.* But see **on tick; tick off.**

tick, half a. See **half a tick.**

tick, on. See **on tick.**

ticket-of-leave, *n.*   **parole**
A *ticket-of-leave man* is a prisoner who has served part of his sentence.

ticket pocket   **change pocket**
Tailor's term.

ticket tout, *Slang.*   *Slang.* **scalper**

tickety-boo, *adj.*   *Slang.* **hunky-dory**
Slang. Also spelled *tiggerty-boo.* All right.

tickler, *n.*   *Inf.* **poser**
Inf. A delicate situation; a tricky problem.

tick off   1. **check off**
                                                                       2. **tell off**
See **tick.**

tick over   **turn over**
Referring to a car or other engine. Extended metaphorically, for example, to
office or business routine: *When he's away on holiday, things just tick over* (activity
slows down).

tic-tac   SEE COMMENT
Inf. An arm-movement signaling system used by *tic-tac men* at racetracks to flash
the changing odds to resident bookies.

tiddler, *n.*   **minnow**
Inf. This word is sometimes used informally as an epithet for little creatures, like
kittens and children, and can even be stretched to cover abstractions, like clues.
"We haven't found a tiddler yet," says the police investigator, meaning, "We hav-
en't found even the most trifling clue."

tiddl(e)y, *adj., Inf.*   *Inf.* **tipsy**
Formerly, a word meaning 'a drink.'

tidy, *adj.*   **neat**
A matter of preference. *Tidy* is not heard much in America except, perhaps, among genteel older ladies. It is common in Britain. KEEP KENT TIDY appeared on signs all over that lovely county. A sign reading PLEASE PARK TIDILY sometimes adorns the parking lot (**car park**) outside a pub. *Tidy-minded* means 'logical,' 'methodical.'

tied, *adj.*   SEE COMMENT
This word has different meanings in Britain depending upon the noun it modifies. A *tied cottage* was one occupied by a farm worker at a nominal or no rent, as a perquisite of his job; but he was not protected by the Rent Act covering most ordinary tenants and making it virtually impossible for landlords to evict them. If he lost his job, he lost his cottage. This semi-feudal system has been abolished, and agricultural workers enjoy the protection of the Rent Act. A *tied garage* is one that serves one company exclusively. A *tied house* is a pub affiliated with a particular brewery and serving only that brewery's brand of beer and ale. It is the opposite of a **free house.**

tie-pin, *n.*   **stickpin**
Synonymous with **breast-pin.**

tiffin, *n., v.i.*   **lunch**
Of Anglo-Indian origin, meaning 'light meal.' Also used as a verb, 'take a light meal.'

tig, *n.*   **1. tizzy**
                                                                          2. tag
1. A *tizzy* in Britain was slang for *sixpence* (now no longer used; see **Appendix II.A**). The British use *tizzy* (in the sense of 'state of agitation') the way Americans do. See also **tizzy.**
2. The children's game, so called from its primary meaning: a *light touch. Tag* is used as well.

tiggerty-boo. See **tickety-boo.**

tights, *n. pl.*   **pantyhose**
A term borrowed from the ballet world. A British saleswoman (shop **assistant**) would understand *pantyhose* but she and the customer would normally say *tights.*

tile-hung, *adj.*   **shingled with tiles**
Describing country houses, the roofs and sides of which are shingled with reddish-brown clay tiles, usually square or rectangular, occasionally rounded at the bottom or top.

till, *conj., prep., n.*   **1. through**
                                                                 2. cash register
1. In expressions of duration of time. *Till* (or *until*) a certain hour or date, in Britain, means 'through,' or, in the awkward American phrase, 'to and including.' At times, however, *till* doesn't literally mean 'through.' Thus, *He'll be away till Sunday* might mean 'He'll return some time in the course of Sunday.' Further questioning is needed to clear up the ambiguity. See also **Appendix I.A.1.**

timber, *n.*   **lumber**
In America *timber* means 'standing trees,' but the British use the term the way Americans use *lumber.* However, see **lumber** for British use of that word.

time!, *interj.*   **closing time!**
Inf. The full phrase is: *Time, gentlemen, please!* See **during hours.** Pub terminology. Closing time is at hand.

time and a half   **(approx.) 150% overtime pay**
Overtime expression.

time-limit, *n.*   **deadline**

The Times   SEE COMMENT
The Times of London.

timetable, *n.*   **schedule**
In British schools the list of periods and subjects is called a *timetable* as is the case with train schedules etc. The Americans refer to it as the *schedule.*

tin, *n.*   **can**
A food container; and naturally the British say *tin-opener, tinned food,* etc.

tinker, *n.*   **itinerant mender**
Not much seen any more except for a mender of pots and pans. In Ireland, the word is used informally as an approximate equivalent of *gypsy.*

tinker's cuss   *Inf.* **tinker's dam(n)**
Inf. The *cuss* is slang for *curse,* of which *damn* is only one example. The British use *damn,* and sometimes even *curse,* in this connection. The thought is that tinkers are free with their cussing.

tinkle, *n.*   *Inf.* **ring; phone call**
Inf. As in, *Give me a tinkle when you're next in town.*

tinpot, *adj.*   *Slang.* **crummy**
Slang. Heard in America in the derogatory expression 'tinpot politician' or 'tinpot gambler.'

tin tack   **carpet tack**
A short, tinned iron tack.

tip, *n., v.t., v.i.*   **dump**
The British *tip* their *refuse* into a *refuse tip.* Americans *dump* their *garbage* into a *garbage dump.* A *tip-truck* is a *dump truck.* An American might well be mystified at the sight of a sign out in open country reading NO TIPPING.

tip down   *Inf.* **rain cats and dogs**

tipped, *adj.*   **favored**
As in *tipped to win the election* (or *the high jump*); or *tipped as the next Prime Minister.* Applied to cigarettes, *tipped* would mean only 'filter tip.'

Tippex, *TM*   correction fluid

tip-top, *adj., Inf.*   first rate

tip-up seat   folding seat

tiresome, *adj.*   tedious; wearisome

titbits, *n. pl.*   tidbits
Both spellings are seen in Britain.

titch, *n.*   a very small person

titchy bit   just a drop
Inf. A *tiny bit* of anything.

tit in a trance   restless soul
Slang. Describes a person who jumps around from one chore to another, not
knowing which to tackle first. Synonymous with **fart in a colander.**

titter, *v.i.*   giggle in an annoying manner

tittup, *n., v.i.*   SEE COMMENT
A word uncommon in America. A *tittup* is an exaggerated prancing and bouncing
sort of movement, characteristic of a spirited horse. To *tittup* is to move that way.

tizzy, *n.*   SEE COMMENT
Slang. The old sixpence, now obsolete. *Tizzy* is a corruption of *teston* (also *tes-
toon*), a term now obsolete meaning certain European coins one side of which
was decorated with a head. The term *teston* was specifically applied to a Henry
VIII shilling, which suffered from inflation and fell in value to sixpence. See also
Appendix, II.A; tig, 1.

toad-in-the-hole, *n.*   sausage in batter
Beef or sausages coated in batter and baked.

toastip   toasted sandwich

tobacconist's shop   cigar store

Toc H. See **as dim as a Toc H lamp.**

tod. See **on one's tod.**

toff, *n.*   *Slang.* **swell**
Slang. A distinguished person. More indicative of a way of life than wealth.

toffee, *n.*   taffy
But *for toffee* means 'at all,' as in, *He can't play bridge for toffee,* i.e., *he plays badly.*

toffee-nosed, *adj.*   *Slang.* **stuck-up**
Slang. Snobbish. *Stuck-up* is used in Britain as well, but see **stick up.**

to hand   **at hand; available**
A shop will have certain merchandise *to hand,* or *ready to hand,* i.e., *available. Your letter to hand,* however, used in old-fashioned correspondence, means 'Your letter received.' A notice on the quarterly telephone bill reads: "Any call charges not *to hand* when this bill was prepared will be included in a later bill." See **Appendix I.A.1.**

toke, *n.*   *Slang.* **grub; chow**
Slang. Food generally, but it has the special meaning of *dry bread.* Synonymous with **tack; tuck.**

tolly, *n., Slang.*   **candle**

Tommy Atkins   SEE COMMENT
Inf. Any private in the British army. The original Thomas Atkins was a private of the 23rd Royal Welch Fusiliers serving under Wellington's command. His name was chosen for a specimen question-and-answer form in a soldiers' handbook around 1815. *Tommy Atkins* has also been used as an epithet for a rank and file member of any type of organization. *Tommy,* by itself, is also slang for *brown bread,* or *rations* generally, of the inferior sort that used to be handed out to privates and laborers.

Tom Tiddler's ground   **red light/green light**
A children's game: one stands in front, all the rest some distance behind him in a line. The ones in back try to sneak forward. The one in front can turn around whenever he chooses and if he sees anyone moving, he sends that one back to the starting line. Also known as *sly fox* or *peep-behind-the-curtain* or *Grandmother's steps or footsteps,* depending on what part of Britain you're in.

ton, *n.* See **Appendix II.C.1.g.**

ton, *n.*   **100**
Slang. The expression *the ton* means '100 m.p.h.' Thus the proud owner of a motorcycle says, *It can do the ton. Ton-up,* as an adjective (e.g., the *ton-up boys*) is a somewhat derogatory term referring to the motorcycle set, the type that do 100 and scare you to death.

tone, *n.*   **whole tone**
Musical term. See **Appendix II.F.**   ·

tongue sandwich, *Slang.*   *Slang.* **soul kiss**

too good to miss   *Inf.* **too good to pass up**
Inf. See also **miss out on.**

toothcomb, *n.*   **fine comb**

toothful   *Inf.* **thimbleful**
Inf. A very small drink (of whiskey, etc.).

top, *n.*   **1. head (beginning)**
                                                              2. blouse
1. As, for instance, in the expression *top of the street.* See also **bottom.**

top, *v.t.*   *Slang.* **kill**
Either oneself or another.

top and tail   SEE COMMENT
Inf. The process of pulling off the inedible extremities of some fruits and vegetables, e.g. **French beans.** This can be done with the help of a knife, or, by the more adept, with the fingers.

top gear   **high gear**
See also **Appendix II.E.**

top-hole, *adj.*   **great**
Slang. Anything the speaker regards as *first rate.*

topliner, *n.*   **headliner**

top of one's bent   **heart's content**

top of the bill, *Inf.*   *Inf.* **headliner**

(at the) top of the tree   **(in the) highest rank**
Slang. At the higher reaches of one's profession.

topping, *adj.*   *Inf.* **great**
Inf. Simply terrific. Rather old-fashioned.

topside, *n.*   **top-round**
Butcher's term, the outer side of round of beef.

top up   **fill**
For example, the gas tank, the crankcase, the battery, a drink. Also used of salary.

torch, *n.*   **flashlight**

(the) Torpids, *n. pl.*   SEE COMMENT
Oxford boat races. These are *bumping races* (see **May Week**). The Torpids are the Oxford equivalent of the Cambridge *Lent Races.* Oxford calls its equivalent of the Cambridge *May Races* the *(Summer) Eights.*

Tory, *n.*   SEE COMMENT
Inf. Member of the Conservative Party. A colloquialism, often used pejoratively.

tossed, *adj.*   *Slang.* **tight**
Slang. In the sense of *drunk.*

tosser, *n.*   *Slang.* **a despicable person**

toss off, *Slang.*   **masturbate**

tosticated, *adj.*   **befuddled**
Slang. Perplexed, usually with the implication of drink. Sometimes *tossicated.* The noun *tostication* means *bewilderment* or *perplexity.* A corruption of *intoxicated.*

tot, *n.*   **dram**
Whiskey is often understood, but it can denote a small portion of any beverage.

to take away   **to go**
Referring to food which, in both countries, is prepared for consumption off
the premises as in, *Sandwiches made up to take away.* Used attributively, without *to,* as in, *take-away coffee,* which would be *coffee to go,* or *takeout coffee,* in
America.

tote betting   **pari-mutuel betting**

totem, *n.*   **hierarchy; order**
Inf. Used in expressions like 'I am a liberal-radical of the old totem,' i.e., *of the old
order.* Apparently derived from the top-to-bottom order on totem poles.

to the wide   **utterly**
Inf. Done to the wide means 'done in' or 'dead drunk,' depending on the context,
so be careful. To distinguish: Use *whacked to the wide* when you mean 'done in'
(but still on one's feet) and *dead to the wide* or *sloshed to the wide* to describe the
condition of extreme intoxication, but *dead to the wide* can mean merely 'uncon-
scious' (without the aid of liquor) if the context makes it clear.

totting-up procedure   **point system**
Whereby, on a cumulative basis, one's driving demerits reach a total sufficient to
result in the suspension of one's license for a given period.

totty, *n.*   *Inf.* SEE COMMENT
A young, sexually attractive person. Applied to men and women, but more often
to women.

touch, *n.*   *Slang.* **thing**
Slang. In the sense of a particular 'sort of thing': *I don't go for the sports car touch.*

touch-lines, *n. pl.*   **sidelines**
Side boundaries in some sports.

tourists, *n. pl.*   *Inf.* **the visiting team**
Used almost exclusively in international cricket; when Australia's cricket team
visits England, they are *the tourists.*

tour of ops. See under **ops room.**

tout, *v.i.*   **scout race horses**
Americans and British are both familiar with the racetrack *tout* who furnishes
advice on how to bet.

tower block. See **block.**

town, *n.*   SEE COMMENT
To someone in England, *town* is *London,* even though London is not a town but a
city. One has, for example, spent the day *in town;* tomorrow one is going *to town*
or *up to town* and the *town* in question is always London.

town and gown   SEE COMMENT
Non-university and university groups, respectively, at Oxford and Cambridge
especially. *Town,* in this phrase, denotes those persons in the town who are not
connected with the university as students, fellows, etc. *Gown* means the 'university people.' The phrase *town and gown,* with the same connotations, is not
unknown in America and is used occasionally in some American college towns
and cities. In Britain, *townee* is university slang for one of those persons who
collectively constitute *town.* In American college towns, *townie* means the same
thing, and like *townee,* is pejorative.

town boundary   city limits

town centre   downtown

track, *n.*   lane
A traffic term, referring to a particular lane of a highway.

trade, *n., v.i.*   (do) business
Trade is often used in Britain where Americans would say *business,* e.g., *He is in
the necktie trade.* A *roaring trade* is a *rushing business. Trader* and *tradesman* mean
'shopkeeper' or 'craftsman,' as opposed to one engaged in a profession. A *trading
estate* is a *business area,* sometimes more particularly a shopping center or a small
factory zone. *Trading vehicles* are *commercial vehicles,* and *trade* plates are *dealer's
plates.* To *be in trade* is to *keep a retail store.*

trade(s) directory book   yellow pages
The American term is now used in Britain as well.

trade(s) union   labor union
Shortened to *union* oftener in America than in Britain. The British name comes
from the fact that membership is based on the worker's craft, rather than on the
industry in which he is employed. See also **T.U.C.; social contract.**

trading, *n.*   SEE COMMENT
In the business pages of British newspapers, you are likely to see the writer say
something like *trading is good/bad/below expectations* at the company being discussed. American papers would say that *business is good, bad,* etc. in the same
discussion.

trading estate. See **trade**

trafficator, *n.*   directional signal
On an automobile etc. See **winker.**

traffic block   traffic jam

traffic lights, *n., pl.*   stop lights

traffic warden   traffic officer
Special officers particularly concerned with parking offenses who also assist the
police in the regulation of traffic.

tram, *n.*   **streetcar**
Short for *tram-car.*

tranche, *n.*   **1. bracket**
                                                                2. block (of stock)
(Pronounced TRAHNSH or sometimes TRONSH in imitation of the French pronunciation of the word.)
1. Fancy equivalent of **slice** and **band,** in tax terminology.
2. Part of a stock issue.

transfer, *n.*   **decal**
Decal is a shortening of *decalcomania.*

transferred charge call   **collect call**
This is the correct technical term for this operation in Britain. *Reverse-charge call* is
a more common variant.

transport, *n.*   **transportation**
A Briton would ask, *Have you got transport?* rather than *Have you (got) transportation?* A sign in an American hotel signifying an office making guests' travel
arrangements would read TRANSPORTATION; in a British hotel, TRANSPORT.

transport café   **truck drivers' all-night diner**
See also **café.**

transport system   **transit system**

trapezium, *n.*   **trapezoid**
In America a *trapezium* is a quadrilateral having no sides parallel. In Britain it
denotes a quadrilateral having two sides parallel, which in America is always
called a *trapezoid.*

traps, *n. pl.*   *Inf.* **gear**
Inf. Traps means 'personal belongings,' especially 'luggage.' Now rare.

traveller   SEE COMMENT
A term used to cover Roman gypsies and Irish travellers, who are recognized
as ethnic groups under the Race Relations Legislation. These groups may travel
around or stay on permanent sites. They live in **caravans** on local-authority-man-
aged or private sites, with a few on unauthorized sites. See also **commercial
traveller.**

travelling rug. See **carriage rug.**

treacle, *n.*   **molasses**

treat   *Inf.* **terrifically**
Inf. An old-fashioned Briton might say to the lady: *You dance a treat,* or he might
say: *My wife is taking on a treat* (i.e., *making a terrific fuss*) about the lack of service.

treble. See under **double, 1.**

trek   *Slang.* **a tiresome journey**
Akin to a mission.

trendy, *adj.*   *Inf.* **faddish, fashionable; with it**
Inf. Applies to clothes, furniture, ideas, anything. Sometimes used as a substantive to mean 'trendy person.' The connotations are usually pejorative.

trews, *n. pl.*   **tartan trousers**
In the old days, short ones were worn by children under kilts. Now only military wear.

trick cyclist   *Slang.* **head shrinker**
Rare. The word also means a 'cyclist who performs tricks.'

trifle, *n.*   SEE COMMENT
A dessert. The base is sponge cake (or ladyfingers, called **sponge fingers** in Britain) soaked in liqueur, wine, sherry, or rum, to which custard and jam and fruit and rich milk or cream are added. Very sweet.

trilby, *n.*   **slouch hat**
Inf. A man's soft felt hat with a lengthwise dent in the crown.

trillion. See **Appendix II.D.**

Trinity. See under **term.**

Trinity House   SEE COMMENT
An institution begun under Henry VIII and still going strong. Responsible for pilotage and aids to navigation around the British coasts, such as lighthouses, pilot boats, beacons, licensing of pilots, etc. It corresponds more or less to the U.S. Coast Guard, without the latter's functions in the military or excise fields. Its members are known as *Trinity Brethren.*

tripe and onions   *Inf.* **trash**
Inf. Like *tripe,* a condemnation of a worthless thing.

tripos, *n.*   SEE COMMENT
(Pronounced TRY'-POSS.) Honors examination at Cambridge University. The term is derived from the three-legged stool *(tripos)* on which the Bachelor of Arts sat to deliver his satirical speech on commencement day. The speech itself was formerly expected to be in Latin.

tripper, *n.*   *approx.* **excursionist**
A pejorative term for those who are having a day out at the shore, in the country, visiting stately homes, etc. The trip occasionally lasts longer than a day.

troilism, *n.*   SEE COMMENT
One ignorant of its pronunciation (TROY'LIZM) might have guessed that this word had something to do with Troilus, the Trojan hero and lover of Cressida. But it is nothing nearly so romantic, but rather sexual activity in which three persons take part simultaneously.

trolley, *n.*   **pushcart**
Trolley in Britain means also a 'hand-lever operated small truck' that carries railroad workers along the rails; but a *trolley-table* (sometimes shortened to

trolley) is a *tea wagon*. *Trolley* is also the name given to the wheeled shopping carts used in supermarkets, as well as the rolling luggage carriers supplied at airports, and in Britain, at some of the railroad terminals. A *sweets trolley* is a *dessert cart*.

trooping the colour(s)   SEE COMMENT
Annual ceremony on the Horse Guards Parade in Whitehall, London. The regimental flag (the *colour*) is borne aloft between lines of troops and handed to the sovereign. This ceremony occurs on the official birthday of the monarch, June 13. (Elizabeth II was born on April 21, a date on which the weather is uncertain.)

trouble and strife, *Rhyming slang.*   **wife**

truck, *n.*   **gondola car**
Truck is the term that would be used by the layman, whereas a more knowledgeable person would call it an *open goods waggon*. What Americans call a *truck* in railroad parlance is a **bogie** in Britain. The American *road truck* is a **lorry** in Britain.

truckle bed   **trundle bed**

trug, *n.*   SEE COMMENT
A convenient flattish garden basket coming in many sizes, made of thin woven wooden strips.

trumpery, *adj.*   **cheap**
In the sense of 'tawdry' or 'gaudy.' Sometimes also used as a noun denoting something that fits the description.

trumps, come up or turn up. See **come up trumps.**

truncheon, *n.*   **billy**
A short club or cudgel, also known in America as a *nightstick.*

trunk call   **long-distance call**

trunk road. See **arterial road.**

try, *n.*   *approx.* **touchdown**
In *rugger.* See under **football.**

try it on   *Inf.* **try it out**
Inf. With the strong implication that one is taking a shot at something in the hope of getting away with it. Hence, the noun *try-on.*

TT, *n., adj.*   **teetotaler; teetotal**
Inf. And the British occasionally say *teetotalist* instead of *teetotaller,* but it all points to the same degree of rectitude.

tube, *n.*   **subway**
Synonymous with **underground. Goggle box** is an equivalent of the American slang use of *tube* for *TV.* But *tube* is also used for *TV* in Britain. See also **subway** for British use.

tub-thumper, *n., Inf.*   *Inf.* **soapbox orator**

T.U.C.   SEE COMMENT
Stands for *Trades Union Congress,* much more closely linked to the Labour Party
than the A.F.L.-C.I.O. is to any American party, and a much more powerful political force. See also **social contract; trade union.**

tuck, *n.*   *Slang.* **eats**
Slang. Variants are *tuck-in* and, less commonly, *tuck-out. Tuck-in* is also a verb meaning to 'put on the feedbag,' that is, 'eat hearty.' A *tuck-shop* is a *pastry shop* and a *tuck-
box* is one for the safeguarding of goodies and is generally school jargon. To *tuck into*
something is to *dig into* it, that is, to *pack in* a hearty meal. See also **tack; toke.**

tumble to   **catch on to**
Inf. To *tumble to* a concept, a hidden meaning, etc. is to *grasp* it, catch on to it, get
the point of it. Synonymous with **twig.**

turf, *n., v.t.*   **sod**
Both terms, in both substantive and verbal uses, are synonymous in both countries, but *turf* is almost always used in Britain. One unit of the stuff (i.e., a standard size piece of ready made lawn) is called *a turf* in Britain, *a sod* in America.
Turves are normally 1' × 3' in Britain; sods 1' × 1' in America. For wholly unrelated
uses of both terms in Britain see **sod,** *n.* and **turf,** *n.*

turf, *n.*   *Inf.* **neck of the woods**
Inf. Preceded by a possessive, an expression that seems to transcend all class bar-
riers, as in, *On me own turf, I sez wot's wot* or, *Let you give me lunch? Oh no, dear boy,
we're on my turf now.*

turf accountant   **bookie**
A euphemism for *bookmaker,* but increasingly rare. **Commission agent** is an
equally euphemistic synonym.

turf out   **throw out**
Slang. Usually applied to rubbish, whether a pile of old magazines or undesirable
people.

turn, *n.*   **1. vaudeville act**
                                                 2. dizzy spell
1. This is a vaudeville term. *Turn* in this sense is short for *variety turn* or *music-hall
turn* and by extension can denote the performer as well. See **star turn.**
2. Turn can mean 'shock' (*It gave me quite a turn*) in both countries. Less educated
Britons also talk of having a *turn* to describe the experiencing of a *dizzy spell.*

turn-about, *n.*   **abrupt change**
Of policy, attitude, etc.

turn and turn about   **alternately**

turncock, *n.*   **water main attendant**

turning, *n.*   **turn**
The *first turning on the right* means the 'first right turn.' The British say, *Take
the first turning on the right* and the Americans, *Take your first right. Turning* has

apparently come to mean *block*, i.e., the space between two *turnings* in the original sense of *turn*. It has been used in such phrases as *a medium length turning, a short turning,* etc. See **Appendix I.A.3.**

turn out, *v.t.*   **clean up**
In Britain one *turns out* a room or a closet by moving everything out of it, cleaning it up, and then moving everything back.

turn the Nelson eye on   **turn a blind eye to**
Inf. To *wink at* (something); to overlook it, act as though nothing had happened. Admiral Nelson (1758–1805) lost the sight of one eye in 1793 during the French Revolutionary Wars. In 1801, he ignored an order to cease action against the Danes at Copenhagen by putting his telescope to his blind eye and claiming that he hadn't seen the signal. He continued the battle and won. Hence, to *turn a Nelson eye* on something is to pay no attention to it, to ignore it, to pretend that nothing has happened.

turn-up, *n.*   **1. trouser cuff**
                                                                            2. upset
1. The term *cuff* in Britain is confined to sleeves.
2. In sports.

turn up one's toes, *Slang.*   *Slang.* **kick the bucket**

turn up trumps. See **come up trumps.**

turtle-neck, *adj.*   **round-neck**
Applied to sweaters with round collars skirting the base of the neck. For the American sense of *turtleneck,* see **polo neck.** See also **roll-neck.**

tushery. See under **Wardour Street.**

twat, *n.*   *Slang.* **fool**
Pronounced like *that,* and likely to be preceded by the adjective *silly.* The same word is used (rhyming with *not*), as in the United States, as a vulgar slang term for the female genitals.

twee, *adj.*   **arty**
Slang. Or *terrible refeened.* Usually seen in the phrase *frightfully twee.* Implies archness, affected daintiness, quaintness-for-quaintness's sake, and so on.

tweeny, *n.*   **assistant maid**
Inf. A maidservant, one who assists both cook and chambermaid, and whose position is thus *between* downstairs and upstairs. Also *tween-maid.*

twelfth man   **standby**
Inf. In **cricket,** the side consists of eleven players and a *twelfth man* who is present to take the place of an injured or otherwise unavailable player. The term has come into general use to signify a *standby* in any situation.

twenty   **a pack of**
Refers to cigarettes. In shops you ask for either *twenty* or *ten.* Thus, *Twenty Players, please.* When you buy from a machine there may be any number of variations, seven, eight, twelve etc., depending on the machine. See also **packet.**

twicer, *n., Slang.*   *Slang.* **double dealer**
A cheat; a deceiver.

twice running   **twice in a row**

twig, *v.t., v.i.*   *Inf.* **catch on (to)**
Slang. In the sense of 'understanding.' *Dig* is a common slang synonym in America; sometimes heard in Britain as well. Synonymous with **tumble to.**

twin-bedded. See under **double-bedded.**

twin set   SEE COMMENT
A matching cardigan and top worn by women. The term *twin set and pearls* is used to describe an affluent suburban woman of conventional views and manners.

twin with . . .   **linked with . . . ; sister-citied with . . .**
Seen on roadside town signs to indicate a special formalized friendly relationship with a town abroad. A variant is the phrase *friendship town* followed by the name of a related community. Thus, driving along, you might see

CHICHESTER
TWINNED WITH CHARTRES

or

ROYAL TUNBRIDGE WELLS
FRIENDSHIP TOWN
WIESBADEN

with the twin town usually chosen on the basis of similar industries or general interests and often quite similar in size.

twist, *v.t., Slang.*   **swindle**

twister, *n., Slang.*   *Slang.* **sharpie**

twit, *n.*   *Slang.* **jerk**
Slang. A foolish or insignificant person.

twitten, *n.*   **alley**
An enclosed type of narrow walk in a village or town, as opposed to open country, where it would be called a *footpath.*

twizzle, *v.t., v.i.*   1. **spin**
                                                               2. **weave**
1. *Slang.* No American slang equivalent. To *twizzle* somebody or something *around* is to *twist* or *spin* him (it) *around,* e.g., in order to examine from all angles.
2. *Slang.* Used intransitively, it means 'weave about,' 'meander.'

two (ten) a penny, *Inf.*   *Inf.* **a dime a dozen**
Something of little value.

twopence coloured   **gaudy**
Inf. Rare. Spectacular, with a slightly pejorative tinge. Cheap. In common speech, the phrase usually comes out *twopenny* (pronounced TUP'-P'NY) *coloured;* its opposite is **penny plain.**

twopenny-halfpenny, *adj.*   *Inf.* **junky**
Inf. (Pronounced TUP'-P'NY HAY'-P'NY.) It can mean 'worthless,' 'negligible,' 'nothing to worry about,' or even 'contemptible,' depending on the context. See also **grotty.**

two pisspots high, *Slang.*   *Slang.* **knee-high to a grasshopper**

two-seater, *n.*   **roadster**
Does anybody still say *roadster?* Maybe *sports car* is closer in feeling, if not as accurate.

two-star. See **four-star.**

two-stroke, *n.*   **oil and gasoline mixture**
Suitable for two-stroke engines. This term formerly appeared on many service station roadside signs.

two-up-two-down, *n., Inf.*   SEE COMMENT
A small house with two floors, each having two rooms.

U

U   See **Appendix I.C.6.**

U.D.I.   **unilateral declaration of independence**

UKIP, *acronym*   SEE COMMENT
Acronym for United Kingdom Independence Party, a political party formed in 1993. Its main mission is to get Britain to withdraw from the European Union.

ulcer, *n.*   **canker sore**
Open sore on a surface of the body, external or internal. Also a corrupting influence.

Ulsterman   **a native of Ulster**

unbelt, *v.t., Slang.*   *Slang.* **shell out**

undercut, *n.*   **1. tenderloin**
                                         2. uppercut
1. Butcher's term. The British use **fillet** (pronounced FILL'-IT) for the same cut. See **Appendix II.H.**
2. Boxing term.

underdone, *adj.*   **raw**
Referring to meat, supposedly rare but really insufficiently cooked.

underground, *n.*   **subway**
Also called the **tube.** A *subway* in Britain is an *underground pedestrian passage.*

underlay, *n.*   **carpet pad**

under observation   **patrolled**

under offer   *approx.* **for sale**
For sale, but with a pending offer.

undertaker, *n.*   **funeral director**

under the doctor   **under the doctor's care**

under the harrow, *Inf.*   *Inf.* **in distress**

unfit, *adj.*   **unable to play**
Because injured or ill. Used in sports reporting and announcements at the game.

unharbour, *v.t.*   **dislodge**
A hunting term: to dislodge a deer from shelter.

unit trust   **mutual fund**
A good way to save for retirement.

unmade road. See under **metalled road.**

unmetalled road. See under **metalled road.**

unofficial strike   **wildcat strike**

unpaved road/track, *n.*   **dirt road**

unseen, *n.*   **sight translation**
In an examination or classroom recitation: *He did well in his Latin unseens.*

unsocial hours   SEE COMMENT
Term used in industrial disputes to describe working hours that interfere with
workers' social lives, like evenings, weekends, and holidays. Not overtime,
which can occur in any job, but the regular hours in jobs like those of bus drivers,
railroad personnel, night watchman, etc.

unstable verge. See **verge.**

up, *adv.*   **to London**
See also **down; down train.**

up, *adj.*   **out of bed**
Up, in America, is ambiguous, in that it can mean 'awake' or 'up and about.' In
Britain it means the latter—'out of bed.'

up a gum tree   *Slang.* **up the creek**
Slang. In a pickle; in a fix. See also **in a cleft stick; on a piece of string; bunkered;
under the harrow; snookered; up the spout.**

up for the Cup   **in town for the big occasion**
Slang. Originated in the North Country, where it is pronounced OOP FOR T'COOP (OO
short as in HOOF, and the T' almost inaudible), and refers to coming up to London to
support the team in the **football** *(soccer)* **Cup Final** at Wembley Stadium.

upper circle   **second balcony**
In a theater. See also **stall; pit; gods.**

upper ten   *Inf.* **upper crust**
Inf. The upper classes; short for the *upper ten thousand,* an analogous phrase that
originated in America.

uppish, *adj., Inf.*   *Inf.* **uppity**
Putting on airs.

upsides. See **get upsides with.**

up-stick, *v.i.*   *Inf.* **pack up and go**
Inf. This can describe moving one's entire ménage or simply clearing up after a
picnic. From former nautical slang meaning 'set a mast.' See also **pull up sticks.**

up stumps *Inf.* **pull up stakes**
Inf. To *clear and leave.* One of the many terms derived from cricket. Not to be confused with **stump up.** *Draw stumps* means the same thing: *clear out. Stumps* are the three uprights in the ground supporting two small cross-pieces *(bails),* the whole structure constituting the *wicket* (See **wicket, 1**). To *up* or *draw stumps* is to close the match, an operation that is extended figuratively to the *winding up* of a situation or phase.

up the duff *Slang.* **pregnant**

up the junction *Slang.* **up the creek**
Slang. In a tough spot; in a fix. The creek in the original reference flowed with human excrement, and those caught upstream were bereft of a paddle.

up the pole **1.** *Inf.* **dead drunk**
2. *Slang.* **in a fix**
3. crazed
1. *Slang.* In this meaning, the very opposite of the American 'on the wagon.'
2. *Slang.* In a predicament.
3. *Slang.* By anything, not merely drink.

up the spout *Slang.* **in a fix**
Slang. Used of any predicament, but, like *in trouble* in America, often understood to mean 'pregnant' when the context permits of the possibility of that interpretation.

up the wall. See **drive (someone) up the wall.**

up to the knocker, *Slang.* *Inf.* **in great shape**

up train. See under **down train.**

U.S., *adj.* **unserviceable**
Slang. The term, always pronounced YOU ESS, originated in the Civil Service, in government laboratories. *Where's the Bunsen burner? Taken away; it's gone You Ess.* If you haven't guessed it, the *U* is the *un-,* and the *S* is for *-serviceable.* Also written *U/S.* Now rare.

V

v. **very**
Common abbreviation in informal correspondence. See also **Appendix I.D.9.**

vac, *n.* **vacation**
(Pronounced VACK.) Also, a school vacation. See also **come down, 2; holiday.**

vacancies *n.* **help wanted**
Also, **situations vacant.** Signifying unoccupied positions.

vacant possession **immediate occupancy**
One sees in most real estate advertisements the expression *vacant possession on* **completion,** meaning 'immediate occupancy on closing title.' This is sometimes qualified by the addition of the phrase *subject to service occupancy* or less commonly, *service occupations,* meaning 'subject to the occupancy of part (rarely all) of the premises by persons living there are rendering services in payment of rent.' The purchaser can get them out by legal means, but it is an arduous process. It almost always applies to agricultural properties.

vacuum flask **thermos bottle**
See also **dewar.** A vessel with a double wall enclosing a vacuum.

vains I! See **fains I!**

value. See **good value.**

value, *v.t.* **appraise**
Whence *valuer,* the usual term for *appraiser,* who makes his livelihood by estimating the value of various objects or land.

Value Added Tax. See **V.A.T.**

value for money **your money's worth**
British shoppers who have found a really good bargain will say they got *value for money* as a way of expressing their approval. It may often be shortened, as in *That skirt was good value.*

valve, *n.* **tube**
Radio term.

van, *n.* **1. closed truck**
2. baggage car
1. Large or small. In America usually restricted to big ones. See also **pantechnicon.**
2. Railroad term.

van, removal. See **pantechnicon; removals.**

(the) V & A   SEE COMMENT
The *Victoria & Albert Museum* in London; almost invariably called V&A. Founded in the mid-19th century, it is the national museum for the decorative and applied arts.

variety, *n.*   **vaudeville**
See also **music-hall.**

variety turn. See **turn.**

varnish, *n.*   **nail polish**

V.A.T.   **sales or excise tax**
(Sometimes pronounced VEE-AY-TEE, sometimes VAT.) Sometimes *VAT,* abbreviation of *Value Added Tax,* which replaced the old purchase tax and the selective employment tax, a sort of payroll tax in the service industries. *V.A.T.* resembles the American Manufacturers' Excise Tax, and derives its *Value Added* label from the fact that at each successive stage of the production of an artifact, the person or entity involved is obliged to add a certain percentage to his charge, which he collects on behalf of Inland Revenue (the national tax authority) and pays over to them at quarterly intervals. At the same time he can recover the V.A.T. amounts that other people have charged him on his acquisitions which go into what he is producing. Thus, a bicycle manufacturer passes on to the Inland Revenue the tax he has collected, but recovers the tax he has paid on, e.g., metal, tires, etc. V.A.T. applies not only to tangibles but to services as well. A writer passes on the percentage he has added to his fee, but gets back the percentage he has paid on writing-paper, telephone, and other things that he has had to pay for in order to perform his professional duties.

V.C.   SEE COMMENT
Stands for *Victoria Cross,* the highest military distinction. Next in order are *C.M.G.* (Companion of the Order of St. Michael and St. George); *D.S.O.* (Distinguished Service Order); *M.C.* (Military Cross). *G.C.* stands for *George Cross,* awarded for extreme civilian bravery (dating from World War II).

verge, *n.*   **grass shoulder**
Verges along roads in Britain vary in width and are favorite spots for picnicking **trippers.** Making oneself at home on the *verge,* however narrow, is a British phenomenon. Americans are amazed to see the equipment employed in this happy activity: folding tables and chairs, ornate tablecloths, electric kettles, elaborate picnic baskets, deck chairs, too; everything but the kitchen sink. In Britain one sees parkway signs reading SOFT VERGES, but, when conditions are appropriate, HARD SHOULDER. Why *shoulder* in this case rather than *verge,* and why the singular, nobody knows. UNSTABLE VERGE, another common road sign, is another term for *soft shoulder.* See also **berm.**

vest, *n.*   **undershirt**
For what Americans mean by *vest,* the British say *waistcoat.* See also **singlet.**

vet, *v.t.*   **check**
Inf. With particular reference to candidates for a job, but now commonly used as well in security checking. By a logical extension, *vet* can mean 'authenticate,' referring to a work of art or a holograph, which is certified genuine after being checked up on. One can also *vet* a manuscript for accuracy. This term is derived

from the practice of sending animals, especially race horses, to a veterinarian surgeon before purchase.

vice-chancellor, *n.*   **president**
A university term denoting the active head of the institution. The *vice-* is used because in Britain the **chancellor** is an honorary officer, always a prominent person, sometimes even royalty.

view, *v.t.*   **inspect**
In connection with selecting a residence. See **order to view.**

viewpoint, *n.*   **lookout point**
A special British meaning in addition to *point of view*, as in America. See **look-out.**

village, *n.*   *approx.* **small town**
Village in Britain is more a description of a way of life than a label applied to a particular political subdivision. The usual demographic distinction between *village* and *town* in Britain is based simply on population, and the break comes somewhere around 3,000.

village shop, *n.*   SEE COMMENT
The local store in a small rural community. A dying institution, as car ownership increases and more rural dwellers shop at supermarkets.

vinaigrette, *n.*   SEE COMMENT
A small box, usually silver, with a fretwork inner lid; frequently Georgian, more often Victorian; now greatly prized by collectors. They originally contained vinegar or salts; ladies carried them to help them through fainting spells. They now make nice pill boxes.

visitors' book   **guest book; register**
The American equivalent at a private home is *guest book;* at a hotel, *register.* The term applies not only to private homes but also to inns and boarding-houses. *Register* is the term commonly used in large British hotels.

viva, *n.*   **oral examination**
Inf. (Pronounced VY'VA.) Short for *viva voce,* Latin for 'aloud.'

voddy, *n., abbrev.*   *Slang.* **vodka**

w.   **with**
Inf. A common abbreviation in informal correspondence. See also **Appendix I.D.9.**

Waac, *n.*   **Wac**
Inf. (Pronounced WACK.) A member of the Women's Army Auxiliary Corps (WAAC) in World War I. This became A.T.S. in World War II and is now WRAC, for Women's Royal Army Corps. The female branches of the air force and navy are, respectively, the W.R.A.F. (rhymes with GRAPH), Women's Royal Air Force, and the W.R.N.S. (pronounced WRENS), Women's Royal Naval Service. See also **Wren.**

waffle, *n., v.i.*   **1.** *n., Slang.* **twaddle**
                                                  2. *v.i., Slang.* **gabble**
                                               3. *v.t., v.i., Inf.* **yelp**
1. *n., Slang.* As a noun *waffle* describes anything silly or useless.
2. *v.i., Slang.* To *waffle* conversationally is to engage in silly chatter; to *gabble, prate.*
3. *v.t., v.i., Slang.* To *waffle* a cry of pleasure is to *yelp* it. Rarely, *woffle.*

wage restraint   **wage control**
Especially as exercised by workers making modest demands on their employer. See also **pay policy; social contract.**

wage-snatch, *n., Inf.*   **payroll holdup**

wages sheet   **payroll**

wage stop, *n.*   SEE COMMENT
The policy of not allowing a person to receive more money from unemployment insurance than he would earn if he were working. Also used as a transitive verb, *wage-stop,* signifying the application of this policy.

waggon, wagon, *n.*   **car**
Railroad term, especially *goods-waggon,* meaning 'freight car.' A *waggon shed* is a *car barn.* The American spelling with one *g* is gaining precedence.

wag it   *Slang.* **play hookey**
Synonymous with **play truant.** Also, *play wag* or *play the wag.*

waistcoat, *n.*   **vest**
Waistcoat is rare in America, and when used is more often pronounced WESKIT than WASTECOTE. In Britain, it should be pronounced as spelled or with the first *t* silent, and the preferred American pronunciation is considered at least colloquial, or even vulgar, though it was considered correct not many decades ago. *Waistcoat* is used in Britain the way *hat* is used in America in expressions like to *wear several*

389

waistcoats or *wear more than one waistcoat,* i.e., to act in a number of different capacities. In America, one is said to wear several *hats* to indicate activity in different capacities. For British meaning of *vest,* see **vest; singlet.**

wait for it! *interj.*   1. *Slang.* **take it easy!; hold your horses!**
                                                    2. *Slang.* **get this!; mind you!**
1. *Slang.* Extended from its use in the army by sergeants teaching new recruits the drill ("Present—wait for it—arms"). Do not begin until you hear my order.
2. *Slang.* Further extended to mean 'wait till you hear this,' and used on the model of the army command as a pause word to underline the irony of the following statement. *The boss told me—wait for it—I had to start working every Sunday.*

waits, *n. pl.*   Christmas carolers
Very rare.

wake-up operator   SEE COMMENT
If you have no alarm clock, or don't trust the one you have, you can dial the hotel operator before retiring for the night and ask to be called at a fixed time next morning.

walkabout, *n.*   campaign stroll
Inf. Taken by candidates for election; also by the monarch, on certain occasions.

walking stick. See **cane.**

walk out, *v.i.*   *Inf.* **go steady**
Inf. A courtship term, very old-fashioned. By contrast, *walk out on* somebody means *desert that person.*

walk slap into. See **slap.**

wallah, *n.*   *approx.* **-man**
A servant or employee charged with the performance of a particular service. Thus, the member of the household staff who worked the **punkah** was known as the *punkah-wallah,* and so on. Applying the term to American situations, *wallah* would appear to come out simply as *-man:* the individual who repairs your typewriter is the typewriter-*man;* e.g., ice*man,* bar*man,* etc. A *bag-wallah,* in the old days, was a traveling salesman. Nowadays the term is either old-fashioned or jocular, depending on the use.

wallpaper music   piped music
Inf. Muzak is the trademark in both countries.

wally, *n.*   *Inf.* **a fool**

wank, *v.i.*   *Slang.* **jerk off**
Slang. Masturbate.

wanker, *n.*   *Slang.* **a foolish or despicable person**
Literally, a masturbator. See **wank.**

want, *v.t.*   1. **take; require**
                                                              2. **need; lack**

1. Example: *It wants a bit of courage to sail the Atlantic alone.*
2. Example: *All the wheels want is a drop of oil; that picture wants to be hung higher; that child wants a good spanking.* In this connection a special use is found in archaic expressions of time: *It wants ten minutes to twelve* meaning 'it is ten minutes to twelve.' The British tend to avoid *want* in the sense of 'desire' or 'wish,' for reasons of politeness. Where an American would say, *I want this changed,* or *Do you want a memo?* a Briton would usually say, *I would like this changed,* or, *Would you like to have a memo?* To Britons, *I want* may sound imperious, and *Do you want?* is considered less polite than *Would you like?* or *Do you wish?* A British usage sometimes heard in America is *want* in the negative, for *shouldn't,* as in, *You don't want to oil this machine too often.* This usage means that 'it is not the best (or the right) way to treat it.'

warder, *n.*   **prison guard**

Wardour Street   *approx.* **movie business**
Inf. A street in London that is the center of the film industry and used figuratively to refer that business, the way Americans use *Hollywood.* The films themselves are shot elsewhere. Wardour Street used to be noted for its antique and imitation-antique shops, especially the latter, giving rise to the term *Wardour Street English,* meaning 'sham-antique diction,' the type common in inferior historical novels. This type of language is also called *gadzookery* or *tushery.*

wardship, *n.*   **custody**
Of minor children, in divorce matters.

warned off   **banned**
A euphemism applied to owners, trainers, jockeys, or bettors (**punters** in Britain) who break the rules of racing and are prohibited from attending races. The banning is effected by the Jockey Club, located at Newmarket, the headquarters of British racing.

wash, *n.*   **use of the bathroom**
Inf. When your host asks whether you would *like a wash* he is offering you the use of *all* his bathroom facilities.

wash, *v.i.*   *Inf.* **stand up**
Inf. Always used in the negative: *It* (that story, that excuse) *won't wash.* See also **wear.**

(The) Wash. See under **(The) Fens.**

wash-cloth, *n.*   **dishrag**
Sometimes called *dish clout.*

washing-book *n.*   **account book**
Slang. An informal *account book,* for instance as between friends on a trip where one pays all the expenses and there is a settlement at the end. It can also mean a 'running score,' as during a social weekend of bridge. No American slang equivalent.

washing things   **toilet articles**

washing-up bowl   dishpan

washing-up cloth   dish towel
Sometimes called a *tea-towel* or *wash-cloth*.

wash leather   chamois
Often shortened to *leather*; also known as *chamois-leather* and *shammy*.

wash up   do the dishes
Do the dishes would confuse a Briton no end because of the restricted meaning of
dish in his country: 'platter' or 'serving-dish.' See **wash,** *n.*

waste bin   wastebasket

waste land   unused land

waste-paper basket   wastebasket

watcher! *interj.*   *Inf.* **hi! howdy!**
Slang. Probably a corruption of *what cheer?*, an old greeting meaning *how's it
going?* There are those who say, however, that it is a running together of *what are
you* (*doing here, up to,* etc.). *Wotcher* is the preferred cockney spelling.

watch-glass, *n.*   watch-crystal
The American equivalent is used in Britain by jewelers, seldom by the general
public.

watching brief, *n.*   SEE COMMENT
A law brief for a client indirectly involved in or concerned with a matter to which
he is not a party. Its technical use refers to the situation of a lawyer charged with
the duty of attending litigation in which the client is not directly involved, where,
however, a point of law affecting the client generally may be involved. To *have*
(or *hold*) a *watching brief*, broadly speaking, is to *keep aware* of a situation that may
ultimately involve your interests.

water, *n.*   river; pond; lake
One sees occasional river, brook, pond, or lake names in which *Water* (with a
capital *W*, as befits part of a proper noun) is used where *River, Brook, Pond,* or *Lake*
would be used in America. Thus, *Aften Water* and *Eden Water* (rivers), *Derwent
Water* (a lake).

water butt   rain barrel

water-cart, *n.*   sprinkling wagon

watersplash, *n.*   ford
Shallow brook running across a road, only a couple of inches high. Sometimes
shortened to *splash*.

waterworks, *n. pl.*   SEE COMMENT
The urinary function and the anatomical organs with which it is carried out. A
euphemism used by some members of the medical profession when talking to
their patients.

waving base   **observation deck**
At an airport. The British expression implies much livelier activity than just looking. At Scottish airports it is called **spectators' terrace.**

Wavy Navy   **Royal Naval Volunteer Reserve**
Inf. Not to be confused with the Royal Naval Reserve. The name comes from the
officers' cuff braid in the form of a wave, as opposed to the straight braid of the
Navy or the approximately diamond pattern of the Naval Reserve.

wax, *n.*   **rage**
Slang. A *dreadful wax* is a *towering rage.* And *waxy* is *jumpy.*

way, *n.*   **dither; tizzy**
Inf. To be *in a way* or *in a great way* is to be *in a dither* or *in a tizzy.*

way, permanent. See **permanent way.**

wayleave, *n.*   **easement**
A right of way rented to a company etc.

Way Out   **Exit**
Ubiquitous sign in public places. *Exit* signs seem to be confined to theaters and
car parks.

wayzgoose, *n.*   **printing company's annual picnic**
Very rare.

wazz, (have a) *v.i.*   *Slang.* **urinate**

W.C.   **toilet**
Stands for *water closet.* One of many euphemisms. See **loo.**

w/e   **weekend**
Common abbreviation in informal correspondence for *weekend* (*week-end* in Britain). Not merely a designation of a part of the week, rather more the name of a
social practice among those who can spare the time. See also **Appendix I.D.9.**

Weald, *n.*   SEE COMMENT
The *Weald* is a district in southern England including parts of the counties of
Kent, Surrey, Hampshire, and Sussex.

wear, *v.t.*   *Inf.* **stand for**
Inf. As in, *Oh no, he won't wear that!* said, for instance, by a lawyer to a client who
suggests an outrageous proposal to be made to the other side. Also in the sense
of 'permit, tolerate': When something slightly irregular, though patently more
efficient, is suggested to a bureaucrat, he won't *wear* it for a minute; or meaning
'accept' or 'see' as in: *I just can't wear him as capable of doing that sort of thing,* when
people are discussing an unsolved murder and someone suggests a suspect. See
also **wash,** *v.i.*

wear off   **wear out**
Of clothes.

weather-board, *n.*   **clapboard**
A *weather-boarded house* is a *clapboard house,* and *weather-boarding* is the *clapboard* itself, also known as *siding.* A *weather-board* is also a sloping board attached to the bottom of a door to keep out rain.

web lettuce   *approx.* **iceberg lettuce**
The web tastes and looks somewhat like iceberg, but has less tightly packed leaves. See also **cos lettuce.**

wedge, *n.*   *Slang.* **wad**
Slang. A *wedge* (of **notes**) is a *wad* (of *bills*). *Wedge* has thus come to mean 'money,' as in, "Got any *wedge?*" *Wodge* and *wadge* are variants. See also **lolly** for slang terms for money.

weed, *n.*   *Slang.* **drip**
Slang. A pejorative, similar to **twit,** for a weak person.

. . . week   **a week from . . .**
The British say *today week* or *a week today* where the Americans say *a week from today; Tuesday week* or *a week on Tuesday* where the Americans say a *week from Tuesday; last Sunday week* where Americans say *a week ago last Sunday;* and the same difference in usage applies to *fortnight.* See also **Appendix I.A.1.**

weekday. See **workday.**

weekly boarder   SEE COMMENT
A student at a boarding school who goes home for the weekends.

weepy; weepie, *n., slang.*   *Slang.* **tear jerker**

weighting, *n.*   **extra salary allowance**
A blanket upward adjustment to cover extra costs of living in certain areas. Under *London weighting,* e.g., government employees living in inner London, i.e., within four miles of Charing Cross, receive a certain increase, those in outer London a somewhat smaller increment, etc.

weigh up   *Inf.* **weigh**
Inf. The British *weigh up* a situation. The Americans drop the *up.* So do the British when they *weight their words.* See **Appendix I.A.3.**

weir, *n.*   **dam**
A *dam* or any fixed obstruction across a river or canal. The water so backed up is directed into a millstream or reservoir, with the excess going over the top of the *weir,* or via a movable sluice gate, or both. On canals, the *weir* is off to one side and the excess water runs down an incline into a reservoir.

well away, *Inf.*   **1.** *Inf.* **tipsy**
                                                         2. *Inf.* **off to a good start**
2. A term borrowed from horse-racing, having made considerable progress. At the outset of a long evening's drinking, one would qualify, it seems, in both senses.

well bowled!   *Inf.* **nice going!**
Inf. The cricket (rough) equivalent of a pitcher in baseball is the **bowler,** and,
like the pitcher, he is a key figure. *Well bowled!* is a phrase borrowed from cricket
which, especially in **public school** and university circles, is used to express
approbation of accomplishments having nothing whatever to do with the game.
Upper class and old-fashioned; synonymous with the more common **well done!**
and **good show!** Another cricket term, applied in its literal sense to fieldsmen
(*fielders*), is *Well stopped, Sir!,* said to someone blocking an absurd proposal.

well breeched, *adj., Inf.*   **well heeled**

well cooked   **well done**
A description of how you would like your meat. The British use *well done* also.
It may be imagined that they would prefer *well cooked* in circumstances where it
was important to avoid giving the waiter the impression that he was being com-
plimented (see **well done!**).

well done!   *Inf.* **nice going!**
Inf. Expressing commendation. *Attaboy!* is not often heard in Britain.

Welliboots, *n. pl.*   **rubber boots**
Slang. Variant of **Wellingtons.**

wellies. See **Wellingtons.**

Wellingtons, *n. pl.*   **rubber boots**
See also **boot; snowboots; galoshes; Welliboots; wellies.**

well-off, *adj.*   **well-to-do**

Welsh dresser, *n.*   **hutch**

Wendy house, *n.*   **play house**
For children, that is. Named after the character in *Peter Pan.*

West Country   SEE COMMENT
This term applies to the southwestern counties, especially Cornwall and Devon.
Englishmen never come from *the west* or have relatives or go on vacations *out
west,* but rather in the *West Country,* and have a *West Country,* rather than a *western* accent. Same goes for *North Country,* but not the South or the East. They also
speak of the *North of England* and the *South of England* (and use *West-of-England*
as an adjective), but never the East of England.

West End   1. SEE COMMENT
                                                               2. *approx.* **Broadway**
1. The shopping and theater center of London.
2. Used figuratively (like *Broadway*) to mean 'the theater,' as in *the West End
season.* But the term is also used in a more general way to denote the way of life
characterized by theater-going, restaurant-dining, and parties. The term *Fringe
Theatre* bears the same relationship to *West End* as *Off Broadway* does to *Broadway,*
in the theater world.

wet, *adj.*   *Slang.* **dumb**
Slang. Both countries use the scornful terms *drip* and *wet behind the ears.* In Britain, *wet* is sometimes used as a noun, synonymous with *dumbbell.*

wet fish   **fresh fish**
Sign in a fish-and-chips luncheon place that also functions as a fish store: OPEN FOR WET FISH 9.00 A.M. TO 3.00 P.M. ONLY. For the periods rather than colons in expressions of time, see **Appendix I.D.4.**

whack, *n.*   **1.** *Slang.* **gob**
                                                              2. *Slang.* **stretch**
                                                              3. share
1. *Slang.* A big *whack* of something is a *gob* of it, i.e., a *large hunk.*
2. *Slang.* Prison term.
3. *Slang.* To *pay your whack* is to *chip in,* as when the class buys the teacher a Christmas gift. For British use of *chip in,* see **chip in.**

whacked   *Inf.* **done in; beat**
Inf. To be *whacked,* or *whacked to the wide,* is to be *beat, pooped,* etc. See **to the wide.**

whacko! *Interj.*   *Inf.* **great!**
An expression of great satisfaction and joy. Little heard nowadays.

whale, *n.*   *Slang.* **shark**
Slang. An American who is expert in a given field is said to be a *shark* at it. A Briton so skilled might be called a *whale on, at* or *for* it. There is an echo of the British usage in the expression *a whale of a* . . . Thus Jones is a *shark at math* in America, a *whale on, at* or *for maths* in Britain, and a *whale of a mathematician* anywhere. For prepositional usages, see **Appendix I.A.1.**

wharf, *n.*   **dock**
See **dock** for British use of the word.

what?   **no?**
Inf. At the end of a sentence expecting the answer *yes,* where Americans would say, *Isn't he?* or *Aren't they?* etc. Example: *"He's a clumsy chap, what?"* Now outdated.

what's the drill?   **what's the ticket?**
Inf. In the sense of 'what is to be done?' *Drill,* apart from its ordinary meaning in the services, is a military term signifying tactics worked out in advance so that everyone knows what to do in a given situation despite the stress of battle. From this background, *What's the drill?* developed the more general meaning 'What is the (proper) procedure?' For example: *What's the drill for getting reservations?* On leaving a restaurant where one has a charge account and usually leaves a 15 percent tip, one might get a nod from the maître d' who regularly murmurs, *The usual drill, sir?* meaning, *Do I charge this to your account, adding the usual 15 percent tip?*

wheeled chair   **wheelchair**
Usually called a **bath chair** or **invalid's chair** in Britain. See **Appendix I.A.3.**

wheelie bin, *n.*   **a garbage bin on wheels**

wheeze, *n.*   **idea; scheme**
Slang. Idea in the sense of *expedient,* as in, *It would be a good wheeze to get an early start.*

When-I, *n.*   SEE COMMENT
Inf. Many Britons, now retired, have spent much of their lives in far-flung places, usually in what used to be the Empire and is now what is left of the Common-wealth. They like to reminisce, and these oral memoirs almost invariably begin, *When I was in Singapore . . . , When I was in Bombay . . . , When I was in Hong Kong . . . ,* etc. A number of these retired gentlemen live in tax-haven parts of the United Kingdom, where the term *When-I* is in current use to describe members of this group fortunate enough to find an audience. An American expression with similar connotations is *Way back when . . .*

when it comes to the bone, *Inf.*   *Inf.* **when you come right down to it**

Where do we go for honey?   **Where do we go from here?**
Inf. What's the next step? (e.g., in an investigation). Its meaning varies with the objective. In bridge, for example, it would mean *How shall I go about playing this hand?*

where the shoe pinches, *Inf.*   **where the difficulty or hardship lies**

Whig, *n.*   SEE COMMENT
Inf. Historically, a member of the political party that was the predecessor of the Liberal Party. It was composed of the aristocratic oligarchy. It is used informally today as a label for one who has faith in progress. Cf. **Tory.**

whilst, *conj.*   **while**
Now used less frequently than *while* in Britain. See also **amongst.**

whin, *n.*   **thorny shrub**
Any prickly shrub.

whinge, *v.i.*   **whine**
Slang. To bewail one's fate, gripe, complain.

whip-round, *n.*   **1.** *Inf.* **passing the hat**
            2. quick tour
1. *Inf.* A collection taken up, usually, for the purpose of purchasing a gift for someone. Note sent around in a factory: 'Jennifer Whalen is getting married next Saturday. There will be a *whip-round* next week to buy her a wedding present.' Also used of a collection in a pub to pay for the next round of drinks.
2. *Inf.* A hurried sightseeing of a place like a museum, a palace, a city, a section of the country. *Let's have a whip-round of Parliament Square.* Or used verbally, as in *We whipped round Bloomsbury.*

whisky, *n.*   **Scotch**
Whisky (no *e* in Britain) is the term for *Scotch whiskey.* There is an *e* in Irish *whiskey. Whiskey,* in America, must be qualified, to distinguish between Scotch and rye, which, like bourbon, is little drunk in Britain. Bourbon, however, is

increasingly found in Britain's pubs and hotel bars. If you ask for 'whisky,' you get Scotch.

whispering cake. See under **schoolboy cake.**

Whit, *adj.*   **Pentecostal**
Whit is short for *Whitsun*, which means 'Whit Sunday,' the seventh Sunday after Easter. It used to be followed by a **bank holiday** known as *Whit Monday*, which has been transferred to an early summer date independent of the religious calendar.

whitebait, *n.*   SEE COMMENT
Very small silvery fish, usually sprat, sometimes young herring, fried whole in batter as caught, without being cleaned. Served in large quantities and extremely tasty when cooked well.

white feather   SEE COMMENT
Slang. During the Boer War, "patriotic" ladies presented white feathers to young men not in uniform. The taunt of cowardice was expected to shame them into enlisting. This practice was revived during World War I. To *show the white feather* means to 'betray cowardice.'

white fish   SEE COMMENT
Generic term for light-colored sea fish, for example, haddock and cod. In America it refers to any one of several distinct freshwater species, written as one word.

Whitehall, *n.*   *approx. Inf.* **Washington (the government)**
Inf. The government, so-called because many government offices are located on *Whitehall*, a London street between Trafalgar Square and the Houses of Parliament. See also **Number 10 Downing Street.**

White Paper. See **Paper.**

white spirit   **methyl alcohol**
Or denatured, for uses other than drinking.

white wax   **paraffin**
In Britain **paraffin** is the material Americans call *kerosene.*

wholemeal bread   **whole wheat bread**

W.I.   SEE COMMENT
Stands for *Women's Institute*, a national women's club with local branches doing charitable work.

wick, get on someone's. See **get on (someone's) wick.**

wicket, *n.*   *approx.* **situation**
Inf. In cricket, *wicket* has two distinct technical meanings:
1. A set of three vertical *stumps* on which rest two horizontal bails that the **batsman** defends against the **bowler.**
2. The space between the two sets of stumps and bails over which batsmen run to score points. See also **cricket; Test Match; sticky wicket.**

widdershins. See **withershins**

wide boy   *Slang.* **sharpie**
Slang. Shady character.

wide, to the. See **to the wide**

wife-battering   **domestic abuse**
The American euphemism covers **child-battering** and *child abuse* as well.

wifey, *n.*   SEE COMMENT
Sometimes *wifie,* occasionally *wify,* a term of endearment for one's wife; but often, especially in Scotland, it appears in the expression *old wifey,* used jocularly and the least bit pejoratively, to describe a somewhat addled woman beyond her first flush of youth.

Wigan, *n.*   SEE COMMENT
Inf. A small manufacturing town in South Lancashire, population about 80,000; used figuratively in music hall patter as a prototype of small city architectural horror and cultural provinciality. To *come from Wigan* is to be *a small town hick,* like one's aunt in Dubuque.

wigging, *n.*   *Inf.* **dressing-down**
Inf. To give somebody a *wigging* is to give that person *hell. Wig* is a transitive verb in both countries and means 'rebuke.' Its use as a verb is rare and it is usually found in the substantive form *wigging.*

Wimpy, *n.*   **hamburger**
Slang. From *Wimpy,* the character in the *Popeye* comic strip, who could eat an infinite number of them. *Wimpy-Bar* is the name of a British fast-food chain of hamburger joints, but the term *wimpy* long remained generic. It has, however, given way to *hamburger* and *beefburger.* And the restaurants have been overtaken by their fast-food American counterparts.

win, *v.i.*   **succeed; gain**
Inf. In the sense of 'making progress,' 'getting there.' A gardener engaged in an unequal combat with weeds might say, "We're winning." In a transitive British use, *win* can mean 'gain' in the sense of 'obtain': through advanced methods of mining, a company can *win* a larger amount of coal from the coal face.

wincey, *n.*   **type of cloth**
Consisting of a mixture of cotton and wool, or wool alone. *Winceyette* is a more finely woven version used for shirts, nightgowns, and so on.

wind, *v.t.*   **crank**
Once upon a time, a Briton still had to *wind* his car, though *crank* was the more usual term. See also **starting handle** and **Appendix II.E.**

wind. See **get the wind up; have the wind up; put the wind up; raise the wind.**

windcheater, *n.*   **windbreaker**
The American form is gaining currency among Britons.

winding point   **turning-around place**
(The first *i* in *winding* is short, as in WINDLASS.) This is a canal term and denotes
the place in a canal wide enough to permit a boat to turn around.

windle, *n.*   *approx.* **3 bushels**
An agricultural measure, used for grain. See also **Appendix II.C.1.h.**

window-gazing, *n.*   **window shopping**
The American term is now coming into general use in Britain.

windscreen, *n.*   **windshield**
See also **Appendix II.E.**

wind (someone) up, *v.t.*   *Inf.* **tease**
The sense is of annoying someone deliberately. *When he heard I was getting
engaged, he wound me up mercilessly.* May also be used as a noun: *Everything he said
about it was a wind-up.*

windy, *adj., Slang.*   **1. flatulent**
                                                                      2. *Inf.* **jumpy**

wine merchant's   **liquor store**
But the term suggests a more **posh** establishment than an **off-license.** Also seen
commonly as *wine merchant.*

wing, *n.*   **fender**
Automobile term; but **fender** in England is *bumper* in America. See **Appendix II.E.**

wing commander   **lieutenant colonel**
In the Royal Air Force. There are *wings* in the U.S. Air Force, too, but the commander of a U.S. wing is called a *lieutenant colonel.*

winker, *n..*   **directional signal; blinker**
Slang. Also *winking lamp.* On a truck, bus, or car, used to indicate an intended turn
left or right.

winkie, *n.*   **weenie**
Slang. Children's slang for *penis.*

winkle, *n.*   **periwinkle**
Or any edible sea snail.

winkle out, *v.t.*   *Slang.* **squeeze out**
Slang. In both senses: for instance, to *winkle out* information by pumping a weak
character previously sworn to secrecy, and to *winkle out* a rival by outmaneu-
vering him. To *winkle* one's way *out* of something is to *wriggle out* of it, and conversely to *winkle one's way in* is to *worm one's way in.*

winkle-pickers, *n. pl.*   SEE COMMENT
Slang. Pointed shoes: the Americans seem not to have coined any slang to describe
this sartorial extravagance.

win one's cap. See **blue,** *n.;* **cap.**

wipe (someone's) eye   *Inf.* **steal a march on (someone)**
Slang. And *get the better of him.*

wipe off a score, *Inf.*   *Inf.* **settle a score**

wireless, *n.*   **radio**
Going out of fashion now in favor of the American term.

wire netting, *n.*   **chicken wire**

witch. See **Appendix II.H.**

with compliments. See under **compliments slip.**

withershins, widdershins, *adv.*   **counterclockwise**
It is said to be bad luck to walk around a church *withershins,* in a direction contrary to the apparent course of the sun.

within cooee (coo-ee) of   **within hailing distance of**
Slang. Within easy reach of (something). *Cooee, coo-ee* or *cooey,* with the *ee* sound
long drawn out, is a very old Australian hailing cry, which spread to England, or
at least London, over a century ago as both noun and verb (to *cooee,* to *hail*). To be
within cooee of something, then, is to be not very far from it.

within kicking distance of, *Inf.*   **anywhere near**
For example, *I never got within kicking distance of that class of jockey.*

within the sound of Bow Bells. See **Bow Bells.**

with knobs on!   *Slang.* **in spades!**
Slang. The same to you with knobs on! is said, especially by youngsters, in retorting
to an insult. 'The same to you and more!'

with respect   **with all due respect**
In the sense of 'Excuse me, but . . .' Americans are careful to limit the degree of
respect in accordance with the qualifications of the individual addressed, while
the British diplomatically sidestep that issue by not modifying the noun, or go to
the other extreme by saying 'with all respect.' When an Englishman begins his
statement with the words *with respect,* you know very well that he disagrees with
you entirely and is prepared to demolish your position.

witness-box, *n.*   **witness stand**
In America one *takes the stand* or is *on the witness stand.* In Britain one *enters the
witness-box* and is *in* it rather than *on* it because literally, one is in an enclosed *box*
(save for the top).

witter, *v.*   **to talk at length about trivial matters**

wizard, *adj.*   *Inf.* **terrific**
Slang. Synonymous with **smashing.** World War II slang in the R.A.F., usually
applied to a successful mission.

wobbly, *n.*   *Inf.* **display of anger or nervousness**
Usually used in the phrase **throw a wobbly.**

wog, *n.*   SEE COMMENT
Slang. A *wog* originally was an offensive term for an 'Arab.' Now it has been extended to include Mediterranean types and other dark-skinned foreigners.

wonky, *adj., Slang.*   *Inf.* **wobbly**
Shaky, groggy. Also unreliable.

won't go   **won't work out**
Example: *Putting Jones in charge of that department just won't go.* Americans would be apt to say, *'Putting Jones in charge is a no-no.'*

wooden house   **frame house**

wooden spoon   *Inf.* **booby prize**
Inf. Derived from the custom, originated at Cambridge, of awarding a *wooden spoon* to the student who came out last in the mathematics **tripos,** a custom that spread to other universities and was applied in other fields.

wood-wool   **excelsior**
The British name has nothing to do with sheep. Shavings of pine and other woods were used for surgical dressing and for packing.

Woollies, *n.*   **F. W. Woolworth & Co.**
Inf. A joke name, like *Marks & Sparks* for Marks & Spencer; for a company no longer in business in America.

woolly, *n.*   **sweater**
Inf. A woolen garment, especially an undergarment. Americans do not speak of a *woolly* but do use *woolies* to mean 'heavy underwear.' See also **jumper; jersey.**

woolsack, *n.*   SEE COMMENT
Seat or divan in the House of Lords for the **Lord Chancellor.** It is stuffed with wool and covered with red baize.

word-spinning, *n.*   SEE COMMENT
Inf. There is no one precise sense in which this expression is used. *Spinning* connotes an endless production of words, and is usually used pejoratively to describe written or verbal verbosity. It can, however, mean 'word play'—using words in novel ways and combinations, in the manner of Joyce or Shakespeare.

workday, *n.*   **weekday**
Interchangeable in Britain with *weekday.* Where an American would use the expression *workday,* the British would say *working day.* It is worth noting that *weekdays* in rail and bus timetables sometimes includes *Saturday.*

workhouse, *n.*   **poorhouse**
Originally a charitable home for the poor, where the able-bodied were given work to do, and tramps could stay for the night in exchange for odd jobs about the place, this institution and the term itself are now obsolete, and the usual term is **almshouse** or *old people's home,* many of which have been converted into apart-

ments for senior citizens who pay nominal rent. See **almshouse**. In America a *workhouse* is a *jail* for petty criminals. No such meaning ever attached to the word in Britain.

working party, *n.*   *approx.* **committee**
An informal group, typically of middle-rank officials, i.e., civil servants, to whom a government official or body refers a question for study and report. Usually, as the term suggests, it is less grand than a committee set up by a **minister** or Parliament. Cf. **Royal Commission.**

works, *n. pl.*   1. **factory**
                                                                    2. **machinery**
                                                                    3. **operations**
A tractor *works* is a tractor *factory*. But the roadside sign ROAD WORKS means 'Men Working'; *sewage works* means a 'sewage system'; and a *spanner in the works* is a *monkey wrench in the machinery*. A *works convener* is a factory union official who *convenes* workers' meetings. Sometimes spelled *convenor*. *Ex-works* means 'from the factory.'

work to rule   **work by the book**
Describing what a union does when it takes advantage of the rule book technicalities to cause a slowdown. A slowdown is form of protest, like a *job action*, short of a strike. See **industrial action.**

work to time, *Inf.*   *Inf.* **watch the clock**

worrying, *adj.*   **troubling**

worth a good deal of anybody's time   *Inf.* **a good sort**
Inf. A highly complimentary description of a person. See also **have no time for.**

wotcher! See **watcher.**

wowser, *n.*   **fanatic puritan; spoilsport; teetotaler**
Slang. (Pronounced WOWZER.) A puritanical type, intent on improving the morals of the community. Also called a *Mrs. Grundy,* from which is derived the word *Grundyism,* synonymous with prudery. Originally Australian, wowser's meaning has tended to narrow to 'teetotaler.'

WRAC   **Women's Royal Army Corps**

wrangler, *n.*   **mathematics honor graduate**
Formerly, at Cambridge University, the Senior Wrangler was the top man. From a sense of *wrangle:* to 'dispute.'

wrap in cotton wool   **spoil; coddle**
Inf. **Cotton wool** is *absorbent cotton.* See also **live in cotton wool.**

wrap up!, *Slang.*   **shut up!**
For synonyms see **belt up!**

Wren, *n.*   **Wave**
Inf. A member of the Women's Royal Naval Service (WRNS).

wrinkly, *n.*   *Slang.* **an old person**

write (someone) down as   **consider (someone) to be**
Inf. As in, *When she heard his reaction to the strike, she wrote him down as another arm-chair reformer.* An approximate informal American equivalent is to *label (someone) as.*

writing down   **depreciation**
Tax terminology.

writ large   **1. (made) obvious**
                                                        2. on a grand scale
1. As in, *He saw the end of his dreams writ large in the new policy.*
2. As in, *His suggestion was no more than the old policy writ large.*

WRNS. See **Wren.**

(get hold of the) wrong end of the stick   **miss the point**
Inf. With the implication that one hasn't got the facts of the case. Sometimes *have* instead of *get,* and sometimes *hold of* is omitted.

(the) Yard SEE COMMENT
Inf. Scotland Yard.

year dot *Inf.* **year one**
Inf. Usually in the phrase, *Since the year dot,* meaning 'for ages.' See also **moons; donkey's years.**

years, donkey's. See **donkey's years.**

yield to redemption **yield to maturity**
Financial language, describing a bond or other financial instrument selling at a discount.

yell pen and ink *Slang.* **yell blue murder**
Slang. Pen and ink is cockney rhyming slang (see **Appendix II.G.3.**) for *stink.* To *yell pen and ink* is to *raise a stink, create an awful fuss, go into hysterics* and indulge in similar types of unpleasant activities.

yeoman, *n.* **1. small farmer**
2. SEE COMMENT
3. SEE COMMENT
1. Who cultivates his own land.
2. Member of the *yeomanry,* a volunteer cavalry force.
3. *Beefeater; informal* for *yeoman of the guard* (see **beefeater**).
As an adjective, *yeoman* is seen almost exclusively in *'yeoman service,'* meaning 'useful help in need.'

yobbo, *n.* *Slang.* **lout; bum**
Slang. An extension of *yob,* **back slang** for *boy.*

yonks **ages**
Slang. A long time, as in *I haven't seen her for yonks.* Much more expressive in Britain than in the United States.

Yorkshire pudding SEE COMMENT
A dish of pancake-like batter baked in muffin tins or a roasting pan till crisp and puffy. Traditional accompaniment for roast beef, and often cooked in the fat (**dripping**) produced by the meat.

Z

Z-car, *n.*   police car
(Pronounced, of course, ZED-CAR.) See also **jam sandwich; panda car.**

zebra crossing   pedestrian crossing
A passage across the road, marked with zebra-like stripes. The *e* is either long
or short. Once a pedestrian sets foot on a *zebra,* traffic must stop to let him or
her cross. See also **pelican crossing** and **belisha beacon.**

zed, *n.*   letter z

Zimmer frame, *n.*   walker
The British term is a trademark that, like **Hoover,** has been applied generically to
any similar piece of equipment.

zip, *n.*   zipper
Also given as *zip-fastener.*

zizz, *n., v.i., Slang.*   *Slang.* **snooze**
Or *catch some Z's.*

APPENDICES

[See Contents, page vii, for outline]

GENERAL DIFFERENCES BETWEEN BRITISH AND AMERICAN ENGLISH

A. Syntax

1. There are many differences between British and American use of prepositions. This is especially true of the prepositions *in* and *on*. Britons live *in* rather than *on* such and such a street (although they do live *on* a road). In Britain animals are *on* heat rather than *in* heat. The British say that predictable events are *on* the cards rather than *in* the cards. Athletes in Britain are *on* form rather than *in* form. Things that are on the way, in a stage of development, are described in Britain as *on* train as well as *in* train.

Different from is heard in Britain but *different to* is more commonly heard, and *other to*, although not frequently met with, is sometimes used where Americans would say *other than*. This usage, incidentally, in both countries may have arisen from the mistaken belief that the ending *-er* in *other* indicated a comparative, and thus gave rise to the apparent solecism *different than*.

Nervous *of* (doing something) for nervous *about*, the advantage *of* for the advantage *over*, an increase *on* rather than an increase *over*, frontage *to* instead of frontage *on*, *by* auction for *at* auction, membership *of* for membership *in* (but one is a member *of*, rather than a member *in* an organization in America as well as Britain), dry *off* for dry *out*, chat *to* for chat *with*, cater *for* rather than cater *to* (in the sense of 'kowtow' or 'pander to'), but sit *to* (in the sense of 'pose') rather than sit *for*, snowed *up* for snowed *in*, haven't seen him *in* rather than *for* six months, Monday *to* Friday (inclusive) for Monday *through* Friday, a week *on* Tuesday (or Tuesday week) instead of a week *from* Tuesday, mad or crazy *on* rather than *about*, *in* the circumstances rather than *under* them, visit *of* London for visit *to* London, infatuated *by*, not *with*, audience *of* the Pope rather than *with* him, the laugh *of* him for the laugh *on* him, liability *to*, not *for* (e.g.) income tax, special charges, etc., a study *of* rather than *in* (e.g.) courage (where *study* is used in the sense of *striking example*), something *on* rather than *along* those lines—these are all further examples. The verb *to notify* presents a special situation, involving something more than a difference in preposition usage. Americans notify someone *of* something. In Britain, one can notify something *to* someone. The subject matter, rather than the person notified, becomes the object of *notify*, thus: 'Please notify any change of address to your local post office.' Some authorities say this is substandard in Britain. It is unthinkable in American English.

2. Usage also differs between the two countries in the matter of the definite article. Sometimes the British leave the article out where Americans put it in. Thus, in Britain, you are *in hospital* or go *to hospital;* and if things are against you, you are *down at heel.* Americans *put on the dog;* Britons *put on dog* (or *put on side*). Sometimes they put it in where we leave it out. Americans, in formal documents, use the term *said* (without the article) as well as *the said* meaning 'aforementioned,' but in Britain the article is mandatory. Thus, a Briton will have *the gift of the gab,* or will visit a shop on *the High Street;* and he or she will call an unidentified person *someone or the other.* **Ministers** *(cabinet members)* are referred to, for example, as *The Foreign Secretary, Lord, Sir, or Mr So-and-so,* or *The American Secretary of State, Mr So-and-So;* never (as in America) *Foreign Minister Lord, Sir or Mr So-and-So* or *Secretary of State So-and-So,* without benefit of the definite article. Sometimes the British use a definite article when we are content with the indefinite one. Thus, Britons go on *the* spree instead of on *a* spree, take *the* rise out of, not get *a* rise out of, someone, and something will cost forty pounds the painting rather than forty pounds a painting. They use both a *hell of a time* and *the hell of a time,* either of which can mean a 'terribly good time' or a 'terribly bad time,' depending on the context and the emphasis: *a hell of a time* usually means a 'rough time' and *the hell of a time* generally means a 'good time.' On occasion the *the* is not omitted but replaced by a possessive pronoun. Thus, *half his time he doesn't know what he is doing.* There is one instance, at least, where the British use the indefinite article in a way that seems peculiar to Americans. Both countries use the term *nonsense* in the same way, but the British also use the expression *a nonsense* in the sense of an 'absurdity,' i.e., a 'piece of absurd behavior,' a *fiasco,* a *muddle,* a *snafu.*

3. The British tend to lengthen the first word of many compound nouns, particularly by adding the ending *-ing.* Thus sail*ing*-boat, row*ing*-boat, dial*ing*-code or tone, bank*ing* account, wash*ing* day, wash*ing*-basin, danc*ing*-hall, spark*ing*-plug, market*ing* research. This happens occasionally to single nouns as well: turn*ing* for *turn,* and part*ing* for a *part* in your hair. Other examples are found in departmental store, cook*ery* book, and high*ly*-strung. A similar practice is the adding of -'s in such Briticisms as barber's shop, tailor's shop, doll's house (any little girl's, not only the Ibsen variety), etc. *Innings* has an *-s* in the singular as well as the plural. There is a tendency often to pluralize, as in brains trust, overhead*s*, removal*s* (the moving business), insurance*s* (as in 'Insurance*s* Arranged' on insurance brokers' letterheads). An *-ed* is often added, as in the stocking*ed* feet, ice*d* water, close*d* company for *close corporation* (in this case the British prefer the participial adjective to the noun phrase), wheel*ed* chair, twin-bedd*ed* room, wing*ed* collar, but *two-room flat* (note absence of *-ed* in *room*), the distinction here being that the *-ed* is used to indicate 'furnished with' but omitted where the concept is 'consisting of.' In the field of music, the British don't sharp and flat notes: they sharp*en* and flatt*en* them; and a music box is a music*al* box. Note, too, the British insistence on adding an object in certain expressions where the American usage is content with the verb alone: to *move house,* to *shower oneself,* although the object of the verb is occasionally omitted. Also note *pour with rain.* However, watch out: sometimes *they* do the shortening, as in *swing door* for *swinging-door, sunk garden* for *sunken garden, spring-clean* for spring *cleaning, long-play* for *long-playing* (record), *punch-bag* for *punching bag, drive* for *driveway.*

4. A singular noun that describes an institution like a university or a political body is followed by a verb in the third person singular in America, third person plural in Britain. Thus, Harvard *plays* Yale, but Oxford *play* Cambridge; the American cabinet *meets,* the British cabinet *meet;* the American public *approves,* the British public *approve.* A headline in the *Daily Telegraph* (London) of August 15,

1981, about England's rout of the Australian side in the fifth **Test Match,** reads: *Australia Crash Again as England Seize Control.*

On the subject of singular nouns followed by plural verbs, see the list in Marckwardt's *American English* (Oxford University Press, New York, 1958), Chapter 4, p. 77. He says that an American would be "downright startled, to see a sports headline reading 'JESUS ROW TO EASY VICTORY.'" (*Jesus* is the name of an Oxford college, and there is a *Jesus* at Cambridge as well). The British often use *look like* followed by a gerund rather than *look as if* or *look as though* followed by a subject and verb: *He never looked like being troubled* rather than . . . *as if he were in trouble,* or, *He looks like being successful in whatever he tries* instead of *He looks as if he would be successful* . . . *One another* incorrectly takes the place of *each other* in Britain when only two persons or things are involved: *Britain and America should treat one another as members of one family.*

5. *Who* has become an acceptable British informal form of *whom.* On the other hand the objective case is used, informally but almost universally, for predicate nominative pronouns as in, *It's me; She's taller than him,* usages popular in America only in less educated circles. But getting back to *who,* the British often use it as a relative pronoun where Americans would use *which* or *that: the companies who pay well, the colleges who admit women.*

B. Pronunciation

1. The spoken language in London and other parts of Britain is often difficult for Americans. There is the matter of intonation generally, and there is a problem with vowels (the broad *a* and the short *o,* which is somewhere between the *o*'s in NOT and NOTE) and the diphthongs AE and OE, which are pronounced like a long E (as in EQUAL) in Britain and a short E (as in GET) in America. Thus, the diphthongs in *oecumenical* and *oedema,* which are variants of *ecumenical* and *edema* in American English spelling, are pronounced EE in Britain and EH in America. The same is true with the second syllable of *anaesthetist* and names like *Aeschylus* and *Aesculapius,* in which the diphthong is not shortened in American spelling, as in the Greek-derived type of word mentioned above. The *time of day* becomes TOYM OF DIE in England's Kent and Sussex; *roundabout* (a 'traffic circle' or 'merry-go-round') comes out RAYNDA-BAYT in those counties; and so it goes. In an amusing article ("Gaffes in Gilead," *The New York Times,* May 12, 1971), Gertrude M. Miller, a BBC pronunciation specialist, listed some horrendous examples, some of which are:

Place-Names

Written:	Pronounced:
Prinknash	PRINNIJ
Culzean	K'LANE
Caius (a Cambridge college)	KEEZ
Magdalen (an Oxford college)	MAWDLIN
Magdalene (a Cambridge college)	MAWDLIN
Belvoir	BEEVER
Wemyss	WEEMZ
Kirkcudbright	KIR-KOO'-BRI
Dalziel	DEE-ELL'

Some notable omissions are:

Written:	Pronounced:
Wrotham	ROOT'M (OO as in BOOT)
Lympne	LIMM

Derby	DARBY
Hertford	HARFORD
Berkshire	BARKSHUH
Thames	TEMZ
Pall Mall	PELL MELL or PAL MAL
Marylebone	MARL'B'N
Beauchamp	BEECH'M
Warwick	WORRICK
Marlborough	MAWL'-BRUH

Family Names

Written:	Pronounced:
Ruthven	RIV'N
Leveson-Gower	LOOS-N-GOR
Menzies	MING-ISS or MINJIES
Cholmondeley	CHUMLEY
St. John	SIN-J'N
Featherstonehaugh	FANSHAW
Cokes	COOKS
Mainwaring	MANNERING
Home	HUME (HYUME)

Note: The Australian statesman and the London stationer's are pronounced *Menzies* as spelled; the -*ng*- in *Mingiss* is sounded as in *singer*.

Caution: To the surprise of some Americans, there are place names that are pronounced the way they are spelled, like Hampstead (pronounced HAMPSTED, not HEMPSTID); Berkhamstead (pronounced BURKHAM'-STED not BURK'-IMSTID); Cirencester (pronounced SIRENSESTER, not half-swallowed like *Worcester, Gloucester*, etc.).

A special note on a few representative county abbreviations (there are many more, and county names are occasionally changed as counties are realigned, eliminated, merged, and renamed for purposes of greater administrative efficiency):

Bucks.	Buckinghamshire
Hants.	Hampshire
Lancs.	Lancashire
Wilts.	Wiltshire

These are Standard English if so written (and analogous to abbreviated American state names), and informal when so pronounced. Bucks., Hants., etc., in the spoken language are as confusing to Americans as Mass. is to a Briton.

For a full treatment of this subject, see the *BBC Pronouncing Dictionary of British Names* (Oxford University Press, Ely House, London, 1971), by G. M. Miller. Walter Henry Nelson, in Chapter V of his admirable *The Londoners* (Hutchinson & Co. Ltd., London, 1975) has some interesting things to say abut the mysteries of British pronunciation of their place names, and refers to Alistair Morrison's most amusing treatment of the pronunciation eccentricities of the denizens or habitués of London's chic West End, in *Fraffly Well Spoken* (Wolfe Publishing Ltd., London, 1968), where Berkeley Square (normally pronounced BARKLY, or more exactly, BARKLIH) becomes BOGGLEY and the British Empire comes out BRISHEMPAH. But these elisions and truncations are not confined to the West End, as any American making a telephone call through a British operator can testify after unraveling the arcana of *trangneckchew*, the solicitous operator's oft-repeated assurance that she is *trying-to-connect-you*.

2. Not only place and family names present difficulty. Many common nouns are normally accented or pronounced differently from the usual American way. Here are a few:

Accent only: *coroll'ary, labo'ratory, metall'-urgy, contro'versy* (the last two also as in America).

Written:	Pronounced:
ate	ETT
clerk	CLARK
figure	FIGGER
herb	sounding the H
lieutenant	LEFTENANT (army); LEHTENANT (navy)
missile	second i rhymes with EYE
privacy	i as in PRIVY
schedule	SHEDULE
solder	sounding the 1
suggest	SUJJEST
vitamin	i as in BIT

Ate, privacy and *vitamin* are also, though not often, pronounced the American way.

The British tend to accent the first syllable of certain words of French origin, where American speech normally refrains from doing so: e.g., *ballet, brochure, café, garage, valet,* and the name *Maurice*. In words of three syllables, like consommé and résumé, they often offend American ears by accenting the *second* syllable: CON SOMM'EE, RAY ZOOM' EE! Differences in the pronunciation of Latin are another matter and of insufficient general interest to go into here. For enlightening discussion of the general area of pronunciation differences, see Marckwardt, *American English* (Oxford University Press, New York, 1958), Chapter 4, pp. 69–75, and Strevens, *British and American English* (Collier-Macmillan Publishers, London, 1972), Chapter 6.

C. Spoken Usage and Figures of Speech

1. Certain usages in the spoken language are foreign to Americans. The telephone rings and the Briton may ask, *Who is that?* never, *Who's this?* Or he may ask, *Is that* (not *this*) *Bob Cox?* An example of this usage is seen in *An Improbable Fiction,* by Sara Woods (Holt, Rinehart & Winston, N.Y. 1971). The English amateur detective says: *". . . It seemed obvious that the [telephone]* **caller** *was an American . . . I never knew an Englishman to say, 'Is this Miss Edison speaking?'"* An Englishman would have used *that,* not *this.* Another British habit is the use of a question to make a statement. Thus, a man who happens to be illiterate, having ignored a printed notice, is called to account and asks (says, really), *Now, I can't read, can I?* Or Little Johnny, signaled by his impatient mother to hurry home, asks (says, really), *I'm coming home, aren't I?* Or a person who has slept through an incident he might have observed if awake, asked about it by a police officer, replies, *Now, I was kipping [napping], wasn't I?* None of these so-called questions implies that the listener knows the answer, nor does the speaker expect one. They are simply statements put in this form for emphasis. And the interrogative form is often used for purposes of delicacy, to underplay a statement: *You've come a long way, haven't you? It's not too difficult, is it?* And often in a shop the salesperson (*shop assistant*), with some knitting of brows, itemizes and tots up your bill, usually mumbling the words and figures with hardly more than a slight movement of lips, and then turns to you brightly and announces the result with eyes opened wide and a rising intonation, as though indicating surprise and apology for the unpleasant tidings.

2. *Do* and *done* keep popping up in Britain in situations where they would be omitted in America. If you ask a British friend whether he thinks Charles has mailed your letters and he is not sure, he will answer, *He may have done.* An American would have said, *He may have.* If you said to a Briton: *Walking two miles before breakfast makes a fellow feel good,* he might reply, *Judging from your rosy cheeks, it must do.* An American would have left out the *do.*

3. American usage tends to be more literal. We say *baby carriage* and the British say *pram* (an abbreviation of *perambulator*). The British would understand *baby carriage* but no recently arrived American would know what a pram was. The same would apply to *cleaning woman* and *char,* or *ball-point pen* and *biro.* There is no hard and fast rule. In general, American expressions are easier for Britons than the other way around. On the other hand, British usage is sometimes more direct: *Cripples' Crossing* (a street sign), where Americans might have preferred the gentler term *Disabled; Limb Fitting Centre* (rather than, perhaps, *Prosthetic Devices?*); *Royal Hospital and Home for Incurables* (would Americans resort to a euphemism like *Chronic?*); *Hospital for Sick Children* (Americans would call it *Children's Hospital,* or, less simply, *Pediatric Hospital); a London charity that sells Christmas cards painted by armless artists, and calls itself, in words sparse but graphic, *Mouth and Foot Painting Artists, Ltd.*

4. Inherent in many units of measure are figurative connotations which exist alongside their scientific functions. Despite the adoption of the metric system in the English-speaking countries, to their citizens things will inch, not centimeter, along; a miss will remain as good as a mile, not 1.609 kilometers; a ton of something will create an image which its metric equivalent won't; 90°F will be a sizzler, while 32.2°C won't alarm anyone. A similar British-American image dichotomy exists in the case of some units. No matter how often an American tells himself a stone (applied to human beings) is 14 lbs., 15 stone does not evoke for him the image of a fat person; and even *a few hundred yards yonder* creates only a fuzzy notion compared with *about a quarter of a mile down the road.* (See also **Appendix II.C.**)

5. In money matters, before decimalization, percentages were often expressed in terms of so-and-so many *shillings in the pound.* Income-tax rates were always so expressed. Since there were 20 shillings to a pound, *40 percent* would be expressed as *8 shillings in the pound.* Although old shillings are no longer circulating, this usage will undoubtedly linger for a time (See also **Appendix II.A.**)

6. For the subleties of variations in the vocabulary of spoken and written British English based on class distinctions, the reader is referred to "U and Non-U, an Essay in Sociological Linguistics," by Prof. Alan S. C. Ross, of Birmingham University (England), which appeared in *Noblesse Oblige,* a collection of articles edited by Nancy Mitford (Hamish Hamilton, London, 1956; Penguin Books Ltd., 1959). His article was commented on by Miss Mitford in *Encounter,* in a piece entitled "The English Aristocracy." She in turn was answered, in *Encounter,* by Evelyn Waugh in "an Open Letter to the Honorable Mrs. Peter Rodd (Nancy Mitford) On a Very Serious Subject." The Mitford and Waugh articles, too, are included in *Noblesse Oblige.* All these comments gave currency to the concept of U and Non-U as linguistic categories constituting "class-indicators." They were followed by Ross's *What are U?* (André Deutsch, Ltd., London, 1969) and *U and Non-U Revisited,* a collection of essays by various authors, edited by Richard Buckle (Debrett's Peerage, Ltd., London, 1978).

D. Punctuation and Style

1. Punctuation in the two countries differs in many respects. The British use the hyphen more frequently than the Americans. *No-one* is a conspicuous case in point, although the *Concise Oxford Dictionary* recommends *no one*. *Loop-hole* and *mast-head* are other examples of this practice. Fowler wrote in 1926, "In America they are less squeamish than we are, and do not shrink from such forms as *coattails* and *aftereffects*." The British still shrink, though *loophole* is now permissible.

2. Parentheses, which they call *brackets* or *round brackets*, are in evidence in company names to designate a particular region or field of activity, like *E.W. Ratcliffe (Timer Merchants) Ltd.; Samuel Thompson (Manchester) Ltd*. This is a useful practice in putting the public on notice and avoiding confusion.

3. The British often use single quotation marks (*inverted commas*) outside the quoted matter and double ones inside; thus, John said, 'Henry told me he had heard Joseph say, "I won't go to school today" '. American usage puts the period (which the British call *full stop*), comma or other mark inside the final quotation mark: John said, "I told him not to worry," and then left. The comma would follow the final quotation mark in Britain: ". . . not to worry", and then left.

4. In telling time, the period, rather than the colon, is used between the hour numeral and the minutes: 6.30 rather than 6:30. When the minutes involved are less than ten, the zero before the digit is omitted: 9.5 rather than 9.05. And while we are speaking of expressions of time, it might be well to note the usage, on invitations, of expressions like *6.30 for 7.15*, which means "Dinner will be served at about 7.15, but come as soon as you can after 6.30 for sherry or cocktails." It is good form to arrive any time between 6.30 and just before 7.15.

5. When dates are expressed in figures, the British follow the European method of day, month, year: thus, 10/27/00 becomes 27/10/00. *Next* often follows the name of the day in the expression of future time, as in, *See you Monday next*. In America it would be *next Monday*.

6. The period is usually omitted in *Mr, Mrs, Messrs, Dr*, but used in such abbreviations as *Prof., Rev., Hon.*, the rule appearing to be to use it where the abbreviation is simply a shortening of the word but to leave it out where the abbreviation consists of omitting letters from the middle of the word, as in *M(iste)r, D(octo)r*. However, it does appear in *St.*, the abbreviation of *Saint*.

7. *Mr* is the title of the common man in both countries. *Mr*, not *Dr*, is also the title of a surgeon or dentist, although Jones, your family physician, is *Dr* Jones. Correspondence that would be addressed to *Mr*. John Smith in America is usually addressed to John Smith, *Esq*. (with a period) in Britain, a quaint practice followed in America only in communications between lawyers. *Junior* (abbreviated to *Jr*.) and *II, III, IV*, etc. following the names of persons in line of descent all bearing the same name are omitted in Britain. One would not address a letter to William A. Jones, Jr., or Samuel B. Smith II, as the case might be. In ordinary speech, if one were to mention a forthcoming visit to Fred Brown (there being a father and son of the same name), the listener might ask, "Senior or Junior?" But in correspondence, or in a formal listing such as a telephone directory, membership list and the like, the *Jr*. and Roman numerals are omitted.

8. In the names of rivers, the British put the word *River* first, the Americans last: *the River Thames*, the *Mississippi River*. The word *River* can of course be omitted in both countries.

9. Abbreviations are common in informal British correspondence. Some, but not all, have been included in the alphabetical listing. Some common ones are:

circs.	circumstances
hosp.	hospital
op.	operation
prb.	probably
s.a.e.	self-addressed envelope
s.a.p.	soon as possible
p.t.o.	please turn (the page) over
v.	very
w.	with
w/e	weekend

People's names are often abbreviated. A Briton in a hurry might write you that M. had been down for the w/e w. N. and would prb. return the favour soon, unless the circs. changed because N. had to go into hosp. for a v. minor op. s.a.p.

For the abbreviation of county names, see **Appendix I.B.1.**

E. Spelling

Spelling differences between the two countries fall into two main categories: word formation groups and individual words. Typical word ending peculiarities (sometimes only preferences) occur in the *-our* group *(colour, honour)*, the *-re* group *(centre, theatre)*; the *-ise* words *(criticise, agonise;* though *-ize* would now appear to be preferred); certain conjugated forms *(travelled, travelling)* or derived forms *(traveller, jeweller)* where the British double consonants; *-xion* words *(connexion* [still used, though *connection* is now preferred], *inflexion,* but *confection, inspection); -ce* words *(defence, pretence; licence* and *practice* as nouns, but *license* and *practise* preferred as verbs); words of Greek derivation containing the diphthongs *ae* or *oe,* from which Americans usually drop the *a* or *o,* like *aetiology, anaesthesia, anaemia, oedema, oenology, oesophagus.* As to the treatment of diphthongs in words derived from the Greek, note the letter that appeared in *The Times* (London) of July 21, 1986:

Unkind Cut
From Dr P. Furniss
Sir, What chance of survival has the diphthong when even you cannot spell "Caesarean" (leading article, July 11)? I note that you also prefer medi*e*val to medi*a*eval.

As an anaesthetist I must declare a partisan interest in the matter, but I am sure Aesculapius would add his support to my plea.

Sir, I beg you to protect the disappearing diphthong; it is an endangered English species!
Yours faithfully,
P. FURNISS.
10 Mile End Road, Norwich.
July 12.

Some common individual differences are found in *cheque* (check), *gaol* (jail), *kerb, pyjamas, storey* (meaning 'floor' of a building), *tyre, aluminium, grey, whisky* (but note *Irish whiskey*—see entry under **whisky**), *manoeuvre,* and again in the consonant-doubling department, *waggon, carburettor* (or *carburetter*), and others.

APPENDIX II
GLOSSARIES
AND TABLES

A. Currency

Up to August 1, 1969, British coins in regular use were the halfpenny (pronounced HAY'PNY), penny, threepence (pronounced THRUH PNY, THRUPPENNY, THRUPPENCE, sometimes THREPPENCE; sometimes called THREPPENNY BIT), sixpence (nicknamed *tanner*, sometimes *bender*), shilling, florin (2 shillings), and half-crown ($2^1/_2$ shillings). Twenty shillings made a pound; 12 pence (plural of *penny*) made a shilling. Thus there were 240 pence in a pound.

The farthing ($^1/_4$ penny) was discontinued years ago; the halfpenny was demonetized on August 1, 1969; the half-crown on January 1, 1970. The *guinea* existed only as a convenient way of denoting 21 shillings, i.e., one pound, one shilling. The symbol for pound is £, placed before the number, like the dollar sign; for shilling (or shillings) it was *s.*, for penny or pence *d.*; but there was also the oblique line and dash meaning *shilling(s)* written after the number; thus: 15/- meant 15 shillings. If there were pence as well, the dash was omitted; thus 15/9, orally *fifteen and nine,* meant 15 shillings and 9 pence.

But on February 15, 1971, the British decimalized their currency, eliminating shillings as such, leaving only pounds and pence (now abbreviated to *p*), with 100 new pence to the pound. What used to be a shilling is now 5 new pence, a florin is now 10 new pence, and so on. (The *new* soon began to be dropped.) The old shillings and 2-shilling pieces (the same sizes as the new 5- and 10-pence pieces but different designs) have become collectors' items. What was one pound two shillings (£1-2-0) is now written £1.10. With the coming of the 100-pence pound, it became the fancy of some merchants, after adding up a column, to announce the total in terms of pence alone; thus: "111 pence" for £1.11 or "342, please," for £3.42. This custom was undoubtedly a hangover from the practice, in the old shilling days, of stating prices in shillings even when they exceeded a pound; thus: 102/6 or 200 s. Apparently, stating the price in smaller units was thought to make things sound cheaper.

On decimalization day ("D-Day") the remaining old coins all became a thing of the past . . . or did they? Although the mint thereafter turned out only the new halfpennies (now discontinued), pennies and 2, 5, 10, and 50 pence pieces, lo! the old pennies, threepences, and sixpences were nevertheless at first allowed to circulate alongside the new coins for a year and a half (the old pennies and threepences were later excommunicated and the sixpences "restyled" $2^1/_2$ p, as of September 1, 1971), either because they went into the old telephone and vending machine coin slots, or out of sentimental attachment to relics of the old regime, or because the British cannot resist the attraction for introducing into almost any situation a bit of amiably maddening confusion or something to grumble about.

With sixpence temporarily worth less than threepence, there was bound to be a fair amount of consternation, indignation, error, high amusement, cries in

Parliament of "Resign!," and general hilarity. Despite all this streamlining, however, things will go on not being worth a farthing and ladies will go on spending a penny albeit a new one. *Pee* is now the familiar pronunciation of *p (penny)*, and 2 *pee* and 3 *pee* have replaced the old *tuppence* and *thruppence*.

B. Financial Terms

For the benefit of those who follow the financial news, *stocks* are called *shares* in Britain, and *stocks* in Britain are *government bonds*. Stock prices are quoted in penny denominations, as are increases, decreases, averages, and the like. Thus, a stock quoted at 150 would be selling at 150 *pence*, or roughly around $2.25 per share (as of June, 2000). A *bonus issue* or *share* is a stock dividend. Preferred stock is called *preference shares*. *Scrip* means a *temporary stock certificate*, not a certificate for a fraction of a share, as in America.

C. Units of Measure
Note: These terms are largely of historical interest, as decimilization and metrification have brought the UK into line with the rest of Europe. But *pint, pound,* and *stone* are still widely used in everyday speech, if more as a reflection of history than of contemporary practice.

1. Dry Measure

a. Barrel
A *barrel* is a varying unit of weight (or other quantitative measure). It depends on what it is a *barrel* of. It works this way:

Commodity	Weight in lbs.
soft soap	256
butter	224
beef	200
flour	196
gunpowder	100

Be careful: Applied to beer and tar, *barrel* is a unit of volume expressed in gallons and works this way:

Commodity	No. of gals.
beer	36
tar	$26^1/_2$

And remember, a *gallon* is an *Imperial gallon*, equal to approximately 120 per cent of an American gallon (120.095 per cent is a little closer). And to make things just a bit less certain, a *barrel* of fish is *500 fish!* For other examples of the British determination to keep things flexible, or doggedly inconsistent, see **e** and **f** below.

b. Hundredweight
112 pounds in Britain; 100 pounds in America.

c. Keel
Weight of coal that can be carried on a *keel*, and still used as a wholesale coal measure. Since a British ton is 2240 lbs. and a British cwt. (hundredweight) is 112 lbs., a *keel* is, in American terms, 47,488 lbs., or a sliver under $23^{3/4}$ tons, all of which is about to become totally immaterial under the fast-encroaching metric system.

d. Quart
1.20095 American quarts. See also **2.a** below.

e. Score
i. 20 or 21 lbs, in weighing pigs or oxen. If you should happen to be in the British countryside and want to buy some pigs, don't think £2.99 a *score* is the bargain it seems: *score* doesn't mean 'twenty' in this usage. It is a unit of weight, regional, and applies especially to pig and cattle raising.
ii. 20 to 26 tubs in dispensing coal. *Tub*, incidentally, in various trades (butter, grain, tea, etc.) is a flexible unit of measure, depending on the commodity. This flexibility seems peculiarly British.

f. Stone
Generally, 14 lbs. British bathroom scales, as well as those in railroad stations and similar public places, are calibrated in *stones*, *half-stones*, and *pounds*, but Americans find it rather difficult to translate *stones* into *pounds* because 14 is a hard number to handle in mental arithmetic. To make things worse, a *stone* of meat or fish is 8 lbs., a stone of cheese is 16 lbs., etc. Eight 14-lb. stones make a *hundredweight*, which is 112 lbs. in Britain (more logically, 100 lbs. in America). Perhaps a table of terms used in the trade would help, showing the meaning of *stone* applied to various commodities.

Commodity	Weight in lbs.
hemp	32
cheese	16
potatoes	14
iron	14
wool	14*
meat	8
fish	8
glass	5

All of this is becoming history with Britain's adoption of the metric system.

g. Ton
2,240 lbs.; an American ton contains 2,000 lbs. Note that a British hundredweight contains 112 lbs. (not 100) so that 20 of them make up a British ton. It may be interesting to note that the Americans adopted British weights and measures in the early years, and then the British upped their "Imperial" standards in the early 1800s. See also **gallon (2.a,** below).

h. Windle
Approximately 3 bushels. An agricultural measure, used for grain.

2. Liquid Measure

a. Gallon
The standard British gallon is the *Imperial gallon*, equal to 277.420 cubic inches. The standard U.S. gallon is the old British *wine gallon*, equal to 231 cubic inches. Thus, the British gallon equals 1.20095, or almost exactly $1^1/_5$ American gallons. This ratio follows through in liquid measure terms used in both countries for parts of a gallon, to wit: quarter ($^1/_4$ gallon); pint ($^1/_8$ gallon); gill ($^1/_{32}$ gallon except that a gill is not uniform in all parts of Britain). And as to terms of dry measure, look out for the British quart, which equals 1.0320, rather than 1.20095, American dry quarts.

---

*-Caution! 14 lbs. in sales to outsiders, but 15 lbs. in the case of sales to other growers or dealers.

b. Gill
(The *g* is soft). When *gill* is used as a liquid measure in Britain, it usually means $1/4$ pint (i.e., $1/4$ of $1/8$ of an *Imperial gallon*) and is therefore 1.2 times as large as an American *gill;* but be careful, because in some parts of Britain it means $1/2$ an *Imperial pint,* or exactly twice as much as in other parts of Britain.

c. Pint. See under **gallon,** above. See also **pint** under alphabetical listing.

d. Quart. See under **gallon,** above.

D. Numbers

Billion
One followed by twelve zeros (called *noughts* or *ciphers* in Britain). An American *billion* is only *one thousand million* (1,000,000,000), which is called a *thousand million* or a *milliard* in Britain. There are wholly different nomenclature systems in the two countries for numbers big enough to be stated in powers of a million. This is important to mathematicians, astronomers, and astronauts, for whose benefit the following partial table is submitted:

English	American	Number	Formation
million	million	1,000,000	1 with 6 zeros
milliard	billion	1,000,000,000	1 " 9 "
billion	trillion	$1,000,000^2$	1 " 12 "
thousand billion	quadrillion	$1,000 \times 1,000,000^2$	1 " 15 "
trillion	quintillion	$1,000,000^3$	1 " 18 "
thousand trillion	sextillion	$1,000 \times 1,000,000^3$	1 " 21 "
quadrillion	septillion	$1,000,000^4$	1 " 24 "
thousand quadrillion	octillion	$1,000 \times 1,000,000^4$	1 " 27 "
quintillion	nonillion	$1,000,000^5$	1 " 30 "
thousand quintillion	decillion—	$1,000 \times 1,000,000^5$	1 " 33 "
sextillion (sexillion)		$1,000,000^6$	1 " 36 "
septillion		$1,000,000^7$	1 " 42 "
octillion		$1,000,000^8$	1 " 48 "
nonillion		$1,000,000^9$	1 " 54 "
decillion		$1,000,000^{10}$	1 " 60 "
centillion		$1,000,000^{100}$	1 " 600 "

Warning note: see the following from *The Times* (London) of November 14, 1974:

How the Treasury Confuses Billions
The Treasury seems to be trying to make a significant change in the English language in a footnote to the Chancellor's Budget speech.

This defines the word *billion* as one thousand million—though since the philosopher John Locke first used the word in the late 17th century it has meant a million million here.

The United States, of course, uses the definition favoured by the Treasury. But the traditional English usage was confirmed in the Supplement to the Oxford English Dictionary published only two years ago.

Asked to explain, the Treasury confused things further. Informally within the Department, it seems, the word means a thousand million, "but the fact that officials use the term does not necessarily mean that it has been officially adopted."

And "it is probably safer to talk about a thousand million or a million million" — which of course is precisely what Locke and his contemporaries were trying to avoid when they coined the word in the first place.

Supplementary warning note: to confound the confusion and enhance the fun, see the following, from *The Times* (London) of October 29, 1975:

Complaint over 'Billion' Dismissed
Exercise in pedantry, the Press Council declares

To uphold a complaint about the misuse of the word "billion" would be no more than an exercise in pedantry, the Press Council said in an adjudication yesterday.

Mr. J. T. Anderson, of Rugby, complained that *The Times* misused the word "billion", having reported remarks by an MP and captain of industry showing "illiteracy and innumeracy."

Mr. A. D. Holmes replied that *The Times* agreed that billion in English meant a million million. However, the Business News section of the newspaper preferred to use the American style (a thousand millions) on the grounds that it was now general and that to translate it into British terms would be misleading. *The Times* was anxious to establish a uniform practice which would be acceptable to scientists, mathematicians, economists and financiers.

Mr. N. Keith, for *The Times*, wrote further to Mr. Anderson saying it was incorrect to say that the business section preferred the American style. In fact it invariably preferred "X,000m", except when reporting a speech or when the term was used figuratively to mean large numbers. The *Financial Times* had formally adopted billion and informed its readers. *The Times* might be forced to do the same if inflation carried on at the present rate.

Mr. Anderson replied with a request that *The Times* should publish his letter but the newspaper replied that it regretted that it had not been possible to find a place for it.

The Press Council's adjudication was:

"The tongue which Shakespeare spoke (although in justice to him he did not employ the word "billion") has been, as some think, much mutilated in the centuries which have passed. The editor who chooses to use a word in a sense different from that accepted by others can hardly be accused of impropriety unless his use of it is calculated to mislead. No doubt the word "billion" as employed in England (but not in America or in the Continental languages) means, in a classical sense accepted here, a million million. In America it means a thousand million and the word is now increasingly used, like other American expressions, in this latter sense in economic and business matters.

"The Press Council notes that the editor of *The Times* seeks to establish a uniform practice, and considers that to uphold this complaint would be no more than an exercise in pedantry."

But wait: see the following, from *The Times* of November 19, 1975:

Billions and Trillions
From Mr. R. H. Ramsford

Sir, Whether or not you were right in refusing to publish a letter criticizing the misuse of the word billion, the Press Council was certainly wrong to dismiss the criticism as pedantry. Regrettably, this misuse is widespread and can—and does—lead to doubt and even outright misunderstanding.

What is particularly disquieting is that a body of the status of the Press Council is apparently so ill-informed that it has no hesitation in stating that billion is not used to signify a million millions in the continental languages. No extensive research would have been needed to reveal its mistake. The oldest edition of *Le Petit Larousse* I have at hand, the 1962 edition, already defines "billion" as "Un million de millions (10^{12}) ou 1-000-000-000-000/

Autref., et encore aux Etats-Unis, syn. de MILLIARD". And its Spanish counterpart in 1972 simply defines "billón" as "Millón de millones".
The two main European countries that formerly used billion in the American sense were France and Portugal, but at a postwar International Con-
ference on Weights and Measures, in 1948 if I remember rightly, they agreed to
fall into line with Italy, Germany, England, and other countries that had always
used it, even in common speech, to mean a million squared—and trillion to
mean a million cubed, and so on. ˙
There is no need to perpetuate the abuse, when we already have an unam-
biguous word for a thousand million: "milliard", which has long been widely
used in Belgium, France and Italy at least. Alternatively, since the metric system is becoming more familiar, why not make use of its prefixes? "Megabuck"
was in vogue some years ago, I have seen "kF" (for "kilo-francs") in official
French writing, and I understand that "kilopounds" is beginning to be used
in English. So why not adopt the prefixes giga (G) and tera (T) to signify the
American and European billion respectively?
I hope *The Times* will decide to set the lead and popularize the use of one or
other of the methods suggested above.
Yours sincerely,
R. H. Ransford,
11 Grovewood Close,
Chorley Wood,
Hertfordshire.
October 29.

And what's more (*Times,* same date):

From Dr. G. B. R. Feilden, FRS
Sir, In the current controversy over the misuse of the word billion it might
help to note the dispassionate advice about the use of such words which is
given in British Standard 350 *Conversion factors and tables.* Part 1 of the standard,
published in 1974, states: "In view of the differences between European and
USA practice, ambiguities can easily arise with the words 'billion', 'trillion' and
'quadrillion'; therefore their use should be avoided."
It is thus encouraging for us to know that *The Times* prefers the form X,000m
and will continue to use it except when quoting less accurate sources.
Yours faithfully,
G. B. R. FEILDEN,
Director of General British Standards Institution,
2 Park Street, W1.
October 29.

The Economist weekly adopted the American usage years ago, to the annoyance
of some readers. One wonders how long it will take for the British public to be
won over to this adoption. As recently as December 7, 1979, the following letter
appeared in *The Times:*

Billion Dollar Blunder

From Señor Francisco R. Parra
Sir, Reference my letter "No 'ulterior motive' behind Venezuelan oil announce-
ment" (November 29), we erroneously addressed you in American and said
"billion" dollars. Understandably believing we were addressing you in English,
you wrote out three more zeros (oops, "noughts"). Correct capital cost figures

should be $3,500m to $4,000m for 125,000 barrels per day by 1988, and $20,000m by the year 2000.
Yours truly,
FRANCISCO R. PARRA,
Managing Director,
Petroleos de Venezeula (UK) SA,
7 Old Park Lane,
London, W1.
November 29.

Philip Howard, in Chapter 4, entitled 'Billion,' of *Words Fail Me* (Hamish Hamilton, London, 1980), favors ending "the dangerous confusion by conforming to the American style of billion." And the BBC is having a hard time forcing *Centigrade* on its listeners and the die-hards are still counting money in shillings and old pence (see **Appendix II.A**). So much for Progress!

The British always put an *and* between 100 and a smaller number, as in *a/one hundred and twenty*, or *a/one hundred and ten thousand*. This *and* is normally omitted in America.

E. Automotive Terms

The British equivalents of automotive terms in common use, such as *boot* ('trunk') and *bonnet* ('hood'), appear in the alphabetical listing below. For the benefit of car buffs or technicians and other specialists concerned with scientific automotive terminology, this list, supplied by British Leyland Motors, Inc., may be of interest. The usual order followed in this book (English-American) is here reversed, on the theory that in this case the American reader knows the American equivalent and might thus more readily locate the relevant pairing.

American	British
Body Parts	
bumper guard	*overrider*
cowl	*scuttle*
dashboard	*fascia panel*
door post	*door pillar*
door stop	*check strap*
door vent *or* vent	*quarter light*
fender	*wing*
firewall	*bulkhead*
hood	*bonnet*
license plate	*number plate*
rear seat back *or* backrest	*rear seat squab*
rocker panel	*valance*
skirt	*apron*
toe pan	*toe board*
trunk	*boot*
windshield	*windscreen*
wheelhouse *or* housing	*wheel arch*
Brake Parts	
parking brake	*hand brake*
Chassis Parts	
muffler	*exhaust silencer*
side rail	*side member*

Electrical Equipment

back up light	*reversing light*
dimmer switch	*dip switch*
dome light	*roof lamp*
gas pump *or* fuel pump	*petrol pump*
generator	*dynamo*
ignition wiring	*ignition harness*
parking light	*side light*
tail light	*tail lamp* or *tail light*
spark plug	*sparking-plug*
turn indicator, blinker	*trafficator*
voltage regulator	*control box*

Motor and Clutch Parts	**Engine and Clutch Parts**
carburetor	*carburetter*
clutch throwout bearing	*clutch release bearing*
engine block	*cylinder block*
hose clamp	*hose clip*
pan	*sump*
piston *or* wrist pin	*gudgeon pin*
rod (control) bearing	*big-end*

Rear Axle and Transmission Parts

axle shaft	*half shaft*
drive shaft	*propeller shaft*
grease fitting	*grease nipple*
ring gear and pinion	*crown wheel and pinion*

Steering Parts

control arm	*wishbone*
king pin	*swivel pin*
pitman arm	*drop arm*
steering idler	*steering relay*
steering knuckle	*stub axle*
tie bar *or* track bar	*track rod*

Tools and Accessories

antenna	*aerial*
crank handle	*starting handle*
lug wrench	*box spanner*
wheel wrench	*wheel brace*
wrench	*spanner*

Transmission Parts	**Gearbox Parts**
counter shaft	*layshaft*
emergency brake	*parking brake*
gear shift lever	*gear lever*
output shaft	*main shaft*
shift bar	*selector rod*
transmission case	*gearbox housing*

Tires

tire	*tyre*
tread	*track*

F. Musical Notation

In musical notation the British have rejected common fractions, as will be seen in the following table of equivalent terms in everyday use in the respective countries:

British	American
breve	double whole note
semibreve	whole note
minim	half note
crotchet	quarter note
quaver	eighth note
semiquaver	sixteenth note
demisemiquaver	thirty-second note
hemidemisemiquaver	sixty-fourth note

The *semibreve* is the longest note in common use. How a half note got the name of *minim* is a great mystery to many people, especially since another (non-musical) British meaning of *minim* is 'creature of minimum size or significance,' and its non-musical American meanings have to do with aspects of minuteness. The answer is that at one time it was the shortest note in use. *Crotchet* is another funny one: it is derived from the Old French *crochet*, meaning 'little hook,' and everything would have been quite neat and tidy if the quarter note had a little hook, but it doesn't, and little hooks don't start until we get to eighth notes. *Quaver* is used in music in both countries to indicate a trill, and one can see a connection between trilling and eighth notes. A final mystery is the connection between *breve*—derived, of course, from *breve*, the neuter form of *brevis* (Latin for 'brief')—and a double whole note, a note no longer used in musical notation, which is the equivalent of two whole notes, and that makes it anything in the world but brief. The explanation is that in the Middle Ages there was a note even longer than the breve, something apparently called a *long*, compared with which a double whole note would seem brief.

G. Slang

1. Cant Terms
No attempt is made to include cant terms in this book. These are terms peculiar to particular groups. The *taxi-drivers* of London have their own code: Charing Cross Underground ('subway') Station, recently renamed *Embankment*, is the *Rats' Hole;* St. Pancras Station, the *Box of Bricks;* the Army and Navy Store in Victoria Street is the *Sugar Box;* the St. Thomas' Hospital *cab-rank* ('taxi stand') is the *Poultice Shop;* the one at London Bridge the *Sand Bin;* Harley Street (where doctor's offices cluster) is *Pill Island;* Bedford Row (where lawyers' offices proliferate) is *Shark's Parade;* and the Tower of London is *Sparrow Corner.*

London busmen have a lingo of their own: The last bus is the *Ghost Train;* to slow up (because of exceeding the schedule) is to *scratch about;* passengers on their way to the greyhound races are *dogs;* a busful is a *domino load,* and a *stone-cold* bus is an empty one; a plainclothes bus inspector is a *spot* and he can *book* ('report') a driver; passengers are *rabbits;* a *short one* is an unfinished trip; an accident is a *set;* to arrive late for duty is to *slip up;* a *cushy road* is an easy trip, and a busy one is known as *having a road on.* In the days when trolley cars competed, the British term *tramcar* became the rhyming equivalent *jam jar.*

Sports talk is another matter. Any newspaper report or broadcast or telecast of a cricket or rugby match would be as unintelligible to an American as an American sportswriter's commentary on a baseball game would be to a Britisher. To understand these categories of terminology, the reader must refer to technical works on the respective subjects.

2. London Slang

London slang is almost a language of its own, and to complicate matters, it keeps shifting all the time. George Orwell in *Down and Out in Paris and London* (1933) gives a list of cant words in this category, including the following:

gagger	beggar; street performer
moocher	beggar
clodhopper	street dancer
glimmer	car watcher
split	detective
flattie	policeman
clod	policeman
toby	tramp
drop	money to a beggar
slang	street-peddler's license
the Smoke	London
judy	woman
spike	flophouse
lump	flophouse
deaner	shilling
hog	shilling
tosheroon	half-crown
sprowsie	sixpence
shackles	soup
chat	louse

3. Rhyming Slang

Rhyming slang is a type of cant that has developed from the peculiarly cockney game of replacing certain common words with phrases ending with a word that rhymes with the replaced word. Thus:

boat race	face
daisy roots	boots
German bands	hands
loaf of bread	head
mince pies	eyes
Mutt and Jeff	deaf
north and south	mouth
plates of meat	feet
tit for tat	hat
trouble and strife	wife
Uncle Ned	head
whistle and flute	suit

And many more. One doesn't run into these expressions very often, but when one does meet them, they can be pretty puzzling, especially when the cant phrase itself becomes truncated or otherwise corrupted through cockney usage. Thus *loaf of bread* is shortened to *loaf*, *mince pies* becomes *minces*, *tit for tat* turns into *titfer*, *whistle and flute* loses the *flute*, *German bands* winds up as *Germans*, and so on. The results: *loaf* for head, *minces* for eyes, *whistle* for suit, etc., come out as quite arbitrary substitutes miles removed from the words they stand for.

One often heard outside the cockney world is *loaf,* particularly in the expression, *Use your loaf! (Use your bean!)* and *Mind your loaf! (Low bridge!).* In certain cases there is a further hurdle in that the replaced word is itself a Briticism requiring explanation, like the case of *daisy roots* for *boots,* where *daisy roots* becomes *daisies, boots* would be shoes in America, and we wind up with *daisies* for shoes, an etymological riddle. For treatment of this subject, see *The Muvver Tongue,* by Robert Barltrop and Jim Wolveridge (The Journeyman Press, London, and West Nyack, N.Y., 1980).

4. Poker Slang

all blue	flush
busted flush	four flush
broken melody	ruptured straight
Colonel Dennison	three tens
Morgan's orchard*	two pair
pea green	flush
running flush	straight flush
stuttering run**	broken straight

*Also means a count of four in cribbage.
**Missing one in the middle, like 7, 8, 9, jack, queen.

5. British Betting Terms
According to Bulletin No. 49 (April 1977) of the American Name Society, quoting *The Daily Telegraph* (London) of March 26, 1976, the British use the following terms in placing multiple race-track bets, which they call *punting:*

each-way: This is a quick way of writing two bets. It means a win bet on a selected horse and also a place bet on the same horse to an equal amount of stake money. Thus, *10p each-way* means a 10p win bet and 10p place bet. Total outlay: 20p.

double: Two horses are linked in one bet. If the first named horse wins, the stake money and the winnings are invested on the other horse.

treble: As a *double,* but with three horses linked together.

accumulator: As a *treble,* but with four or more horses. Advantage: stakes are kept low.

any-to-come (ATC) or **if cash:** Another type of wager where any cash (winning plus stakes) forthcoming from earlier bets finances further bets on selected horses. Examples of *ATC* or *if cash* bets follow:

round the clock: Three or more selections are each backed singly, with ATC bets on the others should there be enough cash available.

up and down: Two horses, each backed singly, with an ATC bet on the other.

rounder: Three horses, each backed singly. If cash, the other two horses are backed in a double.

roundabout: A rounder with double stakes on the double.

patent: Three horses backed in three single-win bets, three doubles, and a treble (seven bets).

round robin: Three horses linked in *up and down* bets on each pair, plus three *doubles* and a *treble* (10 bets).

Yankee: Four horses backed in six *doubles,* four *trebles,* and an *accumulator* (11 bets).

flag: Four horses. Each pair is backed *up and down* as well as all four horses in a *Yankee* (23 bets).

Canadian: Five horses backed in ten *doubles,* ten *trebles,* five four-horse *accumulators,* and one five-horse *accumulator* (26 bets).

Heinz (57 varieties): Name used in Britain for any kind of multiple mixture: a mongrel dog might be a *Heinz hound,* etc. Six horses backed in 15 *doubles,* 20 *trebles,* 15 four-horse and six five-horse *accumulators,* and one six-horse *accumulator* (57 bets).

H. Food Names

Food names are very puzzling and of butchers' terms only a few labels of specific cuts of meat are included. There are a good many that would baffle an American shopper: *rump steak* is top round steak or round steak; *best end* is rack of lamb; *a baron* is a double sirloin; *silverside* is top round (rolled and tied with string); *mince* is chopped meat. It seems worse at the fish store *(fishmonger's):* one can hear of *brill* (similar to a small turbot), *coalfish,* also called *coley* and *saithe* (black cod), *witch* (resembling lemon sole), *John Dory* (a flat fish with a big head), *huss,* also called *dogfish, rig,* and *robin huss* (similar to a small conger eel), and other strange species, to say nothing of unfamiliar seafoods like *winkles* and *prawns.* At the bakery one finds all kinds of goodies with alien names. Many are entries in the book; purchase by sight and smell.

I. Botanical and Zoological Names

Botanical and zoological (especially avian) names present special difficulties, whether they are British names for shared species or simply names for those that do not include the United States in their habitats. There are exclusively British geological terms as well. British apple trees bear fruit called *Beauty of Bath, Cox,* and *queening.* In the floral department, wild or cultivated, one finds the *cuckoobud, buttercress, kingcup, St. Anthony's turnip, blister-flower, horse gold, butter rose, butter daisy,* or *gold cup;* a fair collection of synonyms for the modest buttercup. Moreover, *cuckoobud* is not to be confused with the British *cuckooflower,* a form of wild mustard with white or lilac flowers, and itself synonymous (in Britain) with *lady's smock* and *milkmaid* (actually the *cardamine pratensis*), or with the *cuckoopint* (also known, collectively, as *lords and ladies*), which Americans call *jack-in-the-pulpit,* or with *cuckoospit,* the foamy mass in which various insects lay their eggs, often seen on Queen Anne's lace, which the British call *wild carrot;* and *cuckoospit* itself is usually known in America as *frogspit.* British *orange balsam* flowers, also known there as *swingboats* because the flowers are shaped rather like the carnival boats on some of the giant swings, are known as *jewelweed* or *touch-me-not* in America; *reed mace* is the United States broad-leaved *cattail.* Daffodils are *daffodils* in both countries, but are sometimes called *Lent lilies* by the British because of their time of blooming. *Butterbar, wild rhubarb,* and *bog rhubarb* are British synonyms for American *batterdock* or *umbrella leaves.* Still in the flora division, *wainscot* is the British name for a superior type of oak imported from the Baltic region especially for wainscoting. To go entomological for a moment, the common British butterfly known there as the *Camberwell beauty* is our old friend the *mourning cloak* in America. With respect to avian terminology: a *butterbump* is a *bittern;* a *moorhen* is a *gallinule;* the *tree creeper* is the *brown creeper; windhovers* are *kestrels.* For devotees of the earth sciences we find *beck* and *burn* for *brook, rig* or *rigg* for *ridge, wold* for an open *tract* of uncultivated land, *moss* for *swamp,* nick for a small *valley* or water-cut *gorge, sea-fret* for thick *fog,* and *carr* for a dense *thicket.* Some of these terms are regional, some may be classified as dialect, some are assuredly standard, many will be strange even to British ears, but you never know when you're going to run into them.

J. *Britain, Briton, British, English,* etc.

Except in more or less official contexts, the inhabitants of the British Isles tend to think and speak of themselves as English, Scottish, Welsh or Irish first and British second. In *How to Be an Alien* (André Deutsch, London, 1946), George Mikes told us that an alien may become British, but never English. By *British,* he means a naturalized subject of Great Britain; by *English,* he means English in culture, outlook, heart, and spirit. In a letter to *The Times* (London) on August 25, 1982, the distinction is made quite emphatically:

> **Race and Crime**
> *From Mr D.K. Clarebrough*
>   Sir, Dr Sandra Wallman (August 20) writes that "black people living in Brixton
> . . . are English by objective right as well as subjective preference." British they
> may be but English surely not. If I'm wrong, who then are the black or coloured
> people I see cheering West Indies, India or Pakistan, when they play the England
> cricket team on an English ground?
>   We have a multiracial, multicultural and multinational society.
> Yours faithfully,
> DENIS CLAREBROUGH
> Southwood House,
> Hilltop Road,
> Dronfield,
> Sheffield.
> August 20.

The word *Briton* sounds historical or literary to them, and *Britisher* sounds like an Americanism. The *Concise Oxford Dictionary* says *Britisher* is the U.S. term for a British subject "as distinct from an American citizen" and goes on to say that it is "apparently of American origin but disclaimed by U.S. writers." *Britain* is used in Great Britain, of course, but English people are more likely to refer to it as *England*. To an older generation of the inhabitants of Britain, and still more, perhaps, to those of the white Commonwealth countries, the term *British* covers, as well, the former dominions, colonies, etc., at least those settled from the British Isles. *United Kingdom of Great Britain and Northern Ireland* may still remain the official term for the country, and for alphabetical seating at the United Nations, it is listed as *U.K.*—in convenient proximity to the U.S. Historically, it is *Great Britain,* to distinguish it from Brittany in France. *Briticism* or *Britishism* is a term traced back to 1883 and is handy for distinguishing British idiom from the American, but in distinction to, e.g., French, the term would be *Anglicism*. A final oenological note: *English wine* is made from English grapes, grown on English vines. *British wine* (also called 'made wine') is fermented in Britain from foreign grape-concentrate. Never confuse the two: the English Vineyards Association (EVA) would never forgive you.

As to the inhabitants of Scotland: the variants are Scotch, Scots, and Scottish. According to Fowler (*A Dictionary of Modern English Usage,* 2nd edition revised by Sir Ernest Gowers, Oxford, 1965), *Scottish* is closest to the original form, *Scotch* was the English contraction, and *Scots* the one adopted in Scotland. The current favorite in Scotland is *Scottish,* next, *Scots,* with *Scotch* being more or less discarded. England has gone along with this, but in certain stock phrases, *Scotch* has been retained in both places and the rest of the English-speaking world, thus: *Scotch* whiskey (*whisky* in Britain), broth, tweed, egg, woodcock, mist, terrier, pine, beef; and Scotch House is a famous London shop dispensing Scottish textiles and apparel. The English call the dialect spoken in Scotland *Scotch;* the

Scots usually call it *Scots,* and the dialect of the Lowlands *Lallans,* a corruption of *Lowlands.*

K. Cricket Terms

For the benefit of any Americans who may develop an interest in the English national sport, cricket, there follows a glossary that appeared in a cricket periodical published by *The Sun* (London, 1972). The definitions are couched in cricketese and in turn need defining and translation in many cases:

beamer: a delivery that goes through head high to the batsman without bouncing after leaving the bowler's hand.

blob: one of various words used to denote an innings where the batsman has failed to score.

bosie: the Australian name for the googly, the ball that goes from off to leg instead of turning from the leg as with a normal leg break.

bouncer: has the same end product as a beamer in that the delivery goes through about head high to the batsman but is achieved by pitching short of a length.

boundary: four runs.

castle: the stumps.

century: 100 runs.

cherry: the ball, particularly when new and shiny.

Chinaman: this is bowled by a left-arm spin bowler who makes the ball turn into the right-handed batsman rather than the normal left arm spin delivery, which turns away from the right hander.

Chinese Cut: this refers to the snick off the inside or bottom edge of the bat whereby the ball goes down the leg side close to the wicket instead of towards a third man as the batsman intended.

cutter: a fast spinning delivery that moves quickly off the wicket when it pitches. Can be either off-cutter or leg-cutter.

drag: describes the action of the fast bowler when dragging his back foot along the ground in his delivery stride.

duck: no score.

finger spinner: a bowler who uses his fingers in order to impart spin on the ball, thereby making it change direction when it pitches. A right-handed finger spinner is an off spin bowler, making the ball move in from the off side.

flipper: a delivery from a leg break bowler which has top spin, making it hurry through quickly and straighten when it pitches.

gate: the gap between bat and pad when a batsman is playing a stroke.

googly: the more common term to describe a bosie, also known as "wrong' un."

hob: the stumps as in castle.

inswinger: a ball that swings through the air from the off side to leg.

king pair: falling first ball each innings of a two innings match.

length: the area in which the ball should pitch for a perfect delivery to prevent a batsman playing backward or forward with safety.

long hop: a short-of-2-length delivery that comes through at a nice height for a batsman to hit, generally on the leg side.

Nelson: all the ones as in 111. Considered unlucky for a batsman or a side to be on that figure. Double Nelson is 222.

nightwatchman: a lower order batsman who goes to the wicket just before close of play to save a recognised batsman from having to bat and possibly losing his wicket in the few remaining minutes.

outswinger: a ball that swings through the air toward the off side.

pair: signifies a batsman failing to score in both innings of a match.

sticky dog or **wicket:** a wicket on which the ball turns viciously as the wicket dries out under hot sun after being affected by the rain. It is not often that a true "sticky dog" is found in England but they have been known in Australia, notably in Brisbane.

ton: a century.

wrist spinner: a bowler who uses his wrist to spin the ball, making it come out of the back of his hand as with a leg break.

Yorker: an overhand delivery that pitches near the batting crease and goes that under the bat as the batsman starts to play his stroke generally moving forward.

L. Connotative Place-Names

The use of connotative place-names occurs in every language. The French author placing a character on the rue du Faubourg Saint Honoré, the German writing of the Kurfürstendamm, the Italian locating a scene on the Via Veneto or the Piazza San Marco are all using place-names to create a backdrop, an atmosphere. As for the English, the following might well perplex an American reader unfamiliar with Britain and British life:

Albany. A most exclusive apartment house *(block of flats)* in London, whose occupants always include many distinguished names.

Belgravia. A fashionable district of London. Its name is used metaphorically to mean the very wealthy.

Blackpool. A seaside resort in West Lancashire, in northwest England, known for its appeal to working people.

Bloomsbury. A London district known as an intellectual center. The 'Bloomsbury Group' of artists, writers and intellectuals generally flourished there in the early 1920's and gave this place-name its cachet, implying quality with a hint of preciosity.

Bow Bells. Literally, the bells of Bow Church in the *City* of London (a section of London housing, inter alia, the financial district). This place-name most frequently occurs in the expression *within the sound of Bow Bells,* which means 'in the City of London.' One born within the sound of Bow Bells is said to be a true cockney.

Bow Street. Famed in British detective stories as the address of the principal London police court.

Brighton. A Victorian seaside resort, noted for massive hotels, endless rows of middle-class boardinghouses, the Prince Regent's 'Pavilion,' an antiques section known as 'the Lanes,' and other divertissements.

(The) British Museum. Often shortened to 'The B.M.' Recently remodeled. Britain's great library, museum, and depository of priceless collections in history, art, archeology, etc.

Carnaby Street. A street in the Soho section of London, studded with apparel shops catering to the young with-it crowd in its heyday during the 1960s. The caché has long since migrated to other areas.

Chelsea. A London district, formerly a center of the smart Bohemian set but now inhabited mostly by wealthy people seeking a livelier atmosphere than that of Belgravia or Mayfair—and somewhat cheaper real estate.

(The) City. Short for *the City of London.* See *Bow Bells* (above) and *(the) City* in the alphabetical text.

(The) Connaught. An elegant hotel full of ancient glory and still going strong.

Covent Garden. A London district that once housed London's vast, tumultuous vegetable and flower market, now removed to another part of the city, but still the location of street entertainers, shops, and the long-established theater bearing its name, famous for opera and ballet.

Earl's Court. One of London's major venues for trade and consumer fairs, concerts, and sporting events. (See *White City,* below.) The Earl's Court section of London is known for its proliferation of 'bed-sitters,' tiny one-room housing units cut out of once great mansions.

(The) East End. A poor section of London, which includes the docks. Becoming fashionable.

Eaton Square, Eaton Place. Very fashionable streets in *Belgravia,* London.

(The) Embankment. Road along the north bank of the Thames. Hotel rooms, offices, etc. that overlook it are most desirable, but another connotation arises from the fact that it is the sleeping place of derelicts and tramps.

Eton, Harrow. Leading and venerable *public schools* (i.e., private schools) for ages thirteen to eighteen, whose playing-fields breed 'the future leaders of England,' according to Tory gospel.

Golders Green. A section of north London much favored by middle-class Jews.

Hampstead. An exclusive area of London formerly popular with artists, writers, and intellectuals; now too expensive for all but the most successful.

Harley Street. A London street where many doctors have private consulting rooms. Because these doctors are often the most expensive in London, the term *Harley Street* is almost synonymous with private medicine as used by the wealthiest of the wealthy. Some of the doctors engage only in private practice, but many are also consultants in NHS hospitals. Note: the term *Harley Street* in this sense refers to the street itself and to others in the surrounding area, especially Wimpole Street and Devonshire Place.

Harrods. A universal department store offering just about everything from antiques to food, all at noncompetitive prices.

Harrow. See Eton.

Hyde Park. One of London's many beautiful parks. In one corner (the legendary Speaker's Corner), speakers are permitted to address the public on just about any subject, with the emphasis generally against the **Establishment.**

Kensington Gardens. Another of London's famous parks, formerly part of Hyde Park and forming part of the same expanse of green space; the boundary between the two is indistinct.

Knightsbridge. London area offering elegant shopping, etc.

Lord's. Short for *Lord's Cricket Ground,* the most famous of all cricket fields ('grounds'), home of the M.C.C. (Marylebone Cricket Club), the body that controls and is the arbiter of all things relating to cricket.

Marks & Spencer. A chain store selling wearing apparel, food and drink, and homewares; long known for its competitive prices and high quality, especially in areas such as knitwear and underwear. The name is often shortened to M & S, but its most popular form is *Marks & Sparks,* a sobriquet both jocular and affectionate.

Notting Hill Gate. A socially and economically diverse area in West London, long characterized by a mixture of rich, middle-class, and poor populations and with a large proportion of residents of Afro-Caribbean descent. Increasingly popular with affluent members of the media and other professions, it is now almost synonymous with a certain kind of metropolitan chic.

(The) Old Bailey. The chief criminal court of London.

(The) Old Vic. London's famous old repertory theater, known for its productions of Shakespeare. The scene has in large part shifted to the National Theatre, but

the Old Vic still carries on. It has been refurbished and now enjoys a sparkling façade and elegant interior.

(The) Oval. London's other cricket ground. See *Lord's.*

Oxford Street. London's shopping street devoted to the needs of all people, hard to navigate on foot because of the crowds.

(The) Palladium. London's leading vaudeville house **(music-hall),** scene of generations of memorable variety.

Park Lane. An elegant avenue bordering Hyde Park, location of many great hotels and superior shops.

Piccadilly. London's historic main thoroughfare, with elegant shops and hotels.

Portobello Road. Scene of the historic flea market, a center for relatively inexpensive antiques.

Regent Street. London's most elegant shopping street.

Rotten Row. A fashionable equestrian track in Hyde Park, London. The name has been attributed to a number of derivations, the favorite of which is *route du roi,* the old route of the royal procession from the palace at Westminster to the royal hunting preserve. Others go back to the 18th century word, *rotan,* meaning 'wheeled vehicle' and derived from *rota,* Latin for *wheel.*

Royal Festival Hall. One of London's great concert halls.

Royal Fortnum & Mason. Often shortened to Fortnum's. A department store of great elegance, with a famous tearoom.

Sadler's Wells. A theater, the original location of the ballet company that bore its name and is now the Royal Ballet; still active as a dance center and as a venue for musical and theatrical performances of various types.

Savile Row. A London street, center of elegant *bespoke* (i.e., custom) tailoring for men.

(The) Savoy. One of London's oldest and most expensive hotels.

(The) Serpentine. A lake in Hyde Park, where people love to row.

(The) Tate Gallery. Almost invariably shortened to 'the Tate.' Now officially called Tate Britain, and housing the national collection of British art along with modern art from other countries. The national center for contemporary art has moved to Tate Modern, in a converted power station on the bank of the Thames.

(The) Victoria and Albert Museum. Usually shortened to 'The V. & A.' The national museum for the decorative and applied arts, housing a huge and diverse collection including ceramics, furniture, and photography among many other categories of work.

Wembley Stadium. Always called 'Wembley';.a great *football* (i.e., soccer) field.

(The) West End. A part of London noted as the center of theater and chic restaurant life.

White City. Indoor sports arena in West London.

Wimbledon. A district in South London, home to the All-England Lawn Tennis and Croquet Club, where the annual Lawn Tennis Championships are played.

Winchester. A *public school* (i.e., private school), one of the oldest, with some of the highest academic standards.

Index

Note: This index lists American words, terms, and expressions followed by their British equivalents, which are listed alphabetically in the book; **boldface listings** indicate sections on specialized terms and discussions of British usage.

ambulance chaser; accident
tout
American English 408–415
among; amongst
AM radio; Medium wave
(radio)
amusement park; funfair
anchorman; linkman
And how!; Rather!
. . . and salad; . . . salad
anger, display of; wobbly
angry (get sore); go spare
annex; mediatize
annoyed; shirty
annoying; awkward
Annual Meeting
of Shareholders
(Stockholders); Annual
General Meeting
annuals; bedding plant
annulment; nullity
another drink; (the) other
half
answering machine;
answerphone
antenna; aerial
anxious; in a state
any odd job?; bob-a-job?
anything goes; all in
anywhere near; within
kicking distance of
apartment; flat
apartment; set
apartment, one-room; bed-
sitter
appetizers; starters
applaud; clap
appointment to look at; order
to view
appraise; value
apprentice, law; devil
appropriation bill; supply bill
approximately; query
apron; pinny
architect, licensed; chartered
surveyor
area surrounding; surround
argument, heated; ding-dong
arm of the law; limb of the
law
armpit; oxter
army engineer; sapper
army stew; gippo
around; about
around; round
arouser; knocker-up
arrange; organize
arrange for; lay on
arrest; detain
arrest; take in charge

arrest, justified; fair cop
arrested; done
arson; fire-raising
arty; twee
arugula; rocket
as a matter of fact; actually
as bright as a button; as
bright as a new penny
as dead as a doornail; as dead
as mutton
as easy as pie; as easy as kiss
your hand
as follows; as under
as it turned out; in the event
askew; skew-whiff
as nice as pie; as nice as
ninepence
as of; as from
ass; arse
ass-backwards; arsy-tarsy
ass-freezer; bum-freezer
assistant maid; tweeny
assistant professor; senior
lecturer
assisted living; sheltered
accommodation
ass-kisser; clawback
associate professor; reader
as soon as; directly
assortment; mixed bag
astonished; gobsmacked
as you were; carry on
at a disadvantage; balls to the
walls
at bat; on strike
at full speed; flat out
at hand; to hand
athletic letter; cap
at home; indoors
at one's disposal; in hand
at one's disposal; in one's gift
at the market; best offer
attic; loft
attractive, very; dishy
automatic airplane pilot;
George
Automobile Association;
A.A.
automobile horn; hooter
automotive terms 422–423
autopsy; post-mortem
available; to hand
average; bog-standard
a week from . . . ; . . .week
awful; shocking
awfully; frightfully
awning (shop); sun-blind
(go) AWOL; (go) spare
aye; content
aye; placet

B

babble; chattermag
baby carriage; perambulator
baby carriage; pram
baby carriage; pushcart
baby coat; matinee coat
baby pacifier; comforter
baby pacifier; dummy
babysitter; baby-watcher
babysitter; sitter-in
babysitter, full-time; nanny
Bachelor of Medicine; MB
backdrop; drop-scene
back in civies; bowler-hatted
back kitchen; scullery
back of car seat; squab
backpack; rucksack
backside; fanny
backside; situpon
backstop; long stop
back to business; back to our
muttons
backwards; arsy-versy
bacon; streaky bacon
bacon, Canadian; back bacon
bacon, lean; griskin
bacon, oyster wrapped in;
angel on horseback
bacon, prune wrapped in;
devil on horseback
bacon, slice of; rasher
bacon, strip of; rasher
bad, extremely; diabolical
bad egg; bad hat
bad end; sticky finish
bad form; not on
bad form; off
badger's burrow; set
bad-tempered; liverish
bad-tempered; stroppy
bad-tempered old woman;
boot
(be) baffled; go spare
bagful; shopping-bag
baggage; luggage
baggage car; van
baked; cooked
baked potato; jacket potato
bakery; bakehouse
baking powder; rising
powder
baking powder biscuit; scone
bald man; slap-head
(have a) ball; (have a) rave-up
ballot counter and inspector;
scrutineer
ball-point pen; biro
balls; ballocks
balls; goolies

biting; shrewd
biting cold; as cold as charity
biting cold; monkey-freezing
bits and pieces; odds and
    sods
blabbermouth; pedlar
blab on and on; chunter
blackball; pip
blackberry; bramble
blackjack; cosh
blackjack; pontoon
black magic; devilry
Black or regular?; Black or
    white?
blacktop; macadam
blacktop; tarmac
black woolen cloth;
    broadcloth
blender; liquidizer
blend word; portmanteau
blind drunk; pissed
blinders; blinkers
blinker; winker
block (of stock); tranche
blood; claret
blouse; top
blow; staggerer
blow (squander); blue
blow one's top; do one's nut
blowtorch; blowlamp
blowtorch; brazing lamp
blowtorch; thermic lance
blow up at (someone); blow
    (someone) up
blue-black plum; damson
blue-collar; cloth-cap
(the) blues; hip
blue streak; nineteen to the
    dozen
bluff; fluff
board; join
boarder; P.G.
boat, basket-shaped; coracle
boat pole; quant
bobby pin; hair grip
bobby pin; kirby grip
bodyguard; minder
bomb (a target); prang
bond; loan share (loan stock)
boner; howler
bone to pick; crow to pick
bone up; gen up
boo; barrack
booboo; bloomer
booboo, make a; drop a brick
boob tube; goggle-box
booby prize; wooden spoon
boodle; pot
booger; bogey (bogy)
boogieman; bogeyman

bookie; turf accountant
bookie's joint; (The) Corner
bookmaker; commission
    agent
bookstore; book seller
bookworm; mug
boor; bounder
boost; kiss of life
boot, large; beetle-crusher
boots, rubber; Welliboots
boots, rubber; Wellingtons
booty; pewter
booze, shot of; finger
boozer; battle cruiser
border; frontier
bore; bind
boring; long
boss; gaffer
boss; governor
bosun; Spithead nightingale
botanical names 427
botch job; charley
bother; moider
bothered; arsed
bottom; inside (of a bus)
bouillon cube; stock cube
bounder; chucker-out
bowel movement; motion
bowlegged; bandy-legged
bowl over; knock acock
bowl over; pull up
bow to (someone); give
    (someone) best
box; case
box cutter; stanley knife
box office; pay-box
boy, fair-haired; blue-eyed
    boy
boycott; black
bracelets; darbies
bracket; band
bracket; slice
bracket; tranche
brakeman; brakesman
brakeman; guard
brass knuckles; knuckle
    duster
brass tacks; put-to
bravery, cited for; mentioned
    in dispatches
brawl; dust-up
bread, whole wheat; brown
    bread
bread, whole wheat;
    wholemeal bread
bread-and-butter letter;
    Collins
bread and cheese;
    ploughman's lunch
bread box; bread bin

bread strips; soldiers
break; sit-down
break in; chip in
break in; run in
break things off; part brass
    rags
bribe; bung
bribe; dab in the hand
bribe; dropsy
bricklayer; brickie (bricky)
bridge, removable; denture
bridle trail; gallop
briefed; clued up
brigadier general; brigadier
bring; fetch
bring; make
bring charges against
    (someone); have (someone)
    up
bring (pull) it off; have it off
bring (someone) up to date;
    put (someone) in the
    picture
brisk; parky
brisk; rattling
Britain 428–429
British 428–429
British betting terms
    426–427
British English 408–415
British National Party; BNP
Briton 428–429
broad; Judy
broadcloth; poplin
Broadway; West End
broil; grill
broiler; grill
broke; stony
broken sizes; broken ranges
broken sizes; odd sizes
brokerage firm; broking firm
brood of pheasants; nide
brook; beck
brothel; knocking shop
brush aside; put by
brush (something) off; play
    (something) to leg
brush up on; brush up
brutal killer; butcher
buccaneer; filibuster
buck; jib
(a) buck; bradbury
Buckingham Palace; Buck
    House
buckle under; lie down under
buddy; butty
buddy; mate
buffet; fork supper
buffet; sideboard
bug; beetle

change pocket; ticket pocket
chaotic; shambolic
chapel; bethel
character; blighter
character; bod
charge; book
charge; put down
charge account; account
charter member; foundation
  member
(a) chat; confab
chatter; natter
chatterbox; chattermag
cheap; trumpery
cheap cigarette; gasper
cheap fruit cake; schoolboy
  cake
cheaply; on the cheap
cheap novel; shocker
cheap red wine; red biddy
cheap train fare; APEX fare
cheap wine; plonk
cheat; do the dirty on
cheated; dished
check; bill
check; cheque
check; register
check; tick
check; vet
checkers; draughts
checking account; current
  account
checking account; running
  account
check off; tick off
checkroom; left luggage office
check up; buck up
cheek; cause
cheers!; bung-ho!
cheesecake; maid of honour
cheesecloth; butter-muslin
cheesecloth; muslin
cheese it!; nix!
cheezit!; cave!
chewy candy; stickjaw
chicken; funky
chicken, young; chicken
chicken wire; wire netting
chicory; endive
chief counsel; leader
chief prosecuting attorney, act
  as; lead for the Crown
child beating; child-battering
children's traffic guide;
  lollipop man (woman, lady)
child's bib; feeder
chilly; parky
chimney corner; ingle-nook
Chin up!; Keep your pecker
  up!

chip in; pay one's shot
chocolate candy; Malteser
chocolate sprinkles; chocolate
  vermicelli
chop; cutlet
chopped meat; mince
chow; tack
chow; toke
Christmas carolers; waits
church aisle; aisle
Church of England; C. of E.
church officer; clerk
cigarette; fag
cigarette, cheap; gasper
cigarette butt; dog-end
cigarette paper; skin
cigar store; tobacconist's shop
cilantro; coriander
cinch; doddle
cinch; snip
(a) cinch; easy meat
Circle; Circus
circulation; general post
circumlocution;
  circumbendibus
circumstances; circs
cited for bravery; mentioned
  in dispatches
citizen; subject
city editor; news editor
city hall; guildhall
city limits; city boundary
city limits; town boundary
civilian life; Civvy Street
clamp; cramp
clapboard; weather-board
class; form
class; street
class distinctions 413
classified ad; small ad
cleaning lady; char
cleaning woman; daily
  woman
cleaning woman; Mrs Mop
  (Mopp)
clean up; clear up
clean up; turn out
clearance items; bunches
clear up; fine down
clerk; assistant
clipping; cutting
close; level
close; shut
closed season; close season
closed truck; van
close haircut; short back and
  sides
close order drill; square-
  bashing
closet; cupboard

closing time!; time!
cloth, black woolen;
  broadcloth
cloth, green woolen; Kendal
  green
cloth, type of; wincey
cloth, white cotton; calico
clothespin; clothes-peg
clothespole; clothes-prop
cloture; closure
cloture; guillotine
cloverleaf; spaghetti junction
clumsy; cack-handed
clutter; lumber
coach; carriage
coal, scrap; dross
coal freighter; collier
coarse invective; billingsgate
cockroach; black-beetle
coconut, shredded; dessicated
  coconut
coddle; wrap in cotton wool
coed(ucational); mixed
coffee break, morning;
  elevenses
coffee stand, street; coffee-
  stall
(a) coin of low value; copper
collar button; collar stud
collect call; transferred charge
  call
college department; faculty
college graduate; graduate
college monitor; proctor
college servant; gyp
college servant; skip
college teacher; don
collision; crash
come across; stump up
comedy team; cross-talk
  comedians
come on!; get out of it!
come on!; give over!
come on!; play up!
come out on top; come top
come to a lot; come expensive
come up roses; come up
  trumps
comforter; eiderdown
comfort station; public
  convenience
comic, humorous; comic
coming along; in train
coming attractions; dreadful
  warning
commencement; degree day
commit an error; misfield
committee; working party
common; coarse
common herd; ruck

cubbyhole; cubby
cuff link; sleeve link
cunt; fanny
cup; beaker
cupcake; fairy cake
cup of tea; cuppa
curling iron; curling tongs
currant cookie; garibaldi
currency 413, 416–417
curriculum vitae; CV
curtain material; soft
　furnishings
curve; bend
custard sauce; custard
custodian; keeper
custody; wardship
custom made; bespoke
cut-and-dried;
　straightforward
cutaway; tailcoat
cut down to size; debag
cutie; popsie

D

dad; governor
dainty; dinky
dam; barrage
dam; weir
damages; compensation
dame; bird
dame; broad
damn!; bother
damnable; ruddy
damned; bally
damned; bleeding
damned; blind
damned; blinking
damned; bloody
damned; blooming
damned; dashed
damned; flaming
damned; flipping
damned!; jiggered
damned; rattling
damned good; clinking
damn it!; blast!
dandruff; scurf
Danish; Chelsea bun
darts, the game of; arrows
dates 414
daylight saving time; summer
　time
day nursery; crèche
day's route; country round
day's schedule of doctor
　(dentist); surgery
dazed; knocked off
dead; dead-alive
dead; flat

dead broke; skint
dead drunk; up the pole
dead-end residential area;
　close
dead-end street; cul-de-sac
deadline; time-limit
deaf; cloth-eared
deal; do
dealer; monger
dealer in stocks; stockjobber
dean; doyen
dean; head
Dear . . . ; My dear . . .
decal; transfer
decamp; shoot the crow
decarbonize; decoke
(a) decent person; good egg
(decimal) point; spot
deck; pack
declare; go
declare insolvent; hammer
deduction; allowance
deduction; relief
deduction from wages;
　stoppage
deed, unilateral; deed-poll
deep-dish pie; pie
definite article 409
defroster; demister
degree below 32° F; degree
　of frost
degree removed; remove
dejected; chap-fallen
delay; hold-up
delighted; chuffed
delightful; absolutely sweet
delivery by (refrigerated
　truck); chilled distribution
delivery man; roundsman
dell; dingle
demonstration; demo
den; snuggery
denatured alcohol;
　methylated spirit
dentist's office; surgery
dentist's office hours; surgery
depart; flit
department store;
　departmental store
deposit slip; credit slip
deposit slip; paying-in slip
deprecate oneself; cry
　stinking fish
depreciation; writing down
deputy churchwarden;
　sidesman
derby (hat); bowler
desert; leave in the lurch
desirable residence; Des. res.
desirable woman; crumpet

desist; pack it in
desperate for sex; gagging
　for it
desperate straits, in; past
　praying for
despicable person; tosser
despicable person; wanker
dessert; afters
dessert; pudding
dessert; sweet
destroy; perish
detail; second
detect; catch out
detour; diversion
dial tone; dialling tone
(the) diamond industry;
　Hatton Garden
diaper; nappy
diaphragm; cap
diarrhea; gippy tummy
Dibs on . . . !; bags I!
dicks; busies
die laughing; fall about
　laughing
diet; bant
diet; slim
dig up; rake up
(a) dime a dozen; two (ten) a
　penny
dime novel; penny dreadful
dime novel; shilling shocker
diner; pull-up
dining car; restaurant car
dinner roll; bread roll
diplomat; diplomatist
directional signal; trafficator
directional signal; winker
director; producer
dirt floor; earth floor (earthen
　floor)
dirt road; unpaved road/
　track
dirty (indecent); rude
disagreeable; nasty
disappear; (do a) runner
disappear; go missing
disappointed, very; gutted
disbar; strike off
discard; cast
discharge; demob
discount; concession
discounter; bill broker
disgruntled; choked
disgruntled; chuffed
disgusted; chocker
dish (desirable woman);
　crumpet
dish made of leftovers;
　resurrection pie
dishonest; bent

dune; dene
duplicate; roneo
dust balls; slut's wool

E

early in the picture; early on
earn; knock up
easement; wayleave
easy; cushy
easy does it!; steady on!
easy pickings; money for jam
eat high off the hog; live like a
    fighting cock
eat like a pig; pig it
eats; tuck
eccentric; cranky
(an) edible green plumlike
    fruit; greengage
editor in chief; chief editor
eel, small; grig
eel trap; buck
effective date; tax point
effeminate male; nancy boy
eggplant; aubergine
egg roll; pancake roll
egg roll; spring roll
eggs from uncooped hens;
    free-range eggs
eiderdown quilt; duvet
eighth note; quaver
elastic knit fabric; stockinet
(the) elder; major
elect; return
election, special; by-election
    or bye-election
election day; polling-day
electrical outlet; socket
electrical socket; point
electric cord; flex
electric heater; electric fire
electrician's tape; insulating
    tape
electric tricycle; invalid
    carriage
elementary school; primary
    school
elevator; lift
11 honors; four honors
elimination contest; knock-
    out
embarrassing, painfully;
    Cringe-making
emcee; compère
emergency room; casualty
    ward
employ; engage
employee in charge of
    supplies; storekeeper
empty; peckish

endive; chicory
endless discussion; jaw-jaw
engineer; engine driver
engineer's platform; footplate
English 428–429
English; side
English; spin
English Channel; Silver Streak
English horn; cor anglais
engrave; dye stamp
engraving; copperplate
    printing
enlist; take the shilling
enlisted men; other ranks
enormously; thumping
entail; attract
enter university; go up
enthusiastic; mustard-keen
enthusiastic about; keen on
entitled to the use of; free of
entrance; entry
entrants; intake
eraser; rubber
ER department; accident and
    emergency
erect penis; stiffie
escalator; moving stairway
escritoire; davenport
estate or farm manager; bailiff
Europe, mainland; (the)
    Continent
evading the question;
    ducking and diving
even; level
even; square
even money; evens
even Stephen; honours even
even Stephen; level pegging
everything but the kitchen
    sink; everything that opens
    and shuts
everything's A-OK; Bristol
    fashion
everything's hunky-dory;
    everything in the garden's
    lovely
everything thrown in; all in
excelsior; wood-wool
except; bar
excise tax; purchase tax
excise tax; V.A.T.
exclamation point;
    exclamation mark
excursion bus; charabanc
excursionist; tripper
executive; director
(the) Executive Committee;
    (the) Executive
executive vice president;
    managing director

exemption; relief
exhaust; fag
exhaust; knock up
exhausted; all in
exhausted; hammered
exhaust fan; extractor fan
exhibition game; friendly
exhibitor; renter
Exit; Way Out
expel; sack
expel; send down
expel temporarily from
    university; rusticate
expenses; outgoings
expensive; pricey (pricy)
expensive suburb; gin and
    Jaguar belt
expert, especially in science;
    boffin
explain the situation to
    (someone); put (someone)
    in the picture
express; fast
extension cord; flex
extension courses; extra-
    mural studies
extension school; college of
    further education
extortionate rent; rack-rent
extra; gash
extra measure; long pull
extra measure; pull
extra salary allowance;
    weighting
extremely bad; diabolical
extremely lazy; bone-idle
extremely slow; dead slow
extreme side seat; slip
exult riotously; maffick
eye glasses; spectacles

F

fabulous; snorting
face; Chevy
face; mug
face annihilation; (be) on a
    hiding to nothing
face cloth; flannel
fact-finding board; court of
    inquiry
factor
factory; works
factory whistle; hooter
faddish; trendy
fagged; spun
faintest; foggiest
fair; fête
fair enough; fair do's
fairground; funfair

forward; redirect
foul line; crease
foul up; bugger
(be) found out; (be) blown
Four Corners; Four Wents
4-F; C3
foursome; fourball
frame house; wooden house
frame-up; fit-up
frank; rude
free; gash
free-for-all; Donnybrook
freight; carriage
freight; goods
freight elevator; hoist
freighter; cargo boat
French cuff; double cuff
french fried potatoes; chips
fresh fish; wet fish
freshman; fresher
(be) fresh to; cheek
friends and relations; kith
    and kin
fright; guy
frills; tatt
fringe benefits; perks
fritter away one's time; tatt
frog; rose
from the word go; from the
    off
front desk; reception
front yard; forecourt
frozen food; frosted food
fruit and vegetable pushcart
    vendor; costermonger
fruit and vegetable pushcart
    vendor; pearly
fruit and vegetable store;
    greengrocer's
fruit basket; chip
fruit basket, small; punnet
fruit cake, cheap; schoolboy
    cake
fruit course at end of meal;
    dessert
fruit-seller; fruiterer
fry; fry-up
fuck; shag
full approval; full marks
full of pep; cracking
full-time babysitter; nanny
fully informed; in the picture
fun; all the fun of the fair
fund-raising campaign;
    appeal
funeral director; undertaker
funny; jokes
funny (peculiar); rum
fur hat, tall; busby
furnish; issue

fuss; carry on
fuss; faff
fuss; kerfuffle
futile; fiddling
F. W. Woolworth & Co.;
    Woolies

G

gabble; waffle
gaffe, make a; drop a clanger
gag; rag
(a) gag; funniosity
gain; rise
gain; win
galley; caboose
gallon 418
gallows tree; gallows
galoshes; snowboots
gamble; flutter
gamble; game
game; gammy
game; match
game birds, covey of; brown
(the) game of darts; arrows
gander; shufty
gander (glance); dekko
gander (look-see); recce
gang foreman; ganger
garbage; gash
garbage bin on wheels;
    wheelie bin
garbage can; dustbin
garbage dump; refuse tip
garbage heap; midden
garbage man; dustman
garbage truck; dustcart
garden, family fruit and
    vegetable; kitchen garden
garden area, small rented;
    allotment
garters; suspenders
gasoline; petrol
gas pedal; accelerator
gate; barrier
gate; push
gaudy; twopence coloured
gauge; bore
gear; clobber
gear; traps
gearshift; gear-lever
gee!; coo!
gee!; cor!
geezer; josser
gelatin-type dessert; jelly
general delivery; poste
    restante
general election, have a; go to
    the country
generator; dynamo

genuine; pukka
German shepherd dog;
    Alsatian
get along with; get on with
get a move on; look smart!
get anywhere with; get much
    change out of
get a rise out of; take a rise
    out of
get a rise out of; take the rise
    out of
get away with it; slime
get a word in edgewise; put
    one's hoof in
get back on; get one's own
    back on
get (someone's) back up; put
    (someone's) back up
get by; rub along
get down to brass tacks; come
    to the horses
get even with; get upsides
    with
get forty winks; have a doss
get going; get one's skates on
get going!; get on with it!
get going; get stuck in
get going; get weaving
get going; pull one's socks up
get in (someone's) hair; get
    up (someone's) nose
get killed (be bumped off);
    get the chop
get lost!; cheese off!
Get lost!; On your bike!
get lost!; piss off
get moving; push along
get (someone) out; dismiss
get out of an automobile;
    debus
get (someone) riled up; get
    across (someone)
get settled; smooth
get smashed; go for six
get some shuteye; put one's
    head down
get something going; put up
    the hare
get somewhat tight; have one
    over the eight
get sore (angry); go spare
get the best of; get the better
    of
get the better of; score off
get the gate (be fired); get the
    chop
get things started; open the
    bowling
get this!; wait for it!

grudge match; needle match
gruesome; curly
guard; keeper
guck; jollop
guest book; visitors' book
guest room; spare room
gullible person; mug
gum; chewing gum
gun, soft; fat rascal
gurgle; guggle
guy; bean
guy; beggar
guy; bloke
guy; chap
guy; cove
guy; johnny
guy; stick
gym suit; gym slip (gym tunic)
gypsy; gyppo (gyp)

H

haberdashery; draper's shop
(be) had; (be) done
hairpin; hair grip
hairs, short; curlies
hair spray; lacquer
half a minute (right away); half a tick
half-cocked; at half-cock
halfnote; minim
half past; half
ham; gammon
hamburger; beefburger
hamburger; Wimpy
hand (someone) a line; chat up
handball; fives
handbill; broadsheet
handle; manhandle
handwriting; hand
handyman; odd man
hang around; mouch (mooch)
hang out; cotch
hang up; put the 'phone down
hanky-panky; jiggery-pokery
happy as a clam; happy as a sandboy
hard; shrewd
hard-boiled; hard-baked
hard boiled; hard-cooked
hard cider; cider
hard labor; hard
hard liquor; spirits
hard-luck guy; lame duck
hard sauce; brandy-butter
hard sauce; rum-butter
hard up; in low water

hard up; (in) Queer Street
hardware; fixings
hardware dealer; ironmonger
harum scarum; rackety
hat (derby); bowler
hat, slouch; trilby
hat, tall fur; busby
hat check girl; cloakroom attendant
(have a) ball; (have a) rave-up
have a general election; go to the country
have an affair; have it off
have an alcoholic drink, to; bend the elbow
have a screw loose; have a slate loose
have (someone) at one's mercy; have (someone) on toast
have (something) going; have (something) on
(to) have had it; (to) have had one's chips
have high hopes; fancy one's chances
have it easy; have jam on it
have (something) lined up; have (something) in one's eye
have no use for; have no time for
have plenty to do; have enough on one's plate
have sexual intercourse; go to bed
have sexual intercourse with; bonk
have the inside edge
have your cake and eat it; too; have the penny and the bun
having achieved one's goal; home and dry
having a liquor license; licenced
having a telephone; on the telephone
having made a start; off the mark
hawker; cheapjack
hawthorn; may
hayseed; chaw-bacon
haystack; rick
head; crumpet
head (bean); loaf
head (beginning); top
head (noodle); conk
head (noodle); napper
head (noodle); noddle

headboard; bed-board
head cheese; brawn
headfirst; neck and crop
headlight; headlamp
headliner; topliner
headliner; top of the bill
head nurse; charge-nurse
head over heels; arse over tip
headphones; cans
head shrinker; trick cyclist
health inspector; health visitor
heaping; heaped
hearing aid; deaf-aid
heart's content; top on one's bent
heated argument; ding-dong
heater; fire
heater, electric; electric fire
heaven; Land of the Leal
(peanut) heaven; gods
heavy; double
heavy cream; double cream
heavy favorite; long odds on
heavy food; stodge
heavy goods vehicle; HGV
heavy linen; dowlas
heavy muslin; dowlas
heavy work; rough
hedge clippings; brash
hedge of shrubs bordering a field; hedgerow
held for questioning; assisting the police
hell; bean
hell; rocket
hell-raiser; rip
hell-raiser; tearaway
help wanted; situations vacant
help wanted; vacancies
hem and haw; hum and ha
(hereditary) knight; baronet
here's how!; cheers!
hesitate; jib
het up; in a flap
het up; strung up
hey! hello!; hi!
hey! (what's going on?); hullo!
hi!; watcher!
hideaway; bolt-hole
hideaway; hidey-hole
hiding place; hide
hierarchy; totem
highbrow; Bloomsbury
(in the) highest rank; (at the) top of the tree
high gear; top gear
high rise; multi-storey

Indian summer; St. Martin's summer
in distress; under the harrow
in dutch with (someone); in (someone's) bad books
inexpensive; cheap
infatuate; besot
info; griff
in for it; for it
in for it; for the high jump
inform; bubble
information; enquiries
inform (squeal); grass
in good shape; landed
in great shape; on form
in great shape; up to the knocker
ingrown; ingrowing
in heat; on heat
inheritance tax; death duties
in hot water; in low water
initial; sign off
initiation fee; entrance fee
(The) Inland Revenue; taxman
inlet; creek
inn; hostelry
innards; gubbins
inner-spring; interior-sprung
inning; innings
innkeeper; landlord
in raptures; over the moon
insane; certified
insect; creepy-crawly
inside dope; gen
inside dope; griff
inside of loaf; crumb
in spades!; with knobs on!
inspect; view
installment; plan; hire-purchase
installment plan; tally plan
installment plan; (the) never-never
instant replay; action replay
instruct an expert; teach someone's grandmother to suck eggs
instructions to trial lawyer; brief
instructor; lecturer
insufficient funds; no effects
insufficient funds; R.D.
insufficient funds; refer to drawer
insulating layer; damp course
insurance, liability; third party insurance
(life) insurance; assurance
intensive search; comb-out

inter-city bus; coach
intercity bus; motor coach
interested; bothered
intermission; interval
intern; houseman
internal; inland
international match; Test match
interpolate; spatchcock
intersection; crossroads
intersection area; box
in the cards; on the cards
in the clutch; at the crunch
in the driver's seat; in the driving seat
(in the) highest rank; (at the) top of the tree
in the running; in the hunt
in the same situation; in the same case
in the soup; in the cart
in the works; on the stocks
in town for the big occasion; up for the Cup
in two shakes of a lamb's tail; in two shakes of a duck's tail
investigation; enquiry
investment bank; merchant bank
invisible onlooker; fly on the wall
involve; attract
in wild disorder; all over the shop
I.R.S.; (the) Revenue
Is someone helping you?; Have you been served?
Italian; Eye-tie
itinerant mender; tinker
It's all the same to me; I'm easy (about it)
It's incredible!; It isn't true!
it's unshakable; there's no shifting it
It's up to you; The ball's in your court

J

jabber away; rabbit on
jack; court-card
jack; knave
jacket, light waterproof; anorak
jacket, short tight-fitting; spencer
jacket, velvet; bridge coat
jack-in-the-pulpit; cuckoopint
jack-in-the-pulpit; lords and ladies

jack up; gazump
Jaguar car; Jag
jail; boob
jail; bridewell
jail; shop
jailbird; lag
jalopy; banger
jalopy; granny waggon
Jane Austen fan; Janeite
janitor; caretaker
jelly doughnut; (jam) doughnut
jelly roll; Swiss roll
jerk; charlie
jerk; clot
jerk; git
jerk; hoick
jerk; jobbernowl
jerk; nit
jerk; poon
jerk; swab
jerk; twit
jerk off; wank
jimmy; jemmy
job; job of work
job; lark
job; ploy
jock; hearty
jockey shorts; briefs
jock strap; box
Joe Doakes; Joe Bloggs
john, location of the; geography of the house
john; loo
john; petty
john (toilet); bog
joint; spliff
joint, to smoke; blaze
join up; club together
joke; cod
journalist, political; lobbyist
judge, criminal court; recorder
judgment roll; docket
jug; boob
jug; jankers
juggle; cook
juggle; fluff
jumper cables; jump leads
jumping the gun; early days
jump rope; skipping-rope
jump seat; slit seat
jump the gun; rush one's fences
jumpy; nervy
jumpy; windy
(be) jumpy; get the wind up
June bug; cockchafer
junior varsity player; colt
junk; clutter

letter opener; paper knife
letter z; izzard
letter z; zed
leverage; gearing
liability insurance; third party insurance
library, lending; subscription library
libretto; book of words
licensed architect; chartered surveyor
license plate; number plate
license to sell alcoholic beverages for consumption off the premises; off licence
lickety-split; split-arse
lick (vanquish); flog
lie; fluff
lie low; go to ground
lie low; lie doggo
lieutenant colonel; wing commander
(life) insurance; assurance
life jacket; life vest
life preserver; life-belt
lifesaving service; humane society
lift; elevator
lighting, tubular fluorescent; strip lighting
lightning bug; firefly
light out; bunk
light supper; high tea
light supper; knife-and-fork tea
light waterproof jacket; anorak
like; find
like; sort of thing
like a house afire; like old boots
like it or not; choose how
lima bean; broad bean
lima bean, white; butter bean
limit by cloture; guillotine
limits; boundary
line; free line
line; queue
linear suburban expansion; ribbon development
linen, heavy; dowlas
line of schoolchildren; crocodile
line squall; thundery trough
line up; queue
link arms with; link
linked with . . . ; twin with . . .
linoleum; lino
lint; fleck
lint; fluff

lip balm; lip salve
liquidation sale; closing-down sale
liquid measure 418–419
Liquid paper; Tippex
liquor license, having a; licenced
liquor store; wine merchant's
literary hack; devil
little devil; limb
little hill; molehill
little old lady from Dubuque; Aunt Edna
live; stay
live a sheltered life; live in cotton wool
live like a pig; pig it
liverwurst; liver sausage
livestock farmer; stockholder
live to a ripe old age; make old bones
living room; drawing-room
living room; lounge
living-room; sitting-room
loaded; swacked
load on; skinful
loaf, inside of; crumb
loafer; corner-boy
loafer; layabout
loafers; slip-on shoes
loathe; bar
lobby; foyer
local; branch
local; slow train
local (train); stopping train
local tax; rate
locate; site
location of the john; geography of the house
locker-room; changing-room
lock-up; glasshouse
locomotive fireman; stoker
lodge; slate club
lodging; digs
(the) London Police; (the) Met(s)
London slang 425
long-distance call; trunk call
long-distance information; national enquiries
long run; good innings
longshoreman; docker
long-term; long-stay
long-winded story; circumbendibus
look; look around
look as if . . . ; look like . . .
lookout point; viewpoint
look-see; shufty
loony; dotty

loony; loopy
loophole; let-out
loose gravel; loose chippings
loose-leaf binder; file
loose woman; scrubber
loose woman; tart
Lord; lud
lordy!; lawk(s)!
lose one's balance; overbalance
lose out; kick the beam
lost; landed
lost and found; lost property office
lot; plot (of land)
lotsa luck!; (the) best of British luck!
loud; staring
louder!; speak up!
louse; nasty piece (bit) of work
lousy!; bad show!
lousy; bloody
lousy; filthy
lousy beer; swipes
lout; yobbo
love child; chance-child
love child; come-by-chance
low-class, very; common as muck/brass
lower class; down-market
low gear; bottom gear
lug; hump
luggage rack; roof-rack
lumber; deals
lumber; timber
lump; knob
lunch; tiffin
lunch coupon; luncheon voucher

M

machine operator; machinist
machinery; works
mad; barking
(made) obvious; writ large
(made or become) unemployed; redundant
made to order; bespoke
made vicar; appointed to a cure of souls
made work; hospital job
magazine rack; canterbury
maggot; gentle
magician; conjurer (conjuror)
magistrate; beak
magna; second
magnifying glass; reading glass

money; spondulicks
money (dough); brass
money (dough); dibs
money (dough); lolly
money (dough); £ s.d.
money, paper; folding
moneymaking; money-
  spinning
money market; Lombard
  Street
money pouch; purse
money raising; money-
  spinning
money transfer order;
  standing order
mongrel; Heinz hound
mongrel; pye-dog
monitor; buller
monitor; prefect
more dead than alive; dead-
  alive
more power to you; more
  power to your elbow
morning coffee break;
  elevenses
mortar-board; square
most valuable player; man of
  the match
mother; mater
motorcycle; motor-bike
motorman; driver
mountainside hollow; corrie
mountain slope; scree
mouth; pie-hole
mouth-to-mouth
  resuscitation; kiss of life
move; move house
move on; flit
movie; film
movie business; Wardour
  Street
movie camera; cinecamera
movie house; cinema
movies; flicks
movies; pictures
moving; removals
moving van; pantechnicon
M.P., independent; cross
  bencher
M.P., neutral; cross bencher
M.P.'s (lawyer's) session
  with constituents (clients);
  surgery
M.P.'s (lawyer's) temporary
  outside quarters; surgery
Mr 414
Mr.; Esq.
mucilage; gum
muddle; besot
muddle; cock-up

(a) muddle; (a) nonsense
muddy bottom; putty
muffin stand; curate's
  assistant
mug; beaker
multicolored sprinkles;
  hundreds and thousands
multiple plug; adapter
municipal housing unit;
  council house
municipality; corporation
murder; burke (burk)
Murphy's Law; Sod's Law
mushy; soppy
musical notation 424
music school (conservatory);
  conservatoire
muslin; calico
muslin, heavy; dowlas
mutual fund; unit trust
mutual insurance group;
  friendly society

N

nab; nobble
nag; screw
nailed down; nailed on
nailed down; taped
nail polish; nail varnish
nail polish; varnish
name for; call after
napkin; serviette
national passenger train
  timetable; Bradshaw
Native American; Red Indian
native of Ulster; Ulsterman
navy yard; dockyard
nay-voter; non-content
near; nr.
neat; tidy
neck; snog
neck of lamb; scrag
neck of the woods; turf
need; want
neighborhood bar; local
nerve; neck
nerves; screaming abdabs
nervousness, display of;
  wobbly
net lease; repairing lease
(a) neutral M.P.; cross
  bencher
newscaster; newsreader
newscaster; presenter
newsdealer; newsagent
newspaper, large-sized;
  broadsheet
newspaper editorial; leader
newsstand; bookstall

newsstand; kiosk
nice and . . . ; lovely and . . .
nice going!; well bowled!
nice going!; well done!
nice to hear your voice; nice
  to hear you
nice work!; good show!
nick; middle name
night and day; chalk and
  cheese
night on the town; night on
  the tiles
nightstick; baton
nine of diamonds; curse of
  Scotland
nip; drain
nipple; teat
no?; what?
no answer; no reply
no-building zone; green belt
no damned good; N.B.G
no dice; in the basket
no fuss or feathers; nothing
  starchy
no great catch; not much cop
no holds barred; all in
noisy argument; ding dong
noisy party; ding-dong
no luck; no joy
nominate; adopt
non-Anglican; chapel
non-Anglican; nonconformist
non-profit; not-for-profit
nonsense; flannel
nonsense; rot
nonsense!; rubbish!
nonsense (crap); balls
non-white; coloured
non-white; immigrant
noodle; bonce
noodle (head); conk
noodle (head); napper
noodle (head); noddle
No problem!; Not to worry!
north; norland
nose (beak); conk
nose out; pip
nose out; pip at the post
no soap; in the basket
no-stopping thoroughfare;
  clearway
not a damned thing; not a
  sausage
not a goddamned thing;
  sweet eff-all
not at all; not half
not all there; (a) bit missing
not all there; simple
not applicable; N/A
notary public; Commissioner
  for Oaths

not by a long shot; not by a
  long chalk
not care a rap about; have no
  mind to
not deal with; leave alone
notebook; exercise book
notebook; jotter
not funny; past a joke
nothing; bugger all
nothing; nil
nothing at all; damn all
nothing at all; sweet Fanny
  Adams
nothing to write home about;
  nothing to make a song
  about
no through trucks; except for
  access
notion; clue
notions; fancy goods
notions store; haberdashery
not nearly; not half
not on your life; not on your
  nelly
not so bad; not so dusty
not think much of; have no
  time for
not to mention; let alone
not too happy; not best
  pleased
nouns, compound 409
nouns, singular 409–410
nudist; naturist
(be a) nuisance (put out); put
  about
number; bit of goods
numbers 419–422
number sign; hash mark
nurse, head; charge-nurse
nurse; medic
nurse; sister
nut; chump
nut; nut-case
nut; nutter
nut (head); crumpet
nuts; bonkers
nuts; crackers
nuts; doolally
nuts; stark ravers
nuts about; struck on
nutty; potty

O

oaf; muff
oarlock; rowlock
oatmeal (cooked); porridge
oatmeal (uncooked); oats
observation deck; spectators'
  terrace

obstacle; facer
(obtaining money) under
  false pretenses; (obtaining
  money) by deception
(made) obvious; writ large
occasional; odd
occasional worker; casual
  labourer
occupant; occupier
odd; kinky
oddball; queer card
(any) odd job?; bob-a-job?
odds and ends; oddments
odometer; mileometer
off color; near the knuckle
offer; do
office; reception
office of school principal or
  college dean; headship
officer; official
Officer Commanding; O.C.
officer risen from the ranks;
  ranker
office worker; clerk
official business; statutory
  business
off limits; out of bounds
off one's rocker; off one's
  chump; off one's dot; off
  one's onion
off the rack; off-the-peg
off the record; on a lobby
  basis
off to a good start; well away
oil and gasoline mixture; two-
  stroke
oilcloth; American cloth
oily; smarmy
O.K.; landed
O.K.!; right
old duffer; gaffer
old hand; old soldier
old man; old cock
old people's home; almshouse
(an) old person; wrinkly
old retread; dug-out
old soldier; old sweat
old-timer; old party
old woman, bad-tempered;
  boot
on a grand scale; writ large
on approval; on appro
on a silver platter; on a plate
on a spree; on the loose
once in a while; once in a way
one hell of a hurry; split of a
  hurry
one-horse town; one-eyed
  village
100; ton

150% overtime pay (approx.);
  time and a half
one hundred percent; slap-
  down
100 runs; century
one-lane; single-track
one of a kind; one-off
one-room apartment; bed-
  sitter
one-room cottage; bothy
one's business or occupation;
  line of country
one-story house; bungalow
one-way ticket; single
on one's own; off one's own
  bat
on one's own; on one's pat
on one's own; on one's tod
on sale; on offer
on second thought; on second
  thoughts
on tenterhooks; on thorns
on the cuff; on the slate
on the cuff; on tick
on the double; smartish
on the kitchen counter; on
  the side
on the loose; going spare
on the nose; dead on
on the nose; spot-on
on the payroll; on the strength
on the reverse side; overleaf
on the right track; on the right
  lines
on the wagon; on the hob
on the wagon; on the teapot
on top of the world; cock-a-
  hoop
oomph; comeback
open house; omnium
  gatherum
open one's mouth; say boo to
  a goose
open-toed shoes; peep-toes
open watercourse; leat
operating room; operating-
  theatre
operating room; theatre
operations; works
operations planning room;
  ops room
oppose; take against
oral examination; viva
orchestra; stalls
orchestra seat; stall
order; totem
ordinance; by-law or bye-law
Orient; East
or near offer; o.n.o.
out; get-out

outdo oneself; push the boat out
outdoor painting; external painting
(outdoor) shorts; shorts
outfit; kit
outlook; look-out
out of bed; up
out of luck; landed
outside; outwith
outstanding; corking
outstanding person or thing; oner
over; on
over; P.T.O.
overalls; dungarees
overpass; fly-over
overripe; sleepy
overseas shipping; export carriage
overseer; supremo
overstock; backlog
overthrown; make hay of
oyster wrapped in bacon; angel on horseback

P

P.A. system; Tannoy
pacifier; comforter
pacifier; dummy
pack; look out
pack; shopping-bag
package; packet
package store; off licence
package tour; package holiday
packed full; packed out
(a) pack of; twenty
pack up and go; up-stick
paid hospital bed; pay bed
pain; blighter
painfully embarrassing; cringe-making
pain in the ass; Gawdelpus
paint; decorate
painting, outdoor; external painting
painting of the Last Judgment; doom
Pakistani; Paki
pal; cully
pan; send up rotten
pan; slate
pansy; proof
panties; knickers
pantry; larder
pantyhose; tights
paper, worthless; bumf (bumph)

paper money; folding
paper napkin; square
paper route; paper round
paper towel; kitchen towel
par; level par
paraffin; white wax
parakeet, small; budgie
parentheses 414
pari-mutuel betting; tote betting
parking lot; car park
parking space; parking bay
parlor; saloon
parlor car; saloon-car
parochial school; denominational school
parody; cod
parole; ticket-of-leave
parsnips; neeps
part; parting
partial school promotion; remove
part time; short time
party, noisy; ding-dong
party, riotous; piss-up
party line; shared line
party not in power; (Her Majesty's) Loyal Opposition
(a) party with dancing; knees-up
pass; bung
pass; overtake
passage; passing
passing grade; pass
passing lane; off-side lane
passing the hat; whip-round
pass out; flake out
pass out cold; spark out
pass (something) up; give (someone or something) a miss
past the crisis; off the boil
patrol cars; mobile police
patrolled; under observation
patrolman; constable
paved road; metalled road
pavement; roadway
paving block; set
pawn (hock); pop
pay; pay up
pay a fortune; pay the earth
pay as you go; P.A.Y.E.
pay (someone) peanuts; pay (someone) in washers
payroll; wages sheet
payroll holdup; wage-snatch
pay spot cash; pay on the nail
pay up; stump up
peanut; ground-nut

peanut; monkey-nut
peanut gallery; gods
(peanut) heaven; gods
pear cider; perry
pebble-coated stucco; pebble-dash
peculiar; odd
peculiar (funny); rum
peddler; chapman
peddler of faked merchandise; duffer
pedestrian crossing; pelican crossing
pedestrian crossing; zebra crossing
pedestrian underpass; subway
(take a) pee; pumpship
penalty for delayed delivery; backwardation
pencil, mechanical; propelling pencil
penis; chopper
penis, erect; stiffie
penny-pinching; cheese-paring
pension benefits; pension over
pension plan; superannuation scheme
Pentecostal; Whit
pep; bean
pepper shaker; pepper-castor (-caster)
pepper shaker; pepper-pot
pep talk; ginger-up
perfectly content; happy as Larry
perfectly okay; by all means
perfectly safe; as safe as a bank
perfectly safe; as safe as houses
perfume; scent
period 414
period; full stop
periodical room; news-room
periwinkle; winkle
person, unpleasant; bleeder
person, very small; titch
personal; private
personal baggage; dunnage
personal exemption; personal allowance
personnel; staff
person registered at a hotel; resident
person-to-person call; personal call
pervert; perv

press publication restriction;
    D-notice
pretty; dinky
prick; hampton
prime rate; base rate
prime time; peak viewing time
Prince Albert; frock-coat
principal; head
principal, school; head teacher
printing; impression
printing company's annual
    picnic; wayzgoose
prison guard; screw
prison guard; warder
private hospital; nursing
    home
private line; exclusive line
privy (can); jakes
Privy Councillor; P.C.
prix fixe; set lunch
proctor at school
    examinations; invigilator
prod; job
producer; manager
producer; producer
professor, associate; reader
(a) profitable enterprise;
    earner
promptly; like one o'clock
promptly; sharpish
pronto; bang off
pronunciation 410–412
proofreader; corrector
propane gas; Calor gas
property tax; council tax
prosecuted; done
(be) a prostitute; (be) on the
    game
(be) a prostitute; (be) on the
    knock
provide; lay on
proving-ground; test bed
prune wrapped in bacon;
    devil on horseback
pruning shears; secateurs
pry open; prize (prise)
pub; boozer
pub; pot-house
pubic hair, female; minge
pubic hair; short and curlies
pub keeper; landlord
public, mass-media; admass
    (ad-mass)
public housing unit; council
    house
public issue; off for
    subscription
public office holder; placeman
public open-air swimming
    pool; lido

public room, large; hall
public rubbish receptacle;
    skivvy-bin
public school; council school
public school; state school
pull (bring) it off; have it off
pull (someone's) leg; rally
pullover; jersey
pullover; jumper
pull rank on; pip
pull up stakes; pull up sticks
pull up stakes; up stumps
pump; court shoe
punching bag; punch-bag
punch in the nose; snorter
punctuation 414–415
punishment task; impost
puppet; poodle
puritan, fanatic; wowser
pursue; chivvy
pursue; tail after
push; flog
pushcart; barrow
pushcart; trolley
push-up; press-up
put in place; offer-up
put it over on (someone); sell
    (someone) a dummy
put on the dog; put on side
put out; run out
put out (be a nuisance); put
    about
put (someone) out; dismiss
put (oneself) out to; lay
    (oneself) out to
put together roughly; cobble
put to sleep; put down
put up; field
put up; set fair
put up (for the night); shake
    down
puzzle; stick up

Q

Q-Tip; cotton bud
quality; county
quart 417, 419
quarter note; crotchet
quarter of a pound; quarter
queasy; queer
queen; court-card
quick and lively; like one
    o'clock
quick as a wink; quick as
    thought
quick job; lick and a promise
quick tour; whip-round
quiet down; go off the boil
quiet down; quieten

quilt; eiderdown
quit; pack up
quite a . . . ; fair odd . . .
quite a dish; nice bit of work
quite sure; morally certain
quotation marks 414
quotation marks; inverted
    commas

R

rabbet; rebate
racetrack; race-course
racist; racialist
racket; dodge
racket; ramp
radio; wireless
radio-phonograph; radiogram
rage; wax
railroad switch; point
railroad tie; sleeper
rails; metals
rain barrel; water butt
rain cats and dogs; bucket
    down
rain cats and dogs; rain stair-
    rods
rain cats and dogs; tip down
raincoat; mac
raise; keep
raise; put up
raise; rise
raise an issue; start a hare
rambling; skimble-scamble
    (skimble-skamble)
rambunctious; rumbustious
rancor; gall
range; hob
(the) rank of knight;
    knighthood
rat cheese; mousetrap cheese
rather; -ish
rat on; nobble
rats!; blast!
rats!; bother
rattled; in a flat spin
ravine; gill
raving; staring
raw; underdone
razor, straight; cut-throat
(be) reading; have a read
reading lamp, adjustable;
    angelpoise lamp
read up on (someone,
    something); read (someone,
    something) up
ready-made; reach-me-down
ready to go; ready for off
ready-to-wear; off-the-peg
real; proper

rubbing alcohol; surgical spirit
rubbish; Barry White
rubbish; bumf (bumph)
rubbish; pants
rubbish heap; laystall
rubble; spoil
rube; chaw-bacon
Rube Goldberg; Heath
   Robinson
rub the wrong way; rub up
   the wrong way
ruckus; do
rudeness, piece of; rudery
rugby scrum; ruck
rumble seat; dickey
rummage sale; jumble sale
rumor, plant a; put about
run; ladder
run; stand
run along; cut along
run for office; put up
run into a streak of bad luck;
   shoot a robin
run rings around (someone);
   hit (someone) all over the
   shop
(the) runs; squitters
run through (money); make
   off with
run to ground; earth
run up; cobble

S

sack lunch; packed lunch
saddle; off-load
saddled with; lumbered with
saddle (someone) with; land
   (someone) with
safe cracker; peterman
safekeeping; safe storage
sailors' clothes and bedding;
   slops
salary allowance, extra;
   weighting
saleslady; assistant
salesman; assistant
salesman, door-to-door;
   doorstep salesman
salesman, traveling;
   commercial traveller
salesperson; counter-jumper
sales tax; V.A.T.
sally forth; eddy forth
salmon, young; fingerling
saloon keeper; publican
salt marsh; salting
Salvation Army; Sally Army
same old story; mixture as
   before

sandbox; play-pit
sandpaper; glasspaper
sandwich; butty
sandwich; round
sandwich; sarnie
sandwich box; snap-tin
sandy stretch by the sea; dene
sanitary napkin; sanitary
   towel
Santa Claus; Father Christmas
sarcastic; sarky
sarplike fish, small; roach
sass, to; cheek
sated; full to bursting
sausage; banger
sausage; slinger
sausage in batter; toad-in-
   the-hole
save one's skin; save one's
   bacon
savings account; deposit
   account
savings and loan association;
   building society
savvy; nous
sawbuck; tenner
scab (strikebreaker); blackleg
scab (strikebreaker); knob
scads; lashings
scallion; spring onion
scalper; ticket tout
scarf, woolen; comforter
scavenger; mudlark
schedule; timetable
scheduled sporting event;
   fixture
schedule of charges; tariff
scheme; wheeze
schlepp; hump
schnozzle; hooter
scholarship; studentship
scholarship student; bursar
scholarship student; scholar
school; college
school, divinity; theological
   college
school, elementary; primary
   school
school, extension; college of
   further education
school, grade; elementary
   school
school, parochial;
   denominational school
school, public; council school
school, public; state school
schoolchildren, line of;
   crocodile
schoolmaster; beak
school party; school treat
school principal; head teacher

school prom; school dance
(school) recess; inty
School Zone; Patrol
science expert; boffin
scientist, research; boffin
scold; threap
score 418
scorecard; matchcard
Scotch; whisky
Scotch tape; Sellotape
scoundrel; rotter
scout race horses; tout
scram; buzz off
scram; make oneself scarce
scram!; push off!
scram; scarper
scrambled eggs; buttered eggs
scrap coal; dross
scraper; shave hook
scratch pad; scribbling-block
scrawny; scraggy
screw; diddle
screw; roger
Screw that!; Stuff that for a
   game of soldiers!
scrimmage; scrum
scrounge; cadge
scrounge; nobble
scurry; scutter
scythe, small; bagging-hook
scythe; swop
sea fog; sea fret
seafood; fish
sea inlet; loch (lough)
sea level; ordnance datum
seaman, able; rating
sea mist; haar
seaside promenade; front
secondary issue; offer for sale
second balcony; upper circle
second floor; first floor
second rank; second eleven
second-story man; cat burglar
secretary; bureau
secretary; P.A.
Secretary of Labor;
   Employment Secretary
Secretary of the Treasury;
   Chancellor of the
   Exchequer
sedan; saloon
sedan; saloon car
See?; Follow?
Seeing Eye dog; guide dog
see one in hell; see (someone)
   far enough
see (someone's) point; take
   (someone's) point
see the last of; see the back of
see through; rumble

skip town by night; shoot the moon

slacks; bags

slang 424–427

slash; oblique

sled; sledge

sleep; kip

sleeping sickness; sleepy sickness

sleep in the open; sleep rough

sleep late; lie in

sleep late; sleep in

sleeveless sweater; slipover

slice of bacon; rasher

slicker; loose waterproof

slingshot; catapult

slip (vanishing act); guy

slipcovers; loose covers

slippery; greasy

slip up; put a foot wrong

sloppy clothes; slops

slot machine; fruit machine

slouch hat; trilby

slow, extremely; dead slow

slow lane; near-side lane

slow on the uptake; slow off the mark

slowpoke; slowcoach

sluggish; tardy

sly; pawky

smack; slosh

(a) small alcoholic drink; dram

(a) small blue-black plum; damson

small box; casket

small carplike fish; roach

small eel; grig

small farmer; yeoman

small fruit basket; punnet

small landholding; croft

small parakeet; budgie

small pork sausage; chipolata

small rented garden area; allotment

small scythe; bagging-hook

small spongy cake; muffin

small-time; small beer

small town; village

small wood (wooded area); copse

smart; posh

smashed; sloshed

smash hit; bomb

smashup; smash

smock; overall

smoke marijuana, to / a joint; blaze

snack; munch

snack bar; buffet

snap; popper

snap; snapper

snapper; cracker

snappy; nippy

sneakers; gym shoes

sneakers; plimsolls

sneak off; slope off

snooty; snotty

snooze; zizz

snot; bogey (bogy)

snowed in; snowed up

snow pea; mange tout

soak; rush

soak; sting

soapbox orator; tub-thumper

sob; blub

soccer; football

soccer; footer

soccer team; eleven

social security number; national insurance number

Society for the Protection of the Unborn Child; SPUC

sock on the jaw; fourpenny one

sod; turf

soda cracker; cream cracker

soda pop; squash

soda water; cat-lap

sofa; chesterfield

sofa; divan

soft bun; fat rascal

soft drink; mineral

soft soap; flannel

soft-soap; flannel

soldier in the ranks; ranker

Sold Out; House Full

solicit; importune

solitaire; patience

so long!; bung-ho!

so long!; cheerio!

someone who drinks too much alcohol; boozer

something special; bobby-dazzler

somewhat; -ish

sonar; Asdic

song-thrush; throstle

sonic boom; sonic bang

son of a gun; beggar

soon; sharpish

soothing; balmy

sophisticatedly off-beat; kinky

sop up; mop up

sore; narked

sort of; -ish

so there!; sucks to you!

soul kiss; tongue sandwich

sound; copper-bottomed

south end of a northbound horse; east end of a westbound cow

spank; smack

sparkling wine; fizz

spark plug; sparking-plug

sparrow; spadger

spatula; palette-knife

spay; doctor

speakeasy; shebeen

speak to; have a word with

special delivery; express

special election; by-election or bye-election

specialist (medical); consultant

specialty; speciality

specs; gig-lamps

speed bumps; rumble strip

spelling 415

spending spree; mucker

spiced meatball; faggot

spicy; fruity

spill; mucker

spin; birl

spin; twizzle

spit; gob

split even; fifty-fifty sale

split off; hive off

spoil; rot

spoil; wrap in cotton wool

spoiled; off

spoil one's record; blot one's copybook

spoilsport; wowser

spoken usage 412–414

sponge bath; bed bath

sponge bath; blanket bath

sponge rubber; sorbo rubber

spoof; cod

spool; reel

sporting event, scheduled; fixture

sports; athletics

spree; razzle

spring cleaning; spring-clean

sprinkles, multicolored; hundreds and thousands

sprinkling wagon; water-cart

spud; tater ('tatur, tatie)

spuds; praties

squabble; argue the toss

squabble; barney

squabblers; Kilkenny cats

squander; make off with

squander (blow); blue

squash; marrow

squeal (inform); grass

squeal on; round on

squeal on; shop

squeal on; split on

squeal on (someone); put (someone's) pot on

squeeze-box; squiffer

suffer no harm; take no harm
sugar, finely granulated;
  caster sugar
suit; fadge
suit, lady's; costume
suite; set
summa; first
sunny; sun-trap
superfluous; gash
supermarket, giant; hyper-
  market
supper, light; knife-and-fork
  tea
supply man; clerk of the
  works
supposed to; meant to
suppress; burke (burk)
sure!; right
surely; fair
sure thing; dead cert
sure thing; snip
surgical dressing; lint
surplus; reserve
surplus population; overspill
surprising; random
suspenders; braces
swagger; panache
swanky; cheesy
sweater; jersey
sweater, thin, worn under
  dress; spencer
sweater; woolly
sweet butter; fresh butter
sweetie; poppet
swell; bang-up
swell; swagger
swell; toff
(a) swell; nob
swim; bathe
swimming pool, public open-
  air; lido
swimming pool; swimming-
  bath
swindle; carve up
swindle; do
swindle; fiddle
swindle; swizz
swindle; twist
swinging door; swing-door
swipe; bone
swipe; flog
swipe; pinch
switch; cane
switchback; hairpin bend
switchblade; flick-knife
switchboard operator;
  telephonist
switchman; pointsman
switch tower; signal-box
switchyard; shunting yard
syntax 408–410

T

table d'hôte; set lunch
tadpole; pollywog
taffy; toffee
tag; label
tag; tig
Tag Day; Flag Day
take; screw
take; snaffle
take; want
take (a letter); take down
take (cheat); take down
take a decisive step; put the
  boot in
take a dislike to; take a
  scunner at (against)
take alcohol or drugs in
  excess, to; cane it
take a look at; run the rule over
take an examination; sit an
  examination
(take a) pee; pumpship
take a powder; cut one's lucky
take as a deduction; claim
  against tax
take a shot at; have a bash at
take a tumble; come a cropper
take care of; sort out
take (someone) in; do
  (someone) brown
take it easy!; wait for it!
take it on the lam; bunk
take off; beetle off
take-off; cod
take-off; send-up
take the best (people) out of;
  cream off
take the bull by the horns;
  grasp the nettle
take the cake; take the biscuit
take the lead; make the
  running
take the lead; take (make) up
  the running
take to one's bed; lie up
take turns; take it in turns to
talent scout; talent-spotter
(a) talk; confab
talk a blue streak; talk the
  hind leg off a donkey
talk at length about trivial
  matters, to; witter
talk incessantly (about); bang
  on
talking to; jaw
talk nonsense; haver
talk nonsense on and on;
  blather (blether)
talk one's way out; flannel
talk show; chat show

talk through one's hat; talk
  through (out of) the back of
  one's neck
talk up; ramp
tall fur hat; busby
tamp; pun
tamper with; nobble
tantrum; hissy fit
tantrum; paddy
tape needle; bodkin
taps; last post
target; Aunt Sally
tartan trousers; trews
tax, excise; purchase tax
tax, impose on (something);
  charge (something) to tax
tax, local; rate
tax, property; council tax
taxi stand; cab-rank
tea; char
tea, cup of; cuppa
teacher; master (mistress)
teacher, college; don
teacher, substitute; supply
  teacher
team; side
tea maker; kettle-boy
teams' performance records;
tea party, very large; bun fight
tear down; pull down
tear jerker; weepy (weepie)
tease; chip
tease; cod
tease; rag
tease; wind (someone) up
tedious; long
tedious; tiresome
tedious task; mission
teed off; brassed off
teed off; cheesed off
teeth; choppers
teetotal; TT
teetotaler; TT
teetotaler; wowser
telephone; blower
telephone, upright;
  candlestick telephone
telephone booth; call-box
telephone booth; kiosk
telephone pole; telegraph pole
telephone repair department;
  faults and service difficulties
TelePrompTer; autocue
(be a) television addict; have
  square eyes
teller; cashier
tell off; tick off
temp; casual labourer
temporary mailing address;
  accommodation address

traffic post; bollard
trailer, house; caravan
trailer truck, articulated lorry
trailer truck, bender
train, local; stopping train
train fare, cheap; APEX fare
train timetable, national
    passenger train; Bradshaw
transfer temporarily; second
transient; non-resident
transient; temporary guest
transit system; transport
    system
transmission; gearbox
transmission tower; electricity
    pylon
transom; fair-light
transportation; transport
trap; cakehole
trap; gob
trapezoid; trapezium
trash; tripe and onions
trash basket; litter bin
travel agency; bucket shop
travel at great speed, to; cane it
traveling salesman; bagman
traveling salesman;
    commercial traveller
traveling show; mobile
    production
treasurer; bursar
Treasury; (the) Revenue
Treasury Department;
    Exchequer
treat; jam
treat; push the boat out
treat; shout
treat (someone) right; do
    (someone) well
trellis; pergola
trial balloon; Aunt Sally
trial calendar; cause-list
trial lawyer; barrister
trial lawyer, instructions to;
    brief
tricky; dodgy
tricky job; tease
tricycle, electric; invalid
    carriage
trifle; ha'p'orth
trimester; term
triple achievement; hat trick
trot; crib
trouble; aggro
trouble; bother
trouble; bovver
trouble; snag
troublesome; awkward
trouble spot; black spot
troubling; worrying

trouser, tartan; trews
trouser cuff; turn-up
truck, closed; van
truck, large; juggernaut
truck; lorry
truck drivers' all-night diner;
    transport café
truck farm; market garden
truck (non-driving
    locomotive wheels); bogie
trudge; foot-slog
trundle bed; truckle bed
trunk (of an automobile); boot
try; go
try it out; try it on
try one's luck; chance one's
    arm
T-shirt; gym vest
T-shirt; singlet
tube; valve
tubular fluorescent lighting;
    strip lighting
tuckered out; clapped out
tuckered out; cooked
tuckered out; creased
tuckered out; knackered
turf; manor
Turks, young; ginger group
turn; go
turn; turning
turn a blind eye to; turn the
    Nelson eye on
turned; gone
turned on; switched on
turn in; give in part exchange
turn (someone) in; give
    (someone) in
turning-around place;
    winding point
turnkey deal; package deal
turn on; round on
turn one's back on; send to
    Coventry
turn on/off; switch on/off
turn over; tick over
turnpike; motorway
turn up; knock on
turtleneck; polo neck
tuxedo; dinner-jacket
TV; telly
TV channel; side
twaddle; waffle
£25; pony
21 tons 4 cwt.; keel
twice in a row; twice running
twist; screw
twisted; kinky
two-family; semi-detached
two-toned shoes; co-
    respondent shoes

two weeks; fortnight
type of activity; lark
type of cloth; wincey
typesetter; compositor
type (sort); mark

U

ugly; butters
umbrella; gamp
unable to play; unfit
unconventional and
    uncooperative; bolshy
    (bolshie)
uncouple; hook off
undemanding; cushy
under-drapes; net curtains
(obtaining money) under
    false pretenses; (obtaining
    money) by deception
underhand; hole-and-corner
underpants; liners
underpants; pants
undershirt; singlet
undershirt; vest
undertaker; funeral furnisher
under the doctor's care;
    under the doctor
under the weather; pulled
    down
undesirable; butters
undies; frillies
undies; smalls
undress, to; get one's kit off
    (made or become)
unemployed; redundant
unemployment benefits; (the)
    dole
unexceptional; common-or-
    garden
unexpected; random
unfit; C3
unholy mess; dog's breakfast
uniformed doorman and the
    like; commissionaire
unilateral declaration of
    independence; U.D.I.
unilateral deed; deed-poll
union cost-of-living contract;
    threshold agreement
union protest activity;
    industrial action
union suit; combinations
units of measure 413,
    417–419
university, expel temporarily
    from; rusticate
university head, honorary;
    chancellor
unlisted; ex-directory
unmistakably; nothing (else)
    for it

well-informed; clued up
well nigh; getting on for
well-to-do; well-off
Welshman; Taffy
wet; dabbly
whacky; scatty
wharf; quay
what's fair is fair; fair's on
what's the ticket?; what's the drill?
wheelchair; bath chair
wheelchair; invalid's chair
wheelchair; wheeled chair
when all is said and done; at close of play
when all is said and done; at the end of the day
when the time comes; on the day
when you come right down to it; when it comes to the bone
Where do we go from here?; Where do we go for honey?
where the difficulty or hardship lies; where the shoe pinches
whew!; lumme!
while; whilst
while-U-wait shoe repair shop; heel bar
whimper; grizzle
whimsical structure; folly
whine; whinge
whip; cane
whipping; cat
white cotton cloth; calico
white lima bean; butter bean
whitener; blanco
white out; Tippex
white raisin; sultana
whiz; dab
who/whom 410
whole note; semibreve
wholesaler; merchant
whole tone; tone
whole wheat bread; brown bread
whole wheat bread; wholemeal bread
whopping; swingeing
whorehouse; knocking-house
Who wants this?; Quis?
wicked; naughty
wicket; hoop
wide awake; fly
wife; ball and chain
wife; dutch
wife; trouble and strife

wildcat strike; unofficial strike
wild open land; heath
willies; jim-jams
win a bet; have it off
windbreaker; windcheater
windfall; bunce
winding; crinkle-crankle
windle 418
window shade; blind
window shopping; window-gazing
windshield; windscreen
wine, cheap; plonk
wine, red, cheap; red biddy
wine, sparkling; fizz
wing (wound); pip
wing mirror; off-side mirror
winner; runner
wise guy; clever Dick
(be a) wise guy; come the acid with; w.
with a double bed; double-bedded
with all due respect; with respect
withdraw; stand down
within hailing distance of; within cooee (coo-ee) of
with it; trendy
witness stand; witness-box
wobbly; wonky
wolf; scoff
woman; Biddy
woman; cow
woman, desirable; crumpet
woman, old, bad-tempered; boot
Women's Royal Army Corps; WRAC
wonderful; stonking
won't work out; won't go
wooded area (small wood); copse
wooded vale; dene
wood sliver; chip
woolen helmet; Balaclava
woolen scarf; comforter
woozy; muzzy
word; dicky-bird
work; answer
work by the book; work to rule
work in vain; plough the sand(s)
work like mad; do one's nut
work out; sort out
(the) works; lot
World War I; Great War
World War II; Hitler's War

worn out; frazzled
worn-out rope; junk
worried; in a state
worthless; poxy
worthless paper; bumf (bumph)
wow!; I say!
wow (impress); knock
wrapper; dressing gown
wreck; crash
wreck; crock
wrecking crew; breakdown gang
wrench; spanner
writing table; davenport
written agreement; articles

Y

yard; garden
Yeah; sure!; and pigs might fly!
yearling sheep; hogget
year one; year dot
yell blue murder; yell pen and ink
yellow; amber (of traffic lights)
yellow pages; trade(s) directory book
yellow turnip; swede
yelp; waffle
Yield; Give Way
yield to maturity; yield to redemption
yokel; moonraker
young cabbage; spring greens
young chicken; chicken
young rooster; cockerel
young salmon; fingerling
young tough; cockerel
young tough; skinhead
young Turks; ginger group
you're done!; Bob's your uncle!
you're welcome; not at all
your money's worth; value for money
you win some, you lose some; gain on swings, lose on roundabouts

Z

z (letter); izzard
z (letter); zed
zero; nought (naught)
zip code; post-code
zipper; zip
zoological names 427
zucchini; courgette